W9-DGU-396

610 Opperman Drive
P.O. Box 64526
St. Paul, MN 55164–0526
1–800–328–9352

Library of Congress Cataloging-in-Publication Data

The Career legal secretary / prepared by National Association of Legal
  Secretaries ; edited by ... Kaye Aoki ... [et al.].
— 3rd ed.
    p.   cm.
  Includes index.
  ISBN 0–314–02353–4
    1. Legal secretaries—United States—Handbooks, manuals, etc.
I. Aoki, Kaye. II. National Association of Legal Secretaries
KF319.C37 1993
349.73'024651—dc20
[347.30024651]
                                        93–15370
                                        CIP

ISBN 0–314–02353–4

NALS, Car.Leg.Sec. 3rd Ed.

THE CAREER
LEGAL SECRETAR
Third Edition

Prepared By

NATIONAL ASSOCIATION OF LEGAL SECRET

Edited By

Manual Committee

Composed of

KAYE AOKI, Certified PLS, Chairman

ANN P. ARMSTRONG, Certified PLS

ELSBETH BASKETTE, Certified PLS

CHARLYN BROWN, Certified PLS

AIDA G. DELGADO, Certified PLS, CLA

KATHLEEN B. NEVINS, Certified PLS

ST. PAUL, MINN.
WEST PUBLISHING CO.
1993

PREFACE

For the most part this text is written in the second and third persons. While the third person is often used, the editors feel that exclusive use of the third person would make reading the text unnecessarily stilted. Therefore, the second person is used more often because the editors prefer the informality of the second person.

The National Association of Legal Secretaries (NALS) is aware that the current trend in the use of pronouns is to use his/her or she/he or to rewrite material to avoid completely the use of a pronoun. Both alternatives were considered, and again the editors feel that either alternative would make the text tiresome. Although we recognize that there are lawyers and secretaries of both sexes, the majority of legal secretaries are women and the majority of attorneys are men; therefore, the feminine gender is used for legal secretaries and the masculine gender is used for attorneys. NALS believes that ability—not sex—governs the choice of a career. Therefore, wherever it is used in this book the masculine gender includes the feminine, and the feminine gender includes the masculine. Although the text refers primarily to legal secretaries, the information in the book is in fact of benefit not only to legal secretaries but to all legal support personnel.

*

HOW TO USE THIS BOOK

The Career Legal Secretary is presented by the National Association of Legal Secretaries as a legal secretarial training course at the post-secondary school level as well as the official text for the NALS Legal Training Course and the NALS Independent Course of Study.

It is intended for use as a training aid for people who are entering or have recently entered the legal field. It does not attempt to teach the law.

Because of its nature, the text is broad. Both the workbook and the teacher's manual which accompany the text offer suggestions on how to apply the general material to the local area. However, in spite of its generality, NALS believes that concentrated study of this text will give a good foundation upon which to broaden knowledge and advance careers.

This text is not intended as a legal authority, and it should not be used in that manner. Its intent is purely informational. Likewise, none of the illustrations in the text should be used in the office except under direct supervision of an attorney. Legal procedures change daily, and the support staff in a law office is responsible for keeping abreast of changes, just as attorneys are.

This text emphasizes professionalism. NALS considers the legal secretarial field as a *profession* and strives constantly to achieve the professional recognition it believes this field deserves.

*

ACKNOWLEDGMENTS

NALS acknowledges the following individuals and firms who made especially outstanding contributions to this book:

Members of the Manual Committee

Kaye Aoki, Certified PLS, Salt Lake City, Utah

Ann P. Armstrong, Certified PLS, Greenville, South Carolina

Elsbeth Baskette, Certified PLS, Stafford, Texas

Charlyn Brown, Certified PLS, Dayton, Ohio

Aida G. Delgado, Certified PLS, CLA, San Antonio, Texas

Kathleen B. Nevins, Certified PLS, Catasauqua, Pennsylvania

* * * * *

Barbara Akins, Certified PLS, Carrollton, Texas

Donna Chevalier, Certified PLS, Portland, Oregon

Beverly Comstock, Certified PLS, CPS, Binghamton, New York

Gary R. Henrie, Esq., Salt Lake City, Utah

Jacob S. Kolb, Esq., Bethlehem, Pennsylvania

William B. Long, Jr., Esq., Greenville, South Carolina

John Mauldin, Esq., Greenville, South Carolina

Christopher M. Mislow, Esq., Scottsdale, Arizona

Chris Neely, Greenville Technical College, Greenville, South Carolina

Kathleen K. Quinby, Certified PLS, Portland, Oregon

Rita Reusch, University of Utah College of Law, Salt Lake City, Utah

Daniel A. Ritter, Esq., Salem, Oregon

Margaret J. Scott, Certified PLS, CLA, Traverse City, Michigan

Julie Settimo, Certified PLS, Dayton, Ohio

Judy K. Snider, Certified PLS, CLAS, Sublimity, Oregon

James G. Watt, Esq., Allentown, Pennsylvania

JoAnn Wenmoth, Certified PLS, Chicago, Illinois

*

SUMMARY OF CONTENTS

*

TABLE OF CONTENTS

TABLE OF CONTENTS

TABLE OF CONTENTS

TABLE OF CONTENTS

TABLE OF CONTENTS

TABLE OF CONTENTS

TABLE OF CONTENTS

CHAPTER 6.   WRITTEN COMMUNICATIONS

TABLE OF CONTENTS

TABLE OF CONTENTS

TABLE OF CONTENTS

CHAPTER 7. PREPARATION OF LEGAL DOCUMENTS

TABLE OF CONTENTS

CHAPTER 8.   THE LAW LIBRARY

TABLE OF CONTENTS

TABLE OF CONTENTS

TABLE OF CONTENTS

TABLE OF CONTENTS

TABLE OF CONTENTS

TABLE OF CONTENTS

TABLE OF CONTENTS

CHAPTER 14. CRIMINAL LAW AND PROCEDURE

TABLE OF CONTENTS

CHAPTER 15. FAMILY LAW

TABLE OF CONTENTS

TABLE OF CONTENTS

TABLE OF CONTENTS

CHAPTER 17. REAL ESTATE

TABLE OF CONTENTS

TABLE OF CONTENTS

CHAPTER 18.   ESTATE PLANNING

TABLE OF CONTENTS

TABLE OF CONTENTS

THE CAREER
LEGAL SECRETARY
Third Edition

*

CHAPTER 1

THE CAREER LEGAL SECRETARY

Table of Sections

---

§ 1.1 A Professional Image

One of Webster's definitions of the word secretary is: "One employed to handle correspondence and manage routine and detail work...." The legal profession is set apart in requiring skills and support of the highest quality in order for the attorney to render the finest, most expedient service possible to the clients. As everyone knows, secretaries are employed in most fields of endeavor, and governments and businesses of the world would not function well, if at all, without them. The legal secretary is the very heart of the law office.

Attorneys themselves are unique professionals, each being quite different in personality and work capability, but each having certain things in common. The formal education required of the lawyer is extensive and is the beginning of an education that continues with each case and each client. The attorney is dedicated to the public and serving justice. This often is reflected in his personal activities in the form of community services. The attorney believes in the right of representation of all people in spite of their frailties, gross misjudgments, and even their flagrant violations of the law. The lawyer, so

1

vital to the functioning of our country's judicial processes, requires and deserves professionalism in the legal secretary's image and performance.

There are many factors which distinguish a legal secretary from a secretary simply working for a lawyer, and strict adherence to the Code of Ethics and Professional Responsibility of the National Association of Legal Secretaries (NALS) is essential to the character and behavior of the professional legal secretary.

The image of the legal secretary is composed of many facets and often begins with the visual one. Beyond the outward image, however, imagination is of equal significance in developing the proper atmosphere and impression. It is true that first impressions are lasting, and a negative impact is very difficult to reverse.

Many law offices maintain policies concerning appropriate attire. However, there are certain simple, basic guidelines the legal secretary should follow to achieve the appearance which the position requires. The underlying factor should be to create a picture of professionalism that will encourage the client's confidence in the legal secretary's serious attitude toward the work and the attorneys. Avoid clothing that is too casual, such as jeans. Choose basic styles that can be worn interchangeably, which will lend versatility to a wardrobe if careful planning is used in purchase.

Jewelry, makeup, hair styles, and neat and trimmed beards and mustaches in a law office can be in good fashion, yet tasteful. Take care to avoid extremes in these grooming areas with understatement being preferable to overstatement. A good rule of thumb is "when in doubt, don't."

In addition to appearance, the legal secretary's traits and actions contribute significantly to the image she creates of the attorney and the total office environment. In their dealing with the legal secretary, clients and members of the legal community can sense a legal secretary's respect for the attorney, her work, and herself. Carefully examine any action that could create an impression of lack of respect. In some offices secretaries and other personnel address attorneys on a first-name basis. This practice may portray an unprofessional atmosphere, however, and the legal secretary should avoid addressing the attorney or clients by their first names unless instructed otherwise.

A legal secretary should neither criticize nor condone criticism of the attorney or firm. In spite of her interest in her work and her familiarity with the facts at issue, she does not have the advantage of the extensive legal training necessary to understand why certain decisions are made or positions are taken. As emphasized in the NALS Code of Ethics and Professional Responsibility and in the Code of

Responsibility of the American Bar Association, confidentiality is essential. The etymology of the word "secretary" is from the Medieval Latin word *secretarius* meaning "confidant."

Good manners are a necessary part of civilized living, and we all appreciate those who consistently display them. Application of The Golden Rule is certainly appropriate in relationships with other team members. Promote mutual respect with other staff members by refusing to participate in office politics or gossip. The manner in which the legal secretary deals with clients should always be gracious, yet professional. Treat each client as a special person with an individual problem or situation. Such an attitude is further evidence that the attorney also regards the circumstances as special and deserving of attention. The legal secretary who deals with clients on a direct basis enjoys a very weighty responsibility in that to the clients she is an extension of the attorney. The clients must understand, however, that the legal secretary is prohibited from offering legal advice regardless of circumstances.

In order for a legal secretary, or one aspiring to that position, to convey professionalism to the attorney, the firm, and the clients they serve, there is an essential first step without which she cannot progress beyond the mechanical. She must believe in herself and in her ability to accomplish that goal.

There are many steps to take between leaving the classroom and feeling accomplished as a legal secretary, and these stages of progression vary according to the individual. Occasional discouragement is natural; difficulty makes one proud of an accomplishment.

The primary requirement of a successful legal secretary, which underlies her work and her image on an hourly, daily, and continuing basis, is her *attitude* toward herself and toward her career. Her attitude is reflected in all her dealings with others and in her completion of work assignments, often under troublesome and pressure-filled conditions. The valued legal secretary has learned to remain consistently composed and efficient under the most trying circumstances, knowing that conflicts and deadlines are inevitable. She views her work as her career rather than as a job, recognizing that each experience is a positive contribution to her investment in herself.

A second basic ingredient in the development of the professional legal secretary and a by-product of the proper attitude is *initiative*. A legal secretary can make an appreciable difference in the firm's productivity and in her own career development if she requests additional assignments after she has thoroughly completed delegated work. She should let the attorney know that she is serious about her career and is eager to expand her contribution to his productivity by asking relevant questions, by inquiring about appropriate reading material, and by requesting periodic evaluations of her work. There are excellent legal secretarial training courses and educational materials available through national, state, and local legal secretaries associations, as well as from vocational schools and universities. The motivated legal secretary who wishes to keep abreast of the changing laws and procedures and to expand her knowledge of the legal profession will take advantage of tools available for that purpose. Continuing education is a secure investment that produces earned dividends in proportion to its application.

Development of the proper attitude and strong initiative to accomplish and excel will result in the *self-confidence* that is the third vital factor in the makeup of the professional legal secretary. Real confidence is not automatic—it must be developed over a period of time through a variety of experiences. You will become self-confident by satisfactorily accomplishing tasks you believe too difficult. Excellence in requisite skills will contribute significantly to your feeling comfortable with your work responsibilities and is a definite must if you are to achieve the ultimate performance and recognition in your field. You will know that you have acquired self-confidence when you allow someone else to be given credit for your idea or work product; when you accept sound, constructive criticism graciously and gratefully; and when you admit your mistakes honestly without an attempt to search for an excuse.

Confidence is required for honest self-evaluation. When appraising yourself as candidly and objectively as possible, ask yourself if you fulfill the legal secretary's key responsibility of a professional image.

§ 1.2 Beginning Your Career

You have just finished school and are ready to embark on a career as a legal secretary, or perhaps you are changing positions to become a legal secretary. No matter which situation pertains to you, many of your experiences as a new legal secretary will be the same.

§ 1.3 The Interview

The first active step in becoming a legal secretary is the interview. No matter how much practice you have gone through for this interview, you will probably have "butterflies." You can, however, ease the situation by a calm demeanor. Be courteous, dignified, and pleasant—don't try to "oversell" yourself. Approach the interview with a professional attitude. A courteous, dignified, pleasant, and professional manner is necessary to become a successful legal secretary.

Be yourself. You are not being fair to either yourself or your prospective employer if you try to be something or somebody you are not. Be tidy in your overall appearance; your dress, hair style, and makeup at the initial interview should be an accurate preview of your day-to-day appearance on the job.

Be candid. Ask questions. Find out as much as possible about the job for which you are applying, know what is expected of you, and what you can expect from your employer. Be honest in your responses; clarify matters which you do not understand fully. Remember, your interest—or lack of interest—is on display. It is very possible you might discover you are not compatible with the position being offered. Do not expect the interviewer to indicate immediately to you whether or not the position will be offered to you. The interviewer may have to consult with others or have other interviews scheduled. It is appropriate to inquire as to when you might expect to hear from the firm. If you do not hear at the appointed time, you may call and inquire as to whether or not you are still being considered.

Know when the interview is over—then leave. Don't linger. Be as dignified in your exit as in your entrance. Final impressions are equally as important as first impressions.

§ 1.4   The First Day

If you thought you had the world by the tail, the first few hours at a new job will relieve you of this impression. There are many small ways, however, in which you can eliminate those first doubts and fears that you may never succeed as a legal secretary.

Arrive at work well rested and ready to go. Start out organized from the minute you wake up and carry through to the end of the day. Have a notebook handy when you arrive at work and be ready to use it. Never trust *anything* to memory. Take notes. Learn where the supplies are stored (draw a map if you have to), what type filing system is used, who is in charge of what, and where the form books are.

Ideally, you should have your notebook divided into classifications and take your notes down in proper sections for transcription. Type up your notes and file them in a procedures book in the same manner—by classification. Then, every time something new comes along, you can add it to your notebook. You never know who might have to step into your shoes in an emergency.

Your very first day and you are already preparing an office manual! Even if your office has a procedures manual, it probably doesn't cover nearly enough to get you through those first few days or weeks on a new job.

Your hand will probably have cramps from all the notes you take your first day, but think how much easier the second day will be because you can take your notes home and review them. Do this day after day, until you feel at home in the office and have a comprehensive manual of your duties.

§ 1.5 On With the Job

For a while you may not understand certain methods used by your employer. The best way to learn is by asking and taking notes on the answers for future reference. Let your employer know that your job will be easier and your performance better if you understand what you are doing. The old adage "If you are afraid to ask, you are afraid to learn" is just as true in the office as it is in the classroom.

Get a grip on the filing system immediately. One misplaced file can cause hours of lost time. Misfiling can also cause hours of agonizing search and rescue procedures.

Perhaps one of the most terrifying experiences you can have is the client who calls or comes into the office to ask about a case. You probably have never heard of the client, much less what his case is about; however, the client will expect you to know him and his case. After all, don't you work there? Don't stammer and act foolish. Let him know you are competent. Be calm; be truthful; be confident. Turn on your public relations, for example:

> "I have just begun working here and am not familiar with the case. May I have your name? I will see if someone else can help you."

Occasionally you will get a call or visit from a client who is upset or even irate about the matter that he has pending. Remember that no matter how insignificant a case or problem may seem to you, it is very important to the client. The client may expect you to be able to give him up-to-date information and detailed answers to his problems. The legal secretary cannot and should not give any information that could in any way be considered advice on a legal matter.

Now, follow through. Be sure someone does help the client. Always strive for good public relations. Do not, however, give out information of which you are not sure. Do not be "too" helpful. The client will probably have more respect for you if you are truthful and explain your limitations.

Just remember to take everything one step at a time. Before long, you will be comfortable in the office. That day will arrive sooner if you are calm and matter of fact in your approach to your new situation.

During those first few weeks, keep your notebook handy and build your office manual. Ask questions and get to know the procedures and why they are used. Keep your dictionary by your side—it is probably the best "friend" you will encounter as a secretary. Learn the office machines. Learn the office postal system and use it to the best advantage possible. Learn how the bookkeeping and filing systems work and use them. Be pleasant to all with whom you deal. Remember, you may need their help someday, too.

Perhaps one of the most important things to remember is that each system in the office has been developed to make your job more efficient. Use these systems and make them work for you and with you!

§ 1.6   The Legal Secretary in the Small Firm

Looking for a challenge? That is what you will get if you are the secretary in a small law office—one or two attorneys and you as secretary. The secretary in the small office probably receives a more rounded education on the job than any other secretary. She has to be everything to everybody, an expert in all areas of office relations and office work.

As a secretary in a small office, you deal with the public. You are usually the first person with whom the client or prospective client speaks, either personally or on the telephone. You set the mood. Therefore, you need all of the abilities of a good receptionist, an arbitrator, and a psychologist. You must be interesting and interested.

You get the mail and distribute it, wrap parcels and post the mail. You also take care of postage expenses, collect return receipts, and perform a myriad of other postal duties. You must know the postal system thoroughly and how to make it work for you.

You keep the books, write checks, deposit receipts, send out bills (and the rebillings), and know banking procedures as well. You handle trust and estate accounts and can verify everything you have done. You keep your records in a manner which will expedite your employer's tax preparations. You are competent at accounting and accounting procedures.

You order supplies, take care of the office equipment and necessary repairs. You know where to get what you want at the best price available. You know what equipment and supplies provide the performance required at an economically feasible rate. You have a place for everything and everything well marked for the convenience of everyone in the office.

You take care of the law library by filing new supplements and discarding the old. You keep the library up to date and orderly and keep subscriptions current. You check each supplement before discarding it to determine whether pertinent information has been noted and then transfer these notations to the new supplements in like manner. You have a reference file for articles in law publications and can retrieve information on the basis of this file. You identify all library materials with your employer's name and address.

Since you type everything that leaves the office, you know proper forms for communications, pleadings, and other documents that are drafted. You proofread everything at least once. All corrections are made carefully and neatly. You know proper copying requirements for each matter. You take pride in a job well done and in a document free from error.

As you compose a great deal of correspondence for your employer's signature, you know how your employer likes to express himself and can ghostwrite these letters for his signature. You know the components of a successful business letter and have a thorough knowledge of the English language and how to use it to the best advantage. You know punctuation, spelling, and word division and use all three correctly. You are friends with your dictionary and treat it with the respect due a valued friend.

Every paper coming in or going out of the office has a place, and you make sure it is filed properly for later retrieval. You have a system your employer can use. The files are orderly, and you do the filing on a regular basis.

You may work as an "unidentified" legal assistant. You learn all you can about the mechanics of your employer's practice and relieve him of what work you can. You prepare documents and do research under your attorney's direction to enable him to do his job more effectively. You do not offer legal advice, and you know your limitations in this respect.

You are probably a "jack of all trades." Some of your tasks may include tidying the desks and doing light cleaning. You may even need to fix or replace a screw or oil a squeaking chair.

You know everything that is happening and where everything is. You know what forms to use and what progress is being made in each case. You know what procedures to follow and what comes next. Most important of all, you have this information written in the proper files or in your office manual. You have made it possible for someone to step into your position and do your job with the least disruption necessary if an emergency should arise.

Your professional abilities are challenged every minute of every working day. You have to be the epitome of the truly professional secretary. Your appearance, poise, relations with the public and your employer, as well as your skills, your initiative, and your motivation are all part of this professionalism. You are indeed the well-rounded secretary, and without being conscious of the fact, you are daily grooming yourself to become a Certified Professional Legal Secretary.

§ 1.7   The Legal Secretary in the Large Firm

You now have a new job at a large law firm, and you wonder what to expect.

On your first day, the office administrator will probably give you an employee handbook which explains such things as the office hours, the vacation and sick pay policy, the fringe benefits package, and the conduct expected of all office employees. You will then be given the various local, state, and federal income tax forms and other office forms which are required to place you in the personnel system.

After that, you will be given a tour of the office, and you will be introduced to those members who are available for introductions. Some law firms have a map of the layout of the office to help you find your way around. If the secretaries and other support personnel have nameplates and the attorneys' offices are properly identified, use these to help you learn their names.

Usually the office administrator's secretary or one of the other secretaries in the office will be assigned to assist you in learning how to work efficiently with the support functions of the office. The following functions will be explained:

Telephone Operator—Many offices have special procedures for placing long distance, WATS, and other calls. Some offices have all long distance calls placed by the telephone operator; some may have a call back system to receive long distance charges from the long distance operator; many firms now have an automated system whereby all local, WATS, or long distance calls can be automatically charged to specific files and stored in a computer for automatic recall when billing a file.

File Clerk—All large firms have a special manner of setting up new files and checking for conflicts. It is imperative that you learn the correct procedures for opening and closing files and for maintaining files during the active life of the files.

Bookkeeping—Many offices now have computers and it is important that you learn the best way to utilize the equipment for particular office procedures, especially with regard to maintaining accurate time records for billing clients. You must also learn how to request checks, the turnaround time required to get checks, and how to charge such office expenses as postage, copying, long distance calls, and other out-of-pocket expenses to the individual clients or files.

Word Processing—Documents such as briefs, wills, trusts, profit sharing plans, etc., are now typed in the word processing department, freeing the legal secretary to do more administrative work for the attorney. You may be responsible for getting the work into the proper form to be submitted to the word processing department for actual preparation, or in some instances you may be required to learn to program some of your own work.

Copying—Many firms now have a person who either does all of the copying for the office or who is available to assist with large projects. Additionally, many firms now have several types of copying machines which they utilize for different purposes. If each secretary is responsible for doing her own copying, you will have to learn which type of equipment to utilize for various projects and who the key operators are for the various machines. They can assist if the machine malfunctions. If a record is kept of copies to be billed to clients, you should learn this procedure.

Librarian—The law library will probably be kept up to date by a librarian or by one specific person in the office. It will be your responsibility to learn how to use the office library.

Mail Room—Each firm generally has its own way of handling incoming and outgoing mail. It is important that you learn this procedure so that your mail will be handled timely. Fax transmissions are usually handled by this department, and you must understand the firm's procedures.

Errands—Generally all errands will be handled by a "runner" or some other outside special delivery service in your area. Get the specifics on whom to contact for this service. In an emergency you may have to do the errand yourself.

In addition to having someone explain these various functions to you, the above procedures will probably be set out in the office procedures manual which is available to all employees.

Now that your head is spinning from all of the information you have been given, you will be taken to your desk where you will begin to learn the intricacies of your new job. You will soon learn that each attorney has his own special way of handling matters, and you must now learn how to put your secretarial skills to work for him.

You will find that most firms prefer that their correspondence and legal documents be prepared in a uniform fashion. Fortunately, you will be able to use your office procedures manual to learn how to set up the various documents you will be required to prepare.

By the end of the first day, be assured that you will probably feel very lost, insignificant, and probably incompetent. Each secretary you meet that day seems to know everything, and you are sure you know nothing. If you are new to the legal field, you will have to remember that you have been properly trained, your skills met the tests necessary to be offered the position, and at some time in the past every single one of those "super secretaries" was a "beginner."

If you are an experienced legal secretary, you will have to draw on your past successful experiences and remember that in a very short time you will wonder how you could have doubted your ability to learn this new job.

§ 1.8 The Legal Secretary in the Corporate Environment

The role of the corporate legal secretary is broader in scope than most secretarial roles. There are no routine duties, except perhaps opening the mail.

In the corporate environment the legal department is usually an arm of top management and as such reaches out into every phase of the company's operations. The primary function of the legal department is the practice of preventive law—an effort to perceive, analyze, and correct legally related problems within the organization before they result in litigation. This is, of course, a noble goal, but no large corporation is without its Equal Employment Opportunity (EEO) complaints, workers' compensation claims, unemployment and Department of Labor hearings, union/labor problems, complex contract claims, and liability issues. Corporate legal issues range from small dollar problems to defense of lawsuits involving millions of dollars. The matter is further complicated if the corporation is under prime contract to the government and thus subject to the never-ending rules and regulations which have been promulgated to enforce applicable laws and statutes. These laws have been primarily enacted to assure fairness to labor, equal opportunity, protection of the government's interest, and to absolve the government of any appearance of conflict of interest, corruption, or wrongdoing, but the paperwork and effort to comply are added burdens.

The legal secretary is vital to the proper and effective operation of a corporate legal office. The legal secretary must have excellent secretarial skills, a working knowledge of legal terminology, and good communications skills, both oral and written. In addition, she must have a thorough understanding of the corporate structure and the responsibilities of attorneys in the office in order to direct requests for information to the attorney best able to assist. She must also be sensitive to political issues within and without the company, as good

NALS, Car.Leg.Sec. 3rd Ed.—2

public relations are essential to the smooth operation of the legal department as well as to the corporation. Finally, the legal secretary is often called upon to assist with legal research, which requires a basic knowledge of the legal resources most frequently consulted by the legal department in which she works.

The role of the corporate legal secretary is both administrative and clerical. Corporate legal work is more general than private legal work, and management-related duties often consume as much time as legal duties. A secretarial position in a corporate legal department is challenging, offering the opportunity for learning, variety, high visibility, and a close relationship with top management.

§ 1.9 The Legal Secretary in the Court System

When asked to express his conception of the duties and functions of a court clerk, one judge made the following statement: "It must be borne in mind that the designation court clerk is a complete misnomer, and that the duties of court clerks, regardless of what court they may be in, go far beyond the connotation of clerk, typist, or similar position. The court clerk has great responsibility not only to the court and attorneys but to the public generally. It is the primary responsibility of these individuals to see that the courts run smoothly and that the work is done properly and expeditiously. They are required to have a reasonable understanding of the law, rules of civil and criminal procedure, and other matters that bind the court in its daily work. This is not to say that they must be legally trained, but the clerks certainly must be able to understand statutes and case law as told to them by either the judge or the attorney involved. Therefore, it must be kept in mind that the position of court clerk is one of more responsibility than a clerk, typist, or even a secretary."

Court records are of vital importance in the lives of the general public. Therefore, it is essential that a court clerk have the training and ability to organize and maintain complete, accurate files and dockets. This can at times be repetitious and boring; however, the variety offered in court work more than compensates. The courts handle many kinds of cases, including criminal, juvenile, civil, adoptions, divorces, traffic, etc. The court clerk is responsible for these cases from beginning to end. The clerk assists the courts by swearing in witnesses; operating an electronic recorder; taking orders and motions from the judge verbatim; and receiving, marking, and safeguarding exhibits. The clerk types, compiles, and files minutes of court hearings and trials; issues bench warrants under direction of the judge for persons who do not appear or fail to pay fines imposed by the courts; receives and accounts for fines imposed by the court; maintains a calendar and status file on each active case; types forms, legal documents, and correspondence as directed by the court; compiles and tabulates statistical data and caseload reports; and performs secretarial work for the judges.

A court clerk must have the ability to exercise judgment in proper dissemination of information and to provide good public relations in stressful, sensitive situations. It is a job that is challenging, rewarding, and fascinating. Excellent skills are important, but above all a court clerk is required to be understanding, compassionate, and dedicated to serving the public.

§ 1.10   The Legal Secretary in Federal Government

The duties of secretaries employed in federal service are similar to civil service secretaries with GS ratings. Secretaries employed by a member of Congress are commonly referred to as Hill secretaries. A secretary is normally accorded confidence in all matters relating to the office in which she is employed, and the work is closely identified with the viewpoint and responsibilities of the particular agency or department. An office manager is the person directly answerable to the agency head or member of Congress, and the secretary works under the direction of the office manager.

A secretary performs or supervises the performance of a variety of tasks including:

- Performing telephone and receptionist duties.
- Keeping the calendars and scheduling appointments and conferences.
- Performing liaison duties as necessary between the office manager and other office personnel as well as with other offices.
- Receiving and distributing incoming mail and preparing replies.
- Arranging for recording of proceedings of conferences or hearings.
- Channeling and reviewing outgoing mail.
- Maintaining records and files.
- Making travel arrangements for staff members.
- Assembling and disseminating information.
- Transmitting staff instructions.
- Performing miscellaneous clerical, stenographic, and secretarial duties.

Secretarial positions may or may not require stenographic, typing, computer, or dictating machine transcribing skills.

13

There are significant differences in civil service and federal service jobs. With federal service there is no job security, and salaries may vary a great deal, according to the wishes of the employer, the amount available in the clerk/hire fund of the particular office, or ceilings of grades for certain positions. Service to constituents is the prime reason for hiring of staff in congressional offices. There is a great amount of research and contact with various governmental agencies so that problems may be resolved. Because of these contacts and being "where it is all happening," a certain amount of glamour and prestige is attached to federal service jobs. Many of the secretarial jobs, however, require longer hours than regular civil service jobs or jobs in private industry. No overtime is paid, but in some cases compensatory time off is allowed.

Most federal service secretaries do not come from the civil service registry but are recruited by advertisement or word of mouth. An employment service is also provided for the use of the members of Congress. Secretarial abilities are tested and evaluated in the same manner that private industry employment agencies use. Legal secretarial skills are much in demand. Usually the legal secretary's training has included language skills, such as obtaining information for and composing correspondence and reviewing outgoing correspondence for grammar, spelling, typography, and format. The advancement of the secretary depends on many factors, such as length of time in the job, improved job skills, and ability to work without direct supervision. Other desirable traits essential to performance of secretarial duties are:

- Effectiveness in getting along with others.
- Loyalty, integrity, and discretion.
- Capacity and willingness to accept responsibility.
- Judgment, initiative, and resourcefulness.
- Poise, personal dignity, neatness, and good grooming.

§ 1.11 The Legal Secretary in Specialized Practice

General practice attorneys handle all types of cases—civil and criminal. This means that the attorney might be involved in the defense of a criminal matter one day and in a personal injury trial the next. General practice firms do not limit their practices to trial work. On the contrary, they also usually handle a large volume of nonlitigation work such as property transactions, contracts, estate planning, and tax work. The secretary in a general practice, therefore, must be especially versatile and knowledgeable about all aspects of the law.

Some attorneys thrive on the excitement and challenge of trial work, which is divided into criminal defense and civil trial work.

There are further divisions in these two major areas of trial work. For example, some criminal defense trial lawyers specialize in white collar crime defenses. Likewise, some civil trial attorneys specialize in personal injury cases, tax cases, domestic relations cases, bankruptcy cases, and other types of civil actions.

Other attorneys enjoy the challenge of becoming specialists in one particular phase of the law such as estate planning, property law, probate law, tax law, corporate law, admiralty law, patent law, domestic relations law, and so on. They may rarely engage in trial work but often serve as backup specialists for the trial attorney.

For the legal secretary who works for the specialist, there is a particular challenge to learn the attorney's specialty so that she can become a specialist in that particular phase of the law.

§ 1.12 Career Advancement

Whether you advance your career or remain in the same position year after year while others are advanced before you depends upon many things, one of which is your own frame of mind. Are you willing to learn? Are you able to take instructions gracefully? Are you able to do things the way your present employer desires them to be done without such remarks as "But I've never done it this way before" or "I used to do it this way where I worked before"? Are you able to take constructive criticism without pouting, slamming doors or drawers, or tears? Are you, as a responsible legal secretary, able to make procedural changes to keep in step with modern trends? Keep an open mind—don't let your own attitude keep your career bogged down.

Be ready for career advancement. Perhaps you work in a one-secretary office which does not use information processing at the present time or maybe you contemplate working in a larger firm sometime in the future. If that is so, go to a school that teaches the use of word processors and computers. Attend seminars and workshops. Become an Accredited Legal Secretary as well as a Certified Professional Legal Secretary. Keep abreast of what is happening within the firm and in the world. Read the newspapers, including the news of record columns and obituaries. Do a little bit extra for your employer without being asked. The fact that your employer is aware that you are actually involved in continuing legal education can often make a big difference in who gets the advancement. Be ready!

Some secretaries find that their employers hesitate to promote them into a different position because they feel the secretary is indispensable. The good secretary will have her job so well organized with an office manual, a forms file, a procedures manual, and a systematic training of backup personnel that her employer need not be concerned about promoting her. She can be of even more help to him in an administrative capacity than in a secretarial one. Often the secretary is her own worst enemy when it comes to advancement. She gets caught in a career trap of her own making. She jealously guards her domain and keeps her systems in her head. Yes, she is truly "Old Reliable," but she makes training someone else to take her place such a major event that it is easier to keep her where she is.

Some secretaries have settled for "jobs" instead of careers. Yet, for many of them, a large part of their adult lives were spent in the working world. Planning a career takes just that—planning. Decide on some objectives for your working life and then plan to make them come about. It is up to you whether you have a career or just a job.

§ 1.13 Membership in NALS

The National Association of Legal Secretaries (NALS) began in 1929 when a young legal secretary, Eula May Jett, in Long Beach, California, was encouraged by a court clerk to talk with other legal secretaries about correct preparation of legal documents. As a result of that challenge, NALS was begun. Today NALS is a tri-level organization with membership available in local chapters and associations nationwide.

NALS encourages the personal and professional growth of its members through numerous educational programs and the promotion of professional standards and ethics.

Members support and abide by the Code of Professional Responsibility of the American Bar Association as well as the NALS Code of Ethics and Professional Responsibility.

Membership is available to legal secretaries and any person engaged in work of a legal nature, such as law office administrators, legal assistants, stenographers, or employees of public and private institutions. Attorneys, judges, educators, and students may join NALS as associate members.

NALS, local chapters, and state associations offer many educational materials and programs, such as:

- Texts and handbooks to provide helpful how-to information for the everyday use of legal secretaries in both general and specialty practices.

- Manuals to assist law offices in developing their own procedures and systems as well as tests for hiring support staff.

- Training courses and independent study courses to provide basic and advanced instruction for legal secretaries and educational institutes to assist those preparing for the certification examination.

• Educational conferences and seminars held nationwide at various times of the year.

• *The Docket* which contains educational articles on general trends and emerging issues in the legal field and provides practical information to help achieve and maintain proficiency in the delivery of legal services.

Members have available Specialty Education Sections and Membership Divisions, such as:

> Specialty Education Sections
> • Business/Corporate Law
> • Law Office Management
> • Litigation
> • Probate/Estate Planning
>
> Membership Divisions
> • Legal Secretary
> • Legal Assistant
> • Certified Legal Secretary
> • Young Members

§ 1.14 Certification as an Accredited Legal Secretary

The Accredited Legal Secretary (ALS) designation is achieved after passing a one-day examination. This examination is designed for the individual at the apprentice level—not those veteran members of the legal support staff. The six-hour exam covers three areas:

1. Written Communication Comprehension and Application

2. Office Administration, Legal Terminology, and Accounting

3. Ethics, Human Relations, and Applied Office Procedures

The examination is given concurrently with the Certified Professional Legal Secretary (PLS) schedule—the first Saturday after the first Friday in March and the last Saturday after the last Friday in September. It will also be offered at special times for schools and colleges. Applications and fees must be postmarked by December 1 for the March examination and by July 1 for the September examination.

§ 1.15 Certification as a Certified Professional Legal Secretary

The purpose of the Certified Professional Legal Secretary (PLS) examination is to certify a legal secretary as an executive assistant who possesses a mastery of office and people skills and who demonstrates

17

the ability to interact on a professional level with attorneys, clients, other secretaries, legal assistants, office administrators, judges, and other court officials. Working under the direct supervision of a practicing lawyer or judge, the Certified Professional Legal Secretary is expected to assume responsibility, exercise initiative and judgment, and make decisions within the scope of assigned authority. The Certified Professional Legal Secretary has a working knowledge of procedural law and the law library and is capable of drafting correspondence, legal documents, and court documents with minimal supervision.

The two-day examination is administered at testing centers nationwide the first Friday and Saturday in March and the last Friday and Saturday in September. Applications and fees are due by December 1 for the March examination or by July 1 for the September examination.

Seven areas are tested:

1. Written Communication Skills and Knowledge

2. Ethics

3. Legal Secretarial Procedures

4. Accounting

5. Legal Terminology, Techniques, and Procedures

6. Judgment

7. Legal Secretarial Skills

Hundreds of colleges throughout the country are making available college credits for those achieving PLS certification. The American Council on Education (ACE) has reviewed the examination and recommended credit hours. Acceptance of the credit recommendations is at the discretion of each institution.

Anyone interested in membership or information on programs and available products is encouraged to write or call:

National Association of Legal Secretaries

2250 East 73d Street, Suite 550

Tulsa, OK 74136–6864

918/493–3540

CHAPTER 2

ETHICS

Table of Sections

---

§ 2.1 Definition

According to the dictionary, ethics are "the principles of conduct governing an individual or profession." In law the ethics governing the profession also govern all individuals working in the profession. This must be understood by a secretary entering the field of law as well as secretaries already in the legal field.

§ 2.2 ABA Code of Professional Responsibility and Canons of Judicial Ethics

In 1908 the American Bar Association (ABA) adopted the Canons of Professional Ethics to be used as a guide for attorneys. This set of

19

guidelines, although amended many times throughout the years, left many questions unanswered, and in 1969 the ABA adopted the Code of Professional Responsibility and Canons of Judicial Ethics to replace the Canons of Professional Ethics. Most of the states have adopted the Code of Professional Responsibility with revisions to suit their requirements, since the Code could not reflect local practice, procedures, and traditions. You should consult the Code adopted by the state in which you are employed.

§ 2.3 Canons, Ethical Considerations, and Disciplinary Rules

The Code of Professional Responsibility is interpreted by the ABA's Committee on Ethics and Professional Responsibility which issues formal and informal opinions. It consists of three separate but interrelated parts. They are the Canons, Ethical Considerations, and Disciplinary Rules. The Canons are statements in general terms of professional conduct expected of lawyers from which the Ethical Considerations and Disciplinary Rules are derived. Ethical Considerations represent objectives to which all lawyers should strive. They embody the principles upon which a lawyer can rely for guidelines in many specific situations. Disciplinary Rules are mandatory in character and state the minimum level of conduct below which no lawyer should fall without being subjected to disciplinary action.

§ 2.4 Code of Judicial Conduct

The ABA has also adopted a Code of Judicial Conduct for the United States judges to be used as a guide to the standards judges should observe.

§ 2.5 The Secretary's Role

While a non-attorney employee in a law office cannot be disciplined by a bar association for violating a provision of the Code of Professional Responsibility, the attorney-employer, who is responsible for the conduct of his office staff, would be censured for a violation by an employee. A secretary should be familiar with the Canons set forth in the Code of Professional Responsibility and how she should be guided while employed in a law office. For this reason the Canons are set forth below with an explanation of how they affect a secretary in a law office.

§ 2.6 Canon 1. A Practitioner Should Assist in Maintaining the Integrity and Competence of the Legal Profession

A secretary should also continually upgrade her skills and knowledge in an effort to maintain the competence required in a law office. The legal secretary can accomplish this by attending courses, seminars, and workshops offered for the legal secretary. She should keep available a library of secretarial handbooks for reference and frequent consultation. A secretary should be honest and forthright not only in office matters but in her personal life as well, since this reflects on the office where she is employed.

§ 2.7   Canon 2. A Practitioner Should Assist the Legal Profession in Fulfilling Its Duty to Make Counsel Available

A legal secretary should not be boastful of her employer in public nor try to convince people to use that attorney when they need one because he is "the best." This is a form of solicitation and is not allowed under this canon. If someone asks about your employer, you may certainly answer, but the main thing you must remember is that you may not solicit business.

§ 2.8   Canon 3. A Practitioner Should Assist in Preventing the Unauthorized Practice of Law

A legal secretary should remember that she is not authorized to do those things which the law requires an attorney to do. It is very difficult sometimes to draw a distinction between those things which are allowed and those which are not. It is very important that the new legal secretary not discuss any case with the client or anyone else unless she is specifically authorized by the attorney.

There are times when a relative or friend wishes to discuss a problem he is having which sounds very similar to one which was handled in your office. Although you might be tempted to tell the relative or friend how that matter was handled, you must resist this temptation, as you would be engaging in the unauthorized practice of law. In fact there might be a difference in the facts which would be noticed by an attorney and would require an entirely different approach.

§ 2.9   Canon 4. A Practitioner Should Preserve the Confidences and Secrets of a Client

This canon sometimes proves to be the hardest for the new legal secretary to observe. There is a great tendency to want to talk to your relatives, friends, and at times even strangers about a case in the office which is particularly interesting or "spicy." Whatever you learn about a person or a case while you are working in a law office must be kept confidential. You should not discuss office matters outside the office with office personnel working on the case.

§ 2.10   Canon 5.   A Practitioner Should Exercise Independent Professional Judgment on Behalf of a Client

This canon deals basically with what is called "conflict of interest." A lawyer's judgment should be directed solely to the benefit of his client free from other influences.   If a secretary knows any of the parties on the opposing side of a lawsuit, she should give such information to the attorney so that he can determine whether or not a conflict of interest in fact does exist.

§ 2.11   Canon 6.   A Practitioner Should Represent a Client Competently

This is one canon in which the secretary plays a major role. Perform all work carefully and without error, thus helping the attorney turn out a quality work product.   If a secretary has a question concerning any phase of the paper being prepared, she should consult the attorney so that the matter is handled competently.

§ 2.12   Canon 7.   A Practitioner Should Represent a Client Zealously Within the Bounds of the Law

Under this canon an attorney is to take whatever steps he can to attain the client's advantage, but in doing so he must not act improperly.   Improper conduct might include discussing that case directly with the parties on the opposing side rather than through the attorney representing them (unless permission has been granted by that attorney).   If a secretary screens phone calls, and she receives a call from a person (not an attorney) whom she recognizes to be on the opposite side of a suit pending in the office, she should give such information to the attorney, as it may be that the attorney would not want to take the call.   This canon also imposes certain conduct on attorneys when investigating a case or conducting a trial.

§ 2.13   Canon 8.   A Practitioner Should Assist in Improving the Legal System

A secretary also can assist in improving the legal system by displaying integrity, competence, and an understanding of the judicial system, both in and out of the office, thus inspiring confidence in that system.   She should continue to learn all she can about the system. One method of doing this is by membership and participation in the National Association of Legal Secretaries.   This association conducts seminars on three levels of its association (local, state, and national) and promotes the continuing education of the legal secretary.

§ 2.14   Canon 9. A Practitioner Should Avoid Even the Appearance of Professional Impropriety

If our system of justice is to prevail, the American public must have confidence in the system and all who work in the system. Exemplary conduct should be the hallmark of all legal secretaries as well as that of attorneys, judges, and all who are connected with the administration of justice. The people in our legal system should avoid even the appearance of impropriety.

This canon also requires that all funds of clients paid to a lawyer or a law firm, other than those advanced for costs and expenses, be deposited in an easily identifiable bank account and not be commingled with the funds of the lawyer or the law firm. Therefore, all law firms, regardless of size, maintain a minimum of two bank accounts: one "regular" account in which fees, refunds of advances, and other firm moneys are deposited and one "special" or "trust" account in which all moneys belonging to clients are deposited. The funds in these accounts must never be commingled. This means that the money retained in a special or trust account must not be used by the firm for any reason, and it can only be paid over to, or paid on behalf of, and at the request of the client.

§ 2.15   Model Rules of Professional Conduct

On August 2, 1983, the House of Delegates of the American Bar Association adopted the Model Rules of Professional Conduct to define the relationship of the lawyer to our legal system. These rules consist of eight basic categories, each divided into several subsections.

The first rule deals with client-lawyer relationships, including the competent and diligent representation of the client by the lawyer, scope of representation, fees, communication, confidentiality of information, conflict of interest, organizations as clients, clients under disability, the safekeeping of a client's property, and declining or terminating representation of a client.

The second rule deals with the lawyer in his capacity as an advisor, intermediary, and evaluator.

The third rule deals with the lawyer as an advocate, including bringing or defending only those actions which have a meritorious claim, expediting litigation, candor toward the tribunal, fairness to opposing party and counsel, impartiality and decorum, trial publicity, and the role of the lawyer as a witness.

The fourth rule deals with transactions with persons other than clients, including truthfulness in statements to others and communication with persons represented by counsel, dealing with unrepresented persons, and respect for the rights of third persons.

The fifth rule concerns law firms and associations, including the responsibilities of supervisory and subordinate lawyers, legal support staff, unauthorized practice of law, and restrictions on the right to practice.

The sixth rule speaks to the issue of public service, including pro bono public service, accepting appointments, membership in legal services organizations, and law reform activities affecting client interests.

The seventh rule addresses the issue of advertising and solicitation of business by a lawyer. This rule also deals with the use of firm names and letterheads.

The eighth rule discusses the integrity of the profession, including bar admission and disciplinary matters, reporting professional misconduct, committing misconduct, and the jurisdiction under which the lawyer is subject.

§ 2.16   NALS Code of Ethics and Professional Responsibility

Members of the National Association of Legal Secretaries are bound by the objectives of this association and the standards of conduct required of the legal profession.

Every member shall:

Encourage respect for the law and the administration of justice;

Observe rules governing privileged communications and confidential information;

Promote and exemplify high standards of loyalty, cooperation, and courtesy;

Perform all duties of the profession with integrity and competence; and

Pursue a high order of professional attainment.

Integrity and high standards of conduct are fundamental to the success of our professional association. This Code is promulgated by NALS and accepted by its members to accomplish these ends.

Canon 1. Members of this association shall maintain a high degree of competency and integrity through continuing education to better assist the legal profession in fulfilling its duty to provide quality legal services to the public.

The purpose of continuing legal education, supported by NALS, is to expand and refine the knowledge of a member of this association, both to increase the self-esteem of the member and to make the member of greater assistance to the lawyer in the delivery of legal services. NALS encourages continuing education by offering institutes, seminars, and courses.

The association encourages every legal secretary to become certified as a Professional Legal Secretary or an Accredited Legal Secretary. Certification is used as a standard of measurement that signifies above-average skills and abilities, initiative and good judgment, and dedication to the profession. Certification is a valuable form of career insurance that can be attained once a commitment is made.

The growth of a profession and the attainment and maintenance of individual competence require an ongoing incorporation of new concepts and techniques. Continuing education enables law office staff to become aware of new developments in the field of law and provides the opportunity to improve skills used in the delivery of legal services.

A member of this association recognizes the importance of maintaining an interest in the development of continuing legal education. Professional competence is each member's responsibility. The exchange of ideas and skills benefits the legal profession and the general public.

A member of this association recognizes the necessity of membership and participation in a professional association. One of the hallmarks of any profession is its professional association, founded for the purpose of determining standards and guidelines for the growth and development of the profession. Through professional association, a member is able to promote a cooperative effort with others in the legal community for the delivery of legal services.

The continued and increased contribution by members of this association to the delivery of legal services is dependent upon a further delineation of their skills, qualifications, and areas of responsibility. It is therefore incumbent upon each member to promote the growth of the legal profession through support of and participation in the endeavors of NALS.

For a comparison to other codes and rules of professional responsibilities and ethics, see:

American Bar Association Model Code of Professional Responsibility DR 6–101.

American Bar Association Model Rules of Professional Conduct Rule 1.1.

Canon 2. Members of this association shall maintain a high standard of ethical conduct and shall contribute to the integrity of this association and the legal profession.

The highest degree of ethical conduct and integrity is the backbone of the legal profession. Because of the close professional relationship of a lawyer and a member of this association, it is essential that the member maintain an equally high standard of both ethical conduct and integrity. The public expects and deserves such ethical conduct and integrity by the lawyer and also expects and deserves such conduct by all nonlawyer staff with whom the client comes in contact.

For a comparison to other codes and rules of professional responsibilities and ethics, see:

American Bar Association Model Code of Professional Responsibility DR 1–101, DR 1–102, and DR 9–101.

American Bar Association Model Rules of Professional Conduct Rules 8.1, 8.2, 8.3, and 8.4

Canon 3. Members of this association shall avoid a conflict of interest pertaining to a client matter.

Loyalty is an essential element in the lawyer's relationship to a client. An impermissible conflict of interest may exist on behalf of a member of this association before representation is undertaken. In that event, such conflict of interest must be disclosed to the lawyer because of the lawyer's requirement to avoid such a conflict, even to the extent of declining representation. In the event a conflict occurs after representation has been undertaken, the member must disclose such conflict to the lawyer.

For a comparison to other codes and rules of professional responsibilities and ethics, see:

American Bar Association Model Code of Professional Responsibility DR 5–105.

American Bar Association Model Rules of Professional Conduct Rules 1.7(b), 1.8, 1.9, and 1.10.

Canon 4. Members of this association shall preserve and protect the confidences and privileged communications of a client.

The obligation of a member of this association to preserve the confidences and secrets of a client continues after the termination of employment of the lawyer by the client and after employment of the member by the lawyer.

Both the fiduciary relationship between the lawyer and the client and the proper functioning of our legal system require that the lawyer preserve confidences of the person who employs or seeks to employ the lawyer. A client must feel free to discuss anything and everything with the lawyer, and the lawyer must be equally free to ask the client questions to obtain information beyond that volunteered by the client.

The normal operation of a law office exposes confidential personal information to nonlawyer employees, particularly those having access to files. The requirement of confidentiality obligates a lawyer to exercise extreme care in selecting and training law office personnel so that the sanctity of the client's confidences and privileged communications may be preserved.

Preserving client confidences is a vital part of the relationship between the client and the law office staff in the delivery of legal services. The confidentiality of information must be respected at all times.

For a comparison to other codes and rules of professional responsibilities and ethics, see:

> American Bar Association Model Code of Professional Responsibility DR 4–101, DR 7–102(B), and DR 7–107.

> American Bar Association Model Rules of Professional Conduct Rule 1.6.

> *Canon 5. Members of this association shall exercise care in using independent professional judgment and in determining the extent to which a client may be assisted without the presence of a lawyer and shall not act in matters involving professional legal judgment.*

It is permissible and indeed it often occurs that lawyers delegate tasks to members of the law office staff. In a specific ethical opinion by the American Bar Association, it was held:

> A lawyer can employ lay secretaries, lay investigators, lay detectives, lay researchers, accountants, lay scriveners, nonlawyer draftsmen or nonlawyer researchers. In fact, he may employ nonlawyers to do any task for him except counsel clients about law matters, engage directly in the practice of law, appear in court or appear in formal proceedings as part of the judicial process, so long as it is he who takes the work and vouches for it to the client and becomes responsible to the client.

ABA Comm. on Professional Ethics, Formal Op. 316 (1967).

For a comparison to other codes and rules of professional responsibilities and ethics, see:

American Bar Association Model Code of Professional Responsibility DR 3–101(A) and DR 3–103(A).

American Bar Association Model Code of Professional Conduct Rule 5.5(b).

Canon 6. Members of this association shall not solicit legal business on behalf of a lawyer.

EC 2–8 of Canon 2 of the American Bar Association Model Code of Professional Responsibility best describes the necessity of this canon. EC 2–8 states in part:

> Selection of a lawyer by a layperson should be made on an informed basis. Advice and recommendation of third parties— relatives, friends, acquaintances, business associates, or other lawyers—and disclosure of relevant information about the lawyer and his practice may be helpful. A layperson is best served if the recommendation is disinterested and informed. In order that the recommendation be disinterested, a lawyer should not seek to influence another to recommend his employment. A lawyer should not compensate another person for recommending him, for influencing a prospective client to employ him, or to encourage future recommendations. . . .

For a comparison to other codes and rules of professional responsibilities and ethics, see:

American Bar Association Model Code of Professional Responsibility DR 2–101 and DR 2–103.

American Bar Association Model Code of Professional Conduct Rule 7.2.

Canon 7. Members of this association, unless permitted by law, shall not perform paralegal functions except under the direct supervision of a lawyer and shall not advertise or contract with members of the general public for the performance of paralegal functions.

See discussions under Canons 5, 8, and 9 and the comparisons to other codes and rules of professional responsibilities and ethics referred to in those discussions.

For a comparison to other codes and rules of professional responsibilities and ethics, see:

American Bar Association Model Code of Professional Conduct Rules 5.3 and 5.5.

Canon 8.   *Members of this association shall not perform any of the duties restricted to lawyers or do things which lawyers themselves may not do and shall assist in preventing the unauthorized practice of law.*

Canon 8 above is similar to Canon 9, but Canon 8 specifically states that members may not do or engage in activities "which lawyers themselves may not do . . . ."

For a comparison to other codes and rules of professional responsibilities and ethics, see:

American Bar Association Model Code of Professional Responsibility DR 1–102(A).

Canon 9.   *Members of this association not licensed to practice law shall not engage in the practice of law as defined by statutes or court decisions.*

Although the codes of professional responsibility of the various state bar associations may not directly govern members of this association except through a supervising lawyer, it is incumbent upon a member of NALS to know the provisions of the lawyer's code applicable in the member's state and to avoid any action which might involve a member of this association or a lawyer in a violation of a state code or in the appearance of professional impropriety.

The practice of law includes but is not limited to accepting cases or clients, setting fees, giving legal advice, and appearing in a representative capacity in court or before an administrative or regulatory agency. The definition of the practice of law varies from state to state. A member of this association should consult the appropriate definition in the member's state.

A member of this association may perform tasks assigned by a lawyer so long as the lawyer maintains a direct relationship with the client, supervises the delegated work, and has complete professional responsibility for the work product. The requirement that a lawyer must maintain a direct relationship with the client does not preclude a member of the law office staff from meeting with the client when such a meeting is necessary to carry out the professional duties assigned by the lawyer.

Various states have adopted requirements applicable to the practice of legal assistants. Any member of this association employed as a legal assistant or whose responsibilities include those of a legal assistant should consult the appropriate requirements in that state. Where conflict exists, the requirements of that state shall control.

This canon is intended to protect the public from receiving legal services from unqualified individuals. "The prohibition of lay intermediaries is intended to insure the loyalty of the lawyer to the client unimpaired by intervening and possibly conflicting interest." Cheatham, *Availability of Legal Services: The Responsibility of the Individual Lawyer and of the Organized Bar,* 12 UCLA L. Rev. 438, 439 (1965).

For a comparison to other codes and rules of professional responsibility and ethics, see:

American Bar Association Model Code of Professional Responsibility DR 3–101(A) and DR 3–103(A).

American Bar Association Model Code of Professional Conduct Rule 5.5(b).

Canon 10. Members of this association shall do all other things incidental, necessary, or expedient to enhance professional responsibility and participation in the administration of justice and public service in cooperation with the legal profession.

§ 2.17 Summary

If a legal secretary adheres to this Code of Ethics and Professional Responsibility, she will not subject the attorney or the law firm to censure for a violation of the Code of Professional Responsibility of the American Bar Association.

Simply stated, as a legal secretary you should:

• Work continually to upgrade your skills and knowledge.

• Be honest and forthright in and out of the office; display exemplary conduct; and inspire the confidence of the public in the legal system.

• Be careful not to solicit business for the attorney or the firm.

• Be careful not to practice law by giving advice or preparing documents without the supervision of an attorney.

• Be careful not to discuss any client or case outside the office or discuss a client's case with the client or the opposing counsel unless authorized to do so by the attorney.

• Be certain to advise the attorney or firm if you know any of the parties on the opposing side of a lawsuit being handled in the office.

• Do your work competently.

• Be careful to follow instructions concerning clients' funds.

Working in an atmosphere where all employees, lawyer and support staff alike, are required to adhere to a strict Code of Ethics, which includes a requirement to continue the learning process and to uphold and improve the judicial system under which we live, is both challenging and rewarding. Enjoy it.

CHAPTER 3

THE LAW OFFICE

Table of Sections

---

§ 3.1 Structure

Law firms range in size from a single lawyer and one secretary to hundreds of lawyers and support personnel (senior partners, junior partners, associates, clerks, secretaries, legal assistants, accountants, etc.). Law office support staffs consist of all of these people, and for a law office to function smoothly, everyone must be apprised of his/her lines of authority and responsibility within the structure of the firm. In any office where there is only one lawyer and one secretary, this is seldom a problem, for there is a single chain of command from the lawyer, and the sole responsibility for control and delegation lies with the lawyer. However, in any office where there is more than one lawyer or more than one secretary, it is necessary to define the chain of command and the specific areas of responsibility in planning, procedures, and delegation of work.

Areas of control, unity of command, specific assignments, and delegation of authority commensurate with responsibility are usually detailed in a law office procedures manual. A copy of this manual is given to each new law office employee, and it is up to that individual employee to become thoroughly familiar with the contents of the manual. Not only does it outline the hierarchy of the firm, but it also contains the duties and responsibilities expected of the employee handling the work at each specific desk in the office. In other words, the work assignment depends upon the desk. The manual also sets out firm policy regarding merit increases, sick leave, vacation, and other similar items.

Even if you are in a one lawyer-one secretary firm, you should have at your desk a written list of your duties to guide you in your routine tasks, and if you do not, you should begin work on one your first day on the job.

§ 3.2 Personnel

Depending upon the size of the office, there may be the following:

- Attorney(s)
- Receptionist
- Secretary(ies)
- Legal assistant(s)
- File clerk(s)
- Bookkeeper (accountant)
- Law clerk(s)
- Office administrator
- Administrative secretary(ies)
- Correspondence secretary(ies)

In this chapter discussion is concerned chiefly with the secretary.

§ 3.3 The Secretary's Skills

The basic requirements for this position are good skills in typing, speedwriting (shorthand) of some type, spelling, composition, grammar, and proofreading.

The legal secretary should correct obvious errors in dictation, such as transposing the terms "plaintiff" and "defendant." If information or instructions are questionable, incomplete, or obviously inaccurate, you should obtain the correct data either from the file or from the attorney. Don't make assumptions or try to guess. Asking questions will save everyone's time in the long run, and your conscientiousness will be appreciated.

When transcribing material, do so accurately. Be aware of words and phrases that sound alike but have different spellings and meanings. Proofread very carefully everything you prepare. A misplaced punctuation mark, the wrong word, or an incorrect dollar amount can be catastrophic and irreversible for the client, the attorney, and you.

§ 3.4 Professional Requirements

Perhaps the single most influential element which transforms one from being just a good legal secretary to a professional legal secretary is the attitude of professionalism which the secretary brings to the position. A legal secretary requires not only excellent skills in the basic requirements of the job but also a conscientious attention to detail, creativity, initiative, courtesy, and tact in dealing with associates and clients. These attributes are found in those persons who set their goal to be the best legal secretary possible and keep that goal alive, day after day. No one comes to the position with this knowledge. It must be learned and cultivated. It is a known fact that how you program your thinking is how you will present yourself to others. The human brain is the most complicated computer known and the least used to its capacity.

Take an active interest in your work. Have procedures explained to you if you don't fully understand them. In most instances the attorney will be happy to take a few minutes to answer your questions and can usually refer you to explanatory books or articles for further clarification.

If you wish to be the best legal secretary possible, pursue the education which the position requires and then go further. Continually upgrade that knowledge in all areas of the law, leaving no part of it undiscovered.

Participate in educational seminars and workshops, take evening classes, or study on your own to make yourself more knowledgeable in your profession. Don't allow yourself to wonder why; find out.

Study for and attain certification as an Accredited Legal Secretary (ALS) and a Certified Professional Legal Secretary (PLS). These coveted certifications will help you realize that learning never stops. In doing so, you make yourself an invaluable member of the lawyer/legal secretary team and open endless horizons.

§ 3.5 Getting the Job Done

Much of the work in a law office is done under tremendous pressure. Meeting deadlines is a way of life for attorneys and for their support staffs. The nature of the legal business is such that emergencies are not uncommon, and there are times when there is simply too much to do.

§ 3.6 Establish Priorities

You can eliminate some of these pressures by handling your routine duties in an efficient, orderly manner. Establish priorities for work to be done and do your best to have things completed before the last minute. Supplies, frequently used telephone numbers and addresses, and reference tools should be kept within easy access.

§ 3.7 Keep an Organized Work Area

A good secretary will accept the responsibility of keeping both her work area, as well as the attorney's, neat and orderly. Each secretary should check with the attorney as to his wishes concerning straightening his desk. Some attorneys prefer that the secretary not clean their desks while others enjoy having someone straighten it up for them. If the secretary is also serving as the receptionist, she should keep the reception area in order. A neat work area promotes efficient work. Files should be replaced in cabinets when they are no longer needed, and law books should be returned to the library.

§ 3.8 The Client

At his initial visit to see the attorney, a client generally has not yet had the opportunity to know the attorney personally. He may have been referred by a friend or by a lawyer referral service. He may have even randomly selected the attorney's name from a directory. The client's first impression of what he can expect from the attorney is reflected through the attorney's staff. Be sure your professional attitude reflects the good public image the attorney deserves.

Give the client your full attention when he first arrives. Remember that to the client his time is just as valuable as the attorney's. Make every effort to see that his appointment is kept as near to the scheduled time as possible. If the attorney is going to be very late on his appointments, call the client or inform him of this when he arrives so that he can be doing something else until the attorney is able to see him. If a client must wait, see that he is comfortable. Offer him coffee and a magazine or newspaper.

Before the attorney is ready to see the client, be sure that you locate the file and make it available for the attorney's use during the conference. Escort the client to the attorney's office, announce his arrival to the attorney, and close the door as you leave. Further, you should be available during the course of the conference to provide the attorney with any other material he needs or to perform any services he requests. You should know the client's name and be familiar with the nature of his case. This indicates to the client that he is important enough to have his name remembered. Never allow your personal feelings toward the client to affect your business relationship with him. The client deserves to be treated courteously at all times and should feel that you, as the secretary, care about his case.

Try not to interrupt the attorney and his client during their allotted appointment period; the client is paying for the attorney's time and he should not have to share it. He should be made to feel that his appointment time with his attorney belongs exclusively to him.

§ 3.9 Confidentiality

A client demands and is entitled to complete confidentiality in all matters he discloses to his attorney or with which the attorney or his secretary may come in contact. There can be no compromise on this subject. It is unethical as well as in poor taste for employees to engage in gossip regarding the affairs of clients.

§ 3.10 Privileged Communications

A lawyer is a fiduciary (a person who manages money and property for another), and his relation with his clients is one of trust and confidence. He never discusses a client's business with outsiders. In fact, information a client gives the lawyer is a privileged communication, and a lawyer cannot be compelled to testify concerning it.

The legal secretary is bound by the same code of ethics as her employer. She cannot solicit business for him, and she must regard everything she knows about a client or a case as confidential. Information the secretary receives from a client in the course of her work is also a privileged communication. Serious consequences may result from discussing facts pertinent to a case or revealing information concerning a legal matter.

There must be no office or client business discussed outside the confines of the office. If a secretary is to be trusted—and a legal secretary must be trustworthy—confidentiality must be maintained at all costs.

If your employer calls you into his office to pick up a file and then starts discussing a case with you, be sure you go over and close his door. Do not talk to a client on the telephone about the details of his case if you are sitting in a reception area where other people can hear your side of the conversation.

It is easy to fall into the habit of discussing client affairs when you are in a room away from the client area; but if the door is open, anyone could be standing within hearing distance.

Refrain from even stating to outsiders that a certain person was in your office or is your client. From that simple statement, they could draw conclusions that would make you guilty of a breach of confidentiality.

If you are in an area where clients approach your desk and have conversations with you, be sure that you do not have any open files or documents on your desk. Human nature is such that people will allow their eyes to wander to whatever is available. If you are waiting to have a document signed, keep it in a file folder. If you are working on a document when someone approaches your desk, cover the material so that it cannot be read easily by the person standing there.

The legal secretary should never discuss the client's matter with him while in the presence of other people. Even when alone with the client, she should not discuss his case beyond lending an attentive ear and offering some words of reassurance.

You should not give the client information regarding his case without authorization from the attorney. Some offices make a practice of sending carbon copies of all letters and legal documents relating to a client's case to the client. Others send only copies of certain letters. You should get a clear understanding of the attorney's wishes in this matter before you automatically send out copies to the client.

Too many secretaries feel that if they do not directly and intentionally tell someone about a client's matter, they have not breached the confidentiality code. You must go beyond that and not indirectly or inadvertently convey information to another person about the affairs of a client.

The legal secretary has more occasion to deal with clients than do most secretaries. This requires her to develop good public relation skills and to use them daily.

§ 3.11   The Client's File

Never permit a client to see his file without express permission from the attorney. It is usually permissible to remove his personal papers (not documents, letters, notes, or work products of the attorney) and let him review them in your presence. He should never remove anything from the office without consent of the attorney. It is good practice to establish a policy with the attorney concerning the dissemination of information to clients and others. When in doubt, don't do it.

§ 3.12   Clothing

Your clothing should reflect respect for your office as well as for yourself. You need not have an extensive wardrobe as long as you are neat and clean and dressed suitably. Conservative clothing is the key. Some secretaries wear clothes which are too casual for the office. Your appearance is the first impression that you make on a client. If you look businesslike and neat, he will have more confidence in you.

§ 3.13   Good Grooming

Your hair should be kept clean and neatly styled. Your hands and fingernails should be clean and well groomed.

§ 3.14   Personal Habits

Since you are often with clients and other attorneys, you must be careful not to allow personal habits to offend the people with whom you deal.

Two complaints that employers have about secretaries are that they chew gum in an unattractive and distracting manner and that they smoke in the presence of clients. A good rule is to smoke only in designated smoking areas out of the view of clients.

§ 3.15   Interoffice Relationships

The secretary who approaches the office each morning with anticipation and enthusiasm will find life much more pleasant than the one who arrives ready "to put in her time" and then at 5 p.m. to wake up and start living. A large portion of the secretary's waking hours are spent in the office. She spends more time with her fellow employees and clients than she does with her family. The relationship should be enjoyable for all involved, but it takes effort on everyone's part.

§ 3.16   Loyalty

Loyalty cannot be dictated or decreed. Nevertheless, the primary function of office personnel is to further the business and prosperity of the employer, while serving the needs of the client. The interests of the employer must come first—ahead of the interests of the personnel. The employer should always be referred to with terms of respect, and every secretary should be a one-person publicity campaign for her office. Complete and absolute confidence in the employer's ability should be reflected in the secretary's personal conduct and in the performance of her duties. If you cannot give loyalty to your employer, it is in your best interests as well as his for you to find employment elsewhere. Do not discuss your employer's foibles or idiosyncrasies with other people. Do not downgrade him or your job. Talking disparagingly of your employer or the legal profession is not suitable party conversation, and it is definitely not professional.

Every employee in a law office has a part in the firm's public relations. If people are to have faith and confidence in a law firm, they must have faith and confidence not only in the attorneys, but also in the secretaries and other support personnel. It is at the level of day-to-day contacts with clients or prospective clients (everyone is a prospective client) that the greatest opportunities for good public relations exist. All secretaries and law office personnel should bear this in mind at all times.

§ 3.17   Tact

A good legal secretary uses tact in her relationships with office personnel and clients. Tact is defined as "a quick or intuitive appreciation of what is fit, proper, or right; and a fine or ready mental discernment shown in saying or doing the proper thing, or especially in avoiding what would offend or disturb." Tact is a learned skill that becomes habit. Its elements consist of sensitiveness of feeling, insight into the motives of others, experience as to consequences of conduct, and subtlety of reasoning with reference to detail. Tact is a requirement in the practice of law and in the efficient operation of a law office. It cannot be overrated and is a quality that is required of all personnel.

§ 3.18 Sense of Humor

A sense of humor is a great asset to the legal secretary. It helps in handling people and in interoffice relationships. Do not permit yourself to get emotionally involved in the cases of the office. Treat other members on the staff as friends. Be cooperative, helpful, and thoughtful.

§ 3.19 Evenness of Disposition

Evenness of disposition and personality are distinct business assets and are qualities that are required in legal secretaries. In the office just one mood should prevail—cheerfulness. Minor irritations should be shrugged off and not be allowed to interfere with efficient work. Just as you leave all affairs of the office at the office, leave personal affairs at home.

§ 3.20 Pleasant Personality

Be pleasant to everyone. If your workload is light and you know someone else is getting behind, offer to help. Don't form cliques within an office. This is extremely bad for morale and a detriment to the firm. If there is one person with whom you simply cannot get along, avoid that person as much as possible, but don't try to turn others against her. As long as that person is working smoothly within the firm's structure, you must not be critical. Remember, by criticizing others, you are inviting criticism of yourself.

In your relationships with other employees, maintain a friendly, helpful attitude but not to such a degree that it affects the efficient progress of your duties. Personal conversation can get out of hand and consume too much of the time which should be spent attending to the business of the firm.

No edict concerning interoffice gossip is enforceable. However, you are expected to use sound discretion and good judgment in this regard at all times. Interoffice problems must not extend out of the office or influence the efficient conduct of business.

You are not required to socialize with other office personnel, but you should be sociable. Courtesy takes no more energy than sullenness and is infinitely more pleasant for everyone. Refrain from a "that's not my job" attitude.

§ 3.21 Punctuality

Punctuality is one of the traits lawyers look for in a secretary. Habitual tardiness is a trait that seems to flow over to other areas, and a busy law office cannot tolerate a secretary who does not discipline her time.

§ 3.22 Confidence

A legal secretary should give the impression of confidence to the clients. The beginning secretary should act confident, even if she doesn't feel confident. Of course, she should not communicate incorrect information to the client, but she should give the client the impression that she cares and will get the information for him or have the attorney contact him. It is particularly unnerving for a client to feel that the secretary is uninformed or blundering along.

§ 3.23 Handling Personal Affairs

All personal telephone calls and personal business should be taken care of on the secretary's own time. If personal telephone calls or personal business of an urgent nature must be taken care of during office hours, they should be handled so as not to interfere with the smooth and efficient operation of the office. Discretion and common sense should dictate the course of the secretary's conduct in this regard. Keep foremost in mind the job, its duties, and the fact that you are in a business office, and there will be no problems with abuse of this privilege.

§ 3.24 Addressing the Attorney

In all conversations with the attorney in the presence of any third person and all times over the telephone and while outside the confines of the office, the attorney is to be addressed as "Mr. _____." The law office is a place of business, and the lawyer should be treated with respect. If it is the custom in your office to address the other personnel, including lawyers, by their first names, it is certainly permissible and proper to do so—when not in the presence of outside people or clients.

The secretary should learn to adjust to the moods, actions, and reactions of the attorneys and other members of the staff. Be considerate of other people's feelings. By making allowances for their imperfections, you will find that they are willing to make allowances for yours.

§ 3.25 The Secretary as a Receptionist

The necessary qualities of the receptionist are intelligence, a pleasing appearance, friendliness of manner suitable to the dignity of her position, courtesy, patience, resourcefulness, and attentiveness. She must always keep in mind the lasting effect of first impressions and realize that a client's attitude may be largely influenced by his initial contact with the receptionist.

The receptionist should receive every caller courteously, give him prompt attention, and continue to give him attention until the purpose of his visit is concluded. She should be as pleasant as is consistent with the efficient transaction of business, but she must not waste time by unnecessary visiting.

The receptionist should announce promptly the arrival of the client to the particular attorney's secretary (or to the attorney if that is office practice). This is essential, since it assures the client that his business is being handled. The secretary then immediately notifies the attorney; if the attorney is in conference, she informs the client.

Since the receptionist will be in constant contact with the public and under its scrutiny, she is expected to keep her desk and work area neat at all times. She should practice good housekeeping habits to make sure that the reception area is a pleasant and comfortable place and portrays the professional image expected of law offices.

Many people visit attorneys for personal or financial problems and are often anxious, upset, and nervous. For some, it is their first visit to an attorney, which only intensifies their anxiety. The pleasant, helpful attitude of the receptionist can do much to relieve the situation. The receptionist may find herself in the presence of a tearful, distraught client. She should arrange to have the person taken to a private area.

The receptionist should address and announce callers by titles such as Mr., Mrs., Ms., or Dr. If a client or caller is well known in the firm and has asked that you use his first name, you may do so, but this should be at the request of the client.

Be conscious of reception room behavior, at all times being careful not to perform personal grooming, etc. Avoid engaging in personal conversations either in person or on the telephone in the reception area.

When making appointments, the receptionist or secretary must be sure to get not only the client's name but also his telephone number. It is a good idea to make appointments for the attorneys tentative unless they are available to confirm the appointment. If an attorney is out of the office, there is a good possibility that he may be making an appointment with a judge or a client whom he meets outside the office.

Encourage your attorney to keep you informed of any appointments or hearings that he has scheduled. It is good to check his calendar frequently during the day to make sure that he has scheduled no appointments without your knowledge.

If the client has been into the office, you will have a telephone contact number for him. If he is a new client, you should obtain a call back number when you make the appointment.

Always find out when your attorney wants appointments scheduled. Some prefer to have no appointments until after 10 a.m., so that they can spend the first hours of the morning reading the mail and dictating.

Another function of the receptionist is to know how long the attorney will be gone when he leaves the office. If he has appointments set, she should remind him of those before he leaves.

A good receptionist will use her judgment to determine which clients the attorney will see without appointments, which should be seen by another attorney, and which can be taken care of by the receptionist or a secretary.

When the lawyer will not or cannot see callers, she should make explanations to the callers in such a way that she does not antagonize them. It is always difficult when someone just "drops in" to see the attorney for "a few minutes." She should check with the attorney to see if he can see the caller. She should always respond courteously, but she should also realize that she must protect the attorney from interruption when he requests that she do so.

Salesmen are usually seen by the office administrator.

§ 3.26 The Legal Secretary as a Notary Public

A notary public is a person authorized by law to administer oaths, take and certify depositions, and take acknowledgments of signatures on deeds, mortgages, liens, powers of attorney, and other instruments in writing. The legal secretary may be requested by her employer to become a notary public. In this capacity she can notarize documents for both clients of the law firm and others requesting her services.

§ 3.27 Legal Requirements

The position of notary public is one of great responsibility and is not to be considered lightly. The requirements vary from state to state but usually require a person to be a resident of the state for a stated period of time, to be 18 years of age or older, and to have good moral character. Some states administer examinations to applicants; others require only an application and a bond.

In the performance of your duties as a notary public, you should familiarize yourself with a number of the terms and practices to which you will be exposed. Read the material published by the state on the duties and limitations of a notary public.

§ 3.28   Oath

An oath is a solemn or official declaration by a person before a duly authorized official, such as a notary public, to the effect that the statements which he has just made or is about to make are true.

§ 3.29   Affirmation

Affirmation is similar to an oath in meaning and importance but for religious reasons does not include an appeal to God or any supreme being.

§ 3.30   Affidavit

An affidavit is a written statement sworn to as being true before a notary public or some other officer authorized to perform this function. The affidavit contains the certification of the notary public that the statement was sworn to (or affirmed) and signed in her presence by the affiant (the person who is making the affidavit).

§ 3.31   Acknowledgment

An acknowledgment is required for some documents, such as deeds and mortgages, and consists of a statement that the signer of the document declared to the notary public that he signed the document. The notary public then signs the acknowledgment and dates it as of the day the client appears before her.

§ 3.32   Proper Identification of Affiant

In order to perform her functions properly, the notary public must be familiar with the person who appears before her or be presented with some means of identification establishing the identity of the person. The legal secretary should be very careful to require such identification if she does not know the individual personally. If none is produced, she should refuse to take the acknowledgment. The notary public is also restricted in the performance of her duties in that she cannot act in her official capacity in those instances in which she is personally involved or interested. She is also not permitted to function outside the territorial limits for which she is appointed. (Appointments are made for a county or counties or for the state, depending upon state law.)

§ 3.33   Necessity of Personal Appearance

The notary public should take no acknowledgments by telephone. The person whose signature is on the document and acknowledging such signature should appear personally to make the acknowledgment and/or sign the document. Where an oath is required (as in an affidavit), she should administer the oath, have the person sign in her presence, and then she should sign and affix her seal, if applicable. Some secretaries are reluctant to go through the formality of the oath, but in those instances where the document reads "sworn to before me," or similar wording, it is essential that she perform this function.

The notary public can be liable for damages resulting from the improper performance of her duties. Therefore, upon receiving the appointment of notary public, she should carefully read all information relating to the duties and responsibilities which apply to a notary serving in that state's jurisdiction.

It is not unusual for an affiant to ask a notary to backdate an acknowledgment. The date on which the instrument is acknowledged is the date which must appear on the acknowledgment. To do otherwise is illegal and could result not only in loss of the notary commission but also in a malpractice action against the law firm.

Illustrations 3–1 through 3–9 are general formats of acknowledgments (individual and corporate) and verifications (individual and corporate). Some states use a testimonium clause (In Witness Whereof....) in each acknowledgment; other states omit this clause. The secretary should check to find out what is done in her state.

Illustration 3–1 *

ACKNOWLEDGMENT BY AN INDIVIDUAL

State of (a) _____
County of (b) _____

On this (c) _____ day of (d) _____ in the year (e) _____, before me (f) _____, a Notary Public in and for said state, personally appeared (g) _____, known to me to be the person(s) who executed the within (h) _____ and acknowledged to me that (i) _____ executed the same for the purposes therein stated.

(j) _____

---

* Reprinted from The National Notary. Copyright, 1980. Published by the National Notary Association, 23012 Ventura Blvd., Woodland Hills, CA 91364. Reprinted by permission of the publisher.

INSTRUCTIONS FOR THE NOTARY

(a) *State* in which the notarization is performed.

(b) *County* where the notarization is performed.

(c) *Day of month* the notarization is performed.

(d) *Month* the notarization is performed.

(e) *Year* the notarization is performed.

(f) *Name of the Notary* performing the notarization.

(g) *Name of the individual* who has signed the document and is personally appearing before the Notary. (May contain names of more than one individual if these persons appear before the Notary at the same time and place.)

(h) *Type of document* notarized. (For example, grant deed, homestead affidavit, etc.)

(i) *"He"* or *"she,"* as applicable to the signer; or *"they"* for more than one signer.

(j) The Notary's official *signature,* legibly written, and his Notary *seal,* clearly affixed.

Illustration 3–2

ACKNOWLEDGMENT BY A PARTNER

State of (a) _____
County of (b) _____

    On this (c) _____ day of (d) _____ in the year (e) _____, before me (f) _____, a Notary Public in and for said state, personally appeared (g) _____, of (h) _____ known to me to be the person(s) who executed the within (i) _____ in behalf of said partnership and acknowledged to me that (j) _____ executed the same for the purposes therein stated.

                         (k)_____

INSTRUCTIONS FOR THE NOTARY

(a) *State* in which the notarization is performed.

(b) *County* where the notarization is performed.

(c) *Day of month* the notarization is performed.

(d) *Month* the notarization is performed.

(e) *Year* the notarization is performed.

(f) *Name of the Notary* performing the notarization.

(g) *Name of the partner* who has signed the document and is personally appearing before the Notary. (May contain names of more than one partner if these persons appear before the Notary at the same time and place.)

(h) *Name of the partnership,* as indicated on the proof of partnership.

(i) *Type of document* notarized.

(j) *"He"* or *"she,"* as applicable to the partner; or *"they"* for more than one partner.

(k) The Notary's official *signature,* legibly written, and his notary *seal,* clearly affixed.

Illustration 3–3

ACKNOWLEDGMENT BY A CORPORATE OFFICER

State of (a) _____
County of (b) _____

On this (c) _____ day of (d) _____ in the year (e) _____, before me (f) _____, a Notary Public in and for said state, personally appeared (g) _____, (h) _____ of (i) _____, known to me to be the person who executed the within (j) _____ in behalf of said corporation and acknowledged to me that (k) _____ executed the same for the purposes therein stated.

(l) _____

INSTRUCTIONS FOR THE NOTARY

(a) *State* in which the notarization is performed.

(b) *County* where the notarization is performed.

(c) *Day of month* the notarization is performed.

(d) *Month* the notarization is performed.

(e) *Year* the notarization is performed.

(f) *Name* of the Notary performing the notarization.

(g) *Name of the corporate officer* who has signed the document and is personally appearing before the Notary.

(h) *Corporate title of the person* exactly as it appears on the evidence proving the person's status as a corporate officer (president, vice president, etc.).

(i) *Name of the corporation* exactly as it appears on the document and on the evidence proving the person's status as a corporate officer.

(j) *Type of document* notarized.

(k) *"He"* or *"she,"* as applicable to the corporate officer.

(*l*) The Notary's official *signature*, legibly written, and his Notary *seal*, clearly affixed.

Illustration 3–4

ACKNOWLEDGMENT BY AN ATTORNEY IN FACT FOR PRINCIPAL OR SURETY

State of (a) _____
County of (b) _____

On this (c) _____ day of (d) _____ in the year (e) _____, before me (f) _____, a Notary Public in and for said state, personally appeared (g) _____, Attorney In Fact for (h) _____, known to me to be the person who executed the within (i) _____ in behalf of said principal or surety, and acknowledged to me that (j) _____ executed the same for the purposes therein stated.

(k) _____

INSTRUCTIONS FOR THE NOTARY

(a) *State* in which the notarization is performed.

(b) *County* where the notarization is performed.

(c) *Day of month* the notarization is performed.

(d) *Month* the notarization is performed.

(e) *Year* the notarization is performed.

(f) *Name of the Notary* performing the notarization.

(g) *Name of the attorney in fact* who has signed the document and is personally appearing before the Notary.

(h) *Name of the person or surety* for whom the attorney in fact is acting.

(i) *Type of document* notarized.

(j) *"He"* or *"she,"* as applicable to the attorney in fact.

(k) The Notary's official *signature*, legibly written, and his Notary *seal*, clearly affixed.

Illustration 3–5

ACKNOWLEDGMENT BY A PUBLIC OFFICER, DEPUTY,
TRUSTEE, ADMINISTRATOR, GUARDIAN, OR EXECUTOR

State of (a) _____
County of (b) _____

On this (c) _____ day of (d) _____ in the year (e) _____, before me (f) _____, a Notary Public in and for said state, personally appeared (g) _____, (h) _____, known to me to be the person(s) who executed the within (i) _____ in behalf of said (j) _____ and acknowledged to me that (k) _____ executed the same for the purposes therein stated.

(l) _____

INSTRUCTIONS FOR THE NOTARY

(a) *State* in which the notarization is performed.

(b) *County* where the notarization is performed.

(c) *Day of month* the notarization is performed.

(d) *Month* the notarization is performed.

(e) *Year* the notarization is performed.

(f) *Name of the Notary* performing the notarization.

(g) *Name of the person* who has signed the document and is personally appearing before the Notary. (May contain names of more than one person if they all appear before the Notary at the same time and place.)

(h) *The person's official title,* as indicated on the papers proving his status.

(i) *Type of document* notarized.

(j) *Name of the public corporation, agency, political subdivision, estate, or person* for which the person is signing.

(k) *"He"* or *"she"* as applicable to the signer; or *"they"* for more than one signer.

(l) The Notary's official *signature,* legibly written, and his Notary *seal,* clearly affixed.

Illustration 3–6

ACKNOWLEDGMENT BY A PERSON WHO CANNOT WRITE
HIS NAME (SIGNATURE BY MARK)

State of (a) _____
County of (b) _____

On this (c) _____ day of (d) _____ in the year (e) _____, before me (f) _____, a Notary Public in and for said state, personally appeared (g) _____, who made (h) _____ mark in my presence. I signed (i) _____ name at (j) _____ request and in (k) _____ presence on the within (l) _____ and (m) _____ acknowledge to me and the two witnesses, who have signed and printed their names and addresses hereto, that (n) _____ made (o) _____ mark on the same for the purposes therein stated.

(p) _____ _____

(p) _____ _____

(q) _____

INSTRUCTIONS FOR THE NOTARY

(a) *State* in which the notarization is performed.

(b) *County* where the notarization is performed.

(c) *Day of month* the notarization is performed.

(d) *Month* the notarization is performed.

(e) *Year* the notarization is performed.

(f) *Name of the Notary* performing the notarization.

(g) *Name of the person unable to write his name.*

(h), (i), (j), (k) *"His"* or *"her,"* as applicable to the person unable to write his name.

(l) *Type of document* notarized.

(m), (n) *"He"* or *"she,"* as applicable to the person unable to write his name.

(o) *"His"* or *"her,"* as applicable to the person unable to write his name.

(p) *Signatures of two witnesses and their addresses.*

(q) The Notary's official *signature,* legibly written, and his Notary *seal,* clearly affixed.

Illustration 3–7

JURAT

State of (a) _____
County of (b) _____

    Subscribed and sworn to (or affirmed) before me this (c) _____ day of (d) _____ in the year (e) _____.

                                    (f) _____

INSTRUCTIONS FOR THE NOTARY

(a) *State* in which the notarization is performed.

(b) *County* where the notarization is performed.

(c) *Day of month* the notarization is performed.

(d) *Month* the notarization is performed.

(e) *Year* the notarization is performed.

(f) The Notary's official *signature,* legibly written, and his Notary *seal,* clearly affixed.

NOTE: Unless law prescribes a specific wording for the jurat oath, the following wording may be used: "Do you solemnly swear (or affirm) that the statements made in this affidavit (or deposition) are the truth, the whole truth, and nothing but the truth?" The affiant must answer affirmatively.

Illustration 3–8

ACKNOWLEDGMENT BY A PERSON WHO DOES NOT APPEAR BEFORE A NOTARY (SUBSCRIBING WITNESS ACKNOWLEDGMENT)

I, (a) _____, do solemnly swear (or affirm) that (b) _____, personally known to me, has executed the within (c) _____ in my presence, and has acknowledged to me that (d) _____ executed the same for the purposes therein stated and requested that I sign my name on the within document as a subscribing witness.

                            (e) _____

State of (f) _____ County of (g) _____ Subscribed and sworn (or affirmed) before me this (h) _____ day of (i) _____ in the year (j) _____.

                          (k) _____

INSTRUCTIONS FOR THE NOTARY

(a) *Name of the subscribing witness* who is personally appearing before the Notary to swear (or affirm) that he has seen another person sign the presented document.

(b) *Name of person who does not appear before the Notary,* but who has previously signed the document in the presence of the subscribing witness.

(c) *Type of document* notarized.

(d) *"He"* or *"she,"* as applicable to the person.

(e) *Signature of the subscribing witness.*

(f) *State* in which the notarization is performed.

(g) *County* where the notarization is performed.

(h) *Day of month* the notarization is performed.

(i) *Month* the notarization is performed.

(j) *Year* the notarization is performed.

(k) The Notary's official *signature,* legibly written, and his Notary *seal,* clearly affixed.

Illustration 3–9

CERTIFICATE FOR A CERTIFIED COPY OR FACSIMILE
OF AN ORIGINAL

State of (a) _____
County of (b) _____

I, (c) _____, a Notary Public in and for said state, do certify that on (d) _____, I carefully compared the attached facsimile of (e) _____ with the original I now hold in my possession. It is a complete, full, true and exact facsimile of the document it purports to reproduce. Witness my hand and official seal.

(f) _____

INSTRUCTIONS FOR THE NOTARY

(a) *State* in which the notarization is performed.

(b) *County* where the notarization is performed.

(c) *Name of the Notary* performing the notarization.

(d) *Date* the notarization is performed.

(e) *Type of document* from which the facsimile is made.

(f) Notary's official *signature,* legibly written, and his Notary *seal,* clearly affixed.

NOTE: **(1)** The Notary should ascertain that a certified copy of the document cannot be obtained from a public recording agency, and that reproduction of the document does not violate law or official directive (as is the case with a naturalization certificate).

(2) A hand-written copy is not a facsimile because it does not reproduce the original document exactly.

§ 3.34 Answering the Telephone

The client often gets his first impression of the office from the person answering the telephone. If she answers pleasantly with a "smile in her voice," his impression will be a positive one. Unfortunately, not all secretaries understand the value of this technique. They answer in a very mechanical or impatient tone of voice, which indicates that they feel the caller is interrupting or inconveniencing them. If the secretary has a scowl on her face, she has a scowl in her voice. Remember that the caller cannot see that you are talking to another client or that you are rushing to get out an urgent document for filing before the court closes. His business is very important to him, and he deserves your attention, courtesy, and concern.

§ 3.35 Rules to Follow

Observation of good telephone courtesy will make your day as well as the client's more pleasant. Follow these rules in answering the phone:

- Use a pleasant, positive voice.
- Do not talk too quickly or too quietly.
- Take time to get correct spelling of names and repeat phone numbers to make sure that you have written them correctly.
- Do not bang the receiver when you lay it down on your desk to get information.
- If you must leave your desk to get some information, place the person on "hold" so that the caller does not hear the office conversation.
- Do not have gum or food in your mouth when you answer the phone.
- Make an effort to help the client without giving legal advice.
- Give the client an estimated time when you expect the attorney but avoid being exact.
- Do not tell the client where the attorney is (except when he is in court).
- Do not quote fees or discuss the client's case unless you have been instructed to do so by the attorney in specific situations.
- Conclude a phone call with a friendly "thank you" or "good-bye."
- Use the telephone sparingly for personal calls.
- Be attentive and listen without interrupting.
- Avoid slang in your conversations.
- Convey courtesy, sincere interest, and understanding of the other person's point of view by your voice and words.

§ 3.36 Incoming Calls

Procedures for handling incoming calls vary in firms where there is a central receptionist or operator. In some firms, calls coming through the receptionist or operator are placed directly to the attorney to minimize the amount of time the client must spend on the telephone. Some people resent having to go through more than one person to get to the attorney.

In other firms, the calls are referred to the attorney's secretary rather than placing them directly to the attorney. The secretary can then get any file the attorney might need for the call or handle the call if the attorney is unable to take it.

§ 3.37   Screening Calls

Modern telephone etiquette suggests that calls be answered by the person to whom they are directed, and fewer attorneys have all calls screened as a normal procedure. There will be circumstances, however, when it is necessary to screen calls.

The secretary must be careful not to be rude in an effort to determine who is calling. A simple "May I tell him who is calling?" is usually sufficient to obtain the name of the caller. By knowing in advance who is calling, the attorney can get any information or file he may need to handle the call in a minimum of time. When a call has been screened and the attorney does not wish to take the call, you must be tactful in explaining so the caller does not get the impression that the attorney is "too busy" for him or he is not important to the attorney. The attorney should be advised if the caller appears upset by being unable to speak with him.

§ 3.38   Taking Messages

When the attorney is in but does not wish to be disturbed by calls, the secretary or receptionist must use tact in relaying this information to the caller. She should take a complete message (name, phone number, time of call, and matter called about), assuring the client that she will give this message to the attorney. Some attorneys are very good about returning calls; others are not. The secretary should keep a record of all calls coming in and messages given the attorney. NCR paper or carboned message pads are very useful for this purpose. The secretary can give one copy of the message to the attorney, retaining a copy for herself. Then she has a ready reference of phone numbers and callers.

§ 3.39   When the Attorney Is Out of the Office

If the attorney is out of the office, the secretary should not disclose his location. Most people are satisfied with a standard answer such as "he is in court"; "he is out of the office"; "he is in a meeting." Do not give a specific time when you expect him to return if you can avoid it. Again, deal in generalities.

§ 3.40   Handling the Client

The client, however, does need to feel that you care and are concerned. Instead of just replying that the attorney is not there, you might go on to ask if there is something that you can help with. If you know the nature of the problem, you can then evaluate whether you should attempt to contact the attorney away from the office or refer the client's problem to another member of the firm.

With experience you will learn which clients are persistent callers, which have genuine problems, and which just want a sympathetic listener. For the latter you provide that sympathetic ear. You listen and make comments which are reassuring such as "I know Mr. Attorney is concerned and is working on your case." "Yes, I understand how you feel. I will relay this information to Mr. Attorney and have him get back with you."

The irate client who calls in to berate you and/or the attorney for what he considers your failings or poor handling of his case should be transferred as quickly as possible to the attorney. In the absence of the attorney you should listen and give him an opportunity to clear the air; however, you should not permit this to go on and on. You have work to get done. Interrupt when you can and tell him pleasantly that you will have the attorney call him as soon as he returns. Then do it.

§ 3.41   Answering Promptly

All calls should be answered by the second ring whenever possible. If you are talking to a client, say "Excuse me" and answer the telephone. During office hours, there must always be someone available to answer the telephone; it must never be left unattended. Learn to recognize voices; call clients by name except when other clients or attorneys are present as this may present a breach of confidentiality.

§ 3.42   When the Caller Is on Hold

When the caller has been placed on "hold," check back frequently and remind the attorney if he is too long in answering the call. It is better to call a person back than to have him wait on "hold" for a long period of time. This ties up the phone lines and can be an irritant for the caller.

§ 3.43   Long Distance Calling

Follow your firm's procedures for identifying client-chargeable long distance calls. These calls represent a substantial cost to the firm and should be promptly and carefully recorded.

§ 3.44 Operator–Assisted Calls

Operator-assisted calls are rarely cost effective. You can usually place several direct dial calls for the same cost as one operator-assisted call, and good judgment should be used in determining when an operator-assisted call is necessary. Keep in mind that operator-assisted calls are also more time-consuming for the secretary, the attorney, and the person being called. There are circumstances which justify operator-assisted calls, but they should be rare.

§ 3.45 Checking Time Zones

Be aware of time zones and check before placing a call to another area of the United States to be sure that the office will be open. It does no good to place a call from New York to California when it is 9 a.m. in New York. People in California are in bed. Many companies have an answering service or machine, so the call will be answered and you will be charged for the call.

§ 3.46 Frequently Called Numbers

The secretary should keep an accurate, up-to-date record of names, addresses, and phone numbers of persons who are not clients but with whom the firm does business. These can be kept in a card file or in a notebook. It would include numbers of the courts, process servers, court reporters, insurance adjusters and agents, tax bureaus, office supply firms, home phone numbers of office employees, etc. This would also be a good place to note the attorney's social security number and registration number as issued by the state supreme court.

§ 3.47 Placing Calls to Other Offices

Modern telephone etiquette suggests that calls be placed by the person actually making the call. However, many attorneys prefer not to follow this practice and have their secretaries place their calls for them. Although you must follow the attorney's instructions, you can encourage him to place his own calls whenever possible by seeing that he has telephone numbers readily available at his desk. If the attorney prefers to have you place the call for him, put him on the line as soon as you are being connected with the person you are calling. The person initiating the call should do the waiting, and you should be sure the attorney is aware of any adverse reactions you receive from people who have been kept waiting.

§ 3.48 Summary of Telephone Etiquette

The telephone is the lifeline of the law office. It is the most important method of communication. If it is not answered correctly,

this can create an unfavorable impression on clients and people in the legal community. The secretary or receptionist who has a positive attitude about this important function renders an invaluable service to her firm.

§ 3.49 Copying Machines

A copying machine is an essential piece of equipment in law offices. The secretary keyboards only the original and makes the necessary copies. Most courts permit copies to be used for originals. With the use of bond paper, the copy looks as good as the original; however, the signatures must be original.

§ 3.50 Transcribing Equipment

Another essential piece of equipment found in law offices is the transcriber used in transcribing the machine dictation.

§ 3.51 Dictation Equipment

Dictation equipment permits the attorney to originate documents much faster than by any other method. Dictating material to a secretary, who takes it down in shorthand and then transcribes it, requires the time of two persons for the dictation. If the originator handwrites the material, it is more time-consuming for the writer and is harder for the secretary to transcribe. Handwriting can be difficult to decipher and mistakes can occur. Using machine dictation, the author can dictate whenever he has the opportunity without relying upon someone else to be available. When the secretary is transcribing from machine dictation, she can follow her typing and catch errors as they occur.

Today, dictation equipment is of high quality and can be adapted to meet the needs of any office. An office that is using old equipment which is difficult to operate or not operating properly should consider updating to obtain maximum efficiency.

§ 3.52 Types

There are three basic categories of dictation equipment: desktop models, portable models, and central dictating units which use either endless loop media or discrete media (cassettes, disks, or belts). "Media" is the term used by the word processing industry to identify material used for storing typewritten information on electronic systems.

§ 3.53 Desktop Models

Desktop models are usually located at both the attorney's desk and the secretary's desk. The attorney's unit provides for dictation and is equipped with a microphone; the secretary's unit provides for transcription and is equipped with a headset and a foot pedal. Some offices prefer to have all units equipped for both dictating and transcribing so that during peak periods the machines can be used in any way needed. The desktop units use discrete media cassettes, disks, or belts. Cassettes are easier for the secretary to handle and offer sound quality.

§ 3.54 Portable Models

Portable models are used principally by attorneys who dictate while they are away from the office. They can be purchased in many sizes; some are small enough to fit into a shirt or coat pocket. They are particularly valuable for persons who spend a lot of time in cars, planes, or remote locations. They are also useful in interviewing witnesses both away from the office and in the office. Many people are intimidated by a microphone. After initially telling the individual that the conversation is being recorded, the attorney would place the recorder containing the microphone in his pocket. In a very few minutes, the witness will lose all awareness of the microphone and be able to communicate freely.

Several companies offer transcribers which accept conventional-size cassettes and microcassettes by utilizing an adapter placed on the machine. This is cost-effective because the adapter costs less than a second transcriber, while offering the flexibility of two forms of input.

The portable unit is also useful for recording seminars and speeches. The secretary can then type the material for reference or study by other members of the firm.

§ 3.55 Central Recording Systems

A central recording system is a dictation system with the recorder located in one main area, but with dictating and transcribing units in many locations. Central recording systems are generally classified according to the type of media used in the system—endless loop or discrete, single-unit media. There are numerous advantages to a central system, which are not available in a desktop unit:

- Many dictators can be accommodated at a low cost per unit.
- A variety of dictation can be handled from a short memo or letter to a lengthy brief or document.
- The dictator is relieved of handling the media. Only the transcriber or system attendant handles the media.

- By use of a telephone system, one unit can record dictation by several persons, both inside and outside of the firm, without purchasing several dictation units.
- Input can be through the telephone or a desk microphone.
- The dictator does not have to carry the dictation media to the transcriptionist.

§ 3.56   Endless Loop Media Systems

Endless loop media is a very long loop of tape (usually sealed in a long narrow tank) on which the dictator records dictation for transcription. Systems which utilize endless loop media offer the advantage of non-handling of the media by either the dictator or transcriptionist. As the person dictates, a light appears on the secretary's desk unit, indicating that it is top priority material (red light) or regular dictation (green light). She can begin transcribing within a few seconds after the dictator starts dictating. Both transcription and dictation can occur simultaneously. A disadvantage of endless loop dictation is that it is difficult to process dictation out of sequence. With some systems, it is possible to locate a priority item before the previous material is transcribed, but this is not as easy as on discrete media systems. The dictation cannot be filed and kept for future reference. It is possible to have more than one dictation station and one transcription station using the same endless loop.

§ 3.57   Discrete Media Systems

Discrete media are recording media that are individually distinct—that can be filed, mailed, moved, and otherwise separately handled. The discrete media central recording systems can use minicassettes, microcassettes, belts, or disks. There are three types of hookups which determine how the dictator will have access to the recorder: nonselector, manual selector, and automatic selector. For a firm with several attorneys using the dictation system, the automatic selector is recommended.

The nonselector system is connected to only one recorder, which means that if one person is dictating, another dictator must wait until the first is finished. In a manual selector station, the dictating unit is hooked up to several recorders. The dictator can select a recorder that is not busy by positioning a switch at his station. A light or special telephone tone indicates whether the recorder is busy or free. The dictator would then reposition the switch to another recorder. The automatic selector system is much more sophisticated. There are several recorders, and when the dictator picks up his dictating unit (telephone or microphone), he is automatically tied into a free recorder.

If all systems are in use, he receives a tone and must wait until one of the recorders is free.

§ 3.58 Dual–Track Cassette System

Modern dictating systems offer many features which make transcription and dictation easier. One system offers a dual-track cassette, which permits the dictator to add or modify material without erasing the original recording. Dictation takes place on two tracks. There is a beep programmed into the system which signals the transcriptionist that a modification has been made and that she should switch tracks for the inserted material. A second beep alerts her to return to the original track.

§ 3.59 Automatic Measured Review

An automatic measured review is provided on many systems. The dictator can set the machine for one to nine words (usually four); after an interruption, the dictator can activate the unit to back up the desired number of words automatically.

§ 3.60 Automatic Changer

With an automatic changer on the system, when one cassette or disk is full, another automatically is activated. This provides up to $12\frac{1}{2}$ hours of continuous recording time.

§ 3.61 Electronic Queuing

Some companies offer electronic queuing, which indicates by audible sound the end of the recording or special instructions from the dictator.

§ 3.62 Voice Operated Relay

Telephone or PBX centralized systems can be equipped with a voice operated relay (VOR). These relays stop operation of the unit when the dictator is silent and reactivate the unit at the sound of the voice. This is particularly helpful when the dictator pauses to gather his thoughts or to answer a phone call. Without it, the unit continues running and uses up valuable dictation space on the media.

§ 3.63 Privacy Lockout

A privacy lockout is available for central systems. This ensures that material dictated by one individual is not heard by anyone queuing into the system after the dictator has finished. The sound head automatically moves forward and locks so that no one can access into that dictated material.

§ 3.64 Telephone Input

By using a telephone input system, the dictator can call into the system from outside the firm and from any distance away from the firm. Material can be dictated at any hour of the day or night to be transcribed by the secretary while the dictator is away from the office. No media must be delivered from the dictator to the secretary.

§ 3.65 Selection

In determining which dictation equipment should be purchased by the firm, the amount and type of dictation should be considered. Perhaps a combination of systems would work best for the needs of the firm. The place of origination of documents should be considered. All offices should recognize that the quality of the input directly affects the quality of the output.

§ 3.66 Summary of Law Office Equipment

A secretary is able to produce better work on good quality equipment than on poor, inadequate equipment. It is an investment that will pay for itself many times over in typing, time saved, and quality of product produced.

§ 3.67 Supplies

The secretary is often responsible for ordering supplies and maintaining an inventory of supplies. She should visit the local dealers periodically to learn what is new on the market that would be an improvement over what the office is using. Her office files should contain a list of local dealers with phone numbers and addresses. A word of caution—beware of phone solicitors from out of state offering to sell you office supplies at a large discount because of a close-out, a refused order, a bankrupt business, or an order that was sent to your area by mistake. The reasons they give for offering such savings are numerous, but when you receive your order, you find that the supplies are old, stale, or defective.

A reputable supplier will work with you and replace defective merchandise. Do not order in quantities that are unrealistic for your firm. There are discounts for buying in quantity, but you must be sure of the shelf life of the material purchased before you place a bulk order. A good secretary is cost-conscious.

The supply cabinet should have an inventory on the door listing the minimum amount that is kept on hand so that more can be ordered to maintain that amount. New supplies should be placed behind older supplies so they will be used last. A well-organized supply cabinet can save both money and time.

Following is a list of some of the stationery supplies used by law offices:

Letterhead is used for office correspondence. It is often engraved and states the firm's name, address, telephone and fax numbers, and the individual members of the firm. A high quality bond paper is used.

Continuation sheets (sometimes called second sheets) are of the same paper used for the letterhead. Although they do not have the letterhead on them, they may have the firm's name engraved or printed on them. These are used for additional pages of a letter.

Envelopes to match the letterhead are used for office correspondence.

Manila stock envelopes of various sizes are used to mail bulky documents and papers that cannot be folded.

Letter-size white paper, which may or may not be ruled, $8\frac{1}{2}''\times 11''$, is used in most states for legal documents. This standard is set by the individual states. Federal courts now require all pleadings to be on letter-size paper.

Legal cap is white paper, $8\frac{1}{2}''\times 13''$ or $8\frac{1}{2}''\times 14''$, with a wide ruled left margin ($1\frac{1}{4}''$) and a narrow ruled right margin ($\frac{1}{2}''$). It is used for both legal documents and court papers. In some states legal cap has numbers along the left margin corresponding to the line spaces of typing. Some firms have their legal cap printed at the top with the firm's name, address, and phone number for use as first pages of court documents.

Legal-size paper, $8\frac{1}{2}''\times 13''$ or $8\frac{1}{2}''\times 14''$, unruled, is used in some states for court and legal documents. Some states use legal cap for court documents and unruled legal-size paper for legal instruments such as real estate contracts, agreements, powers of attorney, etc.

A heavier bond paper is used for typing wills. Some firms have LAST WILL AND TESTAMENT engraved at the top for use as first pages and blank paper of the same quality for continuation pages. Will covers, with or without the firm name engraved, are used for binding wills. They are made of very heavy paper. Will envelopes are made of heavy stock and often have LAST WILL AND TESTAMENT engraved on them as well as DATE. They open at the narrow end and are used to hold wills.

Manuscript covers are made of heavy colored paper and are used to bind legal instruments; in some states court documents are also bound in them. Many states do not require any cover or backing on court documents since this takes up unnecessary room in the file.

Legal backs, sometimes printed with the firm name, are used for binding legal instruments and court documents. They cover only the back of the paper and occasionally have a printed panel on the back to identify the document.

Legal pads are tablets of lined paper with a ruled margin. The attorney's desk, briefcase, and conference table should be equipped with these at all times. They are used for making notes and writing longhand drafts.

Law blanks are printed forms used by some offices when the majority of the information can be standardized. Blanks are left to fill in the variable information such as names, addresses, amount of money, dates, and property descriptions. Examples of law blanks would be summonses, deeds, bills of sale, promissory notes, standard forms of leases, and mortgages. These are usually carried by office supply stores or printers. Many offices keyboard such forms into the computer, thus reducing the need for law blanks.

The other supplies maintained in a law office would be the same as those for any other office. What you order would depend on the systems of the firm.

§ 3.68 Handling Office Mail

The following are general procedures for handling incoming and outgoing mail in the law office.

§ 3.69 Incoming Mail

1. Be careful when opening envelopes that you do not slit material in the envelope.

2. Empty each envelope completely; check carefully to see that everything has been removed.

3. Fasten any enclosures to the letter. If the enclosures are small, they should be attached to the front of the letter; larger enclosures are attached to the back of the letter. If any enclosures mentioned in the letter are missing, make note of this on the front of the letter.

4. Before destroying the envelope, check for two things:

a. Be sure the return address and name of the sender are on the letter; if not, staple the envelope to the back of the letter.

b. If the date of the letter is more than one day earlier than the postmark on the envelope, attach the envelope to the back of the letter. If delivery was delayed for any reason, also attach the envelope. If a certificate of mailing or affidavit of mailing states a date that is at variance with the postmark, keep the envelope.

5. Mend the letter or other contents of the envelope with tape if they have been damaged in the process of opening the envelope.

6. Time-stamp the letter with the date the letter is received. Also time-stamp copies of documents received from other attorneys.

7. Read through the letter, underlining or highlighting important points, especially dates. This saves the attorney's time because he has only to review the letter. Enter any important dates in your calendar.

§ 3.70 Outgoing Mail

Procedures for handling outgoing mail vary greatly with the various firms. Large firms often have a central mail department. In other firms the receptionist prepares all mail for the post office. In small firms this is often the responsibility of the secretary.

Each secretary should be responsible for folding and inserting the correspondence she prepares into the envelopes. Being familiar with the letter and enclosures, she will be aware that the right material gets into the envelope. The legal secretary should be very careful that she does not mix up the letters and envelopes. Such a mix-up can be very embarrassing to the attorney and can result in divulging confidential information.

§ 3.71 Domestic Mail

The following are the classes of domestic mail:

1. First-class mail consists of letters, postcards, business reply mail, bills, and checks.

2. Second-class mail includes newspapers, magazines, and other periodicals. There is no weight limit, and it must be unsealed and marked "Second Class." There cannot be any handwritten material enclosed with this mail.

3. Third-class mail is used for material that does not fit the above classes and weighs less than 16 ounces. Circulars, books, and catalogs come under this category. If it is sealed, it must be marked "Third Class"; if unsealed, no marking is necessary.

4. Fourth-class mail is usually referred to as parcel post. The weight must be 16 ounces or over and includes material which does not come under the first three classes of mail. The rates are determined by the weight of the package and the distance it

is being sent. The United States is divided into eight postal zones, and the cost of the mail depends on the zone where the mailing originates and the zone to which it is going.

§ 3.72 Registered Mail

Registered mail provides protection against loss of first-class mail or priority mail up to a maximum of $25,000 except when the insurer carries insurance on the item. In the latter instance, the maximum that can be recovered is $1,000. When sending money and valuable papers such as stocks, bonds, or bids, registered mail is often used.

§ 3.73 Certified Mail

Certified mail is used for first-class mail for which proof of delivery is desired. No insurance is provided, but this service enables the mailer to have a receipt as evidence that the material has been mailed and, for an extra fee, receive a card (return receipt) which shows that the mail was picked up by either the addressee or his agent. It is also possible to stipulate that the letter be given to only the addressee and for the return receipt to show the address of delivery. See the following illustration for an envelope, receipt, and return receipt. Law offices use certified mail a great deal, and the secretary should keep the necessary forms in her desk.

COLVIN, MASON & NORMAN
Attorneys at Law
3005 East Skelly Avenue
Tulsa, Oklahoma 74106-6864

kETURN RECEIPT REQUESTED

MRS JON WILKINSON
222 MASON AVENUE
RIGBY ID   83221-1234

[G14192]

This illustration shows the front of the envelope which has been prepared for certified mail, return receipt requested.

SENDER:
- Complete items 1 and/or 2 for additional services.
- Complete items 3, and 4a & b.
- Print your name and address on the reverse of this form so that we can return this card to you.
- Attach this form to the front of the mailpiece, or on the back if space does not permit.
- Write ''Return Receipt Requested'' on the mailpiece below the article number.
- The Return Receipt will show to whom the article was delivered and the date delivered.

I also wish to receive the following services (for an extra fee):

1. ☐ Addressee's Address

2. ☐ Restricted Delivery

Consult postmaster for fee.

3. Article Addressed to:

MRS JON WILKINSON
222 MASON AVENUE
RIGBY ID   83221-1234

4a. Article Number
    P 301 588 436

4b. Service Type
☐ Registered   ☐ Insured
☒ Certified   ☐ COD
☐ Express Mail   ☐ Return Receipt for
                         Merchandise

7. Date of Delivery

5. Signature (Addressee)

8. Addressee's Address (Only if requested and fee is paid)

6. Signature (Agent)

Is your RETURN ADDRESS completed on the reverse side?

Thank you for using Return Receipt Service.

PS Form **3811**, December 1991   ★U.S. GPO: 1992—323-402   **DOMESTIC RETURN RECEIPT**

This illustration is the return receipt card which is attached to the back of the envelope. This card will show the signature of the person delivered to and the date of delivery.

UNITED STATES POSTAL SERVICE

Official Business

PENALTY FOR PRIVATE
USE TO AVOID PAYMENT
OF POSTAGE, $300

Print your name, address and ZIP Code here

COLVIN MASON & NORMAN
3005 EAST SKELLY AVENUE
TULSA OK   74105-6864

This illustration shows the reverse side of the return receipt card, which is returned to your office acknowledging proof of delivery.   [G14193]

P 301 588 436

**Receipt for
Certified Mail**

UNITED STATES
POSTAL SERVICE

No Insurance Coverage Provided
Do not use for International Mail
(See Reverse)

Sent to
MRS JON WILKINSON

Street and No.
222 MASON AVENUE

P.O., State and ZIP Code
RIGBY ID   83221-1234

Postage	$
Certified Fee	
Special Delivery Fee	
Restricted Delivery Fee	
Return Receipt Showing to Whom & Date Delivered	
Return Receipt Showing to Whom, Date, and Addressee's Address	
TOTAL Postage & Fees	$
Postmark or Date	

PS Form **3800**, June 1991

**STICK POSTAGE STAMPS TO ARTICLE TO COVER FIRST CLASS POSTAGE,
CERTIFIED MAIL FEE, AND CHARGES FOR ANY SELECTED OPTIONAL SERVICES (see front).**

1. If you want this receipt postmarked, stick the gummed stub to the right of the return address leaving the receipt attached and present the article at a post office service window or hand it to your rural carrier (no extra charge).

2. If you do not want this receipt postmarked, stick the gummed stub to the right of the return address of the article, the date, detach and retain the receipt, and mail the article.

3. If you want a return receipt, write the certified mail number and your name and address on a return receipt card, Form 3811, and attach it to the front of the article by means of the gummed ends if space permits. Otherwise, affix to back of article. Endorse front of article **RETURN RECEIPT REQUESTED** adjacent to the number.

4. If you want delivery restricted to the addressee, or to an authorized agent of the addressee, endorse **RESTRICTED DELIVERY** on the front of the article.

5. Enter fees for the services requested in the appropriate spaces on the front of this receipt. If return receipt is requested, check the applicable blocks in item 1 of Form 3811.

6. Save this receipt and present it if you make inquiry.

☆ U.S. GPO: 1991—302-916

PS Form **3800**, June 1991 *(Reverse)*

[G14194]

This is the portion of the receipt which you keep for your file.

§ 3.74 Insured Mail

Insured mail is used for third- and fourth-class mail or priority mail to insure it up to a maximum of $200. It is possible to obtain a return receipt on parcels for an additional fee.

§ 3.75 Special Delivery

Special delivery is used when mail must be delivered sooner than by regular carrier. A special carrier will usually deliver the mail upon its arrival at the addressee's post office. Additional postage is required.

§ 3.76 Express Mail

Many law offices are taking advantage of Express Mail, Express Mail Second Day Service, Custom Designed Service, and Same Day Airport Service. A list of the cities in which these services are available can be obtained from the post office. These are particularly useful when you are trying to meet a deadline.

There are also several commercial courier services which offer next day mail delivery.

§ 3.77 Electronic Mail

Electronic mail is possible through communications equipment instead of lengthy long distance telephone calls or slow mail delivery. Messages or documents can be sent almost instantaneously from one communications device to another, both within the office or to offices down the street or around the world.

§ 3.78 Priority Mail

Priority mail provides air mail service for first-class mail weighing over twelve ounces. When the post office decided to handle all first-class mail by air routes, it did not provide for mail weighing over twelve ounces. This mail would have had to go by fourth-class parcel post. By using priority mail—and paying postage at a higher rate—this mail can now go by air and receive faster delivery. For law offices this is a valuable service. Briefs, depositions, and lengthy documents can all be sent by priority mail for faster service. The maximum weight is 70 pounds. The maximum size and girth combined is 108 inches. The rate is determined by the distance the letter is to travel and by the weight of the letter. The fourth-class mail zones are used to compute postage. A chart can be obtained from the post office which gives the postage rates for all zones and weights.

§ 3.79 Preparation for Mailing

1. When inserting letters into envelopes, verify that the letter has been signed and that all enclosures are in the envelope. If a document accompanies the letter, make sure that the attorney has signed the document as well as the correspondence.

2. Sort mail by class, and separate mail which requires special handling, such as certified mail.

3. Weigh letters that you feel may be overweight, and mark the correct postage in the upper right-hand corner.

4. Run the regular first-class mail through the postage meter if the office uses a meter. Reset the meter for the postage required on the overweight letters.

5. Ascertain the proper postage for letters requiring special handling, and affix the postage to the letter or run it through the meter.

6. Determine weight and postage for the other classes of mail.

7. If a piece of mail is a combination of classes, make proper notations on it and check to see that proper postage is affixed.

§ 3.80   Law Office Filing

Not only is it important to file materials promptly, but it is also important to file using the correct rules. The following is a summary of filing rules.

I. ALPHABETIZING UNIT BY UNIT

File first units letter by letter (alphabetically). Consider second units only when first units are identical. Consider additional units when the first two units are identical.

EXAMPLES:

Name	Unit 1	Unit 2	Unit 3
Allison	Allison		
Barrymore	Barrymore		
Computer Data Association	Computer	Data	Association
Computer Input Association	Computer	Input	Association

II. NOTHING COMES BEFORE SOMETHING

A single letter comes before a name that begins with the same letter. A one-word name comes before a name that consists of the same word plus one or more words. A two- or more-word name comes before a name that consists of the same two or more words plus another word.

EXAMPLES:

Name	Unit 1	Unit 2	Unit 3
K	K		
Kathleen	Kathleen		
Kelly	Kelly		
Diversified	Diversified		
Diversified Consultants	Diversified	Consultants	
Diversified Manufacturers	Diversified	Manufacturers	
Diversified World Consultants	Diversified	World	Consultants

III. DECIDING WHICH NAME TO USE

The Association of Records Managers and Administrators (ARMA) suggests filing "under the most commonly used name or title." For example, given the choice between American Telephone & Telegraph Co. and AT&T, most people would file under AT&T. In these situations, always make a cross-reference card for the alternative name and refer to the law firm's office manual on filing procedures for the firm's preference.

IV. PERSONAL NAMES

Each part of the name of a person should be treated as a separate unit in the order of last name, first name, and middle initial. Any punctuation following the name or within an abbreviation should be ignored.

EXAMPLES:

Name	Unit 1	Unit 2	Unit 3
Brown	Brown		
G. Brown	Brown	G	
G. Mary Brown	Brown	G	Mary
John Browning	Browning	John	
John G. Browning	Browning	John	G

Foreign names are filed the same way, if identifiable. Otherwise, they are filed as written.

EXAMPLES:

Name	Unit 1	Unit 2	Unit 3
Kwon Joo Y	Kwon	Joo	Y
Alice K. Ng	Ng	Alice	K
Ng Keng Choan	Ng	Keng	Choan
Nguyen Truc Duc	Nguyen	Truc	Duc

In names with prefixes, ignore spacing, punctuation, and capitalization. Consider D', L', M', Mac, and Mc as spelled and ignore the apostrophes. Prefixes, such as de, De, La, Los, Saint, San, Santa, Santo, St., Ste., Van, Van di, are filed as spelled.

EXAMPLES:

Name	Unit 1	Unit 2	Unit 3
Ronald DeFosset	Defosset	Ronald	
Susan de Foxxe	deFoxxe	Susan	
Jane Mack	Mack	Jane	
James MacKay	MacKay	James	
Nancy MacKay	MacKay	Nancy	
Peter McKay	McKay	Peter	
William O'Hare	OHare	William	
Edward G. Sahaydak	Sahaydak	Edward	G
John Saint Clair	SaintClair	John	
Eddie Samuels	Samuels	Eddie	
John San Marco	SanMarco	John	
Kaye St. Clair	StClair	Kaye	
F.E. Ste. Joan	SteJoan	F	E

In names with hyphens, ignore the hyphen and consider it a single unit.

EXAMPLES:

Name	Unit 1	Unit 2	Unit 3
Jean–Luc Picard	Picard	JeanLuc	
Albert J. Smith	Smith	Albert	J
Susan Smith–Akins	SmithAkins	Susan	

In abbreviated nicknames or pseudonyms, treat the abbreviated part of a name as written out in its entirety.

When the nickname is used alone, treat it as a separate unit. If the name begins with "The," "The" is considered as the last unit.

EXAMPLES:

Name	Unit 1	Unit 2	Unit 3
Chas. J. Brown	Brown	Chas	J
Diamond Lil	Diamond	Lil	
B. J. Hunnicut	Hunnicut	B	J
The Jackson Five	Jackson	Five	The

Titles and suffixes are considered as a last unit to distinguish between persons with the same names. If the title is used with one part of the person's name, treat it as a first unit. A married woman's first name is used for filing purposes. Only consider the title if her first name is unknown and she uses her husband's name.

EXAMPLES:

Name	Unit 1	Unit 2	Unit 3
Dr. Ruth	Dr.	Ruth	
Dr. Mary Jones	Jones	Mary	Dr
Miss Mary Jones	Jones	Mary	Miss
Princess Diana	Princess	Diana	
Mrs. Jean Short	Short	Jean	Mrs
Mr. Mike Short	Short	Mike	Mr
Mr. Paul Toth	Toth	Paul	Mr
Mrs. Paul Toth	Toth	Paul	Mrs

For seniority terms, such as Jr., Sr., and degrees, the numeric precedes alphabetic; Arabic numbers precede Roman numbers; numbers are sequenced in numeric order; and endings in ordinal numbers are ignored.

EXAMPLES:

Name	Unit 1	Unit 2	Unit 3
John Smith 2d	Smith	John	2
John Smith 3d	Smith	John	3
John Smith III	Smith	John	III
John Smith IV	Smith	John	IV
John Smith Jr.	Smith	John	Jr
John Smith, M.D.	Smith	John	MD
John Smith, Mr.	Smith	John	Mr
John Smith, Ph.D	Smith	John	PhD
John Smith, Sr.	Smith	John	Sr

V. ORGANIZATIONAL NAMES

In names of organizations, treat each word as a separate unit and in the order written. Ignore all punctuation. If the name is joined by a hyphen or a diagonal, treat it as a single unit.

EXAMPLES:

Name	Unit 1	Unit 2	Unit 3
Canadian Data Associates	Canadian	Data	Associates
Canadian Data Company	Canadian	Data	Company
Data Computer Enterprises	Data	Computer	Enterprises
Data Processing Incorporated	Data	Processing	Incorporated
Frank and Johnson	Frank	and	Johnson
Frank's Nursery	Franks	Nursery	
O'Hara's Foods	OHaras	Foods	
O'Hare Airport	OHare	Airport	
Smith–Jones Company	SmithJones	Company	
Smith/Jones Store	SmithJones	Store	

Prepositions, conjunctions, and articles are treated as separate units. However, "the," "a," and "an" are treated as last units when used as the first word of the name.

EXAMPLES:

Name	Unit 1	Unit 2	Unit 3
A New Idea	New	Idea	A
Pen and Ink	Pen	and	Ink
The Trump Hotel	Trump	Hotel	The

Treat a compound expression written as one word or hyphenated as a single unit. If it is written with spaces, then treat it as a separate unit.

EXAMPLES:

Name	Unit 1	Unit 2	Unit 3
East India Company	East	India	Company
Eastwest Airlines	Eastwest	Airlines	
East–West Hotel	EastWest	Hotel	

When personal names are used in an organizational name, consider the name as written and ignore the punctuation.

EXAMPLES:

Name	Unit 1	Unit 2	Unit 3	Unit 4
Ray Bracy Company	Ray	Bracy	Company	
Ray Bracy, Jr., Associates	Ray	Bracy	Jr	Associates
S. Paul Jones Company	S	Paul	Jones	Company
S.R. Stover Flowers	S	R	Stover	Flowers
Sarah Ann Caterers	Sarah	Ann	Caterers	
Sarah J. Holms Inn	Sarah	J	Holms	Inn

When a prefix is used in a personal name, it is not treated as a single unit, but a hyphenated personal name is considered as one unit.

EXAMPLES:

Name	Unit 1	Unit 2	Unit 3	Unit 4
D. de La Vega Homes	D	deLaVega	Homes	
D. D'Ellio Store	D	DEllio	Store	
Simon Saint James Hotel	Simon	Saint	James	Hotel
Simon Sinclair Agency	Simon	Sinclair	Agency	
The Thomas John Inn	Thomas	John	Inn	The
Thomas–Mary Products	ThomasMary	Products		

Titles used in an organization's name are treated as a separate unit and as they are written. Punctuation is ignored.

EXAMPLES:

Name	Unit 1	Unit 2	Unit 3	Unit 4
Capt. Jim Tours	Capt	Jim	Tours	
Captain Tom Cruises	Captain	Tom	Cruises	
Ma Barker's Gun Shop	Ma	Barkers	Gun	Shop
Miss Tuffit's Dairy	Miss	Tuffits	Dairy	

An abbreviation is treated as a single unit exactly as it is written, and punctuation is ignored.

EXAMPLES:

Name	Unit 1	Unit 2	Unit 3	Unit 4
ABC Corp.	ABC	Corp		
Brown Hotel, Incorp.	Brown	Hotel	Incorp	
Brown Metals Inc.	Brown	Metals	Inc	
U.S. Condo Shares	U	S	Condo	Shares
U S Condominiums, Inc.	U	S	Condominiums	Inc
U.S. Condominiums, Ltd.	US	Condominiums	Ltd	
US Delivery Systems	US	Delivery	Systems	

Acronyms and call letters of radio and television stations are treated as single units.

EXAMPLES:

Name	Unit 1	Unit 2	Unit 3
ABC	ABC		
CBS	CBS		
NAACP	NAACP		
NBC	NBC		
WARM Radio Station	WARM	Radio	Station

When an ampersand (&) occurs in a name, it is treated as if it were spelled out.

EXAMPLES:

Name	Unit 1	Unit 2	Unit 3	Unit 4
A & G Company	A	and	G	Company
A&C Hardware	AANDC	Hardware		
AT&T	ATANDT			

Single letters are treated as separate units. If two or more letters in a sequence are written solid or connected by a hyphen or diagonal, the sequence is treated as a single unit.

EXAMPLES:

Name	Unit 1	Unit 2	Unit 3	Unit 4
A & C Books	A	AND	C	Books
A D T Rentals	A	D	T	Rentals
AAA	AAA			
A & D Stores	AANDD	Stores		
ADW Pools	ADW	Pools		
A/P Farms	AP	Farms		
A–Z Caterers	AZ	Caterers		

Geographic names are treated as a separate unit, and hyphenated names are treated as single units. If the name begins with a prefix followed by a space or hyphen, consider the prefix and the following word as a single unit.

EXAMPLES:

Name	Unit 1	Unit 2	Unit 3	Unit 4
Grand Canyon Tours	Grand	Canyon	Tours	
Las Vegas Bank	Las Vegas	Bank		
Los Angeles Realty	LosAngeles	Realty		
New Jersey Cement Co.	New	Jersey	Cement	Co
Wilkes–Barre Coal Mines	WilkesBarre	Coal	Mines	

Arabic and Roman numbers are considered separate units. Ordinal numbers are treated as if they were written 2, 4, and 9. Units that contain Arabic or Roman numbers precede units expressed in words. Units with Arabic numbers precede Roman numbers, and each sequence is arranged in numeric order.

EXAMPLES:

Name	Unit 1	Unit 2	Unit 3
20th Century Fox	20	Century	Fox
1492 Tour Company	1492	Tour	Company
IV Roman Outlets	IV	Roman	Outlets
AAA Travel Club	AAA	Travel	Club
AFL–CIO Local 124	AFLCIO	Local	124
AFL–CIO Local 130	AFLCIO	Local	130

Units that contain numbers written in words are sequenced in alphabetical order. When a hyphen is used in the number, ignore the hyphen and treat it as one unit.

EXAMPLES:

Name	Unit 1	Unit 2	Unit 3	Unit 4
Sixth Avenue Movies	Sixth	Avenue	Movies	
Twelve Fourteen Rental Co.	Twelve	Fourteen	Rental	Co
Twenty–First Century Stores	TwentyFirst	Century	Stores	
The Western 200 Club	Western	200	Club	The
The Western Hotel	Western	Hotel	The	

When the phrase consists of a number linked by a hyphen or diagonal to a letter or word, the punctuation is ignored and is treated as a single unit. Consider only the number that precedes the punctuation when the phrase consists of a figure linked to another figure by a hyphen or diagonal.

EXAMPLES:

Name	Unit 1	Unit 2	Unit 3
1–A Delivery Service	1A	Delivery	Service
1/A Pizza Shop	1A	Pizza	Shop
7–Eleven Stores	7Eleven	Stores	
20/20 Television Show	20	Television	Show

When the phrase consists of a figure plus a letter or word with any space or punctuation, treat it as a single unit.

EXAMPLES:

Name	Unit 1	Unit 2	Unit 3
A–1 Notary Service	A1	Notary	Service
Alice's 15–Minute Service	Alices	15Minute	Service
Alice's One–Hour Photo	Alices	OneHour	Photo

When a symbol appears with a number, treat the two elements as a single unit only if there is no space between the symbol and the number. Consider the symbol as if it were spelled out. When a dollar sign precedes the number, consider the number and then the word dollar or dollars in that order.

EXAMPLES:

Name	Unit 1	Unit 2	Unit 3	Unit 4
The $1 Store	1Dollar	Store	The	
50% Discount Outlet	50Percent	Discount	Outlet	
The 50+ Travel Club	50Plus	Travel	Club	The
The #1 Hair Salon	Number1	Hair	Salon	The

Alphabetize according to address when two organizational names are otherwise the same by city first then by state.

EXAMPLES:

Name	Unit 1	Unit 2	Unit 3	Unit 4
Burger King, Adams, AL	Burger	King	Adams	Alabama
Burger King, Erie, ME	Burger	King	Erie	Maine
Burger King, Erie, OR	Burger	King	Erie	Oregon

If the state and city are the same, then consider the street name. If the street name is a number, treat it exactly as written.

EXAMPLES:

Name	Unit 1	Unit 2	Unit 3	Unit 4
Domino's 15th St. Bangor, ME	Dominos	Bangor	15	Street
Domino's 21st St. Bangor, ME	Dominos	Bangor	21	Street
Domino's Third St. Bangor, ME	Dominos	Bangor	Third	Street

If the street names are the same, alphabetize by direction if it is part of the street address.

EXAMPLES:

Name	Unit 1	Unit 2	Unit 3	Unit 4	Unit 5
Domino's N. 5th St. Bangor, ME	Dominos	Bangor	N	5	Street
Domino's S. 5th St. Bangor, ME	Dominos	Bangor	S	5	Street

If the names of the streets are identical, then consider the building number in numeric order.

EXAMPLES:

Name	Unit 1	Unit 2	Unit 3	Unit 4	Unit 5
Domino's 23 Coal St. Bangor, ME	Dominos	Bangor	Coal	Street	23
Domino's 39 Coal St. Bangor, ME	Dominos	Bangor	Coal	Street	39

VI. GOVERNMENTAL NAMES

The phrase "United States Government" is considered the first three units for any department of the federal government. The name of the department is considered next by moving the words "Department of" to the end. The office or bureau within the department is considered by moving the opening phrases, such as "Office of" and "Bureau of," to the end.

EXAMPLES:

Name	Unit 4	Unit 5	Unit 6	Unit 7
Office of Consumer Affairs	Consumer	Affairs	Office	of
Federal Bureau of Investigation	Federal	Bureau	of	Investigation
Food and Drug Administration	Food	and	Drug	Administration

(Note: Remember, the phrase "United States Government" is considered the first three units.)

For state and local governments, consider the distinctive place name first (except for educational institutions). Then consider the individual department or bureau and moving the standard phrases as was done with the federal departments and bureaus.

EXAMPLES:

Name	Unit 1	Unit 2	Unit 3	Unit 4	Unit 5
Idaho Tax Division	Idaho	Tax	Division		
Iowa State Board of Labor	Iowa	State	Labor	Board	of
Water Department, City of Miami	Miami	City	of	Water	Department
Register of Wills, Miami County	Miami	County	Wills	Register	of

With foreign government names, first consider the name of the country, then the appropriate classification, and finally consider the name of the department or bureau.

EXAMPLES:

Name	Unit 1	Unit 2	Unit 3
Commonwealth of Australia	Australia	Commonwealth	of
Republic of Austria	Austria	Republic	of
Kingdom of Belgium	Belgium	Kingdom	of
State of Israel	Israel	State	of

For more details on filing procedures, *The Gregg Reference Manual, Seventh Edition*, should be consulted.

§ 3.81 Introduction to Files Management

Files management in the law office receives perhaps the least amount of attention, although it may be the most important of all clerical functions. Client files are the inventory and the memory of the law office, and they contain all work in process—a major asset of the firm. In addition, they often contain important client papers and documents, as well as the work product of the firm, and are not always easily replaceable.

Regardless of its importance, however, files management is not popular. Secretaries tend to put off filing because most find it tedious. It is equally difficult to convince law firms that both time and personnel must be allocated for adequate files management.

It is often the legal secretary's responsibility to develop a filing system to control the firm's files. Because it is such an important responsibility, it is necessary for the legal secretary to understand the broad scope of a files management system for the law office.

§ 3.82   Definition

Files management is the control of each file in your office from the time it is opened to the time that it is ultimately closed or destroyed. It is a crucial area of the law practice because handling a file efficiently, generally speaking, impacts on profitability. More important, effective files management provides many of the quality control mechanisms which are essential for ensuring that work is properly handled. It has recently been estimated that 40 percent of all malpractice claims are caused by poor files management.

§ 3.83   Ingredients for Successful Files Management

Files management includes much more than filing papers in a file, although that is important. It also includes checking for conflicts of interest before the file is actually opened; ensuring that work in the file progresses in an orderly fashion by using a docket control system; ensuring that all deadlines are met, whether those deadlines are imposed by law or by a promise to the client; preserving new work products for future use; ensuring that anyone in the office can find the file or any correspondence or document that belongs in the file through centralized files control; closing the file once the work has been completed; and destroying the file once it serves no further useful purpose.

§ 3.84   Centralization v. Decentralization

The major categories of filing systems are centralized and decentralized. Under a highly formalized central filing system, files are removed only to be worked on and are returned to the filing cabinets at the end of each working day, regardless of whether there is still work remaining to be done. In a centralized system there is also controlled access—no one can remove a file from the filing system without "signing out" for it. In a completely decentralized system, work originators maintain their own filing systems, store files in their own work areas, and otherwise have total responsibility and control of the files.

§ 3.85   Centralized System/Decentralized Storage

While totally centralized systems work well in many corporate offices, such a centralized system is difficult to achieve in a law office. Most attorneys like to keep their most active files in their work areas for easy retrieval rather than returning them to the central file room at the end of the working day. There are few totally centralized file systems in law firms.

Centralized control, not necessarily centralized storage, is important. It should be noted that centralized storage makes control easier. Assuming there is sufficient space, file storage in individual attorney work areas is not usually a problem as long as there is centralized control. This means that regardless of where files are physically kept, there is a central *control system* to achieve maximum file efficiency and to maintain control. Although control is more difficult with decentralized storage, in most law firms such a compromise is necessary. Once attorneys gain confidence in the filing system, they soon become willing to turn the majority of their files over to centralized storage.

In most law firms a centralized system means that files which are not being used frequently are kept in the active files area, usually a file room. In other words, there is a centralized *storage area* as well as centralized control, but attorneys and secretaries may store their files in their own work areas at their discretion.

§ 3.86 Necessity for Control

Regardless of whether a firm has centralized storage or decentralized storage, central file control is essential to quality control. As a firm grows, it becomes more and more difficult, if not impossible, to maintain control with a decentralized system.

Since most firms tend to procrastinate in establishing controls, it is not unusual for the file function to get completely out of hand before the problem is addressed. Therefore, a secretary who takes the initiative to develop a controlled system often makes the difference in whether or not the firm has control. While it is important to keep papers in a safe place, the most important criterion in judging the effectiveness of a file system is "findability."

§ 3.87 Classification of Files

In most firms there are several classifications of files. They include:

- *Active.* These constitute the firm's "work in process." They are the files in which there is work to be done and in which there may be unbilled time.

- *Inactive.* These are usually files in which there will be no activity for some time but for which all time has been billed. Additional work is anticipated at some point in the future. In a centralized system, it might not be necessary to differentiate between active and inactive files, as all files are stored together.

If this is done, however, it is critical to have a system for following up on inactive files to ascertain whether they can be "closed" or when they should be pulled for review. There should also be a follow-up system for active files, and there is no reason why the same system cannot incorporate follow-up on the inactive files.

- *Closed Files.* These are usually files where all work has been done and the file has been billed, collected, culled, and marked for destruction, if it can be destroyed, or for permanent retention if it cannot.

While at first glance this may seem relatively simple, in some firms there is more than one classification for the same type of file. Unless there are standardized classifications, it is difficult to determine where a particular file belongs. In addition to the standardized classifications, there should be detailed guidelines for determining into which classification a file falls. For example:

- In some firms there are both "permanent" files and "inactive" files because different attorneys use different words to identify the same type of file. If no one is aware of that, the firm will find itself with both "permanent" files and "inactive" files, resulting in confusion as to which is which and another place in which to look for "lost" files.

- If a file involves a matter in which there may or may not be further action, is it an "active" file or an "inactive" file? In some states there is automatic dismissal of a lawsuit in which there has been no activity for a specified period of time. Therefore, in many situations where a law firm represents the defendant, once a responsive pleading is filed and the services are billed, the attorney hopes that the plaintiff will "lose" its file. At what point does that "active" file become "inactive"?

- Beyond that, when does the file in the above case go from "inactive" to "closed," and when is it scheduled for destruction?

- Is each "closed" file automatically set for destruction at the time it is closed, or is there review at a later date?

- Which files should be destroyed and which should be "permanently" retained?

- Is there automatic review of files which are "inactive"?

The questions go on and on. The point is that there must be written guidelines to prevent confusion and to save time in locating files. The firm's office policy and procedures manual should include detailed explanations of its filing system and the management procedures which are in place. If this is not the case when the secretary begins work in the firm, she should begin putting the procedures in writing once she understands what they are. If there are no standard procedures, she may make suggestions for developing and implementing some.

§ 3.88 File Identification Systems

There are many ways of identifying files. Although some are more effective than others, the "right one" depends upon the needs of the firm. Client files are usually identified in one of three ways:

1. *Alphabetic.* Under an alphabetic system, which is known as a direct filing system, files are labeled and stored in alphabetical order by name, generally of the client, following standard filing procedures. Although many law firms still use alphabetic filing systems, they are the least efficient for law offices because of the necessity of reshuffling files constantly to make room for additional files. Additionally, people rarely interpret filing rules the same way. Even if the firm uses a numeric system, it is not unusual for attorneys and secretaries to file alphabetically in their individual work area.

In some firms the litigation files are filed alphabetically by the name of the plaintiff, regardless of whether the firm's client is the plaintiff, the defendant, or another party to the action. Filing under this system makes controlling and finding files more difficult.

A few firms separate and store files by practice area. For example, all real estate files would be filed together, all litigation files would be filed together, etc. This system is another which is cumbersome and outmoded.

2. *Numeric.* A numeric system is an indirect method of filing, since a cross-index is required. Under such a system, files are assigned a number, are identified by that number, and are stored in numerical order. There is an alphabetic cross-index. This alleviates the problem of reshuffling files. Another big advantage to a well-thought-out numeric system is that the same numbering system can be used both for files and for computerized accounting. This is less cumbersome than having both file numbers and computer numbers. Additionally, with a well-thought-out numbering system through use of a computer, a firm can develop the types of management reports and statistics it needs for assessing profitability and cost controls, and it can store and manipulate data for long-range planning and marketing.

Serial and terminal digit are the two primary types of numeric numbering systems.

Under a serial number system, numbers are assigned in straight sequential order and are filed in straight sequence, one behind the other, so that the most recent number assigned is the last in the file drawer or on the shelf.

With terminal digit filing, numbers are broken down into groups of two digits and are filed in numerical order by the last two digits. (Numbers are read from left to right.) Many terminal digit filing systems are also color coded for increased ease in filing. The advantage of terminal digit filing is that material is evenly distributed through the file storage area so that each drawer or each shelf grows at the same rate. Authorities state that filing is up to 40 percent faster with the terminal digit system. Since only two numbers must be remembered to file the folder, misfiles are less frequent. This system is an indirect system and must have an alphabetic cross-index. The big disadvantage to this system is the inability to accommodate client numbers as well as matter numbers. This disadvantage can be overcome by using the file number as a unique matter number, assigning client numbers as well. Filing then would be by matter number rather than client matter number, and client files would not be filed in the same location.

3. *Alpha-numeric system.* An alpha-numeric system is a combination of an alphabetic filing system and a numeric system. Under this type of system, numbers assigned to files are in blocks according to the letter of the alphabet which identifies the client. The purpose of such a system is to achieve alphabetic filing. Since the number blocks are filed together, the files are also more or less in alphabetic order. In such a system, however, there is still the potential problem of having to reshuffle files constantly to provide for growth. There is also the problem of using up a number block and having to assign a number from another block as near as possible to the desired one. If this happens often enough, the principal reason for the system is defeated.

Other file identification systems include:

• *Subjective system.* A subjective system is one where files are filed alphabetically by the subject matter involved. The firm's general administrative files (accounting, personnel, equipment, insurance, and other files concerning the firm's business affairs) are usually filed by subject matter in a designated area of the file room. Forms files and retrieval systems are also usually filed by subject matter. Needless to say, client files would not be filed by this method.

• *Geographic system.* A geographic system is one where filing is by geographic area, such as a state or a region. Geographic filing would be rare in a law office except that an office which had branch locations might file its general administrative files by location of the office (geographic location) and then by subject. In some corporate law departments that work extensively with various branch offices or subsidiaries, it is not unusual for a geographic system to be used. The geographic system may also encompass a numeric system for ease in identification, but it may be necessary to access files by city, for example.

§ 3.89 How a Numeric Filing System Works

Although many firms continue to use alphabetic systems for filing, and it is still the most common method in the small firm, more and more firms are beginning to convert to numeric filing systems. This is true even for small firms, where the use of microcomputers is common. A numeric system provides a more effective base for control—a number is considerably more specific than an alphabetic designation. The right kind of file numbering system can also be used for the accounting system.

§ 3.90 Client Numbers

To achieve maximum utilization of computerized, statistical information in both short- and long-range planning, a file number should consist of a client number and a matter number. Under this type of system, each client is assigned a unique client number when the firm begins to represent the client. The client retains the same client number no matter how many different matters the firm may handle for the client. These numbers are usually five digits.

§ 3.91 Matter Numbers

A matter number is usually assigned in one of two ways. Either each new file opened is given a unique matter number, or client files are assigned matter numbers in the order in which their files are opened. Matter numbers are usually three or four digits, depending upon computer capability and firm preference.

§ 3.92 Unique Matter Numbers

    EXAMPLE: Using a five-digit client number and a three-digit matter number as an example, the file number for the firm's first client file opened would be 00001–001. Regardless of whether the second file opened is for the same client or a different client, the number would be 00001–002.

§ 3.93   Matter Numbers by Client

If a firm finds it useful to know how many files it has opened for a particular client, it often uses a client matter number system, assigning matters by *client*. Under this system, the client number would still be the same, but matter numbers for all clients would be identical, beginning with 001 or 0001 as the first matter number opened for each client.

> EXAMPLE: If ABC Corporation has a client number of 11000, the first file opened for that client is given matter number 001, making that file number 11000–001; the second file for the same client is given matter number 002, making that file number 11000–002, and so on. (Some firms reserve 001 as a general file for a client, beginning their sequential numbering of matter numbers with 002.)

§ 3.94   Practice Area Designation

Many firms provide codes for practice areas, as these are useful in some management reports. Most computers have the capability to handle this additional number. Sample area of practice designations are:

- 10   General
- 20   Tax
- 30   Pension and Profit Sharing
- 40   Estate Planning
- 50   Real Estate
- 60   Domestic
- 70   Litigation
- 80   Corporation
- 90   Bankruptcy

In some firms the practice area also forms part of the file number, but that is a matter of preference. Depending upon the firm's client and matter number systems, use of the practice area also could make the number too long for computer purposes.

Variations of these systems are limited only by the imagination of the individual who creates the system.

In the final analysis, however, the firm must decide which system will work best for it. A major consideration is whether the system already in place can be adapted to an effective system without starting from scratch.

§ 3.95 Centralized Indexing

The key to a good filing system is a good central index. With a numerical system, there must be an alphabetical index to all files, both active and closed. (Usually the active and closed indexes are maintained separately.) An important aspect of this system is that index cards are never removed from the master index system. Another important aspect is that index cards are automatically prepared in the file opening process.

The key to an effective cross-index system is extensive cross-referencing. This allows location of the file number, regardless of which name in the file is used in checking the index. The master file index is also used for the conflict of interest function, discussed in more detail below.

§ 3.96 Centrally Controlled Files

General files management concepts must be applicable to the law firm—does the system work on a day-to-day basis? Since this is an area that is often left to chance, the legal secretary can make a valuable contribution by developing a system for her office. Let us assume for our case study that there is a file coordinator who is responsible for all aspects of the central system. If you work in an office where there is no one person responsible for the filing function, however, you may assume that you will perform those tasks.

The system described here is not the only kind of files management system that can be effective in a law firm—quite the contrary, there are numerous ways of accomplishing centralized control of a firm's filing system. This system will provide a good basis upon which to grow; a numbering system that works well for a manual system but will easily convert to computerization; an alphabetic cross-index that will work for a manual conflict of interest system and will provide a good data base for a computerized conflict of interest system; a docket control system that will ensure that work is done in the ordinary course and that all deadlines are met; central control of the firm's files; and a procedure for routine file closing and retention.

§ 3.97 Ingredients for Effective Central Control

The following are ingredients for effective central control:

    1. Filing out a new matter report properly

2. Running a conflict of interest check on each new file opened

3. Maintaining a record of the location of every file in the office

4. Maintaining a master index of all active and all closed files including appropriate cross-index entries

5. Maintaining a record of pertinent data of any files that are destroyed

6. Maintaining a Rolodex file index for each attorney's secretary to track the flow of the files among the attorneys in the office

7. Conducting periodic checks of files in various attorneys' offices to verify the accuracy of the file records

8. Preparing and distributing weekly to all attorneys a new file memorandum listing all new files opened the preceding week

9. Maintaining a docket control system

10. Maintaining a retrieval system

11. Keeping written procedures current

§ 3.98   The Master File Index

As previously mentioned, the file opening process must provide for alphabetic cross-index cards for a numeric filing system. The system's master file index provides the information needed to check each new file for a potential conflict of interest. Since the master index will include a listing of all subfiles opened, more than one card might be necessary for one file. This information comes from the new matter report.

In most firms there is a procedure ensuring that an alphabetic cross-index card is made for each party to an action or each name which appears in the name of the file. While this might be enough information for cross-reference purposes, it is not enough for conflicts of interest information. Therefore, many firms now provide a space on the new matter report for inserting names to be entered into the conflicts system and to be checked as part of the file opening process for a new matter.

Cross-reference cards should be made for each plaintiff, each defendant, and any major principals of corporate parties. In the case of corporate subsidiaries, cross-reference cards should be made for the parent company, with appropriate references. These cards enable the file coordinator or secretary to do a manual conflicts check as part of the file opening process.

It is also necessary to maintain a master numerical listing. This numerical list can be kept in a different section of the index card drawer. It is also necessary to keep a master list of matters opened for a particular client. These might be kept in a different section of the numeric master drawer. The master file index will show a listing of all files opened for a particular client.

It is helpful to use colored cards for the indexes.

EXAMPLE:

CARD	COLOR
Master Alphabetic	White
Continuation of Master	Yellow
Alphabetic Cross–Reference	Blue
Master Numeric	Salmon
Master Alphabetic Client Matter	Pink

§ 3.99   New Matter Report

When an attorney accepts a new matter, he provides the legal secretary with the information she needs to prepare a new matter report. Typically the new matter report provides not only pertinent information to the firm for accounting purposes but also provides a brief description of the work to be performed by the firm, perhaps the fee arrangement under which the work will be performed, and the information needed to run a conflict of interest check, as well as any critical deadlines to be entered in the docket control system. (See Illustration 3–10.)

Illustration 3–10

NEW MATTER REPORT

Prepared by: _____ Date: _____ File No. _____

Case name: _____ Client No. _____ Matter No. _____

Court: _____   Docket No.: _____

CLIENT INFORMATION _____ New client _____ Present client

Client: _____

Address: _____

Business phone: _____

Home phone: _____

Person to contact: _____

OPPOSING OR OTHER PARTY INFORMATION

Name: _____   Attorney: _____

Address: _____   Address: _____

Phone No.: _____   Phone No.: _____

MATTER INFORMATION Case Received by: _____ Case Assigned to: _____

File Name: (Client name first) _____

Description of case: _____

Subject indexing: _____

STATUTE OF LIMITATIONS, ANSWER OR   Area of Practice
OTHER CRITICAL DATE TO TICKLE [*specify*]: _____ Code: _____

FEES AND BILLING INFORMATION   Hourly Rate of $_____ per hour

☐ Contingency fee of: _____
☐ Other [*specify*]: _____
   Has retainer agreement been prepared? _____ Yes _____ No
☐ Standard billing (bill fees quarterly and costs monthly)
☐ Other billing agreement [*specify*]: _____

REMARKS (Note additional cross-references or other special instructions in this space):

_____

_____

_____

Names to be run in Conflicts System:	Additional Names to be Cross-referenced:
Shirley Atkinson	Don's Ready Air Cond.
John Smith	_____
Don Atkinson	_____
_____	_____
_____	_____

Conflicts System run by: _____

§ 3.100 Definition of Conflict of Interest

A conflict of interest is being in a position, intentionally or unintentionally, where a person's own needs and desires might lead that person to violate his or her duty to another who has a right to depend on him or her (from *Law Dictionary for Nonlawyers, Second Edition,* West Publishing Company, 1985).

> EXAMPLE: A judge who owns stock in XYZ Company trying a case involving the XYZ Company might have a conflict of interest.

In a law office a conflict of interest arises generally when the law firm (or the individual lawyers in the firm) places itself in the position of representing parties in adverse positions. What is difficult about conflicts of interest is that a conflict may be created by a lawyer's representation of a client years before the current situation. This is especially true if the attorney undertakes representation of one client that places the attorney in the position of divulging a confidence of a former or current client. What is even more difficult is that these guidelines apply to all lawyers in the firm. It is assumed that representation by one attorney in the firm is the same as representation by all, even if they are in different cities.

> EXAMPLE: Mrs. Jane Baker sees a lawyer in the firm about filing for a divorce against her husband, David Baker. Another lawyer in the firm has already agreed to represent David Baker.

> EXAMPLE: The firm is general counsel for XYZ Insurance Company; Jane Baker asks a lawyer in the firm to file a claim against XYZ Insurance Company.

> EXAMPLE: The firm is general counsel for XYZ Insurance Company. Jane Baker sues XYZ Insurance Company and Todd Jones for damages she sustained in an accident in which Todd Jones was driving the car which hit Jane Baker's car. The XYZ Insurance Company is Todd Jones's insurer. XYZ Insurance Company must provide a defense for Todd Jones, but it intends to take the position that Todd Jones violated the conditions of his insurance policy, so the coverage does not apply. In other words, the interests of XYZ Insurance Company and Todd Jones are at odds.

Technically, before a lawyer can undertake representation of a client, he must make certain that he does not already represent another client whose interests are at odds with those of the potential client. It is unethical for a firm to represent clients whose legal positions are conflicting. It is critical, therefore, for every firm to have an index of all clients, present and past, and to check that index when it accepts new work. Unfortunately, it is not always simple to determine whether or not a potential conflict exists, and the decision is a subjective one.

> EXAMPLE: The firm handled an incorporation for XYZ Corporation. One of the firm's clients wants the firm to handle a claim against Jerry Hunt, the vice president of XYZ Corporation. Is there a conflict?

This is a simple example among many gray areas, and only the lawyer or lawyers in the firm can decide whether there is a potential conflict. Even if the firm does not have a conflict, the lawyers may decide that they do not want to accept work as a matter of business practice. From a business standpoint, there are some people against whom the firm will not want to be in an adverse position.

Conflicts of interest are becoming a real problem in many firms. Many do not have effective systems for checking new clients for potential conflicts. There are a number of reasons why, but in most instances the lack of a conflict of interest system results from the failure of the firm to develop such a system when it is small enough to do it easily. As the firm grows, the job becomes more overwhelming, and the result is that one day the firm finds itself in the embarrassing position either of representing clients with conflicting interests, or worse, with a malpractice claim.

It is true that a conflict of interest system is not so critical for a small firm, especially one that has not been in practice for a long time, as for a large firm, since the lawyers in the small firm can remember for whom they've done work in the past. This is a short-sighted position, however, since most firms grow, and new lawyers and new secretaries come into the firm. It is much easier to develop a system when the firm is small. Even if there is only one lawyer, there should be a conflict of interest system.

It is not the duty of the legal secretary or the file coordinator to determine whether a conflict of interest exists. It is necessary only to call to the attention of the attorney opening the file that either a potential conflict or a situation in which the firm might not want to become involved exists. This is done as part of the new file opening process.

Information for conflict of interest purposes is critical. This is true not only for checking the new matter for any potential conflicts when the file is opened, but also for future references. If the attorney does not provide the information to the secretary, she should ask him if there are names in addition to those listed in the file name which must be indexed.

> EXAMPLE: If the firm is representing the estate of a decedent, the name of the personal representative as well as the names of all heirs should be indexed.

If the firm is handling a real estate transaction for a development company, the names of the principals of that company should also be indexed. If the development has a project name, that should be indexed. For example, if the developer is "The Build-it-Fast Company" and the firm is doing the legal work involved in the development of the Josey Ranch Shopping Plaza, there should be a cross-index card made for "Josey Ranch Shopping Plaza."

If the firm represents a bank, the names of the bank officers should be indexed.

If the firm is incorporating a small business, the names of each of the stockholders and officers should be indexed. (Remember that there are times when the firm may not want to be an adverse party against someone for *business* reasons rather than *ethical* ones.)

After the secretary prepares the new matter report, she sends it to the file coordinator for processing.

§ 3.101   Running the Conflicts Check

Running the conflicts check is done at the beginning of the file opening process. Before the file coordinator assigns a number to the file, she checks all names appearing in the file name or on the "conflicts" line of the new matter report against the alphabetic cross-index. The secretary or the file coordinator is trained as to which situations might present potential conflicts. For example, if the firm is opening a new matter for an existing client, that client's name will appear in the index. This is not a problem since the firm is again doing work for the client. If, on the other hand, the person to be sued was a former client, the file coordinator would notify the attorney immediately for further instruction. Determining whether or not a potential conflict exists comes from judgment acquired after a good deal of experience. The safest rule is "When in doubt, ask the attorney." (The file coordinator initials the new matter report to indicate that the conflicts check has been run.)

§ 3.102   Assigning File Numbers

Once the conflict of interest check has been run, the file coordinator can assign the file number (client and matter number). In some firms assignment is made by the bookkeeping department, depending upon the firm's structure. Some computerized systems assign numbers automatically. There is no "best" way to do this, but there must be coordination between the file person and the bookkeeping department.

The file coordinator checks to see whether a client number has already been assigned to the client. This is done simply by checking the client master card index (the pink cards). If the client has a number, only a matter number need be assigned. If the client does not have a number, the next one is selected from the master index (salmon).

Once the file number (client number and matter number) has been determined, the file coordinator prepares the cross-index entries for the master cross index. Each index card gives the name of the file, as well as the file number. The master index card should list all subfiles which are opened and should also either list the other cross-index references or indicate how many cross-index references were made. (See Illustrations 3–11 and 3–12.) When you close the file, you'll know how many cross-index cards must be transferred to the closed file index. The file number (client and matter number) must also be entered in the numerical indexes. If the client is a new client, a "client number" card is prepared. If the client is an existing one, the client number card is updated to indicate the matter number being assigned. (See Illustration 3–13.) An entry is then made for the master file number index. (See Illustration 3–14.)

Once the file clerk assigns the file number, she enters the file number (client and matter number) on all copies of the new matter report, retains one for her central records, forwards one to the book-keeper, and forwards one to the secretary (with the file, etc., described below).

Illustration 3–11

ATKINSON, SHIRLEY vs.	12000–001
John Smith	
Auto Accident—Personal Injury	
Correspondence	12000–001(a)
Pleadings	12000–001(b)
Evidence	12000–001(c)
Discovery	12000–001(d)
Research	12000–001(e)
Briefs and legal memoranda	12000–001(f)
Attorney's notes	12000–001(g)
Miscellaneous	12000–001(h)
1/1/94	

(MASTER ALPHABETIC CROSS–INDEX CARD)

(WHITE)

Cross-reference entries:
Smith, John
Atkinson, Don
Don's Ready Air Conditioning
1/1/94

(CONTINUATION TO MASTER ALPHABETIC
CROSS–INDEX CARD)

(YELLOW)

Illustration 3–12

```
Smith, John

SEE:   ATKINSON, SHIRLEY (vs.) John Smith
       File No. 12000–001

1/1/94
```

(ALPHABETIC CROSS–INDEX CARD)

(BLUE)

Illustration 3–13

```
ATKINSON, SHIRLEY                    12000
Numbers assigned:
12000–001
12000–002
(As new files are opened for this client, the
additional file numbers are noted.  The next
file for Shirley Atkinson would be 12000–003.)
```

(MASTER CLIENT CARD)

(PINK)

Illustration 3–14

```
12000–001


ATKINSON, SHIRLEY v.
Smith, John


1/1/94
```

(NUMERIC MASTER FILE INDEX CARD)

(SALMON)

§ 3.103 Use of a Rolodex

In addition to the master file index maintained by the file coordinator, each secretary should keep a Rolodex file on her desk containing the same information that is shown on the master index file for each active file being handled by her attorney. As part of the file opening process, the file clerk prepares a Rolodex card which will be returned to the attorney's secretary with the new file. (See Illustration 3–15.) In this way, the secretary has a list of the active files being handled by the attorney and will have the file number readily available for use on time sheets and for filing purposes.

Illustration 3–15

```
Client:                    File No. 12000–001

ATKINSON, SHIRLEY
Matter: (v. John Smith)

Auto Accident—Personal Injury
Address:

100 Main Street, Any Where, USA 00000
Phone:   000–622–1111
                          Responsible Atty:  ABC

                          Assigned to:  DEF
```

(ROLODEX CARD FOR SECRETARY'S DESK)

§ 3.104   Preparation of File Folder

The file coordinator prepares the file folder, which contains subfiles and a copy of the new matter report, and which she sends along to the secretary with the Rolodex card described above that gives all pertinent information about the file.

§ 3.105   Subfiles

A common complaint in most law firms is that everyone has his own system for setting up subfiles, so the subfile categories do not necessarily identify the contents of the subfile. Another is that no record is kept on subfiles, so a subfile could be misplaced, and no one would ever know it had existed unless the attorney remembered. This makes control impossible and presents a problem for attorneys and staff when they are looking for a specific document. For that reason, standardized categories for subfiles by area of practice are necessary. For example:

1. *Litigation*
    a. Correspondence
    b. Pleadings
    c. Evidence
    d. Discovery
    e. Research
    f. Briefs and legal memoranda
    g. Attorney's notes
    h. Miscellaneous

2. *General Corporate*
    a. Correspondence
    b. Corporate documents (charter, bylaws, minutes, agreements, etc.)
    c. Client's papers
    d. Attorney's notes
    e. Miscellaneous

3. *Real Estate*
    a. Correspondence
    b. Title search, contract of sale, and survey
    c. Closing papers
    d. Client's papers
    e. Attorney's notes
    f. Miscellaneous

4. *Estates*
    a. Correspondence
    b. Probate pleadings and documents
    c. Assets

     d.   Debts and liabilities
     e.   Will
     f.   Federal estate tax return
     g.   State tax return
     h.   Client's papers
     i.   Attorney's notes
     j.   Miscellaneous

5.   *Tax and Estate Planning*
     a.   Correspondence
     b.   Will for (name of husband)
     c.   Will for (name of wife)
     d.   Drafts
     e.   Client's papers
     f.   Attorney's notes
     g.   Miscellaneous

Each subfile should carry the file number and name and can also be assigned a letter or other identifying mark. The correspondence subfile for File No. 00129–700 might be 00129–700(a); the pleadings file would be 00129–700(b), etc. (See Illustration 3–11.) It is not necessary for the subfile to be entered into the computer records (for accounting purposes), but they are entered in the master index. By keeping a central record of the subfiles, an attorney or a secretary can verify whether he or she has the complete file.

The subfiles can be requested at the time the file is opened or can be opened later. A simple form can be used to advise the file clerk of the subfile which has been opened. (See Illustration 3–16.) In order to keep accurate records, it is essential to have the cooperation of secretaries and attorneys. Once they realize the value of having a central record, they are more likely to make an effort to remember. Opening subfiles at the time the file is opened has the advantage of having a record of every subfile—another important ingredient of file control.

Once the file folders are prepared, the file coordinator returns the file containing a copy of the new matter report to the secretary (if the attorney wishes to keep it in his own office), along with the Rolodex card. The file coordinator also prepares an "out" card and places it where the file would ordinarily be.

Illustration 3–16

SUBFILE OPENED	
Client Number	_____
File Number	_____
Subfile Designation	_____
	Opened By:_____

§ 3.106 File Opening Checklist

At the time she opens a file, the file clerk should utilize a file opening checklist to ensure that all essential steps have been followed. (See Illustration 3–17.)

Illustration 3–17

```
┌─────────────────────────────────────────────────────────┐
│               FILE OPENING CHECKLIST                      │
│                                                           │
│                               Date: _____              │
│  INITIAL WHEN COMPLETED                                   │
│  _____      Files checked for conflict of interest     │
│  _____      File number assigned and added to master   │
│                num-eric list                              │
│  _____      Numeric master card prepared and filed in  │
│                master file                                │
│  _____      File folder and subfolders (if any) prepared│
│  _____      Client and cross-reference index cards      │
│                prepared and filed                         │
│  _____      Tickler established for statute of limita-  │
│                tions, answer date, or other critical dates │
│                and filed in docket system                 │
│  _____      "Out" card inserted on file shelf          │
│  _____      New Matter Report typed and distributed: (a)│
│                Original to master file; (b) copy to        │
│                attorney's book; (c) copy in file; (d) copy │
│                circulated                                 │
│  _____      File returned to attorney's desk           │
└─────────────────────────────────────────────────────────┘
```

§ 3.107 New Files List

As part of the file opening process, a list of all new files should be prepared periodically (perhaps weekly) and distributed to all attorneys. This serves as an additional conflict of interest check and also keeps attorneys informed of what is going on. This is another function that can later be computerized.

§ 3.108 Preparing File Labels

Type the name on the label very close to the top of the label so that it will be visible when materials are placed in the file. Begin typing in the first or second typing space from the left edge of the label so that all labels will be uniform. If the label contains more than one line, indent the second and third lines three spaces so the name on the first line will stand out. It is preferable to type labels with only initial caps instead of solid caps because they are easier to read. Type the file number on the label as well as the name, leaving at least three spaces between the number and words so that the number will stand out.

§ 3.109 Attorney's Approval on Filing

Incoming mail should always be seen by the attorney before it is filed. Some offices require an attorney's initials on all materials coming into the office before the papers are filed in the client folders.

§ 3.110 Organizing the Files

Keep the files neat and orderly. Establish a policy for setting up the files by category: correspondence on the top left side of the file, with the most recent on top; pleadings on the top right side of the file; notes attached at the bottom left of the file. Expandable or multi-part folders, which allow for more division of the file's contents, are available from your office products supplier. Each firm can set up the files so that the contents are available for easy reference. With the exception of clients' personal papers, every piece of paper should be fastened into the file. Metal prongs are excellent for this purpose; some file folders have the prongs permanently attached to the folder. There is no excuse for a sloppy file; the time you spend fastening in papers is more than offset by the time you save in locating materials in the file.

§ 3.111 Use of the File Number

Once the file has been opened and assigned a file number, that number should be shown on all correspondence, statements, and other file documentation. The secretary should note the file number on all pleadings so that the file clerks will have no problem identifying the document for filing. If there are subfiles, the proper subfile identification should also be included. If the document should not be defaced, the file number should be written on a separate note. The secretary should be actively involved in the filing process. She is in a much better position than the file coordinator to identify the files with which she works. For that reason, it is the responsibility of the secretary to see that proper file numbers are noted on all filing material. She is often in a position to do her own filing and should do so as much as possible.

§ 3.112 Preparing Material for Filing

Sort papers by category (client, personal, general correspondence). Check to see if the attorney has initialed papers for filing if this is office procedure. After papers have been sorted by category, sort within the category, placing them in either numerical or alphabetical order, whichever is appropriate for the firm's filing system. Decide where the paper should be filed. (This is known as "indexing.") Mark the paper with the filing notation, such as the file number in numerical filing, or underline the name on the document which indicates in which file it should be placed. (This is known as "coding.") If it goes in a subject file, write the subject in the upper right-hand corner. Carefully punch holes at the top of the paper, placing them so that when the document is placed in the folder, it won't be crowded into the fold of the folder. When placing material in the folder, verify the number and name.

Daily filing means just that—daily. It cannot wait until you have time. An attorney relies on the contents of the file to reflect the file's current status. Therefore, a missing letter or document can have serious ramifications.

Filing should be done by the secretary most familiar with the file (or the file coordinator), not by the part-time clerk or by the newest secretary in the office. The secretary should do the filing daily in those files stored in her or the attorney's work area; the file coordinator should do the filing in the files located in the central file room. The secretary is responsible, however, for giving the file coordinator sufficient, accurate information to ensure that the filing is done properly. (See Illustration 3–18.)

Illustration 3–18

SAMPLE TRANSMITTAL SLIP FOR ITEMS TO BE FILED
TO: _____
FROM: _____
DATE: _____
Attached are the following items
_____
_____
to be filed in the following file:
Client No. _____
Matter No. _____

§ 3.113 When the Client Wants to See His File

If a client asks to see his file, never hand him the file without prior permission from the attorney. Upon direction of the attorney, you may allow him to look at certain papers in the file in your presence. All files which are released from the office should be noted in a "Release File," stating the name of the person to whom the file is released, the date the file leaves the office, and the name of the attorney authorizing release of the file. The person taking the file should sign a receipt for it. This protects the office in the event of future questions on the file.

§ 3.114   Assignment of Files to Other Attorneys

In a firm where attorneys frequently assign work to other attorneys, there must be a system for notifying the file room that another attorney has the file. An easy way to do this is for the responsible attorney's secretary to fill out a transfer slip for the file coordinator so that the "out" card can be changed to show who has the file. (See Illustration 3–19.) Additionally, the responsible attorney's secretary should prepare a Rolodex card for the assigned attorney's secretary for her system. (See Illustration 3–15.)

Illustration 3–19

FILE TRANSFER NOTIFICATION
Client Number _____
Matter Number _____
Transferred by _____ Date: _____
Transferred to _____ Date: _____
File Room Notified _____ Date: _____

Assignment of files to other attorneys is one of the most difficult file functions to control. At the time of assignment, the attorney is thinking only of the necessity of forwarding the file to whoever will do the work. This creates two problems. The first is that the central file records are inaccurate if the assignment notation is not made on the "out" card. The second is that the responsible attorney, particularly if he assigns many files to different attorneys, may forget that he has assigned the file or to whom it was assigned. This makes it impossible to find the file when it is needed.

All attorneys should be encouraged to tell you when they assign a file in order that a transfer form can be prepared and sent to the file room. Secretaries should also look for new files coming to the attorneys. They can then check with the file clerk to see if a transfer slip has been completed.

§ 3.115   Sending Active Files to Central File Room

With centralized storage available, an attorney has the option of storing as many files as he wishes in the central file room. With an effective system, it makes sense to keep as few files as possible in your work area. This alleviates clutter and confusion when you are looking for a misplaced file.

No file should be sent to the central file room unless a review date has been entered into the docket control system. In some firms the docket control date is entered on the file folder so that the file coordinator can verify that a review date has been entered. This is a good procedure to follow. If a file is sent to the central file room without a tickler date, it is returned to the attorney. (In small firms the same person can serve as file coordinator and docket clerk.)

§ 3.116 Retrieving Files From Central File Room

For a more effective system, controlled access to the central file room is critical. "Controlled access" means that only the file coordinator removes files from the file room. This means that the attorney or the secretary tells the file coordinator which file he or she wants, and the file coordinator "checks the file out" to whoever wants it. The obvious reason for this is so that an "out" card can be inserted, which indicates the name of the attorney who has the file. Thus, the file coordinator knows where files are physically located if they are not in the file room.

Controlled access does not usually exist in small firms. Unless the secretaries and attorneys work together to ensure that "out" cards are always inserted when files are pulled, the system will soon lose its effectiveness and its credibility.

Even in firms where there is controlled access, it is impossible for the file coordinator to be in the file room at all times. Therefore, attorneys and secretaries are free to help themselves to files after hours. Problems do arise if the "out" system is not honored.

§ 3.117 Occasional Inventories

At regular intervals, the file coordinator should check attorneys' offices to verify that her records are correct, *i.e.,* the files are where the file room records indicate they are.

§ 3.118 Closing Files

In most law firms attorneys usually feel that it is not necessary to close files as long as there is plenty of filing space available. The crunch comes when there is no longer sufficient space. By then the task is often so monumental that outside help is needed. Unfortunately, closing files is rarely a priority item for attorneys. This is another area where the legal secretary can be of invaluable assistance. The secretary should view it as her responsibility to help the attorney close files on a regular basis. If this is done regularly, the problem of spending months cleaning out file drawers to make room for new files will be alleviated.

Since many attorneys will not cull files, the secretary should review the contents of the file to remove scratch paper, legal pads, and other extraneous material (excluding any legal documents). Before closing the file, the attorney must decide the eventual disposition of the files. (See Illustration 3–20.)

Illustration 3–20

```
┌──────────────────────────────────────────────────────────────┐
│                     FILE CLOSING FORM                          │
│   TO:        File Department            DATE: _____     │
│   FROM:      _____ for _____  │
│                    (Secretary)              (Attorney Initials) │
│   SUBJECT: _____ │
│             File Name                         Our File No.     │
│                                                                │
│                  _____-_____                          │
│                   Client and Matter No.                        │
│          This file has been closed and stripped on this date.  │
│          _____ Destroy file after January 1, _____       │
│          _____ Review file _____ (date)                  │
│          _____ Retain file permanently                      │
│          _____ File checked for retrieval information       │
│   Special Instructions: _____  │
│   Closed File # Assigned: _____  │
│                                                                │
│                              _____  │
│                                     File Coordinator           │
└──────────────────────────────────────────────────────────────┘
```

§ 3.119 Closed File Numbers

Some firms do not renumber files when they are closed. The only disadvantage to this is that constant reshuffling of files may be necessary to make room for files which must be inserted. Therefore, it is usually preferable to have a system under which a new number is given to the file in the file closing process. There are many numbering systems available. One which works well is to have the number relate to the year in which the file is closed. An easy way is to assign numbers in strict sequential order totally unrelated to the numbering system for active files. The file coordinator maintains a register (which can be a card index) for these file numbers. For example:

94–01

94–02

94–03

The first two digits indicate that the file was closed in 1994. The last two digits give the order in which the file was closed in that year.

The file coordinator stamps the closed file number on the master index card and moves it to the closed file index. She also pulls all other cross-index cards pertinent to that file and moves them to the closed file index. This index is also in alphabetical order. The file coordinator notes the file number on the file and moves the file to the closed file area.

§ 3.120   Destruction of Files

Some law firms have never destroyed files and are still storing in expansive storage areas files which are 50 to 100 years old. Many of these firms are now changing their philosophies about the necessity to maintain these files perpetually. Storage of files that will never be used again is expensive. From a business standpoint, some firms are taking the position that it is not a depository for clients' necessary papers—tax returns, wills, etc.—and are now putting the burden of maintaining these necessary papers on the clients themselves. What must be retained from a legal standpoint is a subjective decision which only the firm can make. Generally, firms are taking the position that it is necessary to keep only those documents which cannot be replaced, are not in a court record, or for which they are not protected under the statutes of limitations.

Most firms feel that there are some files which must be retained permanently. As part of the file destruction process, the firm must develop guidelines by which files must be retained permanently. A retention timetable should be developed by area of practice.

§ 3.121   Return of Files to Clients

One way to avoid storage of unnecessary papers is to purge the file of "client" papers when the file goes into inactive or closed status. The file is often composed in large part of documentation furnished by the client for a particular case or contract or as resource material in an estate plan. Once the file is ready for inactive status, there is no reason not to return these papers to the client at that time—when the client can still be contacted. Many firms also offer the file to the client when the file comes up for destruction. Here again, the secretary must be guided by the firm's policy.

§ 3.122   Off–Premises Storage

Particularly in larger metropolitan areas, firms are storing closed and permanent files in commercial file storage facilities. In some instances, commercial storage is less expensive than on-premises storage.

§ 3.123   Microfilm

Some firms are now microfilming files upon closing and destroying the files.

§ 3.124 Filing Supplies and Equipment

In many firms, there is an astounding lack of uniformity in filing supplies. Apparently, those attorneys who prefer particular types of file folders, clamps, subfiles, expandable folders, etc., are accommodated by the firm. Other firms have adopted file procedures which include the use of standardized filing supplies. It is easier to take advantage of volume discounts, and file folders and other supplies are uniform and consistent. This eliminates the question of what supply should be used for which attorney in a given situation. Unfortunately, this is an area in which a secretary often has no control. If she is asked to help standardize firm procedures, she should be aware of the available alternatives in order to be in a position to help.

§ 3.125 Color Coding

Vendors of filing supplies are constantly extolling the virtues of color coding. The extent to which color coding helps is totally dependent upon the individual firm. In firms where there is continuous movement of files among various attorneys, color-coded file folders can be helpful in locating missing files. If color-coded folders are used, color-coded expandable files are also helpful in locating "lost" files. It has been estimated that color coding can reduce misfiling by up to 80 percent. According to some authorities, color coding increases accuracy, speeds up the filing function, and lessens the time spent to find missing files.

Color can be used in a law office in many ways. The following are some possibilities:

- Use a different color for different types of cases, *e.g.*, green for real estate, red for domestic relations, blue for probate, etc.

- Use a different color for the first letter of the last name. Some systems assign colors as follows: The initial letter of B when followed by "a," "b," "c," or "d," is indicated by a green colored tab. When the initial B is followed by "e," "f," "g," or "h," the tab is orange, and so on.

- In numerical filing, a different color can be used for different digits. Generally, the color is determined by the next-to-last digit. Therefore, each group of ten folders is in one color with a second contrasting color for the next ten folders. By using more than one color on the tab of tens, hundreds, and thousands, it is possible to code up to any number.

Four commonly used color filing systems are Varidex and Colorscan, both by Remington Rand; Super–Ideal System by Shaw–Walker;

and Alpha Code System by TAB Products. Others are available at your office store and through business magazine advertisements. Write for information if the system cannot be obtained locally.

§ 3.126 Filing Equipment

Although for many years there was little choice of the type of filing equipment a firm could utilize, this is certainly no longer true. Many vendors are competing to sell their space-saver equipment. As with other types of office equipment, one type is not necessarily better than another. What a firm should use depends upon its needs.

Generally, the types of equipment available include:

- Vertical file drawers. These are the traditional file cabinets which have been in law offices for years. They are the least space efficient and are cumbersome to use, particularly in view of other file equipment currently on the market.

- Lateral file drawers. These are file cabinets, but the files are arranged laterally, providing more space efficiency than vertical file cabinets. They are also more convenient for the user in terms of inserting and removing files.

- Open-shelf filing. Open-shelf filing is also lateral filing, but files are placed vertically on open shelves, which are usually seven feet high. There are no drawers. Open-shelf filing is more space efficient than either lateral file cabinets or vertical file drawers.

- Space-saving retractable shelves. This is the most efficient equipment from a space-saving standpoint. The open shelves are placed on tracks so that an aisle is not required between each row of shelves. There are numerous types available, and each firm must determine which best suits its needs. From a safety standpoint, any firm purchasing this type of equipment should make certain that it is equipped with a slip clutch. This slip clutch causes the movement of the unit to stop when it makes contact with an object. Some manufacturers also feature an optional safety bar that is installed outside the aisle and physically crosses the open aisle. The bar not only locks the equipment but also serves as a visual reminder that the equipment is in use.

Before a firm can make a final decision on conversion of present space or on selection of equipment, it must make sure that the floor load capacity of the area will accommodate any added weight.

§ 3.127 Definition of Docket Control System

A docket control system is a critical ingredient of files management. A "docket" (also referred to as a "tickler," a "calendar," or a "diary") is a reminder system. It provides a means of keeping track of deadlines and court dates for both litigation and non-litigation matters. It should serve not only as a reminder but also as a means of file control, scheduling, and planning. It ensures that work is done in the ordinary course of business rather than at the last minute when someone remembers the deadline. Regardless of the size of the firm, there should be only one system—a firm-wide system. This means that every single file must have an entry in the docket control system.

Missed deadlines or poor follow-through is responsible for many malpractice claims. Malpractice carriers, in an effort to reduce claims, are carefully reviewing docket control systems before issuing insurance. Since malpractice coverage rates are also escalating and coverage is more difficult to obtain, firms are paying much more attention to firm-wide docket control as an effective loss prevention technique. Insurance companies are encouraging lawyers to develop what they are defining as "loss prevention programs" to help reduce malpractice claims.

Some legal secretarial texts (and some law firms) differentiate between the terms "docket," "tickler," "diary," "calendar," and "follow-up." For example, in some firms the word "docket" is used only to identify litigation deadlines. In some instances the word "docket" is used to refer only to the number given a case by a court. The word "docket" is also used to mean a court docket or a list of cases to be tried in a certain court term.

"Tickler" system is used to identify non-litigation matters that require attention in the ordinary course of business, whether those dates are fixed by law, by commitment to the client, or by the attorney who simply wishes to review the file at that time. "Follow-up" system, "suspense file," or "tracer" are synonyms for "tickler" system.

The words "tickler," "calendar," "diary," and "follow-up" are also sometimes used to indicate the specific entry in the docket control system.

> EXAMPLES: The tickler entry shows that a trial is scheduled for May 5, 1994.
> The calendar shows that a trial is scheduled for May 5, 1994.
> The diary shows that a trial is scheduled for May 5, 1994.
> The follow-up entry shows that a trial is scheduled for May 5, 1994.

"Diary" is used to indicate appointments with clients, court dates (a duplication of the docket control entry), and other important matters entered in the docket control system to which the attorney or the secretary refers on a daily basis. The diary may also contain a record of the time an attorney spends on a given appointment or project in order to bill the client for the time spent. This is no longer a common practice as most lawyers use time sheets or time slips on which to record time. The diary is generally an appointment book or calendar. The diary or calendar is one of the tools used in an effective docket control system.

The differentiation described above is often made with the assumption that there will be more than one system to help control the firm's workflow and the attorneys' schedules. The concept is that if one system is used for entering all appointments, deadlines, court dates, and other reminders of work to be done, the system will become too unwieldy. The disadvantage to such an approach is that it is more cumbersome to keep track of several systems when one can accomplish the same objective.

It is important for the legal secretary to determine how these terms are used in her office and to learn as quickly as possible the system the firm or the attorney to whom she is assigned uses to keep track of important dates and critical deadlines. If the system does not provide a method for handling work on which there is no particular deadline, the secretary should ask the attorney how this is done.

§ 3.128 Controlling the Workflow

It is the legal secretary's most important responsibility to see that there is a docket control entry for every file for which her attorney is responsible. The docket control system is one which all attorneys and secretaries refer to on a daily basis. It is the hub from which all work flows.

The ingredients of a good docket control system are:

1. Diaries or calendars for the secretary and the attorney

2. A tickler card file or a follow-up folder system

3. A central office calendar

Although a firm-wide system is preferable, there are still many firms in which each attorney has responsibility for his own docket control systems. If the firm or attorney does not have an organized system of docket control, this is a good opportunity for the legal secretary to show her creativity.

§ 3.129 Types of Systems

There are several types of docket control systems used in law offices, and different secretarial texts and law office management experts recommend different ones. What is important is that there be a system in writing and that the system be used and maintained religiously.

§ 3.130 Essential Ingredients

The essential ingredients of a docket control system are:

1. Immediate and automatic calendaring

2. A cross-check on entries and notifications

3. Sufficient lead time to accomplish the task

4. A follow-up on actual performance of the task

§ 3.131 Responsibility for the System

Although primary responsibility for the docket control system rests with the attorney, the legal secretary is responsible for its administrative aspects. She is responsible for getting the information into the system. To the extent that the secretary has access to the information, she is often expected to make entries into the system without the necessity of instruction from the attorney. Therefore, this responsibility carries with it the need for the legal secretary to be resourceful in determining important dates that should be entered into the system. It is better to have more entries than are necessary than to risk missing an important date.

§ 3.132 Items to Be Calendared

Any type of future commitment belongs in the docket control system. Examples are:

• All dates related to litigation, including statutes of limitations dates; due or deadline dates for various pleadings and briefs; deadlines for notices of appeal and renewals of judgments; deposition dates; due dates for answers to interrogatories; dates by which certain discovery material must be made available; dates by which subpoenas must be issued and served; and trial and hearing dates.

• Dates by which adverse parties in litigation have agreed to provide material, data, or information.

• Dates by which service of process is expected to be made.

• Dates by which the receipt of certain documents or requested information—medical opinions, accident reports, weather reports, certified copies of documents, checks for advanced costs—is expected.

- Filing and hearing dates for various estate matters, such as federal estate tax returns, state inheritance tax returns, notice dates required by law, and dates of annual and final accountings.

- Follow-up dates for annual reports, minutes of meetings, etc., provided for corporate clients.

- Dates by which clients must meet the requirements of a contract provision.

- Proof of publication from newspapers on advertisements required in various types of actions.

- Follow-up dates for work in progress on all files.

- Follow-up dates for review of inactive files or review of files labeled for destruction.

- Appointments.

- Professional and personal commitments.

- Accounting and administrative deadlines, such as personnel and expense accounting, tax returns and other tax-related reports, supply ordering, lease renewals, maintenance contract renewals, insurance policy renewals, etc.

§ 3.133 Calendar Systems

Some firms employ double calendar systems. Two calendar or diary entries are made for each transaction or date which requires a reminder. One entry is made on a calendar or diary kept by the attorney who is responsible for meeting the deadline, and the other entry is made on a central calendar kept by a secretary or docket clerk. Both the attorney and the secretary are responsible for checking the calendar or diary each day to be sure all deadlines and appointments are kept. A major drawback to this type of system is that the calendars used may become full and run out of space in which to record new entries.

§ 3.134 Perpetual Calendars

A system employed by many firms—and one which overcomes the problem of the full calendar—is a perpetual calendar system. This system employs a standard pocket or desk calendar or diary kept by the attorney, but the central calendar maintained by the secretary is kept on index cards and can grow with the firm—it never gets full. The secretary may also keep a desk calendar also as a supplement to the perpetual calendar.

A perpetual calendar can be kept in a 3″ × 5″ index card file or in "follow-up" file folders. An index card file consists of:

1. Twelve major guides labeled January through December.

2. A set of numerical guides marked from 1 through 31 for the days of the month.

3. A set of blank index guides to provide dividers for at least five future years.

4. Tickler form cards. (See Illustration 3–21.)

Illustration 3–21

TICKLER FORM

Date to be reminded: _____
IMPORTANT REMINDER
To Attorney(s): _____
Re:　　　　_____
_____
Message:　_____
_____
_____

(May be used for follow-up request and as reminder memorandum from Docket Coordinator)

The pertinent information is placed behind the proper day of the month (if in the current month) or behind the guide for the month in which action is to be accomplished. A tickler file does not take the place of a diary or a calendar; it supplements it. Recurring items such as rent payments can be entered on one card and moved from month to month as they are paid. Only one card needs to be prepared. These entries do not need to be made 12 times in the diary. Tickler cards are particularly useful when a follow-up date is indefinite. A good example is a file on which there are no critical deadlines but there is work to be done. A simple entry of "review file" can be moved ahead easily.

§ 3.135 Follow–Up File Systems

Some offices prefer a follow-up file system to a tickler card system. With follow-up files, the secretary prepares file folders in the same manner as she would guide cards for the tickler system. Materials are placed in the proper file folder. Offices using this system make an extra copy of any letter requiring a follow-up (such as collection letters) and place a copy of the letter in the file folder. The office file copy still goes to the client file in case it is needed before the follow-up date. Copies of short documents are also placed in the folder. In lieu of placing the document in the folder, a slip stating the name of the client, the type of response due, and the date when it is due can be used.

When sending certified or registered mail, keep the receipt in the follow-up file until you receive the return receipt or you are notified of receipt. For matters referred to other attorneys, a slip can be made giving a follow-up date for checking on progress.

§ 3.136   Automated Calendars

Many firms now have computers which have records management capabilities. Reminder dates and pertinent information are fed into the machine, recorded, and later retrieved by date, by attorney, by file, or other sequence. At regular intervals, perhaps weekly, semi-weekly, or monthly, a master, or office, calendar (list of reminder dates) is printed for each lawyer individually and one for the entire firm. Friday is a popular day for distributing the calendar, since it is useful to attorneys in planning their work schedules for the upcoming weeks. The calendar lists by date every future commitment of all firm attorneys. In some firms file review items are not included on the master calendar.

§ 3.137   Calendaring Incoming Mail

For the system to be effective, ALL incoming mail must be opened and processed by the secretary. Under no circumstances should any mail be removed from her desk prior to processing.

The secretary sets up ticklers from all incoming mail which notify an attorney of any due date, such as a hearing date, brief deadline, trial date, etc. She writes "Noted" and initials it.

The attorney is equally responsible for seeing that any items in the mail requiring ticklers or calendar notations are properly handled. Any piece of mail requiring a tickler which is not marked "noted" should be returned to the secretary with instructions to set up the proper ticklers. Depending upon the nature of the deadline, it is critical that the docket control entries be current. Docket control requires constant attention. It is not something you can put off until later. Make the entry as soon as you learn of the date, regardless of how you learn about it. For instance, as you are reviewing the mail, enter right then dates mentioned in letters or in notices. Calculate the return time on summonses, interrogatories, etc., and enter them in the diary. If you do not know how to calculate these dates, ask the attorney. When you are typing notices, interrogatories, or material requiring a response by a certain date, log these in the system. The secretary may also enter the date in both her desk calendar or diary and the attorney's. Deciding how much or how little should also be

113

entered on the desk calendars is a matter of judgment which the secretary will acquire as she gains experience. Examples of what should be entered in the desk calendars or diaries include appointments, meetings, court dates, birthdays and anniversaries, etc., and any *critical* deadline dates. Don't clutter the calendar. On the other hand, it is better to have too much than too little.

§ 3.138   Calendaring Telephone Calls and Office Conferences

Often a hearing date or other matter requiring a tickler or calendar entry results from an office or telephone conference with another attorney, judge, clerk, etc. It is imperative that the attorney scheduling a hearing or other appointment tell the secretary of the hearing or due date so that she can set up a tickler or calendar entry. Be sure there is a supply of tickler forms on the attorney's desk for his convenience.

In the event an attorney sets a hearing date, deposition, appointment, or some other event of which he wishes to be reminded, he should note the date on his own calendar and on a tickler card to give to the secretary for filing. Attorneys also use the tickler forms for establishing recall dates for files by noting the date on a tickler form and attaching it to the file folder.

Prior to filing the tickled file in the central files, the secretary notes the tickler date in the upper right-hand corner of the face of the file folder. Thus, if a tickled file is removed from the central files for a conference, reference, or the like, it is readily apparent that the file is tickled and can be refiled.

Prior to filing a tickler prepared by an attorney, the secretary should check the tickler to determine if additional lead time will be needed. For instance, any item tickled that requires a written document or a personal appearance will require several tickler slips—the last of which is always the due date.

EXAMPLES:

- Statute of Limitations
  No less than five tickler slips are set up to tickle a statute of limitations as follows:
  1. Three months prior to expiration of the statute
  2. Two months prior to expiration
  3. One month prior to expiration
  4. One week prior to expiration
  5. Date of expiration
- Answer (to complaint, interrogatories, motion to produce, etc.)

114

No less than four tickler slips are set up to tickle an answer due date as follows:

1. Fifteen days prior to answer date
2. Ten days prior to answer date
3. Five days prior to answer date
4. Answer due date

- Hearing dates

    There must be at least three tickler slips as follows:

    1. One for a date sufficiently ahead of the actual due date to allow for necessary preparation (dependent upon the nature of the hearing)
    2. One for the day before the hearing
    3. One for the date of the hearing

When a document being prepared necessitates typing, there should be at least two full working days allowed for typing of the document. For particularly lengthy briefs, contracts, and the like three full working days should be allowed. If a document requires outside printing, sufficient time should be allowed. These deadlines must be kept in mind when setting up tickler dates. The due date means that the attorney's work product must be completed and the final document out of the office by that date.

§ 3.139 Responsibility for Docket Control System

Some offices entrust the docket control system to one individual (often referred to as a "docket clerk" or "docket coordinator"), who is responsible for reminding all attorneys of deadlines a minimum number of days in advance. With this system all secretaries and attorneys are required to furnish the pertinent information to the docket coordinator. This can be done using the form shown as Illustration 3–21. In some firms all mail and all pleadings (whether coming into the firm or leaving the firm) are routed to the docket coordinator to ensure that all critical dates are entered into the system. The docket coordinator then sends written reminders of all deadline dates. Attorneys responsible for the work must then notify the docket coordinator that the work has been completed. If the docket coordinator has not been notified of the completion of the work by the deadline dates, she follows up to be sure the work was done.

§ 3.140 Final Responsibility With Secretary

The secretary must always remember that the final responsibility for reminding the attorney of deadlines rests with her. Even if there is a central reminder system operated by one member of the staff, she must monitor it carefully, making sure that the attorney receives the reminder and that the work has been done.

§ 3.141 Daily Checking of Diaries/Calendars

The first thing the secretary should do in the morning and the last thing she should do at night is to check her diary with the attorney's. They should correspond, but often she will find that he has made appointments without notifying her, or she has made appointments without entering them on his diary. She should then make them correspond with each other. By checking the diaries for the next several days, she will be "on top" of things. Knowing what may come up tomorrow will make life easier today. She can anticipate and plan ahead.

§ 3.142 Calendaring of Unscheduled Appointments

If a client drops in without an appointment, the legal secretary should make note on the attorney's calendar because it may later be necessary to verify that the client was in the attorney's office on that particular day. If she also notes this information on her calendar, the legal secretary can check with the attorney to see what work must be done for the client.

§ 3.143 Retention of Diaries/Calendars

After the year is completed, diaries should be retained with the accounting records. They serve as a handy reference to determine who was in on what date and what business might have transpired. Many attorneys have had to go back to their diaries to recreate a sequence of events for a client.

The legal secretary's diary contains all the information that the attorney's does. It also includes her personal deadlines, reminders, and appointments. This might seem like a duplication of effort, but it provides good backup for the reminder system.

§ 3.144 Reminder System

A formal reminder system should be established, as should a good working rapport with the attorney. Some attorneys postpone projects until the last minute. This means that you will be putting in a lot of overtime unless you develop the knack of getting him to do the work sooner. You can leave reminders on his desk or chair, taped to his briefcase, or pinned to his overcoat. Use bright paper so the message will be obvious. Some secretaries become very original and creative in their reminders. The important thing is to get action.

An attorney might unconsciously play "hide-and-seek" with the secretary. He leaves his office and disappears. If there are several attorneys in the firm and more than one is familiar with each case, this disappearance act is not too drastic. In a small firm, however, it is essential that the secretary be able to reach the attorney on matters which might arise in his absence. When the attorney leaves the office, ask him where he can be reached. If he is going out of town, obtain a copy of his itinerary, including lodging. He should understand that you are not checking up on him; you just want to be prepared for any emergency which might occur.

You might find when you are establishing a new client file that you do not have all of the necessary information you need, such as complete names, addresses, ages, phone numbers, and so on. This might be just an oversight. If it occurs often, you need to arrange with the attorney to sit in on the latter part of the initial interview so that you can obtain the information. In the alternative, you might prepare a checklist or client interview sheet for his use in obtaining needed information.

The good secretary complements the attorney by filling in any gaps. They work as a team and everyone benefits. The word "synergy" means making the whole equal to more than the sum of its parts. In the law office, this means that when you take one good attorney and add one good secretary, with both working as a team, you get a work output that is greater than the total of what each could do separately. One plus one can equal three.

§ 3.145   Summary of Docket Control System

It is critical to the functioning of a docket system that the secretary receive notice of all deadline dates, appointment dates, court appearances, etc., in order that every future commitment is automatically and immediately calendared. Input must come from each staff member.

§ 3.146   Retrieval System

A retrieval system is one designed to preserve material that might be helpful to the firm in the future. The preservation of legal research, briefs, and forms can save a tremendous amount of time on future work. Not only does it save time in preparation of a document or in doing legal research, but it also saves time the attorney and the secretary might otherwise spend looking for a form "we used in that Jones case two years ago." Legal work received from other law firms or legal departments may be put into the system for future reference. This obviates the necessity of trying to remember where someone has seen a particular form or legal opinion about a particular topic, etc.

Retrieval systems are considered an important ingredient of files management and would become more efficient if the work product were integrated into the system immediately. The tendency is to postpone development of a system "until I have more time." In the meantime, there is more material which should be integrated into the system, the task becomes overwhelming, and it doesn't get done.

As with a filing system, the key to an effective, useful retrieval system is a good index with extensive cross-indexing. A subjective filing system (and most retrieval systems are) requires extensive cross-indexing. Most such systems are indexed by major practice area categories and then by subtopics. Some are tied to the West Key Number System, but that numbering system is controlled by an extensive subject matter index.

Documents in the system are considered *masters* and are not removed from the system. Anyone who wants to work from the document makes a photocopy so the original is always in the system. In some firms the work product is not physically maintained in a separate system, but rather there is an index which identifies the file in which the work product can be found.

One of the things most systems lack is a weeding process. Should a document be pulled and should the attorney working on it feel that it is obsolete or is a poor work product, he should either weed the document and remove the index cards or attach a note indicating that the document may no longer be applicable because of a change in law (or whatever the reason may be). In a small firm the system tends to be relatively simple and flexible. All attorneys contribute items to the system, update material, and even weed. In larger firms, however, one attorney (or the librarian, if there is one) is given the responsibility for maintenance of the system. Substantive changes cannot be made to the system without approval of the person responsible.

§ 3.147 Summary

The practice of law requires close cooperation and teamwork between the lawyer and the secretary. It is the function of the secretary to save the lawyer time and to fulfill his stenographic and administrative requirements. The practice of law is a business, and the law office is a business office. Only through teamwork, cooperation, and strict compliance with duties can progress be made.

CHAPTER 4

COMPUTERS IN THE LAW OFFICE

Table of Sections

----

§ 4.1 Concept

Information management is a system of processing all types of information (written text, statistics, voice communications, and any other form of data) at top speed with the highest accuracy, least effort, and lowest cost utilizing modern automated equipment, standardized procedures, and specialized personnel. Equipment used in the processing of information is known as a computer. A computer can be programmed to perform specific tasks, such as word processing, accounting, data base management, etc.

It is important, therefore, to understand the basic components and concepts of a computer before any discussion on law office applications.

§ 4.2 Major Computer Components

A computer system is made up of hardware and software. The hardware consists of all the equipment and devices discussed in this section that make up the computer system.

All computers have three major components:

1. Input Device—Keyboard, optical character reader, floppy disk, magnetic tape, voice recognition, or any other device that allows an operator to get information or data into the computer.

2. Central Processing Unit (CPU)—Part of the computer where all computations, sorting, selecting, and all data manipulation takes place. The CPU consists of three components:

   • Main Memory—The staging area for information or programs waiting to be processed either as input or output. Memory size is expressed in megabytes (MB) where one MB equals approximately one million characters or bytes of information.

   • Control Unit—Basically the brain of the computer, which directs the operations of the computer by following the instructions programmed into it. It references main storage for the next instruction to be executed and the next batch of data to be processed. It then retrieves the data from storage, reads the instructions, and executes in the arithmetic/logic unit.

   • Arithmetic/Logic Unit—Performs all computations and processing of information.

3. Output Device—Printer, video display, magnetic tape or disk, floppy disk, microfilm, or any other device that accepts the output or results of the computer processing. Storage capacity on storage devices utilized for output is usually expressed in "MB" or "megabytes." One megabyte of storage equals one million bytes or characters of information. For example, a storage device which can store 60 MB can store 60 million characters of information.

(See Illustration 4–1.)

Illustration 4–1

MAJOR COMPONENTS OF A COMPUTER

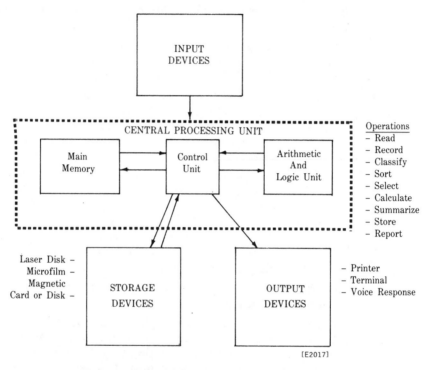

[E2017]

The computer's input devices translate coded data into electrical impulses which are sent to the computer's memory. The data is processed by the CPU and then sent to the output device, which translates the electrical impulses into output data such as a printed report. Such devices as magnetic cards and disk drives are classified as both input and output devices.

§ 4.3 Major Software Components

Software is a term used to describe all the various types of programs or sets of instructions which direct the hardware to perform the data processing function. There are two types of software:

1. The software that makes up the operating system of the computer that allows the computer to run itself automatically and perform housekeeping and utility programs.

2. The software or software package, which is a set of programs that performs specific functions or applications, such as word processing, accounts receivable, spreadsheeting, etc. There are

virtually thousands of application software packages available to run on various operating systems.

§ 4.4 Computer Classifications

Computers can be classified as mainframe computers, minicomputers, or microcomputers. The distinction between these classifications is becoming blurred, with microcomputers becoming more powerful every day.

- Microcomputer—The microcomputer is revolutionizing offices and homes. The microcomputer utilizes a microprocessor, a silicon chip smaller than a fingernail. Although very small, the microprocessor has a control unit and an arithmetic/logic unit. Microprocessors can be found everywhere, in microwave ovens, automobiles, watches, etc. More important, however, is that the microprocessor has made computers much smaller and more affordable. The impact of the personal computer, which is based on microprocessor technology, has revolutionized information processing both in the office and at home.

  Microcomputers can be used in a standalone mode, in a communications mode with other microcomputers or larger minicomputers or mainframe computers, or as a terminal in a network of microcomputers to allow the electronic sharing of information and output devices.

- Minicomputer—The minicomputer is a small/large computer with multiple input, output, and storage devices. Minicomputers are most prevalent in law offices with more than 15 to 20 attorneys. Companies such as Hewlett Packard, Digital Equipment, Data General, and IBM all provide a wide selection of minicomputer configurations.

- Mainframe Computer—A very large computer with virtually unlimited expansion capabilities.

§ 4.5 Computer Configuration Classifications

Computer systems can be configured in one of four ways:

1. Standalone System—One central processing unit with internal memory and an internal disk drive and/or floppy disk drive, one input device (usually a workstation that includes a keyboard and a video display), and one output device (printer). It may be able to send or receive information through communications, but it basically cannot share information or devices with other computers.

2. Shared Logic System—One central processing unit with internal memory and multiple internal and/or external disk or tape

drives, multiple input devices (workstations), and multiple output devices (printers). The operation of all devices is dependent on the central processing unit. (See Illustration 4–2.)

Illustration 4–2

SHARED LOGIC SYSTEM

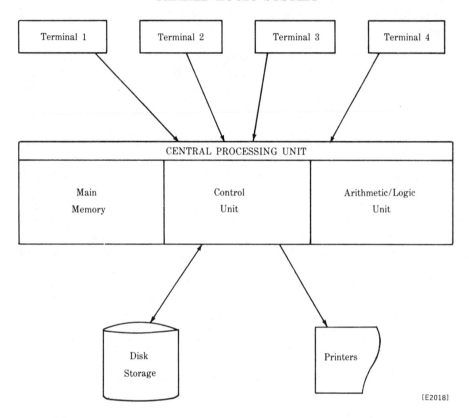

[E2018]

3. Distributed Logic System—Similar to a shared logic system except that, in addition to the internal memory in the CPU, each workstation has its own internal memory. This decreases the number of times the workstations must interact with the CPU, thereby freeing up the CPU to perform other tasks more quickly. (See Illustration 4–3.)

Illustration 4–3

DISTRIBUTED LOGIC SYSTEM

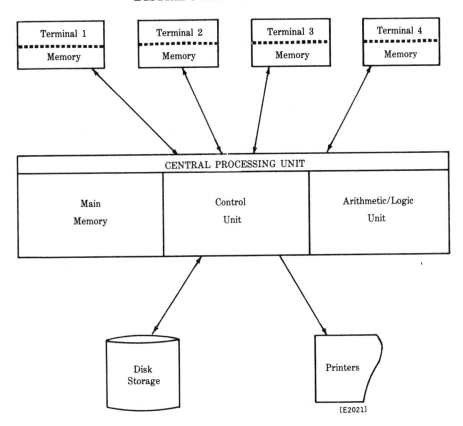

[E2021]

4. Shared Resource System—Similar to a distributed logic system except that, in addition to each workstation's having its own memory, workstations may have their own storage (floppy diskettes or hard disk drive) as well as their own microprocessors. The more sophisticated systems provide multiple microprocessors within the main CPU to handle various functions. For example, a microprocessor may be assigned to monitor all system printers; another microprocessor may be assigned to monitor all input and output functions of the CPU; another microprocessor may be assigned to monitor all communication functions; etc.

The increase in the number of microprocessors within one computer results in faster processing time of all functions. It also allows those workstations with their own microprocessors to operate independently of the main CPU. (See Illustration 4–4.)

Illustration 4–4

SHARED RESOURCE SYSTEM

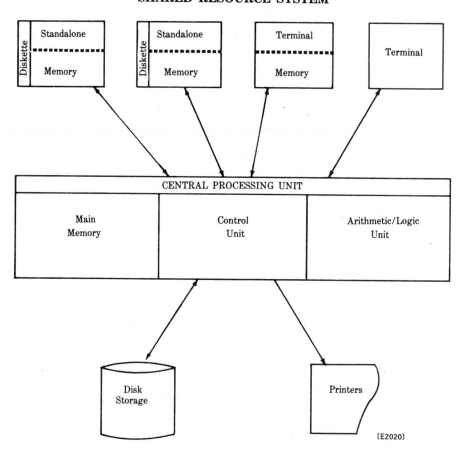

[E2020]

§ 4.6 Data Organization Within the Computer

Data is only meaningful if it can be saved and recalled in an orderly manner. The typical data or memory hierarchy is shown below:

- Bit—The smallest element of computer memory and storage. A bit can represent 1 or 0 ("on" or "off" electrical pulse) in computer memory. The word "bit" is a contraction of the word "binary digit."

- Byte—Normally one byte represents one character or number. Seven or eight bits usually make up a byte, depending on the manufacturer of the computer.

- Field—A group of bytes or characters make up a field. For example, a client number is treated as one field in a computer record.

- Record—A group of related fields. For example, a client record might consist of the client number field, the client address field, client telephone field, etc.

- Block—A group of related records.

- Data File—A group of related blocks or records. For example, a client master file would be considered a data file.

- Volume—All the data on one disk or tape.

- Data Base—A group of associated data files would make up a data base. For example, a client master file, an attorney master file, etc., may make up the firm's time and billing data base.

In a typical law office, the major application is the processing of words. Word processing, therefore, has become a natural application for the law office to automate.

§ 4.7 Definition of Word Processing

Word processing is a method of producing written communication at top speed, with the greatest accuracy, the least effort, and the lowest possible cost through the combined use of proper procedures, automated business equipment, and trained personnel.

§ 4.8 Introduction

Word processing has introduced equipment and management techniques which increase the productivity of typewritten work with a corresponding improvement in typewritten quality. Word processing equipment and procedures are office tools which help law firms serve their clients more efficiently, allowing them to deliver typewritten communications promptly. Since the typewritten word is the most frequent form of communication between lawyers and clients, speed, time savings, and error-free pages are of significant importance in the law office. Word processing should be viewed by legal secretaries as the means of achieving faster completion of typewritten work, reduced proofreading, and reduced overtime. The arrival of automatic typewriters in law offices during the late 1960s transformed the preparation of typewritten work. The rapid technological progression of automatic typewriters, dictation, and copier equipment continued through the

1970s. Because of the impact of these machines, the traditional office had to be reorganized to utilize equipment effectively.

The introduction of the personal computer in the early 1980s made word processing affordable for all offices.

In the law office where there is a considerable amount of repetitive typing and a need for a high degree of accuracy, use of word processing equipment can result in a 300 percent increase in productivity. Equipment is now priced to fit the budget of any law office and, if properly utilized, can pay for itself in a very short period of time.

For the legal secretary, there are numerous benefits to be derived from the use of automatic typing equipment. The secretary can type material onto the equipment at rough-draft speed, make corrections easily, and store the copy for revision at a later date. If the material is revised, the secretary does not need to retype the entire document. She can very quickly locate the material to be revised and make corrections, deletions, or additions. The turnaround time on documents is decreased, proofreading is confined to that portion which has been revised, and error-free copy is produced each time.

§ 4.9 Typing Repetitive Material

Much of the typing done by a legal secretary is repetitive typing using standardized paragraphs. With a conventional typewriter, the secretary must keyboard the same material time after time. With automated equipment, the repetitive material is keyboarded once and played back in the sequence needed for future documents. If there are variables (names, amounts of money, dates), the material can be keyboarded to allow the variables to be typed in on succeeding documents.

§ 4.10 Advantages of Using Automated Equipment

For the attorney, word processing offers minimal proofreading, rapid production of boilerplate (form) documents, easy revision of documents, and an increase in the quantity of error-free legal papers. His proofreading is confined to the first keyboarding of repetitive material and the revisions on revised material. He has the option of making changes on documents without being concerned about the retyping required by the secretary or the time involved in making revisions. Documents can be drafted quickly for his review without concern for getting it "just right" the first time. The final document can be worded exactly as he prefers. While the attorney is conferring with the client about a drafted document, the secretary can be making necessary revisions as she receives them; she can have the finished document ready by the end of the conference.

§ 4.11 Essential Parts of a Word Processing System

The essential parts of a word processing system are Input, Process, Storage, and Output; these are commonly known as "IPSO," with a fifth function being Distribution, "IPSOD."

§ 4.12 Input

Input consists generally of words or information in raw form, *e.g.*, in handwritten drafts, dictation tapes, or shorthand notes. In a law office it may consist of a list of the variables to be incorporated into form paragraphs or form documents which are referenced to a forms book or file.

The human factor must be considered when updating the input operations of an office. Many attorneys are reluctant to give up dictating to their secretaries because they like the one-to-one relationship and the immediate feedback from the secretary. Nevertheless, it is certainly more cost-effective to use dictation equipment.

§ 4.13 Keyboard

The most common method of inputting data into a computer is by means of a keyboard. Most keyboards have an alphabetical and numerical format similar to that on typewriters. (Some of the keys, however, have different uses. For example, the carriage return key enters data, and the backspace key deletes data.) In addition, they have function keys which, when pressed, will cause the computer to perform one or more specific functions (the function will differ with the computer involved), thereby saving the necessity of multiple keystrokes for commonly used procedures.

§ 4.14 Mouse

A mouse is a hand-sized device, flat on the underside and convex on the top, which can be rolled about on a table. A rotating ball on the underside registers the movement and displays a corresponding pointer to various options on the screen. When the pointer designates a function that the user wishes to implement, the user presses a button on the top of the mouse, thereby causing the function to be performed. The advantage of a mouse is its speed (it does not require a series of multiple keystrokes) and its ease (the user need not remember a host of commands, but can simply choose from a menu of options on the screen). One disadvantage is that it requires users to interrupt typing by taking their fingers from the keyboard.

129

§ 4.15   Optical Character Reader

Optical character reader (OCR) equipment is similar to the office copier in appearance; it has the capability to "read" a typewritten page onto word processing systems, providing another means of compatibility between systems.

OCR equipment is a "peripheral" device which may be added to the word processing equipment configuration, providing a means of input to a word processor. Pages may be typed on manual typewriters or printed from automatic typewriters; it is necessary that the typewritten characters are in a type style which is readable by the OCR unit. The copy is then read by the OCR scanner, which converts the black/white variations on the printed page into electrical signals and transfers these to a magnetic medium such as a diskette, which can be utilized by the word processor.

§ 4.16   Advantages

Each secretary in the office with a typewriter can keyboard material using an OCR font. This material is then read into the word processing equipment for storage and revision. Since the original keyboarding of material is the most time-consuming, use of OCR equipment frees the word processing operator and equipment from this initial operation.

Over the past few years, OCR devices have come down in price to the point where even small law offices can consider OCR devices for their operations.

§ 4.17   Disadvantages

With some systems, the error rate is very high when transferring material to magnetic media, resulting in the necessity for a large number of corrections. The time saved in keyboarding is offset by the time spent in correcting the material. The requirements for preparing the material for conversion by the OCR are sometimes so cumbersome that it does not justify the cost involved.

In many areas of the country, OCR devices are marketed by local office equipment dealers. Sometimes these dealers do not have the expertise necessary to assist the law office in successfully interfacing the OCR device to the word processor. It is important to obtain local customer references that have a similar configuration to determine the quality of the technical support provided by the local dealer.

§ 4.18   Process

The process portion of the IPSOD acronym could more accurately be described as a conversion function. The secretary converts the informal input into formal, print-like, understandable output. The outputs are generally typewritten original documents. A word processor captures a document on magnetic media; the document then can be manipulated in many ways before it is transferred to hard copy (output).

§ 4.19 Types of Word Processing Equipment

The general categories of word processing equipment are standalone, clustered, shared logic, and shared resource.

§ 4.20 Electronic Typewriters

Electronic typewriters are suitable for many purposes in a law office. While it is not recommended that they be the only word processing machines, they are very practical for letters, checks, and short documents which do not need revision. The electronic typewriter has many features which benefit the legal secretary, such as lift-off correction, automatic centering, a decimal tab (used in typing columns of figures), and storage of short phrases or small portions of a document. Short form letters can also be stored.

§ 4.21 Intelligent Typewriters

Some electronic typewriters can be upgraded into a display machine with external minidisk media which offers a larger range of capabilities, such as storage of multi-page documents and revisions. These typewriters have a partial line display at the top of the keyboard so that the typist can see what has been typed before the characters are actually printed on the page. The printing is delayed by several characters so the typist can make any change before the characters are printed.

The upgraded electronic typewriter with external storage, though more expensive, is still within the reach of most law office budgets.

Intelligent typewriters are not intended for heavy text editing. They bring such features as automatic centering and underlining and perform in error-free form, reusing the storage space daily.

§ 4.22 Standalone Automatic Typewriters

The term "standalone" means that the system does not require processing power of a central computer. The standalone mechanical, text-editing typewriter consists of a keyboard printer (usually a modified electronic typewriter) that is coupled with a storage console containing edit and central logic, internal memory, and a magnetic media recorder (such as card, cassette, tape cartridges, or diskette). These are usually found in one-secretary offices, centralized correspondence cen-

131

ters, and work clusters. Sometimes they are used as additional input machines for larger text-editing systems. They are quite capable of producing original and repetitive documents. They are suitable for performing limited revisions of short documents but are not recommended for lengthy documents requiring major revisions because of the limited movement within the text. They are basically page-oriented machines.

§ 4.23   Text–Editing Typewriters

Text-editing typewriters usually provide storage plus memory. Text may be stored internally or on discrete (removable) media. Text editing is accomplished by bringing stored text into memory either by recalling it from memory or reading media into memory, where additions, deletions, etc., may be accomplished. The newly edited text can be stored in the same space or another space in memory, on the same or on a second piece of media, thereby retaining the old version, creating a new version, or both.

The volume of characters which may be placed in memory at one time may range from 2,500 to 5,000 characters (from one to two pages). Since the memory is invisible, unless a visual display is available, access through memory to the point of change in a document is usually accomplished by keyboard buttons, which can move through pages, paragraphs, lines, words, and characters.

These machines range from standalone units to computer time-sharing devices.

Text-editing memory typewriters providing discrete media are most productive when used for editing short documents (five to six pages in length). They are also useful for producing originals from stored forms. The internal memory is useful for editing or personalizing short documents of one to three pages in length.

Those linked to computers may provide fast, unattended printout of lengthy documents. The self-contained systems require monitoring during printing and are relatively slow (15 characters per second—cps) by today's standards. They can print unattended if continuous form paper is used.

§ 4.24   Special Features

Each unit or machine has two disk drives for handling text. Documents may be transferred from one station to the other during the editing process, recording new media to match the new hard copy while retaining the old.

An advantage of a dual-disk drive is that the variables needed to personalize and complete forms may be prerecorded, placed in one station, and then merged with a prerecorded form placed in the second drive during printing. Prerecording of variables ensures that all text, including variables, is error-free before it becomes hard copy. The same variables may be stored and reused with other forms, thus eliminating their retyping.

Some text-editing typewriters are available with a one-line display. This permits one line of memory to be visible during draft typing or text editing.

Dual-drive machines are more flexible than single-drive machines; however, productivity is still relatively low because of printing speed (15 cps), the fact that the keyboard is locked while the printer is in operation, and because the playout sometimes requires monitoring. With some models, printing may be accomplished on a separate, fast printer (55 cps or more).

§ 4.25 Standalone Visual Display Typing Systems

Since display standalones are basically computers programmed to do one application—word processing—they differ from mechanical standalones in that they have additional equipment components and are capable of performing more automated functions. They have a visual cathode ray tube (CRT) screen located above the keyboard, a storage console, and a separate printer. Standalone displays are more expensive than mechanical standalones, because they have more sophisticated logic and can perform a greater number of functions at much faster speeds. The media used are typically capable of storing a large volume of text.

These machines offer three important advantages:

1. Since draft typing takes place on a video screen, errors are corrected before printing takes place.

2. Since text is visible during draft typing and text editing, the point of change may be located faster. A "cursor" may be moved up, down, left, or right through a document to the point of change.

3. The printer is a separate unit, providing the simultaneous use of the keyboard/screen and the printer for either related or unrelated work.

On the CRT, the size and number of lines displayed ranges from as few as eight lines up to a full page. The printers most often employ a daisy wheel (impact printing wheel), which is from three to four times faster (45–55 cps) than the text-editing typewriters (15 cps). Other printers utilize the "golf ball" element (15 cps), inkjet (90 cps), or laser technology, producing anywhere from eight to hundreds of pages per minute. They each have their place, depending upon the number of pages of typewritten work to be produced, the quality of appearance of typed characters needed, the number of copies or multiple copies needed, and the method of distribution of the copies.

The storage media are usually a 3½-inch or 5¼-inch floppy diskette, holding from 70,000 to 325,000 characters. Newer models offer a larger, computer-type "hard" disk storing 10 million characters (ten megabytes) or more. Along with more advanced features for draft typing (automatic page numbering, headers, footnotes, etc.), they offer advantages for text editing such as "search and replace," "global search," and numbered variables.

These machines handle small and large jobs equally; the convenient limit on document length is equal to the total volume of storage and the total volume of memory. Many of these machines permit the use of the keyboard and screen for draft typing or text editing at the same time the printer is operating.

§ 4.26 Advantages

Display standalones utilize either magnetic floppy disks or diskettes, tapes, or cassettes for storage. They are particularly suitable to lengthy projects, which require major revision. The large working memory allows the versatility of moving text throughout a document. The visual display screen permits the operator to verify that the changes have been made correctly so the material will play back correctly. This is a decided advantage over the mechanical standalone where the operator is working "blind" throughout the text.

§ 4.27 Cluster Systems

These machines are identical to the standalone machines described above except that a "cluster" (a number of keyboards, each usually equipped with its own CRT) is grouped with one or more printers. The cluster approach is extremely cost-effective compared to standalones which require a printer for each CRT. Cluster systems may or may not share a central processing unit and programming.

Because the printers are separate and extremely fast (55 to 90 cps), one printer can support two to three secretaries, even when each of them works on lengthy documents, permitting the installation of word processing equipment for several secretaries at lower cost than standalone equipment.

Care must be taken to locate printers so that paper handling can be managed easily; time should not be wasted by secretaries walking to and from the nearest printer. In large firms, a printer monitor (someone who handles all phases of printing, including delivery of finished work) may be justified. It is not necessary for the printer monitor to have either legal or word processing experience.

§ 4.28 Shared Logic Systems

Outwardly, shared logic systems are identical to standalone, video display machines, and the cluster machines. The difference is that they share a microprocessor (the brains of the system) as well as the printer. The microprocessor may be visualized as a box providing power, programming, and memory. The bigger the box, the larger and more powerful the system, and the more workstations it can support. The microprocessor may be placed near a word processing supervisor or in an out-of-the way location.

Small shared logic systems use 3½-inch to 5¼-inch floppy disk storage media; larger systems utilize a computer-type hard disk or magnetic tape providing millions of characters of storage. It is desirable and often necessary to provide an extra floppy disk drive for a supervisor's use in removing some documents from the hard disk and storing (archiving or filing) them on floppy diskettes, either for later use or permanent storage. That space on the hard disk then becomes available for new work. On smaller systems utilizing only floppy disk storage, archiving is a must so that there is enough working-disk space and memory available for daily use.

Since the microprocessor represents a major part of the word processing investment, shared logic systems are often the most economical even when as few as three machines are in use. If more workstations (CRTs and keyboards) are needed, they may be added to existing equipment with no further financial outlay for microprocessors and printers.

Firms using three or more automatic typewriters or word processors should investigate shared logic systems when upgrading or adding equipment.

In addition to the cost savings achieved from sharing the microprocessor and printer, shared logic systems offer several other advantages:

- The microprocessor's capacity may be expanded to provide for growth of the system.

- The hard disk, by providing a permanent directory, eliminates media handling for all operators other than a supervisor.

- Any operator at any CRT can direct printing requests to any printer in the firm.

• Documents may be broken down, so text editing may be performed by several secretaries if necessary.

• In an emergency, draft typing may be shared by as many typists as there are CRTs.

The two major disadvantages of a shared logic system are that the more input and output devices attached to the one processor, the slower the processing speed becomes. In addition, all devices attached to the central processor are totally dependent on the processor. This means that if the central processor should fail or go down, all attached devices would also go down. Unless the law office has some standalone word processors and has backed up information onto floppy diskettes, the law office could not produce any documents stored on the system.

§ 4.29 Software Programmable Systems

Many of the standalones, video display machines, cluster machines, and shared logic systems are programmed through a special disk or a group of program disks. This is a distinct advantage because it provides for the addition of new programs and features to existing equipment as technology progresses. The machine installed today may have several new features added before it is a year old, if it is programmable. The advantages become clearer when programmable systems are compared to those which are not programmable. In the latter case, the features and the machine you purchased will be the same next year and the next and the next. In the rare event that the manufacturer offers to retrofit the machine with a new feature, a sizeable charge for the feature and the service can be expected.

Programmable systems vary in the type of language used to program them. For example, a system using an industry-known language, such as BASIC, COBOL, or FORTRAN, may be programmed by either the vendor or your own programmer. Systems programmed by a special language known only to the vendor can be programmed only by that vendor. They should be considered programmable only to the extent the vendor will provide new programs.

§ 4.30 Information Processors

Information processors are word processors with some added functions, the most common being the ability to create files and then to sort and select information from those files, providing printed lists for various purposes. Example of law office lists are office directors, client names and addresses, client active files, closed files, destroyed files, time and charges billing, ticklers, etc.

Some of the information processors provide simple mathematical functions, *i.e.*, add, subtract, multiply, and divide. Time and charges billing can then be automated.

A major difference between these machines is how the memory is utilized for sorting. Some handle sorting in the foreground (active memory) while others sort in the background. When sorting takes place in the foreground, the machine is essentially locked; it cannot be used for other purposes while it is sorting. If sorting takes place in the background, the foreground is still available for other functions, such as draft typing and text editing.

Another major difference is the speed with which the system can perform its records processing (sorting and selecting from stored files). If records processing takes place in the background, the speed may not be critical because the foreground is available for the continuation of daily work; however, if sorting takes place in the foreground and is slow, a machine may be tied up for several hours or days per week while it performs records processing applications.

On a standalone system, the ideal information processor is one with a hard disk drive, which can sort in the background. This permits all data to be sorted from one drive while text editing, typing, and printing continues.

It is important to note that on most systems, word processing and information processing functions are separate. Information files are not available except through printed lists. Documents may not be catalogued or "filed" in the same way that time and charges files are handled.

§ 4.31   Integrated Systems

Outwardly integrated systems are identical in appearance to stand-alones, video display systems, cluster systems, shared logic systems, and information processors. The differences are:

- They perform full word processing and data processing functions.
- They can perform word processing functions on data processing applications.

Often data available from a computer must be retyped on another machine to create typewriter-quality copy. An integrated system eliminates the retyping—the data processing files are available for word processing functions and vice versa.

Obviously an integrated system is more powerful than a word processor or an information processor. In law offices, the equipment can be used for accounting, payroll, billing, communications, and text editing. Any workstation (CRT or keyboard) can be used to perform any of these functions. In that case, management of information, including controlled access and security, must be considered.

§ 4.32 Glossary or Library Capacity

Most word processors today have a glossary or library capacity which permits frequently used words, phrases, or paragraphs to be instantly retrieved and incorporated into the document being keyboarded. For example, the word "plaintiff" or "defendant" could appear on the screen automatically by touching two keys rather than nine. Whole documents can be put together by using individual paragraphs stored in the glossary and compiled by using a few keystrokes for each paragraph.

§ 4.33 Vertical Scrolling

Most CRT machines have vertical scrolling which means the operator can go through the document from one page to another. Horizontal scrolling is for wide documents. If there are charts with several columns to be printed out on wide paper, horizontal scrolling is essential.

§ 4.34 Display Highlighting

Display highlighting is used to brighten the words being deleted, moved, or copied. This enables the operator to be certain of her corrections before she takes the step necessary to delete, move, or copy material.

§ 4.35 Justified Right Margins and/or Proportional Spacing

Justified right margins and/or proportional spacing are available on most word processors.

§ 4.36 Format Storage

Formats can be stored and recalled as you need them for a document. Format includes margin and tab settings, line length, etc. Automatic line spacing allows a document to be typed in double spacing and then switched to single spacing at certain locations within the document by queuing it to do so. The printer responds to that queue and adjusts the spacing accordingly. This is useful in typing quoted material within a document.

§ 4.37 Automatic Carrier Returns (Wraparound)

Automatic carrier returns on the CRT machines and some of the standalones reduce keyboarding time. The operator does not touch the carrier return except at the end of paragraphs. The machine automatically makes the right margin decision and returns the cursor (indicator of typing position) to the beginning of the next line. This is referred to as "wraparound" because it appears that the end of the line wraps around and begins the next line.

§ 4.38 Automatic Decimal Tabs

Automatic decimal tabs are useful in typing columns of numbers. The tab stop is placed at the position of the decimal. This feature automatically keeps decimal points in vertical alignment while columns of numbers are being typed. It aligns whole numbers on the right-most digit.

§ 4.39 Automatic Underlining

Each machine has some form of underlining which is automatic and relieves the secretary of doing it stroke by stroke.

§ 4.40 Search and Replace

Search and replace allows the operator to queue the machine to search for one word and replace it with another. If the secretary has a habit of typing "palintiff" instead of "plaintiff," she can queue the machine to search for the incorrect spelling and replace it with the correct spelling whenever it appears in the document. A document programmed with one name can be used for another party by searching and replacing with the new party's name.

§ 4.41 Delete Capability

The delete capability is on all machines. This permits the operator to remove any letters, words, paragraphs, or pages in the document. Material can also be inserted anywhere in the text by using the insert feature. The line endings will automatically be adjusted after an addition or deletion.

§ 4.42 Block Move

Block move is useful when a section of material such as a citation is to be moved from one page or document to another. The usual procedure is to queue the machine that certain material is to be moved. After the material has been removed from its location, the text automatically adjusts to close up the space left by the move. The new page containing the moved material automatically adjusts itself to accommodate the material, and the document may need to be repaginated after such moves.

§ 4.43 Copy Feature

The copy feature allows the operator to take the material from one page or document and copy it into another page or document without deleting it from the first one. This is particularly useful for property descriptions, citations, etc.

§ 4.44 Automatic Footnoting

The automatic footnote feature assures that a footnote remains on the same page as the quoted material when the document is printed. Many systems will automatically renumber the footnote if it is moved.

§ 4.45 Hard Disk

A hard disk is a magnetic storage medium capable of storing large amounts of text, as well as system information. It is usually a fixed part of the word processor but in some cases may be physically removed from the system. The advantages of using a disk for work processing applications are its large storage capacity and its ability to allow a faster random access method of document retrieval.

§ 4.46 Floppy Disks

Floppy disks (also called diskettes) arrived during the mid-1970s and are available in $5\frac{1}{4}$ inches square and $3\frac{1}{2}$ inches square; most are dual-density floppy disks, which record on both sides. They are ideal for use in law offices for many typewritten applications ranging from short memos and correspondence to lengthy briefs and trusts. Since they hold from 70,000 to 325,000 characters of stored text (40 to 100 pages), they are particularly valuable for lengthy work. Transmission of text or data to and from larger systems may be available either through disk-to-disk conversion or through electronic communications. This feature varies widely among vendors.

§ 4.47 Filing

Each office develops its own system for filing the media. If a law firm is still using a mag card system, it is essential to keep a hard copy of the programmed material which corresponds to the cards, noting the margin settings, tab stops, spacing, and locations for variable data. A reference to the card number should be noted on the top of the hard copy. It is recommended that a forms file of all recorded material be kept on both the attorney's desk and the secretary's desk so that both can refer to it when creating documents. Some offices use different colored binders for each type of matter, such as wills, contracts, divorces, discovery documents, etc.

Secretaries with CRT equipment do not need to keep a hard copy file at their desks because they can call the copy up on the screen and see exactly what has been programmed. It is wise to have a copy of each document or paragraphs (for boilerplate material) printed out and kept in a binder for the attorney to use when he is dictating.

Diskettes or hard disks used in CRT machines print an index listing everything that is programmed on the diskette or hard disk by author and title. This listing can be stored with the diskette or in a separate file. Some offices prepare an index card for each item programmed on a diskette, stating the name of the document, the client (if applicable), and the number of the diskette. These are then filed by document title or client name.

Some secretaries use a separate diskette for each attorney and color code the diskette by attorney. Other secretaries use a different diskette and color code for each type of document, such as wills, contracts, probate, etc.

All diskettes must be stored away from anything that is magnetic. Diskettes cannot be stored flat; they must be stored in a rack standing up, just as phonograph records are stored. Diskettes are very susceptible to dust.

It is worth taking the extra time to set up media and hard copy filing systems.

§ 4.48   Types of Printers

There are various types of printers used in conjunction with word processing equipment. In some instances, there is only one printer available for the equipment. With some of the more sophisticated machines, the purchaser has several options regarding the printer. The amount of use, the quality of the documents to be produced, and cost all affect the decision.

§ 4.49   Electronic Typewriters

On standalone mechanical text editors, the electronic typewriter is the most common printer. It is combined with the input function and cannot be used at the same time that the operator is keyboarding material.

§ 4.50   Daisy Wheel Printer

The daisy wheel printer uses a flat disk with characters around its circumference and is commonly used with CRT equipment. It has several advantages:

   • It prints forward and backward (bidirectional).

- The output speed is faster than with an electronic typewriter.

- A variety of type styles and type sizes is available.

- The ribbons and fonts are easily changed.

- Proportionally spaced printing fonts are available if the input equipment is set up for this spacing.

- With a dual-head printer, it is possible to mix type styles and fonts.

§ 4.51 Ink Jet Printer

The ink jet printer "spits" a stream of tiny, electrostatically charged ink drops at the page as its head moves across the paper. Its print speed is exceptionally high. As with a dual-head printer, the output can be in a variety of formats and type styles and sizes. The most significant advantage is the exceptionally high quality of the final copy.

§ 4.52 Laser Printer

Laser printers have become very popular for high-quality, high-speed printer output. The first models introduced in the market were very expensive and could be justified only in larger firms with very high printing production. Recent models are now affordable by many firms.

The laser printer also uses a stream of tiny, electrostatically charged ink drops that are guided to the paper by a laser beam. The result is a very high-quality product produced at high speed with little noise.

§ 4.53 Justified Printout

Justified printout is available on most of the printers by either interword spacing or intercharacter spacing with a proportionally spaced font.

§ 4.54 Sub/Superscript Printout

Sub/superscript printout allows characters to be printed one-half space (occasionally one-third or one-fourth) above or below the typed line; footnotes, chemical formulas, and the like can be automatically printed without stopping the printer for adjustment.

§ 4.55 Bold Print

Bolding allows characters to be overstruck slightly off exact alignment to produce a shadow or bold print effect on the paper. This feature is activated by the operator providing a simple command to begin bolding and to end bolding.

§ 4.56 Simultaneous Printout

Simultaneous printout allows the system to print one document while recording new text or revising previously recorded text. Some systems accept only one page or one document at a time for simultaneous (also called background) printing; others allow a queue of documents to be created. If a queue is created, it may print out on a first-in, first-out basis, or it may have a priority arrangement so that an urgent document can be moved ahead of the others. This is an important feature for a law office to have. If a complaint is queued into the printer and must be filed by the end of the day, the operator could move it ahead of a large brief that is not urgent.

§ 4.57 Copiers

Copiers are becoming more and more important to the law office. With the use of word processing equipment, carbon copies are nearly a thing of the past. In addition to a central copier, many offices now have small copiers utilizing fiber optics which are easily accessible to the secretary. Fiber optics are small in size but produce a very good quality copy. Many of the new desktop laser printers are also capable of making photocopies.

§ 4.58 Distribution

Distribution, the fifth portion of the IPSOD acronym, is a relatively recent addition. Communicating and networking word processing equipment is rapidly becoming widespread. Through the use of telecommunications, data can be typed on the word processing equipment and printed out on equipment located miles away. It offers the speed of the telephone without the necessity of the recipient's being present. It is printed out or stored on the receiving equipment until it is collected. The time required for mail delivery is reduced to minutes. Electronic mail merges a number of technologies, such as telephones, word processing terminals, copiers, printers, and satellite communications. Some large companies utilize electronic communications within the office or company organization. One machine communicates with another, thereby reducing the need for messengers, intercoms, or message slips. With satellite communications, firms can contract to utilize satellites and transfer data independent of the telephone system. With telecommunications, it is possible for law offices to tie in with legal research systems, such as LEXIS, WESTLAW, ABA/net, The Source, etc.

§ 4.59   Rent, Lease, or Purchase of Equipment

If you are helping the attorney investigate the possibility of installing word processing and are uncertain about exactly which equipment you should recommend, then you may want to suggest that he rent the equipment for a period of time.   If you are certain about which equipment you wish to recommend, you will still want to suggest that he investigate the advantages of a lease-purchase agreement.

§ 4.60   Renting and Leasing

With rental, ownership of the equipment remains with the supplier.   When renting from manufacturers, the equipment remains the equipment of the manufacturer, who provides maintenance and service on the equipment during ordinary business hours.   These leases are of a short-term nature, allowing some flexibility in changing equipment. The rates are usually higher because the manufacturer has to face the possibility of obsolescence, which is one of the reasons for the user's renting the equipment—so he won't have a large investment in obsolete equipment.

Check the agreement for breach of contract clauses; a cancellation charge (which can be extremely high) may be due if the equipment is surrendered before the rental term has run.   One feature of many rental plans is the possibility of building equity in the equipment, working toward an eventual purchase.

When leasing, the user is usually working through a third-party firm.   The supplier buys the equipment and then leases it out to the lessee, making the supplier the owner of the machine rather than the manufacturer.   A third party can offer a lower monthly rate than the manufacturer, partly because as an owner, it can take advantage of depreciation for tax purposes; however, a maintenance charge is usually added to this type of contract.

§ 4.61   Types of Leases

There are two types of leases: partial pay out, which is known as an operating lease, and full pay out, which is a financial lease.   The operating lease and financial lease differ in that with an operating lease, the lessor keeps the large equity in the equipment and does not recover his full costs until the end of the contract period.   Usually maintenance is provided by the lessor on this type of lease, although the lessee can contract with the manufacturer for maintenance.   With a financial lease, the customer agrees to make periodic payments which in the end total something in excess of the purchase price, often 10 percent more.   The 10 percent is essentially a financing charge.   The purchaser can buy the machine for a small additional amount.   This is a method of conserving cash by paying the cost of the machine over a period of time. However, an agreement should be made at the outset as to who is considered the owner of the machine. If the purchaser or lessee is going to be the owner (considering this as a conditional sale agreement), he would get the income tax advantages of ownership, the investment tax credit, and the depreciation credit. If the lessor remains the owner during the payment period, the lease payments would be considered business expenses for tax purposes. On a rental, the price can always go up; on a lease, the price usually remains the same.

§ 4.62   Availability of Repair Service

Before purchasing or leasing a machine, you should investigate the reputation of the dealer. Find out about repair services. Check with other companies which have the machines to ask what the downtime (time machine has been unusable while waiting for service) has been on that particular machine. Sometimes the machine is an excellent one with great capabilities, but the dealer has poor repair service. A nonworking machine is worse than no machine. Investigate before you invest.

§ 4.63   Ease of Operation

One other feature that should be considered is ease of operation. Check into the time required to learn the operation of the machine. Often the more sophisticated the equipment, the easier it is to use. This is not always true, but manufacturers are realizing that complicated coding operations are not necessary.

§ 4.64   Conclusion

Word processing, information management, information processing—no matter what you call it—is here to stay. It is really not a question of "Will your office invest in this equipment?" but "When will you invest and what equipment should you purchase?" What was envisioned only a few years ago as "The Office of the Future" is here today. Word processing equipment can be cost-effective and productive for any office, large or small. The wide variety of equipment assures that there is a machine to fit the need of every office. For the sake of the lawyer, client, and secretary, you should carefully investigate the market and determine what will best meet your office's needs.

Once you have obtained the equipment, allow adequate learning time not only for the person operating the equipment but for backup personnel, who will use the equipment in the absence of the word processing operator. Time spent in learning all the applications of the equipment will pay off in increased production.

CHAPTER 5

ACCOUNTING

Table of Sections

146

§ 5.1 Introduction

The practice of law, like any other type of income-earning business or profession, must be run in a businesslike manner. The law office or firm maintains an orderly system of accounts that shows the attorney many things he must know to continue to realize a profit. All but the beginning firms already have a system established for handling the accounting and recordkeeping. The purpose of this chapter is to assist the legal secretary by refreshing her memory on some of the fundamentals of bookkeeping in order that she can maintain the system in use.

§ 5.2 Bookkeeping in a Law Office

A personal service enterprise is one in which the principal source of revenue is compensation for personal services rendered. The practice of law, like many other professions, is based upon the fact that the compensation received for personal services rendered is the source of revenue. There are generally two systems of bookkeeping used by personal service enterprises: one is called cash basis, and the other is called accrual basis.

§ 5.3 Cash Basis

The cash basis of accounting is widely used in the small- to medium-sized law offices. Accounting for revenue on a cash basis generally means no record of revenue is made in the accounts until cash is actually received for the services performed. In most cases, this causes the revenue for services rendered in one period to be accounted for in another period. Since the attorney cannot spend the promise-to-pay money, he waits until it is in his possession in a form that can be spent. This eliminates the need for many of the more complicated bookkeeping items caused by services billed and not paid, causing bad debts to be charged off, income tax to be paid on moneys not actually received, and other more advanced forms of bookkeeping. The cash basis set of books usually consists of a cash journal, general ledger, payroll record book, invoice file, and sometimes a petty cash record book.

Accounting for expenses on a cash basis generally means that expenses are not recorded in the records until they are paid.

§ 5.4 Accrual Basis

The accrual basis of accounting consists of recording revenue in the period in which it is earned and expenses in the period in which they are incurred. Revenue is considered to be earned when, in exchange for something of value, money is received or a legal claim to money comes into existence. Since the lawyer's invoice to a client is a legal claim to money and the invoice is not always paid immediately, the accounts receivable ledger becomes necessary to keep track of the amounts which the client owes and pays. Under this system the accounts payable ledger comes into being and is used only by the attorney or firm (*not for the client accounts*) to show financial obligations for equipment, supplies, buildings, libraries, and other amounts that are paid in installments. The accounts payable ledger shows the attorney what the firm owes at any given time.

The accrual basis is widely used because it shows a period-by-period matching of revenues and expenses, and therefore, the profit and/or loss for that period. The accrual method recognizes changes in many types of assets and liabilities in computing net income for a specific period, not just changes in the cash account. Under this method, the firm's accountant usually charges off many so-called bad debts before closing the books so that the Internal Revenue Service (IRS) will not have a claim to moneys that may never be received by the firm. Law firms usually use a modified accrual system, since a true accrual system requires accounting for inventories and other retail sales types of bookkeeping not required in a professional office.

§ 5.5 Journal

The first formal double-entry record of a transaction is usually made in a journal. The act of recording transactions in a journal is called journalizing. Journalizing involves analyzing each transaction and entering the significant information concerning the transaction either (1) at the time the transaction occurs or (2) subsequently, but in the chronological order in which it and the other transactions occurred. The purpose of journal entries is to provide a chronological record of all transactions completed, showing the date of each transaction, titles of accounts to be debited or credited, and amounts of the debits and credits.

Journal pages are numbered in sequence, and the appropriate number is entered after the word "page" in the upper right-hand corner of each page of the journal. A two-column journal has two amount columns, one for debit amounts and one for credit amounts.

The first column is the Date column. The year is entered in small figures at the top of the column immediately below the column heading and needs to be repeated only at the top of each new page unless, of course, an entry for a new year is made further down on the page. Next, enter the abbreviation for the month to the right of the line. The number designating the day of the month should be entered to the right of this line. The name of the month needs to be shown only for the first entry on a page unless an entry for a new month is made further down on the page.

Column 2 is generally referred to as the Description column. This column is used to enter the titles of the accounts affected by each transaction. The titles of the accounts debited are entered first at the extreme left of the column, followed by the titles of accounts credited usually indented one-half inch. A separate line should be used for each account title. The description should be entered immediately following the credit entry and indented an additional one-half inch.

Column 3 is the Posting Reference column, which is sometimes referred to as a folio column. No entries are made in this column at the time of journalizing the transactions. Entries in this column are made only at the time of posting.

Column 4, the Debit amount column, is a column in which the amount that is to be debited to an account should be entered on the same line on which the title of that account appears.

Column 5, the Credit amount column, is a column in which the amount that is to be credited in an account should be entered on the same line where the title of that account appears in the description.

Journal

Date	Description	Post Ref	Debit	Credit
1	2	3	4	5

§ 5.6 Ledger

Since the purpose of the journal is to provide a chronological record of all transactions and the accounts to which debits and credits have been made, the accounts kept to supply the desired information collectively are described as the general ledger.

Subsidiary ledgers are used to supply itemized information necessary to support the information found in the general ledger. The usual subsidiary ledgers found in law offices are accounts receivable, accounts payable, trust fund ledger (for client funds), payroll record book, and a petty cash ledger. If the lawyer or firm has considerable investments, then several investment ledgers may have to be kept.

§ 5.7 Basic Principles of Double–Entry Bookkeeping

The basic reason behind double-entry bookkeeping is that each entry has a *dual effect* on a transaction. A change in any asset, any liability, or in owner's equity is always accompanied by an offsetting change within the basic accounting elements. It is that dual effect that provides the basis for what is called double-entry bookkeeping.

§ 5.8 Accounting Equation

The accounting equation is the relationship between the three basic accounting elements. The equation is:

$$\text{ASSETS} = \text{LIABILITIES} + \text{OWNER'S EQUITY}$$

The balance sheet is set up as follows:

ASSETS	LIABILITIES
	+
	OWNER'S EQUITY
SAME	SAME

The simplest way to remember the equation is to picture mentally the balance sheet format. The equation can be turned around different ways, *i.e.*, Assets − Liabilities = Owner's Equity, which gives the same answer but is harder for the novice bookkeeper to remember.

When the amounts of any two of the equation elements are known, the third can always be calculated. For example, L.G. Lambert, Attorney, invests $30,000 to open a private practice. After purchasing office supplies and equipment for $4,820 and a law library for $8,600, his business liabilities are $13,420, and his equation is:

ASSETS   =   LIABILITIES   +   OWNER'S EQUITY
$30,000 $13,420 $16,580

In order to increase his equity in the business, Mr. Lambert must either increase the assets without increasing the liabilities or decrease the liabilities without decreasing the assets. In other words, he will have to operate his practice at a profit. For example, if one year later the assets amount to $78,000 and the liabilities to $2,400, the status of the business would be as follows:

ASSETS   =   LIABILITIES   +   OWNER'S EQUITY
$78,000 $2,400 $75,600

It is essential that the business records show the extent to which the change in owner's equity is due to the regular operation of the business and the extent to which increases and decreases in owner's equity are due to the owner's investing and withdrawing assets.

In order to maintain the equality of this equation, the sum of the debit entries must always be equal to the sum of the credit entries. If the totals of the debit and credit entries are equal, the accounts are said to be in balance, but if one aspect of a transaction is properly recorded while the other part is overlooked, the records will be out of balance. The bookkeeper then knows that something is wrong and must recheck the work to discover the trouble and make the needed correction.

§ 5.9   Debits and Credits

To debit an account means to record an amount on the left or debit side of the account. A debit is always the first entry. To credit an account means to record an amount on the right or credit side of the account. The abbreviation for debit is Dr. and for credit, Cr. The difference between the total debits and total credits in an account is called the "balance."

§ 5.10   Increases and Decreases

Accounts have two sides so that increases can be recorded on one side and decreases can be recorded on the other side. The nature of the account determines the side to be used for increases and the side to be used for decreases.

Assets are shown on the left side of the balance sheet. Consistency suggests that asset accounts should therefore have balances on the left or debit side. An asset account may be increased in any of the following ways:

1. Additional cash or other property may be invested by the owner.

2. Liabilities of the business may increase.

3. Revenues may be derived from services or from other sources.

4. Another asset may be decreased.

Decreases in assets are called credits and are recorded on the right side of the account. An asset may be decreased in any of the following ways:

1. Cash or other property may be withdrawn from the business by the owner.

2. Liabilities of the business may decrease.

3. Expenses may be incurred in operations.

4. Another asset may be increased.

Since the liabilities and owner's equity are shown on the right side of the balance sheet, consistency also suggests that increases are recorded on the right side (Cr.) of the account and decreases are recorded on the left (Dr.) side. Liabilities may be increased in any of the following ways:

1. Assets may increase.

2. Expenses may be incurred.

3. Other liabilities may be decreased.

Liabilities may be decreased in either of the following ways:

1. Assets may decrease.

2. Other liabilities may increase.

Owner's equity, on the other hand, can be increased only in the following ways:

1. The owner may invest additional cash or other property (assets) in the business.

2. Revenue may be derived from services or from other sources.

Owner's equity can also be decreased in only two ways:

1. Cash or other property (assets) may be withdrawn from the business by the owner.

2. Expenses may be incurred in the operation.

152

Illustration 5–1

		ASSETS		=		LIABILITIES + OWNER'S EQUITY	

All Asset Accounts		All Liability Accounts	
Debit to enter increases (+)	Credit to enter decreases (−)	Debit to enter decreases (−)	Credit to enter increases (+)

All Owner's Equity Accounts	
Debit to enter decreases (−)	Credit to enter increases (+)

All Revenue Accounts		All Expense Accounts	
Debit to enter decreases (−)	Credit to enter increases (+)	Debit to enter increases (+)	Credit to enter decreases (−)

REVENUE > EXPENSES = NET PROFIT
EXPENSES > REVENUE = NET LOSS

§ 5.11 Sources of Information

Before recording transactions in the journal, it is necessary to analyze each transaction so that it can be recorded properly. The term *source papers* or *source documents* covers a wide variety of forms and papers. Any document or paper that provides information about cash received, cash disbursed, fees charged, or purchases charged can be called a source document or paper.

EXAMPLES:

- Check stubs or carbon copies of checks

- Receipt stubs or carbon copies of receipts, cash register tapes, copies of invoices marked "paid" by clients' checks, or any other document used by the law office to record receipts

- Purchase invoices received from vendors

- Lawyer's time sheets for services to be billed or invoices as billed to clients

- Sources of interest earned on savings accounts, certificates of deposit, or other asset accounts invested for profit

- Documents used to record funds expended on behalf of clients

§ 5.12   Multicolumn Journal

The multicolumn journal (sometimes known as combined journal) usually consists of from four to twelve or more columns spread across two facing pages. This type of journal saves a great deal of time in the journalizing as well as in posting accounts to the general ledger. In a multicolumn journal, items that have a great number of entries during a month are placed in an appropriately titled column, and only the total at the end of the month is posted to the general ledger.

A law office multicolumn journal usually includes the following columns for the purposes indicated:

Cash (Firm Bank Account), Debit. All deposits of moneys belonging to the firm are entered in this column.

Cash (Firm Bank Account), Credit. All checks drawn on the firm bank account are entered in this column.

Trust Bank Account, Debit. All moneys received belonging to clients are entered here. Advances made by clients for expenses are also usually deposited in the trust account, as are collections of commercial items for clients, and therefore both are entered in this column.

Trust Bank Account, Credit. All checks drawn on the trust account are entered in this column.

Accounts Receivable, Debit. All charges made to clients are entered here.

Accounts Receivable, Credit. All payments made by clients are entered here.

Accounts Payable, Debit. All payments made on accounts owed are entered here.

Accounts Payable, Credit. All accounts owed are entered here.

Services Billed, Debit. All payments made by clients are entered here. Items entered here must also be credited to the clients' account in the Accounts Receivable column.

Services Billed, Credit. All charges made to clients' accounts are entered here. Items entered here are also debited to the clients' account in the Accounts Receivable column.

General Ledger, Debit and Credit. These columns are for accounts in the general ledger that do not have separate columns of their own in the cash journal. The items in these columns must be posted individually to the accounts in the general ledger, whereas the other columns in a multicolumn journal can be posted by a total only for the period.

Taxes Withheld Columns, Credit. Credit only columns are used to record the Social Security and Medicare taxes and income tax withheld from salaries. In a state or city requiring income tax to be withheld, another credit column is also used. (The offsetting debits appear when the quarterly payroll taxes are paid. When all of the taxes withheld have been paid, these accounts in the general ledger are in balance.)

Income From Fees, Credit. This account may be titled "Professional Fees," "Attorney Fees," or a variety of other names. All income from fees is posted in this column, which is a credit column only. (The offsetting debit appears as a debit to the firm's bank account at the time of deposit.) If the income is a payment by a client on an account previously billed and appearing on the Accounts Receivable account, a double entry whereby the Services Billed account is debited and the Accounts Receivable account is credited is necessary.

The multicolumn or combined journal can be reduced to as few as four to six columns showing simply the debit and credit columns for the bank accounts and everything else in the general ledger column. This system is simple, yet eliminates the large number of cash deposits and withdrawals necessary in the simple journal system.

§ 5.13   Helpful Rules to Remember in Journalizing

Since almost all transactions in a law office involve either bank deposits and withdrawals or charging clients and receiving payments from them, the following rules are helpful:

1.   CASH RECEIVED (bank deposits) is always debited to the bank account in which it is deposited and therefore must be credited to another account.

2.   CASH PAYMENTS (bank withdrawals) are always credited to the bank account on which they are drawn and therefore must be debited to another account.

3.   ACCOUNTS RECEIVABLE is always debited when the bill for services is sent to a client, and the amount charged is credited to the Services Billed account.

4.   ACCOUNTS RECEIVABLE is always credited when payment is received from a client, and the payment must be debited to the Services Billed account.

§ 5.14 Compound and/or Double Entries in Journalizing

A compound entry is used when it becomes necessary to show a distribution of an amount to different accounts. A compound entry may be used in either debit or credit amount columns or both.

A double entry is almost the same as a compound entry with the exception that instead of distributing one amount between accounts, it lists the same amount twice with two debits and two credits of the same amount. This occurs most often when Accounts Receivable and Services Billed accounts are affected. For example, if a client has been billed $500 in one month, the journal entry would look like this:

```
Accounts Receivable—Client's Name        $500.00
    Services Billed                                   $500.00
```

When the client makes the payment of that amount, the following entries are made:

```
Services Billed                           $500.00
    Accounts Receivable—Client's Name                 $500.00
```

In order to get the cash into the bank and into the income accounts, the following entry is made:

```
Cash in Bank (Firm Account)               $500.00
    Attorney (Professional) Fees                      $500.00
```

A single explanation would follow the two entries to explain that payment had been received from the client. The client's Accounts Receivable and the Services Billed accounts would be decreased and the Cash in Bank and Attorney Fees would be increased, while the entries balance each other out.

§ 5.15 The Chart of Accounts

In analyzing a transaction, the bookkeeper or accountant must know which accounts are being kept. In setting up a new set of books, the first step is to decide which accounts are required. Regardless of the number of accounts kept, they can be segregated into the three major classes and should be grouped according to these classes in the ledger. The usual custom is to place asset accounts first, liability accounts second, and owner's equity accounts, including revenue and expense accounts, last. It is common practice to prepare a chart of accounts in outline form in the front of the general ledger for easy reference. Each account is given a number to keep the accounts in order, and the accepted pattern of coding is to assign the number "100" to asset accounts, the number "200" to liability accounts, the number

"300" to owner's equity accounts, the number "400" to income or revenue accounts, and the number "500" to expense accounts. Illustration 5–2 is an example of L.G. Lambert's Chart of Accounts.

Illustration 5–2

L.G. LAMBERT
ATTORNEY AT LAW
Chart of Accounts

Asset Accounts		Expense & Income Summary	314
		Income Accounts	
Cash in Bank	111		
Trust Account—Bank	112	Professional Fees	411
Office Furn. & Equip.	113	Earned Interest	412
Library	114		
Accts. Receivable–Services	115	**Expense Accounts**	
Prepaid Rent	116		
Prepaid Insurance	117	Rent	511
Savings Account	118	Salaries	512
Petty Cash Fund	119	Telephone	513
		Books and Periodicals	514
Liability Accounts		Insurance	515
		Petty Cash	516
Accounts Payable	211	Postage	517
Social Security and Medicare		Travel	518
Taxes Payable	212	Office	519
Withholding Taxes Payable	213	Client Entertainment	522
Notes Payable	214	Payroll Tax	523
Trust Acct.—Client Funds	215	Unrecovered Cost	524

Owner's Equity Accounts	
Services Billed	311
L.G. Lambert, Capital	312
L.G. Lambert, Drawing	313

§ 5.16 The General Ledger

The process of recording (entering) information in the ledger from the journal is known as posting. Each amount in the journal must be posted to the proper account daily or at frequent intervals in order to summarize the results.

Since the accounts provide the information needed in preparing the financial statements, a posting procedure that will ensure accuracy in maintaining the accounts must be followed. Posting from the journal to the ledger involves recording the following information in the accounts:

1. The date of each transaction

157

2. The amount of each transaction

3. The page of the journal from which each transaction is posted

As each amount in the journal is posted to the proper account in the ledger, the number of that account should be entered in the Posting Reference (Folio) column in the journal so as to provide a cross-reference between the journal and ledger and a quick-check method of ensuring proper posting to the accounts.

§ 5.17 Ledger Sheets

There are two forms of ledger sheets in use. One has three amount columns for debit, credit, and balance. The other is divided into two equal parts or sections which are ruled identically to facilitate recording debits and credits. The left side is the debit side, and the right side is the credit side. Date and item columns are used on both sides for recording the dates of the transactions and when necessary a brief description. This divided form is the more widely used.

§ 5.18 Subsidiary Ledgers

In every type of business, it is necessary to keep one or more subsidiary ledgers. Each ledger contains like information so that totals or breakdowns can be seen at a glance. These ledgers may pertain to accounts receivable, payroll, petty cash, or other desired information.

§ 5.19 The Trial Balance

Since the fundamental basic equation of accounting is that the sum of the assets equals the sum of the liabilities and owner's equity, a list of all the debit and credit balances must be prepared to check equality. This list is called a trial balance. A trial balance can be placed on standard two-column forms or typed on plain paper.

It is important that the procedure set forth below be followed in preparing a trial balance:

1. The heading of the trial balance should show the name of the firm, the title of the report "Trial Balance," and the date. The date shown is the day of the last transaction that is included in the accounts, which is usually the last day of the month.

2. List the account titles in order, showing each account number.

3. Enter the account balances, placing debit balances in the left amount column and credit balances in the right amount column.

4. Add the columns and enter the totals, placing a single line across the amount columns above the totals and a double line below the totals in the manner shown in Illustration 5–3.

Illustration 5–3

L.G. LAMBERT, ATTORNEY AT LAW

Trial Balance

As of June 30, 19__

	Debit	Credit
Cash in Bank	$14,812.95	
Trust Account—Client Funds	1,075.00	
Office Furniture and Equipment	4,820.00	
Library	8,600.00	
Accounts Receivable—Clients	2,175.00	
Prepaid Rent	650.00	
Prepaid Insurance	429.17	
Professional Fees		$ 3,715.00
Rent Expense	650.00	
Salaries Expense	850.00	
Telephone Expense	116.00	
News Services, Periodicals and Magazine Expense	16.85	
Insurance Expense	85.83	
Social Security and Medicare Taxes Payable		51.42
Withholding Taxes Payable		64.38
Services Billed		3,250.00
L.G. Lambert, Capital		30,000.00
L.G. Lambert, Drawing	2,800.00	
TOTALS	$37,080.80	$37,080.80

§ 5.20   Financial Reports

Periodic reports must be prepared according to the needs of the attorney or firm. These may be monthly, quarterly, annually, and so on. The two types of financial statements are the income statement (profit and loss) and the balance sheet (statement of financial position).

§ 5.21   The Income Statement

The income statement is an itemized statement that provides information regarding the profit and loss of the operation during a specific period of time. It is a statement of the changes in owner's equity resulting from the revenue and expenses of the specific period (month, quarter, year). Only those accounts involved in income or expense are included in the statement, and the difference between the two is known as the net income or net loss. When the periodic closing of the books takes place, it is the net income or net loss that is added to or subtracted from the owner's equity or divided among partners, etc., as the case may be. Since the figures for the income statement are in the trial balance, it is not necessary to take time to look up individual accounts in the ledger. (See Illustration 5–4.)

Illustration 5–4

L.G. LAMBERT
ATTORNEY AT LAW
INCOME STATEMENT
For the Month Ended June 30, 19__

Income

Professional Fees		$3,715.00
Expenses		
Rent Expense	$650.00	
Salaries Expense	850.00	
Telephone Expense	116.00	
News Services, Periodicals and		
Magazine Expense	16.85	
Insurance Expense	85.83	
Total Expenses		1,718.68
NET INCOME		$1,996.32

§ 5.22 The Balance Sheet

The balance sheet is an itemized statement of the assets, liabilities, and owner's equity of a business enterprise as of a specified date. Its purpose is to provide information regarding the status of these basic accounting elements. The heading of a balance sheet contains the following:

1. The name of the firm

2. The title of the statement

3. The date of the statement as of the close of business on that day

The trial balance is the source of the information needed in listing the assets and liabilities in the balance sheet. The income statement is the source of information for obtaining the net loss or net profit figures. (See Illustration 5–5.)

Illustration 5–5
L.G. LAMBERT
ATTORNEY AT LAW
Balance Sheet
As of June 30, 19__

Assets		Liabilities		
Cash in Bank	$14,812.95	Social Security and Medicare Taxes Payable	$51.42	
Trust Acct—Client	1,075.00	Withholding Taxes Payable	64.38	
Office Furniture and Equipment	4,820.00			
Library	8,600.00	Total Liabilities		$ 115.80
Accounts Receivable	2,175.00	**Owner's Equity**		
Prepaid Rent	650.00	Services Billed		3,250.00
Prepaid Insurance	429.17	L.G. Lambert Capital	$30,000.00	
		Less Drawing	2,800.00	
			27,200.00	
		Plus Net Income	1,996.32	
				29,196.32
		Total Owner's Equity		32,446.32
		TOTAL LIABILITIES AND		
TOTAL ASSETS	$32,562.12	OWNER'S EQUITY		$32,562.12

In a law firm with more than one owner or partner, the net income is divided according to the agreed percentages among the owners, with each owner having his or her own capital and drawing accounts. The services billed amount remains intact in the owner's equity section of the balance sheet, as this amount has not yet been paid by the clients and upon payment will be reflected in the net income and divided at that time. This simply shows that an ownership exists in the amount billed but not yet paid.

§ 5.23 Other Periodic Financial Statements

Some offices require analysis of all action on each client's account quarterly or for other periods of time, but mostly the attorneys want to know who owes what to whom. Some offices also break down the costs recovered from each client in the analysis.

§ 5.24 End-of-Period Worksheet

To enable preparation of the financial statements, first adjustments in the accounts, as well as closing the temporary owner's equity accounts, are necessary steps to take to prepare a worksheet. Usually worksheets, like the other financial statements, may not be necessary more than quarterly, semi-annually, or annually, depending on the desire of the attorney.

Let us use an eight-column worksheet for Mr. Lambert's business. The first pair of columns of the worksheet is used to show the trial balance taken after the routine posting for the month has been completed. The second pair of headings would be adjustments and would be used to show the manner in which the expenses of estimated depreciation of office equipment for the period affects the accounts. These depreciation figures will be determined by the firm's accountant or by the attorney on a periodic basis and entered into the adjustment columns of the journal at closing time. The third and fourth sets of columns are headed "Income Statement" and "Balance Sheet." The figures for these columns are obtained by extending the revenue and expense account balances to the income statement and balance sheet account balances to the balance sheet columns. When the total of the Income Statement Credit column exceeds the total of the Income Statement Debit column, bring the pair of Income Statement columns into balance by calculating the difference (net income), which will then bring the two columns into total balance. When the same amount of net income is placed in the Balance Sheet Credit column, the last pair of columns will be brought into balance. The final totals of the last four columns are recorded at the bottom of the worksheet. Once the worksheet is completed, it is a simple matter to type the fiscal period financial reports because if something is out of balance, it will appear first on the worksheet and can be corrected easily. (See Illustration 5–6.)

Illustration 5–6
L.G. Lambert
Attorney At Law
Worksheet
For Period Ended June 30, 19__

Account	Acct. No.	Trial Balance Debit	Trial Balance Credit	Income Statement Debit	Income Statement Credit	Balance Sheet Debit	Balance Sheet Credit
Cash in Bank—Firm	111	13,812.95				13,812.95	
Trust Account—Bank	112	1,000.00				1,000.00	
Office Furniture and Equipment	113	4,820.00				4,820.00	
Library	114	8,600.00				8,600.00	
Accounts Receivable—Clients	115	3,250.00				3,250.00	
Prepaid Rent	116	650.00				650.00	
Prepaid Insurance	117	429.17				429.17	
Social Security and Medicare Taxes Payable	212		51.42				51.42
Withholding Taxes Payable	213		64.38				64.38
Trust Account—Client Funds	215		1,000.00				1,000.00
Services Billed	311		3,250.00				3,250.00
L.G. Lambert, Capital	312		30,000.00				30,000.00
L.G. Lambert, Drawing	313	2,800.00				2,800.00	
Professional Fees	411		2,715.00		2,715.00		
Rent Expense	511	650.00		650.00			
Salaries Expense	512	850.00		850.00			
Telephone Expense	513	116.00		116.00			
News Services, Periodicals and Mag. Exp.	514	16.85		16.85			
Insurance Expense	515	85.83		85.83			
		37,080.80	37,080.80	1,718.68	2,715.00	35,362.12	34,365.80
NET INCOME				996.32			996.32
				2,715.00	2,715.00	35,362.12	35,362.12

§ 5.25 Adjusting Entries for a Personal Service Enterprise

The financial statements must agree with the ledger accounts. To speed up the preparation of the statements, a worksheet is used with the needed adjustment included. Subsequently, this adjustment has to be recorded formally in the journal and the general ledger accounts by a debit to depreciation expense and a credit to the accumulated depreciation account for each depreciable item in the assets. The percentage of depreciation will be given by the accountant or the attorney on a periodic basis.

§ 5.26 Closing Entries

The attorney or the accountant will decide the fiscal period for the closing entries, and a time schedule will be established. Closing the accounts means that the revenue and expense accounts and the drawing accounts of owners will have served their purpose for that fiscal period and the balance of each of these accounts needs to be brought back to zero in order to make the accounts ready for entries in the following period. Since the means of closing a ledger account under the double-entry procedure is to add the amount of the account's balance to the side of the account having the smaller total (so that the account will have no balance), each of the owner's temporary equity accounts will have to be closed this way. The net effect is an increase in the credit balance of the account for the owner's capital account (the excess of his net income over his withdrawals). The result is accomplished by means of four entries in the journal as follows:

1. The credit balance of Professional Fees is closed to Expense and Revenue Summary. (Debit Prof. Fees. Credit Expense & Revenue Summary.)

2. The debit balances of all expense accounts are closed to Expense and Revenue Summary. This may be done as a compound total or singularly (referred to as posting in detail). (Debit Expense & Revenue Summary with the total. Credit each expense account individually.)

3. The result of entries 1 and 2 is usually a credit balance and represents the net income for the period. This balance is closed to the owner's capital account. (Debit Expense & Revenue Summary. Credit Owner's Capital.)

4. The debit balance of the owner's drawing account is closed to the owner's capital account. (Debit Owner's Capital. Credit Owner's Drawing.)

The Expense and Revenue Summary account is given a "300" number with the owner's equity accounts. Depreciation expense accounts are assigned "500" numbers when the books are set up. An accumulated depreciation account bears a "contra account" number and appears immediately following the asset which it depreciates. A contra account is an asset account with a negative balance which always represents a credit entry offsetting a specific plant asset, *i.e.*, accumulated depreciation equipment. A contra account number is one beginning with "0" and a number. The purpose of the Expense and Revenue account is to summarize the amounts of expenses and revenue which are reasons for changes in the owner's equity that were not the result of investments and withdrawals by the owner.

§ 5.27 Ruling the Closed Accounts

After posting the closing entries, all of the owner's temporary equity accounts (expense accounts and revenue accounts) are in balance (closed), and they are then ruled in the following manner:

1. Where two or more amounts have been posted to either side of an account, the amount columns are footed to be sure that the total debits are equal to the total credits.

2. A single line is ruled across the debit and credit amount columns immediately below the last amount of the side with the most entries.

3. The totals of the debit and credit amount columns are entered on the next line in ink.

4. Double lines are ruled just below the totals. These rulings extend through all but the Item columns.

If an account had only one item on each side, only the double ruling is necessary. If an account page is not filled, it may be used for recording the transactions of the following period.

§ 5.28 Balancing and Ruling Open Accounts

After the owner's temporary equity accounts are closed, the open accounts (assets, liabilities, and owner's capital) are balanced and ruled where necessary to prepare them to receive entries in the next fiscal period. The procedure for this is:

1. Enter the amount of the balance of the account on the side having the smaller total to equalize total debits and total credits. The word "Balance" is then written in the Item column.

2. Foot the columns to prove the equality of the debits and credits.

3. Draw a single line across the debit and credit amount columns immediately below the line with the last amount.

4. Enter the totals of the debit and credit amount columns on the next line in ink.

5. Draw double lines just below the totals extending through all but the Item column.

6. Make an entry on the next line under the next date with the amount of the balance—so labeled in the Item column—entered in the Amount column on the proper side (the debit side for the asset accounts and the credit side for owner's equity and liability accounts). If the account page has been filled, enter the balance at the top of a new page.

§ 5.29 Post–Closing Trial Balance

Once the posting of the closing entries has been accomplished, it is advisable to take what is called a post-closing trial balance to prove the equality of the debits and credits of the accounts left open. This trial balance reflects the beginning balances of all open accounts for the ensuing period.

§ 5.30 The Accounting Cycle

The steps involved in handling all of the transactions completed during the fiscal period, beginning with recording in a book of original entry and ending with a post-closing trial balance, are referred to collectively as the accounting cycle. A brief summary of those steps is as follows:

1. Journalize the transactions from source papers.

2. Post journal entries to the ledger accounts.

3. Take a trial balance.

4. Determine needed adjustments, such as depreciation, etc.

5. Complete the end-of-period work sheet.

6. Prepare income statement and balance sheet.

7. Journalize and post adjusting and closing entries.

8. Rule the closed accounts.

9.   Balance and rule the open accounts.

10.   Take a post-closing trial balance.

§ 5.31   The Petty Cash Fund

A petty cash fund, sometimes called an imprest fund, is usually established for paying small items. Such a fund eliminates the necessity of writing checks for relatively small amounts. The fund is usually established for $50, $100, $200, or any amount considered necessary. The check to establish or replenish the fund is made payable to "Cash." Only one person should be responsible for accounting for these funds. Payments from the fund should not be made without obtaining some sort of receipt in return. This is usually known as a "petty cash voucher" and shows the name of the payee, the purpose of the payment, and the account to be charged.

The check written to establish the petty cash fund may be entered in the journal by debiting Petty Cash Fund and by crediting Cash. When it is necessary to replenish the fund, the person responsible for the fund prepares a statement of the payments properly classified. A check is then written for the exact amount of the total payments. This check is entered in the journal by debiting the proper "expense" account(s) and crediting cash.

Illustration 5–7

Jan. 1	Petty Cash Fund	$200.00	
	Cash		$200.00
	To establish petty cash fund		
Mar. 1	Automobile Expense	$ 22.00	
	Supplies Expense	32.00	
	Postage Expense	26.00	
	Miscellaneous Expense	5.25	
	Cash		85.25
	Replenish petty cash fund		

The petty cash fund is a revolving fund. The petty cash account balance does not change in amount unless the fund is increased or decreased.

A statement of petty cash disbursements or trial balance of petty cash is typed for the period and kept in the front of the subsidiary ledger with copies to the owner and bookkeeper according to office practice. Vouchers for the period are filed in a dated envelope and kept in a safe place.

§ 5.32   Petty Cash Subsidiary Ledger

It is good practice to keep a subsidiary ledger in which all the expenditures and reimbursements to the fund are listed. This ledger can be either bound or loose-leaf sheets with as many columns as are deemed necessary. Each petty cash expenditure falls into one of the expense account categories listed in the general ledger or into one titled "Miscellaneous Expenses." Each column bears the title of the account, and at the end of the accounting period, totals are taken (unless replenishment is needed sooner). These totals are then journalized as if there had been but one disbursement for the period, rather than many small ones. For this reason a trial balance of the petty cash ledger is kept at the end of the petty cash period because the trial balance shows the amount for which a check must be written to replenish the fund. It also shows the control figures to balance with the journalized figures. This trial balance is also referred to as a petty cash statement.

As expenses occur in an area for which no account has already been designated, set one up or place the item in a miscellaneous expense account which serves as a catch-all for minor expenses. It is advisable to pencil in a brief description of each item placed in the miscellaneous account. Expenses chargeable to clients or to owner's drawing accounts must be journalized individually, but the other columns may be journalized by the total for the period with a reference noted as to the page number of the petty cash disbursement ledger.

Even though there are many ways of accounting for petty cash, Illustration 5–8 is given to assist in understanding the petty cash fund.

Illustration 5-8

PETTY CASH DISBURSEMENTS

FOR THE MONTH OF: JUNE, 19___

Page 1

Day	Vou. No.	Description		Total Amt.	Postage	Donations	Advances	Travel	Office	Misc. Exp.
1		Received in fund	100.00							
3	1	Client luncheon		11.50						11.50
5	2	C.O.D. Postage		4.65	4.65					
7	3	Messenger to courthouse		5.00						5.00
8	4	Emergency supply-typewriter ribbons		28.00					28.00	
14	5	L.L. Lombard, Banking-Personal use		10.00			10.00			
15	6	Light bulbs-office		3.50					3.50	
18	7	Gas secretary to airport for packet		7.50				7.50		
19	8	Postage stamps		15.00	15.00					
24	9	Retirement fund, Medical-Clerk, Gordon, Adv. for		3.00			3.00			
28	10	C.O.D. Postage-Letter tests		2.29					2.29	
29	11	Reference for client		4.26						4.26
				94.70	19.65		13.00	7.50	33.79	20.76
				94.70	19.65		13.00	7.50	33.79	20.76
		Balance	5.30							
29		Received in fund	94.70							
29		Total	100.00							

(E2011)

§ 5.33 Handling Attorneys' Fees

The only saleable commodity in a law office is the lawyer's time. A good time reporting system that will not prove burdensome to the lawyer must be adopted. Because law firms differ so much, there is no one system suitable to all. Any time system that works is a good one. "Timekeeping pays" is a cardinal rule in any law office.

No matter who is given the responsibility for billing in a law office, duplicates of all time and costs billed must be given to the bookkeeper, who in turn journalizes the entries by debiting Services Billed and crediting the client's Accounts Receivable—Services account. When a cost check is written or the amount paid out of petty cash, the costs advanced appear as a debit to the client's Accounts Receivable—Costs and a credit to the bank account.

When the client pays the bill, the bookkeeper must break down the amount to determine how much of the amount is for costs advanced and how much is for services and make double journal entries as follows:

Debit Cash In Bank (Deposit)

Credit Accounts Receivable—Client's name—Costs

Credit Accounts Receivable—Client's name—Services

Debit Professional Services (amount of services only)

Credit Services Billed (amount of services only)

NOTE: The amount of the Costs were never debited to the Services Billed account, only to the Accounts Receivable—Costs account for that client.

Any combination of these entries accomplishes the same figures in the accounts.

§ 5.34 Handling Trust Accounts

Trust funds in a law office must be handled meticulously. Canon 9 of the ABA Code of Professional Responsibility sets out the itemized requirements for handling these funds. Unfortunately, many lawyers have found to their dismay that slipshod recordkeeping or commingling of funds belonging to the firm and the clients can result in serious complications with lasting effects.

The main admonishment of Canon 9 is for the lawyer to keep all funds of clients paid to a lawyer or law firm, other than advances for costs and expenses, deposited in one or more identifiable bank accounts maintained in the state in which the law office is located, and no funds belonging to the lawyer or law firm are deposited therein except as follows:

1. Funds reasonably sufficient to pay bank charges.

2. Funds belonging in part to a client and in part or potentially to the lawyer or law firm, but the portion belonging to the lawyer or law firm may be withdrawn when due unless the right of the lawyer or law firm to receive it is disputed by the client, in which event the disputed portion is not to be withdrawn until the dispute is finally resolved.

The Canon goes on to set out that clients must be notified immediately of receipt of funds, securities, or other property and that the attorney must maintain complete records and render a complete accounting to the client. The attorney must promptly pay to or deliver to the client all funds, securities, or other properties in his possession to which the client is entitled.

There are many printed forms on the market for trust accounts, and the large firm keeps a subsidiary ledger of these accounts; but the smaller firm can maintain accurate records by establishing a separate checking account, preferably in a different bank from the firm's account. Trust accounts should be maintained separately from the firm's regular account. If trust moneys cannot be kept in a different bank from the firm's account, the trust account might use different-colored checks from the firm's regular checks. It should also be designated as "Trust Account," with the firm's or attorney's name printed above the signature line. The pages in the accounts receivable ledger under each client's name reflect all services charged, costs advanced and repaid, payments received, and balances remitted to the client. Listings of the other negotiable instruments or properties received for or remitted to the client can also be made somewhere on his ledger page. When these items are delivered to the client, the signed receipts can be attached to the ledger page.

Remember that when funds are received as a retainer, they are to be placed in the firm's trust account. Monthly, prepare a statement of services and costs expended by the firm to the client and show what portion of the retainer has been used. At this point, transfer funds from the trust account to the firm's general account to cover those fees earned and expenses advanced. By following this method, you will never commingle clients' funds with firm funds, thereby not violating Canon 9 of the ABA Code of Professional Responsibility.

§ 5.35 Cash Systems, Checking Account, Endorsements

Most businesses make payments by checks drawn on local commercial banks. Many individuals now use checking accounts drawing on funds in savings banks and/or in money funds. A check is a written order directing the "drawee" (the bank) to make payment to the "payee" (the party indicated by the words "Pay to the order of") from the account balance of the "drawer" (the party who signs the order or check).

When a checking account is opened, each person authorized to sign checks completes a signature card. A deposit slip is used to list items to be added to the account, including checks received from others—paychecks, amounts collected from clients, and so on.

Each check deposited must be endorsed. Endorse a check in ink across the reverse left end, never across the right end. Endorse it exactly as the name appears on the face, even though incorrect. If incorrect, write the correct signature immediately below. It is not necessary to write the explanation of the two signatures; they will be understood by the bank. Do not write the correct signature first and the incorrect one below in parentheses. This violates the banking rule that the last endorser must be the person to whom the money is paid. There are several types of endorsements:

1. Endorsement in blank. This is a simple signature of the payee, which makes the check payable to bearer. It should be cashed or deposited immediately.

Donna Smith

[G13489]

2. Special (or Full) endorsement. This states to whom a check is to be paid, *i.e.*, "Pay to the order of ..." above the payee's signature. This requires the designated person's endorsement but is still negotiable.

Pay to the Order of
Karl Hodges
Donna Smith

[G13490]

3. Restrictive endorsement. This limits the further purpose or use of the check, *i.e.*, with just "Pay to ..." above the payee's signature. The check is then nonnegotiable—it must be paid to the designated person and no one else.

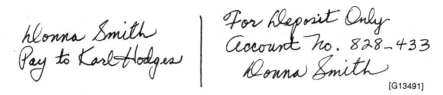

[G13491]

4. Qualified endorsement. The endorser assumes no legal responsibility for payment should the drawer have insufficient funds to honor his/her own check by using the words "Without recourse" written above the payee's signature in the endorsement. This relieves the endorser of any future liability on the check.

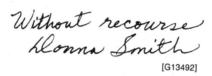

[G13492]

5. Deposit endorsement. This is a form of special or restrictive endorsement, which may be typed or stamped.

Pay to the order of Portland Branch U.S. National Bank The Jones Company 828–433

For deposit in The U.S. National Bank to the credit of The Jones Company

The restrictive endorsement should be used on checks to be deposited. The blank endorsement should be used only when presenting a check for immediate payment, such as when cashing one's paycheck.

Checks for deposit by a firm are, preferably, endorsed with a rubber stamp. A customer's number is assigned by the bank. The date is also carried on some rubber stamps.

In the absence of a rubber stamp, type "For deposit only" and below it the payee's name.

All checks for deposit should be endorsed immediately to safeguard them in case they are lost while being taken or mailed to the bank.

When preparing to write a check, be sure the stubs are completed first, showing all information; then complete each check using pen and ink. When making deposits, be sure to enter the deposit on the check stub and carry the balance forward. The check stubs can be used to prepare the journal entries.

§ 5.36 Certified Check

When a check is deposited, the bank credits the account subject to collection of the check. To ensure that a check is good, you may ask the drawer to have the check certified by his bank, or you may have it certified by his bank. To certify a check, the teller stamps "Certified" and the date on the check, and the certification is then signed by an authorized bank officer. After the check is certified, the bank reduces the drawer's account by the amount of the check and holds the funds for payment. The bank then becomes responsible for the payment of the certified check.

In reconciling the bank balance, a certified check which is outstanding is listed separately from the other outstanding checks because it has already been charged to the account by the bank and deducted as a payment. Certified checks are recorded like ordinary checks by both drawer and payee in the Cash Journal.

§ 5.37 Cashier's Check

A check drawn by a bank on its own funds is called a cashier's check. This check may be used when a depositor, in closing out his checking account, requests a cashier's check so that he does not have to carry cash. If the depositor's credit is not established, the cashier's check will be accepted as payment where the depositor's personal check might not be. Cashier's checks are recorded as ordinary checks by both buyer and seller in the Cash Journals.

§ 5.38 Bank Draft

A bank draft is a check issued by a bank upon its funds in another bank, usually located in some other city. The bank draft is used chiefly in buying goods from out-of-town concerns with whom the buyer has no credit but from whom he wishes immediate delivery. If the purchaser had sent his personal check in payment, the seller would not ship the goods until the check was honored, a procedure which might take from four to fourteen days. The seller will generally make immediate shipment against a bank draft because the bank is responsible for its payment.

To obtain a bank draft, the buyer draws a check to the order of his bank for the amount he needs plus the bank charge for the service. The bank then gives him a bank draft for the required amount, drawn on a bank in the city where the seller resides. The bank draft should be made payable to the buyer; he then endorses it in full to the seller. The reason is that this procedure makes it easy to secure the canceled bank draft from the bank as evidence of payment.

The purchaser of the bank draft enters the check in the Cash Disbursement Journal; Accounts Payable is debited for the amount of the invoice, the Bank Charge Expense account is debited for the amount of the bank charge, and the Cash Account is credited for the total. The seller treats the bank draft as any other check from a customer and records it in his Cash Receipt Journal.

§ 5.39 The Money Order

If a person does not have a checking account and wants to make a payment other than in currency, he can purchase a money order for that purpose at a United States post office, bank, and many grocery stores. The amount for which a money order can be bought is limited. In the books, money orders are treated in the same manner as ordinary checks.

§ 5.40 Reconciling the Bank Statement

When a bank statement is received, the bookkeeper's agent should check it immediately with the balance record on his check stubs or the bank account in the general ledger. The procedure known as reconciling the bank statement is simply one of making sure the record of the bank and the record of the depositor are in agreement. The balances may not be the same for one or more of the following reasons:

- Some of the checks issued during the period may not have been presented to the bank for payment by the date the statement was prepared.

- Deposits made may not have been recorded in time to appear on the bank's statement.

- Bank services charged to the depositor may not appear on the depositor's record. (In fact, the bank statement is usually the source paper for such charges unless a carbon copy of such debit has already been received and journalized.)

- Errors may be made by either party.

Most bank statements contain a form on the reverse side for the depositor's use in reconciliation, and after completion these forms are filed in a predetermined place in the depositor's office.

A suggested procedure for reconciliation of a bank statement is as follows:

1. Check the amount of each deposit on the bank statement with the check stubs, duplicate deposit tickets, or the general ledger account. If any outstanding deposits are found, they should be enumerated and added to the bank's total.

2. Check the amount of each canceled check and the numbers of the checks returned by the bank to be sure all checks issued have been paid and the amounts entered properly in the check stubs or ledger. Any checks not paid should be enumerated as outstanding and deducted from the bank's balance shown on the statement.

3. Any amounts of bank service charges or debits to the depositor not already shown on check stubs or the ledger account must be enumerated and deducted from the depositor's record total. These items must be journalized as a debit to an expense account (usually Office Expense) and a credit to the Cash In Bank account.

After these adjustments are entered on the reconciliation form, the two balances should be in agreement. If not, the depositor's records should first be checked for errors in addition, subtraction, and posting (such as a transposition of figures). If the error still cannot be found, a check of the bank's statement may reveal an error. Bank errors should be reported to the bank at once. If a depositor still is unable to reconcile the bank statement, he should report it to the bank immediately. (Note: Errors in transposition are divisible by 9. Divide the amount out of balance by 9, and if it is divisible evenly, the problem very easily could be a transposition error.)

§ 5.41 Payroll Records and Tax Reports

Since accurate accounting for employee's earnings preserves the legal right of each employee to be paid according to his employment contract and the laws governing such employment, there is absolutely no margin for error in payroll accounting.

§ 5.42 Earnings and Deductions

The first step in determining the amount to be paid an employee is to calculate the total or gross earnings. The second step is to determine the amount of deductions that is required either by law or agreement. The third step is to pay the employee the difference between the two, the net pay.

§ 5.43 Determination of Total Earnings

An employee in a law office will be paid either an hourly, weekly, semimonthly, or monthly rate. Wages by the hour are governed by the Fair Labor Standards Act (minimum wage laws). An employee may be entitled to overtime pay in some cases. Wage and hour cases usually involve time cards and time clocks or a computer-based timekeeping system in the larger firms. Regardless of the method the employer uses to determine pay scales and dates, the bookkeeper must maintain an accurate record of the gross amount paid, the deductions (itemized), and the net amount paid.

§ 5.44 Deductions From Total Earnings

With few exceptions, employers are required to withhold portions of each employee's total earnings for both federal income tax and Social Security taxes. Certain states and cities also require income or earnings tax withholding on the part of employers. Besides these deductions, an agreement between employer and employee may call for amounts to be withheld for any one or more of the following reasons:

- To purchase United States savings bonds for the employee
- To pay life, accident, or health insurance premiums for the employee
- To pay the employee's union or other professional dues
- To add to a pension or profit sharing plan
- To pay to some charitable organization, such as United Way
- To repay a loan from the company or the company credit union

§ 5.45 Social Security and Employer's Identification Numbers

Each employee is required to have a social security number for payroll accounting purposes. To obtain this number, a Form SS–5 may be secured from the Social Security office and completed.

Just as each individual must have a reporting number, so must the employer have a number with which to identify his tax reports. All but the new employer will have these numbers. In the case of new employers, the bookkeeper must obtain an application form (SS–4) from the Internal Revenue Service (IRS). After the number is obtained, it must be used on all reports submitted to the IRS.

§ 5.46 Circular E—Employer's Tax Guide and Federal Employment Tax Forms

The IRS publishes a booklet for the employer's use entitled "Circular E—Employer's Tax Guide." This booklet is revised periodically and supplemented regularly as tax laws change. The bookkeeper must obtain a copy of this booklet for the files. Once a mailing is established with the IRS, the subsequent editions are automatically sent to the employer.

Circular E provides the bookkeeper with the following information and instructions:

- Income tax withholding and payment to the IRS
- Form W–4
- Withholding Allowance Certificates
- Combined Annual Wage Reporting
- Form W–2
- Wage and Tax Statements
- Form W–2P
- Statements for Recipients of Periodic Annuities, Pensions, Retired Pay, or Individual Retirement Account (IRA) Payments
- Form W–3, Transmittal of Income and Tax Statements
- Which forms are transmitted to the Social Security Administration
- Which forms (941, 941E, 943, etc.) are to be filed with the IRS
- Charts of amounts to be withheld for both income tax and Social Security and Medicare taxes
- Tax withholding by the percentage method

The secretary-bookkeeper must be alert to the changes in these laws and should inquire of the IRS periodically as to whether or not there have been revisions.

There also is literature on Social Security and Medicare taxes included in the booklet. The bookkeeper must be aware of the maximum amount an employee must pay on for the year and the current percentage rate for both employee and employer.

Federal Unemployment Tax Act (FUTA) taxes must be sent in at the close of each year, or quarterly if required, on the form provided.

A few states require employers to withhold a percentage of wages for unemployment compensation benefits as well as a percentage for state and local income taxes. Payroll files must contain the latest literature, forms for reporting, deposit slips, and percentage rates from the state, if any, required for these taxes. An accurate record of all payments made must be kept for at least four years or the length of time specified by the IRS.

The government also publishes on an annual basis a booklet entitled "Federal Employment Tax Forms" (Publication 393). This booklet contains a supply of the routine forms needed to report taxes as well as an order blank for more forms. Instructions are included for filling out each type of form. Usually these items are mailed to the employers well in advance of the due dates, but the bookkeeper must be aware of the dates and should obtain a supply from the local IRS office if she does not receive them.

§ 5.47   Payroll Register

There are many types of payroll registers on the market in bound, spiral, and loose-leaf forms. As long as the form contains necessary information, any type is satisfactory.

§ 5.48   Journalizing the Payroll

Payroll Expense. This is an expense account which is debited for the total amount of the gross earnings of all employees for each pay period.

Payroll Expense	
Debit	
to enter gross earnings of employees for each pay period	

Social Security and Medicare Taxes Payable. This is a liability account which is credited for (1) the Social Security and Medicare taxes withheld from employees' earnings and (2) the Social Security and Medicare taxes imposed on the employer. The account should be debited for amounts paid to the Internal Revenue Service. When all of the Social Security and Medicare taxes have been paid, the account should be in balance.

Social Security and Medicare Taxes Payable	
Debit	Credit
to enter payment of Social Security and Medicare taxes previously withheld or imposed	to enter Social Security and Medicare taxes (1) withheld from employees' earnings and (2) imposed on the employer

Employees Income Tax Payable. This is a liability account which should be credited for the total income tax withheld from employees' earnings. The account is debited for amounts paid to a bank depository for the Internal Revenue Service. When all of the income taxes withheld have been paid, the account will be in balance.

Employees Income Tax Payable	
Debit	Credit
to enter payment of income tax previously withheld	to enter income tax withheld from employees' earnings

Other Deductions. Pension Plan Deductions Payable is a liability account which is credited with amounts withheld from employees' earnings for pension plan contributions. The account should be debited for the subsequent payment of these amounts to the pension plan trustee. Accounts for health insurance premiums payable, credit union contributions payable, and charitable contributions payable are other examples of accounts.

Journalizing Payroll Transactions. The information needed to properly enter the payment of employee wages and salaries is contained in the payroll register.

Payroll Taxes Expense. All of the payroll taxes imposed on an employer under the federal and state social security laws are an expense of the employer. For the purpose of this discussion, it is assumed that a single account entitled Payroll Taxes Expense is used to summarize these taxes. This is an expense account that is debited for all payroll taxes imposed on the employer.

Payroll Taxes Expense	
Debit	
to enter Social Security and Medicare, FUTA, and state unemployment taxes imposed on the employer	

Social Security and Medicare Taxes Payable. This is the same liability account that was illustrated above. The account is credited to enter the Social Security and Medicare taxes imposed on the employer. The account is debited when the taxes are paid to the Internal Revenue Service. When all Social Security and Medicare taxes have been paid, the account should be in balance.

Social Security and Medicare Taxes Payable	
Debit	Credit
to enter payment of Social Security and Medicare taxes	to enter Social Security and Medicare taxes (1) withheld from employees' earnings and (2) imposed on the employer

FUTA Tax Payable. In entering the federal unemployment tax, it is customary to keep a separate liability account entitled FUTA Tax Payable. This is a liability account that is credited for the taxes imposed on employers under the Federal Unemployment Tax Act. The account is debited for amounts paid to apply on such taxes. When all FUTA taxes have been paid, the account should be in balance.

179

FUTA Tax Payable	
Debit	Credit
to enter payment of FUTA tax	to enter FUTA tax imposed on the employer

State Unemployment Tax Payable. In entering the tax imposed under the state unemployment compensation laws, it is necessary to keep a separate liability account. This is a liability account that is credited for the tax imposed on employers under the state unemployment compensation laws. The account is debited for the amount paid to apply on such taxes. When all of the state taxes have been paid, the account should be in balance.

State Unemployment Tax Payable	
Debit	Credit
to enter state unemployment tax paid	to enter state unemployment tax imposed on the employer

Journalizing Employer's Payroll Taxes. The payroll taxes imposed on employers may be entered periodically, such as monthly or quarterly. It is common to enter such taxes at the same time that wages are paid so that the employer's liability for such taxes and related expenses may be entered in the same period as the wages on which the taxes are based.

The information needed to enter employer payroll taxes properly is contained in the payroll register.

Strict adherence to state and federal deadlines and amounts to be deposited at certain intervals is absolutely essential, and the penalty for not doing so can be severe.

§ 5.49   The Write–It–Once Principle as a Labor–Saving Device

There are many systems on the market today that make the life of a bookkeeper much easier. These systems employ computers, electronic posting machines, or pegboard-type operations. The main advantage of all these systems is that figures are placed into the system only once, thus eliminating the chance of transposition errors and the tedious routine of posting incoming and outgoing cash figures to the journal, general ledger, and subsidiary ledgers.

The mechanics of the pegboard system are basically:

    1.   Cash disbursements—checks with a carbon strip on the back are placed over a disbursements journal (subsidiary ledger

showing cash disbursements only). Individual client ledger sheets are inserted between the checks and the journal page so that when a check is written the entry is made from check to ledger sheet to journal.

2. Cash Receipts—follows the same principle as disbursements. (Again, a cash subsidiary ledger—usually with both receipts and disbursements in one journal—is used.) The client ledger card is placed on top of the journal sheet. Receipts are journalized as fee income, reimbursement for advances, etc., and at the same time entered on the bank deposit form. The deposit total is added to the disbursements journal, providing a current balance.

3. Payroll Records—the employee payroll card is placed between the check and the disbursement journal. The check is written in the net amount due the employee. The payroll information is entered on the payroll card and journalized at the same time. At the end of the month the journal is totaled, and records are immediately available for preparing payroll tax forms.

Much has been written on the pegboard systems so that instructions for their use are available from the suppliers.

The important thing for a beginning bookkeeper is to learn the basics first. After obtaining a thorough knowledge of double-entry bookkeeping, learn the many ways of making it easier and more error free.

§ 5.50   Computing Interest

There are three factors that must be considered when computing interest: (1) principal, (2) interest rate, and (3) time period.

The principal is the amount of money borrowed. The amount of interest is based on this figure.

The interest rate is usually given on the face of the note. If the note is interest bearing and the interest rate is not given on the face of the note, the legal rate must be used. The legal rate varies among the different states. The interest rate shown on the face of the note is always an annual percentage rate unless stated otherwise.

The time period of the note is determined by the number of days or months from the date of the note until the date of maturity. Interest computations are based on this time period. When the maturity date is specified in months, the fraction of the year and months represented is used to calculate interest. For example, if a note specifies maturity in four months, interest is calculated on $4/12$ or $1/3$ of a year. If maturity is specified in days, interest is calculated based on the fraction of the year those days represent. Three hundred sixty days is customarily used to compute interest for one year. For example, if a note matures in 60 days, interest is based on $^{60}/_{360}$ or $^1/_6$ of a year.

If the due date is specified on a note, the exact number of days from the date of the note through the due date or maturity date must be determined. For example, if a note is issued on January 1 and is due on March 17, the time period is computed as follows:

Days in January	31
Date of note, January 1	−1
Days remaining in January	30
Days in February**	28
Days in March	17
Time period in days	75

** Do not assume February to be leap year in your computations unless you are told it is.

Notice in the above computation that the date of maturity is included but the date of the note is excluded.

After determining the proper factors, interest is calculated using the following formula:

Principal × Rate × Time Period = Amount of Interest.

Remember, the time period is usually a fraction of a 360–day year.

EXAMPLE: The principal amount is $500; the interest rate is 8%; the time period is three months. The interest payable is $10, computed as follows:

$500 × 8% × $^3/_{12}$ = $10 interest.

Assume the same facts as in the above example except that the note matures 90 days after issuance instead of three months. The interest is $10, computed as follows:

$500 × 8% × $^{90}/_{360}$ = $10 interest.

CHAPTER 6

WRITTEN COMMUNICATIONS

Table of Sections

---

§ 6.1 Introduction

One of the most valuable skills you will ever acquire is proper use of English grammar. We spend over 70 percent of our day using the English language. Much of our business success is in direct proportion to the manner in which we communicate. Although both oral and written communications are important, this chapter deals mainly with written communications.

In order to be an effective secretary, you must master the basic grammar skills. The next step is to learn how to use these skills effectively in creating written communications.

This chapter is not intended to offer a complete course in grammar. It is expected that the reader has some background knowledge of grammar; this chapter provides only a cursory review. If you need additional help, consult grammar textbooks or even take a class in grammar. Your local college bookstore can offer many suggestions about good handbooks. Keep a good reference handbook on English usage at your desk and consult it often.

§ 6.2 The Basics of English Grammar

There are eight parts of speech; these are names given to words according to their usage in the sentence. The eight parts of speech are verbs, nouns, pronouns, adverbs, adjectives, prepositions, conjunctions, and interjections. The role the word plays in the sentence determines the form of the word which should be used. Each of these parts of speech is examined in this chapter.

§ 6.3 Verbs

A *verb* is a word or word group that tells what the subject does or is or what happens to the subject. A sentence is not complete without a verb. Some writers define *verb* as an action or state of being. There are two types of verbs: *transitive* and *intransitive*.

§ 6.4 Transitive Verbs

A *transitive verb* is one which shows physical or mental action and has a direct object when the subject is the doer of the action. If the subject is the receiver of the action, the verb is also transitive.

EXAMPLES: Mary read the book. (*Book* is the direct object.)
The table was repaired by Kris. (*Table* is the subject and receives the action.)

§ 6.5 Voice

A transitive verb is either *active* or *passive*. In the active voice someone or something acts. In the passive voice someone or something is acted upon.

EXAMPLES: The secretary typed the letters very quickly. (Active.)
The letters were typed very quickly by the secretary. (Passive.)

In business writing active voice is preferred to passive voice. It is direct and concise. It is more personal and conversational. It is easier for the reader to follow the sequence of thoughts when active voice is used. Passive voice is impersonal; however, it does tend to sound less blunt than active voice. Therefore, it is often used for making suggestions or recommendations.

§ 6.6 Intransitive Verbs

An *intransitive verb* shows physical or mental action but does not have a direct object.

EXAMPLE: Charlie snored during the night.

Some intransitive verbs show a state of being rather than action. These are called *linking verbs* and link the subject to a word or words which are the same as the subject or describe the subject.

EXAMPLES: *Gerry* is very *efficient*. (*Efficient* describes *Gerry*.)
Gerry is *president* of the club. (*Gerry* and *president* are the same person and are linked by the verb *is*.)

Depending upon the grammar book you are reading, *efficient* is a *predicate adjective* or *subject complement*, and *president* is a *predicate nominative* or *subject complement*.

§ 6.7 Verb Tense

The *tense* of a verb refers to the time an action or event takes place or the time of the state of being.

When we speak of verbs, we generally refer to them in three forms. These are called the three principle parts of the verb and are the present tense, past tense, and past participle.

Depending on how the past tense and past participle are formed, verbs are divided into two categories: regular and irregular.

§ 6.8 Regular Verbs

A *regular verb* is one which forms its past tense and past participle by adding *d, ed,* or *t* to the present tense of the verb.

§ 6.9 Irregular Verbs

Verbs which do not form their past tense and past participle in this manner are called *irregular*. Illustration 6–1 shows several of the irregular verbs in their three forms. (The past participle is used in forming the perfect tenses.)

Illustration 6–1

COMMONLY USED IRREGULAR VERBS		
Present Tense	Past Tense	Past Participle (have, has, had)
become	became	become
begin	began	begun
bite	bit	bitten
blow	blew	blown
break	broke	broken
bring	brought	brought
buy	bought	bought
come	came	come
do	did	done
draw	drew	drawn
drink	drank	drunk
drive	drove	driven
eat	ate	eaten
fall	fell	fallen
fight	fought	fought
fly	flew	flown
get	got	got or gotten
give	gave	given
go	went	gone
grow	grew	grown
hear	heard	heard
hit	hit	hit
know	knew	known
lay	laid	laid
lead	led	led
leave	left	left
let	let	let
lie (recline)	lay	lain
lose	lost	lost

Present Tense	Past Tense	Past Participle (have, has, had)
put	put	put
ride	rode	ridden
ring	rang	rung
run	ran	run
say	said	said
see	saw	seen
show	showed	showed or shown
sing	sang	sung
sink	sank or sunk	sunk
sit	sat	sat
sleep	slept	slept
speak	spoke	spoken
swim	swam	swum
take	took	taken
teach	taught	taught
tell	told	told
think	thought	thought
throw	threw	thrown
wear	wore	worn
write	wrote	written

NOT SO COMMONLY USED IRREGULAR VERBS		
Present Tense	Past Tense	Past Participle (have, has, had)
arise	arose	arisen
awake	awoke or awaked	awaked or awoke
beat	beat	beaten
burst	burst	burst
choose	chose	chosen
cling	clung	clung
cost	cost	cost
drag	dragged	dragged
fling	flung	flung
forget	forgot	forgotten or forgot
freeze	froze	frozen
hang	hung	hung
hang (death)	hanged	hanged
hurt	hurt	hurt
pay	paid	paid
read	read	read
rise	rose	risen
set	set	set
shake	shook	shaken
spring	sprang or sprung	sprung
steal	stole	stolen
swear	swore	sworn

Present Tense	Past Tense	Past Participle (have, has, had)
swing	swung	swung
tear	tore	torn
wake	woke or waked	waked or woken
wet	wet	wet

§ 6.10 Present Tense

Present tense refers to the present time—now.

EXAMPLES: I am happy. (Shows state of being is now.) The baby plays with the ball. (Action is occurring now.)

In the present tense if you wish to show that the action is continuous and moving forward (progressive), use the *ing* form of the verb and add the proper form of the *be* verb.

EXAMPLES: I *am dancing.*   We *are dancing.*
You *are dancing.*   You *are dancing.*
He *is dancing.*   They *are dancing.*

If you want to emphasize the action taking place in the present tense, use the emphatic verb *do* as the helping verb.

EXAMPLES: I *do dance.*
You *do dance.*
He *does dance.*

§ 6.11 Past Tense

Past tense shows that something took place at some time in the past or that the state of being was in the past.

EXAMPLES: He *left* at five.
He *was* there all night.

In the past tense to show action that was continuous or moving forward, use the *ing* form of the verb (progressive form) with the past tense of the *be* verb.

EXAMPLES: I *was filing.*   We *were filing.*
You *were filing.*   You *were filing.*
She *was filing.*   They *were filing.*

To emphasize the action in the past tense, add the past tense of the *do* verb (*did*) to the verb.

EXAMPLES: I *did file.*   We *did file.*
You *did file.*   You *did file.*
He *did file.*   They *did file.*

§ 6.12   Future Tense

Future tense tells that the action or state of being will occur at some future time. To express future tense, use *shall* (with first person pronouns) or *will* (with second and third person pronouns) followed by a main verb.

EXAMPLES: He *will leave* tomorrow.
We *shall go* with you.

In the future tense show the progressive form by adding the *be* verb.

EXAMPLES: I *shall be singing.*   We *shall be singing.*
You *will be singing.*   You *will be singing.*
He *will be singing.*   They *will be singing.*

§ 6.13   Present Perfect Tense

Present perfect tense indicates that the action or state of being is complete (perfect) at the present time. This tense is always written with *has* or *have* preceding the past participle of the main verb.

EXAMPLES: Mary *has danced* all night.
Jon and Fred *have* already *left.*

§ 6.14   Past Perfect Tense

Past perfect tense shows that the action or state of being was completed at some particular time in the past. It denotes action or being begun in the past and completed at some stated past time or before some other implied time. It is always formed by using *had* with the past participle of the main verb.

EXAMPLES: Sarah *had sung* by the time I arrived.
By the time of her divorce, she *had lived* with him for two years.

§ 6.15   Future Perfect Tense

Future perfect tense shows that the action will be completed by a certain time in the future. It indicates action will be completed in the future before some other future action takes place. It is formed by using *shall have* and *will have* with the past participle of the main verb.

> EXAMPLES: By the time I am 21, I *shall have* bought my own car.
> By the end of next year, they *will have* completed the merger.

§ 6.16   Agreement of the Subject and Verb

A subject must agree with the verb in person and number. A singular subject must have a singular verb. A plural subject must have a plural verb.

> EXAMPLES: He *does* it. (singular)
> We *do* it. (plural)

You is considered to be a plural word and always takes a plural verb even when it is understood that only one person is being referred to.

> EXAMPLES: *You* are the only *secretary* for me. (singular)
> *You* are the only *girls* for me. (plural)

Two or more singular subjects connected with *or* or *nor* take a singular verb.

> EXAMPLE: Either Sally *or* Mary *plans* to meet you there.

When a singular subject and a plural subject are joined by *or* or *nor,* the plural subject should directly precede the verb and a plural verb should be used.

> EXAMPLE: Either Mary *or* the boys *plan* to meet you there.

A collective noun requires a singular verb if the noun is considered as a single unit; a plural verb should be used if the persons or things are being considered as individuals within the unit.

> EXAMPLES: The jury *delivers its* verdict to the judge. (singular)
> The jury *sleep* in separate rooms. (plural)

When the word *number* is preceded by *the,* a singular verb is used. If *a* precedes the word, a plural verb is used.

EXAMPLES: *The* number of boys *was* large this year. (singular)
             A number of girls *were* present. (plural)

Sums of money used as subjects require a singular verb.

EXAMPLE: *Fifty dollars is* a lot to spend on a present for her.

§ 6.17 Agreement of Pronouns and Antecedents

The word to which a pronoun refers must be clear to the reader. Maintain a consistent viewpoint by making sure that the pronoun agrees in number with the word to which it refers.

EXAMPLES:

Incorrect: Students learning to type must be careful to type his papers accurately.

Correct: Students learning to type must be careful to type their papers accurately.

Incorrect: I enjoy eating in restaurants because you get such a wide variety of food.

Correct: I enjoy eating in restaurants because I get such a wide variety of food.

Incorrect: Alice wants to know where you can buy a set of striped seatcovers.

Correct: Alice wants to know where she can buy a set of striped seatcovers.

The biggest difficulty seems to occur when indefinite pronouns are used. See Illustration 6–5 to determine whether the pronoun is singular or plural. Be sure that any reference back to the indefinite pronoun is also singular or plural.

EXAMPLES:

Incorrect: Everyone going to the picnic should bring their lunch.

Correct: Everyone going to the picnic should bring his (or her) lunch.

Incorrect: All employees working on the night shift should be sure to bring his lunch.

Correct: All employees working on the night shift should be sure to bring their lunches.
                         (or)
  Each employee working on the night shift should bring his lunch.

§ 6.18 Verbals

There are three types of verbals: *infinitives, gerunds,* and *participles.* The word *verbal* is derived from the word *verb;* it is not a verb but a form of a verb.

§ 6.19 Infinitives

An infinitive is created by placing the word *to* in front of the verb, as in *to go.* An infinitive may be used as a noun, an adjective, or an adverb. It may be modified by adverbs and may have subjects and objects just as a verb has. The infinitive phrase consists of the infinitive and the word or words that are closely related to the infinitive.

> EXAMPLE: *To read* a book is an interesting pastime. (*Book* is the direct object of the infinitive *to read.*)

Do not be guilty of using a split infinitive. This occurs when a modifier is placed between "to" and the verb. Some writers say that splitting the infinitive helps the reader. Knowing, careful writers, however, not only believe that it hinders the reader, but that splitting the infinitive is "language deterioration." If the sentence is awkward without placing the modifier before the word it describes, revise the sentence.

> EXAMPLES: To improve slowly, not *to slowly improve.*
> You have the right not *to see it,* not ...
> You have the right *to not see it.*

Many words are merely verbose.

Rescue the split infinitives that are smothered with unnecessary adverbs.

> EXAMPLES: To efficiently maintain
> To successfully complete
> To officially thank
> To publicly express
> To completely eliminate
> To effectively promote

§ 6.20 Gerunds

A *gerund* is the present participle form of the verb used in the sentence as a noun.

> EXAMPLE: *Singing* gives me great pleasure. (*Singing* is a gerund and is the subject of the sentence.)

A gerund phrase consists of the gerund and the adverbs, adjectives, and words closely associated with it. It can take an object and an indirect object.

> EXAMPLE: *Writing Alice a letter* was a generous gesture. (*Writing* is the gerund; *Alice* is the indirect object; and *letter* is the direct object of the gerund. The gerund phrase, *Writing Alice a letter,* is the subject of the sentence.)

When a noun or pronoun precedes the gerund, the possessive case of the noun or pronoun is generally used.

EXAMPLES:

Incorrect:	I look forward to *him* going.
Correct:	I look forward to *his* going.
Incorrect:	I objected to *Mary* leaving.
Correct:	I objected to *Mary's* leaving.

§ 6.21   Participles

A *participle* is a verb form which cannot stand by itself as a verb. It must have a helping verb in order to function as a verb.

The *past participle* is the third principle part of the verb. A fourth verb form is the *present participle,* which is formed by adding *ing* to the present form of the verb. In regular verbs the past participle ends in *ed, d,* or *t* (walk, walked, walked). In irregular verbs there is no consistency in forming the past participle. Consult the irregular verb chart (Illustration 6–1) for past participles of irregular verbs. The *perfect participle* is formed by adding *having* or *having been* to the past participle.

A participle may function as an adjective when it is used without a helping verb.

> EXAMPLES: The *dancing* bear stole the show. (*Dancing* is the present participle.)
> The *tired* old woman walked slowly. (*Tired* is the past participle.)
> The watch, *having been broken,* no longer worked accurately. (*Having been broken* is the perfect participle.)

A *participle phrase* consists of the participle and words closely associated with it. The phrase should be placed close to the word it modifies. When it is incorrectly placed, it distorts the meaning of the sentence and is known as a dangling participle.

EXAMPLE:

Incorrect: *Leaping nimbly across the stage,* the aged woman envied the teenage dancers.

Correct: The aged woman envied the teenage dancers *leaping nimbly across the stage.*

§ 6.22   Nouns

A *noun* is a word that names a person (dancer), place (town), thing (table), or idea (beauty). There are two types of nouns: *common* and *proper.*

§ 6.23   Common Nouns

A *common noun* is a name given to a general class of person (lady), place (city), thing (chair), or idea (success).

§ 6.24   Proper Nouns

A *proper noun* is the name of a particular person (Alice), place (Utah), or thing (Park Building). Proper nouns are always capitalized.

Nouns are also categorized as *concrete, abstract,* and *collective.*

§ 6.25   Concrete Nouns

A *concrete noun* is one that can be experienced by one or more of the five senses, such as *car, building, vase, baby.*

§ 6.26   Abstract Nouns

An abstract noun is one that cannot be experienced by any of the five senses. It cannot be seen, heard, touched, tasted, or smelled, such as *happiness, logic, luck, wisdom.*

§ 6.27   Collective Nouns

A *collective noun* is one that names a group of persons or things, such as faculty, orchestra, jury, family.

§ 6.28   Plurals of Nouns

When forming the plural of a noun, you may use one of the following guides or consult the dictionary. When you are in doubt, use the dictionary.

- Add *s* to most common nouns (cat/cats, boy/boys, chair/chairs).

- Add *es* to nouns ending in *s, x, ch, sh,* or *z* (glass/glasses, box/boxes, waltz/waltzes, wish/wishes, crutch/crutches).

- When nouns ending in *o* have a consonant preceding the *o,* add *es* to the noun (potato/potatoes, veto/vetoes); exceptions to this rule are nouns dealing with music, such as piano/pianos, solo/solos; silo/silos is another exception.

- When nouns ending in *o* have a vowel preceding the *o,* add *s* to the noun (radio/radios, ratio/ratios).

- When nouns ending in *y* have a consonant preceding the *y,* change the *y* to *i* and add *es* (fly/flies, company/companies, secretary/secretaries).

- When nouns ending in *y* have a vowel preceding the *y,* leave the noun the same and add *s* (attorney/attorneys, honey/honeys, gray/grays).

- When forming the plural of abbreviations and letters, the rule is that you add an apostrophe and an *s* (*'s*) to lower case letters and abbreviations (*p's* and *q's, r.p.m.'s, c.o.d.'s*); for capital letters and abbreviations ending in capital letters, add just the *s* (M.D.s, Ph.D.s, ABCs).

- Nouns ending in *f* or *fe* are made plural by changing the *f* to *v* and adding *es* (wife/wives, life/lives); an exception is chief/chiefs.

There are exceptions to the above rules, such as man/men, woman/women, child/children, mouse/mice, sheep/sheep, tooth/teeth, foot/feet, corps/corps. Most of these exceptions are fairly well-known. If you are in doubt, consult the dictionary.

§ 6.29　Compound Words

When forming the plural of compound words, such as *attorney general* or *notary public,* make the most descriptive word plural. For instance, *attorney* more nearly describes the function of the attorney general, so you would use *attorneys general* for the plural. This rule is not so hard and fast as it used to be, and the dictionary now recognizes both *attorneys general* and *attorney generals* as well as *notaries public* and *notary publics.* The first form is probably the most widely accepted, however. With hyphenated compound words, such as *mother-in-law* and *brother-in-law,* you again make the plural on the most descriptive word; *mothers-in-law* and *brothers-in-law* are correct. Once again, consult the dictionary when you are in doubt.

§ 6.30   Possessive Nouns

To show ownership or possession, use an apostrophe with the noun. There are three basic rules governing the form of possessives. (See Illustration 6–2).

Illustration 6–2

POSSESSIVE CASE OF NOUNS		
Singular	Plural	
To all singular nouns, add 's	To all plural nouns ending in s, add '	To all plural nouns NOT ending in s, add 's

§ 6.31   Singular Possession

Add an apostrophe and an s ('s) to the end of a singular noun (Mary's, secretary's, today's). The exception to this rule is that when a proper noun ends in s and the addition of 's would make the word hard to pronounce, only an apostrophe is added (Moses'). Since opinions vary as to what is hard to pronounce, it is difficult to know when to omit the added s. When in doubt, add 's.

§ 6.32   Plural Possession

First, make the word plural; then look at the end of the word. If it ends in s, you should add only an apostrophe. If it does not end in s, you should add 's just as you did in the singular (boy/boys/boys', child/children/children's). It is essential that you do not omit the first step of forming the plural word. Once you have done this, you can decide which method to use for showing possession—' or 's.

§ 6.33   Three Steps to Forming Possession

1. Ask yourself, "Do I really need the apostrophe? Does this word show possession?"
2. If the answer is yes, spell out the singular or plural noun first.
3. Apply the rules in the chart above.

Following are some additional rules for forming possessive nouns:

- When you have a compound word and need to show singular possession, add an apostrophe and s ('s) to the last word (brother-in-law's).
- When you have a compound word and need to show plural possession, make the plural word first; then add apostrophe and s ('s) to the end of the compound word (mothers-in-law's).

- To show separate ownership of two or more things, add an apostrophe and *s* (*'s*) to each name (Sue's and Mary's cards).

- To show joint ownership, add the possessive only to the last owner (Fred and Robyn's house).

- On personal and company names, add the apostrophe and *s* (*'s*) at the end of the name (John Q. Smith III's, Stacy & Stacy's).

§ 6.34   Pronouns

A pronoun is a word used in place of a noun. There are

- Personal pronouns
- Relative pronouns
- Indefinite pronouns
- Possessive pronouns
- Interrogative pronouns
- Demonstrative pronouns

§ 6.35   Personal Pronouns

Personal pronouns are used for the person speaking, the person spoken to, and the person spoken about.

EXAMPLE: *He* told *her* about *me*. *(He, her, me*—personal pronouns)

§ 6.36   Person and Case

Pronouns are classified as first person (person or persons doing the speaking), second person (person or persons being spoken to), and third person (person or persons being spoken about).

First person pronouns are I, we, me, us, my, mine, our, ours.

Second person pronouns are you, your, yours.

Third person pronouns are he, she, it, they, him, her, it, them, his, hers, its, their, theirs.

There are three case forms of personal pronouns: *nominative, objective,* and *possessive.* Illustration 6–3 shows the pronouns in each case. The part the pronoun takes in the sentence determines which case you should use. Note that in the possessive case there are two forms of pronouns. When the pronoun precedes a noun, it is known as an adjective. When it stands alone and shows possession, it is a possessive pronoun.

199

Illustration 6–3

CASES AND FUNCTIONS OF PRONOUNS			
Nominative	Objective	Possessive	
I, we	me, us	my our	mine ours
you he, she it, they	you him, her it, them	your her, his its, their	yours hers, his its, theirs
	FUNCTIONS IN THE SENTENCE		
1. Subject She is home. 2. Predicate nominative (sub- ject complement) The owner is he.	1. Direct object Ray told her. 2. Indirect object Ray told me the news. 3. Object of preposition Give the food to him. 4. Object of infinitive Jay wanted to send me instead of Alice. 5. Subject of infinitive The teacher wanted them to do the act- ing. (Pronouns preceding and following an in- finitive are in the objective case.)	1. Possessive pronoun as adjective This is your book. 2. Possessive pronoun Is the book yours?	

§ 6.37 Possessive Pronouns

A *possessive pronoun* does not contain an apostrophe. Do not confuse *it's* with *its*. *It's* is a contraction of it is; *its* is a possessive pronoun.

§ 6.38 Compound Personal Pronouns

A *compound personal pronoun* is one ending in *self* or *selves,* such as *myself, ourselves.* These are used only when they refer back to a noun in the sentence meaning the same person. It is a reflexive pronoun—it reflects back.

EXAMPLES: I gave *myself* a haircut. (*Myself* refers to I.)
Incorrect: Mary and myself went shopping.
Correct: Mary and I went shopping. (In the incorrect sentence there is no one to whom the pronoun *myself* can reflect back.)

§ 6.39 Relative Pronouns

A *relative pronoun* joins dependent clauses to independent clauses (a subordinate clause to a main clause). It begins the subordinate clause and is related to another word or idea in the sentence. It also serves as either the subject, direct object, or object of the preposition in the dependent clause.

EXAMPLES: The secretary *who* types the fastest will get the job. (*Who* is a relative pronoun and is the subject of the verb *types.*)

The secretary *whom* you hired is very efficient. (*Whom* is a relative pronoun and is the direct object of the verb *hired.*)

The secretary to *whom* you refer is my wife. (*Whom* is a relative pronoun and is the object of the preposition *to.*)

In each of the above examples the dependent clause is related to "the secretary" by the relative pronoun.

Illustration 6–4 shows the relative pronouns.

Illustration 6–4

RELATIVE PRONOUNS		
Pronoun	Use in Sentence	Examples
Who	*Nominative case* Used as a subject of a clause	The girl *who* gave you the package left quickly.
Whom	*Objective case* Used as a direct object Used as an object of the preposition	The teacher *whom* I knew well quit teaching. The lady to *whom* I gave your name will call you tomorrow.
Whose	*Possessive case* Used as an adjective (NOTE: WHO, WHOM and WHOSE refer to persons only)	The man *whose* dog was lost lives on your street.
Which	Refers to animals or things Used for clauses that are non-essential (non-restrictive) Used as a subject Used as a direct object Used as an object of a preposition	The desk *which* was broken was sold. The speech *which* I heard was dull. The chair on *which* I stood fell.
That	Refers to persons, animals, or things Used for essential (restrictive) clauses Used as a subject Used as a direct object	I think *that* will do for now. The girls *that* I know will do it for you.

§ 6.40   Indefinite Pronouns

Indefinite pronouns are those that do not stand for a particular person or thing. Some of them are always singular; others are always plural; others may be either singular or plural depending upon the noun to which they refer. (See Illustration 6–5.)

Illustration 6–5

INDEFINITE PRONOUNS		
Use a Singular Verb	Use a Plural Verb	Use Either a Plural or Singular Verb
another, anybody, anyone, each, everybody, everyone, either, neither, someone, somebody	both, few, many, others, several	all, any, more, none, some

§ 6.41   Interrogative Pronouns

Interrogative pronouns are used in asking questions. *Who, whom, which, what,* and *whose* are the most common ones. Do not confuse *whose* with *who's; who's* is a contraction of *who is* and *whose* is possessive.

EXAMPLES: Whose car is that?
What are you doing?
Who is going with me?
Whom shall I appoint?
Which of the books do you want?

§ 6.42   Demonstrative Pronouns

Demonstrative pronouns are used to modify a noun or take the place of a noun. They point out.

Singular   **Plural**
This   These   Refer to objects near at hand.
That   Those   Refer to objects at a distance, either a slight or great distance

§ 6.43   Adverbs

Adverbs are words which describe or limit a verb, an adjective, or another adverb. They also modify verbals (infinitives, gerunds, and participles). They answer the questions of:

Where?	He works downtown.
When?	Mother left today.
To what degree?	She worked considerably harder than Mary.
How?	The snow melted quickly.
Why?	She worked so she would not starve. (Adverb clause)

§ 6.44   Comparison of Adverbs

Illustration 6–6 shows the three degrees of comparison of adverbs.

The *positive* expresses no comparison.

EXAMPLE: The boy worked hard.

The *comparative* compares two persons or things.

EXAMPLE: The boy worked harder than his friend.

The *superlative* compares three or more persons or things.

EXAMPLE: Of the three boys, Jack worked hardest.

Illustration 6–6

COMPARISON CHART FOR ADVERBS		
Positive	Comparative	Superlative
No comparison	Compares two persons or things. Add *er* to positive form. Use the word *more* before the positive form. Use the word *less* before the positive form.	Compares three or more persons or things. Add *est* to the positive. Use the word *most* before the positive. Use the word *least* before the positive.
EXAMPLES		
efficiently	more efficiently	most efficiently
efficiently	less efficiently	least efficiently
soon	sooner	soonest
obvious	more obvious	most obvious
much	more	most
bad	worse	worst
slowly	more slowly	most slowly

§ 6.45   Adjectives

Adjectives are words which modify, describe, or limit nouns, pronouns, and gerunds. They answer questions such as:

Which one? The red car is mine.

How many? The two books are his.

What kind? The wooden chair is broken.

Most people are familiar with adjectives preceding nouns such as those in the examples given above. There are also adjectives which follow linking verbs (forms of verbs such as *be, appear, seem*). These are called *predicate adjectives.*

> EXAMPLES: The dress is *beautiful.*
> She seems *happy.*
> He appears *exhilarated.*

Occasionally an adjective follows a noun.

> EXAMPLES: His wife found the restaurant *dirty.* (*Dirty* modifies restaurant.)
> A dress *six inches longer* would not look nice on her. (*Six inches longer* modifies dress.)

Adjectives are sometimes created from proper nouns. These are called proper adjectives.

> EXAMPLES: An *English* actor
> A *European* car

Some proper adjectives are no longer capitalized because they are no longer associated with the proper names from which they were derived.

> EXAMPLES: pasteurized milk (Louis Pasteur)
> herculean task (Hercules)

§ 6.46   Compound Adjectives

Compound adjectives are those that consist of two or more words that function as a unit and express a single thought. The words in a compound adjective are hyphenated when they occur directly before the noun. When they occur elsewhere in the sentence, they may or may not be hyphenated depending on how they are used.

EXAMPLES: This is a *first-class* restaurant.
                   She is a *well-informed* reporter.
                   The *up-to-date* report was given to the manager.

When they follow the noun, they are not hyphenated.

EXAMPLES: The restaurant was *first class.*
                   The reporter was *well informed.*
                   The report was *up to date.*

Sometimes what looks like a compound adjective is in reality an adverb-adjective combination. The adverb ends in *ly*. These should never be hyphenated. The test is to see if you can omit the word immediately preceding the noun and still have a combination that sounds correct.

EXAMPLES: The *friendly-acting* man sold teapots.
                   The *privately owned* yacht was luxurious.

If you can say *friendly man,* you need a hyphen. If you cannot, you do not need a hyphen. You cannot say *privately yacht;* you do not need the hyphen. The reasoning behind this is that the *ly* ending on the adverb shows the relationship of the two words without the hyphen. But two adjectives with the force of one thought, as in *worldly-wise person,* needs the hyphen to tie the two words together.

A noun followed by a gerund (*profit-taking, price-cutting*) needs a hyphen when it is used as an adjective preceding a noun.

EXAMPLES: She did her *letter writing* late at night.
                   He entered the *letter-writing* contest.

Most words ending in *-ing, -ed, -d, -en, -n* when used in compound modifiers are hyphenated.

EXAMPLES: Far-reaching
                   Old-fashioned
                   Soft-spoken
                   Half-grown

The general rule is that if the phrase is out of its normal order, it should be hyphenated.

EXAMPLES: The outfit looked odd.
                   The odd-looking outfit ...
                   The woman was stricken with panic.
                   The panic-stricken woman ...

When the comparative or superlative forms are used in a compound adjective, no hyphen is used; however, a hyphen is used in the positive form.

EXAMPLES: a low-priced house   a lower priced house
              a slow-burning fire   the slowest burning fire

§ 6.47 Comparison of Adjectives

Adjectives are compared in the same manner as *adverbs—positive, comparative,* and *superlative.*

Positive—pretty, graceful

Comparative—prettier, more graceful

Superlative—prettiest, most graceful

Consult the chart on adverbs for additional information. (See Illustration 6–6.)

§ 6.48 Distinguishing Between Adverbs and Adjectives

Adverbs are often formed by adding *ly* to adjectives (courteous/courteously, direct/directly, real/really). Occasionally, when the adjective ends with *y* preceded by a consonant, the *y* is changed to *i* and *ly* is added (ready/readily, happy/happily).

Some adverbs and adjectives are confusing. *Good* is an adjective and *well* is an adverb, except in matters of health; then, *well* is an adjective. *Bad* is an adjective and *badly* is an adverb; when you are talking about any of the five senses, be sure that you use the correct word.

EXAMPLES: I smell *bad.* (The person has a bad odor.)
              I smell *badly.* (The person does a poor job of sniffing.)
              I feel *bad.* (I am not well.)
              I feel *badly.* (I do a poor job of touching.)

Real is an adjective; *really* is an adverb. *Real* is not a substitute for the word *very;* neither is *really* a good substitute for *very.* It may be used, but it gives the impression of *actually* rather than *very.*

EXAMPLES:

Incorrect: I worked *real* hard.

Correct: I worked *very* hard.

Incorrect: She is a *real* happy person.

Acceptable: She is a *really* happy person.

Correct: She is a *very* happy person.

Some adjectives form their degrees in an irregular manner. The following are some of the common irregular adjectives:

Positive	Comparative	Superlative
bad, ill	worse	worst
good, well	better	best
little	less, lesser	least
many, much	more	most
far	farther, further	farthest, furthest

Most adjectives which end in *ful* or *less* and all adjectives of more than two syllables form their degrees by adding *more* or *less* for the comparative and *most* or *least* for the superlative.

Farther and *further* are the comparatives for *far*. *Farthest* and *furthest* are the superlatives for *far*. *Farther* and *farthest* are preferred when referring to measurable distance; *further* and *furthest* are preferred when referring to degree or quantity, as in the sense of additional or figurative distance.

Later is used to refer to time; *latter* means near the end or the second of two items.

Less and *least* are used to describe nouns that are concerned with amount and quantity; *fewer* and *fewest* are used to emphasize number by actual count. If you could replace the word *fewer* with "a smaller number of," then you should use *fewer*. It is used chiefly before plurals; *less* and *least* are used chiefly before singular words.

§ 6.49　Prepositions

A *preposition* is a word used to show the relationship of the noun or pronoun which follows it to some other word in the sentence. The prepositional phrase may be used to modify other words in a sentence. It helps connect the thoughts in a sentence and offers clearer writing.

COMMONLY USED PREPOSITIONS

about	between	off
above	but	on
along	by	over
after	except	through
against	for	under
among	from	up
at	in	upon
before	into	with

NOTE: *But* is usually a conjunction but may also serve as a preposition. Everyone left *but* him.

§ 6.50　Conjunctions

A *conjunction* is a word used to connect two or more words, phrases, or clauses. There are two main classes of conjunctions: *coordinating* and *subordinating*.

§ 6.51　Coordinating Conjunctions

Coordinating conjunctions connect words, phrases, and clauses of equal value (two independent clauses, two subjects, two verbs, two dependent clauses). The common ones are *and, but, or, nor.*

§ 6.52　Subordinating Conjunctions

Subordinating conjunctions join dependent clauses (subordinate clauses) to independent clauses (main clauses).

Following is a list of subordinate conjunctions:

after	in order to	whether
although	if	whereas
as	since	unless
as if	until	than
as though	when	provided
because	while	inasmuch as
before	where	so that

§ 6.53　Conjunctive Adverbs

Conjunctive adverbs also join clauses, words, and phrases which are grammatically equal. The following is a list of conjunctive adverbs:

however	moreover	thus
therefore	nevertheless	too
consequently	likewise	hence

§ 6.54　Correlative Conjunctions

Correlative conjunctions are *either/or* and *neither/nor.* They also join equal sentence elements such as two subjects, two verbs, two independent clauses, or two dependent clauses.

§ 6.55　Interjections

An interjection is a word used to express strong feeling or emotion. It does not change the basic meaning of the sentence. It is usually followed by a comma or exclamation mark.

EXAMPLE: Help! I'm being robbed! (*Help* is the interjection.)

§ 6.56 Sentence Structure

Every English teacher frequently hears the question, "Why do we need to learn parts of a sentence?" The main reason is that it is difficult, if not impossible, to use pronouns correctly if one does not know how they are used in the sentence.

If a pronoun is used as a subject or predicate nominative, the nominative case must be used (I, you, he, she, they, we).

If a pronoun is used as the direct object, indirect object, or object of the preposition, the objective case must be used (me, you, him, her, them, us).

The same is true of *who* and *whom*. *Who* is in the nominative case and is used for subjects and predicate nominatives; *whom* is in the objective case and is used for direct objects, indirect objects, and objects of prepositions.

Many people pick up poor speaking habits from their associates; although it may "sound right," it may be wrong. "It's me" sounds good, but it should be "It's I." If you truly understand the nominative and objective cases, a large percentage of your grammar errors will disappear.

Another reason for learning sentence structure is so that you can punctuate correctly.

Correct usage of adverbs and adjectives also depends on the structure of the sentence.

§ 6.57 The Sentence

A *sentence* expresses a complete thought; it contains a *subject* and a *predicate* (verb plus associated words). The *subject* is the person, place, or thing being told about or doing the action. The *verb* tells something about the person, place, or thing.

There are four types of sentences: *simple, compound, complex,* and *compound-complex.*

§ 6.58 The Simple Sentence

The *simple sentence* contains a subject and a verb.

EXAMPLE: Allen sings.
                      S   V

A simple sentence may also contain a compound *subject* (more than one doer) and a *compound verb* (more than one action). It still is a simple sentence because there is just one element for the subject and one for the verb.

EXAMPLE: <u>Fred and Alice</u>   <u>danced and sang</u>   in the show.
                        S   **V**

(*Fred and Alice* = subject; *danced and sang* = verb)

A simple sentence may also contain a direct object, indirect object, predicate nominative, predicate adjective, and other parts of speech.

The *direct object* is the person, place, or thing receiving the action.

EXAMPLE: Ralph   pounded   the   table.
                   S   **V**   **DO**

The *indirect object* is the person, place, or thing receiving the direct object.

EXAMPLE: Rosalie sold Alice   the   necklace.
                   S   **V**   **IO**   **DO**

A *predicate nominative* means the same thing as the subject and is connected to the subject by a linking verb. The sentence can be reversed without changing the meaning.

EXAMPLE: Mrs. Smith is   the   teacher.
                        S   **V**   **PN**
                 The   teacher is Mrs.   Smith.
                        S   **V**   **PN**

A *predicate adjective* describes the subject and is connected to the subject by a linking verb.

EXAMPLE: The   sunflowers are yellow.
                      S   **V**   **PA**

A simple sentence does not need any other element to complete its meaning. It could be called an *independent clause*.

§ 6.59 The Compound Sentence

The *compound sentence* consists of two or more independent clauses connected in one of the following ways:

1. By a coordinating conjunction preceded by a comma
     EXAMPLE: Alice rode the horse, and John cleaned the stable.
2. By a semicolon
     EXAMPLE: Alice rode the horse; John cleaned the stable.

3. By a conjunctive adverb preceded by a semicolon and followed by a comma
   EXAMPLE: Alice rode the horse; however, John cleaned the stable.

If there are more than two independent clauses and they are short, they may be joined with commas. This would make a series of clauses.

EXAMPLE: I cleaned, Ray cooked, Sally scrubbed, and John mowed the lawn. (Note the coordinating conjunction preceding the last clause.)

When joining more than two independent clauses, use semicolons between each clause. Place a semicolon followed by *and* between the last two independent clauses.

EXAMPLE: The boys went fishing in the morning; the girls prepared the picnic lunch; and they ate together in the afternoon.

When joining clauses which contain commas, use a semicolon at the joining place rather than a comma. This prevents confusion and clearly establishes the break between the clauses.

EXAMPLE: Harry, Martha, and Fred went looking for Alice; but they did not find her until the movie had already started.

NEVER join two independent clauses with a comma. This is known as a *comma splice* and is absolutely incorrect. Use one of the three methods shown above, or put a period at the end of each clause, making two sentences.

§ 6.60 The Complex Sentence

The *complex sentence* consists of one independent clause and one or more dependent clauses. In order to understand this type of sentence, you must have a good understanding of dependent clauses.

The *dependent clause* contains a subject and a verb; it may also contain any or all of the other sentence parts as well. It cannot stand by itself; it needs the independent clause to complete its meaning.

EXAMPLE: While the attorney was in court, Sally did the filing.
         Dep. Cl.   Indep. Cl.

Dependent clauses can serve as nouns, adverbs, or adjectives in relation to the main clause.

A *noun clause* functions as a noun; it serves as the subject, direct object, or object of the preposition.

> EXAMPLES: *Who is going to be president* is anybody's guess.
> (The noun clause is the subject of the sentence.)
> Jack said *that Mary would not be here today.*
> (The noun clause is the direct object of the verb *said.*)
> Please give the promotion to *whomever you choose.*
> (The noun clause is the object of the preposition *to.*)

There is no punctuation separating the noun clause from the remainder of the sentence.

An *adverb clause* functions in the same manner as an adverb; it modifies or limits verbs, adjectives, or other adverbs. It answers the questions of Where? When? How? Why? It is connected to the main clause by a subordinating conjunction. The subordinating conjunctions are:

after	before	so that	whereas
although	if	than	whether
as	in order to	unless	while
as if	inasmuch as	until	
as though	provided	when	
because	since	where	

If the adverb clause precedes the independent clause, the two clauses are separated by a comma. When the subordinate clause follows the independent clause, it is not preceded by a comma unless it is not essential to the sentence. When an adverbial clause ends the sentence, check to see if it is restrictive (essential to the meaning) or nonrestrictive. If it is nonrestrictive, place a comma between it and the main clause.

> EXAMPLES: Please decide if you wish to purchase the suit, *inasmuch as we have other interested buyers.*
> *If we cannot agree,* we must submit to arbitration.
> We must submit to arbitration *if we cannot agree.*
> *Before he gets home,* she wants to leave.
> She wants to leave *before he gets home.*

Adjective clauses are generally introduced with *relative pronouns* (who, whom, whose, which, and that). They modify, limit, or describe nouns and gerunds. They are directly related to a noun or gerund in the sentence.

212

EXAMPLE: She cried because the tree *that* she loved was struck by lightning. (This has two dependent clauses in it: *that she loved* is part of the dependent clause beginning with *because. That she loved* modifies tree.)

A modifier clause can be either essential or nonessential to the meaning of the sentence. If it is essential, no commas are used to separate it from the independent clause; if it is nonessential, it is set off by commas. Some books refer to these as restrictive and nonrestrictive modifiers. If necessary for identification, commas are not used.

EXAMPLES: Her brother, *who lived in Albany,* was sent to prison. (She has only one brother; therefore, the clause is nonessential.)
Her brother *who lived in Albany* was sent to prison. (She has more than one brother; therefore, the clause is essential to identify which brother was sent to prison.)

§ 6.61   The Compound–Complex Sentence

A *compound-complex* sentence consists of two independent clauses, one of which contains a dependent clause.

EXAMPLE: They hired a new secretary who had excellent train-
                IC   DC
ing, but she came in late every morning.
              IC

§ 6.62   Phrases

Do not confuse phrases with clauses. A *phrase* is a group of words without a subject and verb. Phrases usually serve as modifiers in the sentence, but infinitive and gerund phrases can also serve as nouns. Probably the most common phrase is the prepositional phrase. It can serve as an adverb or adjective in the sentence. It consists of the preposition and its object (a noun or pronoun); it may also contain several related words which serve as modifiers in the phrase itself.

EXAMPLES: During the long, dark night, she cried continuously.
           PREP   ADJ   ADJ   OB PREP   S   V   ADV
           He   gave   it   to   the   very   pretty   girl.
            S   V   DO   PREP   ADV   ADJ   OB PREP

§ 6.63 Summary

In determining the role of the various words in the sentence, there are some basic steps you can follow:

1. Locate the verb or verbs in the sentence.

2. Identify a subject for each verb.

3. Find the direct object and indirect object, if any.

4. Locate the predicate nominative or predicate adjective, if there is one.

5. Determine the correct case for Items 3 and 4 above.

6. Look for the prepositions and the nouns following them. Some people prefer to locate the nouns in the sentence and check to see if they are preceded by a preposition.

7. Then look for the adverbs, adjectives, and connecting words.

8. With sentences containing *who* or *whom,* you may need to rearrange the sentence in order to identify the case correctly.

EXAMPLES: The man (who/whom) I gave it to was very handsome.

The man to *whom* (object of preposition) I gave it was very handsome.

Who/Whom are you going to call?

You are going to call *whom?* (object of the infinitive *to call*)

COMMON ERRORS TO AVOID

1. A prisoner is hanged, not hung. A picture is hung.

2. Something is unique but not very unique or most unique. The same is true for words like *certain* and *perfect.*

3. He was graduated from college, will be graduated, is to be graduated; not he graduated, will graduate, is to graduate.

4. There is a difference between a house and a home. A home is not sold. A house can be sold.

5. He is a sort of radical, not sort of a radical. There is a difference.

6. Injured refers to persons; damage refers to objects.

7. A resolution is adopted. An ordinance is passed.

8. Don't say a person broke his arm unless he did so deliberately.

9. A person doesn't sustain a fatal injury. Sustain means to bear up under; to support by adequate proof.

10. Webster says *all right* is all right. *Allright* and *alright* are not all right.

11. The man who got married is a bridegroom, but it is permissible to refer to the couple as bride and groom. When mentioning the man alone, he is the bridegroom unless he takes care of horses.

12. Take it for granted that a marriage is consummated, but don't discuss the matter in print. Do not say, "The marriage was consummated."

13. The thing about which you write is the wedding ceremony. An event that has not been arranged or planned occurs. A wedding, a party, or a conference takes place.

14. *Afterward, forward, toward,* and similar words with the suffix *ward* take no *s*.

15. Go a short way, not a short ways.

16. *Headquarters, molasses,* and *whereabouts* all take singular verbs.

17. Fifty persons were present, not fifty people. *The people of the United States* is correct.[1]

18. Mrs. Jones is the widow of John Jones, not the late John Jones. He leaves his widow; his widow survives.

19. A person died of pneumonia, not from pneumonia.

20. Rosary was recited or said; Requiem Mass was celebrated.

21. Make it miles an hour, not miles per hour.

22. It is proved, not proven.

23. Collective nouns generally take singular verbs, but there are exceptions. The pair were married. The pair spent their honeymoon in San Francisco. The public is alert. The American people are dependable.

24. A scholar is a learned person. A child in school is a pupil. A person attending high school or college is a student.

25. Heart disease is an ailment of the heart; heart failure is what occurs whenever anyone dies.

26. Murder is a technical term denoting a degree of guilt and should be used advisedly.

27. Not all real estate brokers are realtors. A realtor is an active member of the local real estate board having membership in the National Association of Real Estate Boards.

28. Character is what one really possesses; reputation is what one is reputed to have.

29. State presidents from every state association attended the Round Table conference, not Roundtable.

---

1. Some authorities no longer distinguish between *persons* and *people* and use them interchangeably.

30. Many well-known organizations are usually identified only by their initials: YWCA for Young Women's Christian Association. Such abbreviations are written without periods or spaces in all capitals. Certain professional designations are also written in this way. In describing a Certified Professional Legal Secretary, use the full identity initially; thereafter the abbreviated Certified PLS will not be misunderstood.

31. A turkey is red-headed, but a legal secretary is red-haired.

32. The adverb *only* has slipped its moorings and now drifts anywhere in a sentence. Why do most people say, "I only have ..." when they mean, I have only ...? Instead of the faulty, "I only have eyes for you," the songwriter could have written any of three other versions:

> "I have eyes only for you."
> "I have eyes for only you."
> "I have eyes for you only."

Most people would understand the four versions to mean essentially the same thing; however, don't allow the lonely *only* to float too far. "Only I have eyes for you" means something very different and is certainly less flattering!

§ 6.64 Punctuation

The purpose of punctuation is to assist the reader to understand the written material. When a person is speaking, he lowers or raises his voice and pauses for emphasis or clarity. Punctuation accomplishes this for the reader. There are certain accepted rules and principles for punctuation that are understood by the majority of writers and readers. A good secretary should be familiar with the rules of punctuation and refer to them periodically for reinforcement.

§ 6.65 The Period

The period indicates a full stop. It is used:

- At the end of a sentence except for questions or exclamatory sentences
- After abbreviations, except when several initials are used together and do not require periods (YMCA, AAA)
- After initials in a name
- Between dollars and cents ($1.89)
- To indicate a decimal (10.9 inches)

§ 6.66 The Comma

The *comma* is a partial stop. It gives pause and helps clarify the meaning of the sentence. Commas should be used only when there is a reason for using them. Some writers insert so many commas in their writing that the reader finds he cannot follow the flow of the sentence. The comma is used:

1. To separate words, phrases, or short clauses in a series of three or more. A comma is placed before the *and.* In legal papers it is often omitted.

   EXAMPLE: A secretary needs to be prompt, efficient, and trustworthy.

   In the names of business firms, *do not use a comma before an ampersand* (&) in a firm name.

   EXAMPLE: Jackson, Hall, Roe & Stone

2. To separate clauses connected by conjunctions unless they are short and closely related.

   EXAMPLES: The attorney was in court all day, and the secretary had to work late.
   Kristen rowed and Robyn bailed.

3. To set off a subordinate clause that precedes the main clause.

   EXAMPLE: Since she locked her key in the car, she couldn't open the door.

4. After an introductory phrase which contains a verb form.

   EXAMPLE: After skiing all day, he was too tired to go to a movie.

5. To set off a nonessential (nonrestrictive) clause from the rest of the sentence.

   EXAMPLE: The baby, who had never spoken a word, suddenly screamed.

6. To set off parenthetic and transitional words from the rest of the sentence when pauses are clearly indicated. The following is a list of some of these expressions or words.

accordingly	more or less
all in all	namely
also	needless to say
as a matter of fact	of course
by and large	otherwise
by the way	so it seems
for example	therefore
however	though
if possible	too
in brief	unfortunately
meanwhile	usually

   The test is whether or not a pause is indicated.

7. To set off an intervening phrase or clause which breaks the continuity of the sentence.

   EXAMPLE: These men, even though they were very hungry, gave the food to the children.

8. To set off contrasting phrases or clauses.

   EXAMPLE: What we need is justice, not just trite promises.

9. To set off "*or* phrases" which mean the same as the preceding word.

   EXAMPLE: Indexing, or coding, of the material to be filed is necessary.

10. To separate two or more adjectives.

    EXAMPLE: The tall, lovely woman came to my table.

11. To set off names that are used in a direct address.

    EXAMPLE: Do you believe, Dr. Jones, that I will live?

12. To set off phrases or words used to identify a preceding word when they are not essential to the meaning.

    EXAMPLE: My mother, Madeline, was here this evening. George Washington, the first president, wore wooden teeth.

13. To set off quotations from the rest of the sentence.

    EXAMPLE: Charlie said, "Don't count on me for more money."

14. To set off explanatory words such as *Inc.*, *Jr.*, names of states when used with the city name, and the year when used with the month and day.

    EXAMPLES: I will be there on August 11, 19__, to see you perform.
    Mason & Jones, Inc., is open for business.
    Did you go to Denver, Colorado, on your birthday?
    Lee James, Jr., is not my husband.

15. To set off *etc.*, a comma is placed before and after it.

    EXAMPLE: Paper, pencils, pens, etc., will be sent tomorrow.

16. To separate a title or degree from a name.

    EXAMPLE: John Jones, Ph.D., will speak at our next luncheon.

§ 6.67 The Semicolon

The *semicolon* is used between parts of a sentence to separate phrases, clauses, and enumerations. It is used:

1.　To separate independent clauses joined by a connective when one or more of the clauses contain internal commas.

　　EXAMPLE:　The shipment of coats, suits, and skirts will be ready tomorrow; and they will be sent air express.

2.　To separate two independent clauses when no connective is used.

　　EXAMPLE:　I plan to leave at nine on the plane; I'll be in New York by ten.

3.　To precede expressions such as *that is, namely,* or *for example* when they introduce a clause.

　　EXAMPLE:　I plan to quit for two reasons; namely, because the hours are long and the pay is poor.

4.　To set off a phrase when words are missing but understood, a comma may also be used; but if there are other commas, a semicolon makes the meaning clearer.

　　EXAMPLE:　To some teachers, it was a catastrophe; to others, a minor nuisance.

5.　Between independent clauses of a compound sentence that are joined by a conjunctive adverb (however, therefore, etc.).

　　EXAMPLE:　We had car trouble; therefore, we did not arrive on time for the depositions.

§ 6.68　The Colon

The *colon* is used:

1.　After the salutation in a business letter.

　　EXAMPLE:　Dear Mr. Jones:

2.　In stating clock time.

　　EXAMPLE:　12:10 p.m.

3.　After introductory expressions preceding an enumeration, such as *the following, thus, as follows.*

　　EXAMPLE:　Please order the following:

The colon may follow a verb, preposition, or conjunction when it introduces a tabulation, but in running text no colon is used.

EXAMPLES: Among those present were:
Sam Brown
George White
James Black
Among those present were Sam Brown, George White, and James Black.

4.   To introduce a long quotation.

EXAMPLE: Lincoln's Gettysburg address read: "Fourscore and seven...."

§ 6.69 The Question Mark

The *question mark* is used in the following ways:

1.   After a direct question.

EXAMPLE: When are you sending my next shipment?

A question mark should not be used after a request which is phrased in the form of a question.

EXAMPLE: Will you please send me a corrected billing.

2.   After each question in a single sentence.

EXAMPLE: How do you feel about *Time? Newsweek? Fortune? Good Housekeeping?*

§ 6.70 The Exclamation Point

The *exclamation point* may be used internally in a sentence or at the end of a sentence. It is used after a word or group of words expressing a strong command, strong feeling or emotion, or an excited exclamation.

EXAMPLE: Help! He stole my purse!

§ 6.71 The Dash

The *dash* is used:

1.   To set off a single word or expression for emphasis.
EXAMPLE: Her work lacked only one thing—accuracy.

2.   To set off or segregate a change of thought or side command from the rest of the sentence.
EXAMPLE: His whole unlucky life—or so it seemed to me—was wasted on that woman.

3. To take the place of parentheses.

EXAMPLE: The five senses—smell, touch, sight, hearing, and taste—are like gems of great value.

4. To substitute for a colon where the word *namely* has been omitted.

EXAMPLE: There are two crying needs—prevention of crime and a balanced economy.

5. To replace the semicolon before words such as *namely, for instance,* and the like.

EXAMPLE: The house needed three things—namely, a roof, a porch, and a front door.

6. To set off a repetition, variation, explanation, or summary of what has gone before.

EXAMPLES: Give money—dollars and cents—right now.
They have acquiesced—given in—to our demands.
I went to that movie—one I had seen before—and sat through it again.
To give your money and your life for a cause—that is dedication.

7. For emphasis (as in sales letters).

EXAMPLE: This is not the same offer we made last year—it is a brand new plan especially created for the consumer of today.

§ 6.72 Parentheses

Parentheses are a strong mark of punctuation used when it is necessary to separate certain information from the rest of the sentence. Parentheses need no additional punctuation, such as commas, to set them off. All marks of punctuation, such as the ending period, question mark, exclamation point, or semicolon, should be placed outside the parentheses; the exception to this rule is when the material contained in the parentheses requires its own internal or ending punctuation. If the sentence in the parentheses stands alone and is not a part of another sentence, a period is used within the parentheses.

1. Place only material in parentheses which could be removed from the sentence without impairing the meaning of the sentence.

2. A complete sentence in parentheses which is part of another sentence should not start with a capital letter or end with a period.

EXAMPLE: His luck was running out (he lost all the money he had), and he had to sell his car.

3. Parentheses are used when writing figures after words.

EXAMPLE: We are enclosing a check for Twenty-five Dollars ($25).

4. Use parentheses when enumerating in running text.

EXAMPLE: There are three kinds of ending punctuation marks: (1) period, (2) question mark, and (3) exclamation mark.

5. Use parentheses around explanatory or illustrative words or phrases.

EXAMPLES: The three secretaries (Miss Jones, Mrs. Smith, and Ms. Bills) were at the meeting.
Water (H_2O) is essential to all human beings.

§ 6.73 Quotation Marks

There is a difference in the way certain authorities handle periods and commas with quotation marks. The "inside method" requires that all commas and periods be placed inside the quotation marks (", " ".")." The "outside method" places the commas and periods outside the quotation marks unless they are part of the quotation itself (" ". " ",). The more commonly accepted practice is the inside method.

1. When a quotation mark is used with a semicolon, colon, or dash, the quotation mark comes before the punctuation.

EXAMPLE: She was told "A stitch in time saves nine"; she did not believe it.

2. A question mark or exclamation point should be placed after the quotation mark unless the quoted material itself ends in a question mark or exclamation point.

EXAMPLES: She asked, "Where did you buy the blouse?"
Why didn't she ignore his "idiosyncrasies"?

3. Only one ending punctuation mark should come at the end of the sentence, either before or after the quotation mark. If the quotation ends in a period, question mark, or exclamation point and is followed by a quotation mark, no further punctuation is needed.

4. When there is a quotation within another quotation, the single quotation marks are used for the internal quote. On the typewriter use the apostrophe for the single quotation marks.

5. Quotation marks are used to indicate conversation.
A new paragraph should be made each time the speaker changes.

222

EXAMPLES: "I would like to see Mr. Mason," said the client.
"He is in court today. May I make you an appointment for tomorrow?" asked the secretary.
"No," answered the client, "because I will be in the hospital tomorrow."

6. Place quotation marks around slang or coined words if they might give a poor impression. By the use of quotation marks, the reader is made aware that the writer knows the words are poor but is using them for effect.

EXAMPLE: Granny says things "ain't like they uster be."

7. Words which are referred to as words are placed in quotation marks to identify them as words and not part of the sentence.

EXAMPLES: Place the comma before "and" in a compound sentence.
The word "beautiful" was misleading when applied to Lisa.

8. Use quotation marks to indicate the title of a published article. In typewritten work there are three methods for indicating titles of books: (1) placing quotation marks around the title, (2) typing the title in solid caps, (3) underlining the title. Articles are still placed only in quotation marks.

EXAMPLES: Have you read "The Organization Man" yet?
Have you read THE ORGANIZATION MAN yet?
Have you read <u>The Organization Man</u> yet?

(Underlining stands for italics in printing.)

§ 6.74   The Apostrophe

The apostrophe is used

1. To form contractions of words and figures. The apostrophe is used in place of omitted letters or figures.

EXAMPLES:

is not	isn't	wherever	where'er
cannot	can't	you have	you've
'76	'50s		

2. To form possessives. Never use an apostrophe with pronouns showing possession.

EXAMPLES: Robyn's hair looks very nice.
Its color is red.

3. To form plurals of lower case letters.

EXAMPLE: Watch your p's and q's around here.

§ 6.75 The Hyphen

There is a great deal of disagreement over just when and where a hyphen should be used. Many words that were once hypenated are now joined as one word or separated into two words without the hyphen. The following is a list of general usage rules. The main rule to remember is that a hyphen pulls things together into a single thought.

1. Use the hyphen for one-thought expressions (two or more words functioning as one word).

    EXAMPLE: He has the know-how to do the job.

2. Use the hyphen to join two or more words which modify a noun and act as a single thought.

    EXAMPLE: She had blue-green eyes.

3. When two or more words modify a noun and are not in their normal order, they are hyphenated. The test is to place them after the noun to see if the words then have separate force. If so, then they are not hyphenated after the noun and are hyphenated before the noun.

    EXAMPLES: a well-known author   author was well known
               an up-to-date proce-   the procedure was
               dure   brought up to date

If the one-thought idea is still retained when it is placed after the noun, however, it is still hyphenated.

    EXAMPLE: a never-ending job   the job was never-end-
                                     ing

4. Three or more words serving as a single modifier are usually hyphenated.

    EXAMPLE: change-of-address cards

5. An adverb ending in *ly* preceding an adjective is not connected to the adjective with a hyphen. To test to see if it is an adverb, try to use it with just a noun and not the adjective. If you cannot use it with the noun, then you do not use the hyphen.

    EXAMPLES: a highly respected em- (a highly employee)
               ployee
               a homely-looking girl   (a homely girl)

6. Use the hyphen when verbs are composed of two or more words (not including helping verbs) and have a single thought.

    EXAMPLES: Double-space the rough draft.
               She cross-referenced the material.

224

7. Suspended hyphens occur when two or more words share an additional word with a hyphen. Each of the words must have a hyphen following it.

    EXAMPLES: the five- and ten-cent store
    at three-, six-, and twelve-month intervals

8. When the prefix *re* is added to a word and the resulting word means to do something *again,* you add a hyphen between the *re* and the word if the unhyphenated word would be confused with another word.

    EXAMPLES: recover   re-cover   (cover again)
                  reform   re-form   (form again)
                  resign   re-sign   (sign again)

9. Words preceded by the prefixes *ex-, self-,* and *quasi-* are hyphenated.

    EXAMPLES: ex-wife, self-sacrificing, quasi-legal

10. A civil or military title which stands for a single office should not be hyphenated.

    EXAMPLES: Vice President   Attorney General
                  Secretary of State

11. When an office consists of two functions, it is hyphenated.

    EXAMPLE: secretary-treasurer

12. A letter meant to designate shape before a word is hyphenated to the word.

    EXAMPLES: An S-curve   A-bomb   T-square

13. A hyphen should be used to clarify meaning.

    EXAMPLES: fifty one-dollar bills
    one half-cooked chicken or
    one-half cooked chicken

§ 6.76   Ellipses

These are known as omission marks and are used to denote omission of a word or words in quoted material.

1. If the quoted material is in the middle of the sentence, three periods with intervening spaces (. . .) are used. If the quoted material ends with a period, four periods with intervening spaces (. . . .) are used. Some authorities do not use spaces between the periods; others recommend them. Spacing the periods seems to make the omission stand out more clearly.

2. When you have an unfinished sentence and wish to indicate that the sentence breaks off, you can use three dashes.

3. In quoted material, omissions of paragraphs are indicated by inserting and indenting four periods (. . . .) on a new line.

§ 6.77 Capitalization

The selected summarized rules for capitalization will be convenient for reference purposes.

§ 6.78 Common Usage

The following are examples of the most common usage of capitalization:

1. The first word of every sentence is capitalized.
2. The first word of a complete direct quotation is capitalized.
3. The first word of a salutation and all nouns used in the salutation are capitalized.
4. The first word in a complimentary close is capitalized.

§ 6.79 First Word After a Colon

Capitalize the first word after a colon only when the colon introduces a complete passage or sentence having independent meaning.

> EXAMPLE: In conclusion I wish to say: "The survey shows that...."

If the material following a colon is dependent on the preceding clause, the first word after the colon is not capitalized.

> EXAMPLE: I present the following three reasons for changing: the volume of business does not justify the expense; we are short of people; the product is decreasing in popularity.

§ 6.80 Capitalizing Names

1. Capitalize the names of associations, buildings, churches, hotels, streets, organizations, and clubs.
   EXAMPLES: The Business Club, Merchandise Mart, Central Christian Church, Peabody Hotel, Seventh Avenue, Administrative Management Society, Chicago Chamber of Commerce
2. All proper names should be capitalized.
   EXAMPLES: Great Britain, John G. Hammitt, Mexico
3. Capitalize names that are derived from proper names.
   EXAMPLES: American, Chinese, English, Chinese noodles, English grammar, Italian spaghetti

Do not, however, capitalize words that are derived from proper nouns and that have developed a special meaning.

> EXAMPLES: pasteurized milk, china dishes, morocco leather

4. Capitalize special names for regions and localities.

> EXAMPLES: North Central states, the Far East, the East Side, the Hoosier State

5. Capitalize names of government boards, agencies, bureaus, departments, and commissions.

> EXAMPLES: Civil Service Commission, Social Security Board, Bureau of Navigation

6. Capitalize names of the Deity, the Bible, holy days, and religious denominations.

> EXAMPLES: God, in His kingdom, Easter, Genesis, Church of Christ

7. Capitalize the names of holidays.

> EXAMPLES: Memorial Day, Labor Day

8. Capitalize words used before numbers and numerals, with the exception of common words such as page, line, and verse.

> EXAMPLES: He found the material on page 3, line 3, Part 3 of Chapter X.
> The reservation is Lower 6, Car 27.
> The class will meet in the Fine Arts Building, Room 114.

9. Capitalize names of the days of the week and months; do not capitalize names of seasons unless they are personified.

> EXAMPLE: I can arrange for a showing of fall styles on Tuesday, August 28.

§ 6.81   Capitalizing Titles Used in Business and Professions

The following are rules for capitalizing titles in business and professions.

1. Any title that signifies rank, honor, and respect and immediately precedes an individual's name is capitalized.

> EXAMPLES: She asked President Harry G. Sanders to preside.
> He was attended by Dr. Howard Richards.

2. Academic degrees are capitalized when they precede or follow an individual name.

> EXAMPLES: Mrs. Constance R. Collins, Ph.D., was invited to direct the program.

             Fred R. Bowling, Master of Arts

3. Capitalize titles of high-ranking government officers when the title is used in place of the proper name in referring to a specific person.

    EXAMPLES: Our Senator invited us to visit him in Washington.

                   The President will return to Washington soon.

4. Capitalize military and naval titles signifying rank.

    EXAMPLES: Captain Meyers, Lieutenant White, Lieutenant Commander Murphy

§ 6.82   Word Division

Whenever possible, avoid dividing a word at the end of a line. The printed document should flow for easy reading, and a divided word may cause the reader to become confused or have to slow down in reading. When dividing a word is unavoidable, there are certain basic rules that should be followed. With widespread computer use, word division has been altered somewhat. Also, typesetters may take great liberties in dividing words. Whenever unsure of correct division of a word, consult a current dictionary.

§ 6.83   General Principles of Word Division

1. Divide only when absolutely essential.

2. Divide between syllables only. The addition of the past tense does not necessarily add an extra syllable.

    EXAMPLE: *guessed*

3. Put enough of the word to be divided on the first line to suggest what the completed word will be.

4. It is permissible to have a right margin that is approximately five spaces shorter or five spaces longer than the desired length of line if this avoids the necessity of dividing the word.

5. In many cases syllable division of words as found in dictionaries is to be avoided, if at all possible, because the dictionary division shows each syllable and does not show the exact or best place to divide. This is indicated in the next section.

§ 6.84   How to Divide Words

1. As a rule divide between a prefix and the letter following it.
    EXAMPLE: *pre-sumed*

2. Divide a word with a suffix as follows:

A. When a root word ends with the double consonant, separate the suffix from the root word.

   EXAMPLE: *express-ing*

B. When a consonant is doubled before a suffix, the added consonant goes with the suffix.

   EXAMPLE: *stop-ping*

C. For words ending in *cian, cion, gion, sion, tion,* and *sive,* divide between the stem of the words and the suffix.

   EXAMPLE: *progres-sion*

3. When a word containing three or more syllables is to be divided at a one-letter syllable, divide as follows:

A. For most words, type the one-letter syllable on the first line.

   EXAMPLE: *sepa-rate*

B. For words to be divided at a point where two vowels that are pronounced separately come together, divide between the vowels.

   EXAMPLE: *gradu-ation*

C. For words ending in such terminations as *able, ible,* and *ical,* divide between the stem of the words and the suffix.

   EXAMPLE: *remov-able*

   NOTE: This rule applies only when the vowel is typed correctly as a syllable by itself and does not apply to such a word as *feasible* (feasi-ble) in which the vowel is a part of the syllable *si.*

4. Divide hyphenated words and compounds at the hyphen only

   EXAMPLE: *self-explanatory*

§ 6.85 When Not to Divide Words

1. Do not divide a word of one syllable.

2. Do not divide a two-syllable word of four letters.

3. Do not separate a single-letter syllable at the beginning or end of a word.

   EXAMPLES: *around, steady*

4. Do not separate a two-letter syllable at the end of a word.

   EXAMPLE: *difficulty*

5. Avoid separating a two-letter syllable at the beginning of a word.

   EXAMPLE: *defended*

6. Do not separate a syllable that does not contain a vowel from the remainder of the word.

EXAMPLE: *wouldn't*

§ 6.86 Word Division to Avoid

1. Do not divide words at the ends of more than two consecutive lines of typing if you can avoid it.
2. Do not divide a word at the end of the first line of a personal or business letter if it is possible to avoid it.
3. Do not divide the last word on a page. Carry the entire word to the following page.
4. Do not divide a five- or six-letter word.
5. Do not divide a proper name if it is possible to avoid it, and do not separate titles or initials.

EXAMPLE: Dr. John C. Crosby
When necessary, divide at the surname. Keep the initial with the first name.

6. Do not separate abbreviations and numbers.

EXAMPLES: YMCA, 13,000,000

7. Do not separate dates if you can avoid it. If you cannot avoid the division, retain the numeral representing the day of the month with the whole name or a syllable division of the month.

EXAMPLES: March 7, 1994; Sep/tem/ber 23; Janu/ary 15, 1995

§ 6.87 Compound Words

There are numerous compound words which are used by the legal profession. Give careful attention to their proper usage. They offer exact reference with the use of a minimum of words.

AFORESAID — Stated before or stated earlier in this document.
FOREGOING — What precedes or has gone before.
HEREAFTER — After this present point in time.
HEREBY — By this or by this document.
HEREINABOVE — Within this document; however, before this point in this document.
HEREINAFTER — Within this document; however, after this point in this document.
HEREOF — Of this.

HERETO	To this.
HERETOFORE	Before now or prior to this point.
HEREUNDER	Under the conditions in this document; following this point in this document.
HEREUNTO	To this.
HEREWITH	With this document or enclosed with this document.
NOTWITHSTANDING	Regardless or however.
THENCEFORTH	Following that condition or that time.
THEREAFTER	After that condition or that time.
THEREFOR	For it.
THEREFORE	Because.
THEREFROM	From that.
THEREOF	Of that.
THEREON	On that or on it.
THERETO	To that.
UNDERSIGNED	One who signed at the end of a document (under the document).
WHATSOEVER	What or whatever.
WHEREAS	Considering or when in fact.
WHEREFORE	For those reasons or for that reason.
WHERESOEVER	A place or where it is.
WHEREWITHAL	Resources, means, or money.
WHOMSOEVER	Whomever.
WHOSOEVER	Whoever.

Watch these common compound words and their problems:

- Inasmuch as

- Insofar as

- In fact (is not a compound word)

- A lot (is not a compound word)

§ 6.88   Spelling

1. Be sure to complete your root word before you add a suffix beginning with a consonant (ly, less, ful, ment).

EXAMPLES:	EXAMPLES:	EXCEPTIONS:
additional-ly	financial-ly	true—truly
accurate-ly	grate-ful	argu-ment
agree-ment	immense-ly	acknowledg-ment
accidental-ly	immediate-ly	judg-ment
achieve-ment	incidental-ly	
adjust-ment	install-ment	
advertise-ment	misstate-ment	
allot-ment	occasional-ly	
approximate-ly	sincere-ly	

arrange-ments	undoubted-ly
develop-ment	force-ful
final-ly	

2. Remember, "*i* before *e* except after c, or when sounded like a, as in neighbor and weigh." This means that when the sound of the diphthong is a long *e*, as in receive, believe, etc., *c* is followed by *ei* and other letters are followed by *ie*. When the sound of the diphthong is a long *a*, as in neighbor, the spelling is *ei*.

EXAMPLES:	EXAMPLES:	EXCEPTIONS:
anxiety	cashier	either
audience	fierce	neither
believe	grief	financier
boundaries	niece	weird
convenience	pier	species
efficiently	pierce	seize
grievous	relieve	leisure
necessities		forfeit
ninetieth	**EXCEPT AFTER C**	ancient
siege	ceiling	foreign
sieve	conceive	height
achieve	deceit	their
apiece	deceive	
chief	receive	

3. A word ending in silent *e* generally drops the *e* before a suffix beginning with a vowel.

EXAMPLES:

admire	admiration	arrive	arriving
admire	admirable	believe	believing
arrange	arranging	desire	desirous

4. Words ending in *ce* or *ge* to which is added a suffix beginning with *a* or *o* (*able* or *ous*) retain the silent *e* in order to preserve the soft sound of the *c* or *g*.

EXAMPLES:

advantage	advantageous	notice	noticeable
change	changeable	peace	peaceable
courage	courageous	service	serviceable

5. Only one word in our language ends in "sede"—supersede. Three words end in "ceed"—exceed, proceed, succeed. The rest end in "cede."

EXAMPLES:

accede	cede	concede
precede	recede	intercede

6. In words of one syllable and words accented on the last syllable ending in a single consonant preceded by a single vowel, double the final consonant before adding a suffix beginning with a vowel unless adding the suffix will change the accented syllable.

EXAMPLES:

Suffix begins with a vowel (one syllable)

cut	cutting
plan	planning
stop	stopped
quit	quitting

(Accent on last syllable)

admit	admitted	equip	equipped
begin	beginning	commit	committed
remit	remitted	occur	occurred
confer	conferring	compel	compelled

(No accent on last syllable)

prefer	preference	benefit	benefited
refer	reference	marvel	marvelous
happen	happened		

(Suffix begins with a consonant)

glad	gladness
fat	fatness
man	manhood

§ 6.89   Words That Are Frequently Misspelled

absorbent	bankruptcy
accessible	believable
accidentally	benefited
accommodate	category
accumulate	coliseum
acknowledge	concede
acknowledgment	consensus
announced	definitely
appearance	develop
assistance	disappointed
athletic	dissatisfaction
auxiliary	

drastically	occurred
eligible	occurrence
embarrass	personal
exaggerate	personnel
existence	perseverance
extension	phenomenal
extraordinary	precede
facetious	principle
February	privilege
forty	procedure
governor	proceed
grammar	prominence
guarantee	questionnaire
harass	recommend
hemorrhage	referring
incidentally	relevant
inoculate	rhythm
insistence	resistance
intercede	safety
jeopardize	scissors
judgment	seize
justifiable	separate
knowledgeable	similar
laid	singular
liaison	soluble
license	superintendent
likelihood	surreptitious
maintenance	transferable
manageable	usage
mathematics	various
miscellaneous	vicinity
ninety-ninth	weird
occasionally	wrought

§ 6.90   Vocabulary Improvement

Whether you have had any college training or not, and whether you are young or old, it is never too late to develop the language skills that will mark you as an educated person. How do people form an impression of you when they meet you? How do they judge you from the material you write? What indicates that a person is educated?

   1.   An educated person does not use a word if she does not know its meaning. It is never safe to assume that you know the meaning of words that look easy or familiar. Look up the meaning of any word which puzzles you. The meaning may surprise you.

2. An educated person does not misspell words. Misspelling often gives you another word with a different meaning. Using *principle* when you mean *principal* is an obvious spelling mistake. So is writing *capital* when you mean *capitol*. Spelling mistakes result from either carelessness or ignorance. Both can be remedied. Go over any final copy you expect others to read to make sure it is free from spelling errors. *If you have any doubt about the spelling of any word, use your dictionary.*

3. An educated person does not mispronounce words. As you read, you encounter more and more words that you have never used yourself. You may know the meanings of these words, but be sure you can pronounce them. Test yourself. Try reading these sentences aloud:

    The gourmet appreciates culinary excellence.

    Police attempts to corral the blackguard proved a lamentable fiasco.

4. An educated person increases her vocabulary. When you encounter words that can be useful to you in speaking, use them. Don't ignore such useful words if you cannot pronounce them. Look them up; pronounce them to yourself. When you are sure of their meaning and pronunciation, you are ready to use them in speaking.

5. An educated person becomes an expert in her career field— yours is as a legal secretary. You wouldn't trust your life to a doctor or nurse who could not describe an illness exactly or did not know the name of a drug that could cure it. Enrich your legal vocabulary by using a specialized legal dictionary. Black's Law Dictionary published by West Publishing Company is excellent.

6. An educated person must be an intelligent citizen. You must be familiar with political tides and events and the words that describe them. As a citizen you have a right to demand that leaders define their terms. It is your responsibility as a citizen to know political vocabulary, to be wary of slogans and catchwords, to think straight, and to act only on the basis of factual information.

7. An educated person looks for various ways to increase vocabulary. Learn the vocabulary of various hobbies. Plan your recreational reading to embrace as many areas as possible. Keep up to date with new events. Listen to educated people. Take advantage of worthwhile television and radio programs. Make use of fine books available on vocabulary development.

Take word tests; play word games; do acrostic puzzles. Above all, use all the resources that your dictionary offers.

§ 6.91 Confusing Words

ACCEDE	To express approval or give consent as a result of urging.
EXCEED	To be greater than; to go beyond a set limit.

> EXAMPLES: He acceded to the demands of his public and ran for office.
> His vote total exceeded that of his opponent.

ACCEPT	To receive with consent; to endure without protest; (must always be used as a verb).
EXCEPT	verb: To take or leave out from a number. preposition: with the exclusion or exception of.

> EXAMPLE: I hope you will accept all the gifts except the mink coat.

ACCESS	Permission; liberty or ability to enter.
EXCESS	More than the usual or specified amount.

> EXAMPLE: The farmer allowed them access to his property as long as they didn't use it to excess.

ADAPT	To make, fit, adjust, conform.
ADOPT	To take as one's own; to take by choice into a relationship. To accept formally and put into effect.

> EXAMPLE: The child found it hard to adapt to the decision of his parents to adopt a second son.

ADVISE	To give information; to inform or recommend; (always used as a verb).
ADVICE	Recommendation; information given; (always used as a noun).

> EXAMPLE: I advise you to take your attorney's advice.

AFFECT	To produce an influence upon or alteration in; to act upon; (always used as a verb).
EFFECT	noun: Result of a change or influence; result, consequence, outcome. verb: To cause to come into being.

> EXAMPLE: The new office manager will effect a change in office procedures which

236

will affect all secretaries. Hopefully, the effect of the change will be good.

AID	verb: To give help.
AIDE	noun: Assistant.
	EXAMPLE: The teacher's aide tried to aid the child in reading.
ALL READY	All prepared.
ALREADY	By this time; prior to some specified or implied time.
	EXAMPLE: The packages are all ready for mailing; the letters have already been mailed.
ALTOGETHER	Wholly, thoroughly, in all.
ALL TOGETHER	Collectively.
	EXAMPLES: They are altogether too frail. Were the school children all together?
AMONG	Used when three or more persons or things are involved.
BETWEEN	Used when two persons or things are involved.
	EXAMPLE: The cake was divided among the four boys, and the pie was divided between the two girls.
ANTE–	A prefix which means *before* when added to the beginning of a word.
ANTI–	A prefix which means *against* when added to the beginning of a word.
	EXAMPLES: An antecedent is a word which is referred to by a following word. An anticoagulant is a substance which hinders (works against) the clotting of the blood.
ANYONE	Any person at all; anybody.
ANY ONE	Any individual person.
	EXAMPLE: The winner can be any one of the three candidates; not just anyone can win.
APPRAISE	To set a value on; to evaluate the worth, significance, or status.
APPRISE	To give notice; to tell; to inform.
	EXAMPLES: Please apprise the attorney of the value of the estate. He is the one who will appraise the assets.
APPROXIMATE	Nearly correct or exact.

PROXIMATE   Very near, close.

                  EXAMPLE: The proximate cause of the accident
                  was that he was traveling approxi-
                  mately 120 miles an hour.

AS—AS   Usually used with positive statements.

SO—AS   Usually used with negative statements.

                  EXAMPLES: She was nearly as talented as he.
                  The amount was not nearly so large
                  as she said it was.

ASSISTANCE   Help that is given.

ASSISTANTS   Plural of assistant; those giving help.

                  EXAMPLE: The legal assistants offered their as-
                  sistance with his problem.

BESIDE   At or to the side; by the side of; disjoined from.

BESIDES   Over and above; moreover, else, in addition to.

                  EXAMPLES: She sat beside the road, but that is
                  beside the point. Besides that, she
                  was hurt.

BIANNUAL   Occurring twice a year.

BIENNIAL   Occurring every two years.

BIMONTHLY   Occurring every two months.

                  EXAMPLES: The biennial meetings will be held
                  in 1994 and 1996; however, the
                  board meetings will be held biannu-
                  ally.
                  The bimonthly newsletter will be
                  published in January, March, May,
                  July, September, and November.

CAPITAL   Chief in importance or influence; related to mon-
                  ey; seat of government; a city serving as a seat of
                  government.

CAPITOL   A building in which a legislative body meets.

                  EXAMPLE: The legislature voted a capital appro-
                  priation of $750,000 to build the new
                  Capitol for the state government.

COMPLIMENT   An expression of esteem, respect, affection, or
                  admiration.

COMPLEMENT   Something that fills in, completes, or makes per-
                  fect; one of two mutually completing parts; coun-
                  terpart.

                  EXAMPLES: The dark blue tie complemented
                  the light blue shirt. Everyone likes
                  to receive a sincere compliment.

238

COURTESY	Refers to manners.
CURTESY	Interest a husband has in the property of his wife.
	EXAMPLE: He had the courtesy to give up his curtesy in her property.
DECENT	Fitting, worthy, honorable.
DESCENT	A downward step, as in station or value; a derivation from an ancestor; process of descending from a higher to a lower level.
DISSENT	Disagree.
	EXAMPLE: There was dissent that her descent down the stairs on her hands was the decent thing to do.
DESCENDANT	One descended from another (having to do with family).
DECEDENT	A deceased person.
	EXAMPLE: The descendant of the decedent was Christopher Columbus.
DEVICE	A scheme to deceive; a piece of equipment or mechanism designed to serve a special purpose or function.
DEVISE	The act of giving or disposing of real property in a will; property devised by will; to plan to obtain or bring about.
	EXAMPLE: A will is a device by which a person can devise his real property to his heirs.
DISCREET	Having or showing good judgment in conduct and speech; capable of preserving silence.
DISCRETE	Individually distinct; constituting a separate entity.
	EXAMPLES: The secretary should be very discreet when discussing clients. Magnetic cards and diskettes are discrete media.
DIVERS	Various.
DIVERSE	Differing from one another.
	EXAMPLE: She discovered the divers objects to be very diverse in design.
EMINENT	Prominent, standing out, distinguished.
IMMINENT	Ready to take place; hanging threateningly over one's head.
	EXAMPLE: The eminent senator believed death to be imminent.

ENVELOP	To enfold or enclose completely.
ENVELOPE	A container, usually for a letter.
	EXAMPLES: The fog threatened to envelop the airport.
	She forgot to put the letter in the envelope.
FORMERLY	Refers to a previous time.
FORMALLY	In a formal, conventional manner.
	EXAMPLE: The initiation was more formally conducted than formerly.
GUARANTEE	verb: To assure the fulfillment of a condition; to promise performance.
GUARANTY	noun: Something given as security; a pledge to answer for the payment of a debt; an assurance of performance.
	Guarantee and guaranty are often used interchangeably; the dictionary uses them both as nouns.
WARRANTY	A binding legal covenant of assurance of facts.
	EXAMPLES: Can you guarantee the merchandise and is there a guaranty in writing?
	You have my warranty on the property.
ILLICIT	Illegal.
ELICIT	To draw forth or bring out.
	EXAMPLE: Did the detective elicit any information from the man about illicit activities?
IMPLY	To express indirectly; to indicate by association.
INFER	To derive a conclusion from facts; to deduce, conclude.
	EXAMPLE: From what you say, I infer that you mean to imply she is incapable.
INSURE	To make certain by taking necessary precautions or steps; to obtain or give insurance on.
ENSURE	To make sure, certain, or safe.
ASSURE	To make safe from risks; to inform positively.
	EXAMPLE: I assure you that I have ensured your safety by carefully checking your parachute; however, the company has refused to insure you when you are jumping.

240

INTERSTATE   Between two or more states.

INTRASTATE   Within one state.

     EXAMPLE: He runs an interstate trucking service in the Pacific Northwest; his brother has an intrastate service in Idaho.

LATER   At a future time; more recent.

LATTER   Relating to the second of two groups or things or the last of several things referred to; near the end.

     EXAMPLE: Later I will serve pie and coffee; the latter will be decaffeinated.

LATEST   Most recent; after all others; at the end; following.

LAST   All the rest; the only remaining; final, terminal. These two words are generally used interchangeably.

     EXAMPLE: The latest edition was the last one sold.

LIABLE   Obligated according to law; responsible. (Do not use *liable* for *likely*.)

LIBEL   A written defamation or attack of another person.

     EXAMPLE: Newspapers are liable if they publish a libel of a person.

LIKE   Takes an object; can substitute *similar to* or *similarly to* for *like*.

AS, AS IF   Used as a conjunction and introduces a clause with a subject and verb.

     EXAMPLE: The fabric looks like suede, but it washes as if it were cotton.

LOSE   verb: To miss from one's possession; to suffer deprivation of.

LOOSE   verb: To release, untie;
adj: Not rigidly fastened or attached.

     EXAMPLE: Do not loose the reins from the post. The horse has a loose shoe; he might lose it if he runs away.

MAY BE   This is a verb phrase.

MAYBE   An adverb meaning perhaps.

     EXAMPLE: Maybe the attorney may be able to win the case.

PRECEDENTS   Something done or said that may serve as an example or rule to authorize or justify an act of similar nature. In law, those previous court decisions which influence all later cases of a similar kind.

PRECEDENCE　　Priority of importance.

EXAMPLE: The case which took precedence on the calendar was based on precedents established in California.

PRINCIPLE　　A rule or code of conduct; a fundamental law, doctrine, or assumption; the laws or facts of nature.

PRINCIPAL　　A person who has controlling authority; a chief or head, man or woman; one who employs another to act for him; a capital sum placed at interest; the corpus of an estate.

EXAMPLE: The school principal invested his principal at five percent interest because he was devoted to the principles of saving money.

PROCEEDING　　A form of the verb "proceed" meaning to go forward; move along a course.
A noun meaning events, happenings; a legal action.

PRECEDING　　A form of the verb "precede" meaning to be, go, or come ahead or in front of; to be earlier than.

EXAMPLE: The divorce proceeding will be held preceding the criminal trial.

RECENT　　Refers to time not long past.

RESENT　　A verb meaning to feel or express annoyance or ill will at a person or event.

EXAMPLE: I resent your recent attacks on my honesty.

RESIDENCE　　A dwelling place.

RESIDENTS　　Those who reside in a place; physicians serving residencies.

EXAMPLE: Who are the residents of that two-story residence on the corner?

RESPECTIVELY　　In the order given.

RESPECTFULLY　　With respect or deference.

EXAMPLE: The employer respectfully requested George Brown and Sally Smith, the president and vice president respectively, to report to him in his office.

SOME TIME　　A period of time.

SOMETIME	At some not specified or definitely known point of time.
SOMETIMES	At times; now and then.
	EXAMPLE: Sometimes quite some time elapses between visits, but I plan to remedy that sometime.
SPECIALLY	In a special manner.
ESPECIALLY	Particularly; usually great or significant.
	EXAMPLE: The specially prepared foods were a delight to the palate, especially since the cook had so little experience.
THAN	A word used in making comparisons.
THEN	At that time.
	EXAMPLE: It was later than I thought. I decided to leave then.
THEIR	Possessive pronoun.
THERE	Indicates a place or points out.
THEY'RE	A contraction of *they are*. Do not confuse with *there*; used as a subject and verb.
	EXAMPLE: The attorneys left their briefcases in the car, and now they're unable to proceed with the trial being held there in the city.
THEREFOR	For it.
THEREFORE	Because.
	EXAMPLE: The debtor was unable to pay the $1,000; therefore, the attorney agreed to accept $750 in full payment therefor.
TRUSTEE	One to whom something is entrusted.
TRUSTY	A trusted person.
	EXAMPLE: No one realized that the jail trusty had appointed a trustee for his child's estate.
WHOSE	A possessive pronoun.
WHO'S	Contraction of *who is;* should be used as a subject and verb.
	EXAMPLE: Who's going to tell me whose coat this is?
YOU'RE	A contraction of *you are;* must be used as a subject and verb.
YOUR	A possessive pronoun.

EXAMPLE: Did you tell me that you're going to your office this afternoon?

§ 6.92 Abbreviations

Abbreviating in the body of any written communication is considered incorrect and in poor taste. A trained writer knows where abbreviations are permissible. In written communications the following are satisfactory to use.

1. The title that precedes a person's name is abbreviated.
   EXAMPLES: Ms., Mrs., Mr., Dr.

2. Titles or degrees written after names are abbreviated.
   EXAMPLES: Jr., B.A., M.D., PLS.

3. Titles before surnames are never abbreviated.
   EXAMPLES: Governor Ray, Professor Smith.

4. Titles before full names can be abbreviated.
   EXAMPLES: Gov. Robert Ray, Prof. Sam Smith.

5. Titles of respect or dignity are never abbreviated.
   EXAMPLES: The Honorable Robert Ray, the Reverend Doctor Bennett.

6. Firm names are not abbreviated unless the company prefers the abbreviation and uses it in its communication.

7. Names of agencies, organizations, or associations are abbreviated using the first letter of each word in the title. These are generally written "solid" with no space or punctuation.
   EXAMPLES: FBI for Federal Bureau of Investigation, UAW for United Auto Workers, NALS for National Association of Legal Secretaries.

8. Technical terms such as chemical symbols or formulas which are used many times in business communications are abbreviated with no punctuation.

9. When letters are substituted for names, punctuation is unnecessary.
   EXAMPLES: Mr. A, Exhibit D, Mister X.

10. Certain words in our vocabulary which have been shortened through usage are not followed by punctuation.
    EXAMPLES: Ad for advertisement, lab for laboratory, gym for gymnasium.

11. Always abbreviate A.D. and B.C. in dates and use the punctuation. Use a.m. and p.m. to designate afternoon and forenoon; use punctuation but no spacing. Use a numeral for the hour.

EXAMPLES: 10 a.m.; never use 10 o'clock a.m.

12. Use No. or Nos. before a numeral except when it occurs at the beginning of the sentence; then spell "number." If the numeral is specifically identified, No. or Nos. should be omitted.

13. Fort, Point, Port—which are parts of place names—should never be abbreviated.

14. Directions written in context should never be abbreviated. N, NE, NNE can be used for real estate descriptions, however.

15. Terms of measurement should not be abbreviated except in technical writing, invoices, etc. This rule applies to weight, length, capacity, area, volume, temperature, time, etc.

16. If possible, the following words should be spelled out in full:

president	building	street
superintendent	association	boulevard
honorable	department	avenue
reverend		east
professor		west
		south
		north

The rule is that if you are in doubt, spell out the word completely.

17. Generally, city and state names should be spelled out completely; however, in the inside address the two-letter ZIP Code abbreviation may be used so that it will correspond to the address on the envelope. You may use the two-letter ZIP Code abbreviation only when it is followed by the ZIP Code. If you do not use the ZIP Code, you must type out the state name in full.

18. When an abbreviation is followed by a period, the period should be retained even if other punctuation follows the abbreviation. If the abbreviation ends the sentence, however, only one period is necessary. The plurals of abbreviations are generally formed by adding an *s* to the abbreviation before the period. Exceptions are as follows:

   - in. for inch or inches
   - mi. for mile or miles
   - oz. for ounce or ounces
   - pp. for pages
   - ll. for lines

Spacings between the parts of an abbreviation are usually omitted to save space except in the instance of initials.

EXAMPLE: E. R. Farris

A list of commonly used abbreviations follows:

@	at
ab ex.	from without (L. ab extra)
ab init.	from the beginning (L. ab initio)
abst.	abstract
A.D.	in the year of the Lord (L. Anno domini)
acct., a/c, A/C	account
addl., add.	additional
ad fin.	to the end (L. ad finem)
Adm.	administration, administrative, Admiral
Admr.	Administrator; Admx.-trix
agt.	agent
a.m.	before noon
amt.	amount
anon.	anonymous
approx.	approximate
appt.	appointment
Apt.	Apartment
arr.	arranged
art.	article
Assn.	Association
assoc., asso.	associate
Asst.	Assistant
Attn.	Attention
Atty.	Attorney
Atty. Gen.	Attorney General
Ave., Av.	Avenue
avg., av.	average
bal.	balance
bbl.	barrel(s)
bf.	boldface
B/L, b/l	bill of lading
Bldg.	Building
Blvd.	Boulevard
bu.	bushel(s)
bus.	business
Bus. Mgr.	Business Manager
bx.	box
C.	Celsius (centigrade), hundred
cap.	capital, capacity
caps	capital letters
Capt.	Captain
cat.	catalog
cc, cc.	carbon copy
C/D, CD	Certificate of Deposit
cert.	certificate, -tion, certified
cf.	compare (L. confer)
cfm, cfs	cubic feet per minute, per second

chg.	charge; change
ck.	check
cm	centimeter
c/o, %, c.o.	in care of; carried over
Co.	Company; County
c.o.d.	cash on delivery
com., comm.	committee; commission
Corp.	Corporation
C.S.T., CST	central standard time
Dept.	Department
E.	East
ea.	each
e.g.	for example (L. exempli gratia)
enc.	enclosure
e.o.m., EOM	end of month
Esq.	Esquire
et al.	and others (L. et alia, et alii)
E.S.T., EST	eastern standard time
etc.	and so forth (L. et cetera)
F., Fahr.	Fahrenheit
ff.	and following page(s); folio(s)
fac.	facsimile
f.b.o., FBO	for the benefit of
fig.	figure
f.o.b., FOB	free on board
ft.	foot, feet
fwd.	forward
FY	fiscal year
FYI, fyi, f.y.i.	for your information
g	gram (metric)
gal.	gallon(s)
govt.	government
gr. wt.	gross weight
guar., gtd.	guarantee; -ed
hdbk.	handbook
hdqrs., HQ.	headquarters
hp, HP	horsepower
hr.	hour
ht.	height, heat
ibid., ib.	in the same place (L. ibidum)
id.	the same (L. idem)
i.e.	that is (L. id est)
Ill., illus.	illustration; illustrated
in.	inch(es)
Inc.	Incorporated
incl.	inclusive, including
inst.	instant, installment
inv.	invoice
ital.	italics

J.D.	Doctor of Jurisprudence (L. juris doctor)
JJ.	Justices
kc	kilocycle
kg	kilogram
km	kilometer
kw	kilowatt
L.	Latin, law, ledger
l	liter (metric)
l., ll.	line, lines
lab.	laboratory, labor
lb., lbs.	pound(s)
L/C	Letter of Credit
l.c., lc.	lower case
liq.	liquid
LL.B.	Bachelor of Laws (L. legum baccalaureus)
LL.D.	Doctor of Laws (L. legum doctor)
loc. cit.	in the place cited (L. loco citato)
L.S.	place of the seal (L. locus sigilli)
ltr.	letter
lv.	leave
m	minutes, meter
mdse.	merchandise
memo	memorandum
Messrs.	plural of Mr. (F. Messieurs)
mfg.	manufacturing
mi.	mile(s)
min.	minute(s)
misc.	miscellaneous
Mlle.	Mademoiselle
mo.	month
MS., ms.	manuscript
M.S.T., MST	mountain standard time
Mt.	mount, mountain
mtg.	mortgage
n.	note, net, new, noun, noon, name
n/30	net in 30 days
N.	North
No., Nos.	number(s) (use before figures only)
obs.	obsolete
op. cit.	in the work cited (L. opere citato)
oz.	ounce, ounces
p., pp.	page, pages
pat.	patent
P.C.	Professional Corporation
pd.	paid
PBX	Private Branch Exchange (telephone)
pfd., pf., pref.	preferred (stock)
pkg.	package
p.m.	after noon (L. post meridiem)

pmt., payt.	payment
p.p.	parcel post
pr.	pair, pairs
prox.	of the next month (L. proximo)
PS.	postscript
P.S.T., PST	Pacific standard time
qt.	quart
recd.	received
ref.	reference, referee, refining, refunding
retd.	returned
Rev.	Reverend
rev.	revised
R.F.D.	Rural Free Delivery
rm.	ream, room
R.N.	Registered Nurse
rpt.	report
R.S.V.P.	please reply (F. repondez s'il vous plait)
Rte., Rt.	Route
Ry.	railway
S.	South
Sec., Secy.	Secretary
sec.	section
seq.	the following (L. sequens)
ser.	series
sic	so written, thus (L.)
sim.	similar
sing.	singular
Soc.	Society, Sociology
sq. ft.	square foot (feet)
Sr.	Senior
SS.	To-wit (L. scilicet)
St.	Street, Saint, Strait, Statute(s)
Ste.	Sainte (feminine for St.), Suite
Supt.	Superintendent
syl.	syllable(s)
sym.	symbol
T., Tp., Twp.	township (pl. Tps., Twps.)
tab.	table(s)
T.B.	trial balance
tech.	technical
tel.	telephone, telegraph, telegram
tp	title page (cap.) township
TWX	teletypewriter exchange
u.c.	upper case
ult.	last month (L. ultimo); ultimate, -ly
Univ.	University
U.T., UT, u.t.	Universal time
viz.	namely (L. videlicet)
vol., vols.	volume, volumes

v., vs.	versus
whsle.	wholesale
wk., wks.	work, week, weeks
wpm	words per minute
wt., wts.	weight, weights, warrant, warrants
yd., yds.	yard, yards
yr., y.	year
z., Z	zone, zero, zenith distance

NOTE: Authorities differ as to the correct form of some abbreviations. Therefore, you should select one authority and follow it.

STATE ABBREVIATIONS *

		ZIP			ZIP
Alabama	Ala.	AL	Missouri	Mo.	MO
Alaska	—	AK	Montana	Mont.	MT
Arizona	Ariz.	AZ	Nebraska	Nebr.	NE
Arkansas	Ark.	AR	Nevada	Nev.	NV
California	Calif.	CA	New Hampshire	N.H.	NH
Canal Zone	C.Z.	CZ	New Jersey	N.J.	NJ
Colorado	Colo.	CO	New Mexico	N. Mex.	NM
Connecticut	Conn.	CT	New York	N.Y.	NY
Delaware	Del.	DE	North Carolina	N.C.	NC
District of			North Dakota	N. Dak.	ND
Columbia	D.C.	DC	Ohio	—	OH
Florida	Fla.	FL	Oklahoma	Okla.	OK
Georgia	Ga.	GA	Oregon	Oreg.	OR
Guam	—	GU	Pennsylvania	Pa.	PA
Hawaii	—	HI	Puerto Rico	P.R.	PR
Idaho	—	ID	Rhode Island	R.I.	RI
Illinois	Ill.	IL	South Carolina	S.C.	SC
Indiana	Ind.	IN	South Dakota	S. Dak.	SD
Iowa	—	IA	Tennessee	Tenn.	TN
Kansas	Kans.	KS	Texas	Tex.	TX
Kentucky	Ky.	KY	Utah	—	UT
Louisiana	La.	LA	Vermont	Vt.	VT
Maine	—	ME	Virgin Islands	V.I.	VI
Maryland	Md.	MD	Virginia	Va.	VA
Massachusetts	Mass.	MA	Washington	Wash.	WA
Michigan	Mich.	MI	West Virginia	W. Va.	WV
Minnesota	Minn.	MN	Wisconsin	Wis.	WI
Mississippi	Miss.	MS	Wyoming	Wyo.	WY

* The ZIP abbreviation MUST be used with ZIP Codes and should be used ONLY with ZIP Codes; the other abbreviations should be used whenever there is a need to save space in informal writing.

§ 6.93   Number Usage

    1.   Spell out a number beginning a sentence. If the number is large, it is best to rearrange the sentence. It is now considered acceptable to begin a sentence with a year.

EXAMPLES: Two hundred members were expected to attend.
1929 was a disastrous year for many people.

2. Spell out approximate numbers if they are "rounded off" in even units.

EXAMPLE: There were approximately five hundred persons at the wedding.

3. Numbers ten and below are spelled out; numbers above ten are written in numerals.

EXAMPLE: I have three coats.
John has 14 shirts.

4. When two numbers follow each other in a sentence, use numbers for the larger one and spell out the smaller number. If both numbers contain three or more numerals, use figures for both.

EXAMPLES: He ordered 12 two-piece suits from his client in New York City.
They sent us 175 500–page manuals.

5. Use figures for dimensions, measurements, distances, weights, and capacities.

EXAMPLES: 8 × 11 inches   4 ft. 3 in. or 4'3"
2 lbs. 15 oz.   6 mi.

If a weight or capacity is written before a noun, it is hyphenated to the singular word. If it is after the word, the plural word is used.

EXAMPLE: a 15–gallon jug
a jug holding 15 gallons

6. Use figures for page numbers and divisions of books.

7. Use figures for temperatures, election returns, and chemical terminology.

8. When writing a fraction, use a hyphen (one-half). Some authorities omit the hyphen if the fraction stands alone in the sentence; they include the hyphen if the fraction is a modifier. In general business usage, however, all fractions in sentences are written in words with a hyphen. If the fraction accompanies a whole number, the whole thing is written in figures.

EXAMPLES: There was two-thirds of the pie left. She sent one-half of the merchandise. She sent half of the merchandise. His hat size was 6⅞.

9. Fractions ¼ and ½ should be written the same as other fractions when mixed:

EXAMPLES: ¼, ½, ⅔, ¾

10. Alignment of Numbers. Columns of whole numbers are aligned on the right; decimals are aligned on the decimal

point; Roman numerals and ordinal numbers are aligned on the right; dates and words are aligned on the left; and mixed items are aligned on the left or centered.

11. Use figures before the word "percent" or the percent symbol (%). The symbol should be used only in tables or in technical writing. Spell out "percent" in all formal writing.

    EXAMPLE: He gave me a 20 percent discount on the damaged goods.

12. Spell out numbers referring to decades and centuries.

    EXAMPLE: twentieth century

13. Use figures for a series of numbers in a sentence even though some of the numbers may be below ten.

    EXAMPLE: I sent 20 letters, 2 postcards, and 6 packages.

§ 6.94 Dates

1. When writing dates, use figures without ordinal endings (st, nd, rd, d, or th) unless the day precedes the month.

    EXAMPLES: We will send the money on January 25, 1994.
    We will send the money on the 25th of January, 1994.

2. There is a difference between the first or last of the month and the 1st and 31st of the month. The latter two are definite days; first and last apply to a general period.

3. When the name of the month is not given, spell out the date.

    EXAMPLE: He will be leaving for Europe on the tenth.

4. Never indicate the month in figures except in tabulations.

    EXAMPLES: 8/11/94
    August 11, 1994

5. There is disagreement among references about spelling out the day of the month when it precedes the month. Some state that if the date is over ten, use figures; under ten, words.

    EXAMPLES: The eighth of May.
    The 25th of October.

6. In formal invitations, spell out the dates.

    EXAMPLE: On the twelfth day of May, nineteen hundred ninety-four.

§ 6.95 Age

1. When stating age, the general rule is that when the age is definite and given as a statistic or for quick reference, use

figures; if the age is indefinite or is used in formal writing, use words.

> EXAMPLES: He was dating a girl who was about sixteen years old.
> Judge John J. Bell, 56, is an authority on family law.
> She will be 39 on her next birthday.

2. When writing the age in years, months, and days, use figures and no commas. The whole phrase is considered as one unit.

> EXAMPLE: His age is 87 years 9 months and 5 days.

§ 6.96 Time

In stating time, the following rules apply:

1. Use figures preceding a.m. and p.m.
   > EXAMPLES: 10 a.m.
   >   9 p.m.

2. Use words or figures preceding o'clock.
   > EXAMPLE: ten o'clock or 3 o'clock
   > Words are more commonly used.

3. To express noon or midnight, do not use a.m. or p.m. Instead use 12 noon or 12 midnight.

4. Write a.m. and p.m. in small letters with a period after each letter and no space between them.
   > EXAMPLES: 3:10 p.m.
   >   8:30 a.m.

5. Do not use morning and a.m. in the same phrase.
   > *Incorrect:* I will see you this morning at 10:30 a.m.
   > *Correct:*   I will see you this morning at 10:30.
   >   OR
   >   I will see you at 10:30 a.m.

(The same is true of afternoon and evening and p.m.)

6. Do not use a.m. or p.m. with o'clock.

7. When you are using an even hour, it is not necessary to add the colon and two zeros unless you are typing a tabulation. Use 3 a.m. or 8 p.m. rather than 3:00 a.m. or 8:00 p.m.

§ 6.97 Money

1. In legal documents amounts of money are often written in words and figures. Be careful that the figures in the parentheses are an exact summary of the words.

EXAMPLES:

Incorrect: Twenty-five Dollars ($25.00).   Incorrect because the No/100 was not included before the parentheses.

Correct: Twenty-five Dollars ($25)

Incorrect: Twenty-five and No/100 ($25.00) Dollars.   Incorrect because dollars must come before the parentheses.

Correct: Twenty-five and No/100 Dollars ($25.00).   Correct because ciphers are included in the preceding phrase.

2.   In correspondence, amounts of money are written in figures.

EXAMPLE: The estimated fee for processing your claim is $585.   The cents ciphers are unnecessary for even dollar amounts: $25, not $25.00.

3.   Separate hundreds from thousands with a comma.

EXAMPLE: His annual membership fee was reported to be $1,800.

4.   Spell out an amount of money if it occurs at the beginning of a sentence.

EXAMPLE: Sixty cents is really a trifling amount.

§ 6.98   Addresses

1.   Spell out numbered street names from one through ten; use figures for numbered streets over ten.

EXAMPLE: 15550 Eighth Street

When figures are used, the ending st, th, nd, rd, or d is omitted when the words *North, East, South* or *West* separate the street number from the house number.

EXAMPLE: 2400 North 32 Street

If no such word intervenes, use the ordinal ending to prevent misreading.

EXAMPLE: 234 34th Street

2.   Do not use # or No. in addresses.   When an apartment number is needed, use the abbreviation, *Apt.,* after the address.

EXAMPLE: 600 Lake Shore Drive, Apt. 280 or
             1400–B College Drive

3.   Never use commas in address numbers.

§ 6.99 Roman Numerals

The rules for reading Roman numerals are as follows:

1. A repeated letter multiplies the value.
    EXAMPLE: II = 2   XX = 20
2. A letter occurring *after* one of higher value is added to the preceding one.
    EXAMPLE: VI = 5 + 1 = 6   LX = 50 + 10 = 60
3. A letter occurring *before* one of higher value is subtracted from the higher letter.
    EXAMPLE: IV = 5 − 1 = 4   XL = 50 − 10 = 40

The numbers and corresponding Roman numerals are as follows:

1 I	30 XXX
2 II	40 XL or XXXX
3 III	50 L
4 IV	60 LX
5 V	70 LXX
6 VI	80 LXXX or XXC
7 VII	90 XC or LXXXX
8 VIII	100 C
9 IX	150 CL
10 X	200 CC
11 XI	300 CCC
12 XII	400 CD or CCCC
13 XIII	500 D
14 XIV	600 DC
15 XV	700 DCC
16 XVI	800 DCCC
17 XVII	900 CM or DCCCC
18 XVIII	1000 M
19 XIX	1500 MD
20 XX	2000 MM

§ 6.100 The Creative Aspects of Written Communications

Writing, like many other forms of work, is a process. To accomplish it well, you should plan to complete each one of its five stages.

The time allocations may vary with the deadline, subject, and purpose; but the work schedule should generally follow this pattern:

1. Thinking   15%
2. Planning   10%
3. Writing   25%
4. Revising   45%
5. Proofreading   5%

Note that only 25 percent of the time should be spent in writing; the rest should be spent in getting ready for the task and perfecting the initial effort. Observe also that more time is spent in revising than in any other stage, including writing.

§ 6.101 Stage One—Thinking (15%)

You should be concerned—always—with human relations and public relations in organizing your thoughts, or clarifying your thoughts, for written communications. Some people interpret this first process as "worrying," rather than "thinking." In either event this is a vital process. You can proceed only if you have some ideas of something to write about.

§ 6.102 Stage Two—Planning (10%)

Planning is another term for organizing. When you force yourself simultaneously to conceive of ideas, to arrange them in logical order, and to express them in words, you cannot perform all of these complex activities as effectively as if you had concentrated on each one separately. By dividing the writing process into five stages and by focusing on each one individually, you increase the odds that the result will be much better than you thought possible.

Of course, you will hear about people who never plan their writing and do well anyway, just as you may know someone who skis or plays golf well without having had a lesson. There are always some naturals who can flaunt the rules, but perhaps these people could have significantly improved their writing, golf, or skiing if they had received some formal instruction and proceeded in the prescribed manner.

Perhaps you, through years of experience, follow the processes mechanically, unaware that you are doing so. If you fit into this category, admit it without loss of modesty and humility, but be honest about the labor along the way. Think of the waste of paper and other supplies and the personal frustration in starting over one, two, or more times to achieve the desired results.

To be an efficient person, you must plan your work. Many executives take a few minutes before leaving the office or retiring at night to jot down problems to attend to the following day. Many vacationers list tasks to do before leaving. Of course, you can go on vacation without planning—you do not have to stop the newspaper, turn down the refrigerator, inform the letter carrier, cut off the hot water, check the car, mail the mortgage payment, and the like. You can write without planning; but the chances are that the more carefully you organize, the better the results will be.

Planning consists mainly of examining all your ideas, eliminating the irrelevant ones, and arranging the others in a clear, logical order. Whether you write an informal outline or merely jot down your ideas on a scrap of paper is up to you. As you write, you can concentrate on formulating sentences instead of being concerned with thinking of ideas and trying to organize them.

§ 6.103   Stage Three—Writing (25%)

When you know what you want to say and have planned how to say it, then you are ready to write. This third step in the writing process is self-explanatory. Now put your thoughts on paper.

§ 6.104   Stage Four—Revising (45%)

Few are so talented that they can express themselves clearly and concisely in a first draft. Most know that they must revise. Revision is painful: removing pet phrases and savory sentences is like getting rid of cherished possessions. You must accomplish this without appearing curt or blunt.

Only by attacking your paper objectively can you revise it effectively. You must be eager to find fault, and you must be honest with yourself.

One method of saving time and energy is to utilize your shorthand skill in the processes of writing and revising.

§ 6.105   Stage Five—Proofreading (5%)

The final task, although not as taxing as others, is just as vital. If words are missing or repeated, letters are transposed, sentences are incoherent, or one misspelled word appears on the paper, a reader may be perturbed enough to ignore or resist your ideas or information. Carelessness in your writing antagonizes readers and raises questions in their minds about your competence.

§ 6.106   Utilizing Outlines

You may find that your writing process is simplified by use of an outline. Illustration 6–7 provides an informal outline using the five-step concept. Illustration 6–8 shows the correct format of an outline which you will use in formal writing.

Illustration 6–7

A JOB RESPONSIBILITY: WRITTEN CORRESPONDENCE

General Idea

Main Thrust (summary of purpose) In one sentence what do I want to say

A paragraph or two setting forth main ideas/points

What kinds of research needed

Basic outline or approach

Illustration 6–8 *
TOPIC OUTLINE

I. IDENTIFYING DIVISIONS OF OUTLINES
    A.   Roman Numerals for Major Divisions
    B.   Capital Letters for Subheadings (First Order)
    C.   Arabic Numerals for Items Under Subheadings (Second Order)
    D.   Lowercase Letters for Third Order Subheadings

II. CAPITALIZATION OF HEADINGS IN OUTLINES
    A.   Major Headings in All Caps
    B.   First–Order Subheadings with Important Words Capped
    C.   Second–Order Subheadings with Only First Word Capped
    D.   Third–Order Subheadings with Only First Word Capped

III. SPACING AND PUNCTUATION IN OUTLINES
    A.   Spacing
        1.   Horizontal spacing
            a.   Title typed either solid or as spread heading
            b.   Other headings typed solid
            c.   Two spaces after identifying designation
        2.   Vertical spacing as indicated in this outline
    B.   Punctuation
        1.   Except for abbreviations, no end-of-line punctuation in topic outlines
        2.   Appropriate end-of-line punctuation in sentence outlines

§ 6.107 The Paragraph

Each of your ideas may need its own paragraph, or you may wish to put them in groups in a logical combination.

1. Start with the topic you used in your plan. Put it into sentence form. Develop your topic with another sentence, two, three, or whatever it takes. Then, move on to your next topic and develop it the same as you did your first.

2. Keep your paragraphs reasonably short. Long ones are discouraging to the reader. Try to make the first and last in letters and memos short—not more than three or four lines. Elsewhere, if a paragraph gets to be more than eight or nine lines (100 words), consider breaking it up. Also ignore the idea that a paragraph has to be more than one sentence long.

3. Your paragraphs should be developed adequately to clarify and back up points. Use explanations, facts, illustrations, and examples.

4. Make sure each paragraph is unified and coherent. Take out anything irrelevant to the subject. To be in the same paragraph, your ideas should be closely related. The topic sentence or a summary sentence helps to keep out the irrelevant.

* Reprinted from *College Typewriting, Ninth Edition,* by Lessenbery, Wanous, and Duncan, with permission of the publisher, South–Western Publishing Company.

5. Use transitional words to move from one paragraph to the next. Use words such as *next, moreover, besides, nevertheless, on the other hand, first, second, third. If your ideas are logical, these words will not sound phony.*

6. Don't forget your reader.

§ 6.108   The Letter

There are many good books available in this field of writing. Some are very detailed and leave one really wondering how to go about the task. If you want simple, easy-to-understand steps for this process, see *The Gregg Reference Manual,* Seventh Edition.

Your first step for letter or memo writing should be planning and organizing. Answer the following questions on paper:

1. What is the purpose of the letter or memo?

2. To whom are you writing?

3. How much are you going to tell? List each item (you may have 2 or 40).

4. What do you wish to accomplish by writing this letter?

By now you should have a relatively good outline; but rearrange, add items, enlarge with details, statistics, and examples to get your idea across.

Next, decide on your conclusion and make sure at this point that you do not bring up a new idea.

If you are answering a letter, keep the letter in front of you while you compose. (Always answer promptly—don't sit on it, as that invites the person on the other end to sit on whatever you want from him.) So plunge right in!

1. Start your first paragraph by writing what your letter is about in one or two sentences. Don't keep the reader guessing, or he might file it before he finishes reading it.

2. If you're answering a letter, refer to the date; the reader can then pull his letter.

3. Write from the reader's point of view. Put the "you" into it, not "I," "me," or "we." Visualize the reader's way of life.

4. Be positive—your reader will be more receptive.

5. Be nice—it's not easy when you have a gripe. It's an art to be agreeable when disagreeing.

6. Be natural—write just the way you would talk. Imagine the reader sitting in front of you and you saying, "I acknowledge receipt of your letter" or "we transmit herewith." The acid test is to read your letter out loud when you're finished. Don't sound like a computer—sound like a human being.

7. Don't be cute or flippant—but don't be dull either. These hints may help:
   a. Have a sense of humor—it's refreshing and in a business letter, a surprise.
   b. Be specific—say something the reader can sink his teeth into.
   c. Lean on nouns and verbs—let up on adjectives. Use the active voice instead of the passive.

§ 6.109   The Three Cs of Written Communications

The three Cs of written communications are correctness, conciseness, and clarity.

§ 6.110   Correctness

Some people have a distorted concept of the correctness principle. They think it comprises only proper grammar, punctuation, and spelling. The fact is that you can be correct grammatically and mechanically in every respect and fail to use the correct level of language. There are three overlapping levels of language: formal, informal, and substandard.

The first two—formal and informal language—are both correct; but they are quite different from one another, have different uses, and should not be interchanged.

The formal level of language is used for writing a scholarly dissertation, a legal document, or other material for which formality is expected. The expressions used are often long, unconversational, and impersonal—just what the term "formal" implies.

In contrast, the informal level refers to the language of business— the language of letters, reports, and other business communications. Such language is alive and ever-changing. Instead of formal words you should use short, well-known, conversational words as the following illustrates:

Formal	Informal
domicile	home
deem	think (believe)
edifice	building
procure	get
remunerate	pay
Will attain the age of eighteen years	Will be 18 years old

The legal profession has the great failing of using the identical phraseology in business letter writing as is used in legal pleadings.

§ 6.111 Conciseness

Many business executives believe that conciseness is the most important writing principle because a wordy message requires more time (and money) to type and to read. Conciseness is saying what you have to say in the fewest possible words without sacrificing completeness and courtesy.

To achieve conciseness—the opposite of wordiness—observe the following suggestions:

- Omit trite expressions
- Avoid unnecessary repetition and word expressions
- Include only relevant facts

EXAMPLES:

Not this	But this
Enclosed herewith please find	Enclosed is
At this time	Now
Consensus of opinion	Consensus
Pursuant to your inquiry	As you requested
Please don't hesitate to write	Please write us
The undersigned (the writer)	I, me, or we
Please be advised that	(four wasted words)
The above subject matter	Unnecessary. The subject line is enough.
According to our records	Implies that the other person is wrong. Reword.
Acknowledge receipt of	The answer itself is an acknowledgment.
Advise	Tell or inform
As per	According to
At an early date	Vague. Use a definite time period: within the next 10 days, for example.
At the present time	Unnecessary. A verb tense says the same thing.
At your earliest convenience	This could be never. State a date or definite time period.
Attached please find; attached hereto; enclosed please find	Enclosed or attached is
By return mail	Meaningless. Say: right away or immediately
Under date of January 15	January 15

Don't hesitate to call	Please call
Due to the fact that	Because
For your information	Obviously the purpose of the communication; omit the phrase
Hoping to hear from you soon, I remain	Old-fashioned; poor grammar; do not use.
I have your letter	Naturally, or you wouldn't be answering. Do not use.
a check in the amount of $50	A check for $50
Kindly	Say: please
Our Mr. Jones	You don't own him. Omit "our."
Recent date	Use the specific date.
We take pleasure	We are glad.
We take the liberty	Do not use.
We take this opportunity	Obviously you are.
Thank you in advance	Presumptuous. We should appreciate.
Under separate cover	We are sending

Another caution is to begin the letter directly with the subject. Avoid beginnings that merely tell readers what they told you.

> EXAMPLE: "I have your letter of June 13 in which you informed me that Mr. John Smith called on you for the first time a few weeks ago and that he appealed to you as a capable and intelligent young man."

Organize effectively. Conciseness contributes to emphasis. By eliminating unnecessary words, you help make important ideas stand out.

§ 6.112　Clarity

Clarity involves most of the other principles of business writing—especially correctness, conciseness, completeness, consideration, and concreteness. Clarity means getting across your message, so the reader will not misunderstand what you are trying to convey.

Choose short, familiar, conversational words. Avoid professional jargon. Your professional vocabulary contains words you've been accumulating since you began your business career, and these words are quite clear to you. Furthermore, your colleagues easily understand you when you use technical terms, so it is all right to use them when talking or writing to people who also use them. You should, however, avoid professional jargon when you talk or write to a person who is not acquainted with such words.

If you must use technical words that the reader may not understand, define them briefly and clearly.

EXAMPLES:

Technical jargon	Expressions familiar to the layperson
Easement for ingress and egress	Agreement allowing passage in and out
Escrow account	Reserve account for taxes and insurance
Conveying title	Signing and recording a deed

In summary, make your writing clear by using words that are familiar to your reader.

§ 6.113 Finishing Touches

Now, you are ready for some finishing touches.

1. Make your letter look appealing. You can strike out here if you aren't careful. Use good quality stationery, 8½″ × 11″. Keep it neat and use paragraphing that makes it easy to read.

2. Keep your letter short, one page if possible. Keep the paragraphs short. Underline for emphasis. Indent sentences as well as paragraphs. (Save these tricks for something special.)

3. Make it perfect, or the reader will think you don't know better or don't care. And you do care, don't you?
    a. No typos
    b. No misspellings
    c. No factual errors

4. Be crystal clear. If the reader doesn't get the message, you won't get what you want.

5. Use good English.

6. Don't put on airs. Pretense won't impress anyone.

7. Don't exaggerate. Do it once and your reader will suspect everything else you write.

8. Distinguish opinions from facts. You may have the best opinion in the world, but your opinion is not gospel. You really owe it to your reader to let him know which is which. He'll appreciate it and admire you for it. The dumbest people are the people who "know it all."

9. Be honest. It will get you further in the long run.

10. Edit ruthlessly. Weed out all extras.

11. The windup is last. Your last paragraph should tell the reader exactly what you want him to do or what you are going to do. Close with something simple, like "sincerely." The biggest ego trip is the signature that is completely illegible.

12. PROOFREAD by reading aloud. Errors will pop up immediately. Check spelling, punctuation, and tenses of verbs.

13. Take the time to revise and rewrite. It will pay in the long run.

§ 6.114   Review Points for a Letter

1. Did you make the most important point first?

2. Did you anticipate any objections that the reader might have and then answer those objections in your letter?

3. Is the language of your letter suitable to your reader's location, education, and background?

4. Does your letter make it easy, logical, and advantageous for the reader to respond as you would like him to?

5. Does your letter contain complete information so that the reader will not have to write you or call you for further information?

6. Does your letter sound stilted, calculatingly businesslike, boring, pretentious, negative, or cold?

7. Is your letter conversational and warm? Does it sound like you are interested in the person to whom you are writing?

8. Are the facts accurate? Is the statement of your position clear?

9. Have you checked your letter for spelling, punctuation, and grammar?

10. Does your letter have the effect of building goodwill but still accomplish the purpose for which it is intended?

11. Is it tactful?

12. If you were the recipient of the letter, what would be your reaction?

§ 6.115   First Aid for Writing Problems

A major fault with letterwriting is the tendency to smother the reader with words. Don't make your reader work hard to find out what you are saying. Repeating words and phrases is not good word economy—it is redundancy.

There was a time when the language of letters was in a far different style from the spoken language. Today we make every attempt to write as we talk. When you edit your writing, weed out every trite expression that flows from you to the paper. Be careful, though, that you don't begin to ramble.

Always "accentuate the positive" in your letters. Every piece of correspondence that goes from your office can make friends or alienate clients—so stress the positive. Think of your reader, the "you" out there who is going to react to your message. Eliminate "I," "me," and "we" and accentuate the "you" attitude.

Make yourself clear by using the right words and spelling them correctly. Master the spelling errors that are most commonly made in writing. If you still have a problem after studying, then at least admit you have a spelling problem; doubt everything and use your dictionary.

Along with spelling goes vocabulary improvement. In your office something new comes across your desk every day. Know what you are doing and look the words up in the dictionary. Don't just hear them; look at them in print.

§ 6.116 The Memo

Memorandums, or memoranda, are the means organizations use to communicate internally. Used within an organization, memoranda serve the same purpose as a letter does to the outside. A memo will never be directed to anyone outside your office. Remember, don't rely upon what you may "tell" someone—"put it in writing." Use a memo.

The tone of your memo will depend upon the relationship between you and the recipient, the nature of the subject, and organization policy. In some organizations the policy is that memos be written in the third person to avoid the mixing of facts with opinions. A memo addressed to top management should be more formal than to someone of equal rank with the writer. You can gain formality by not using contractions such as "here's," "can't," "you'll." Using them sets the informal tone.

When you organize the contents of your memo, keep in mind that you are conveying a message, and brevity is the rule; but don't be so brief that you come across as being curt or impolite. Your message is selling a point of view or explaining a situation. State your purpose in the first paragraph. Deliver your message using the same rules you do for a letter. Use separate paragraphs for each idea or point. In a separate paragraph close with a statement of future action or your conclusions.

Don't take for granted that your subject line will cover the purpose of your memo. Always state your reason for writing. It may be here that you need to refer to a memo received, to a meeting, or perhaps to a telephone conversation.

An excellent method for stating your message briefly and quickly is to use enumerations. Use numbered paragraphs, one for each point. If you have several topics to discuss, you may use a method of bold side headings. Type the topic in all capitals or underline for emphasis.

Memos need to be as courteous as letters. Your closing should include a last paragraph with a short statement concerning future action or a request.

Rely upon the same sentence and paragraph construction and all the other rules for writing letters, and you will produce an excellent product.

§ 6.117   The Informal Report

You will have many occasions where you need to "put in writing" some information that the attorney or others have requested. The practice of writing informal reports is also a form of self-protection. If you tell the attorney something, he may forget; however, if you report on it, he has a paper to refer to. Informal reports also stand as visible proof of your efficiency, and your efficiency is not so much an intangible thing if you report "on paper."

There are essentially three parts to the report:

1. In the introduction state your purpose with points to support the purpose.

2. In the body refer to any background necessary for clarity; then begin a discussion of each of the major points, giving details, examples, and facts. Reports rely very heavily on descriptive data.

3. The conclusion summarizes and gives results or findings. Recommendations you may have are put in at this point.

First, prepare your outline. This can be very short or very detailed depending upon the assignment. An attorney may need to have a report on the kind of typewriter each of the twelve secretaries in your office is using. He is planning to make replacements to the extent the budget will allow and needs prices also. In this situation you really have two things to investigate.

1. The types of machines the secretaries are using, including the age and condition of the typewriters

2. The prices of new equipment from two or more suppliers

When you have gathered all the details, place the facts in the two categories. Arrange the items in each group in the order in which you should present them. You can proceed to write at this point.

In an informal report of this type, you will set it up as a memo to the person requesting the information. Whenever you make an informal report, no matter how minor you think it is, make a copy for your files. Your attorney may misplace his.

In choosing your words, be clear, correct, complete, and concise. Say everything which needs to be said in the fewest number of words possible, using the same rules of grammar, punctuation, spelling, etc., used for letter writing. In a report, accuracy in giving your information is more important than correctness. You need not give as much attention to the tone of your report as you do when writing a letter to a client. In a report you should be factual and straightforward.

A very effective way to present information is to tabulate or chart. The reader has the advantage of seeing everything at a glance without wading through a maze of words.

After all the information in your research has been included in your report, you should summarize. In this situation you may recommend keeping some of the older machines and adding to the total number, particularly if the trade-in prices are not very good. Remember, the attorney is too busy to know many of these details, and you owe it to him to put these ideas and facts on paper. Isn't this part of his reason for asking you to make the report?

Another type of report you might want to write is an unsolicited report. This is a situation where you take the initiative to write. In business any idea that you might have for increasing efficiency and productivity or changing procedures is more than welcome. You will want to put your idea or ideas in writing in a complete, logical, and effective manner.

Be careful to direct your idea to the person who has the authority to put it into effect.

Your subject line should be chosen carefully to describe what the report is about in a very few words.

The wording in the report should be slanted so that it will appeal to the reader's interest. You are, in effect, doing a selling job. Go about the planning as you do for the informal research report. Rely on facts and not on your judgment. Give alternatives, good and bad, and back up the strong points with criteria you have gathered. In your conclusion reemphasize the strong points you have presented.

§ 6.118　The Formal Report

Formal business reports concern themselves with more complicated problems and may require weeks of extensive research. The finished product may contain anywhere from one or two pages to well over a hundred. If a company is basing a decision concerning the expenditure of a great amount of money on this report, it must be very carefully and expertly done.

Before starting the report, the purpose and scope of the project must be set out. Also, it will have more parts: introduction, summary, body, conclusions, and recommendations, plus supplementary information such as an appendix and bibliography.

As the researcher gathers information, he must make special notes as a formal report is made up of information from many sources. The ideal way to catalog this information is through the use of note cards or note sheets, one sheet for each item of information along with its source. After all collecting of information is complete, the writer then studies the material and begins the task of organizing in a logical sequence for presentation.

A good report writer is careful to avoid any expressions which might imply that his personal opinions are the basis for the evaluations presented in the paper. The important factor in the success of a business report is separating reasoning from facts.

§ 6.119　Proofreading

Poor proofreading results from failure to realize its importance, from inadequate time, and from improper effort. Unless you are convinced that scrutinizing your final copy is important, you cannot proofread effectively. Like most things, proofreading takes time, but lack of time is seldom a legitimate excuse for doing it badly.

To proofread well, focus on the words. Slow down your reading speed, stare hard at the black print, and search for trouble rather than a way to finish quickly.

If interruptions occur while you are proofreading, place a check in the margin where you stopped reading. When you return to the proofreading, go back two or three sentences preceding the checkmark; you will then pick up the flow of the words.

When proofreading numbers, difficult copy, or property descriptions, you should check carefully with the original copy. Check dates with a calendar to be sure that you have them correct.

Carefully proofread letters that you type routinely, such as form letters. There is the tendency to see what is expected to be there rather than what is actually there.

Following are 13 troublespots in proofreading:

1. Headings, subheadings, and inside addresses often contain errors. The proofreader assumes they are correct and spends time on the body of the material. Headings which are typed in all capital letters or are underlined are often skipped over. There seems to be the assumption that they are correct because they look different.

2. Errors in proofreading often occur at the beginnings and ends of lines. There is a natural tendency to read more quickly as you approach the end of a line. You may pass over the beginning of the next line before you consciously realize that you haven't read carefully the beginning of the line.

3. Missed proofreading errors occur often at the bottom of the page. If things have gone well that far, the proofreader has a tendency to rush to finish and skips over errors.

4. When typing, the typist might omit or insert a line of text or one or more words. When proofreading, read for the sense of the sentence. The text should follow logically. If you are reading only for the spelling of the words, you may miss insertions or deletions.

5. Another proofreading problem arises in long words which are very familiar to the reader. There is a tendency to expect the word to look right. Readers have mental pictures of words and recognize words without spelling them. If the word is very familiar or is repeated often in the text, it is easy to miss the omitted letter in the word. There is a tendency to assume the word is correct because it appears so often.

6. Transposed letters are easy to skip over. Sometimes the transposed word creates another word that is correct, and it is easy to pass over it. *From* can be transposed to *form*. Since both words are correctly spelled, the eye passes over the word even though it is not the correct word for the sentence. Transposed vowels occur frequently and are easy to miss unless you are analyzing carefully the syllables of the word.

7. Errors often go undetected in captions and footnotes because the proofreader has a tendency to ignore them when proofreading. Once again, there is an assumption they are correct, and they are only glanced at by the proofreader.

8. Always verify the spelling of proper names. There are several spellings for certain names. Do not assume that the spelling is correct. The typist may have typed *Petersen* instead of *Peterson*. In proofreading the error would probably go unde-

tected unless the proofreader checked the name against the source.

9. When proofreading vertical enumerations, check the continuity of the numbers. In outlines check the continuity of the letters and numbers. It is not unusual to see a list of numbers as 1, 2, 3, 4, 4, 5. Check numbers both horizontally and vertically to find all errors.

10. Number combinations cannot be proofread without checking them with the original source. Any number can look correct when in reality the numbers may be transposed.

11. One of the most common errors in proofreading occurs with the repeated word or letter. It occurs in the middle of a line, as *and and.* It occurs at the end of one line and the beginning of the next. It is very easy for the typist to type a word, carriage return, and type the same word at the beginning of the next line. This is also difficult for the proofreader to spot. The repeater can occur in the middle of words, such as *bottom, boookkeeper.*

12. Check divided words carefully. It is easy to miss a mistake when half of the word is on one line and the other half at the beginning of the next line. Make sure the second half is there. Words can be divided incorrectly; or they may have letters left out when they are divided, such as *immed-* on one line and *ate* on the next. In proofreading, it is hard to recognize that the *i* is missing.

13. Words which contain double letters are common sources of typing errors. These are also difficult to spot in proofreading. *Bookeeping* is easy to pass over.

Some professional proofreaders start with the last sentence and read backward to the first. Then they read it again from beginning to end. Whatever technique you adopt, work painstakingly, so that a few careless errors will not spoil your efforts. If you realize the importance of proofreading, view it as one of the stages in the writing process, and labor at it conscientiously, your communication will reflect your care, concern, and competency.

§ 6.120   Mailability

The standard for preparation of all written communications is mailability. Mailability means that the letter or document is suitable to be sent through the mail. It is in a form that represents the high standards of the office. To judge mailability, use the following checklist:

1. *Is the content accurate?*

   It is not always necessary to follow the dictator's words verbatim, but it is essential that the exact meaning be conveyed. There will be times when you will substitute one word for another to clear up the meaning or to fill in for a word you omitted in your shorthand notes. Be sure that you have the correct name, title, and address of the addressee. A reader is quick to notice a mistake in his name, title, or address. This creates a negative impression.

2. *Does the letter have a good appearance?*

   Is the layout of the letter attractive, or is it too high or low on the page? Are the margins even or nearly so? Are the paragraphs too long? (Break up the body of the letter into paragraphs that are easy to read.)

3. *Have all errors been corrected?*

   Check the spelling. A spellcheck program will not highlight a correctly spelled word incorrectly used. Spelling errors damage the firm's prestige and divert attention from the message.

Remember, your letter is *not* mailable if it has misspelled words or faulty punctuation.

§ 6.121 The Letterbank

Your attorney is, no doubt, a very busy person. Time is at a premium, so your being able to handle routine correspondence in an effective manner will free some of his precious time for other duties.

Once you get your lawyer's approval to handle some of his correspondence, you will be looking for ways to slash hours off the time you spend writing letters. You can do this with a "letterbank."

Your bank can be a folder, series of folders, or a notebook. Break it up into categories such as appointments, collections, statements, executive's personal correspondence, and then divisions of the types of law your lawyer practices. As letters enter and leave the office, cull out the most useful and make a copy to deposit in the appropriate category of your letterbank. As a result you have timesaving, ready-to-use model letters at your fingertips. As your file builds up, you increase your value to your lawyer by taking on more and more of his letterwriting tasks.

If you find yourself referring to a certain form letter many times, put it through the tests of good letterwriting rules. Work on it, polish it. Then you will have more confidence in your skills, and it is much more likely that your reader will react favorably. Once you have created a few good letters, you have a pattern established; and you'll be surprised to see that the letters you write in the future will seem to fall in line and be good letters, too.

§ 6.122 Parts of a Business Letter

There are 15 parts to a business letter. Some are found in nearly all business letters; others are used in special circumstances. The parts of a business letter are as follows: (Asterisked items are optional).

1. Printed letterhead
2. Date line
3. Inside address
4.* Attention line
5. Salutation (omitted on AMS Simplified letter)
6.* Subject line (must be included on AMS Simplified letter)
7. Body
8. Complimentary close (omitted on AMS Simplified letter)
9.* Company name
10. Signer's identification
11. Reference initials
12.* Enclosure notation
13.* Mailing notation
14.* c or cc (copy) notation
15.* Postscript

Each of these parts is illustrated on the letter shown in Illustration 6–9.

Illustration 6–9

COLVIN, MASON & NORMAN ①

Kay Colvin
Jerry Mason
Scott Norman

Attorneys at Law
3005 E. Skelly Avenue
Tulsa. Oklahoma 74105

Telephone
Area Code 918
749–6423

August 3, 19--②

Office Supply Company ③
3399 Notation Boulevard
Tulsa, OK 74105

Attention Mr. S. E. Tedesco ④

Gentlemen: ⑤

SUBJECT: Purchase Order No. 8843 ⑥

Thank you for rushing to us our order for two secretarial desks and two posture chairs. They arrived yesterday in time for the opening of our new offices.

There has been a mistake, however, in the order. We requested ⑦ two posture chairs, Catalog No. A67D, with dark blue upholstery. The ones we received are listed as Catalog No. A68D; they have light blue upholstery.

These chairs will not be suitable as they do not match the color scheme of our offices. Do you have the chairs we ordered in stock? If so, would you please ship them to us immediately. We are enclosing a copy of our order form.

We appreciate your assistance in this matter. By copy of this letter, we are notifying your local sales representative of the problem.

Sincerely, ⑧

COLVIN, MASON & NORMAN ⑨

P. M. Martell   ⑩
Office Manager
mm ⑪
Enclosure ⑫
By messenger ⑬
cc: Sarah Wilkins   ⑭
P. S. The chairs which we received cost $12 more than the ⑮ ones we ordered. We would appreciate your revising the billing.

                     P.M.M

                         [C4074]

§ 6.123   Letter Styles

There are four basic letter styles:

- Modified block (also known as blocked)
- Modified block with indented paragraphs (also known as semi-blocked)
- Full block (also known as extreme block)
- Simplified (also known as AMS Simplified)

§ 6.124   Modified Block

The *modified block* is the most commonly used letter style. The date line, the complimentary close, and the signer's identification all begin at center. The remainder of the letter begins at the left margin. (See Illustration 6–10.) Some firms prefer the date to be centered under the firm name or at the right margin. The subject line may be centered for emphasis.

Illustration 6–10

COLVIN, MASON & NORMAN

Kay Colvin   Attorneys at Law   Telephone
Jerry Mason   3005 E. Skelly Avenue   Area Code 918
Scott Norman   Tulsa, Oklahoma 74105   749–6423

October 9, 19___

Mrs. Jon Wilkinson
222 Mason Avenue
Rigby, ID 83221

Dear Mrs. Wilkinson:

Re: Modified Block Letter Style

This letter is written in the modified block style. The first line of each paragraph begins at the left margin. Mixed punctuation is used. Note that a colon follows the salutation, and a comma follows the complimentary close.

The date and complimentary close, as well as the writer's name and identification, begin at the horizontal center of the page.

The subject line may be typed even with the left margin, indented five or ten spaces, or centered.

Sincerely,
COLVIN, MASON & NORMAN

Trema Kuchenbecker
Office Manager

mm
cc: Kristen Saunderson

MODIFIED BLOCK

§ 6.125 Modified Block With Indented Paragraphs

The *modified block with indented paragraphs* is the same as the modified block style except that the first line of each paragraph is indented five or ten spaces. (See Illustration 6–11.)

Illustration 6–11

COLVIN, MASON & NORMAN

Kay Colvin	Attorneys at Law	Telephone
Jerry Mason	3005 E. Skelly Avenue	Area Code 918
Scott Norman	Tulsa, Oklahoma 74105	749–6423

June 26, 19___

Mr. Joe Kelly, President
Ace Electronics
445 Tudor Square
Boise, ID 83702

Dear Mr. Kelly:

     This is a modified block style letter with indented paragraphs. It is the same format as the modified block letter except the paragraphs are indented five spaces. The date and closing information begin at the horizontal center.

     If the letter contains an enclosure, the enclosure notation is placed one space below the reference initials. The copy notation should be placed one space below the enclosure notation.

     Postscripts are not common in business letters, but when they do occur, they are placed at the end of the letter following the copy notation.

Sincerely,

COLVIN, MASON & NORMAN

Lila Smith
Secretary to Jerry Mason

mm
Enclosure
cc: Loren Siddell (w/enc.)

MODIFIED BLOCK WITH INDENTED PARAGRAPHS

§ 6.126 Full Block

The *full block* is used in many offices because it is the fastest to type. Each line begins at the left margin, including the date and signature lines. (See Illustration 6–12.)

Illustration 6–12

A.G. LAMBERT
Attorney at Law   Telephone
741 Main Street   (918) 749–5826
Tulsa, Oklahoma 74105

July 6, 19__

Mr. Lee James
900 Spring Place
Rexburg, Idaho 83440

Dear Mr. James

Re: Full Block Style Letter

In this type of letter, all lines begin at the left margin. The letter can use either open or mixed punctuation. This letter uses open punctuation; there is no mark of punctuation after the salutation and complimentary close.

This form of letter saves typing time because no tab stops or indentions are required for paragraphs, datelines, or closings.

Sincerely

Sally Johnson
Office Manager

mm

FULL BLOCK

§ 6.127   Simplified

The *simplified* letter is preferred more by business than by law firms. Law firms might use it for corresponding with suppliers but rarely for writing to clients or other attorneys. It was designed by the Administrative Management Society and is, therefore, referred to as the AMS Simplified style. All lines begin at the left margin. The salutation is omitted and replaced with a subject line typed in solid capital letters. The word *subject* is not used. The complimentary close is omitted, and the writer's identification line is typed in solid capital letters. The writer's name is usually followed by a hyphen and then his title is typed in all capital letters. (See Illustration 6–13.)

EXAMPLE: JOHN J. JONES—VICE PRESIDENT, MARKETING

Illustration 6–13

A.G. LAMBERT
Attorney at Law
741 Main Street
Tulsa, Oklahoma 74105

Telephone
(918) 749–5826

August 11, 19__

Mr. Gary Ryan
123 Fifth Avenue
Pocatello, ID 83201

AMS SIMPLIFIED LETTER STYLE

This letter is typed in the simplified letter style. This format was developed by the Administrative Management Society and has been accepted by business because it takes less typing time.

The letter is typed in full block format. The salutation is omitted and replaced by a subject line which is typed in solid capital letters. The subject line is placed three spaces below the inside address and three spaces above the body of the letter.

The complimentary close is omitted. The writer's name and title are typed in solid capital letters at least four lines below the body of the letter.

Although this letter style is popular in business, most law firms have been reluctant to adopt it. They prefer the more traditional letter styles.

ALICE WHITE—OFFICE MANAGER

mm

AMS SIMPLIFIED

§ 6.128   Punctuation

The most common style of punctuation in business correspondence is *mixed punctuation,* also known as *standard punctuation.* A colon (never a comma) is placed after the salutation and a comma after the complimentary close.

§ 6.129   Open Punctuation

Open punctuation is more common in business, but law firms have generally resisted it. No punctuation is used at the end of any line other than in the body of the letter unless the line ends with an abbreviation.

§ 6.130   Closed Punctuation

Closed punctuation is rarely used. Each line outside of the body of the letter ends with a punctuation mark, either a period or a comma. This includes the date and each line of the inside address.

§ 6.131   Letters of Two or More Pages

In typing a multipage letter, do not end a page with a divided word. Leave at least two lines of a paragraph at the foot of the page and carry at least two lines to the next page.

Use plain paper of the same color and quality as the letterhead for the second and subsequent pages of a letter. However, some law firms have the firm name engraved on the continuation pages as in Illustration 6–14. Use the same margins and letter style that you used on the first page.

The second page should contain a heading giving the name of the addressee, the date, and the page number. This heading should start approximately six line spaces from the top. At least two lines should be left between the heading and the first line of the resumed letter. Some software programs with a header feature allow only one blank line between the header and the text of the letter.

There are two methods for heading continuation pages:

1. All information begins at the left margin.
2. The addressee's name is at the left margin, the page number is centered, and the date ends at the right margin.

The page number usually precedes the date, although some firms prefer that the page number be placed last when the items are placed in three lines. The numeral is preferred to the word for the page number, although some firms feel that the spelling out of the page number looks more formal.

Illustration 6–14

William E. Kerr, Ph.D.
Page 2
April 14, 19__

food is delicious, the fireplace is bright and warm in the evenings.

BLOCK STYLE OF SECOND–PAGE HEADING

William E. Kerr, Ph.D.   2   April 14, 19__

food is delicious, the fireplace is bright and warm in the evenings, and the fishing stories exchanged by the guests are among the best I have heard anywhere.

HORIZONTAL STYLE OF SECOND–PAGE HEADING

§ 6.132   Appearance of the Letter

The appearance and mechanics of the letter are what the reader sees first when the letter is opened. A pleasing appearance invites the reader to investigate the contents. Here are some dos and don'ts.

1. The side margins of your letter will depend on the kind of stationery you are using, size of type, space taken by the letterhead, and the length of your message. Many tables, formulas, and measurements for calculating margins have been published; however, with all the instructions and guidelines you can have, there is one basic rule you must follow for a neat appearance—*your finished letter must look like it is sitting in a frame of white space.* Eye it from start to finish, and if your result does not satisfy you, redo it.

2. Plan to leave a bottom margin of at least six line spaces (or one inch). If you have a long letter continuing to a second page, the bottom margin can increase to about twelve line spaces—but watch your side margins also; you want it framed.

3. You can spread a short letter over a page by using several techniques:
   • Lower the date line.
   • Allow more space between the date and inside address.
   • Allow more space for the signature.
   • Put signer's name and title on separate lines.
   • Lower reference initials, *cc* notation, and enclosure notation.

4. You can shorten a long letter on a page by using these techniques:
   • Raise the date line.
   • Allow only two or three blank spaces between date and inside address.
   • Allow only two or three spaces for the signature.
   • Raise the reference initials one or two lines.

5. Ordinarily, all letters should be single-spaced. If the message is very, very short you may double space; however, this will call for paragraph indentation.

6. If you are writing as an individual without a letterhead, put your return address in the upper right-hand corner. You may begin at the center; or for the best appearance, start about nine line spaces from the top and have the longest line of your address even with your right-hand margin. If you are using full block or simplified style, you will start at about line nine flush with the left-hand side.

7. The date line is never abbreviated. Avoid using 6/23/94. Military or international form—5 June 1994—is acceptable, although it is not common.

8. With a letterhead, position the date line three line spaces below the letterhead. This may vary with letter length and style of letterhead, so don't feel you must adhere to this rule of three line spaces. Remember, it must look right.

9. If you send a letter of a personal or confidential nature, type the appropriate notation on the second line below the date *at the left margin.* It may be in all capital letters or with capital and small letters and underlined.

10. The inside address in a letter being sent to an individual's home should include (1) name, (2) street address, (3) city, state, and ZIP. If the person lives in an apartment, the apartment number should appear after the street address on the same line. If the person lives in a small town and the address is only two lines, do not separate the city from the state to make three lines.

11. For a letter going to a company, organization, or school, use the above arrangement. If possible, address to a particular individual and place this above the company name along with that person's title. If you do not have a specific name, address it to a title, such as *Personnel Director.*

12. When a room number or suite is given, use the same form as on the letterhead or envelope.

    EXAMPLES: 416 12th Street, Room 12
               Suite 1200
               103 Ryan Center

               Room 228, Financial Center
               890 Locust Street

13. The inside address should begin about five spaces below the date line; use single spacing.

14. If a letter is addressed to two people at different addresses, type each name and address either one under the other, with one blank line between, or side by side, with one address aligned at the left margin and the other at center.

    EXAMPLES: Dr. J.W. Cooper
               123 Mustard Avenue
               Greenwood, MO 45983

               Dr. Jane Melody
               432 Levon Creek, Suite 22–B
               Jefferson City, MO 45976

    Dr. J.W. Cooper   Dr. Jane Melody
    123 Mustard Avenue   432 Levon Creek, Suite 22–B
    Greenwood, MO 45983   Jefferson City, MO 45976

    Dear Dr. Cooper and Dr. Melody:

    If a letter is addressed to two people at the same address, list each name on a separate line of the same inside address.

EXAMPLE: Dr. J.W. Cooper
Dr. Jane Melody
123 Mustard Avenue
Greenwood, MO 45983

15. Use a form of address before the name of a person (*Mr., Mrs., Ms., Miss, Dr.*). If you do not know whether the person addressed is a man or a woman, do not use a courtesy title; the salutation should read *Dear Madam* or *Sir*.

16. Consult the original correspondence for a person's preference in spelling. Do not abbreviate names or omit initials.

17. People who have ambiguous names like Marion, Leslie, Carol, or Lee should use courtesy titles when they sign their letters so that others may be spared the confusion when replying.

18. When *Jr., Sr.*, or a Roman numeral, such as *III*, is part of the name, omit the comma after the surname, unless that person prefers the use of a comma.

19. Do not use a form of address before a name if *M.D.* follows the name. Write it either *Dr. John Jones* or *John Jones, M.D.*

20. Abbreviations of religious orders, such as *S.J.*, are typed after names and preceded by a comma. An appropriate title should precede the name even though the abbreviation follows the name:

EXAMPLE: *Reverend Neil Cahill, S.J.*

21. If a person's title is very short, it should be placed with his name. If the title is very long, you may need to put it on a separate line and also divide it. In this case be certain that the second line of the title is indented at least two spaces beyond the first line of title:

EXAMPLE: Vice President and
General Manager

22. If a letter cannot be sent to the addressee but must be directed through a third person, use *In care of* ... or *c/o* John Doe.

23. When writing the name of an organization in an inside address, follow the organization's letterhead style for spelling, punctuation, capitalization, spacing, and abbreviation. If you do not have a way to determine the official form, consult the phone book or call the library. If you are still without information:

- Spell out the word *and*—don't use *&*.
- Write *Inc.* for Incorporated and *Ltd.* for Limited.
- Spell out Company or Corporation; however, if the name is extremely long, abbreviate it.
- Do not use *The* at the beginning of the name unless you are sure it is a part of the official name.

24. If an address contains a building name and a street address, type the building address on the line above the street address. See the examples in item 13 above.

25. The street address should always be on a line by itself on the line preceding the city, state, and ZIP.

26. Do not abbreviate directions that appear before a street name: 1668 Southeast 14th Street, but use abbreviations if directions represent a section of a city.

    EXAMPLE: 1668 Ninth Street, SE

27. Use the word *and* and not & in a street address:

    EXAMPLE: Tenth and Maple Streets.

28. Never abbreviate *Street, Avenue,* or *Boulevard* in an inside address.

29. A post office box number may be used in place of a street address. Use Post Office Box 521 or P.O. Box 521. A station name, if needed as in some larger cities, should appear after the box number on the same line and before the line for city and state.

30. If an address shows both a street address and a box number in its mailing address, whatever information appears in the line preceding the city and state is where the mail will be delivered.

31. The city, state, and ZIP must always be typed on one line:

    EXAMPLE: Des Moines, IA 50322

    Use one or two spaces between the state abbreviation and the ZIP Code.

32. In an address never abbreviate the name of a city or words like *Fort* and *Mount.*

    EXAMPLES: Fort Dodge, Mount Vernon

    Abbreviate the word *Saint* in names of American cities.

    EXAMPLES: St. Louis, St. Paul

33. When an address is given in a sentence, insert a comma after the street address and after the city. Leave one space between the state and the ZIP Code. Insert a comma after the ZIP Code unless a stronger mark of punctuation is required.

34. When addressing mail to foreign countries, type the name of the country in all capital letters on a separate line. Do not abbreviate the name of the country.

35. An attention line can be used; however, it is better to address the letter to a particular person named in the first line of the inside address. In either case, in the absence of a notation of *personal* or *confidential,* the communication will be presumed to be company business and may be handled by others.

36. Make certain that the spelling of the name in the salutation is the same as the spelling in the inside address.

37. There are a few instances where a person's title or gender is unknown.

    EXAMPLES: To a person with name known, gender unknown:
Dear Pat Black, Dear C.L. Blue

    To a person with name and gender unknown:
Dear Sir or Madam

    To a woman, title unknown:
Dear Ms. Black or Dear Mary Black

    To an organization composed of all men or all women:
Dear Gentlemen or Dear Ladies

    To an organization composed of both men and women:
Dear Ladies and Gentlemen

Another alternative in situations like those above is to use the simplified letter style.

38. In all other letter styles when a subject line is used, it is placed on the second line below the salutation. In most cases it will start at the left margin; however, in the semi-blocked style it may be indented the same as the paragraphs. (The reference books agree in most cases with the above; however, your office may have another method or style, so use it. Many offices still have their subject line appear before the salutation.)

39. The term "Subject" is not necessary. *In re:* or *Re:* may also be used. (These are used mainly in legal correspondence.)

40. The message will start on the second line below the subject line or salutation, whichever precedes your message. If the simplified style is used, start your message on the third line.

41. All letters except the semi-blocked style will have paragraphs flush with the left margin. The semi-blocked style paragraphs should be indented from five to ten spaces. If your letter is double spaced, you must indent each paragraph.

42. If you need to insert a quotation or other material in a display, indent the material five spaces or the same as your paragraph, leaving a line above and below. The material should be centered in this space with even margins left and right.

43. If you have a list of numbered items appearing in the body, leave a line before beginning the items and begin either at the left margin or at the point of paragraph indentation. Follow the item number with a period, and start the item even with

the paragraph indentation or five additional spaces to the right. If any item requires more than one line, indent the second line so that it begins under the first word of the line above. You may wish, in this situation, to leave a line between items.

44. Capitalize only the first word of the complimentary close, placing a comma after the last word (except when open punctuation is used).

45. The complimentary closing you choose will express the tone of your letter. For a personal tone use "Sincerely," "Cordially yours," "Sincerely yours," "Cordially." Your reader will feel a more formal tone if you use "Yours truly," "Yours very truly," "Very truly yours," "Very sincerely yours," "Very cordially yours," "Respectfully yours." If you use an informal closing phrase ("Best wishes," "Warmest regards," or "See you next week"), follow it with a comma. If you use one of these phrases with a complimentary close that is more formal, insert the informal phrase at the end of the last paragraph or as a separate paragraph.

46. Watch your pattern of closings in writing to the same people. In a later letter if you resort to a more formal closing, your reader may wonder what has happened to the relationship.

47. The company or firm name may be used to follow the complimentary close. Its use emphasizes the fact that the letter represents the views of the company as a whole. If used, the name should be typed in all capitals on the second line below the complimentary close and beginning at the same point as the complimentary close.

48. A general rule for typing the writer's name is on the fourth line after the complimentary close or company name, whichever is the last typed. Here is where you take a good look at the placement of your letter. If you are high on the page, extend to five or six line spaces. If you are running near the bottom, close in two or three line spaces. Start your typing in line with the complimentary close. The exception to this will be for the simplified letter when you will type the writer's name on the fifth line below the last line of the body in all capital letters and flush with the left margin.

49. If the writer prefers to omit his name in the signature line, and use only his title, then his name should be spelled out in the reference initials. Copies would not show the writer's name and poor handwriting in the signature could leave doubt in the addressee's mind about the correct spelling of the writer's name.

50. Take care to set up the writer's name and title so that it has good balance. If the title takes more than one line, use two

lines and block the second line with the left margin of the title.

51. A person with a special title should set up the signature block as he wishes to be addressed. A person wishing to be addressed as Dr. should use the degree initials after the name:

EXAMPLE: Marie Smith, M.D.

A person wishing to be addressed by a title of academic or military rank should include the title after the name or on the next line:

EXAMPLE: Marie Smith, Dean of Students

Some titles like Rev. and Mother cannot be placed after the surname and should be typed:

EXAMPLES: Rev. Marion Smith, Mother Marie Smith

52. Men's signatures do not require that *Mr.* be written before the name; however, in the case of a questionable gender name such as Lynn, Leslie, or Shirley, he should either have *Mr.* typed in the typewritten line or *Mr.* written in parentheses before his name as he signs the letter.

53. A woman may include a courtesy title with her signature so the reader is not put in the awkward position of wondering if she is *Ms., Miss,* or *Mrs.* If the courtesy title is left for the handwritten signature, it should be written in parentheses.

54. A woman in business should not use her husband's name as a courtesy title. She should use Mrs. Marie Smith, not Mrs. Frank Smith.

55. If a secretary signs a letter at the attorney's request, the preference of the attorney should be followed. There are two good ways: Ms. Marie Smith, Secretary of Frank Mullen (using her own signature above the title), or the boss's name and title with her own handwriting signing *his* name with her initials penned underneath the last part of the signature she has affixed.

56. If a letter is to be signed by two people, type each name and title either one under the other, with three blank lines between, or side by side, with one name aligned at the left margin and the other aligned at center.

EXAMPLES: Sincerely,

Ann A. Pitts
Office Manager

Joan D. Moseley
Patient Representative

Sincerely,

Ann A. Pitts   Joan D. Moseley
Office Manager   Patient Representative

57. Reference initials of the typist are typed at the left margin on the second line space below the writer's name and title. If the writer's initials are included here, they will precede the typist's initials. Here again, you may have an opportunity to do more "framing" work. If you have everything high on the page, you may extend to a three-line space; if you are nearing the bottom of the page, close in. There are several commonly used styles for the typist only: *trs, TRS, t;* for using the writer's and typist's initials together: *L:S, FLR/ts, FLR:TRS, FLR:trs.* If the writer's name is not typed in the signature block, use *FLRyan/ts.*

58. When writing and typing your own personal letter, do not include reference initials.

59. If the letter mentions that one or more items are to be included with the correspondence, indicate that fact by typing *"Enclosure," "Enc.," "Check enclosed," "Enc. 2,"* or other appropriate identification at the left margin one space below the reference initials. (Here is another place to spread if your letter is very short.)

60. If the items are to be sent under separate cover, indicate by typing *"Separate cover,"* or *"Under separate cover."*

61. If the letter is to be delivered in a special way, type the appropriate notation after the last notation line, flush with the left margin:[2]

EXAMPLE: *Special Delivery, Certified*

62. Copy notations let the reader know that one or more other persons will receive a copy of the letter. Use the initials *c* or *cc.* Type at the left margin under the mailing notation, if used. If more than one person receives a copy, type *c* or *cc* only once; then line the second name under the beginning of the first name. Type either in order of rank or alphabetically.

63. The initials *c* or *cc* are typed in small letters and with or without a colon. (See Illustrations 6–9, 6–10, and 6–11 for a sample of each.) You need not use courtesy titles when indicating copies.

64. When an addressee is not to know who received copies of the letter, type *bcc* on the copies to the individuals who need to know in the upper left corner, starting on the seventh line. Your file copies should show all the blind copies, even though

---

2. Some authorities recommend placing these notations immediately following the date line. Therefore, it appears that usage permits the placement of these special notations in either place.

the individual copies do not.   Use the style you used for the other copy notations.

65.   Copies of letters are not signed unless the person has been named in the salutation.   A checkmark should be made to the right of the person's name for whom the copy is intended.   In a situation where an unsigned copy might strike the receiver as impersonal or cold, it is appropriate to add a brief hand-written note at the bottom and sign with your initials.

66.   Postscripts are used to express an idea that has been inten-tionally or inadvertently omitted from the letter.   Use *"PS:,"* *"PS.,"* or *"Postscript"* with or without punctuation.   If punc-tuation is used, leave two spaces after the period or colon.   For a second postscript, use *"PPS:,"* *"PPS,"* and type as an entirely additional paragraph.

67.   Never use the second page of a letter only for the closing section of a letter.   You should have at least two lines of the body of the letter on the second page before the complimenta-ry close.

68.   Leave a margin of from 6 to 12 lines at the bottom of each page.   Make every attempt to have uniform bottom margins on each page except the last.

69.   Never divide the last word of a page.

§ 6.133   Addressing Envelopes

Single-space and block the address lines.   The bottom line must include the city and state names and the ZIP Code in that sequence. Leave one or two spaces between the state names or abbreviation and the ZIP Code.   (See Illustration 6–15.)

When the ZIP Code is known, use the two-letter abbreviation in all caps without punctuation.   If the ZIP Code is unavailable, call the post office if your office does not have a ZIP Code Directory.

For a small envelope, start the address lines 2″ from the top and 2½″ from the left edge.

For a large envelope, start the address lines 2½″ from the top and 4″ from the left edge.   (See Illustration 6–15.)

§ 6.134   Return Address

Start the return address on the second line from the top and three spaces from the left edge.

§ 6.135   Postal Notations

Type postal notations such as SPECIAL DELIVERY below the space required for the stamp.   (See Illustration 6–15.)

§ 6.136   Addressee Notations

Type HOLD FOR ARRIVAL, PERSONAL, PLEASE FORWARD, and the like, a triple space below the return address and three spaces from the left edge.

Illustration 6–15

COLVIN, MASON & NORMAN
Attorneys at Law
3005 East Skelly Avenue
Tulsa, Oklahoma 74106–6864   SPECIAL DELIVERY

HOLD FOR ARRIVAL

           ACCOUNTS PAYABLE
           XYZ CORPORATION
           10 ELM AVE
           ANYTOWN ST 01234–5678

---

§ 6.137   Automated Mail Processing

The United States Postal Service has an electronic scanner machine which speeds up the processing of the mail by rapidly reading and sorting the mail with an Optical Character Reader.

Getting your mail ready for machine processing actually involves few steps beyond what you are already doing. Most necessitate just a little more attention to detail. Here are the items to watch:

1. ZIP Codes

    ZIP Codes must be included in addresses, return addresses, and on pre-addressed business reply mail and should be placed right after the state name. An envelope address which lacks a ZIP Code is put aside until a post office employee can look it up and add it. This can delay a letter for several days.

2. Addresses
    (a) Addresses should be in block form with a uniform left margin.
    (b) Print the address in block-style type fonts, preferably in upper case letters without punctuation. Try to avoid use of italic, artistic, script, or proportionately spaced fonts.
    (c) In the last two lines of the address include only the street address or box number on the next-to-last line, and the city, state, and ZIP Code on the last line.

(d) Spell street, city, and state names correctly. Some equipment depends on finding an exact match of names with those already stored in memory.

(See Illustration 6–16.)

Illustration 6–16

SECRETARIAL ADDRESSING FOR AUTOMATION
(POST OFFICE RECOMMENDATION)

1. BASIC FORMAT

The address area should be in block form with all of the lines having a uniform left margin. It should be at least ⅝ inch up from the bottom of the envelope. No print should appear to the right or below it.

6. ACCOUNT NUMBERS, DATES, ATTENTION LINES, etc.

Enter these on any line of the address block above the second line from the bottom.

2. UNIT NUMBER

Mail addressed to occupants of multiunit buildings should include the number of the apartment, room, suit, or other unit The unit number should appear immediately after the street address on the same line never above, below, or in front of the street address.

ATTN MR C P JONES
GENERAL XYZ CORP
1000 MAIN ST ROOM 4325
DETROIT MI 48217–1234

5. STREET ADDRESS OR BOX NUMBER

These should be placed on the line immediately above the city, state, and ZIP Code. When indicating a box number at a particular station, the box number should precede the station name.

Correct spelling of street names is essential since some machines match the names in the address to those like it on the machine's memory.

4. WINDOW ENVELOPES

Inserts and envelopes must be matched so that the address will show through the window no matter how much the insert slides around in the envelope. There should be at least ¼ inch between the address and the left, right, and bottom edges of the window whatever the position of the insert.

3. CITY, STATE, AND ZIP CODE

These should appear in that sequence on the bottom line of the address block. This is where automatic sorting equipment is instructed to look for this information.

Mail presorted by ZIP Codes bypasses many processing steps in the post office and can get to its destination quicker.

FORMS OF ADDRESS

Addressee	Form of Address	Salutation
Federal, State, and Local Government Officials		
alderman or city councilman	The Honorable John Smith	Dear Mr. Smith:
cabinet officers (as the Secretary of State and the Attorney General)	The Honorable John Smith Secretary of State The Honorable John Smith Attorney General of the United States	Dear Mr. Smith:

chief justice, Supreme Court	The Chief Justice of the United States	Dear Mr. Chief Justice:
commissioner	The Honorable John Smith	Dear Mr. Smith:
former U.S. president	The Honorable John Smith	Dear Mr. Smith:
governor	The Honorable John Smith Governor of _____	Dear Governor Smith:
judge, federal	The Honorable John Smith United States District Judge	Dear Judge Smith:
judge, state or local	The Honorable John Smith Chief Judge of the Court of Appeals	Dear Judge Smith:
lieutenant governor	The Honorable John Smith Lieutenant Governor of _____	Dear Mr. Smith:
mayor	The Honorable John Smith Mayor of _____	Dear Mayor Smith:
president, U.S.	The President	Dear Mr. President:
representative, state (same format for assemblyman)	The Honorable John Smith House of Representatives State Capitol	Dear Mr. Smith:
representative, U.S.	The Honorable John Smith The United States House of Representatives	Dear Mr. Smith:
senator, state	The Honorable John Smith The State Senate State Capitol	Dear Senator Smith:
senator, U.S.	The Honorable John Smith United States Senate	Dear Senator Smith:
speaker, U.S. House of Representatives	The Honorable John Smith Speaker of the House of Representatives	Dear Mr. Speaker:
vice-president, U.S.	The Vice President United States Senate	Dear Mr. Vice President:

Clerical and Religious Orders

archbishop	The Most Reverend Archbishop of _____ or The Most Reverend John Smith Archbishop of _____	Your Excellency: Dear Archbishop Smith:
bishop, Catholic	The Most Reverend John Smith Bishop of _____	Your Excellency: Dear Bishop Smith:
bishop, Episcopal	The Right Reverend John Smith Bishop of _____	Right Reverend Sir: Dear Bishop Smith:
bishop, other denomination(s)	The Reverend John Smith	Reverend Sir:

		Dear Bishop Smith:
cardinal	His Eminence John Cardinal Smith	Your Eminence:
		Dear Cardinal Smith:
clergyman, Protestant	The Reverend John Smith	Dear Mr. Smith:
	or	Dear Sir:
	The Reverend Dr. John Smith (if having a doctor's degree)	or Dear Dr. Smith:
dean (of a cathedral)	The Very Reverend John Smith	Very Reverend Sir:
	or	
	Dear John Smith	Dear Dean Smith:
monsignor	The Right Reverend Monsignor Smith	Dear Monsignor Smith:
patriarch (of an Eastern church)	His Beatitude the Patriarch of _____	Most Reverend Lord:
pope	His Holiness Pope _____	Your Holiness:
	or	or
	His Holiness the Pope	Most Holy Father:
priest	The Reverend Father Smith	Dear Father Smith:
	or	
	The Reverend John Smith	Dear Father:
rabbi	Rabbi John Smith	Dear Rabbi Smith:
	or	or
	Rabbi John Smith, D.D. (if having a doctor's degree)	Dear Dr. Smith:
sisterhood, member of	Sister Mary Angelica, S.C.	Dear Sister Mary Angelica: Dear Sister:
sisterhood, superior of	The Reverend Mother Superior, S.C.	Reverend Mother: Dear Reverend Mother:

College and University Officials

dean of a college or university	Dean John Smith	Dear Dean Smith:
president of a college or university	President John Smith	Dear President Smith:
professor at a college or university	Professor John Smith	Dear Professor Smith:
administrator at a college or university	Robert K. Wales, Ph.D.	Dear Dr. Wales:

Miscellaneous Professional Ranks and Titles

attorney	Mr. John Smith Attorney at Law or John Smith, Esq.	Dear Mr. Smith:
dentist	John Smith, D.D.S. (office address) or	Dear Dr. Smith:

	Dr. John Smith (home address)	
physician	John Smith, M.D. (office address)	Dear Dr. Smith:
	or	
	Dr. John Smith (home address)	
veterinarian	John Smith, D.V.M. (office address)	Dear Dr. Smith:
	or	
	Dr. John Smith (home address)	

§ 6.138 Memo Format

Most organizations have memo forms printed, carrying the company name and the designation that it is a memorandum. If your organization does not have a printed form, it is easy to set one up when you need one. There are four basic elements you must include in your form:

TO:

FROM:

DATE:

SUBJECT:

These words should be typed in all caps followed by a colon. The arrangement is optional. The elements can be divided with two positioned on the left side and two at the center, or all four can be listed at the left margin. Double spacing should set them apart to allow space for long names, titles, addresses, etc.

Write dates just as you would in a letter.

When you address your memo, use a professional title for the addressee, such as Dr., but you may omit Mr., Mrs., Ms., or Miss. If your organization is large, you may wish to add the addressee's title, room number, or other identification for faster delivery.

If your memo is being sent to a number of people, opposite the "TO" type "See below." Then at the bottom of the memo, include the names at the left margin. If you have only one *cc* notation, include it directly underneath the addressee's name. If additional *cc's* are sent, because of space you will need to place these after the body of the memo just as you would for a letter.

On the "FROM" line, the writer does not include a courtesy title before his name, but might include a job title, department, or some other information. An additional courtesy item would be to include the writer's telephone extension number.

The subject line should be filled in with as few words as possible. Style may vary; however, most subject lines have only the first letter of the first subject word capitalized.

The body or message should start three or four spaces below the subject line. Use single spacing unless your message is very, very short. Organizations usually have both short and long memo forms. If a short memo (8½ × 5½) is available, it will look best if single-spaced. Paragraphs may be blocked or indented. In either paragraph style you should leave one space between paragraphs.

Complimentary closings are omitted in memos, but many people prefer to have the initials or full name typed below the message. Others feel it is unnecessary to repeat the reference to the writer when his name appears at the beginning of the memo.

§ 6.139 Facsimile or Fax

Facsimile or fax machines are electronic machines used to transmit over standard phone lines reproduced images of documents or photographs. The machine optically scans the document to be sent and converts the image into digitized data that is transmitted by means of a modem over the phone to a compatible fax machine on the receiving end which converts the data back into its original image. Plug-in circuit boards are also available for personal computers. With the speed and ease of a phone call, documents are now transmitted by fax to anywhere in the world within a few minutes rather than taking days by mail.

§ 6.140 Teleconferencing

Teleconferencing once meant more than two persons sharing a phone conversation. Today, however, it includes video conference with the use of computers and television cameras to transmit the video images and sound to others at remote locations. The video image is not as clear as television for moving objects. Video conferencing is used to transmit and receive video and audio signals over standard communication channels.

§ 6.141 Voice Mail

Voice mail is the ability to leave a message, similar to leaving a message on an answering machine. The message is digitized so that it can be stored on a disk like other computer data. This allows the receiver to hear the message later (by reconverting it to an audio form) and, if desired, to add comments and forward the message to someone else who has access to the voice mail system.

§ 6.142 Summary

Skilled writers are highly valuable in any business. The reason is obvious. The spoken word evaporates in air; the written word stands as a permanent testimony. That is why in business where large sums of money hinge on people's understanding each other—to produce items, deliver goods, promote goodwill, or render services—the accurately written word is essential.

Writing is affected by your environment, education, and intelligence. You can LEARN to write competently if you desire to do so, receive proper instruction and supervision, and then continue to practice in improving the skill. You should also realize that you can handicap yourself by depending upon certain skills and techniques that may be obsolete. You should be curious, interested, and flexible enough to adapt to changes in forms, formats, and the mechanics of written communications.

CHAPTER 7

PREPARATION OF LEGAL DOCUMENTS

Table of Sections

---

§ 7.1 Introduction

The competent legal secretary takes pride in her work product. It reflects on her, the attorney, and the law firm. Her typewritten documents are neat, unsmudged, and attractively arranged on the page; they conform to the specifications of the courts for preparation of documents; they have been proofread and contain no misspelled words.

You should understand the contents of legal documents. If you do, you can catch errors in grammar or content. If the attorney has dictated "plaintiff" when he means "defendant," you should correct it.

An excellent background in the mechanics of English grammar and in punctuation techniques is essential. Punctuation in legal documents should be logical and conform to general standards of punctuation; however, some attorneys have very definite ideas about the use of punctuation and dictate all commas and other marks of punctuation.

If the office has a procedures manual, you should read it and then consult it often for office format in preparing letters and court and non-court documents. Most states have a prescribed procedure for the preparation of documents, and the secretary should read this carefully. When in doubt, consult a good legal procedures book.

If you are working from a previously prepared document and find errors in format, do not perpetuate the errors. Just because the office "has always done it that way" does not make it correct. Of course, there are many ways of doing things, all of which may be equally correct. It may be different from the way you have done it before, but it is still correct. So, before you make any sweeping changes, make sure that the difference is an error and not just a difference in procedure.

A common error in legal documents is the repetition of the word "that" when introducing a phrase or clause having intervening words coming between the conjunction "that" and the remainder of the clause.

EXAMPLES:

Incorrect: "I know that in spite of all the errors that I have made in my marriage thus far, that my husband will give me another chance."

Correct: "I know that in spite of all the errors I have made in my marriage, my husband will give me another chance."

There are many pairs of words that sound alike or very nearly alike but which convey completely different meanings.

EXAMPLES:

Affect/effect, advise/advice, principal/principle, proximate/approximate, praecipe/recipe, and abjure/adjure. Make sure that the word you use is the correct one by checking the meaning of the sentence. When in doubt, check the dictionary.

Following are some general procedures used in preparing legal documents.

§ 7.2 Paper and Number of Copies

Generally, bond paper is used for the original copy and a lighter weight paper is used for copies. The usual practice is to prepare one original and make any copies needed on the copying machine. Most court systems, whether local, state, or federal, now require all documents filed to be on 8½– by 11–inch paper. Ascertain the size of the paper required for the court in which you plan to file the document. Because of this court requirement, many law offices now use the 8½– by 11–inch paper for the preparation of all noncourt documents also.

When preparing court papers, determine the number of copies to be made as follows: original for the court, a copy for each attorney representing a party to the action, a file copy, and a copy for the client (if this is office practice). If this is the first time you have prepared a document of this type, make a copy for the form file.

When preparing noncourt papers, prepare a copy for any party signing the papers as well as a file copy. In some instances it is necessary for the parties to sign more than one copy. The original and one or more of the copies will be designated as duplicate or triplicate originals. These will be executed just as the original and will be treated in all respects as original copies.

When the attorney dictates material or asks you to prepare a document, he will usually tell you how many copies to make. He may ask for "two plus four," meaning an original, a duplicate original (a copy), and four copies. Alternatively, he might request one plus two which means an original and two copies. Some offices make it a practice to keep a photocopy of all executed documents if a signed original will not be retained.

§ 7.3 Margins

Documents typed on legal-size paper are bound at the top. Those on letter-size paper are bound either at the left or at the top. Some papers are not bound but are stapled in the upper left-hand corner only. Use a one-inch margin at the top of the page and start the text on line 7.

If the office uses ruled legal paper (legal cap), the left margin should be one or two spaces to the right of the ruled line. The right margin should be a justified margin.

The bottom margin should also be one inch. If using legal cap, type a test copy to determine your margins. All documents should begin on the same line space from the top and end on the same line space from the bottom. This format should be followed whenever

NALS, Car.Leg.Sec. 3rd Ed.—8

possible. The documents look neater and there is no question about inserted lines.

When typing on plain letter-size paper, use the margins as mentioned above. The legal secretary should avoid excessive use of hyphenation. Do not hyphenate the last word on a page.

§ 7.4 Tab Settings

A ten-space paragraph indention is usually used on legal documents. Set a tab at this position and subsequent tabs at five-space intervals. These stops will be convenient and useful in typing subheadings.

§ 7.5 Spacing

Generally, all legal documents and court papers are double spaced. Some material within the document, such as property descriptions and quotations, is usually indented and single spaced. An acknowledgment or verification at the end of a document may be single spaced depending on office preference. Caution: do not begin a new page with the signature line, separating it from the text. Adjust the lines accordingly.

After typing the court heading on a document, double space to the caption. After the caption, double space to the body of the court document.

§ 7.6 Incomplete Pages

A paragraph that is divided at the bottom of a page should have at least two lines of the paragraph on the end of the page and at least two lines at the top of the next page. A three-line paragraph should not be divided.

At least two lines of the body of the document in addition to the testimonium clause (paragraph just before the signatures) must be on the page with the signatures. This occasionally presents a problem. If you are working from a rough draft, it is relatively easy to plan for the signatures. If not, you may have to insert a hard return on the appropriate line in order that at least two lines move to the following page.

There are several ways to adjust the page or pages prior to the signatures either to get the signatures on the page or some of the body of the document onto the page with the signatures:

• Use wider top and bottom margins.

• Shorten the lines slightly, thereby creating an additional line.

- If one line has only one word on it, move that word up to the line above by lengthening the lines.

- Leave less space between the signatures or between the testimonium clause and the signatures.

- It is also possible to put half of the signature lines on the left side of the page and half of them on the right side of the page rather than aligning them vertically on the right side of the page.

Some offices use a Z line for incomplete pages. A Z line or Z rule is used to cover the blank space at the end of a page so that no material can be inserted between the last line of typing and the beginning of the next page. (See Illustration 7–1.) With the use of word processing equipment, which makes it easier to retype a page, this practice is fading from use. Most offices prefer to retype and balance out the pages rather than use a Z line.

Illustration 7–1

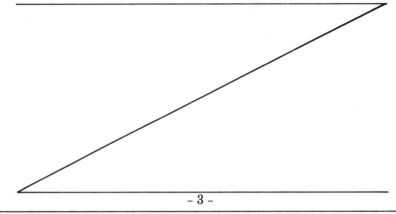

    7. Employee agrees that neither during nor after his employment with DANIEL MANUFACTURING, neither directly nor indirectly, will he reveal or furnish any information relating to the business or transactions of DANIEL MANUFACTURING. Employee further agrees never to divulge the names or addresses of any of the customers of DANIEL MANUFACTURING nor any details of any business transactions or negotiations with customers or suppliers and that he will treat all trade secrets as confidential and never will, either during or after his employment with

– 3 –

DANIEL MANUFACTURING, reveal to any person or business entity such trade secrets.

    IN WITNESS WHEREOF, the parties have signed this agreement the day and year first above written.

DANIEL MANUFACTURING

By_____
Vice President

_____
Employee

§ 7.7 Typing Drafts

    Drafts are typed on inexpensive paper. The word DRAFT as well as the date should be typed at the top of the page. When possible, double spacing is used for drafts so that revisions and corrections can be made. However, any material directly copied from another source, such as a citation, can be single spaced because it will not be revised.

Speed and accuracy are more important than neatness on drafts. The lawyer expects to make changes on the draft. However, he also expects that what has been typed is accurate. So be careful about citations, numbers, names, descriptions, and the like. If you make a draft of the revised first draft, mark it SECOND DRAFT and date it so that the two will not get mixed up.

§ 7.8   Signatures

The testimonium clause is the last paragraph on a legal document (noncourt) before the signatures.

EXAMPLE:

"IN WITNESS WHEREOF, the parties hereto have hereunto set their hands the day and year first above written."

If the testimonium clause states that the parties have "set their hands and seals," you know that the document is to be sealed. In the case of a corporation, the corporate seal would be affixed.

EXAMPLE:

"IN WITNESS WHEREOF, the parties hereto have caused this instrument to be executed properly the day and year first above written."

Not all states require corporations to have seals, so that if the corporation does not have a seal, only the signature of the person signing for the corporation will appear.

EXAMPLE (for individual signature lines):

_____ L.S.

or _____ (SEAL)

The document itself gives you the clue as to who will sign it. Prepare the proper number of signature lines. Usually three or four line spaces between lines is sufficient. However, two-line spaces would also be permissible if necessary to conserve space. The standard seems to be whatever permits sufficient space for the signature.

Under each line is usually typed the designation of the signing party, such as "seller," "lessee," and the like. Some offices prefer to have the name of the party typed below the line, along with the designation.

EXAMPLE: _____

E.G. Smith, Lessor

This is useful for the persons signing the document. They are less likely to sign the wrong line.

When a corporation is a party to an instrument, the instrument is signed in the name of the corporation. On the left hand side of the page, type "(CORP. SEAL)" in all caps. On the same line, space to the center of the page and type the name of the corporation; return to the left side of the page after spacing down two lines and type "ATTEST:" in all caps; space down two more lines and set up the signature line by aligning it under the corporation name. Return to the left side of the page after spacing down one line and type another signature line. Space to the center of the page, which should place you under the signature line for the corporation, and type the name of the officer, if known, and "President." Return to the left side of the page, which should place you under the second signature line, and type the word "Secretary." If you know the name, type it in.

EXAMPLE:

(Corp. Seal)   ABC CORPORATION

ATTEST:

_____   By: _____
Jane Jones, Secretary   Mary Smith, President

§ 7.9 Collating

Collating is the process of placing the pages of a document in proper sequence. Many copying machines have the collating feature. If not, you must do it manually.

§ 7.10 Executing Documents

Executing a document is a term used for signing the document. It includes the procedure of affixing a seal if required, acknowledgment, and notarization. The latter two steps are described in the section on notaries public in The Law Office chapter. To be legally binding, a document must bear the signatures of the parties named in the document. When the document is properly signed, it is said that it has been executed, and it is then legally enforceable.

§ 7.11 Conforming

Every copy of a document must contain all of the information that has been written, stamped, or typed on the original after the documents were prepared. This is an important responsibility of the legal secretary. You type in the name as it is written on the original and precede the name with an "s" inside two diagonal marks. Some firms make a photocopy of the executed document and use it for the file copy. This should have "COPY" stamped on it so it will not be confused with the original executed document.

EXAMPLE: /s/ Sarah Bridger

§ 7.12 Date Blanks

When preparing a document, you do not know the exact date on which it will be executed. Therefore, you must leave the date blank. The usual procedure is to leave a space sufficient to insert a date.

EXAMPLE: the   day of July, 19___
          or the _____ day of July, 19___

Six spaces are left so that there would be a space before the day, four spaces for the day and ordinal ending (12th), and a space following the day. Some firms prefer to have lines instead of blank spaces. A line ending in a space is hard to recognize and may be overlooked in executing the document. If it is near the end of the month and you do not know in which month the document will be executed, leave sufficient space for the name of the longer month.

§ 7.13 Legal Backs

In some states all legal documents, including court documents, must have legal backing. This is a heavy sheet of paper, longer than the document, and often of colored stock. The extra length of the backing sheet ($^3/_4$ to 1″) is folded over at the top, and the document is inserted under the fold and stapled into the backing sheet with two staples about ½ inch from the top. Often, on one-fourth of the backing sheet is typed the name of the parties, date of execution, and the printed name and address of the law firm. Office file copies are not backed.

In most states a legal backing sheet is used for noncourt documents. The backing sheet offers protection for the document as well as identification when the document is folded.

§ 7.14 Law Blanks (Printed Forms)

The use of law blanks varies from state to state. All states use some printed forms and fill in the variable information. Law blanks are used less and less, yielding to forms in the computer. Material typed on printed forms is generally single spaced due to the space restrictions on the form. Be very careful when preparing printed forms. Read through the form carefully, filling in all blanks. It is easy to miss a small space after a partial word, such as ha___; either an "s" or "ve" must be filled in to make a complete verb. Also punctuate the law blank just as if it were typed completely. Too often secretaries fill in the blank and do not place a comma or period after the entered material, although they would have done so if they had typed the whole document. Law blanks should be punctuated just as accurately as typed papers.

§ 7.15 Capitalization

It is traditional that certain phrases and words are typed in solid caps.

- IN WITNESS WHEREOF,
- THIS INDENTURE,
- FOR VALUE RECEIVED,
- RESOLVED,
- WHEREAS,
- NOW, THEREFORE,
- WHEREFORE,
- KNOW ALL PERSONS BY THESE PRESENTS,
- THIS AGREEMENT

You capitalize the same words in legal documents that you do in regular typewritten work. Proper nouns and words beginning sentences are capitalized. In addition, in legal papers other words may be capitalized. When "court" refers to the courtroom or the organization dealing with a matter, the word is not capitalized. When you refer to a specific court by title, it is capitalized. When court means the judge hearing the case, it is capitalized. For example, "The Court hereby orders" would mean that the judge does the ordering. If you can substitute "judge" for "court" and retain the meaning, you will generally capitalize "Court."

In many offices whenever a party's name is mentioned in a document or pleading, it is typed in solid caps. Some secretaries capitalize the first letter of "plaintiff" and "defendant" when they are used in the document without a proper name following the designation. Some attorneys prefer that the name of one document be capitalized when referred to in another document, such as "in answer to the Complaint filed herein." Other offices do not capitalize in that instance. One method is probably no more correct than the other. The principal thing to remember is that you must be consistent throughout the document. Establish the rule for yourself and follow it in all instances.

"City," "County," and "State" are not capitalized as in the following expression: city of Idaho Falls, county of Bonneville, state of Idaho. Unless directed otherwise, you should not capitalize these words.

§ 7.16 Numbers and Amounts of Money

The term "words and figures" is used in dictation by attorneys when they want the secretary to type a number or amount of money in words followed by the figures in parentheses.

EXAMPLE:

"Under the age of twenty-one (21) years."

Money is written with the initial letter of the major words being capitalized. Some offices prefer not to include the cents fraction if the dollar amount is even.

EXAMPLE:

Twenty-five Thousand Dollars ($25,000)

Twenty-five Thousand and no/100 Dollars ($25,000.00).

The rule to remember is that the material in the parentheses summarizes what precedes the parentheses.

Incorrect: Twenty-five Thousand Dollars ($25,000.00) (The parentheses show the cents fraction but the preceding words do not.)

Correct: Twenty-five Thousand Dollars ($25,000)

Occasionally, you will see the following expression of money.

Incorrect: Twenty-five Thousand and no/100 ($25,000.00) Dollars (This is incorrect because the word "Dollars" comes after the parentheses but is included in the $ sign in the parentheses.)

Correct: Twenty-five Thousand and no/100 Dollars ($25,000.00)

§ 7.17 Legal Citations

A citation is a legal authority, such as a constitution, a statute, a case, or other authoritative source, which is used to support a written legal document.

A brief is a memorandum of the material facts, the issues, the applicable law, and an argument to show the court how the law applies to the facts supporting the client's position and the law of the case.

The contents of a brief are the responsibility of the lawyer. The secretary is responsible for typing the brief in an attractive and accurate manner. She must be knowledgeable regarding correct citation practices, including proper abbreviations, punctuation, capitalization, etc.

Although all legal secretaries may not type briefs, citations also appear in correspondence, in written advice to clients, and in the preparation of a case for trial. Therefore, all legal secretaries should be familiar with correct citation practice.

After typing any citation, it is important that you check your work very carefully. Since an incorrect citation is unforgivable, all citations should be verified with their actual sources. No matter how attractive your brief or legal opinion is, the effectiveness of its attractiveness is lost if it contains an incorrect citation. Judges expect accuracy in the briefs they read and look upon incorrect citations with great disfavor. The importance of checking all citations cannot be overemphasized. The legal secretary is in a position to save the attorney embarrassment by verifying every citation that leaves the office.

A Uniform System of Citation (15th ed. 1991), compiled by the editors of the Columbia Law Review, the Harvard Law Review, the University of Pennsylvania Law Review, and The Yale Law Journal (often referred to as "The Bluebook"), is the most widely accepted guide for legal citations. An excellent course book on legal citation and style is *Citing & Typing the Law, A Course on Legal Citation & Style,* by C. Edward Good, who used The Bluebook as his authority.

Some states have developed their own citation practices, which should be followed where appropriate. The important thing is to be consistent, particularly within any one brief. It should be noted, however, that the name of the case must ALWAYS be underscored or italicized.

Other helpful handbooks are *Citations Manual* by Norma Jean Miles, Certified PLS, which is published by the National Association of Legal Secretaries, and the *United States Government Printing Office Style Manual,* which is available from the Superintendent of Documents, U.S. Government Printing Office, Washington, D.C. 20402.

§ 7.18 Order of Citations

If one authority is more helpful or authoritative than the others, it should be listed first. Otherwise, they should be in the following order:

1. Cases—in reverse chronological order
    a. Federal
        i. Supreme Court
        ii. Courts of Appeals
        iii. District Courts
        iv. Claims Court
        v. Specialty Courts
        vi. Bankruptcy appellate panels and judges
        vii. Administrative agencies (alphabetically by agency)

    b. State
        i. Courts (alphabetically by state and then by rank within each state)
       ii. Agencies (alphabetically by state and then by rank within each state)
    c. Foreign

2. Constitutions (federal, state [alphabetically], and then foreign [alphabetically by jurisdiction])

3. Statutes (federal, state, and foreign)

4. Treaties and other international agreements

5. Legislative materials

6. Administrative and executive materials

7. Records, briefs, and petitions (in that order)

8. Secondary materials
    a. Books and essays
    b. Articles
    c. Student-written law review materials
    d. Signed book reviews
    e. Student-written book notes
    f. Newspapers
    g. Annotations
    h. Unpublished materials and other materials of limited circulation.

§ 7.19 Citation Sentences

When joining citations in a sentence, begin with a capital letter, separate individual citations by means of a semicolon, and end with a period.

EXAMPLE:

    McClanahan v. American Gilsonite Co., 494 F. Supp. 1334 (D. Colo. 1980); *Shibuya v. Architects of Hawaii, Ltd.,* 647 P.2d 276 (Hawaii 1982); *Kallas Millwork Corp. v. Square D Co.,* 225 N.W.2d 454 (Wis. 1975); *Phillips v. ABC Builders Inc.,* 611 P.2d 821 (Wyo. 1980).

§ 7.20 Elements of Case Citations

A complete citation contains:
1. The volume number of source in Arabic numerals;
2. The abbreviated name of the volume;
3. The page upon which the cite begins;

4. Parenthetical information which identifies the court making the decision and the date of the decision: *Wyant v. SCM Corp.,* 692 S.W.2d 814 (Ky. Ct. App. 1985).

In addition, many citations include the following information:

- A "pinpoint cite" or "page cite" (page(s) particularly referred to): *Curtiss v. Hubbard,* 703 P.2d 1154, 1155 (Alaska 1985).
- A parallel citation—official reporter first: *State v. Reed,* 237 Kan. 685, 703 P.2d 756 (1985).
- Other parenthetical information regarding the decision (in parentheses): *State v. Story,* 646 S.W.2d 68 (Mo. 1983) (en banc); *State v. Brewer,* 247 N.W.2d 205 (Iowa 1976) (maximum age of 65 is reasonable limitation).
- Subsequent case history: *Daniel v. International Brotherhood of Teamsters,* 561 F.2d 1223 (7th Cir. 1977), *rev'd on other grounds,* 439 U.S. 551 (1979).
- Other related authority: *Memphis Bank & Trust Co. v. Garner,* 459 U.S. 392 (1983) (construing 31 U.S.C. § 742).

§ 7.21 Case Material

The full case name appears at the beginning of an opinion in the official reporter. In citations in text the case names should be altered as follows:

1. If a case is a consolidation of two or more actions, cite only the first listed parties:

EXAMPLE:

Keller v. Holiday Inns, Inc., NOT *Keller v. Holiday Inns, Inc.* and *Burman v. Holiday Inns, Inc.*

2. Omit all parties but the first listed on each side:

EXAMPLE:

Porter v. Johnson, NOT *Porter et al. v. Johnson et al.*

3. Abbreviate "on the relation of," "for the use of," "on behalf of," etc., to "ex rel." Do not omit the first-listed relator or any part of a partnership name.

EXAMPLES:

State ex rel. Clark v. Pratt, NOT *State v. Pratt* or *State ex rel. Clark, Wilson & West.*

Hochfelder v. Ernst & Ernst, NOT *Hochfelder v. Ernst.*

4. Abbreviate "in the matter of" and "petition of" to "in re."

EXAMPLE:

In re Cooper.

5.   When adversary parties are named, omit all procedural phrases except "ex rel."

EXAMPLE:

Cooper v. Harris, NOT *In re Cooper v. Harris,* BUT *Idaho ex rel. Evans v. Oregon.*

6.   Do not abbreviate the first word of a party's name unless the full name of a party can be abbreviated by commonly known initials.

EXAMPLE:

Blackstone Co. v. NLRB, NOT *Blackstone Co. v. National Labor Relations Board.*

7.   In briefs and memoranda do not otherwise abbreviate words in case names except for "Co.," "Corp.," "Inc.," "Ltd.," "No.," and " & ."

8.   Omit given names or initials of individuals except in names of business firms.

EXAMPLES:

Chavez v. Chenoveth.

Carley v. A.H. Robins Co.

9.   Omit "The" as the first word of a party name except as the part of the name of the object of an in rem action or in cases in which "The King" or "The Queen" is a party.

EXAMPLE:

The Steamer Daniel Ball v. United States.

10.   Do not omit any part of a surname made up of more than one word.

EXAMPLE:

Van DeVelde v. Running Wolf.

11.   Given names that follow, rather than precede, a surname should be retained.   Retain the full name where the name is entirely in a language in which the surname is given first.   If in doubt about a foreign name, use the name under which it is indexed in the reporter.

EXAMPLE:

Chun Ming v. Kam Hee Ho.

12. Omit "City of" and like expressions unless the expression begins a party name.

EXAMPLE:

Johnson v. Mayor of Clarkston, NOT *Johnson v. Mayor of City of Clarkston,* BUT *Schmidt v. City of Clarkston.*

13. Omit "State of," "Commonwealth of," and "People of" except in citing decisions of the courts of that state, in which case only "State," "Commonwealth," or "People" should be retained.

EXAMPLES:

People v. Lucky (when cited in California).

California v. Lucky (when cited outside California).

14. In business firm designations omit "Inc.," Ltd.," etc., if the name also contains the word "Co.," "Bros.," "Ass'n," etc., indicating the party is a business firm.

EXAMPLE:

Land v. Twin City Insurance Co., NOT *Land v. Twin City Insurance Co., Inc.*

15. Omit such terms as "administrator," "appellee," "executor," etc., that describe a party already named.

EXAMPLES:

Gold v. Sullivan, NOT *Gold, Trustee v. Sullivan, Executor.*

Silkwood v. Kerr–McGee Corp., NOT *Silkwood, Administrator v. Kerr–McGee Corp.*

16. "Estate of" and "Will of" are not omitted.

EXAMPLE:

In re Estate of Freeburn.

17. Phrases or party names that would aid in identification of the case may be appended in parentheses after the formal case name.

EXAMPLE:

Morse v. Barnard (In re Ramsey) [bankruptcy proceeding].

18. When referring to a railroad company omit "Co." unless the full party name in the official report is "Railroad Co."

EXAMPLE:

Burlington Northern Railroad v. United States.

19. Omit all prepositional phrases of location not following "City," etc., unless the omission would leave only one word in the name of a party or of a corporate or other entity.

EXAMPLES:

Hall v. Department of Human Resources, NOT *Hall v. Department of Human Resources of State of Oregon.*

Chavez v. Industrial Commission, NOT *Chavez v. The Industrial Commission of Arizona.*

City of Somewhere v. Thomas.

20. Include designations of national or larger geographical areas except in union names, but omit "of America" after "United States." NEVER abbreviate "United States" when it stands for "United States of America."

EXAMPLES:

Smith v. Prudential Insurance Co. of America.

United States v. Widgets of America.

21. Commissioner of Internal Revenue is cited simply as "Commissioner."

22. A union name should be cited exactly as given in the official report except that only the smallest unit should be cited. All industry designations except the first full one should be omitted, and all prepositional phrases of location should be omitted. Widely recognized abbreviations (CIA, UAW, etc.) may be used.

EXAMPLE:

International Brotherhood of Teamsters v. NLRB, NOT *International Brotherhood of Teamsters, Chauffeurs, Warehousemen & Helpers of America v. NLRB.*

23. Case names may be abbreviated more extensively in footnotes to save space. Acceptable abbreviations are listed in The Bluebook. Remember, NEVER abbreviate United States.

EXAMPLE:

Pennsylvania Nat'l Mut. Casualty Co.

§ 7.22   Federal Court Cases

Federal court cases should be cited as follows:

- United States Supreme Court: *Hunter v. Erickson,* 303 U.S. 385, 89 S. Ct. 557, 21 L. Ed. 2d 616 (1969). A recent unreported case may be cited as *United States v. Leon,* ___ U.S. ___ (No. 86–1771, decided July 5, 1987).

- United States Court of Appeals: *Haley v. United States,* 739 F.2d 1502 (10th Cir. 1984).

- United States District Court: *Brady v. Hopper,* 570 F. Supp. 1333 (D. Colo. 1983). A recent unreported case may be cited as *Hawks v. Ingersoll Johnson Steel Co.,* U.S. District Court, S.D. Ind., No. IP 82–793–C, Apr. 4, 1984, OR *Perry v. Rockwell Graphic Systems,* ___ F.Supp. ___ (D. Mass. 1985).

§ 7.23 State Court Cases

In briefs and memorandums to be filed in state courts, cases should be cited to both the official reports (*United States Reports, Washington Reports,* etc.) and the unofficial reports (*Supreme Court Reports, Pacific Reporter, Atlantic Reporter,* etc.).

EXAMPLE:

> *Quinn v. Southern Pacific Transportation Co.,* 76 Or. App. 617, 711 P.2d 139 (1986).

If your state does not publish an official reporter or has adopted the unofficial National Reporter System as its official reporter, the court must be identified in parentheses at the end of the citation, followed by the year of the decision.

EXAMPLE:

> *State v. Twoteeth,* 711 P.2d 789, 794 (Mont. 1985).

When the court report identifies the state but not the court, the state abbreviation may be omitted in the parenthetical.

EXAMPLE:

> *Lang v. Lang,* 109 Idaho 802, 711 P.2d 1322 (Ct. App. 1985).

Only the jurisdiction must appear at the end of the citation if the court of decision is the highest court thereof.

EXAMPLE:

> *Miller v. Ottman,* 136 N.E.2d 17 (Ind. 1956).

If the jurisdiction is not the court of decision, cite as follows:

EXAMPLE:

> *Mathes v. Ireland,* 419 N.E.2d 782 (Ind. App. 1981).

If the decision has just been filed and it does not appear in the state reporter, it may be cited in one of the following ways:

EXAMPLE:

> *Wing v. Martin,* 688 P.2d 1172 (Idaho 1984), OR *Wing v. Martin,* ___ Idaho ___, 688 P.2d 1172 (1984), OR *Wing v. Martin,* 84 Idaho Supreme Court Reports [I.S.C.R. when cited in Idaho] 1117, 688 P.2d 1172 (Idaho 1984).

If the advance sheets are not yet available, cite as follows:

EXAMPLE:

> *Wing v. Martin,* No. 14790, Idaho Supreme Court (Sept. 25, 1984), OR *Wing v. Martin,* ___ Idaho ___ (1984).

§ 7.24 Citation of Constitutions, Statutes, Session Laws, Ordinances, Rules, Etc.

The following are the accepted formats of citing the various authorities:

- Constitutions
  U.S. Const. art. II, § 4.
  U.S. Const. amend. XIV, § 1.
  Idaho Const. art. I, § 3.
- Federal Statutes
  Official Code: 28 U.S.C. § 2105(a)(1)–(3) (1964).
  Uniform Commercial Code: U.C.C. § 4–109 (1962).
  Code of Federal Regulations: 24 C.F.R. § 202.13 (1949).
  Internal Revenue Code: Int. Rev. Code of 1986; § 12.
- State Statutes

Since the statutes are not cited the same in all states, consult the most recent edition of *A Uniform System of Citation* for the correct way to cite state statutes. An example of a citation to your own state statutes should be placed in your procedures manual for future reference.

EXAMPLE:

> Wyo. Stat. § 7–13–904 (1977).

- Session Laws
  United States Statutes at Large: Federal Land Policy and Management Act of 1976, 90 Stat. 2769, 43 U.S.C. § 1744 (1982).

Since the state session laws are not cited the same in all states, consult the tables in the The Bluebook for the correct way to cite your state session laws and type the correct citation in your procedures manual for future reference.

EXAMPLES:

> Act of July 1, 1972, ch. 202, 1972 Idaho Sess. Laws 535.
> Michigan Sesquicentennial Act of 1984, Pub. Act No. 266, 1984 Mich. Legis. Serv. 37 (West).
> • Ordinances

Cite by name of code (including municipal unit, not abbreviated, followed by state, abbreviated), section, and year of publication of the code.

EXAMPLE:

> Chicago, Ill., Municipal Code § 155–1 (1931).
> • Miscellaneous Codes
> Model Penal Code § 303.5 (1962).
> • Restatements
> Restatement (Second) of Torts § 324A.
> • Federal Rules
> Federal Rules of Civil Procedure: Fed. R. Civ. P. 23(b).
> Federal Rules of Criminal Procedure: Fed. R. Crim. P. 12.
> • State Rules

Consult your own state code to determine the correct way to cite the civil, criminal, and appellate rules in your state.

> • Jury Instructions

Citation forms are usually suggested in the volumes cited. If you are going to cite a jury instruction in a foreign jurisdiction, a more detailed citation must be given for state jury instructions.

EXAMPLES:

> Ninth Circuit Court: Model Jury Instr., 9th Cir. 3.08.
> California Jury Instructions: BAJI (6th ed.) No. 4.01; CALJIC (4th ed.) No. 7.07.
> Illinois Jury Instructions: IPI—Criminal 3d 20.02.
> • Legislative Materials
> Bills

> > Senate Bill: S. 507, 94th Cong., 1st Sess. § 311 (1975).

House Bill: H.R. 507, 95th Cong., 1st Sess. (1977).

Resolutions

Senate Resolution: S. Res. 50, 99th Cong., 1st Sess. (1983).

House Resolution: H.R. Res. 50, 98th Cong., 1st Sess. (1983).

• Committee Hearings

Give title of hearing (underlined) and add which Congress, which session, page, date, and attribution.

EXAMPLE:

Age Discrimination in Employment: Hearings on S. 830 and S. 788 before the Subcommittee on Labor of the Senate Committee on Labor and Public Welfare, 90th Cong., 1st Sess. 23 (1967) (statement of Sen. Javits).

• Committee Reports
Senate Report: S. Rep. No. 583, 94th Cong., 1st Sess. 65 (1975).

EXAMPLE:

Criminal Code Reform Act of 1977: Report of the Committee on the Judiciary, United States Senate, to accompany S. 1437, S. Rep. No. 605, 95th Cong., 1st Sess. 911 (1977).

House Report: H.R. Rep. No. 1724, 94th Cong., 2d Sess. 62 (1976).

H.R. Rep. No. 805, 90th Cong., 1st Sess. 4 (1967), 123 Cong. Rec. 34295 (1977) (remarks of Sen. Williams).

H.R. Rep. No. 867, 97th Cong., 2d Sess. 7, *reprinted in* 1982 U.S. Code Cong. & Ad. News 3362.

• Floor Debates
124 Cong. Rec. 8218–8219 (1978) (remarks of Sen. Javits).
• Congressional Records (daily edition)

130 Cong. Rec. H1847–48 (daily ed. Mar. 21, 1984) (statement of Rep. Kindness).

• Dictionaries
Black's Law Dictionary 912 (6th ed. 1991).
Stedman's Medical Dictionary 783 (4th Unabridged Lawyers' Ed. 1976).
7 Am. Jur. Proof of Facts *Last Clear Chance* (Supp. 1990 at 45).
49 Am. Jur. 2d *Eviction* § 300 (1970).

86 C.J.S. *Torts* § 61 n. 9.
• Treatises

Cite by volume (use Arabic numerals); author (initial and last name); full title; serial number (if any); page, section, or paragraph; edition (if more than one); and year.

EXAMPLES:

R. Hunter, *Federal Trial Handbook* § 15.26 (1984).

2A A. Larson, *The Law of Workmen's Compensation* § 68.21 (1976).

• Law Review Articles

If written by a student, give a designation, such as "Note" or "Comment," instead of a student author's name.

EXAMPLE:

Note, *Employee Handbooks and Employment-at-Will Contracts,* 1985 Duke L.J. 196 (1985).

Other authors are identified by last name only.

EXAMPLE:

Strauss, *Mining Claims on Public Lands: A Study of Interior Department Procedures,* 1974 Utah L.Rev. 185, 193, 215–19.

• Services

Services (cases, administrative materials, and brief commentaries that are published periodically in loose-leaf form) are cited by volume, abbreviated title, publisher, subdivision, and date.

EXAMPLES:

United States v. Leon, Search & Seizure L. Rep. (Clark Boardman) 53 (Aug. 1984).

O'Brien v. Dean Witter Reynolds, Inc., [Current Binder] Fed. Sec. L. Rep. (CCH) ¶ 91,509 (D. Ariz. 1984).

• Periodicals

Cite by author (last name only), title of article in full, volume number of periodical, name of periodical found on title page (abbreviated), page on which article begins (and page or pages specifically referred to), and year of publication.

EXAMPLE:

Rothstein, *Amendments to the Federal Rules of Criminal Procedure,* 69 A.B.A. J. 1938 (1983).

A table of frequently used American abbreviations is found in the Harvard Bluebook.

- Annotations

Give the date of the volume, not of the case.

EXAMPLES:

American Law Reports, Fourth Edition: Annot., 41 A.L.R. 4th 131 (1985).

American Law Reports, Federal: Annot., 74 A.L.R. Fed. 505 (1985).

- Newspapers

News reports are cited without title or byline.

EXAMPLE:

Lewiston Morning Tribune, June 18, 1986, at 2A, col. 1.

A signed article (not a news report) is cited by author and title.

EXAMPLE:

Ammons, *Hanford,* Lewiston Morning Tribune (Idaho), June 18, 1986, at 1, col. 5.

§ 7.25 Citation Abbreviations, Spacing, Punctuation, Capitalization, Numbers, Quotations, Sections and Subdivisions, and Underlining

The following are rules for citation abbreviations, spacing, punctuation, capitalization, numbers, quotations, sections and subdivisions, and underlining.

- Abbreviations
  "And" is always abbreviated to "&."
  "United States" is never abbreviated when it refers to the United States of America.

Abbreviations for states, months of the year, subdivisions, and some reporters are included at the end of this chapter.

- Spacing

A space should precede and follow all abbreviations that consist of more than one letter and the ampersand; close up single capitals.

EXAMPLES:

Ariz. St. L.J. [Arizona State Law Journal].

Fla. St. U.L. Rev. [Florida State University Law Review].

An exception to the spacing rule is when an entity is abbreviated by widely recognized initials and a combination of those initials with others would be confusing.

EXAMPLE:

A.B.A. J. [American Bar Association Journal].

There must be a space between the symbols "§" and "¶" and a number.

• Punctuation

Periods may be omitted from widely recognized initials that are read out loud as initials (NLRB, CBS, IRS) in case names but not when they refer to reporters, codes, or courts. If initials are read as words (N.D., S.C.), the periods should not be omitted.

A comma should not precede "note," "n.," and "nn."

A comma should not precede the symbols "§" and "¶" unless they are preceded by a number.

Multiple citations in a sentence are separated by semicolons.

Commas and periods are always placed inside quotation marks. All other punctuation is placed outside unless it is part of the quoted material.

Citations should never appear within parentheses.

• Capitalization

Generally, follow the "Guide to Capitalization" in the *United States Government Printing Office Style Manual.*

"Act," "bill," "rule," "statute," etc., are capitalized only when used as part of a proper name given in full.

"Court" is capitalized only when naming a specific court, when referring to the United States Supreme Court, or when referring to a specific judge (and the judge's name could be used in its place).

"Circuit" is capitalized only when used with a circuit number.

"Constitution" is capitalized only when used in the full name of a constitution or when referring to the Constitution of the United States. Parts of a constitution are not capitalized.

"Judge" and "justice" are capitalized only when giving the name of the judge or justice or when referring to the Chief Justice of the United States Supreme Court.

The abbreviation for "number" (No.) is always capitalized.

When used alone, a word which refers to people or groups is capitalized only when it is used as the shortened form of a specific group or body.

- Numbers

Spell out the numbers zero to ninety-nine in text and zero to nine in footnotes.

Spell out all numbers that begin a sentence.

Round numbers may be spelled out (three hundred).

Use numerals in a series that contain any numbers.

Use numerals for numbers that include decimal points.

Do not use periods after 1st, 2d, 3d, 4th, etc.

Pages may be cited as follows:

EXAMPLES:

Pages 416 through 433: 416–33

Pages 1476 through 1517: 1476–517

Sections must be cited as follows:

EXAMPLES:

Sections 416 through 433: 416–433

Sections 1476 through 1517: 1476–1517

- Quotations

Quotations of fifty or more words are usually indented, and quotation marks should not be used. Quotations of forty-nine or fewer words should be enclosed in quotation marks but not set off from the rest of the text. Commas and periods are always placed inside the quotation marks.

When a letter is changed from lower to upper case or from upper case to lower case, enclose it in brackets. All substituted words or letters and added material should be placed in brackets.

Do not use ellipses to begin a quotation or when a word is merely altered. An omission of language from the middle of a quoted sentence is indicated by three periods separated by spaces between them. A fourth period is used to indicate the end of a sentence. Do not indicate deleted material after a period or other final punctuation that ends the quotation.

Indicate paragraph structure by indenting the first word of a paragraph. If the quotation begins in the middle of a paragraph, do not indent the first line. Omission of one or more paragraphs is indicated by inserting and indenting four periods on a separate line. Mistakes in the original of quoted material should be followed by "[sic]."

The citation should not be indented. It should appear at the left margin immediately following the quotation. Omitted footnotes, omitted citations, and change in emphasis of certain words in a quotation should be indicated in a parenthetical after the citation.

• Sections and Subdivisions

The following demonstrates the proper way to cite sections and section subdivisions in citations (do not use section symbols in text).

EXAMPLES:

Section 1414: § 1414

Section 1414 through section 1452: §§ 1414–1452

Section 1414, subsections a and 3: § 1414(a)(3)

Sections 2.15–312, 2.15–314, and 2.15–320: §§ 2.15–312, –314, –320 [drop identical digits preceding a common punctuation mark]

Subdivision designations should be enclosed in parentheses even if printed in the source without.

EXAMPLE:

§ 145(a)(1)(iii)
• Underlining
In briefs and legal memoranda underline:
1. Case names
2. Book and treatise titles
3. Titles of articles in periodicals and newspapers
4. Congressional publications (including committee hearings)
5. When referring to a publication rather than citing to it (*Yale Law Journal, Pacific Reporter,* etc.)
6. Names of titles or topics within encyclopedias
7. Introductory signals (*E.g., See,* etc.)
8. Id. and supra

9. The letter "l" when it is used to identify a subsection so it will not be confused with the number "1"

10. Letters used to designate people in hypothetical situations (*A* filed suit against *B*.)

11. Foreign words not incorporated into the English language

12. For emphasis

Extend the underscore beneath the period ending an abbreviation. Do not extend the underscore beneath the period that ends a sentence.

§ 7.26 Abbreviations for Reporters, States, Months of the Year, and Subdivisions

The following are rules for abbreviations for reporters, states, months of the year, and subdivisions.

REPORTS:

American Law Reports Annotated	A.L.R.
American Law Reports Annotated, Second Series	A.L.R.2d
American Law Reports Annotated, Third Series	A.L.R.3d
Atlantic Reporter	A.
Atlantic Reporter, Second Series	A.2d
Automobile Cases (CCH)	Auto. Cas.
Automobile Cases, Second Series (CCH)	Auto. Cas. 2d
Bankruptcy Reporter	Bankr.
California Appellate Reports	Cal. App.
California Appellate Reports, Second Series	Cal. App. 2d
California Reporter	Cal. Rptr.
Commissioner of Patents, Decisions	Dec. Com. Pat.
Court of Customs Appeals Reports	Ct. Cust. App.
Federal Cases	F. Cas.
Federal Reporter	F.
Federal Reporter, Second Series	F.2d
Federal Rules Decisions	F.R.D.
Federal Supplement	F. Supp.
Lawyers' Edition, United States Supreme Court Reports	L. Ed.
Lawyers' Edition, United States Supreme Court Reports, Second Series	L. Ed. 2d
Lawyers Reports, Annotated	L.R.A.
Lawyers Reports, Annotated, New Series	L.R.A. (n.s.)
Negligence Cases (CCH)	Negl. Cas.
Negligence Cases, Second Series (CCH)	Negl. Cas. 2d
New York Criminal Reports	N.Y. Crim.
New York Supplement	N.Y.S.
New York Supplement, Second Series	N.Y.S.2d
North Eastern Reporter	N.E.

North Eastern Reporter, Second Series	N.E.2d
North Western Reporter	N.W.
North Western Reporter, Second Series	N.W.2d
Pacific Reporter	P.
Pacific Reporter, Second Series	P.2d
South Eastern Reporter	S.E.
South Eastern Reporter, Second Series	S.E.2d
South Western Reporter	S.W.
South Western Reporter, Second Series	S.W.2d
Southern Reporter	So.
Southern Reporter, Second Series	So. 2d
Supreme Court Reporter [United States]	S. Ct.
United States Supreme Court Reports	U.S.
United States Tax Cases (CCH)	U.S. Tax Cas.

STATES:

Ala.	Ill.	Mont.	R.I.
Alaska	Ind.	Neb.	S.C.
Ariz.	Iowa	Nev.	S.D.
Ark.	Kan.	N.H.	Tenn.
Cal.	Ky.	N.J.	Tex.
Colo.	La.	N.M.	Utah
Conn.	Me.	N.Y.	Vt.
Del.	Md.	N.C.	Va.
D.C.	Mass.	N.D.	Wash.
Fla.	Mich.	Ohio	W.Va.
Ga.	Minn.	Okla.	Wis.
Hawaii	Miss.	Or.	Wyo.
Idaho	Mo.	Pa.	

MONTHS OF THE YEAR:

Jan.	Apr.	July	Oct.
Feb.	May	Aug.	Nov.
Mar.	June	Sept.	Dec.

SUBDIVISIONS:

The following terms are always abbreviated as indicated below in full citations, but never in text—except that "section" is written § in textual footnotes when followed by the number of the section and not the first word of a sentence:

amendment(s)	amend., amends.
appendix(es)	app., apps.
article(s)	art., arts.
book(s)	bk., bks.
chapter(s)	ch., chs.

clause(s)	cl., cls.
column(s)	col., cols.
folio(s)	fol., fols.
footnote(s)	n., nn.
number(s)	No., Nos.
page(s)	p., pp. [or, at]
paragraph(s), subparagraph(s)	para., paras., ¶, ¶¶
part(s)	pt., pts.
section(s), subsection(s)	§, §§ [space between § and number]
series, serial(s)	ser.
title(s)	tit., tits.
volume(s)	vol., vols.

CHAPTER 8

THE LAW LIBRARY

Table of Sections

---

§ 8.1   Why an Attorney Must Have a Law Library

The essential tools of the lawyer are libraries—generally, a personal collection of law books, plus access to the larger holdings of an academic, bar, or government law library. However, it is very difficult for a lawyer to develop or keep a successful law practice without the use of law books. Because the law library is very important to the attorney's practice, it is essential for the legal secretary to understand the contents of the books used in legal research and the concepts behind that legal research. Very often the attorney must do some preliminary legal research before he can advise his client. It is not that he does not know the law (or at least have a relatively good idea of what it is). What he must ascertain is how the law is applied to the facts of his client's case.

§ 8.2   Authority

This information is the authority which a lawyer uses to convince a court how to apply the law to the facts of his client's case. Legal authority is divided into two classes—primary and secondary.

§ 8.3   Primary Authority

Primary authority is the text of the law itself. The sources of primary authority are:

1. Constitutions, codes, statutes, and ordinances.
2. Cases (court decisions).

Constitutions, codes, statutes, and ordinances are laws which are enacted by Congress, state legislatures, and local governing bodies. The cases are court decisions of how these various constitutions, statutes, and codes are interpreted when disputes arise as to the meaning of the laws. The cases, then, give examples of how laws were applied to the facts of a particular situation. The lawyer compares the situation in the case to his client's situation and makes a decision as to whether the facts are similar enough that the doctrine of stare decisis will control in his case. (Stare decisis, as you will learn from the chapter on courts, is the doctrine by which courts are bound to apply the same principle of law to a similar fact situation.) In legal research the attorney attempts to find primary authority to support the client's position.

327

§ 8.4 Secondary Authority

Books of secondary authority are writings setting out the opinion of the writer as to what the law is. Secondary authorities include legal encyclopedias, treatises, legal texts, law review articles, restatements, and essays. Courts are not bound by secondary authority. However, if a lawyer cannot locate primary authority, he often quotes secondary material in the hope that he will be able to persuade the court that his position is correct. Further information about secondary authorities may be found in section 8.21.

§ 8.5 Dignity Accorded Authorities

Within the distinctions of primary and secondary authorities, there are further distinctions which accord greater dignity to some authorities than to others. For instance, a constitutional provision is superior to any other kind of law.

The United States Constitution (as amended) is the supreme law of the land. Neither the Congress nor any of the states may enact a constitutional provision or a statute or code which conflicts with the United States Constitution.

EXAMPLE:

The United States Constitution has a provision which declares that all persons are given equal protection of the laws. If the Congress enacts a statute that purports to give one class superior protection, it would be unconstitutional because it is in conflict with a superior authority (the United States Constitution).

In those instances where the United States Supreme Court is, under its power of judicial review, interpreting the effect of statutory provisions, federal or state, affecting the United States Constitution, its decisions control; and such statutory provisions, if in conflict with the United States Constitution, are rendered void.

Each state may adopt its own constitution without regard to the constitutions and laws of other states. These constitutions may not conflict with the United States Constitution, United States Supreme Court decisions construing the federal Constitution, or federal statutes.

The legislature of each state may enact statutes and codes. These may not conflict with the United States Constitution, United States Supreme Court decisions construing the federal Constitution, federal statutes, or the constitution of that particular state.

§ 8.6   Constitutions

You will learn in the chapter on Courts that our form of government—both federal and state—provides for three branches: executive, legislative, and judicial. The organization of the government and the rules for operation are established by constitution. The United States Constitution is the supreme law of the land, but each state has its own constitution which acts as the fundamental law for that state.

§ 8.7   Statutes

The legislative branches of the government—both state and federal—meet on a regular schedule. It is from the legislative branches of the governments that we get our statutes and codes. A member of a legislature introduces a bill which if passed becomes an act after it is approved by the President or a state governor. At the end of each legislative session—state or federal—the acts are published in chronological order.

The collected work of each legislative session is reproduced in volumes known as session laws. Congressional session laws are called the Statutes at Large. All of these laws are very important, but they become impossible to find when they are published in chronological order, for there is no rhyme or reason to their placement. It is necessary, therefore, to consolidate these acts in some logical order. This is usually done according to subject matter by either the legislature itself or by a private publisher or by both. This process is known as codification. The statutes are referred to as Revised Statutes, Compiled Laws, or other similar designation. You will note as you become familiar with the law library that the terms "revised," "compiled," "consolidated," and "code" are often used interchangeably in referring to codifications.

§ 8.8   Ordinances

Local ordinances are similar to state statutes. In fact, they can be thought of as local statutes. Towns and cities usually come into existence with state government approval, either under a specific act dealing with each municipality or under general authority which sets out the procedure for incorporation by a municipality. When a town or city is recognized as a municipality, that recognition carries with it the right to enact certain legislation. Usually, municipalities adopt their own traffic ordinances, zoning ordinances, tax ordinances, Sunday closing laws (blue laws), and other laws of that nature. They usually develop their own election procedures and their own licensing procedures as well.

§ 8.9 Administrative Agency Rules

The executive and legislative branches of federal and state governments have created administrative agencies and empowered them to enact rules and regulations to carry out their functions. These administrative rules have the effect of law.

The federal administrative rules and regulations are printed in the Federal Register and the Code of Federal Regulations.

§ 8.10 Court Rules

Each court may adopt rules for conducting business in the court. Usually these rules deal with the mechanical processes of prosecuting and defending a legal matter.

§ 8.11 Court Decisions

All lawsuits brought to trial result in court decisions. Therefore, court decisions come from all kinds of courts—both state and federal. A lawyer often relies upon court decisions to support his legal position, so it is important to have court decisions published in such a manner that a researcher can find them. Court decisions are published in books called reporters. Although most trial court decisions on the state level are not reported, many United States District Court cases are reported. The reports do include those state intermediate appellate and highest appellate court decisions officially released for publication and all decisions of federal appellate courts officially released for publication. Cases decided by the United States Supreme Court are reported in the United States Reports (U.S.), in the West system in the Supreme Court Reporter (S. Ct.), and in the Lawyer's Edition (L. Ed.) of the United States published by the Lawyers Co–Operative Publishing Company Reports. Decisions of the 13 United States Circuit Courts of Appeal are reported in the Federal Reporter (F. and F.2d). The Federal Supplement contains reported decisions of the United States District Courts (F. Supp.). Federal District Court cases dealing primarily with the construction of the federal rules are reported in Federal Rules Decisions (F.R.D.).

At one time each state published its own reports, and those reports were known as official reports. West Publishing Company published reports containing the same cases known as unofficial reports. However, an increasing number of states have discontinued publishing their own reports and rely solely on the West Reporter System. West does publish separately the official reports of some of the states, and about one-fourth of the states which no longer publish their own official reports have officially adopted or rely on the decisions reported in the West regional reporters.

About 1880 West Publishing Company undertook the publication of all decisions reported out of state appellate courts in the United States. While the statutes of each state provided for the publication of all decisions of the highest appellate court in an official reporter, the reports were often tardy and generally were not well proofread. Consequently, the West Publishing Company had an open door with its accurate and fairly quick reporting service. These state appellate court decisions are published by West Publishing Company in regional reporters. At present West's National Reporter System is comprised of seven regional reporters as follows:

ATLANTIC: Maine, Vermont, New Hampshire, Connecticut, Rhode Island, Pennsylvania, New Jersey, Delaware, Maryland, District of Columbia

NORTH EASTERN: Illinois, Indiana, Massachusetts, New York, Ohio

NORTH WESTERN: North Dakota, South Dakota, Nebraska, Minnesota, Iowa, Wisconsin, Michigan

PACIFIC: Washington, Oregon, California, Idaho, Nevada, Montana, Wyoming, Utah, Arizona, New Mexico, Colorado, Kansas, Oklahoma, Alaska, Hawaii

SOUTHERN: Louisiana, Mississippi, Alabama, Florida

SOUTH EASTERN: West Virginia, Virginia, North Carolina, South Carolina, Georgia

SOUTH WESTERN: Texas, Missouri, Arkansas, Kentucky, Tennessee

(See Illustration 8–1.)

For court opinions issued prior to the beginning of the National Reporter System, one must consult older volumes of official state reports or the set called Federal Cases for lower federal courts.

Illustration 8–1

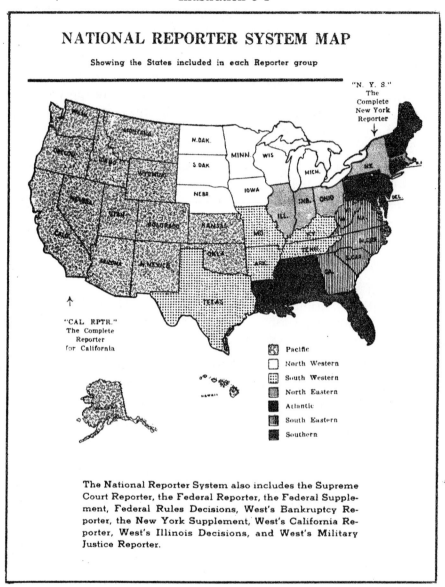

NATIONAL REPORTER SYSTEM MAP

Showing the States included in each Reporter group

"N. Y. S."
The
Complete
New York
Reporter

"CAL RPTR."
The Complete
Reporter
for California

Pacific
North Western
South Western
North Eastern
Atlantic
South Eastern
Southern

The National Reporter System also includes the Supreme
Court Reporter, the Federal Reporter, the Federal Supplement, Federal Rules Decisions, West's Bankruptcy Reporter, the New York Supplement, West's California Reporter, West's Illinois Decisions, and West's Military
Justice Reporter.

The reporter listed next to the states includes all appellate decisions from those states. Many states have adopted the National Reporter System as their official state reports.

§ 8.12 The Decision

It is the decision of the court itself (written by one of the judges) that is reported—not a transcript of the trial or briefs of attorneys. The opinion of the court (the decision) is the primary authority that an attorney seeks in his research. (See Illustration 8–2.)

Illustration 8–2

Case Name ↘   Headnotes ↙

Earl D. JOHNSON, Plaintiff-Appellee,

v.

GALLATIN COUNTY, ILLINOIS, a municipal corporation, and Herman Watters, Deputy Sheriff of Gallatin County, Illinois, Defendants-Appellants.

Earl D. JOHNSON, Plaintiff and Cross-Appellant,

v.

Vernon Eugene HISE, Defendant and Cross-Appellee,

and

Gallatin County, Illinois, a municipal corporation, and Herman Watters, Deputy Sheriff of Gallatin County, Illinois, Defendants and Cross-Appellees.

Nos. 17575, 17576.

United States Court of Appeals
Seventh Circuit.

Nov. 4, 1969.

Case Synopsis →

Action against county, its deputy sheriff and suspect who had escaped from custody for personal injury sustained when suspect shot plaintiff during escape attempt, wherein county and deputy counterclaimed against plaintiff and deputy cross-claimed against suspect. From judgment of the United States District Court for the Eastern District of Illinois, Henry S. Wise, J., county and deputy appealed and plaintiff cross-appealed from denial of post-trial motion for judgment against all defendants for combined sum of judgments. The Court of Appeals, Kiley, Circuit Judge, held that questions of deputy's negligence in way he handled lockup of suspect or manner in which he conducted himself after allowing himself to be kidnapped and whether deputy's negligent conduct was proximate cause of plaintiff's injury were for jury, that county was liable for negligent personal injuries proximately caused by its officers, and that as matter of law plaintiff was not negligent in throwing can of paint thinner into suspect's face in emergency.

Affirmed.

1. Assault and Battery ☞26
Counties ☞223
Sheriffs and Constables ☞138(1)

Plaintiff suing county, its deputy sheriff and suspect to recover for personal injury sustained when he was shot by suspect, escaping from officers, after plaintiff had thrown can of paint thinner into suspect's face had burden of proving his own due care and negligence of county, its deputy sheriff and suspect proximately causing injury.

2. Sheriffs and Constables ☞140

In suit against county, its deputy sheriff and suspect for personal injury sustained when plaintiff was shot by suspect fleeing from law officers, deputy sheriff was not entitled to instruction that he had no duty to resist suspect while being held hostage because trial court had directed verdict for other law officer.

3. Municipal Corporations ☞189(1)

Where a policeman has duty to exercise reasonable care, he is liable for injuries proximately caused by neglect of that duty, as same general rules of negligence law which apply to others are equally applicable to police.

4. Municipal Corporations ☞189(1)

Under Illinois law, a policeman, under proper circumstances, can be held liable for negligence committed in performance of his duty which proximately causes injury to a third person.

5. Sheriffs and Constables ☞140

Question whether deputy sheriff should have foreseen that if he permitted suspect to leave his presence in courthouse, while taking him to lockup location, suspect might attempt an escape, taking deputy hostage and, in making his eventual getaway, could injure a third person, and question of proximate cause of injury of third person shot by suspect were properly for jury.

6. Municipal Corporations ☞745

Under Illinois law, municipality is liable for negligent personal injuries proximately caused by its officers.

Excerpt taken from 418 Federal Reporter, 2d Series 96

[C4061]

Illustration 8–2 (CONTINUED)

7. Negligence ⬤⟞12

Airport employee, from whom deputy sheriff sought to recover for injuries suffered when suspect holding officers hostage shot deputy, was not negligent in throwing can of paint thinner into suspect's face and scuffling with suspect in emergency which could have reasonably led employee to believe he and others were being forced into danger of their lives.

8. Witnesses ⬤⟞388(2)

Where suspect had testified that it was his idea to charter airplane for escape, testimony by state trooper that suspect had told him that defendant deputy sheriff had initially suggested idea of getting suspect to airplane was properly admitted despite alleged lack of proper foundation where plaintiff's attempt to lay foundation for impeaching suspect was circumvented by trial court's erroneous sustaining of deputy's objection.

9. Federal Civil Procedure ⬤⟞2195

Where verdicts were returned in favor of plaintiff against suspect, county and its deputy sheriff and in favor of deputy against suspect on cross claim in action for injury sustained when plaintiff was shot by suspect making an escape, plaintiff's prejudgment motion for entry of a nolle prosequi as to suspect and to affirm judgment against county and deputy removed basis for any claim of impropriety between verdicts as improper attempt to apportion damages against joint tort-feasors.

10. Federal Civil Procedure ⬤⟞2342

There was no inconsistency in verdicts for plaintiff against county and its deputy sheriff and for deputy against suspect which required new trial in action for damages sustained when plaintiff was shot by suspect making an escape after taking deputy and police chief hostage.

11. Federal Civil Procedure ⬤⟞2195

Where jury in personal injury action returned separate verdicts for plaintiff against suspect who shot him and county and its deputy sheriff from whose custody suspect had fled, denial of plaintiff's post-trial motion for judgment against all three defendants for total of verdicts was not error, in absence of indication that jury intended to award sum total of damages against all defendants.

———◆———

Maurice E. Gosnell, Gosnell, Benecki & Quindry, Lawrenceville, Ill., for Earl D. Johnson.

Everett L. Laury, Hutton, Hegeler, Buchanan & Laury, Danville, Ill., for Gallatin County, Illinois and Herman Watters.

Before KILEY, SWYGERT and CUMMINGS, Circuit Judges.

KILEY, Circuit Judge.

This is a personal injury action based on diversity jurisdiction. The district court directed a verdict against plaintiff Johnson, an Indiana resident, and in favor of defendants Shawneetown, Illinois and its police chief Paul Wood. It also directed a verdict against Gallatin County, Illinois and its deputy sheriff Herman Watters upon their counterclaim against plaintiff. The jury returned verdicts for plaintiff against defendants Gallatin County and Watters for $22,500 and against defendant Hise for $25,000; and for Watters on his cross-claim against Hise for $15,000. The court entered judgments on the verdicts. Watters and Gallatin County have appealed from the judgment entered against them, and plaintiff Johnson has cross-appealed from the denial of his post-trial motion that judgment be entered on the verdicts in favor of him against all three defendants in the sum of $47,500. We affirm.

Hise was in Watters' custody in the courthouse in Shawneetown. He managed to seize a gun, and took Watters and Wood hostages. They drove to an airport at Lawrenceville, Illinois, where Johnson was in charge. In a corridor of the airport building, a scuffle ensued in which Hise shot both Watters and Johnson. This suit followed. Plaintiff sued

[C4062]

§ 8.13 Case Finding

Several specialized publications are devoted to finding cases and to verifying the current validity of cases already found.

§ 8.14 Citators

A citator is used to verify legal authorities and to locate additional, more recent cases, so it is an essential tool in legal research. Before a lawyer can depend upon a particular case as authority for a legal proposition, he must be certain the authority is still valid. What would happen to his argument if the case upon which he relies had been reversed? He would be a very embarrassed attorney with an upset client. The use of a citator eliminates the possibility of this ever happening.

Making certain that the primary authority, whether statutory or case law, is still valid after a lapse of time is a task which often is assigned to a legal secretary or paralegal. Shepard's Citations is a series of volumes divided in areas generally on the same lines as the reporter and digest systems. A Shepard's Citations is published for each unit of the National Reporter System.

§ 8.15 Importance of Shepardizing

Shepard's Citations actually gives a history of each reported case. It contains every instance in which one particular case has been cited by a court in another case. It uses a system of abbreviations for evaluating a certain case. Once you are familiar with the abbreviations, you can tell at a glance whether or not the case you've found is still good law. This process is called Shepardizing. Unless the researcher takes the time to Shepardize the cases and statutes she finds as a result of the research, she may find that her work was in vain. It is absolutely essential that authority upon which an attorney takes a legal position be verified. A legal secretary who Shepardizes the relevant cases and statutes will save the attorney time and possibly great embarrassment. The original concept of the citator was that it was to be used as an evaluator. However, as researchers began to use it, they discovered that it was a good search tool, as it disclosed additional cases on point.

By using a state citator, most often consisting of two units—one for statutes and one for cases—one can determine all legislative and judicial action concerning the particular holding or statute. The citation to the case or statute appears at the top of the appropriate book, and columns of figures announce revisions of a statute or the subsequent modification of a ruling. (See Illustration 8–3.)

Illustration 8-3

PACIFIC REPORTER, 2d SERIES								Vol. 440
Pa	**– 32 –**	Fla	f517P2d¹60	65FRD¹636	d533P2d³52	489P2d³170	470P2d⁴380	
268A2d93	(7AzA396)	268So2d555	532P2d¹398	82Æ1429s		489P2d⁴170	470P2d⁵380	
321A2d882	445P2d¹188	Iowa	480F2d¹1020		**– 158 –**	489P2d⁵170	471P2d⁴443	
17Æ146s	453P2d¹232	202NW76	402FS98	**– 124 –**	(165Col475)	489P2d⁷170	471P2d¹833	
	459P2d¹323	Me	L402FS¹99	(84Nev298)	498P2d¹951	494P2d	471P2d⁵836	
– 1020 –	370FS¹867	249A2d757	Ore	495P2d¹633	o498P2d²952	[¹¹1021	471P2d²837	
(103Az260)	Mass	14Æ605s	462P2d673			495P2d¹678	475P2d994	
444P2d¹450	277NÆ118		Fla	**– 129 –**	**– 162 –**	495P2d²678	478P2d⁴650	
535P2d²48	42Æ31n	**– 65 –**	294So2d78	Case 2	(73W582)	507P2d¹167	j485P2d²417	
q390FS⁴1161	42Æ81n	(68C2d547)		(151Mt574)		507P2d²167	j485P2d¹417	
Fla	42Æ97n	(68CaR1)	**– 95 –**		**– 164 –**	523P2d⁴1199	f485P2d⁴1239	
260So2d253	42Æ153n	447P2d¹654	(50H298)	**– 129 –**	(73W608)	530P2d¹312	e485P2d	
Va	42Æ157n	447P2d⁵654	408FS⁴51	Case 3		538P2d¹³852	[⁴1240	
165SÆ409	42Æ168n	d449P2d⁵211		(151Mt574)	**– 167 –**	544P2d¹777	486P2d⁴590	
95Æ1122s		454P2d⁶695	**– 100 –**		(73W634)		Colo	486P2d⁵1314
	– 39 –	457P2d¹580	(103Az267)	**– 130 –**	462P2d²⁰986	470P2d¹⁴40	487P2d¹109	
	(7AzA403)	458P2d¹505	s463P2d65	(79NM92)	466P2d¹⁷129	Nev	489P2d⁹975	
Vol. 440	v449P2d596	459P2d¹259	447P2d¹³555	s418P2d545	471P2d¹⁰136	444P2d¹⁸897	j491P2d²1001	
		465P2d²27	455P2d¹³458	cc467P2d27	476P2d⁸130	Md	j491P2d³1001	
– 1 –	**– 44 –**	506P2d¹1009	464P2d⁸827	490P2d³464	476P2d¹⁰130	340A2d369	494P2d¹468	
441P2d²328	(7AzA408)	j506P2d³1012	474P2d²865	j506P2d²353	544P2d⁷775	NJ	494P2d⁴468	
446P2d²556	452P2d²724	j506P2d	479P2d¹⁴729		Kan	247A2d12	495P2d³290	
463P2d¹28	j452P2d⁹726	[¹¹1013	485P2d⁷812	**– 133 –**	551P2d⁸833	21Æ1088s	500P2d⁵477	
464P2d³534	457P2d⁸347	f514P2d⁸1209	490P2d⁵563	(79NM95)	Iowa	31Æ620n	520P2d⁴469	
476P2d¹484	457P2d⁸348	f514P2d⁹1209	492P2d²1166	465P2d¹286	190NW404		521P2d⁴1322	
486P2d¹239	459P2d²319	537P2d¹910	NM	491P2d¹538	Miss	**– 199 –**	527P2d⁴425	
549P2d³1171	459P2d¹⁴320	537P2d⁹910	508P2d⁴31		301So2d863	(73W653)	527P2d⁵425	
550P2d²1117	480P2d⁹1006	e537P2d⁹910	20Æ1421s	**– 136 –**	NY	444P2d⁵159	528P2d²95	
j550P2d²1124	485P2d⁸569	e537P2d¹⁷911		Case 1	256NÆ174	477P2d⁷6	530P2d²546	
j550P2d²1126	500P2d⁷1134	537P2d⁸917	**– 105 –**	(79NM98)	307S2d860	479P2d¹950	550P2d¹747	
NM	500P2d⁸1134	70CaR¹¹25	(103Az272)		338S2d801	499P2d²904	551P2d⁴493	
484P2d¹342	500P2d	73CaR¹414	473P2d¹⁷788	**– 136 –**	SD	508P2d⁵1402		
j484P2d¹349	[¹²1135	73CaR⁴414	489P2d¹⁷16	Case 2	163NW546	518P2d⁸700	**– 229 –**	
	511P2d⁷183	d74CaR⁵275	493P2d¹⁷498	(79NM98)	17Æ146s	20Æ3473s	(250Or54)	
– 7 –	f524P2d³1317	75CaR⁵56	d458F2d	s439P2d567	31Æ594n		471P2d2849	
s441P2d320	f524P2d⁵1317	77CaR⁸799				**– 204 –**	527P2d²135	
d464P2d¹534	f524P2d⁷1317	78CaR¹29	[¹⁰1267	**– 136 –**	**– 175 –**	v395US161	534P2d²192	
d464P2d⁵543	f524P2d⁸1318	79CaR⁸748	63Æ1160s	Case 3	(73W601)	v23LÆ175	549P2d²513	
475P2d¹549	f524P2d	80CaR⁴593		(79NM98)	472P2d⁴396	v89SC1647	551P2d²458	
	[¹¹1318	81CaR⁹5	**– 113 –**		474P2d²108	s456P2d570	Idaho	
– 15 –	524P2d⁵1320	83CaR⁵129	Case 1	**– 136 –**	f492P2d²1374	o450P2d²906	509P2d³1322	
(21U2d40)	f536P2d²241	84CaR⁸139	(7AzA429)	Case 4	499P2d¹876		NJ	
458P2d¹875	f536P2d⁴241	85CaR¹¹754		(79NM98)	j500P2d⁸86	**– 211 –**	342A2d167	
517P2d²1023	f536P2d⁸241	90CaR⁴321	**– 113 –**		510P2d²1121	481P2d²187	24Æ986s	
	537P2d⁸935	91CaR⁵793	Case 2	**– 137 –**	521P2d²215	482P2d²954		
– 17 –	537P2d¹²936	91CaR¹¹794	(7AzA429)	(73W629)	536P2d²584	490P2d¹256	**– 231 –**	
(21U2d43)	539P2d545	s436P2d942	s450P2d722	442P2d¹778	549P2d²24		(250Or196)	
s374P2d254	Okla	103CaR⁸103	8Æ6s	44Æ349n		**– 212 –**	s417P2d1002	
	509P2d¹903	103CaR⁷106		44Æ365n	**– 179 –**	(249Or633)		
– 23 –		103CaR⁴681	**– 117 –**		(73W629)		**– 233 –**	
(21U2d51)	**– 54 –**	d103CaR⁸682	(21U2d60)	**– 141 –**	499P2d¹236	**– 214 –**	(68C2d563)	
d465P2d⁴176	(7AzA418)	106CaR²633	508P2d²542	(92Ida208)	491F2d⁸439	(250Or19)	(68CaR161)	
504P2d37	465P2d¹593	j106CaR⁸636	Nev	547P2d549	29Æ530s	US cert den	US cert den	
526P2d⁴1189	506P2d¹1088	j106CaR¹¹637	472P2d¹337			in393US891	in393US1057	
		108CaR675		**– 143 –**	**– 182 –**	479P2d³511	s64CaR625	
– 29 –	**– 58 –**	f110CaR⁸¹29	**– 119 –**	(92Ida210)	(73W671)		cc464F2d	
(103Az264)	(7AzA422)	f110CaR⁹129	cc409P2d847	59Æ1299s	444P2d¹693	**– 219 –**	[1293	
463P2d⁶111	450P2d⁶713	110CaR¹211	453P2d⁴472	89Æ1040s	f453P2d¹858	(250Or140)	o453P2d⁴359	
469P2d⁸850	451P2d⁸647	114CaR864	d456P2d¹454		465P2d¹689	451P2d⁸117	464P2d⁵79	
471P2d⁶714	f468P2d²595	115CaR¹136	468P2d²49	**– 151 –**			481P2d⁴242	
471P2d⁷714	f468P2d³595	116CaR⁴725	470P2d¹271	(165Col500)	**– 184 –**	**– 224 –**	493P2d²1193	
483P2d²557	477P2d²751	121CaR56	488P2d⁴722	71Æ284s	(73W596)	(250Or39)	j508P2d²1140	
494P2d¹378	488P2d¹¹507	122CaR¹790	489P2d⁴459			440P2d867	f70CaR³62	
502P2d1334	492P2d⁶1190	122CaR⁸790	490P2d⁶909	**– 152 –**	**– 187 –**	444P2d¹946	f70CaR⁴62	
502P2d⁷1353	504P2d²957	e122CaR⁹791	494P2d⁸792	(165Col514)	(73W751)	444P2d²946	70CaR⁶613	
506P2d¹645	506P2d⁶652	e122CaR	494P2d⁹792	458P2d⁵78	95Æ351s	445P2d²488	72CaR⁵628	
508P2d³339	f512P2d	[¹¹791	514P2d238	458P2d⁷79		459P2d²995	72CaR⁴749	
510P2d⁵51	[¹²1228	122CaR⁸797	520P2d²95	502P2d³1121	**– 192 –**	461P2d¹269	73CaR⁴504	
510P2d⁷51	q547P2d¹²479	Alk	520P2d⁸95	511P2d¹922	(73W660)	461P2d²269	74CaR⁴763	
511P2d⁸626	f548P2d	f526P2d¹¹22	520P2d⁹95	513P2d¹1086	US cert den	464P2d⁸843	75CaR865	
511P2d⁹695	[¹¹1203	f526P2d¹²23		516P2d¹¹143	in393US1096	d463P2d¹877	o76CaR⁴815	
549P2d²229	f548P2d	Ariz	**– 122 –**		cc446F2d861	d463P2d²877	77CaR⁵537	
j549P2d²232	[¹²1203	468P2d¹¹563	(84Nev300)	**– 155 –**	444P2d¹655	465P2d241	80CaR⁸206	
Wis	j549P2d¹²232			(165Col371)	447P2d¹⁸608	j465P2d242	80CaR⁵797	
230NW903		**– 76 –**	f442P2d²913	506P2d²414	477P2d⁸187	f466P2d¹621	81CaR⁹712	
65Æ1102n		(50H314)	f533F2d¹489	f389FS²851	486P2d¹¹120	470P2d²378	*Continued*	
		(50H452)		d533P2d²52				
							963	

Volume 2, Part 2, Page 963, Citing Volume 440,
Shepard's Citations

§ 8.16   Digests

Digests are detailed indexes by subject on points of law contained in reported cases. The American Digest System published by West Publishing Company is the master index to all cases reported in the National Reporter System. The method for compiling this index is described below in Sections 8.17 and 8.18.

Sets of digests include the comprehensive Decennial and General Digests; regional digests that correspond to some of the regional reporters (Atlantic, North Western, Pacific, South Eastern); state digests for most states (not including Delaware, Nevada, or Utah; there are combined digests for North and South Dakota and Virginia and West Virginia); and the federal digest covering all of the federal courts.

§ 8.17   Headnotes

When the publisher receives a decision from a court, its staff reviews it for the points of law decided in that case. A brief summary of each point of law is then written, and these summaries appear at the beginning of each reported case.

§ 8.18   Topic and Key Number System

The Topic and Key Number System is a master index of case headnotes. West has devised a list of over 400 general areas of law, such as Mortgages and Wills, and has further divided each of these topics into a numbered outline ("key numbers"). Every headnote composed by a West editor is assigned a topic and key number. The headnotes appear at the beginning of the reported case with the topic and key number designation and are then collected by topic, or subject, in the digests. Once a researcher has identified the pertinent topic and key number that collects headnotes on the point of law she is researching, she can consult any unit of the American Digest System to locate additional cases on point. (See Illustration 8–4.)

§ 8.19   American Law Reports

American Law Reports (A.L.R.), originally a selective approach to court reports, is used today for the annotations or legal memoranda following the reported case. Each annotation focuses on a specialized issue of law and summarizes pertinent cases and other authority from all jurisdictions. A.L.R. annotations are located through the A.L.R. Index, American Jurisprudence, Shepard's citators, and other cross-references.

Illustration 8–4

OUTLINE OF THE LAW

*Digest Topics arranged for your convenience
by Seven Main Divisions of Law
and their numerical designations*

---

1. **PERSONS**

2. **PROPERTY**

3. **CONTRACTS**

4. **TORTS**

5. **CRIMES**

6. **REMEDIES**

7. **GOVERNMENT**

---

1. PERSONS
RELATING TO NATURAL PERSONS IN GENERAL

Civil Rights 78
Dead Bodies 116
Death 117
Domicile 135
Drugs and Narcotics 138
Food 178
Health and Environment 199
Holidays 201
Intoxicating Liquors 223
Names 269
Poisons 304
Seals 347
Signatures 355
Sunday 369
Time 378
Weapons 406

PARTICULAR CLASSES OF NATURAL PERSONS

Absentees 5
Aliens 24
Chemical Dependents 762
Children Out-of-Wedlock 76H
Citizens 77
Convicts 98
Indians 209
Infants 211
Mental Health 257A
Paupers 292
Slaves 356
Spendthrifts 359

PERSONAL RELATIONS

Adoption 17
Attorney and Client 45
Employers' Liability 148A
Executors and Administrators 162
Guardian and Ward 196
Husband and Wife 205
Labor Relations 232A
Marriage 253

Master and Servant 255
Parent and Child 285
Principal and Agent 308
Workers' Compensation 413

ASSOCIATED AND ARTIFICIAL PERSONS

Associations 41
Beneficial Associations 54
Building and Loan Associations 66
Clubs 80
Colleges and Universities 81
Corporations 101
Exchanges 160
Joint-Stock Companies and Business Trusts 225
Partnership 289
Religious Societies 332

PARTICULAR OCCUPATIONS

Accountants 11A
Agriculture 23
Auctions and Auctioneers 47
Aviation 48B
Banks and Banking 52
Bridges 64
Brokers 65
Canals 68
Carriers 70
Commerce 83
Consumer Credit 92B
Consumer Protection 92H
Credit Reporting Agencies 108A
Detectives 125
Electricity 145
Explosives 164
Factors 167
Ferries 172
Gas 190
Hawkers and Peddlers 198
Innkeepers 213
Insurance 217
Licenses 238
Manufactures 251
Monopolies 265
Physicians and Surgeons 299
Pilots 300
Railroads 320
Seamen 348
Shipping 354
Steam 362
Telecommunications 372
Theaters and Shows 376
Towage 380
Turnpikes and Toll Roads 391
Urban Railroads 396A
Warehousemen 403
Wharves 408

2. PROPERTY
NATURE, SUBJECTS, AND INCIDENTS OF OWNERSHIP IN GENERAL.

Abandoned and Lost Property 1
Accession 7
Adjoining Landowners 15

Confusion of Goods 90
Improvements 206
Property 315

PARTICULAR SUBJECTS AND INCIDENTS OF OWNERSHIP

Animals 28
Annuities 29
Automobiles 48A
Boundaries 59
Cemeteries 71
Common Lands 84
Copyrights and Intellectual Property 99
Crops 111
Fences 171
Fish 176
Fixtures 177
Franchises 183
Game 187
Good Will 192
Logs and Logging 245
Mines and Minerals 260
Navigable Waters 270
Party Walls 290
Patents 291
Public Lands 317
Trade Regulation 382
Waters and Water Courses 405
Woods and Forests 411

PARTICULAR CLASSES OF ESTATES OR INTERESTS IN PROPERTY

Charities 75
Condominium 89A
Dower and Curtesy 136
Easements 141
Estates in Property 154
Joint Tenancy 226
Landlord and Tenant 233
Life Estates 240
Perpetuities 298
Powers 307
Remainders 333
Reversions 330
Tenancy in Common 373
Trusts 390

PARTICULAR MODES OF ACQUIRING OR TRANSFERRING PROPERTY

Abstracts of Title 6
Adverse Possession 20
Alteration of Instruments 25
Assignments 38
Chattel Mortgages 76
Conversion 97
Dedication 119
Deeds 120
Descent and Distribution 124
Escheat 152
Fraudulent Conveyances 186
Gifts 191

Lost Instruments 246
Mortgages 266
Pledges 303
Secured Transactions 349A
Wills 409

3. CONTRACTS
NATURE, REQUISITES, AND INCIDENTS OF AGREEMENTS IN GENERAL

Contracts 95
Customs and Usages 113
Frauds, Statute of 185
Interest 219
Usury 398

PARTICULAR CLASSES OF AGREEMENTS

Bailment 50
Bills and Notes 56
Bonds 58
Breach of Marriage Promise 61
Champerty and Maintenance 74
Compromise and Settlement 89
Covenants 108
Deposits and Escrows 122A
Exchange of Property 159
Gaming 188
Guaranty 195
Implied and Constructive Contracts 205H
Indemnity 208
Joint Adventures 224
Lotteries 247
Principal and Surety 309
Rewards 340
Sales 343
Subscriptions 367
Vendor and Purchaser 400

PARTICULAR CLASSES OF IMPLIED OR CONSTRUCTIVE CONTRACTS OR QUASI CONTRACTS

Account Stated 11
Contribution 96

PARTICULAR MODES OF DISCHARGING CONTRACTS

Novation 278
Payment 294
Release 331
Subrogation 366
Tender 374

4. TORTS

Assault and Battery 37
Collision 82
Conspiracy 91
False Imprisonment 168
Forcible Entry and Detainer 179

§ 8.20   Words and Phrases

Words and Phrases is a work that compiles, in dictionary form, judicial definitions of a word or phrase. The state and federal cases from which these definitions are taken are identified. In a number of instances, this method of initiating legal research may be quite effective. (See Illustration 8–5.)

Illustration 8–5

CERTIFICATE OF STOCK

Cross References

In general

A "certificate of stock" expresses the contract between corporation and stockholders. Jay Ronald Co. v. Marshall Mortg. Corp., 40 N.Y.S.2d 391, 398, 265 App.Div. 622.

A "certificate of stock" is not the stock itself, but simply evidence of title to an interest in corporation. Lake Superior Dist. Power Co. v. Public Service Commission, 26 N.W.2d 278, 282, 250 Wis. 39.

"Certificates of stock" in a corporation are the paper representation of the incorporeal property right. Crocker v. Crocker, 257 P. 611, 617, 84 C.A. 114.

A certificate issued as part of an attempted fraudulent overissue of stock is not a "certificate of shares of stock." Smith v. Worcester & S. St. Ry. Co., 113 N.E. 462, 463, 224 Mass. 564.

In a remote sense, a "certificate of stock" is an interest in the property of the corporation, which might be in other states than either the corporation or the certificate of stock. Warner v. Brown, 121 N.E. 69, 70, 231 Mass. 333.

A "stock certificate" is merely a muniment or representative of title. The stock which it represents exists apart from the certificate, and its existence is contemplated to endure so long as the corporation continues. Zander v. New York Security & Trust Co., 70 N.E. 449, 451, 178 N.Y. 208, 102 Am.St.Rep. 492.

A certificate of stock is simply a written acknowledgment by a corporation of the interest of the holder in its property and fran-

In general—Cont'd

chises, and has no value except that derived from the company issuing it, its legal status being in the nature of a chose in action. Person v. Board of State Tax Com'rs, 115 S.E. 336, 346, 184 N.C. 499.

"Certificates of stock" take on the character of the stock in the corporation and are "choses in action" within statute providing that choses in action are not liable to be seized and sold under execution unless made so especially by statute. Tow v. Evans, 20 S.E.2d 922, 924, 194 Ga. 160.

Where debenture certificates issued by corporation, although payable out of earnings, were payable irrespective of sufficiency of earnings or surplus and there was a fixed maturity date when owner could demand payment, a finding that the certificates represented "indebtedness" rather than "stock ownership" was justified. Washmont Corp. v. Hendricksen, C.C.A.Wash., 137 F.2d 306, 308, 309.

A "certificate of stock" is a written acknowledgment by a corporation of the interest of the stockholder in its property and franchises. It has no value except that derived from the company issuing it, and its legal status is in the nature of a chose in action. The value of all the property owned by a corporation, including its franchise, is the value of all of its stock. Rhode Island Hospital Trust Co. v. Doughton, 121 S.E. 741, 747, 187 N.C. 263.

Receipt given by depositary for stockholders' committee, representing stock in bank and bank's affiliate, which was transferable on depositary's books and gave depositary power of attorney to transfer stock on corporate books, was not a "certificate of stock" within meaning of Uniform Stock Transfer Act. Commissioner of Banks v. Chase Securities Corp., Mass., 10 N.E.2d 472, 485, 298 Mass. 285.

A "certificate of stock" is, from one point of view, a mere muniment of title like a title deed. It is not the stock itself but evidence of the ownership of the stock; that is to say, it is a written acknowledgement by the corporation of the interest of the shareholder in the corporate property and franchises. It operates to transfer nothing from the corporation to the shareholders but merely affords to the latter evidence of his rights.

72

Excerpt taken from Words and Phrases Legally Defined   [C4065]

§ 8.21   Sources of Secondary Authority

Sources of secondary authority are very diversified. They include legal encyclopedias, legal texts, restatements, and treatises. Secondary sources are very important in legal research, as they provide background and analysis of the law and often lead to primary sources or verify primary sources.

§ 8.22   Legal Encyclopedias

Legal encyclopedias are books that state principles of law supported by footnote references to pertinent cases from throughout the United States. The law topics contained are arranged alphabetically. The principal encyclopedias used in the United States are Corpus Juris Secundum (C.J.S.) and American Jurisprudence Second (Am. Jur. 2d). (See Illustration 8–6.)

Illustration 8-6

| 65A C. J. S. | NEGLIGENCE §§ 116–117 |

reasonable and ordinary care for his own safety;[82] and that it is an application of the rule, expressed in the maxim, Volenti non fit injuria, that one who invites an injury cannot make it the basis of a recovery.[83] Still another view finding favor with the courts is that the rule precluding recovery is in the nature of a penalty, established by public policy, to admonish all to use due care for their own safety.[84] In other words, the doctrine is said to be founded on the impolicy of allowing a person to recover for his own wrong, and the policy of making personal interests of men dependent on their own prudence and care.[85]

§ 117. Contributory Negligence Distinguished from Assumption of Risk and Other Doctrines

While the doctrine of assumed risk and the doctrine of contributory negligence are closely associated, and the former may be held in some cases to be a form or phase of the latter, they are nevertheless distinct doctrines of law and are not synonymous.

Library References

Negligence ⬤65.

Under certain circumstances the same acts or conduct may render one guilty of contributory negligence or give rise to the defense of assumption of risk or incurred risk.[86] Moreover, the defense of assumed or incurred risk has been held to be closely associated with contributory negligence,[87] and to be

---

82. La.—**Corpus Juris Secundum cited in** Normand v. Piazza, App., 145 So.2d 110, 113.

Tex.—Magnolia Petroleum Co. v. Owen, Civ.App., 101 S.W.2d 354, error dismissed.

Wash.—Hauswirth v. Pom-Arleau, 119 P.2d 674, 11 Wash.2d 354—Morris v. Chicago, M., St. P. & P. R. Co., 97 P.2d 119, 1 Wash.2d 587, opinion adhered to 100 P.2d 19, 1 Wash.2d 587—Chadwick v. Ek, 95 P.2d 398, 1 Wash.2d 117.

83. N.J.—Kimpel v. Moon, 174 A. 209, 113 N.J.Law 220—Schnackenberg v. Delaware, etc., R. Co., 93 A. 701, 86 N.J.Law 517, affirmed 98 A. 266, 89 N.J.Law 311.

N.Y.—Zurich General Accident & Liability Ins. Co. v. Childs Co., 171 N.E. 391, 253 N.Y. 324.

Relation voluntarily assumed

Maxim, Volenti non fit injuria, applies equally to any relation voluntarily assumed, contractual or otherwise.

N.Y.—Zurich General Accident & Liability Ins. Co. v. Childs Co., 171 N.E. 391, 253 N.Y. 324.

84. Wash.—Alexiou v. Nockas, 17 P. 2d 911, 171 Wash. 369.

45 C.J. p 942 note 34.

85. Ariz.—MacDonald v. Eichenauer, 269 P.2d 1057, 77 Ariz. 252—Womack v. Preach, 165 P.2d 657, 64 Ariz. 61.

N.H.—Niemi v. Boston & M. R. R., 173 A. 361, 87 N.H. 1, affirmed 175 A. 245, 87 N.H. 1.

Tex.—St. Louis Southwestern R. Co. v. Arey, 179 S.W. 860, 107 Tex. 366, L.R.A.1916B 1065.

86. U.S.—Krolikowski v. Allstate Ins. Co., C.A.Wis., 283 F.2d 839.

Cal.—Vierra v. Fifth Ave. Rental Service, 383 P.2d 777, 60 C.2d 266, 32 Cal.Rptr. 193.

Hedding v. Pearson, 173 P.2d 382, 76 C.A.2d 481.

Conn.—Zullo, v. Zullo, 89 A.2d 216,

138 Conn. 712—L'Heureux v. Hurley, 168 A. 8, 117 Conn. 347.

La.—Benedetto v. Travelers Ins. Co., App., 172 So.2d 354, application denied 175 So.2d 108, 247 La. 872.

Md.—Wiggins v. State, Use of Collins, 192 A.2d 515, 232 Md. 228.

Mo.—**Corpus Juris Secundum cited in** Terry v. Boss Hotels, Inc., 376 S.W. 2d 239, 247.

Neb.—Darnell v. Panhandle Co-op. Ass'n, 120 N.W.2d 278, 175 Neb. 40 —**Corpus Juris Secundum cited in** Brackman v. Brackman, 100 N.W.2d 774, 780, 169 Neb. 650—Landrum v. Roddy, 12 N.W.2d 82, 143 Neb. 934, 149 A.L.R. 1041.

Ohio.—Centrello v. Basky, 128 N.E.2d 80, 164 Ohio St. 41—Morris v. Cleveland Hockey Club, 105 N.E.2d 419, 157 Ohio St. 225—Masters v. New York Cent. R. Co., 70 N.E.2d 898, 147 Ohio St. 293, certiorari denied 67 S.Ct. 1519, 331 U.S. 836, 91 L.Ed. 1848, rehearing denied 68 S.Ct. 33, 332 U.S. 786, 92 L.Ed. 369.

Straley v. Keltner, 164 N.E.2d 186, 109 Ohio App. 51.

Tenn.—**Corpus Juris quoted in** Gargaro v. Kroger Grocery & Baking Co., 118 S.W.2d 561, 564, 22 Tenn. App. 70—**Corpus Juris quoted in** Loew's Nashville & Knoxville Corporation v. Durrett, 79 S.W.2d 598, 607, 18 Tenn.App. 489—**Corpus Juris quoted in** John Bouchard & Sons Co. v. Keaton, 9 Tenn.App. 467, 481.

Vt.—Bouchard v. Sicard, 35 A.2d 439, 113 Vt. 429.

45 C.J. p 944 note 50.

Assumption of risk in law of negligence generally see infra § 174(1) et seq.

Defenses not inconsistent

"In actions based on negligence the defense of assumption of risk under the maxim 'volenti non fit injuria' is not inconsistent with the defense of contributory negligence."

Neb.—O'Brien v. Anderson, 130 N.W. 2d 560, 567, 177 Neb. 635—Landrum

v. Roddy, 12 N.W.2d 82, 84, 143 Neb. 934, 149 A.L.R. 1041.

Independent defenses

Doctrine of assumed risk is independent of defense of contributory negligence.

U.S.—Western Contracting Corp. v. Odle, C.A.Neb., 331 F.2d 38.

Neb.—Darnell v. Panhandle Co-op. Ass'n, 120 N.W.2d 278, 175 Neb. 40.

Conduct not mutually exclusive

Conduct which may be termed "assumption of risk" and conduct which constitutes contributory negligence are not mutually exclusive.

Wis.—Meyer v. Val-Lo-Will Farms, Inc., 111 N.W.2d 500, 14 Wis.2d 616.

87. Cal.—Hedding v. Pearson, 173 P. 2d 382, 76 C.A.2d 481—Coole v. Haskins, 135 P.2d 176, 57 C.A.2d 737.

D.C.—Harris v. Plummer, App., 190 A.2d 98.

Kan.—**Corpus Juris Secundum cited in** Shufelberger v. Worden, 369 P. 2d 382, 386, 189 Kan. 379—**Corpus Juris Secundum cited in** Taylor v. Hostetler, 352 P.2d 1042, 1051, 1052, 186 Kan. 788—**Corpus Juris Secundum cited in** Kleppe v. Prawl, 313 P.2d 227, 230, 181 Kan. 590, 63 A.L. R.2d 175.

Ky.—**Corpus Juris Secundum cited in** Dean v. Martz, 329 S.W.2d 371, 374 —Entwistle v. Carrier Conveyor Corp., 284 S.W.2d 820—Gates v. Kuchle, 134 S.W.2d 1002, 281 Ky. 13.

Md.—Evans v. Johns Hopkins University, 167 A.2d 591, 224 Md. 234— Peoples Drug Stores v. Windham, 12 A.2d 532, 178 Md. 172—Warner v. Markoe, 189 A. 260, 171 Md. 351.

Mass.—Silver v. Cushner, 16 N.E.2d 27, 300 Mass. 583.

Mo.—**Corpus Juris Secundum cited in** Bullock v. Benjamin Moore and Company, App., 392 S.W.2d 10, 13.

Neb.—**Corpus Juris Secundum cited in** Brackman v. Brackman, 100 N.W.2d 774, 780, 169 Neb. 650.

Excerpt from 65A Corpus Juris Secundum 25

§ 8.23 Legal Texts and Treatises

Legal texts and treatises are books prepared by legal scholars and practice experts that cover specific areas of the law. Legal texts usually deal with a single topic, such as contracts, torts, bankruptcy, trusts, evidence, and civil and criminal law and practice. Information about texts and treatises may be obtained through the catalog of a law library.

§ 8.24 Legal Periodicals

Articles from legal periodicals also discuss specific areas of the law and are particularly useful for prediction and analysis of trends in the law. Treatment of the subject ranges from scholarly to practical to news reporting. Information about articles can be located by subject, author, or title through legal periodical indexes, such as Index to Legal Periodicals or Legaltrac.

§ 8.25 Restatements

The restatements are publications setting out and explaining, by practical examples, the law in particular fields. Restatements covering various areas of the law, including agency, conflict of laws, contracts, judgments, property, restitution, security, torts, and trusts have been published. The purpose of the American Law Institute, the prestigious group responsible for the restatements, is to restate the common law (as reflected both by case decisions and statutory interpretation); to that end the Institute appoints committees to study and draft restatements covering assigned law topics, and eminent legal scholars are appointed to be reporters for each one of the restatements being prepared, and as a practical matter they principally prepare the drafts. The restatements are not adopted in whole by the highest appellate courts in the states, but they are referred to and in many instances are approved on a section-by-section basis in the written opinion. Therefore, to that extent, they do become law. Information about court opinions that have interpreted restatement provisions is contained in the Appendix volumes of the restatement set.

§ 8.26 Uniform Laws Annotated

Individual lawyers, judges, and law professors are selected as commissioners to sit with the National Conference of Commissioners on Uniform State Laws. They then research and draft model legislation covering law topics dealing with specific legal problems. Their goal is to make uniform, as far as possible, many of the major areas of the law that can be codified. The state legislatures may or may not adopt the law, but the books are valuable for a comparison of case law interpretations from various states. Many of the uniform laws, for example, the Uniform Commercial Code, have been adopted by practically all of the states.

§ 8.27   Other Research Aids

Law book publishers offer additional aids to legal researchers, the most important of which are discussed and illustrated as follows.

§ 8.28   Annotated Statutes

While official editions are published of the federal and various state codes and statutes, *i.e.,* United States Code (U.S.C.), it is important for a lawyer to know of any court interpretations of specific code or statutory provisions that will help in an understanding of those provisions. Accordingly, there have been published annotated code and statute editions that contain not only the code and statutory provisions but also digests (abstracts) of court decisions construing those provisions; the annotations are conveniently classified and appear under the code and statutory provisions to which they pertain. In addition, the annotated editions contain legislative history and cross-references to other applicable provisions and to other publications as well.

On the federal level, there are two annotated editions of the official United States Code, the United States Code Annotated (U.S.C.A.) [West Publishing Company] and the United States Code Service, Lawyers Edition (U.S.C.S.) [Lawyers Cooperative Publishing Company].

On the state level, most states have annotated statutes or codes similar in style to the annotated editions of the United States Code described above. Annotations to the codes are helpful toward a start in research, although they cannot, of course, be complete. The meaning of a statute must be explored through examining the intent of the legislators (this is known as legislative intent) and also with respect to its application and interpretation by the courts subsequent to its passage.

Annotations give some legislative history, if only reference to the session law number. That number and its date provide access to journals of both houses, and debate on the floor can be obtained through recordings at the House and Senate chambers.

The legislative history of a United States law, as annotated in United States Code Annotated, often refers to a House Report, a Senate Report and a Joint Committee Report. It often includes regulations enacted under authority of the statute. (See Illustration 8–7.)

Illustration 8-7

Official Text of the U. S. Code

Ch. 9   FOOD, DRUG, AND COSMETIC ACT   **21 § 355**

§ **355.**   **New drugs—Necessity of effective approval of application**

(a) No person shall introduce or deliver for introduction into interstate commerce any new drug, unless an approval of an application filed pursuant to subsection (b) of this section is effective with respect to such drug.

Filing application; contents

(b) Any person may file with the Secretary an application with respect to any drug subject to the provisions of subsection (a) of this section. Such person shall submit to the Secretary as a part of the application (1) full reports of investigations which have been made to show whether or not such drug is safe for use and whether such drug is effective in use; (2) a full list of the articles used as components of such drug; (3) a full statement of the composition of such drug; (4) a full description of the methods used in, and the facilities and controls used for, the manufacture, processing, and packing of such drug; (5) such samples of such drug and of the articles used as components thereof as the Secretary may require; and (6) specimens of the labeling proposed to be used for such drug.

Period for approval of application; period for, notice, and expedition of hearing; period for issuance of order

(c) Within one hundred and eighty days after the filing of an application under this subsection, or such additional period as may be agreed upon by the Secretary and the applicant, the Secretary shall either—

(1) approve the application if he then finds that none of the grounds for denying approval specified in subsection (d) of this section applies, or

(2) Every person required under this section to maintain records, and every person in charge or custody thereof, shall, upon request of an officer or employee designated by the Secretary, permit such officer or employee at all reasonable times to have access to and copy and verify such records.

Citations to original and amending Acts of Congress in U. S. Statutes at Large

June 25, 1938, c. 675, § 505, 52 Stat. 1052; 1940 Reorg.Plan No. IV, § 12, eff. June 30, 1940, 5 F.R. 2422, 54 Stat. 1237; June 25, 1948, c. 646, § 32(b), 62 Stat. 991; May 24, 1949, c. 139, § 127, 63 Stat. 107; 1953 Reorg.Plan No. 1, § 5, eff. Apr. 11, 1953, 18 F.R. 2053, 67 Stat.

Citation to Reorganization Plan in Federal Register

Excerpt from 21 U.S. Code Annotated § 355

[C4066]

Illustration 8–7 (CONTINUED)

Ch. 9   FOOD, DRUG, AND COSMETIC ACT   **21 § 355**

631; June 11, 1960, Pub.L. 86–507, § 1(18), 74 Stat. 201; Oct. 10, 1962, Pub.L. 87–781, Title I, §§ 102(b)–(d), 103(a), (b), 104(a)–(d) (2), 76 Stat. 781–783, 784, 785.

Historical Note

Notes explaining Historical Development of Act

1962 Amendment. Subsec. (a). Pub.L. 87–781, § 104(a), inserted "an approval of" preceding "an application."

Subsec. (b). Pub.L. 87–781, § 102(b), inserted "and whether such drug is effective in use" following "is safe for use."

Subsec. (c). Pub.L. 87–781, § 104(b), substituted provisions requiring the Secretary, within 180 days after filing an application, or such additional period as the Secretary and the applicant agree upon, to either approve the application, if meeting the requirements of subsec. (d) of this section, or give notice of opportunity for hearing on question of whether such application is approvable, and providing that if applicant requests hearing in writing within 30 days, the hearing shall begin within 90 days after expiration of said 30 days, unless the Secretary and applicant agree otherwise, that such hearing shall be expedited, and that the Secretary's order shall be issued within 90 days after date for filing final briefs, for provisions which had an application become effective on the sixtieth day after filing thereof unless prior thereto the Secretary postponed the date by written notice to such time, but not more than 180 days after filing, as the Secretary deemed necessary to study and investigate the application.

Subsec. (d). Pub.L. 87–781, § 102(c), inserted references to subsec. (c), added cls. (5) and (6), provided that if after notice and opportunity for hearing, the Secretary finds that cls. (1)–(6) do not apply, he shall approve the application, and defined "substantial evidence" as used in this subsection and subsec. (e) of this section.

Subsec. (e). Pub.L. 87–781, § 102(d), amended subsection generally, and among other changes, directed the Secretary to withdraw approval of an application if by tests, other scientific data or experience, or new evidence of clinical experience not contained in the application or available at the time of its approval, the drug is shown to be unsafe, or on the basis of new information, there is shown a lack of substantial evidence that the drug has the effect it is represented to have, and provided that if the Secretary, or acting Secretary, finds there is an imminent hazard to public health, he may suspend approval immediately, notify the applicant, and give him opportunity for an expedited hearing, that the Secretary may withdraw approval if the applicant fails to establish a system for maintaining required records, or has repeatedly or deliberately failed to maintain records and make reports, or has refused access to, or copying or verification of such records, or if the Secretary finds on new evidence that the methods, facilities and controls in the manufacturing, processing, and packing are inadequate to assure and preserve the drugs' identity, strength, quality and purity, and were not made adequate within a reasonable time after receipt of written notice thereof, or finds on new evidence, that the labeling is false or misleading and was not corrected within a reasonable time after receipt of written notice thereof.

Change of Name. Act June 25, 1948, eff. Sept. 1, 1948, as amended by Act May 24, 1949, substituted "United States District Court for the District of Columbia" for "District Court of the United States for the District of Columbia."

Effective Date of 1962 Amendment; Exceptions. Amendment of section by Pub.L. 87–781 effective on the first day of the seventh calendar month following Oct. 1962, see section 107 of Pub.L. 87–781, set out as a note under section 321 of this title.

Effective Date. Section effective June 25, 1938, see section 902(a) of Act June 25, 1938, set out as a note under section 392 of this title.

Legislative History. For legislative history and purpose of Act May 24, 1949, see 1949 U.S.Code Cong.Service, p. 1248. See, also, Pub.L. 86–507, 1960 U.S.Code Cong. and Adm.News, p. 2356; Pub.L. 87–781, 1962 U.S.Code Cong. and Adm. News, p. 2884, and part 2 of Senate Report No. 1744, set out as a note under section 321 of this title.

Reference to Legislative History and Purpose in U. S. Code Congressional and Administrative News

[C4067]

§ 8.29   Martindale–Hubbell Law Directory

The law directories and digests published by Martindale–Hubbell are comprised of several volumes. The Martindale–Hubbell Law Directory contains names, addresses, specialties, and ratings of United States lawyers while the International Law Directory lists lawyers and law firms worldwide.

The Martindale–Hubbell Law Digests summarize the statutory laws in each of the United States, the District of Columbia, Puerto Rico, the Virgin Islands, and Canada as well as over 60 other countries. The complete texts of many Uniform Acts including the Uniform Commercial Code and the Uniform Probate Code, and four Model Acts including the Revised Model Business Corporation Act are included, as are selected international conventions to which the United States is a party. Besides presenting the substantive law controlling the grant of copyright, patent, and trademark rights, the digests of these subjects provide information as to the practice to be followed in obtaining, protecting, and enforcing such rights, the fee schedules of the respective bureaus, examples of forms in use, and other practical assistance. The Law Digest also contains information on the federal judiciary and the Model Rules of Professional Conduct and the Code of Judicial Conduct of the American Bar Association.

§ 8.30　Form and Practice Books

Form books are specialized publications that provide suggested text for various legal forms, such as contracts, leases, and procedural pleadings. Large sets of form books cover an encyclopedic range of forms on virtually all subjects. Smaller sets can focus on particular areas of law, e.g., real estate forms. Although these forms are very useful for guidance in drafting legal documents, care must be taken to verify that the suggested language is in fact applicable to the specific case.

Many other practical publications exist to assist the attorney in procedural, evidentiary, and trial practice areas. Some examples are AmJur Trials, AmJur Proof of Facts, Causes of Action, and Cyclopedia of Federal Procedure.

§ 8.31　Keeping the Library Current

In order for an attorney to be able to rely on the books in his library, he must be certain that they are absolutely current. There are several services provided by law book publishers which help the attorney keep his library current.

§ 8.32　Pocket Parts

Most law books are equipped with pockets in the inside back covers which accommodate pamphlet inserts. All statutes and codes are kept current in this manner, normally issuing new pocket parts after each legislative session. In doing legal research it is very important to check the pocket parts for recent changes.

In many offices it is the responsibility of the legal secretary to keep the pocket parts current. Generally, these are published once a year.

When new pocket parts arrive, they should immediately be placed in the pertinent volumes and the old pocket parts destroyed. The pocket parts are clearly labeled, so there can be no mistake as to where they belong.

§ 8.33 Replacement Volumes

When the pocket part becomes so bulky that the book no longer closes properly, the volume is replaced. Replacement volumes usually come with instructions on which book or books are being replaced. It is not unusual for one volume to be replaced by two. Be guided by the publisher's instructions, as they usually are very specific.

§ 8.34 Bound Supplements

These may be of a temporary nature, to be used because a pocket part would be too bulky or because the particular book being updated is not equipped with a pocket part, or they may be permanent updates to the main volume. Here, again, rely on the publisher's instructions for guidance.

§ 8.35 Advance Sheets

The National Reporter System is crucial to legal research. The volumes are published as soon as there are a sufficient number of cases to fill a bound volume. Often, however, an attorney must know about the most current cases more quickly than that. To alleviate the problem, West Publishing Company issues advance sheets weekly in a paperback pamphlet. The advance sheets carry the correct volume numbers and page numbers of the National Reporter volume of which it will become a part. Once you receive the bound volume, you may destroy the advance sheets.

§ 8.36 Loose–Leaf Services

Loose-leaf services are used extensively in administrative law areas. Changes occur at a rapid rate, but the materials must be kept current to be of any value.

These services are kept current by the publication of replacement pages or additional pages. It is a good idea to replace substitute pages as soon as they arrive, as it can be very confusing to attempt the insertion of more than one group of changes. Be very careful to follow the publisher's instructions about the replacements.

§ 8.37 Computer–Assisted Legal Research

A substantial proportion of the publications described in this chapter are located in the large computer-assisted research systems of

LEXIS and WESTLAW. These two databases contain the full text of federal and state case law (both current and historical), statutes and regulations, legal periodicals, and other publications. Both systems utilize open-ended "keyword" search techniques, which facilitate location of pertinent materials without resort to indexes and digest and multiple sources for updating.

For the attorney these computer systems can be a cost-effective approach to legal research. Shepardizing cases on-line, for instance, is far faster and easier than using the citator volumes. Because the user is charged on a per-search basis, however, the attorney must be careful to utilize his time carefully and consider useful book alternatives.

Another recent development in computer research systems is in local and specialized Compact Disk–Read Only Memory (CD–ROM) databases. State databases on CD–ROM are a cost-effective alternative to LEXIS and WESTLAW because they provide unlimited access to all of the primary legal authority from that state. Drawbacks of these systems include the inability to consult legal authority from other states and, in some cases, poorly designed search and retrieval software.

§ 8.38 WESTLAW

WESTLAW is the computerized research system of West Publishing Company. In addition to the features described above, WESTLAW permits a combination of keyword and digest searching using the West Key Number digest system.

§ 8.39 LEXIS

LEXIS is the computerized research system of Mead Data Central, Inc. In addition to the features described above, LEXIS provides access to associated databases of NEXIS (news services) and MEDIS (medical literature).

§ 8.40 Learning the Law Library

To become an efficient researcher, the legal secretary must become familiar with the books in the law library. Knowing where the books are and why they are there makes the legal secretary much more helpful to the attorney.

The art of effective legal research requires concentrated study and practice. As you learn your way around the library:

• Take the time to study some of the books.

• Read the table of contents, introduction, and foreword of some of the books.

- Study the indexes. Use your imagination. Try to find a key word listed for a current legal problem in the office.

- Study the topics of the Key Number System. Many legal indexes may use the same topic designations.

- Always check pocket parts.

- Read some of the headnotes in your state's reporter. Can you find references to the same key number anywhere else?

- Find a case in the reporter and Shepardize it. Pull one of the cases referred to. Can you tell that it is on the same point of law?

- Do the same for one of your statutes.

- If your office has access to LEXIS or WESTLAW, become familiar with the dimensions of these databases.

§ 8.41 Summary

The career legal secretary feels at home in the law library and realizes the importance of the library and assumes responsibility by helping keep it current. After becoming familiar with the books in the library and understanding their contents, the legal secretary is ready to undertake the challenge of legal research.

CHAPTER 9

THE COURTS

Table of Sections

---

§ 9.1 Introduction

From your study of government, you know that the government of the United States is based on the concept of separation of powers. That separation of powers is accomplished by a delicate system of checks and balances in our three branches of government. Each of the three branches—the executive, the legislative, and the judicial—is completely independent of the other, but each is a vital part of the whole. Each performs its own function and when combined with the others provides us with our system of government, but under our system one branch cannot dominate another.

It is the judicial branch of the government which administers justice. Its power to do so comes ultimately from constitutional authority. Its financial and other resources to administer justice come from the legislative branch. However, the legislative branch in no way controls the actions of the judicial branch.

§ 9.2 History of the Law

It is difficult to point to a beginning date of the development of our legal system as we know it today. In prehistoric times there were no written laws, but there were established modes of conduct. In highly developed civilizations as early as 2100 B.C., codes of conduct actually were written and enforced. Religion played an important part in the history of the law after the decline of the Roman Empire when the ecclesiastical courts handled most legal matters. Hence, many ancient civilizations had relatively sophisticated written laws. Eventually all of the concepts embodied in these ancient laws evolved into the two legal systems which dominate the Western world today—civil law and common law.

§ 9.3 Civil Law

Civil law derives from the Roman law. Most of the countries in Western Europe today operate under civil law systems. In the United States, Louisiana operates under a civil law system greatly influenced by France's Code Napoleon (also known as the Napoleonic Code). California and Texas law are heavily influenced by Spanish law. Some of the Spanish law influence is evident also in New Mexico and Arizona.

§ 9.4 Common Law

Except for a few civil law states as mentioned above, the remainder of our states operate under a common law system which is an adaptation of England's common law. Common law evolved in England after the Norman Conquest. At that time there were no written rules to govern conduct. When disputes arose, the people involved appeared before a tribunal or a judge, and a decision was reached based upon the evidence and the facts at hand. Under that system two different courts could reach completely different conclusions in a similar fact situation because there was nothing in writing to guide the judge to a decision.

§ 9.5 Distinction Between Civil Law and Common Law

Civil law is based on a series of written codes or laws. These written codes are interpreted by courts if disputes arise, but it is the written law itself that is binding. On the other hand, common law has evolved from earlier decisions made by courts. To solve the problem of inconsistency in decisions reached in similar fact situations, these decisions have been reduced to writing, and the courts are bound by them. This concept is known as the doctrine of stare decisis (to stand by decisions). For that reason, it often is said that common law is based on the law of precedent. One court sets a precedent, and courts making decisions later relating to similar fact circumstances are required to abide by the precedent. The primary distinction, then, between the two systems is that civil law is based on written codes, while common law is based on precedent.

§ 9.6 The American Judicial System

The distinction between civil law and common law is now primarily a historic one because our legal system today is a meld of both systems. For example, no longer does common law in the United States rely merely upon case decisions. All states, whether civil- or common-law oriented, have written laws. The Constitution of the United States became effective in 1788 and, of course, is a written law. The civil-law states use written law, but case law has become a very important part of the whole of civil law. Tort law (thoroughly discussed in the chapter on Torts) is a common law concept, but in Louisiana (a civil law state) the law of torts for the most part is applied as it is in the rest of the United States. Most commercial laws in force in the United States today, although written in commercial codes, have found their origin in common law.

§ 9.7   The Law

The law orders, permits, forbids, rewards, and punishes. It establishes rules of conduct that define what is legally right and what is legally wrong. Laws are nothing more than rules of human behavior enforced by the state or federal government by means of various penalties for their violation. To a great extent laws are influenced by moral and social habits or customs. Therefore, as society changes its customs and traditions, laws change. These changes are accomplished by enactment of new laws by the legislative branch of government or by interpretation of existing laws by the judicial branch.

§ 9.8   Significance of the Law

Regardless of whether or not one is employed in the legal field, it is very important that everyone understands the basic elements of our judicial system. Unfortunately, many people do not realize the extent to which laws affect their daily lives. Common events, such as a birth, a death, applying for a driver's license, buying or selling a house or a car, paying taxes, buying a bus or airplane ticket, banking, and using electricity or other utilities, are all governed by specific laws. Many laymen have the mistaken impression that laws apply only to people who commit violent crimes. That simply is not the case. The law affects everyone, and all of us should have some idea as to our legal rights so that we are in a position to know when to consult an attorney. As a matter of fact, the law encompasses such a broad spectrum of our daily activities that even categorizing it for ready reference is difficult.

§ 9.9   Categorizing the Law

Generally, there are two types of legal actions—criminal and civil.

§ 9.10   Criminal Actions

Criminal actions generally are brought by the people through a government (either federal, state, or local) against the person or persons accused of a crime. Because society is wronged by the commission of a crime, the government prosecutes the wrongdoer on behalf of society. Therefore, in a criminal action the government is always the plaintiff.

EXAMPLES:

> *United States of America v. Albert Jones*
>
> *State of Texas v. John Smith*
>
> *County of Tulsa v. Barry Green*
>
> *City of Apple Grove v. June Collins*

§ 9.11 Civil Actions

Civil actions generally are brought by one party against another to resolve a controversy. These actions include any kind of legal action which is not a criminal action but typically fall within one of the following categories:

1. For money

2. For specific performance

3. For stay of performance

In actions for performance or for a stay of performance, the relief usually requested is in the form of a restraining order or an injunction.

§ 9.12 The Individuals Involved

The law can be classified as either public law or private law. Public law applies to everyone. It governs the rights and obligations of individual citizens in relation to other citizens and to their government. It also governs the divisions of government and delegates power to those divisions.

EXAMPLE:

> Criminal law—A person who steals commits a crime against all other people. A public law has been violated. The crime is against all of society and not only against the victim.

Private law applies to individuals who subject themselves to it by their actions or by agreement.

EXAMPLE:

> Two people enter into a contract for the sale of a house. Only they are involved. If one person does not honor the terms of the agreement, only the other person to the contract has been damaged.

§ 9.13   Nature of the Law

We have discussed law by separating it into two types of legal systems (civil and common) and by categorizing it based upon the people involved. The law is also separated based upon its nature (substantive law) or how it is applied to the situation at hand (procedural law). Substantive law tells us what to do, and procedural law tells us how to apply the law and how to get relief.

§ 9.14   Substantive Law

Substantive law sets out the rights and obligations of individuals. It tells us what we can legally do or what we cannot legally do.

§ 9.15   Procedural Law

Procedural law defines and describes the process which we must follow to enforce the substantive law.

EXAMPLE:

A, who owns property, has the right to enjoy it without interference from anyone else. (This right comes from substantive law.) B installs a fence which is partly on A's property. When B refuses to remove the fence, A sees an attorney, who files a lawsuit asking the court to force B to remove the fence from A's property. (The attorney knows in which court to file the suit and what remedy to seek by referring to applicable procedural law.)

§ 9.16   Source of the Law

Law is often classified on the basis of where it is found. Constitutional law is that which is set out in the Constitution of the United States and in the 50 state constitutions. Statutory law is that body of laws promulgated by the United States Congress, by the 50 state legislatures, and by local governments. However, rules and regulations promulgated by governmental agencies and commissions which receive their power from statutory law are given the force of statutory law. Case law is that body of court decisions resulting from legal controversies over interpretations of substantive and procedural law. Remember that the doctrine of stare decisis binds a court to follow a decision made previously in a similar fact situation. This doctrine adds stability to our legal system.

§ 9.17   United States Constitution

Constitutional law regulates and governs public law. The Constitution of the United States is given the greatest degree of dignity of any law in this country. No other law—regardless of whether it is adopted by Congress or by a state legislature—can conflict with the United States Constitution.

§ 9.18 State Constitutions

Each one of our 50 states has its own constitution. However, those constitutions may not contain any provision that is contrary to a provision in the United States Constitution.

§ 9.19 Statutory Law

Statutory law is that enacted by Congress, by the 50 state legislatures, and by local governments. Many local governments also have charters which control their form of government and establish their local governmental agencies.

§ 9.20 Summary of Classification of Laws

Any specific law must be considered from several different viewpoints. A law can be classified as a private law or as a public law; as a constitutional law, a statutory law, or case law; as a substantive law or a procedural law. (See Illustration 9–1.)

Illustration 9–1

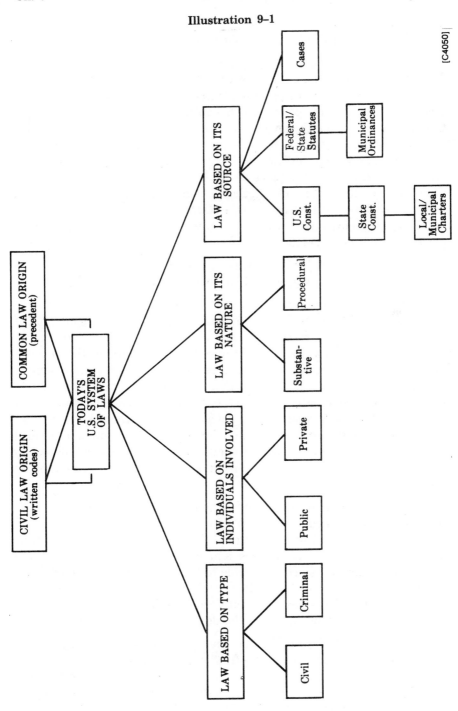

[C4050]

§ 9.21 Creation of Court Systems in the United States

Courts are created by constitutional authority. The Constitution of the United States is the primary source of the judicial powers of federal courts. No state constitution or legislative body can create any court or give authority to any court which conflicts with the United States Constitution. The state constitutions do create courts for their states, and the legislative bodies, both federal and state, have the power to create courts and give judicial authority to those courts subject to any restrictions set forth in the state constitutions or the United States Constitution. Regardless of whether a court is established pursuant to the United States Constitution or a state constitution, that court has authority to decide only those cases which the constitution ultimately gives it authority to decide.

The basis of the judicial authority of federal courts is found in Article III, § 2 of the United States Constitution.

Without authority granted in the state's constitution, a legislative body may not alter, abolish, or restructure a constitutional court, but it may alter, abolish, or restructure any court that it has created pursuant to constitutional authority. State courts are not under the authority and control of Congress, but Congress may authorize state courts to enforce federal laws. Both federal and state legislative bodies may increase, decrease, create, or change the number of judicial districts or circuits as long as they act under constitutional authority. They also may divide a court into divisions or departments. A court so divided remains a single court, and any decisions or judgments rendered by that division or department are considered as having been rendered by the whole court.

Courts, whether federal or state, apply the laws created by constitutions, legislative bodies, and all administrative agencies having authority to enact rules and regulations. They do this in two ways: they adjudicate or settle controversies and disputes between parties, and they decide which laws are applicable to the cases that are before them. Once their decisions are final, they are binding and the interpretation and application of the laws indicate how similar cases will be determined in the future pursuant to the doctrine of stare decisis.

In addition to the application and interpretation of laws, courts may adopt rules that have the effect of procedural law within their jurisdiction. These court rules cannot conflict with the Constitution of the United States, the state's constitution, or any law enacted by Congress or state legislatures.

§ 9.22   Determining the Correct Court

To determine whether a case should be brought in federal court or in state court, the following is considered:

- If the subject matter involved is covered by state law, the case usually is brought in a state court.

- If federal law is involved or if a federal court has original jurisdiction (discussed later), the matter usually is brought in federal court.

Remember, however, that this is just a general rule to which there are many exceptions, as you will see in the discussion of jurisdiction of state and federal courts.

§ 9.23   Jurisdiction

Jurisdiction is the authority given a court to hear and decide certain cases. There are many limitations placed on a court when it is given such authority, and very often those limitations are defined by the kind of jurisdiction granted to the court by a constitutional or a legislative body. Just as it is necessary to understand the many classifications of law, you must also understand the many facets of jurisdiction. Before a court may hear a particular case, it must have the authority or jurisdiction over that case. Whether a particular court has jurisdiction over a certain case depends upon many factors.

§ 9.24   Original Jurisdiction

Original jurisdiction is the authority granted a court to hear and determine a matter for the first time. Actions are begun in courts of original jurisdiction. It is in the court of original jurisdiction that the lawsuit is filed and where the trial is held or the matter is otherwise resolved.

§ 9.25   Jurisdiction Over the Subject Matter

Jurisdiction over the subject matter is authority given a court to render binding decisions over the matter in dispute, and lack of such authority usually cannot be waived by the court or by the parties. In fact, if a court lacks jurisdiction over the subject matter, any judgment rendered by it is void.

EXAMPLE:

Some state courts handle only divorce matters. Therefore, a defendant charged with a crime could not be tried in such a court because it does not have jurisdiction over criminal matters.

§ 9.26   Jurisdiction in Personam (Over the Person)

Jurisdiction in personam is the power of a court to render a judgment against a person or to subject the disputing parties to the decisions and rulings made by it. Ordinarily this means that a defendant has the right to be tried in his own geographic location. This is only a general rule, however, and other types of in personam jurisdiction may preempt that general rule. A person may be subjected to the jurisdiction of a court by statute, by agreement, or if he does not file a formal objection to the jurisdiction. In order for the judgment to be valid in such an instance, however, the court must also have subject matter jurisdiction.

EXAMPLES:

A lives in Tulsa and owes $10,000 to B, who lives in Oklahoma City. B must sue A in a Tulsa court which has authority to hear matters involving at least $10,000. An Oklahoma City court may have subject matter jurisdiction over the $10,000 debt, but it does not have in personam jurisdiction over A.

Assume the same facts. B sues A in Oklahoma City, where A spends a lot of time on business. A employs the services of an Oklahoma City attorney to defend the suit which B files. When A makes an appearance in that matter through his attorney and does not dispute the jurisdiction, he has subjected himself to the jurisdiction of the Oklahoma City court. Therefore, if the Oklahoma City court has jurisdiction over the subject matter, a judgment it renders against A is valid.

§ 9.27   Jurisdiction in Rem (Over the Thing)

Jurisdiction in rem is the authority of a court to render a judgment concerning property over which it has jurisdiction. Ordinarily, this means that the court and the property are in the same geographic location, but the owner of the property is not subject to personal jurisdiction in that court. When a court renders an in rem judgment, that judgment attaches only to the property which is the subject of the court's jurisdiction. The judgment does not apply to the owner of the property if the court does not have in personam jurisdiction over the owner. This means that any such judgment would have to be satisfied from the property subject to the court's jurisdiction. Other personal assets and property of the owner which are located elsewhere beyond the court's jurisdiction could not be seized by a court which did not have in personam jurisdiction over the owner.

EXAMPLE:

A lives in Tulsa and owes B, who lives in Oklahoma City, $10,000, which is secured by a mortgage on property located in Oklahoma City. B must sue A in Oklahoma City if he wishes to regain possession of the property in payment of the mortgage, since only the Oklahoma City court has jurisdiction in rem. However, if B is not interested in the property but only wants to get his money back, he may sue A in a Tulsa court which has in personam jurisdiction over A so that, once he has a judgment, he can seize other assets owned by A to satisfy his judgment.

§ 9.28   Limited Jurisdiction

A court of limited jurisdiction is one which is restricted in the type of case it can hear or in the amount of money involved in the litigation.

EXAMPLE:

A juvenile court, probate court, or a family court can hear only cases involving that particular subject matter. Its jurisdiction is very limited.

Many municipal courts (or other state courts) are limited by the amount of money involved in a particular lawsuit.

EXAMPLE:

A owes B $10,000. B wishes to sue A. If the municipal court where A lives does not have a monetary jurisdiction of $10,000, B must sue A in the appropriate court having monetary jurisdiction of that amount.

§ 9.29   Exclusive Jurisdiction

Exclusive jurisdiction is the authority granted to a court to hear certain matters to the exclusion of all other courts. No other court within the same territorial limits may hear any matter for which there is a court with exclusive jurisdiction. The court also may be restricted to that type of case.

EXAMPLE:

A juvenile court, a family court, or a probate court has exclusive jurisdiction to hear only those matters for which it is established.

§ 9.30   Territorial Jurisdiction

Territorial jurisdiction applies to the actual geographic area over which the court has authority. Both the federal and state court systems have various divisions which limit jurisdiction to specific geographic areas.

§ 9.31　General Jurisdiction (Sometimes Referred to as Unlimited Jurisdiction)

If a court has general jurisdiction, usually this means that the court has no limitation as to the types of cases it can hear and no limitation on its monetary jurisdiction. Since there is no limit as to subject matter or as to the amount in controversy, it is often referred to as a court of general or unlimited jurisdiction. However, in the strict sense of the word "unlimited," all courts are limited in some regard because most court systems have some courts of special exclusive jurisdiction; courts of general jurisdiction cannot hear cases over which special courts have exclusive jurisdiction.

EXAMPLE:

Many states have juvenile courts which handle all matters concerning juveniles. In such a jurisdiction the courts of general or unlimited jurisdiction could not hear any matters concerning juveniles. Therefore, the courts of general jurisdiction are limited to that extent.

§ 9.32　Concurrent Jurisdiction

Concurrent jurisdiction refers to jurisdiction granted to different courts at the same time over the same matters and within the same territorial limit. This means that in certain situations, the plaintiff has a choice of the court in which he wishes to file his suit. This is particularly true, for example, where municipal or small claims courts are established to alleviate crowding the court dockets of the courts of general jurisdiction. Usually, the jurisdiction of the small claims court is concurrent with that of the court of general jurisdiction. The whole purpose of the small claims court is to give claimants a faster, more efficient, more economical court than the court of general jurisdiction in which to process claims which do not involve a large amount of money.

§ 9.33　Monetary Jurisdiction

Monetary jurisdiction refers to the limitation on dollar amount that a court may award. Usually, courts of general jurisdiction are not limited by monetary jurisdiction, but municipal courts and small claims courts are. Federal district courts have jurisdiction in certain types of cases only when the amount in dispute is more than $50,000.

366

§ 9.34   Appellate Jurisdiction

Appellate jurisdiction grants the authority to a court to review cases tried in lower courts. Some courts have both original jurisdiction and appellate jurisdiction.

EXAMPLES:

Very often, a judgment of a municipal or small claims court can be appealed to a court of general or unlimited jurisdiction. In that instance, therefore, the court of general jurisdiction, which is usually a trial court, becomes an appellate court.

Most states have a court of last resort (often called the Supreme Court). Often, these courts have a right to decide whether or not they will even hear an appeal. In addition, it often is the court of last resort which handles disbarment cases against attorneys. In that instance the court may act as a trial court of original jurisdiction, although it is usually an appellate court.

§ 9.35   Venue

Venue refers to various factors in determining the geographical location of a particular dispute and is very important in determining where lawsuits are to be filed. For example, in a state having a trial court of general jurisdiction encompassing four counties, the court has the same subject-matter jurisdiction and thus can hear the same type of disputes in all four counties, but venue differs from one county to the next. Even if the four counties share one judge, each county has its own courthouse and personnel. Venue determines in which county a particular dispute is to be tried. Generally, but subject to many exceptions, venue is proper only in the county in which the defendant resides. In federal courts the general rule is that venue is proper only in the federal district and division in which the defendant resides.

EXAMPLE:

Assume that the counties of Bonneville, Jefferson, Madison, and Fremont share the District Court of the Seventh Judicial District of Idaho. A wishes to sue B, who lives in Jefferson County. A lives in Bonneville County, so it would be more convenient for him to file suit in Bonneville County, which is in the same court. Generally, he cannot sue in Bonneville County, because only the Jefferson County court has proper venue, as well as in personam jurisdiction over B.

§ 9.36   Dual System of Courts

You now have seen several references to state courts and federal courts. There are actually two court systems in the United States.

Although there are many similarities in the two systems, they work independently of each other. There are instances when the United States Supreme Court might review a judgment rendered by a state court, but those instances are rare, occurring only when there has been a final judgment or decree of the highest court of the state in which a decision could be had involving a substantial federal question. You will find that lawsuits which are initiated in either the state or federal system will remain there and that lawsuits usually are not switched from one system to the other. There are exceptions to this rule, of course, but federal courts are very hesitant to interfere in state court matters.

Historically, there are certain types of legal matters which are exclusively reserved to state courts in which federal courts are very hesitant to intervene.

EXAMPLES:

Matters of marriage, divorce, custody, probate proceedings, and property.

On the other hand, there are matters over which federal courts have exclusive jurisdiction.

EXAMPLES:

Criminal matters involving violation of federal laws, admiralty and maritime matters, United States copyright matters, bankruptcy proceedings, proceedings against ambassadors, consuls, and ministers.

Intervention by a federal court in a state court matter would occur most likely if a federal constitutional right of a party were at issue.

§ 9.37   Concurrent Jurisdiction of State and Federal Courts

There are times when state courts and federal courts have concurrent jurisdiction. The most common instance is where there is diversity of citizenship (citizens of different states or of a state and foreign country) and where the amount in dispute is more than $50,000. In such a situation, if a lawsuit is filed in the federal court, the federal court applies state law. Since the federal court and the state court have concurrent jurisdiction, the plaintiff may file his suit in either court, but once he selects the court, he usually brings his suit to conclusion in that court.

§ 9.38   Federal Court System

We will discuss the judicial system starting with the highest court down through the lowest court. This is opposite to the way a matter moves through the courts. Most actions are started in the lowest court authorized to hear the matter. If the parties are dissatisfied with the result, they can appeal to the next higher court authorized to hear appeals, and they may be able to have their case heard by an even higher court. As you can see by referring to Illustration 9–2 showing the federal judicial system, the United States Supreme Court is the highest court in the United States.

Illustration 9–2

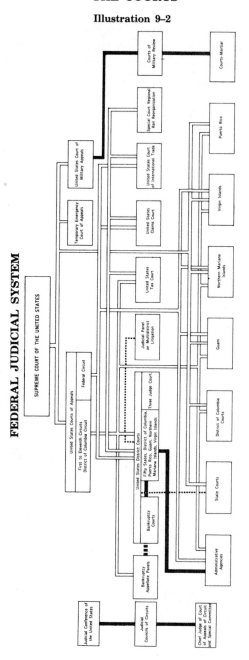

§ 9.39 The United States Supreme Court

The United States Supreme Court is the only court created by the United States Constitution. Its jurisdiction is varied and usually of an appellate nature. There are three principal ways in which a case is heard by the United States Supreme Court:

1. In most instances the United States Supreme Court may decide whether or not it will hear a particular case. This discretion is very similar to that of state courts of last resort which are discussed below. Once there has been a decision in a trial court and in an appellate court, the losing party may petition the United States Supreme Court for a writ of certiorari (review). If the Supreme Court wishes to hear the case, it grants the writ. If it does not, the writ is denied.

2. There are some cases which the Supreme Court is obligated to hear. These cases come to the Supreme Court on appeal rather than by petition for a writ of certiorari.

3. Interestingly enough, however, there are instances in which the United States Supreme Court has original jurisdiction.

EXAMPLE:

Texas and Louisiana have a dispute over their common boundary along the Sabine River. Only the United States Supreme Court has jurisdiction to hear this dispute.

Since it has original jurisdiction over disputes between states, it is a trial court in this instance. Because the United States Supreme Court is the highest court in the land, there is no right to appeal from its decision.

The other federal courts established by legislation are:

• United States Courts of Appeals—These courts hear appeals from various federal district courts, bankruptcy courts, and tax courts. They also review decisions of federal administrative agencies. In many cases that are appealed to a United States Court of Appeals, the losing party may petition the United States Supreme Court for a writ of certiorari. However, the Supreme Court does not have to hear such cases. There are 13 circuit courts of appeals, including one for Washington, D.C. (See Illustration 9–3.)

371

Illustration 9–3

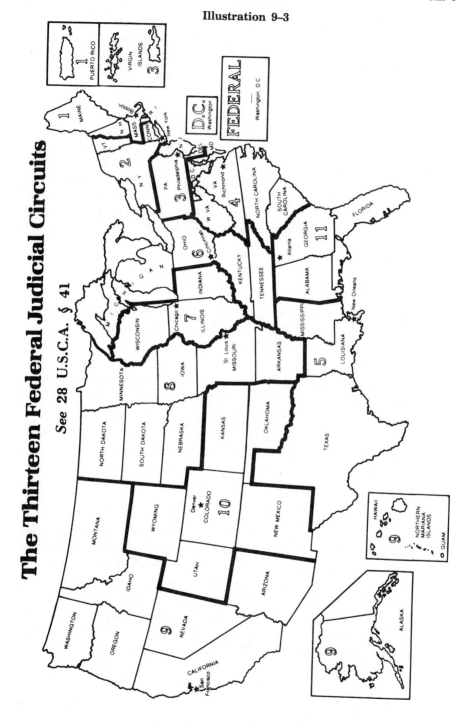

- United States Court of Appeals for the Federal Circuit—This court replaced the United States Court of Customs and Patent Appeals effective October 1, 1982. It hears appeals from the United States Claims Court, the United States Court of International Trade, the Merit Systems Protection Board, and appeals in cases relating to patents, copyrights and trademarks, among others. Its decisions may be appealed to the United States Supreme Court on certiorari.

- United States Court of Military Appeals—This court hears appeals from court martial decisions. Its decisions may be reviewed by the Supreme Court by writ of certiorari in certain cases.

- United States Claims Court—This court, formerly called the United States Court of Claims, hears actions against the United States Government. These cases may be appealed to the United States Court of Appeals for the Federal Circuit.

- United States District Courts—These courts try both criminal and civil actions and sit as admiralty courts. They may also review decisions of federal administrative agencies. There is at least one United States District Court in each state. Their decisions may be appealed to the United States Courts of Appeals.

- United States Tax Court—This court, formerly called the Tax Court of the United States, hears cases concerning federal tax laws. Its decisions may be appealed to the United States Circuit Courts of Appeals (other than the Court of Appeals for the Federal Circuit).

- United States Court of International Trade—This court replaced the United States Customs Court effective October 1, 1982. It hears cases concerning federal tariff laws. Its decisions may be appealed to the United States Court of Appeals for the Federal Circuit.

- United States Bankruptcy Courts—These courts are units of the United States District Courts and hear bankruptcy and reorganization matters referred to bankruptcy judges by the District Courts. Their decisions may be appealed to the United States District Court and, in some cases, to the United States Circuit Courts of Appeals or a bankruptcy appellate panel, if one has been established in the particular circuit.

§ 9.40   United States District Courts

These federal courts have both civil and criminal jurisdiction. They have original jurisdiction in the following types of actions:

- Civil actions arising under the Constitution, laws, or treaties of the United States

- Actions where the matter in controversy exceeds the sum or value of $50,000, exclusive of interest and costs, and is between citizens of different states; citizens of a state and foreign states or citizens or subjects thereof; or citizens of different states in which foreign states or citizens or subjects thereof are additional parties

- All criminal offenses against the laws of the United States

- Admiralty, maritime, and prize cases

- Bankruptcy matters and proceedings

- Actions of interpleader involving money or property of the value of $500 or more claimed by citizens of different states

- Actions to enforce, enjoin, set aside, annul or suspend, in whole or in part, any order of the Interstate Commerce Commission

- Actions or proceedings arising under any act of Congress regulating commerce or protecting trade and commerce against restraints and monopolies

- Any civil action arising under any act of Congress relating to the postal service

- Actions arising under any act of Congress providing for internal revenue or revenue from imports or tonnage except matters within the jurisdiction of the Court of International Trade

- Any civil action authorized by law to be commenced by any person dealing with civil rights, election disputes, and voting rights

- All civil actions, suits, or proceedings commenced by the United States or by any agency or officer thereof

- Actions for recovery of taxes levied by the Internal Revenue Service or actions not exceeding $50,000, founded upon the Constitution, any act of Congress, or any regulation of any executive department (The Claims Court has concurrent jurisdiction in those actions.)

- Actions for the partition of lands where the United States is one of the tenants in common or joint tenants

- Actions involving banks and other corporations

- Actions involving labor disputes by specific statute

- Aliens' actions for torts

- Actions and proceedings against consuls or vice consuls of foreign states

- Actions on bonds executed under any law of the United States (State courts have concurrent jurisdiction in those actions.)

- Actions involving Indian allotments and land grants from different states

- Actions involving injuries under federal laws

- All proceedings to condemn real estate for the use of the United States or its departments or agencies

§ 9.41 State Court System

Because each state has the authority to create its own courts, there are more differences among state courts than federal courts.

Generally, each state has:

- A court of last resort which is the highest court in the state from which there is no appeal, except in certain instances when a decision may be reviewed by the United States Supreme Court.

- An intermediate appellate court or courts to which most appeals are brought before reaching the court of last resort.

- Courts of original jurisdiction having general jurisdiction with no monetary jurisdictional limitations. These courts may also have a division which has appellate jurisdiction to hear appeals from lower courts.

- On a level with these courts, there may be courts with limited jurisdiction, such as a court for family matters, a separate court to handle estate matters, and perhaps a separate criminal court. There also may be a court of claims to hear and determine claims by or against the state.

- The lowest courts in a state are typically courts with lesser monetary and territorial jurisdictions, such as small claims courts and traffic courts. See Illustration 9–4 for a typical state court system.

Illustration 9–4*

B. DIAGRAM OF A "TYPICAL" STATE JUDICIAL SYSTEM

STATE JUDICIAL SYSTEM ††

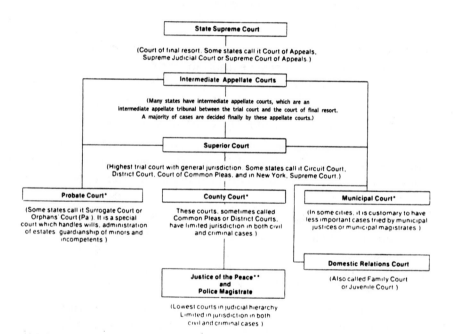

State Judicial System

State Supreme Court

(Court of final resort. Some states call it Court of Appeals, Supreme Judicial Court or Supreme Court of Appeals.)

Intermediate Appellate Courts

(Many states have intermediate appellate courts, which are an intermediate appellate tribunal between the trial court and the court of final resort. A majority of cases are decided finally by these appellate courts.)

Superior Court

(Highest trial court with general jurisdiction. Some states call it Circuit Court, District Court, Court of Common Pleas, and in New York, Supreme Court.)

Probate Court*	**County Court***	**Municipal Court***
(Some states call it Surrogate Court or Orphans' Court (Pa.). It is a special court which handles wills, administration of estates, guardianship of minors and incompetents.)	These courts, sometimes called Common Pleas or District Courts, have limited jurisdiction in both civil and criminal cases.)	(In some cities, it is customary to have less important cases tried by municipal justices or municipal magistrates.)

Domestic Relations Court

(Also called Family Court or Juvenile Court.)

Justice of the Peace** and Police Magistrate**

(Lowest courts in judicial hierarchy. Limited in jurisdiction in both civil and criminal cases.)

†† [The names of courts are illustrative. Others are used.]

*Courts of special jurisdiction, such as Probate, Family or Juvenile, and the so-called inferior courts, such as Common Pleas or Municipal courts, may be separate courts or may be part of the trial court of general jurisdiction.

**Justices of the Peace do not exist in all states. Their jurisdictions vary greatly from state to state where they do exist.

* Reprinted from "Law and the Courts," A Layman's Handbook of Court procedures, with a Glossary of Legal Terminology. Copyright 1980, American Bar Association.   Reprinted by permission of the publisher.

[B3904]

§ 9.42   Who May Sue?

Virtually anyone can sue anyone else. The important thing is whether or not the lawsuit has merit. Most lawsuits arise out of legitimate controversies where one party believes that he is entitled to some kind of relief, the other party disagrees, and they cannot come to terms through negotiation. Therefore, they must rely on a decision of a court to determine which party has taken the correct position.

§ 9.43   Standing

The Litigation chapter explains "standing" as being the requirement that the person injured be the one who must sue. The word "person" here includes many legal entities, including corporations and partnerships, and is not limited to a human being (which is how we ordinarily define "person"). Additionally, in order for a person to have standing, he must have the legal capacity to sue.

§ 9.44   Legal Capacity

Legal capacity refers to whether a person may sue in his own right without being represented by someone else. Each state sets the age at which a person reaches what is known as "the age of majority." Until a person reaches majority (usually 18 to 21 years of age), he is a minor. A minor is someone under the age of majority whose legal affairs must be handled by a parent or a guardian. Therefore, the law considers minors as being children. Once a minor reaches majority, he then may handle his own legal affairs because he then has legal capacity.

Most states have a provision which allows a minor to be emancipated before he reaches the age of majority. This is most often accomplished by a petition of the parent or the minor asking that the court grant an order relieving the minor of the "legal disabilities which attach to minors." Although there is usually a minimum age at which a state will allow a minor to be emancipated, once that emancipation is granted, the minor has legal capacity and the legal authority to handle his own legal affairs.

§ 9.45   Corporations and Other Business Entities

In law the word "person" has many meanings. Various business entities which are not really persons (humans) are recognized in the law as being legal persons. A corporation, for example, is a person (legal entity) which is separate and distinct from the people who run it; for purposes of "standing," it is a person, and it has legal capacity to sue.

§ 9.46   Minors, Legal Incompetents, and Estates

Because a minor does not have legal capacity, he does not have standing to sue in his own name. Any claim that he has must be pursued through his legal guardian. Similarly, an adult who is mentally incapacitated cannot sue except through a guardian who has been appointed by the court to handle the legal affairs of that person. A deceased person's estate has standing to be a party to a lawsuit only through a fiduciary (administrator, executor, or personal representative) appointed by a court.

§ 9.47   Parties

Often, the people or corporations or other legal entities involved in a lawsuit are referred to as "parties." The word "parties" is not limited only to humans but includes corporations, guardians of minors, estates of deceased persons, etc. The parties involved in a lawsuit depend to a large extent upon their standing and legal capacities, the nature of their dispute, and their roles in the lawsuit, such as plaintiff or defendant.

§ 9.48   Parties to an Action

The person (party) who files the lawsuit is usually called the plaintiff, or is also sometimes known as the petitioner. The word "plaintiff" is most commonly used to refer to the party who files a lawsuit. The term "petitioner" is more often used to refer to a party who files a nonlitigious legal proceeding (such as an adoption or probate matter) or the party who initiates dissolution proceedings in states having no-fault divorce laws.

The defendant is the party who is sued. In states having no-fault divorce laws, the party being sued is called the "respondent."

After the complaint has been filed, many other pleadings involving additional claims may ensue. The defendant may file a counterclaim against the plaintiff; in this instance, the defendant would then become the counter-plaintiff, and the plaintiff would be the counter-defendant.

When a case is appealed, the party appealing is referred to as the appellant; the party against whom the appeal is filed is known as the appellee or, in some states, as the respondent.

EXAMPLES:

Alice Williams, Defendant–Appellant
> v.

Sam Jones, Plaintiff–Respondent
Jack White, Plaintiff–Appellant
> v.

Sandra Black, Defendant–Appellee

§ 9.49   Pleadings

Written statements called "pleadings," such as complaints and answers, are made by each side of a lawsuit concerning the respective claims and defenses which will be decided in court. Other papers filed in court—including petitions, orders, motions, memoranda, and affidavits—generally also are referred to as pleadings.

§ 9.50   Filing and Recording

To have a pleading placed in the court file by the clerk or deputy clerk is called "filing" the pleading. If it is the first pleading in the case, the clerk opens a new file and issues a docket number (also sometimes known as a civil number, a case number, or an index number). The case number is to be used on all future pleadings filed in that case.

Some courts charge a fee in order to file certain types of pleadings. Some courts charge a fee only for the initial pleading of a party to an action (such as complaints); others charge a fee for each additional pleading initiating action (such as counterclaims); others charge for filing certain other papers (such as jury demands). Most courts require the correct filing fee to be paid at the time the applicable pleading is filed.

When a document or court paper is sent to a county recorder with the request that notification of the paper be registered in the county records (such as liens, deeds, mortgage records, corporation and partnership records, notary bonds, and declarations of homestead), the document is said to have been "recorded." Some recorders retain the original document in the county records; others microfilm it and return the original document to the owner with the recording information stated on the document.

§ 9.51   Summons and Subpoena

After a complaint has been filed, the clerk generally will sign and "issue" a summons which must be served on the defendant. In some states the summons may be signed and issued by the plaintiff's attorney. After a case is filed, the clerk can issue subpoenas summoning witnesses to testify at depositions or at trial. These subpoenas usually are prepared by the attorney for issuance by the clerk.

§ 9.52 At Issue

A case is said to be "at issue" when the complaint and a responsive pleading (usually an answer) have been filed. It then is said that "the issues have been joined," which means, for example, that the plaintiff has pleaded his claims and the defendant has pleaded his defenses and both are ready to proceed.

§ 9.53 Default

In some instances after a complaint is filed, the defendant enters no defense. After the time set by rule or statute (usually 20 days) has passed, the defendant is said to be in "default." The plaintiff, through his attorney, then can receive a default judgment against the defendant from the court.

§ 9.54 Service

Court rules require that each party to an action must be provided with copies of all court papers filed in the lawsuit. Except for the service of summonses, complaints, and subpoenas, this is usually accomplished by mailing or hand delivering copies to the attorneys of record (or to defendant if there is no attorney of record). A certificate of service is usually typed at the end of the pleading stating that the appropriate copies have been provided to the attorneys for the parties. A copy of the certificate of service is filed with the court.

EXAMPLE:

I certify that on the _____ day of _____ 19__, I mailed (or hand delivered) a copy of the foregoing Answer to John Q. Jones, Esq., 999 Tudor Avenue, Salt Lake City, Utah 84111, attorney for plaintiff.

_____

(name of attorney)
Attorney for Defendant

This method of service does not apply to complaints, summonses, and subpoenas, because they must be served personally by an authorized person. In some jurisdictions service may be obtained by certified mail, return receipt requested. If personal service is not possible, upon approval of the court, service usually can be accomplished by publication of appropriate notice in a newspaper.

§ 9.55 Leave of Court

In the course of a lawsuit, it may become necessary to obtain permission of the court to take some action, such as, for example, permission to amend a complaint. This is referred to as obtaining "leave of court."

§ 9.56 The Court

Technically, the word "court" means a tribunal with judicial authority to handle the administration of justice. That administration requires a meeting place, a system for meeting at particular times, and administrative personnel. Therefore, when a person is said to be "in court," that usually means he is attending a formal court hearing. However, day-to-day usage of the word "court" also includes:

1. Reference to a hearing date or place.
   EXAMPLE:
   > Court will be held on June 10; or court will recess and reconvene at 2 p.m.

2. Reference to the judge who presides at a hearing or over a particular court.
   EXAMPLE:
   > The Court believes; or may it please the Court; or if the Court please; or with the Court's permission. (All these remarks are made by or to the presiding judge.)

3. Reference to the physical facility which houses the court (the courtroom or the courthouse).

4. Reference to a specific court.
   EXAMPLE:
   > Court of Common Pleas; or Probate Court, Tulsa County.

§ 9.57 Term of Court

Court rules sometimes designate the period of time during which a court sits to conduct business. This is known as a "term of court." A term may be divided into different periods which are referred to as sessions. These terms are often given a name related to the time of year, such as "spring term" or "October term." Some courts use a descriptive name such as "general term" or "trial term."

§ 9.58 The Bar

In a courtroom, there is usually a railing dividing the area where the attorneys, witnesses, court reporters, jury, and judge sit from the spectators' area. This railing is generally referred to as "the bar." When an attorney is licensed to practice, he is permitted to go beyond the railing into the privileged area. Hence, being licensed to practice law is known as being "admitted to the bar," and the "Bar" refers to attorneys, and their organization is known as the "Bar Association."

§ 9.59   The Bench

The raised podium at the front of a courtroom behind which the judge sits is known as "the bench." During a trial attorneys may request permission to "approach the bench," meaning that they wish to confer privately with the judge out of the hearing of the jury.

§ 9.60   In Chambers

In some instances a judge may meet with the attorneys and parties in his chambers (office) rather than in the courtroom. These meetings usually are more informal than hearings in open court.

§ 9.61   In Open/Closed Court

Hearings conducted in the courtroom at which members of the general public may be present as spectators are said to be "open." In contrast, hearings excluding spectators are "closed" hearings. A judge in some instances may use his own discretion as to whether or not to close a hearing. Generally, however, unless a closed hearing is ordered by law (such as juvenile hearings and adoptions), court hearings are open to members of the public.

§ 9.62   Ex Parte

In some instances a judge can sign an order "ex parte" (without the presence of attorneys from both sides of a case). This usually occurs when immediate action must be taken to obtain an order from the court. Such an order, for example, would extend a deadline which is about to expire or to stop someone from doing something which might be injurious to person or property (such as a restraining order). This order would be entered prior to a complete hearing on the merits of a dispute. It might also result from application to the court for a form of relief such as continuance of a hearing date or permission to file an over-length brief.

§ 9.63   Show Cause

An order granted ex parte may generally make provision for a date and time at which the opposing side may appear before the court to present arguments against entry of such order. This generally is referred to as appearing to "show cause" why the order should not be granted.

§ 9.64   Contempt of Court

When an individual refuses to obey either a written or oral order of the judge, the judge may find him "in contempt of court." The judge usually has the option of levying a fine or imposing a jail sentence, or both, upon the person who is in contempt of court.

§ 9.65   Pro Se (In Proper Person)

When a person decides to represent himself rather than have an attorney represent him, he is said to be appearing "Pro Se" or "In Proper Person," and he uses that designation when signing pleadings.

§ 9.66   Law and Motion Day

A court generally sets aside a specific time or day to hear routine matters such as show cause orders, motion hearings, and default judgments. Hearings at which only the attorneys but not the parties need appear or which, by their nature, will be of short duration are usually set for these days or times.

§ 9.67   Court Officers

Most of the people involved in the administration of justice are known as "officers of the court." Courts require attorneys appearing before them also to be officers of the court as well as advocates for their clients.

§ 9.68   Judge

The judge is the presiding officer of the court. Most state judges are elected, although some are appointed. All federal judges are appointed. A judge's major duties are to preside over the hearings and trials in a case and to rule on issues raised by pleadings or that come up during a hearing or trial. He instructs the jury on matters of law in jury trials. The number of judges which a given court has depends upon the workload of that court.

§ 9.69   Clerk of Court

The court clerk is the administrator or chief clerical officer of the court. He is responsible for the clerical details of a case. In most jurisdictions the clerk of the court is the custodian of all public records filed with the court. Sometimes the clerk of court is ex-officio recorder of conveyances and of mortgages, and in this capacity he may keep records of sales and mortgages on property.

§ 9.70 Secretary/Deputy Clerk/Law Clerk

Each judge has at least one secretary or deputy clerk or law clerk. This person may function as a secretary or as a courtroom or research assistant to the judge. This person may sit in the court while it is in session, and may be responsible for the judge's calendar, files, and exhibits. Judges in federal courts and in the higher state courts usually have at least one law clerk in addition to a secretary.

§ 9.71 Minute Clerk or Court Reporter

A court generally has a court reporter who sits in court while it is in session and records all legal proceedings verbatim with some type of recording equipment. The court also may have a courtroom deputy clerk or minute clerk to keep track of files, exhibits, and proceedings, and to administer oaths.

§ 9.72 Bailiff

The bailiff is the peace officer of the court and is responsible for keeping order. He also is responsible for the protection of everyone in the courtroom and for maintaining appropriate decorum during proceedings.

§ 9.73 Sheriff or Marshal

The sheriff or marshal is the law enforcement officer for the court who serves summonses and citations and executes court orders. The sheriff is a county officer, and the marshal is a federal officer. Their duties are similar, although the marshal also transports federal prisoners. Some lower state courts also have constables, whose duties are the same as those of the sheriff. In many jurisdictions the sheriff or marshal makes seizures to satisfy judgments, holds public auctions, and reports back to the court regarding these matters. In a few jurisdictions there are civil sheriffs and criminal sheriffs, so in such systems the civil sheriff handles only civil matters and the criminal sheriff handles only criminal matters.

§ 9.74 Attorneys

Each attorney is also an officer of the court and as such is obligated to uphold the dignity of the court and to abide by the rules of the court.

§ 9.75 Complaint/Petition

The pleading that is filed to initiate an action is usually called a complaint or a petition. In some jurisdictions the term "complaint" is used in litigated matters, reserving the term "petition" for legal proceedings that do not involve a contest.

384

§ 9.76 Caption

The caption of the case is the title of the case. The actual form of the caption varies from jurisdiction to jurisdiction, but it usually sets out:

1. The full name of the court in which the action is filed.

2. The full names of the parties involved, with the plaintiff's name listed first. If there are numerous plaintiffs involved, on all pleadings after the initial pleadings, only the name of the first plaintiff usually must be given followed with the designation "et al." to indicate that there are other plaintiffs. The same procedure generally is used for cases having numerous defendants.

3. The number of the case. On initial pleadings the court usually will assign a docket or case number when the action is filed.

4. The name of the pleading.

EXAMPLE OF COMPLETE CAPTION:

IN THE DISTRICT COURT OF THE SIXTH JUDICIAL
DISTRICT OF THE STATE OF IDAHO, IN AND FOR
BANNOCK COUNTY

JOHN DOE, FRED WHEELER,)
SAM SMITH, GEORGE AL-)
COTT, ACE LINCOLN, and) Civil No. _____
JOHN BRYAN,)
           Plaintiffs,) COMPLAINT
    vs.)
)
JANE X. BROWN,)
         Defendant.)

§ 9.77 Opening Paragraphs

The opening paragraphs of a complaint usually give introductory information about the name, legal capacity, domicile of the parties, and the legal basis for jurisdiction and venue.

§ 9.78 Allegations/Claims

The opening paragraphs are followed by numbered paragraphs setting forth the background and reasons for filing the suit. These paragraphs are referred to as "allegations," which must set forth a short, plain statement of the claims or causes of action.

§ 9.79   Prayer

The complaint usually ends with a "prayer" which sets forth a summary of what the plaintiff or petitioner is asking the court to do.

§ 9.80   Verification

A complaint generally must be signed by the plaintiff's attorney. Because it contains allegations of fact, it is preferable (required in some jurisdictions) that the complaint contain a statement by the plaintiff asserting that the allegations are true and correct to the best of his knowledge. This is called a "verification" and is placed at the end of the complaint following the attorney's signature. (See Illustration 9–5.)

Illustration 9–5

NO. _____

JANE DOE,	)	IN THE DISTRICT COURT
Plaintiff	)	
	)	_____ JUDICIAL DISTRICT
v.	)	
	)	
ALEX PRINCE,	)	BEXAR COUNTY, TEXAS
Defendant	)	

COMPLAINT

Plaintiff herein for her cause of action respectfully shows to the Court that:

I.

The plaintiff is a resident of the City of _____, County of _____, State of _____, and the defendant is a resident of _____ County, residing at _____ Street, _____, _____. [*If either party is a corporation, give place and where incorporated.*]

II.

On or about the _____ day of _____, 19__, a _____ automobile owned by plaintiff was being driven by _____ in a _____ direction on _____ Street, in the City of _____. [*Here set out facts upon which the plaintiff bases his cause of action.*]

III.

The defendant was negligent in the operation of his automobile immediately preceding and at the time of the collision in the following particulars: [*here state facts indicating negligence*].

Each of the foregoing acts of omission and of commission were negligent, and each was a proximate cause of the accident which is the basis of the suit.

IV.

As a result of the collision, plaintiff has been forced to spend the sum of $_____ in order to repair her automobile.

V.

Plaintiff's automobile prior to said collision had a reasonable market value of $_____, and just after the collision it had a reasonable market value of $_____. Therefore, the plaintiff has been damaged in the amount of $_____.

WHEREFORE, plaintiff prays that defendant be cited to appear and answer herein; that upon final hearing, the plaintiff recover her damages as hereinabove alleged, together with all costs; and for such other, further, and general relief to which she may be entitled.

_____
(name and address of attorney)
ATTORNEY FOR PLAINTIFF

STATE OF TEXAS   )
)   ss.
COUNTY OF _____)

JANE DOE, being duly sworn, deposes and states that she is the plaintiff in the above entitled action, that she has read the foregoing complaint and that every statement contained therein is within her personal knowledge and is true and correct.

_____
JANE DOE

Subscribed and sworn to before me the _____ day of _____, 19__.

_____
Notary Public, State of Texas

My commission expires:

§ 9.81   Relief Sought

What the plaintiff hopes to gain by filing the lawsuit is referred to as "relief sought by the plaintiff," or in a counterclaim "the relief sought by the defendant."

§ 9.82   Remedy

In assessing the validity of a claim for his client, the attorney may refer to whether there is an adequate, available remedy at law. A typical remedy at law is a recovery of money damages.

§ 9.83   Types of Relief or Remedies

Although most lawsuits seek awards of money, some seek other types of relief.

EXAMPLES:

Assume A and B entered into a contract in which B agreed to begin building a residence for A within 90 days after execution of the contract. B does not begin the work as he promised. A sues B for specific performance. He wants B to perform the terms of the contract.

A is demolishing a building in a residential area using explosives. B is concerned that his building next to A's also will be demolished by the explosion. B may seek injunctive relief asking the court to issue an injunction preventing A from using explosives to demolish his building.

Injunctive relief also may be sought to require that something be done rather than to stop something.

EXAMPLE:

A and the phone company are involved in a dispute over the nonpayment of a commercial account, a portion of which A guaranteed. A refuses to pay the disputed portion of the bill, so the phone company terminates A's phone service at his residence. A seeks injunctive relief asking the court to issue an injunction requiring the phone company to restore his service.

§ 9.84   Alternative Relief

In suits that seek one type of relief, it is not uncommon to ask for alternative relief.

EXAMPLE:

Assuming the facts in the house construction contract example above, A's complaint could contain a plea in the alternative that if the court decides he is not entitled to specific performance, then he should be awarded a sum of money for the damages he sustained in not having his residence timely built.

§ 9.85   Docket or Case Number

When a legal proceeding is filed with the clerk of court, it is given a docket or case number. Most courts having numbering systems assign numbers in numerical order, but sometimes the numbering systems are divided into various subject matters. Some courts use their numbering systems to keep track of the number of lawsuits filed in a particular category each year. Docket numbers may be referred to in different jurisdictions in pleadings as Civil No. _____, Criminal No. _____, or Case No. _____.

§ 9.86 Filing Pleadings

With exceptions in some courts (especially federal trial courts) concerning certain discovery requests, the original of the pleadings generally is filed with the clerk of the appropriate court. These pleadings are placed in the court record. In addition to the complaint, other pleadings which might be filed during the course of an action include: answers, motions, notices, petitions, orders, memoranda, and affidavits.

§ 9.87 Motions

Often during the course of a legal proceeding, one of the parties to the proceeding must seek some type of interim order. This is usually done by a pleading moving (asking) the court for some specific relief. This is known as a written motion.

EXAMPLE:

If there is a hearing set in a case on a date when one of the attorneys already has a trial scheduled, he can file a motion for continuance. (He asks the court to continue the trial to another date.)

Some courts require supplementary papers supporting the request, such as an affidavit, memorandum of law, or legal brief.

§ 9.88 Notices

Whenever a hearing is scheduled, all parties must be informed of the date, time, place, and subject matter to be heard. This is accomplished by sending a notice of hearing to all attorneys involved. The attorney requesting the hearing generally prepares and sends the notice.

§ 9.89 Orders

When a motion and notice of hearing are filed, the judge may hold a hearing and issue an order on the motion. In some instances, no hearing is held because the motion is routine, opposing counsel does not object, or the particular court does not have hearings on motions. The order usually is prepared for the judge's signature by the attorney who prevails on the motion.

§ 9.90 Answer

The answer is a responsive pleading in which the defendant answers the allegations of the complaint. This response to the complaint must be filed within a statutory period of time (usually 20 days from the date he is served with the summons) unless he is given additional time by the plaintiff's attorney and/or by the court. An extension may be accomplished informally and, in some instances, an answer may never be filed because:

• The defendant is agreeable to a default judgment, or

• The case has been settled out of court.

A trial cannot be held until the answer is filed.

§ 9.91 Summons

When a lawsuit is filed in a court, the clerk generally issues a notice of the suit to the defendant called a "summons." In some states the summons may be signed and issued by the plaintiff or his attorney. The summons and a copy of the complaint, if any, may be served by the sheriff, his deputy, or by any other authorized person who is not a party to the action.

§ 9.92 Judgment

When a court issues a decision, it is said that the court "renders judgment."

When a plaintiff sues a defendant, that plaintiff is seeking a judgment or order of the court granting him some type of relief. It may be that the defendant owes him money, or it may be that he wishes the defendant to do some particular thing. If the judge believes that the plaintiff is entitled to the relief he seeks, the judge signs a judgment or order.

If the judgment rendered is against the defendant and is for a certain sum of money, then in most jurisdictions the plaintiff can seek satisfaction of his judgment by seizing assets which belong to the defendant. The plaintiff might seize the defendant's bank account, his wages, a car, or anything of value which the defendant owns. There are many variances from state to state as to what exactly can be seized in satisfaction of a judgment and the procedures that must be followed to accomplish the seizure. For example, some states do not allow seizure of wages.

In most states a judgment is placed of record and becomes a lien attaching to any property owned by the defendant in that county. This means that the plaintiff might have an opportunity to collect his judgment if the defendant were to attempt to sell his property. Once a judgment has been paid, it is said to have been satisfied. Once a judgment has been satisfied, evidence of satisfaction is recorded so that the judgment can be canceled. The mechanics of recording and canceling judgments vary considerably from state to state.

§ 9.93   Findings of Fact and Conclusions of Law

Except for uncomplicated cases and jury trials, most courts give written reasons for judgment. This is a writing by the judge which sets out the factual and legal reasons why he arrived at his decision. This is generally known as "Findings of Fact and Conclusions of Law" but may be called "Written Reasons for Judgment" in some states.

§ 9.94   Appeals

Once a judgment is rendered by the court, the losing party may appeal. Except for rare instances, the losing party has the right to one automatic appeal. If the appeal is filed within the statutory time period, the appellate court must review the law as applied to the facts of the case by the jury or trial judge. The procedure in the appellate court is quite different from that in the trial court because there is not another trial. The appellate court reviews the court record of the entire proceeding (in some states a shortened version of the record). When the record has been prepared and delivered to the appellate court, it is said to have been "lodged" or "filed." The attorneys for the parties file briefs and may later appear before the court for oral argument. No witnesses appear at such a hearing. After it has studied the record of the case, the briefs filed by the parties, and the oral arguments, if any, the appellate court renders its decision. The appellate court usually issues a written opinion when it reaches a decision. The appellate court can issue one of several opinions:

1. It can affirm the judgment of the trial court. This means that the appellate court agrees with the decision.

2. It can amend the judgment of the trial court. This means that the appellate court believes that all or a portion of the judgment of the trial court was in error and it therefore amends (changes) it.

3. It can remand the case to the trial court. This means that the appellate court believes that the trial court failed to consider an important point, so the case is sent back to the trial court for reconsideration. This may result in a complete new trial or a partial retrial.

4. It can reverse the judgment of the trial court. This means that it believes that the trial court reached the wrong decision, and

the appellate court completely reverses the trial court's decision (reaches the opposite decision).

5. It can affirm in part and reverse in part.

After the appeal court renders its judgment, the losing party may request a rehearing.

In states having intermediate courts of appeal, there is a court of last resort (most often called the supreme court) which has the right of review of appellate court decisions. In those instances, however, that court usually has the right to decide whether or not it will review the decisions of the intermediate courts of appeal. The party seeking the review (the losing party in the intermediate appellate court) applies to the supreme court for a writ of certiorari (review). The supreme court, on the basis of the application, decides whether or not it will grant the writ. If it does, the entire court record of the proceeding up to that point (from the initial pleading in the lawsuit to the decision of the intermediate appellate court) is sent to the supreme court. The same procedure as in the intermediate appellate court then is followed. The attorneys for all parties involved file briefs; there may be oral argument before a panel of judges; and after reviewing the entire record with the additional briefs and arguments, if any, the supreme court reaches a decision, usually set forth in a written opinion. In some states once the supreme court has reached its decision, a party may petition the court for a rehearing. Even when a court has the right to grant a rehearing, it rarely does. Rehearings are granted if the losing party can convince the court that it made a grave error or failed to consider an important legal point.

Once a legal matter has been heard by the court of last resort or once that court has refused a further hearing of a case, the judgment in that case is said to be res judicata. This means that the particular dispute has been resolved once and for all, and neither party to the suit can sue the other again regarding the same dispute.

§ 9.95 Nonlitigated Matters

Not all court proceedings are litigated matters. As a matter of fact, unless your firm specializes in litigation, it is possible that the majority of court proceedings handled by your office will not be litigated matters. Many legal matters involve only the client, his attorney, and the judge. In these instances the hearing is usually a very informal meeting in the judge's chambers (office) and is much like a conference in your office.

It is possible that a defendant who has been sued will not attempt to defend the lawsuit. If so, assuming the plaintiff can prove his case to the judge's satisfaction, the plaintiff will get a judgment by default.

The defendant is given a specified period of time within which to present a defense to a suit against him. If he fails to do so, a default judgment can be taken against him. The plaintiff accomplishes this by appearing in court with his attorney and presenting his case to the court. Most courts have designated times for handling this type of hearing.

§ 9.96   Decorum in the Courtroom

While most court proceedings are not conducted as portrayed on television, judges and courts are entitled to be treated with respect. Each time a court convenes, the bailiff generally enters the courtroom immediately before the judge, asks that all stand, and makes an announcement, such as: "Oyez, oyez (or Hear ye, hear ye), the Honorable 19th Judicial District Court in and for the County of Tulsa, State of Oklahoma, is now in session, the Honorable Mary Ann Spencer presiding."

The judge also stands, as it is the court itself (the tribunal) which is being honored, not the judge.

In most cases, spectators are allowed in the courtroom, but if the spectators are disruptive, the judge may have them removed.

§ 9.97   Contact With Courts

In performing your daily tasks, you will often find it necessary to talk with personnel in the clerk's office or the judge's office. Having a friendly relationship with these people can make your job much easier. Remember that they are the people who process most of your work. Because they are thoroughly familiar with the procedural aspects of what they handle, you should seek guidance from them when you are uncertain as to how you should proceed. Set up an index card system of names, addresses, and telephone numbers of the people with whom you deal with a notation of what that person handles. It is helpful to address the clerks and their staffs by name. Displaying such initiative also will demonstrate to your employer that you are interested and know how to do a good job.

§ 9.98   Court Records

Courts, both federal and state, must keep a record of all judicial proceedings. The record is the written history of all proceedings in a legal matter, regardless of whether it is tried or not. A court record is opened or begun when the complaint or petition is filed. All subsequent pleadings in that case, all actions taken by the court, all written material filed for discovery or evidence, and the transcript of the trial, if there is one, are filed in the record. If an appeal is taken, then that appeal also forms part of the record. In the event of an appeal, the entire record, or some designated portion, is sent to the appellate court; the proceedings in the appellate court become part of the record; and when all appeals have been exhausted, the record on appeal is sent back to the trial court, where it remains. Some courts, such as justice of the peace courts, however, do not keep written records of all proceedings in a legal matter.

When a court takes action in a case without issuing an order or judgment, the action often is noted in the record as a minute entry or simply as a docket entry.

§ 9.99   Rules of Court

Each court, whether federal or state, has its own rules and procedures to follow when filing legal pleadings. These rules have the effect of law, and they are very important to the efficient preparation of pleadings. It is essential that you have a copy of the court rules for each court in which you will file pleadings. Copies of these rules usually are available from the clerk of court's office. If your firm subscribes to publications of West Publishing Company, your office each year receives from West a pamphlet giving the court rules of the United States Supreme Court, the United States Courts of Appeals in which your state is situated, the federal district courts for your state, and the major state courts of your state. Look for this publication in your library and become familiar with it.

The rules of court also give the court's requirements as to the number of copies of pleadings which must be filed, how much advanced costs are required, information about getting orders signed by the judge, priority of some kinds of cases, how to get on the trial docket, and other useful information.

Although the federal district courts are governed by the rules of procedure set forth in the Federal Rules of Civil Procedure, Criminal Procedure, and Evidence, each federal court also may adopt its own local rules. Therefore, you must have a copy of the local rules for your district.

§ 9.100   Uniform Laws

The National Conference of Commissioners on Uniform State Laws develops model laws in various areas of the law. Their goal is to attain some uniformity among state laws. These model acts are made available to state legislatures for their consideration. The model acts often are adopted by the state legislatures but usually with some modification. Examples of such acts are the Uniform Probate Code, the Model Business Corporation Act, and the Model Penal Code.

§ 9.101   Summary

Although the subject of courts is very broad and sometimes difficult to comprehend, it is essential for a secretary to have a thorough understanding of court structure and procedure. Court rules and procedures change constantly. You can keep current by reading bar association publications and by attending workshops and seminars sponsored by your local chapter of the National Association of Legal Secretaries and by the local and state bar associations. Often notice of changes in court rules and procedures comes through the mail from law book publishers. You should study these changes before routing them to your attorney, and you should make notes of any important changes. If you do not have time to look at the changes when they are received in your office, write a note to your attorney that you would like to see them once he has read them. It is your responsibility to be aware of current rules and procedures.

CHAPTER 10

ADMINISTRATIVE AGENCIES

Table of Sections

---

§ 10.1 Introduction

Administrative agencies are created by the legislative branch of government to administer a specific law or group of similar laws. That is their only function. Federal agencies are created by Congress, and state agencies are created by individual state legislatures. Legal secretaries must cope almost daily with a multitude of these agencies and should have a general knowledge of the functions performed by those agencies they frequently encounter.

§ 10.2 Federal Agencies

The legal secretary employed in a large city is often able to secure information she needs from local branches of the various agencies. Local offices are listed under United States government offices in the telephone directory. However, for special kinds of information it may be necessary for the legal secretary to communicate directly with the main office in the Washington, D.C., area. Of course, if there is no local office in her area, the legal secretary will have to deal directly with the Washington office for any information she needs. Some of the agencies which the legal secretary is most likely to encounter are:

1. Bureau of Land Management
   Department of the Interior
   Washington, DC 20240

The Bureau of Land Management has jurisdiction over approximately 450 million acres of public lands, which it manages. Its objective is to achieve maximum benefit from these lands for the public. The lands may be opened up for use by the public by the issuance of permits for grazing of sheep and cattle or by leasing the rights to mineral resources or timber. The lands may also be withdrawn from public use in order to conserve natural resources, prevent soil erosion, or protect watershed areas.

2. Consumer Product Safety Commission
    1111 Eighteenth Street, NW
    Washington, DC 20207

The purpose of this commission is to protect the public against unreasonable risks of injury from consumer products and to assist in the evaluation of the comparative safety of consumer products.

3. Department of Veterans Affairs (VA)
    810 Vermont Avenue, NW
    Washington, DC 20260

Veterans' benefits, administered by the Department of Veterans Affairs (formerly the Veterans Administration), include cash benefits and services for veterans and their dependents and survivors. Among these benefits are compensation for service-connected disability or death; pensions for non-service-connected disability or death, based on age and financial need; medical benefits including nursing home, domiciliary, or hospital care; burial benefits; and life insurance. Except for life insurance, these benefits do not create vested rights in the recipients and can be withdrawn by Congress or forfeited.

4. Environmental Protection Agency (EPA)
    401 M Street, SW
    Washington, DC 20460

The EPA works to protect and enhance our environment now and for the future by a coordinated effort with state and local governments to abate all forms of environmental pollution.

5. Equal Employment Opportunity Commission (EEOC)
    1801 L Street, NW
    Washington, DC 20507

The purpose of this commission is to eliminate discrimination in employment in all areas and to promote voluntary compliance by employers.

6. Federal Aviation Agency (FAA)
    800 Independence Avenue, SW
    Washington, DC 20591

The FAA is charged with regulating air commerce to foster aviation safety.

7. Federal Bureau of Investigation (FBI)
   Ninth Street and Pennsylvania Avenue, NW
   Washington, DC 20535

The FBI investigates all violations of federal laws except those specifically assigned to other federal agencies. Some of the areas in which the FBI is involved are espionage, sabotage, kidnapping, extortion, bank robbery, civil rights matters, interstate gambling violations, and assault or killing of the President or a federal officer.

8. Federal Communications Commission (FCC)
   1919 M Street, NW
   Washington, DC 20554

The FCC licenses and regulates interstate and foreign communications by radio, television, wire, and cable.

9. Federal Deposit Insurance Corporation (FDIC)
   550 17th Street, NW
   Washington, DC 20429

   and

   Federal Savings and Loan Insurance Corporation (FSLIC)
   1700 G Street, NW
   Washington, DC 20552

The FDIC and FSLIC provide insurance coverage for bank and savings and loan depositories up to a specific amount set by law in the event of financial failure of a financial institution.

10. Federal Mediation and Conciliation Service
    2100 K Street, NW
    Washington, DC 20427

This agency promotes the development of equitable and stable labor-management relationships and assists in settling disputes in the event of work stoppages or threatened work stoppages.

11. Federal Trade Commission (FTC)
    Pennsylvania at Sixth Street, NW
    Washington, DC 20580

The basic objective of the FTC is to maintain a free and fair competitive enterprise system within the American economic system.

12. Food and Drug Administration (FDA)
     5600 Fishers Lane
     Rockville, MD 20852

FDA activities are directed toward protecting the public against impure and unsafe drugs, food, and cosmetics.

13. Government Printing Office (GPO)
     710 North Capitol Street, NW
     Washington, DC 20401

The GPO is in charge of all printing, binding, and sales of government publications. Inquiries regarding the purchase of government publications should be directed to:

> Superintendent of Documents
> Government Printing Office
> 941 North Capitol Street, NE
> Washington, DC 20401

A free informational brochure, *Consumers Guide to Federal Publications,* designed to familiarize the public with the material is available from this address.

14. Immigration and Naturalization Service (INS)
     425 I Street, NW
     Washington, DC 20538

This agency is charged with the administration of immigration and naturalization laws relating to the admission, exclusion, deportation, and naturalization of aliens.

15. Internal Revenue Service (IRS)
     1111 Constitution Avenue, NW
     Washington, DC 20224

The IRS administers all federal tax laws except those relating to alcohol, tobacco, firearms, and explosives.

16. Interstate Commerce Commission (ICC)
     12th Street and Constitution Avenue, NW
     Washington, DC 20423

The ICC regulates interstate surface transportation, including trucks, trains, buses, inland waterway and coastal shipping, freight forwarders, and express companies.

17. National Labor Relations Board (NLRB)
    1717 Pennsylvania Avenue, NW
    Washington, DC 20570

NLRB is vested with the power to safeguard employees' rights to form bargaining units and to prevent and remedy unfair labor practices.

18. Occupational Safety and Health Administration (OSHA)
    200 Constitution Avenue, NW
    Washington, DC 20210

OSHA develops and regulates occupational safety and health standards.

19. Patent and Trademark Office
    Washington, DC 20231

The Patent and Trademark Office examines and issues design patents, plant patents, and utility patents and registers trademarks.

20. Resolution Trust Corporation (RTC)
    801 Seventeenth Street NW
    Washington, DC 20434

The Resolution Trust Corporation was established to manage and resolve failed savings associations that were insured by the Federal Savings and Loan Insurance Corporation before the enactment of the Financial Institutions Reform Recovery and Enforcement Act of 1989, and for which a conservator or receiver was appointed between January 1, 1989, and August 9, 1992.

The corporation will terminate all functions no later than December 31, 1996.

21. Securities and Exchange Commission (SEC)
    450 5th Street, NW
    Washington, DC 20549

The SEC monitors the securities industry by providing disclosure to the investing public and protects the interests of investors against malpractices in the securities and financial markets.

22. Small Business Administration (SBA)
    409 Third Street, SW
    Washington, DC 20416

The SBA provides assistance of all kinds, including loans, to small businesses.

23. Social Security Administration (SSA)
    6401 Security Boulevard
    Baltimore, MD 21235

This agency administers social security and Medicare programs.

24. United States Customs Service
    1301 Constitution Avenue, NW
    Washington, DC 20229

The Customs Service administers and enforces customs laws, which includes the collection of revenue from imports.

25. United States Marshals Service
    One Tysons Corner Center
    McLean, VA 22101

The U.S. Marshals Service shares the responsibility for maintaining the integrity of the Federal judicial process by insuring the security of court facilities and the personal safety of judges, including around-the-clock protection when a real or apparent threat has been made because of court action. The Marshals Service has the primary responsibility for tracking and apprehension of fugitives, assists other law enforcement agencies in apprehending fugitives, and is the principal contact for all international investigations and extraditions. This agency provides protection to witnesses whose testimony endangers their own lives or lives of their families. It maintains custody of federal prisoners after arrest and during transport and also houses approximately 16,000 unsentenced prisoners each day in federal, state, and local jails throughout the nation. It is responsible for seizing, managing, and disposing of forfeited properties and assets from major drug and criminal cases. The Special Operations Group of the Marshals Service is a highly trained, self-supporting mobile (within six hours from anywhere in the United States) reaction force designated to provide federal assistance in emergency situations of national significance.

26. United States Postal Service
    475 L'Enfant Plaza West, SW
    Washington, DC 20260

The Postal Service provides mail processing and delivery to individuals and businesses within the United States.

§ 10.3 State Agencies

Each state government and many local governments have their own administrative agencies. As a matter of fact, you may have had occasion to deal with some of your local or state administrative agencies.

EXAMPLES:

Public service or public utilities commissions regulate utilities (water, telephone, electricity). Workers' compensation boards or industrial commissions handle claims of workers injured on their jobs. Civil service commissions regulate the hiring of government employees.

Licensing boards regulate the issuance of licenses for any specific field designated by the acts which create these boards. (For example, the Licensing Board for Contractors would regulate licenses to contractors, and the Licensing Board for Realtors would regulate the issuance of licenses to realtors.)

Boards of health regulate matters concerning the health and well-being of the public.

Zoning commissions regulate the use of property under their jurisdiction.

School boards regulate matters involving the public school system.

Banking boards regulate certain aspects of the banking business under their jurisdiction.

§ 10.4 Importance of Having a Contact Within the Agency

It would probably be safe to say that you will have the experience of calling an administrative agency to secure information and be shifted from department to department before being able to reach the person who has the information you need. It is important to write down the name, title, telephone number and extension of this person. Otherwise, you may need additional information a few days later with reference to the same matter and run into the same problem, even though you ask for the person with whom you had previously talked. At this point you end up talking to an entirely different person and of necessity repeating the entire matter instead of simply requesting the additional information.

Thus, the importance of having a contact within the agency is fairly obvious. Making a call directly to the contact will get you either the needed information or a transfer to the proper person in the proper department. Future calls on the same matter can then be handled much more efficiently. It is important that you strive at all times to keep a good business relationship with that contact. If a problem arises from either your office or that of the administrative agency concerning a particular matter, you and the contact should be able to work together to arrive at a satisfactory answer or solution.

Many state and local governments publish a directory or manual that lists the various agencies and their functions. Try to locate such a directory and become familiar with it. Your Secretary of State should be able to provide you with such a directory if your state publishes one or tell you where you can secure such a list. The time you invest now in establishing a contact and locating this information will result in saving time later.

CHAPTER 11

LITIGATION

Table of Sections

405

––––––––––

§ 11.1　Definition

Webster's Dictionary defines the word "litigation" as "the act or process of litigating; a suit at law." Litigation is the means of resolving a dispute between parties in a court of law. Simply stated, litigation is the handling, preparation, and trial of lawsuits.

This chapter offers a discussion of the steps in a civil lawsuit where a private party brings suit against another to resolve a dispute or a controversy.

§ 11.2   How Lawsuits Arise

The American legal system provides that any person injured by another may bring a civil suit seeking damages for that legal wrong. The reason for the lawsuit, then, arises when one party suffers an injury or damage as a result of a legal wrong committed by another. These factors are basic to any lawsuit—a wrong done by one and an injury or damage suffered by another.

§ 11.3   A Cause of Action

Generally, a person who suffers an injury from an automobile accident or a physical attack realizes that he has a reason for suing to seek damages from the person who caused the injury. Even though the ordinary person may not know anything about the law, he realizes that this cause of action is something for which he has a right to recover damages. He usually seeks an attorney for advice and to handle his case.

§ 11.4   Res Judicata

Parties to a dispute have the right to have their case tried. However, under normal circumstances it may be tried only once. This rule is known as the res judicata principle. As you learned from your study of courts, this rule means that once there has been a final judicial decision (usually by a court of last resort), the same matter cannot be litigated again. That matter has been set to rest forever. It is necessary to have such a rule so that the losing party will not return to court to keep asking for his case to be retried in the hope that he will find a sympathetic judge or jury to grant his request for the relief he wants. If that were to happen, the losing party would attempt retrials until he could get the results he wanted, and the matter would go on and on.

§ 11.5   Beginning a Lawsuit—Initial Client Interview

The attorney's first interview with the client is to determine whether there is a cause of action. He is sometimes able to decide during the course of the interview if he wishes to accept the case. Other times, he may want to research the problem before deciding to handle the matter.

The attorney will then answer the client's questions about the matter, explain how the case will be handled, the length of time it may take to resolve the matter, and the fee arrangement.

§ 11.6 The Fee Arrangement

Legal management experts recommend that an attorney have a full understanding with the client of the fee arrangement. Most attorneys recognize the value of this advice and make it a point to reach an agreement on the fee and obtain it in writing during the first interview.

§ 11.7 Contingency Fees

When a client's case involves one in which he may recover damages, the most common fee arrangement is a contingency fee. Under a contingency fee arrangement, the client pays a specified percentage of the total recovery as a fee. Usually, the percentage is less if the case is settled before a suit is filed. Under a contingency arrangement, if there is no recovery, there is no fee. However, the client is still responsible for costs because it is unethical for the attorney to absorb these. Costs include all of the attorney's expenses, such as service and filing fees, witness fees, etc.

§ 11.8 Fees Based on a Flat Fee or on an Hourly Basis

Depending on the kind of case involved, the fee may be an agreed amount for the work to be done. Often, the client is billed on an hourly basis, particularly in legal matters where it is difficult to assess how much time will be involved.

Regardless of the fee arrangement, the attorney will want to have it in writing and may ask you to prepare the usual fee agreement letter while the client waits. Some offices have forms for this purpose. With the use of computers in most legal offices, it is easy to tailor a form agreement to fit a particular situation.

§ 11.9 Authorization by Client

Depending upon the nature of the legal matter involved, there are probably several forms which the client will need to sign. It is usually more convenient for both the attorney and the client to do this at the time of the initial client interview. Most offices use printed forms for this purpose.

§ 11.10 Medical Authorization

This form is necessary to secure medical reports and other medical data from doctors and hospitals. They do not release this information without a signed authorization by the patient. You will need to prepare a medical authorization for each doctor who treated the client and for each hospital or clinic in which he was a patient.

§ 11.11 Employer Authorization

Employers need authorization to release payroll information, and it may be necessary to have this information to establish lost wages.

§ 11.12 Request for Copies of Income Tax Returns

Income tax returns may also be needed to establish damages or lost wages.

§ 11.13 Authorization for Attorney to Settle

An authorization for the attorney to settle the claim for a specified amount is sometimes signed by the client. Once the attorney assesses the value of the claim, he can have the client authorize settlement for that amount.

§ 11.14 General Authorizations

The contents of general authorizations vary with each situation and are written to suit a particular need. The attorney usually dictates the contents of these documents.

§ 11.15 Organizing the File

One of the most valuable services that you can render to the attorney in litigation matters is to learn to organize the contents of the client's litigation file. From the client's information obtained during the initial interview, prepare client cards for the Rolodex files, the client billing card, and the ledger sheet. Different offices have different systems for opening files. Familiarize yourself with the system used in your office and follow that procedure.

If there is no specific system used in your office for litigation matters, you may wish to consider the system discussed below. Ask the attorney for permission to use it.

In organizing the file, separate folders for different types of information are extremely helpful. An exhibit folder, for instance, holds photographs, drawings, documents, and other materials the attorney uses as exhibits at the trial of the case. An investigation folder holds accident reports, investigation reports, statements, and other items of that nature. A folder for depositions and statements of witnesses is also helpful and allows easy reference to those items. A folder or a notebook for all medical reports and bills may be kept up-to-date easily as the case progresses. In addition, depending on the complexity of the case, folders may be prepared for briefs or memoranda concerning the law applicable to the case.

If the attorney uses a trial notebook, keep a supply of three-ring binders on hand so that the notebook can be prepared step by step as the case progresses.

Careful organization of the file will keep it in instant readiness for the attorney's review at any time. Using this system, he will always be able to find the information he needs at any stage of the case, and you will always be able to locate quickly any items and will be able to file any new materials in the proper place. By following this system throughout the course of the case, when trial time arrives, the file will be in excellent condition and the attorney will have available everything he needs to present his case in an orderly fashion.

§ 11.16   Types of Litigation

The notes which the attorney makes during the initial client interview will probably include a reference to the type of litigation involved in that particular case. The type of litigation is important because many decisions must be made to see that the lawsuit is properly filed and that proper proof is accumulated for the file.

For purposes of litigation, there are basically three general categories of lawsuits—workers' compensation suits, damage suits, and equity suits.

§ 11.17   Workers' Compensation Suits

Workers' compensation suits are processed under the workers' compensation act of each individual state and are handled initially by a state administrative agency, such as an industrial accident board or industrial commission. A workers' compensation action is one which grows out of an on-the-job injury in which an employee is covered by workers' compensation insurance. Most employers are required by state law to provide insurance to cover these claims unless they receive special permission to be self-insured. However, to qualify for self-insurance status, employers usually must prove that they are able to pay any workers' compensation award granted. Following the filing of notice by the employee and the compilation of various medical reports, the agency conducts a hearing and enters an award. In most states the award rendered by the board or commission is directly appealable to a state trial court and is then handled in the same manner as other lawsuits.

§ 11.18 Damage Suits

Damage suits cover a wide range of subject matter. A damage suit seeks an award of money. Some examples of damage suits seeking money damages are those arising from tortious acts, such as automobile accident cases and slip-and-fall cases; contract disputes; title actions (boundary disputes and other land matters); consumer actions (often coming under Deceptive Trade Practices Act, both state and federal); civil antitrust actions; and professional malpractice.

§ 11.19 Equity Suits

Rather than seeking monetary judgments, equity suits seek some specific action coercive in nature. Included are actions for injunction (to prevent a party from committing some action or requiring him to perform some action) or specific performance as, for instance, on a contract.

>EXAMPLE:

>A, whose land borders B's land, is digging postholes for a fence. B is sure that the holes are on his property. He seeks an injunction preventing A from further digging until the property can be surveyed and the property lines established.

§ 11.20 Role of Attorney as a Negotiator

Regardless of the kind of litigation that might be involved if a lawsuit is filed, a lawyer always seeks an amicable solution to his client's problem before he files the lawsuit. Litigation is expensive and time-consuming; and, therefore, the art of negotiation plays a vital role in trial practice. Negotiation and settlement of controversies consume a large percentage of an attorney's time. Even if a matter cannot be settled before the lawsuit actually is filed, negotiations between the attorneys usually continue throughout the course of the litigation up to the trial itself. It is not unusual for attorneys to reach a settlement the day of the trial.

If negotiations break down, the attorney must file the suit because no purpose could be served by further negotiation. Some of the factors that must be considered in preparing the suit are discussed below.

§ 11.21 Factors to Be Considered Before Filing the Lawsuit

When an attorney decides to file a lawsuit on behalf of a client, he must be certain that the lawsuit is properly brought. It must be filed by the correct parties in the proper court within the legal time periods. Following is a discussion of some of the factors which influence the attorney's decision as to:

Who may sue?

Where must the suit be filed?

What is the statute of limitations involved?

§ 11.22　Who May Sue

The injured party (or the party who has a claim) is the person best able to determine whether to seek a recovery through the legal system to rectify the wrong he feels was done to him. Therefore, there is a concept in the law called standing, which means that only the party injured by another may bring a civil suit. This rule of standing is designed to control the amount of litigation which might arise from one incident or wrong by letting only the injured party sue. Anyone else would be denied the right to bring suit.

In the case of a minor child, his parents may bring suit on his behalf; the legal guardian of a ward of the court may sue on behalf of that ward; a fiduciary appointed by the court might sue on behalf of a deceased person's estate; and a shareholder might sue on behalf of a corporation in which he owns stock.

To summarize, the one who has standing to bring a suit is the claimant.

§ 11.23　Jurisdiction

The jurisdiction of the courts is set forth by Congress or by the legislatures of the various states and is the authority of a court to hear a matter. If the complaint or petition is not filed in a court having jurisdiction, then the lawsuit is worthless and any action by the court is void. Venue, often referred to as geographical jurisdiction, is the place of the lawsuit—the county, or parish. Congressional statutes or the statutes of the various states govern the place of an action. Usually it is where the incident causing the lawsuit occurred or where the parties reside. An important difference to consider between jurisdiction and venue is that venue may be waived by the parties, but jurisdiction may not be conferred upon a court by agreement of the parties.

Jurisdiction covers both the parties and the subject matter as well as the amount or value in controversy and other relevant factors. As you will recall from your study of courts, courts may be said to have original jurisdiction or appellate jurisdiction. A new lawsuit may be brought only in a court of original jurisdiction. (For a more complete discussion of jurisdiction and venue, see the chapter on Courts.)

Often, courts have concurrent jurisdiction; that is, an action may be filed properly in any of several courts. For instance, some suits may be filed either in an appropriate state court or in a United States district court, provided the jurisdictional requirements of both courts are met.

§ 11.24   Statute of Limitations

Each state as well as the federal government has a statute of limitations, or time limit, within which a particular type of lawsuit must be filed. This does not mean that the suit cannot be filed. Anyone can file a lawsuit. It does mean that a defendant can ask to have the suit dismissed on the grounds that the statute of limitations has run. Most of the limitations statutes do have exceptions which toll (delay) the running of the period of limitations. Such a tolling would have the effect of an extension of time in which to file the suit. However, if a defendant can show that his situation is not covered by an exception, the suit will probably be dismissed.

Note that the statute of limitations does not require that the litigation be completed within that time period; the lawsuit simply must be filed within that time period.

There are many statutes of limitations, and they vary in length of time. The statutes usually fix the time limits based on the kind of claim or lawsuit involved. These vary considerably from state to state; within states they vary considerably among the types of claims. The statute of limitations might be one year for one kind of claim and ten years or even thirty years for another.

§ 11.25   The Importance of Diarying the Statute of Limitations

Most malpractice claims arise out of missed statute of limitations dates. You can play a significant role in not allowing the statute of limitations to run against a client; do this by keeping an accurate tickler (reminder) system. As you open each file (or work in it for the first time), ask the attorney to help you determine the statute of limitations date so that you can enter it on the calendar. You will find it beneficial to be thoroughly familiar with the statutes of limitations in your state.

§ 11.26   Filing the Complaint or Petition

The first pleading filed in any lawsuit is the complaint or petition. This is filed with the clerk of the court having venue and jurisdiction over the parties and the subject matter. The person who files the lawsuit is known as the plaintiff, and the person sued is the defendant. The action may be by one or more plaintiffs against one or more defendants.

The complaint must follow a certain format when it is prepared. It begins with the jurisdiction of the case, *i.e.*, the name of the state and court. Next are the names of the parties involved in the suit, beginning with the plaintiff.

(Note sample complaint printed for reference. See Illustration 9–5 in The Courts chapter.)

The court assigns a case number to every complaint that is filed. You should prepare a place for this number to be entered on your complaint form. The name of the document should be spelled out; then the allegations of the plaintiff regarding his cause of action are set forth in numbered paragraphs. The complaint ends with a prayer for relief from the defendant, usually in a specific amount, and is signed by an attorney.

Make enough copies of the complaint for each defendant, the client, and for the attorney's file. The original is filed with the clerk of the court having jurisdiction of the case. You will also want to make a copy for your forms manual if it does not yet contain a sample of this kind of form. A filing fee is required at the time of filing the complaint.

§ 11.27   Verification

Since the complaint is signed by the attorney and he does not have first-hand knowledge of the case, it may be necessary in some jurisdictions for the plaintiff to sign a verification stating that the allegations of the complaint are true and correct. In some jurisdictions, this must be sworn to before a notary public. (See Illustration 9–5 of The Courts chapter for the form of an individual verification.)

§ 11.28   The Summons

A resident defendant must be served with the complaint, since he must be officially notified that he has been sued. The official notification to the defendant that he has been sued is called a summons. It should be noted that some jurisdictions do not use a summons. The summons also advises the defendant that there is a time limit in which he must appear in court to answer the complaint or a default judgment can be taken against him.

In some jurisdictions the suit is not considered filed until the defendant has been served with the summons and complaint because it is the service upon the defendant that brings him within the jurisdiction of the court. Failure to make proper service on the defendant within a prescribed time period can cause the complaint to be dismissed. This could cause the claimant to lose his right to sue if, by that time, the statute of limitations has run.

§ 11.29   Preparation of the Summons

The summons is prepared by the legal secretary or by the clerk of court, depending upon the rules of the court. In some jurisdictions, even if the secretary prepares the summons, it must still be issued by the clerk. In such cases, the clerk must sign it, seal it, and date it before it is served on the defendant.

You must prepare sufficient copies of both the complaint and the summons for service upon each defendant named in the complaint. You should prepare two copies for each defendant if in your jurisdiction the attorney must provide an extra copy for the return of service (discussed below).

§ 11.30   Information for Service

Since it is vitally important that the summons and complaint be served promptly once the complaint has been filed with the court, you should be certain that you have given the process server correct information to help him locate the defendant. Some persons are very hard to locate, and any information about those persons, such as their place of employment or working hours, can be extremely helpful in arranging for prompt service. As a rule you should make a point of providing the following information about each defendant: complete name, gender, race, home address, and place of employment including address, work hours, and telephone number. Any other information you may have about the person, such as the type of car he drives or places he frequents, is helpful to the process server. If you make the extra effort to have all the above information available, the process server will stand a much better chance of making quick, effective service without incurring additional costs.

§ 11.31   Service on Corporations

Service on corporations is made through an agent for service, who may be an officer of the corporation, at its corporate offices within the state where the suit is instituted or upon a separate professional agent for service, registered with the designated office of that particular state, commonly known as the "registered agent." Call the office of the corporate department or division of the secretary of state's office or the lieutenant governor's office to ask whether there is an agent for service within the state. When the defendant is a corporation, it is important to learn the name and address of the registered agent or the officers of the corporation so that the proper person may be served on behalf of the corporation.

The defendant corporation is often a foreign corporation, particularly in the case of insurance companies. A foreign corporation is a corporation that is domiciled in another state. It is important to determine whether that company has designated a registered agent to accept service of process in your state. This information is usually available from your secretary of state with whom foreign corporations must register or with the insurance commissioner for insurance companies. Most states provide for service through the secretary of state or insurance commissioner if no agent has been designated.

§ 11.32 Delivery to the Court Clerk

In preparing the complaint for filing with the clerk, check to see that the original complaint is signed by the attorney and notarized, if applicable; that you have sufficient copies for service and return of service; that you have the appropriate number of summonses prepared for issuance by the clerk, if appropriate; and that you have a check for the filing fee.

The court clerk assigns a new file number for the case, stamps the complaint to indicate the filing date, and prepares a file folder for the new case. The clerk then puts the court seal on the summonses, signs and dates the summonses, and returns them to you to make arrangements for service on the defendants or delivers them to the sheriff if that is the procedure for your state.

§ 11.33 Service of Process

The method of service on defendants varies from state to state. In state courts service is made by a sheriff, a constable, or other authorized person. Service is made by delivering a copy of the summons, together with a copy of the complaint, to each defendant. The process server then completes his return on the original of the summons or the copy you have prepared (depending upon the jurisdiction) which shows the name of the person served, the place, the date, and time of service. (See Illustration 11–1.) The summons showing the return of service is then filed with the clerk of the court.

In some jurisdictions the process server prepares a separate certificate or affidavit as to the service which has been accomplished.

Illustration 11–1

RETURN OF SERVICE

STATE OF _____   )
) ss.
COUNTY OF _____   )

_____, being duly sworn, states that he is a person of suitable age and discretion and that on the _____ day of _____, 19__, he served the Summons and the Complaint, a copy of which is attached hereto, upon _____,
                                                    (name of defendant)

at _____, by personally delivering same to said defendant.

_____

Subscribed and sworn to before me
this _____ day of _____, 19__.

_____

Notary Public
My commission expires:

§ 11.34 Service on a Nonresident

For service of a defendant who is a nonresident, many states have a long arm statute, according to which service may be made on the office of the secretary of state, who forwards the suit papers by certified mail, return receipt requested, to the out-of-state defendant at his last known address. A small fee is usually charged by the secretary of state at the time service is made. In some states long arm statute service can be made by the attorney's office by certified mail, return receipt requested.

§ 11.35 Other Types of Service

Some states also provide, under certain circumstances, for:

- Service on a third party at the residence of defendant
- Service by posting the summons on the door of the defendant's residence or in a public place
- Service by publication of a notice in a newspaper of general circulation

Affidavits as to the necessity of service by one of these means are usually required, and the court grants an order giving permission for service by one of these methods.

§ 11.36 Response or Answer to Complaint

The defendant has a specific time after he has been served within which to present an answer or other response to the complaint. The time varies from state to state and even from court to court within a state. In the federal courts the time is 20 days unless the United States is a party defendant, in which case the answer date is extended to 60 days.

The summons usually specifies the time within which the defendant must respond to the complaint. Failure to respond within the time specified can result in a default judgment against the defendant. There are various responses or defenses which a defendant can advance. Since some responses could result in dismissal of the suit, they are filed before an answer is filed, often with a special appearance for that purpose only. Ultimately, however, if the defendant is unsuccessful in having the suit dismissed, he must file an answer.

The defendant's answer tells his version of the lawsuit. Often the defendant simply denies all allegations of the complaint.

EXAMPLES:

> The defendant John Good, by and through his attorney of record, for answer to the complaint filed herein, denies each and every allegation as though his denials were set out at length herein.

> The defendant John Good, by and through his attorney of record, for answer to the complaint filed herein, denies the allegations of paragraphs 1 through 10, inclusive, as though his denials were set out at length herein.

Sometimes the allegations contain information about which the defendant has no knowledge. However, he must answer each of the allegations. In this situation those allegations are denied for lack of information sufficient to justify a belief as to the truth or falsity of a particular allegation in the complaint. (When the attorney dictates such an answer to you, he may simply say, "Deny number 3 for lack" and will expect you to be able to put it in the form he uses.)

EXAMPLE:

> The defendant denies the allegations of paragraphs 5, 6, 7, 9, and 10 and states he does not have sufficient information or belief to answer those allegations.

Note that in federal court, and in most state courts, each specific allegation of the plaintiff's complaint must be either denied or admitted. Those allegations not specifically denied are deemed admitted unless the defense counsel can show good cause why he can neither admit nor deny (usually due to lack of sufficient information with which to respond). Consequently, it is good practice to include in the answer a general denial to the effect that "All allegations not specifically admitted herein are denied."

§ 11.37   Affirmative Defenses

There are special defenses available by law to certain types of actions. These special defenses are called affirmative defenses, and to be considered by the court, they must be asserted in the defendant's answer. If they are not included in the answer, the affirmative defenses are, in most courts, waived and may not be asserted later.

Examples of these defenses are set forth below in §§ 11.38 through 11.41.

§ 11.38　Contributory Negligence

The defendant specifically pleads the contributory negligence of the plaintiff as an affirmative defense. Contributory negligence means that the injuries and damages complained of by the plaintiff were caused in whole, or in part, or were contributed to as a result of plaintiff's own negligence.

§ 11.39　Comparative Negligence

The defendant specifically pleads comparative negligence as an affirmative defense. Comparative negligence means that if an accident was caused in part by the negligence of plaintiff, any award to the plaintiff should be diminished in the proportion of his negligence.

§ 11.40　Assumption of Risk

The defendant specifically pleads assumption of risk as an affirmative defense. Assumption of risk means, for example, that the plaintiff was fully aware of the icy condition of the sidewalk and made a conscious decision to attempt to negotiate it.

§ 11.41　Statute of Limitations

The defendant specifically pleads as an affirmative defense that plaintiff's claim is barred by the applicable statute of limitations.

§ 11.42　Special Exceptions

The defendant may specially except and object to specific allegations in the plaintiff's complaint and may ask the court either to strike (eliminate) such allegations or require the plaintiff to replead more specifically. This is an objection to the form of the complaint.

§ 11.43　Plea to the Jurisdiction (Sometimes Called Special Appearance or Notice of Appearance)

A plea to the jurisdiction is filed, when appropriate, in lieu of an answer; it sets out that the court has no jurisdiction over the party filing it and states the reason for such lack of jurisdiction. Its purpose is to prevent the entering of a default judgment pending decision by the court on the jurisdictional question. Usually this pleading must be sworn to and filed before any answer is filed, or the party entitled to file such appearance may waive his right to file it.

§ 11.44   Plea to the Venue (Sometimes Called Plea of Privilege)

A plea to the venue must be filed before an answer is filed, must be sworn to, and must give reasons why the case should be transferred to another county or parish.

EXAMPLES:

The incident occurred in a different county from where the suit is filed, so this court does not have venue.

The residence of the parties is in a different county, so the court does not have venue.

The plaintiff, within a time set out by statute, may file a sworn controverting (opposing) plea, setting out any exceptions under the statutes which would allow the lawsuit to remain in the county where it was originally filed. If the plaintiff does not timely file such a plea, the court may automatically transfer the case to the county requested by the defendant (usually the county of his residence). After the time for filing such controverting plea has passed, the order of transfer is prepared by the defendant's attorney and submitted to the court for entry. Unlike a plea to the jurisdiction, an answer to the petition or complaint must be filed in addition to the plea to venue, and such answer should always contain language to the effect that the answer is subject to the plea to venue and does not waive that issue.

§ 11.45   Motion to Quash Service

If service is improperly made, the wrong party is served, or the summons does not show the date of service, a motion may be made to quash service (declare the service invalid). This requires the plaintiff's attorney to have the summons reissued and new service attempted.

§ 11.46   Removal to Federal Court

If the plaintiff's action was filed in a state court and jurisdiction would be valid in federal court, the defendant may, within 30 days, file a petition to remove the case to the United States district court for the particular district having jurisdiction. This petition must be filed in federal court prior to filing any other defensive pleading, must be sworn to, and must be accompanied by notice to the plaintiff's attorney of the removal, notice to the clerk of the state court, and the filing fee. If the plaintiff's attorney desires, he may file a motion to remand (return) the case to state court. The federal court then determines whether the case should remain in federal court or be returned to state court. If the plaintiff's attorney does not file such a motion to remand and jurisdiction is proper in federal court, the removal is good and the case remains in federal court. The defense attorney must then file an answer and a demand for jury trial if he wants a jury trial, and the case is handled as any other federal court case.

§ 11.47   Third–Party Complaint

During the preparation of the defense of the lawsuit, it may become evident that a party not named as a defendant may be responsible for the cause of action. The defendant (becoming the third-party plaintiff) files a third-party action against the additional party. In some jurisdictions leave of court may be required. The defendant (now the third-party plaintiff) files his third-party complaint, and the new party (the third-party defendant) is served with the summons in the same manner that an original defendant is served. The third-party complaint must be complete in its allegations as to the third-party defendant. Within the time limit shown on the summons, the third-party defendant must file responsive pleadings. This situation occurs frequently in products liability cases.

EXAMPLE:

A buys a car from B, a car dealer. The car simply will not run, and B's service department cannot get it to run. A sues B to rescind the sale and get his money back. When B answers A's suit against him, he admits that he sold A the car but since he did not manufacture the car, he files a third-party complaint against C, the manufacturer of the car.

§ 11.48   Counterclaim

The defendant as a counter-claimant may file an action for damages (counterclaim) against the plaintiff, who then becomes a counter-defendant. This claim is usually a claim that would reduce the amount owed by the defendant to the plaintiff if the defendant is successful in establishing the claim.

EXAMPLE:

A hires B to install bathroom plumbing and agrees to pay $500. A pays $250 and does not pay the rest. B sues A for the $250. A counterclaims against B for $1,000, stating that the plumbing leaks and has destroyed his flooring worth $750 and he should have the $250 back.

§ 11.49   Cross–Claim (Also Called Cross–Complaint or Cross–Action)

Where there is more than one defendant, any defendant (who then becomes a cross-plaintiff) may file an action against any other defendant (who then becomes a cross-defendant) alleging that the cross-defendant was responsible for the matter which is the subject of the complaint. When a defendant files a cross-claim, he is taking the position that if he owes the plaintiff any money, then the cross-defendant owes him that same amount (or some portion of it). Therefore, if a cross-plaintiff is successful in presenting his cross-claim, he will probably get a judgment against the cross-defendant similar to the one granted the plaintiff against him.

EXAMPLE:

A owns a building which he leases to B for $30,000 per year, payable in monthly installments. After B has been in the building two months, he subleases the building to C for the same rental. C pays the rent for one month and moves out of the building. A sues B and C for all unpaid rent under the lease. B files a cross-claim against C. A gets a judgment against B and C, and B gets a judgment against C on his cross-claim. B must pay A but he can collect from C.

§ 11.50 Distinction Between Cross–Claim and Counterclaim

Cross-claims are litigated by parties on the same side of the main litigation, while counterclaims are litigated between opposing parties to the principal action.

§ 11.51 Amended and Supplemental Pleadings

There are times when it is necessary to amend a pleading. Under the Federal Rules of Civil Procedure and in most state courts, any change in pleadings can be made once without court order at any time before responsive pleadings are filed. Afterward, either leave of court or consent of opposing counsel is needed to amend or supplement pleadings. The amendment changes the original pleading.

A supplemental pleading supplements or adds to the original pleading facts or events which have happened since the original pleading was filed.

§ 11.52 Distinction Between an Amended Pleading and a Supplemental Pleading

An amendment to a pleading involves the correction of the pleading. The content of the amendment was in existence at the time the original pleading was filed. On the other hand, a supplemental pleading involves events which were not known or not in existence at the time the original pleading was filed.

§ 11.53   Interventions

An additional party (intervenor) having an interest in the outcome of the lawsuit may attempt to intervene by filing a written petition in intervention, setting out the reasons why the intervenor has an interest and the amount the intervenor seeks.

EXAMPLES:

An insurance company, which has paid money damages to the plaintiff for injuries growing out of the same cause of action, may seek to recover its payment.

Where several parties claim injuries in the same incident and only one party has filed suit, others may petition to intervene, claiming they also were damaged and thus are entitled to recover damages.

In wrongful death cases which are usually filed by the spouse or an heir at law of the deceased, other heirs may intervene, claiming a legal interest in the estate of the decedent. This often happens in cases of prior marriages, where children of the prior marriage intervene for a portion of the recovery.

§ 11.54   Discovery

Evidence is needed by each party to a lawsuit to support its side of the case, and both attempt to gather by means of discovery all the necessary evidence for their use at trial. Discovery is the vehicle by which one party to a lawsuit is entitled to obtain certain facts, documents, and other information to help it prepare for trial. The purposes of discovery are to clarify the issues, to eliminate surprise in the courtroom, and to avoid wasting the time of the court.

Every attorney knows that lawsuits usually are not won in the courtroom by brilliant trial tactics; rather, lawsuits are won in advance of trial by thorough preparation. Preparation may include use of any or all of the discovery procedures available under the law.

Discovery procedures include request for admissions of fact, interrogatories, request for production of documents and other things, and depositions.

§ 11.55   Request for Admissions

As the name of the instrument implies, either party may request the other party to admit or deny certain facts in regard to the lawsuit which are not in dispute. The reason for using such requests for admissions is to avoid having to prove such undisputed facts at the trial.

EXAMPLES:

1. Admit you were the owner of a blue automobile, license No. 0000, on the date of the incident which is the basis of this suit.

2. Admit you were the operator of that vehicle on the occasion in question.

OR:

1. Admit that you were a partner in the firm of Smith and Smith on August 1, 1993.

2. Admit that the firm of Smith and Smith entered into a contract (a copy of which is attached) on August 1, 1993, with the Jones Construction Company.

NOTE: In each of the sample requests, the admissions requested are easily established by testimony. However, to call witnesses at trial and ask of them a series of questions designed to show those facts would be needlessly time-consuming and expensive. Note that the first two sample requests do not ask whether an accident took place and that the second two requests do not ask whether there was a problem concerning the contract because these likely would involve disputed facts. The requests simply resolve some basic, undisputed issues.

Requests for admissions of fact are served on counsel for the opposing party and consist of:

1. The caption or style of the case

2. The title of the pleading

3. The name of the party to whom such requests are directed

4. An opening paragraph setting out the state or federal rule under which the requests are made and the time within which to respond

5. The requests

6. The signature of the attorney requesting the admissions

7. A certificate that the request was served on the opposing attorney and the method of service (mail or in person)

§ 11.56   Responses to Request for Admissions

When the attorney receives a request for admissions on behalf of the client, you should stamp it with the date it was received and place a note in your tickler system in advance of the date the response is due. This is a very important service that you perform because failure to respond (usually within 30 days) results in a finding that the requests are admitted. There are several possible responses to such requests, but each separate request must be answered. For example, the attorney responding may:

- Admit any statement.

- Deny any statement.

- Neither admit nor deny. (This must be done specifically and a reason given for the refusal to admit or deny must be given; this typically is due to lack of sufficient information with which to respond.)

- Omit any statement in the request. (This last method, however, must not be an oversight on the part of the typist or word processor, but must consciously be made by the attorney because failure to respond to any statement in the request results in that statement's being deemed admitted.)

The response may be short and need contain only the caption, title, and the responses, which may be shortened. An example of responses to the four sample requests set out above might be:

1. Admitted.

2. Denied.

3. Admitted.

4. Neither admitted nor denied due to lack of information at this time with which to respond.

The response must be signed by the attorney, and a verification (sworn statement) by the person making the response of the truth of the responses must be attached. A certificate that the response has been served on opposing counsel also is necessary.

§ 11.57 Interrogatories

One of the simplest and most economical discovery tools is the use of interrogatories (questions). At any time after the suit is filed, either party may propound (file) interrogatories to the opposing party and/or his attorney. It should be noted that some jurisdictions no longer require the filing of interrogatories with the court. Instead, a certificate of service signed by the attorney indicating service on the opposing counsel should be filed (this corresponds to the federal rules). The secretary should check the local court rules to determine which documents need not be filed with the court. Interrogatories include:

- The caption or style of the case

- The title of the pleading

- The name of the party to whom the interrogatories are directed

- An opening paragraph setting out the state or federal rule under which the interrogatories are propounded and the time within which to answer
- The interrogatories
- A statement that the interrogatories are ongoing and that the answering party must supply additional information as it becomes available in the future
- The signature of the party serving the interrogatories
- A certificate of service on the opposing attorney and the method of service (mail or personal delivery)

It is good practice when preparing interrogatories to leave sufficient space after each question for the opposing party to type in his answer, which may then be photocopied and returned. Some states now require this procedure.

Parties generally are not limited in the types of interrogatories which may be asked but the number of interrogatories may be limited. Some states, however, allow only certain specific interrogatories to be asked. Some typical interrogatories, in a personal injury case, include questions about

- Name
- Address
- Marital status
- Previous marriages
- Social security and driver's license numbers
- Previous accidents
- Version of the incident
- What is claimed by the other party as the cause of the incident
- Injuries
- Amount of time lost from work
- Whether the injured party has returned to work
- Lost wages
- Names of doctors
- Location and custodian of records
- Names of hospitals
- Amount of medical expenses to date
- The existence and limits of coverage on insurance policies
- Names of witnesses to be called at trial

• Names of experts consulted and their fields of expertise

§ 11.58 Answers to Interrogatories

On receipt of interrogatories, the legal secretary should note both the date received and the date answers are due and make a tickler notation. The client should be contacted and an appointment made for him to come in and provide answers to the interrogatories. If the client lives in another city, a copy of the interrogatories should be forwarded to him immediately requesting that he obtain all information needed to prepare the answers. Provide him with a date by which to respond so that the attorney may timely file the answers.

Answers to the interrogatories may be read at the trial of the case and must be sworn to by the person answering the interrogatories. Some states require the answers to be signed by the party, while other states permit the attorney to respond for his client.

Some courts do not want interrogatories filed with the court. Instead, a certificate of service signed by the attorney indicating service on the opposing counsel should be filed (this corresponds to the federal rules). The secretary should check the local court rules to determine which documents need not be filed with the court.

§ 11.59 Objections to Interrogatories

In some instances the attorney may file objections to some of the interrogatories on various grounds. However, a good faith effort must be made to answer the remaining interrogatories within the time allowed. Occasionally the attorney filing the interrogatories may grant additional time in which to answer if there is a real difficulty in obtaining the information requested, but this is an agreement between the attorneys.

After the answers are typed, they are signed and sworn to, and a certificate of service is attached showing the answers have been served.

§ 11.60 Continuing Interrogatories

In many states interrogatories, once served, are continuing; that is, if after answers are made initially, there is a change in the situation (for example, an additional witness is located or a new expert is employed, etc.), supplemental answers must be served upon the initiating party to reflect the changed situation.

§ 11.61 Request for Production of Documents and Things

While one party cannot secure privileged communications in the file of the opposing attorney or any materials considered to be the attorney's work product, there are numerous documents, photographs, and other materials which may be obtained through discovery. This is accomplished by filing a request for production listing each item requested. The request is then served upon opposing counsel. Such request for production does not require leave of court. Samples of discoverable documents include: photographs, contracts, corporate records, income tax records, and drawings and plans of equipment or buildings involved in the litigation. The request should be addressed to the party from whom the materials are requested, show the federal or state rule under which the request is filed, specify the time within which to respond, and list each item requested. The request, like all other pleadings, must be signed by the attorney and must show a certificate of service on opposing counsel.

Some jurisdictions do not require the filing of requests for production but do require filing a notice that the request has been made.

§ 11.62 Responses to Request for Production of Documents and Things

As soon as such a request is received, the secretary should prepare a tickler entry noting the date the response is due. She should then draft for the attorney's approval a letter to the client, enclosing a copy of the request, with instructions to produce the requested documents.

§ 11.63 Objections to Request for Production of Documents and Things

The party on whom the request is served (through his attorney) may file objections, for example, that the requests are unduly oppressive or that the materials requested are irrelevant to any issue in the lawsuit. Upon motion the court rules on the validity of the objections. If the objections are overruled, the materials must be produced within a specified period of time. If the objections are sustained, those particular documents need not be produced.

If a written response to a request is not received in the specified time limit, the requesting party may file a motion asking the court to compel compliance and to award costs of filing the motion.

§ 11.64 Subpoena Duces Tecum

The subpoena duces tecum is authorized by Rule 45 of the Federal Rules of Civil Procedure, and most states have a similar provision. Such a rule authorizes the issuance of a subpoena to custodians of certain documents to appear at a designated time and place with certain records described in the subpoena for the purpose of producing them. Often, since these are ordinary business records of the custodian, by agreement of the parties, they are simply copied and supplied to the requesting party. Since some of the material so produced is of a technical, statistical nature, it is often time-consuming to analyze the information contained in them, and the legal secretary can play an important part in the preliminary review of the data contained in the records.

§ 11.65　Depositions

One of the most useful discovery tools is the deposition, either oral or written. Each side in a lawsuit has the right to question the parties on the other side, as well as other persons who are not parties, such as eyewitnesses, doctors, and experts employed by either side to investigate and give an opinion in the case.

An oral deposition may be taken by either party after the lawsuit is filed and consists of sworn testimony in the presence of counsel for all parties before a court reporter, who transcribes the testimony verbatim. The testimony is as binding as any testimony given at the actual trial of the case, and often entire depositions or portions of depositions are read during the course of trial.

§ 11.66　Setting the Depositions

Depositions are usually set by agreement between the attorneys as to time and place. It is the responsibility of the secretary, once depositions are set, to calendar the time and place on both the attorney's calendar and her own. She should draft a follow-up letter to the opposing attorney confirming the date and time. In addition, she should inform the deponent (witness) or his attorney of record, if represented by counsel, both by telephone and letter of the time and place advising him to be present. A court reporter must also be contacted; therefore, it is necessary to verify which side will obtain the reporter to avoid duplication of effort and to ensure that a reporter will be available to take the testimony. The party requesting the deposition usually makes the arrangements for the court reporter. If the deposition is to be taken in the office, the secretary should reserve a conference room or other suitable place for the deposition. The room should be large enough to accommodate the attorneys for each side, the person whose deposition is being taken, and the court reporter. Shortly before the scheduled time of the deposition, the legal secretary should inspect the room where the deposition will be taken to ensure that it is ready.

§ 11.67　Notice of Depositions

If your state requires it, notice to take the deposition is filed, setting out the time and place of the deposition, and any subpoenas or subpoenas duces tecum (commanding the deponent to produce specified items) are issued. The notice is served on opposing counsel well in advance of the date of the deposition.

§ 11.68 Use of Checklists

Many attorneys use a checklist during depositions to make certain all pertinent information is obtained. This checklist should be placed in the file shortly before the deposition for the attorney's use. In addition, the secretary should make certain the attorney has a legal pad, pens, and pencils for taking notes during the deposition.

§ 11.69 Meeting With Client and Opposing Attorney

Time should be allotted prior to the deposition for the attorney to discuss the case with the deponent to explain the procedure and purpose of the deposition. To prepare the deponent properly, the attorney should explain to him the manner and method of responding to questions and the necessity of answering such questions. The deponent often is nervous when he appears for the deposition, and the secretary can help to put him at ease by using tact and courtesy.

Following a deposition, attorneys sometimes discuss the possibility of settlement. Therefore, the attorney's calendar for the date of deposition should allow sufficient time for both the deposition and for discussion with the opposing attorney afterward.

§ 11.70 Transcription of Depositions

The verbatim written transcript of the testimony is prepared by the court reporter. The original copy is sent to the attorney for the deponent or directly to the deponent if he is not represented by counsel. The deponent is then asked to read the transcription of his testimony, make any corrections necessary, and sign it before a notary public who will notarize his signature. It is then returned to the court reporter who, in some jurisdictions, files it with the clerk of the court and also provides copies of the transcription to the parties who requested them.

§ 11.71 Videotape Depositions

Use of videotape depositions is extremely valuable when it is anticipated that a witness will be unavailable to testify at the trial of the case. This is especially appropriate if the client or witness is due to leave the country or is terminally ill. Use of a videotape deposition enables the trier of fact to see the witness's demeanor and thus evaluate his credibility. There are some jurisdictions, however, where videotape depositions are not admissible.

§ 11.72   Written Depositions

Written depositions may also be taken and generally are less expensive than oral depositions. Notice of taking a written deposition, together with a list of the questions to be asked by the reporter, must be sent to all opposing counsel, and sufficient time must be allowed (usually 10 to 15 days, according to the rules of the jurisdiction) for the opposing attorney to file cross-questions. These questions are mailed to the reporter, who sometimes obtains any necessary subpoenas or subpoenas duces tecum, contacts the witness, and makes an appointment with him. At the time of the appointment, the reporter asks the questions and obtains any records requested by the questions. The answers are sworn to by the witness and are filed by the reporter in the same manner as an oral deposition.

Written depositions are often used to obtain a doctor's testimony, employment records, income tax records, and other information, but they also may be used in the case of a witness who is in a distant city or state, thereby avoiding the expense of both attorneys traveling to the deposition.

§ 11.73   Motions Prior to Trial

After pleadings are filed and during the course of discovery, various facts may come to light which require the necessity of filing motions with the court. In some jurisdictions, a courtesy copy of the motion must be delivered to the judge. This is in addition to the original which is filed with the clerk of the court. Some common pretrial motions are discussed below.

§ 11.74   Motion for Continuance

This is simply a motion to postpone or continue a trial date. The content of the motion and requirements for filing vary considerably from jurisdiction to jurisdiction.

§ 11.75   Motion to Compel

This motion is filed to require the opposing party to perform some act, usually to answer interrogatories or to produce documents in accordance with a motion for production. The motion, if not responded to or if the action sought in the motion is not performed, is set for hearing; and the court may impose any of numerous sanctions (relief), including an order that the act be performed. If this order is not obeyed, the disobedient attorney may be held in contempt of court, or certain pleadings of the disobedient party may be stricken or removed by the court. The court also may impose a money penalty on the disobedient party and may require him to pay the costs of the hearing, including a reasonable attorney's fee, to the other side.

§ 11.76   Motion for Protective Order

A motion for protective order is filed in response to some action by the opposing side, requesting the court to take some action. For example, such a motion can be filed regarding a notice to take a deposition if the distance involved in travel or the shortness of time of the notice makes it difficult or impossible for the deponent or the attorney to appear at the time and place of the deposition. It also may be used when interrogatories are oppressive or when requests for production are unduly burdensome.

A protective order may also be used to specify who may see confidential documents and/or the handling of "for attorney's eyes only" documents.

§ 11.77   Stipulations

A written stipulation is an agreement made and signed by the attorneys for both sides of a case regulating any matter pertaining to the proceeding or trial which is within their ability to agree. This may be used to dispose of or narrow certain issues so that trial time and proof are not required for those issues. A stipulation can be used also in an attempt to have the court vacate a trial date, reset a hearing date, or extend time for response to a pleading.

§ 11.78   Motion to Dismiss for Want of Jurisdiction

A defendant may file a motion to dismiss the case for want of jurisdiction because he believes that the court does not have authority to hear or decide the case.

§ 11.79   Motion to Dismiss for Lack of Prosecution

A defendant's motion to dismiss a case for lack of prosecution may be made after a case has been filed for a long period of time with no action on the part of the plaintiff's attorney to prepare it for trial. Granting such a motion is within the discretion of the court if there is no specific length of time within which to file such a motion. Most judges, however, are reluctant to grant such motions unless the case has been inactive for a very long time.

§ 11.80   Motion for Nonsuit

This is a plaintiff's motion which requests the court to dismiss the case either with prejudice or without prejudice and can be presented any time before the case goes to the jury. In some states it is called simply a voluntary dismissal. When such a motion is granted without prejudice, the plaintiff may later refile the same action. However, if the case is dismissed with prejudice, the plaintiff is prevented from again filing the same cause of action. In federal court this motion is known as a motion for dismissal pursuant to Rule 41 of the Federal Rules of Civil Procedure.

§ 11.81   Motion for Summary Judgment

If, during preparation of the case, it becomes obvious to either party that there is no real issue of fact to be decided at trial, a motion for summary judgment may be made. This motion requests the court to grant judgment in favor of the party filing the motion. It usually is accompanied by affidavits or answers to discovery stating the undisputed facts which entitle the party to a judgment in his favor. In many jurisdictions it is difficult to obtain a summary judgment, and the party filing such a motion has the burden of proving that there is no genuine issue of fact in dispute. The opposing party has time in which to respond, and the court usually holds a hearing on the motion. If the court determines that there is no fact issue, it can grant judgment to the moving party. However, if in the court's opinion there is any factual question which is in dispute, the court may deny the motion; and the case is then tried on its merits.

§ 11.82   Pretrial Hearings

A pretrial hearing is held in many jurisdictions for the purpose of clarifying the issues which will be tried and for determining the approximate length of time which will be necessary for the trial of the case. A pretrial conference is a meeting with the trial judge at which each counsel states the basis of his case and how he intends to prove it. The pretrial conference serves as a clearinghouse at which the attorneys discuss the discovery that must be completed and disclose exhibits or witnesses they might use for trial.

A pretrial conference helps to speed up the court procedures because it establishes ground rules for the trial and helps to eliminate courtroom surprises and delays.

§ 11.83   Pretrial Orders

A pretrial order usually is agreed to by both sides and is presented to the court for entry, or a pretrial summary is prepared by the court. Such pretrial orders typically contain a basic statement of the contested and uncontested issues and facts, a stipulation of agreed facts, a list of witnesses to be called by each side, exhibits to be introduced by each side, and the date of trial.

§ 11.84   Trial Notebooks

In organizing the file for trial, the legal secretary may assist in indexing the file or trial notebook for the attorney's use during trial. The attorney will likely include the following instruments and/or items:

- All pleadings filed in the case, with the first pleading filed being labeled "No. 1"

- All depositions clearly indexed for easy access by the attorney, along with any summaries of the depositions which may have been prepared

- All interrogatories and answers, request for admissions, any other discovery materials and photographs

- Any other documents which the attorney will present for evidence during trial

Certain motions which will be presented by the attorney during the trial may be prepared in advance so the attorney will have them ready at the proper time.

In addition to organizing the file with the pleadings and documents, a list of witnesses and their telephone numbers should be placed in a convenient place for the attorney's use. The witness list should enumerate the names in the order their testimony will be presented. Likewise, the documents to be presented as evidence should be placed in the order in which they will be introduced. If the court rules permit, the legal secretary could mark the documents with exhibit stickers obtained from the court clerk. (See Illustration 11–2 for a trial notebook checklist.)

A more comprehensive discussion of a trial notebook is found in the *Manual for the Lawyer's Assistant* and the *Litigation Handbook for the Lawyer's Assistant.*

Illustration 11–2

CLIENT _____

Our File No. _____

TRIAL NOTEBOOK CHECKLIST

_____ Check pleadings for amendments.
_____ Pleadings amended.
_____ Amend prayer to: _____
_____ Prepare subpoena for each witness.

_____ Basic information sheet prepared.
_____ All witnesses listed.
_____ List all expenses.
_____ Copies of all bills.
_____ Exhibits numbered and listed.
_____ Medical and/or other expert reports.
_____ All doctors and/or other expert witnesses alerted.
_____ Depositions read and marked.
_____ Case law, law notes inserted.
_____ Requested instructions prepared.

NOTE: This is a sample list and may be adjusted to include/delete other items applicable and pertinent to your particular case.

§ 11.85　Settlement

At any time during the course of a lawsuit, the parties may be open to an agreeable settlement. If settlement can be reached prior to the filing of the lawsuit by the plaintiff's attorney, costs can be minimized, and the plaintiff may realize more actual money than he would if the case is ultimately tried and appealed.

Once a lawsuit is filed, attorneys for both sides evaluate the case at various points throughout the course of the matter. Factors which enter into such evaluations, among others, are:

- Extent of injuries or damages
- Duration of injuries or damages
- Time lost from work, if any
- Medical or other expenses in connection with the incident
- Probable cost of trial
- Liability (fault)
- Credibility (believability) of the parties or witnesses
- Recent decisions on similar matters in the area

Settlements are often reached shortly after the depositions of all parties are obtained when both attorneys have had an opportunity to assess the credibility of the witnesses as well as other factors.

At any time during the course of a case, the settlement value may go up or down. Changes in the valuation may be brought about because the plaintiff incurs additional medical or other expenses. For example, an additional operation may be necessary. If he returns to work or presents a poor impression as a witness, the attorney may recommend acceptance of a settlement offer. Other factors affecting settlement would be an extremely large verdict in a similar case, a total loss by a plaintiff in a similar case, or favorable or unfavorable facts ascertained in a deposition. Each factor, while not controlling in itself, becomes part of the overall picture to the attorneys, who place evaluations on the case and make recommendations to their respective clients based on such evaluations. Occasionally, a client refuses the recommendations and insists the case be tried unless the case can be settled for a different amount than that recommended by the attorneys.

Settlement negotiations are usually conducted up until the time the trial begins, and it is not unheard of for a lawsuit to result in settlement after the jury retires to deliberate, but before the verdict is reached (often to the disappointment of the jury members). Settlement may also be reached after judgment is entered and during the course of an appeal.

Once a settlement has been agreed to by all parties, the papers reflecting the settlement must be prepared, usually by the attorney for defendant. These include a judgment dismissing the lawsuit and a release of all claims which will be signed by the plaintiff and possibly by his attorney. In some matters (workers' compensation and cases involving minor plaintiffs), court approval is necessary; consequently, a hearing is held before the trial judge to approve the fairness of the settlement. These hearings are usually informal hearings; the judge hears testimony regarding the injuries, the amount involved, the amount of expenses, and then may enter an order granting judgment. In some cases, the court allows the use of interrogatories in place of a hearing to determine the fairness of the settlement; these are filed by the defendant's attorney and answered by the plaintiff.

The judgment in a settlement case reflects who pays the costs of court. In a judgment which is based on a jury verdict, the costs may be taxed against the losing party at the court's discretion.

After releases are executed and the judgment is entered by the court, the amount of settlement is paid to the prevailing party and his attorney. The case can then be closed. If the prevailing party is a minor, however, the award is handled through a guardian or next friend and deposited according to the order of the court for the use and benefit of the minor. The guardian or next friend of the minor must post a bond with the court to ensure proper handling of the minor's funds. The court, however, retains jurisdiction over the disbursement of funds in most cases until the minor reaches majority.

§ 11.86 The Trial

At the trial of the case the dispute of the parties will be settled. The plaintiff is given his opportunity in court to present his case and his evidence. The defendant also has that opportunity.

§ 11.87   Role of the Judge

The judge presides in the courtroom and ensures that only proper evidence and arguments are presented. In a jury trial he instructs the jury on issues they will consider. This is called a "charge." A judgment will be entered based on the jury's verdict. In a nonjury trial the judge is both the trier of law and the trier of fact. His role is that of judge and jury. Judgment is entered on the evidence and arguments presented to the judge.

§ 11.88   Role of the Jury

The jury listens to the testimony, reviews all the exhibits, and considers the arguments of counsel and the instructions from the judge. At the conclusion of the trial, and after final arguments by both sides, the jury retires to deliberate what has been presented to them and arrives at a verdict. After returning to the jury box, the juror who was chosen foreman announces the verdict to the court.

§ 11.89   Selection of the Jury

A jury trial begins when the first prospective juror is called for voir dire (examination). Both plaintiff's and defendant's attorneys have the right to examine the prospective jurors after they are sworn. This questioning is called the voir dire examination of the jurors. The court may disqualify a prospective juror from service in a particular case when, for any reason, doubt exists as to his competency to serve in the case. After the juror is questioned, either attorney may accept him, challenge him for cause, or reject him by use of a peremptory challenge. In federal court, the judge conducts the voir dire.

§ 11.90   Challenge for Cause

During voir dire, either the plaintiff or defendant may challenge for cause when the prospective juror lacks a qualification required by law, is not impartial, is related to any of the parties, or will not accept the law as given to him by the court.

§ 11.91   Peremptory Challenge

During voir dire, each party has a given number of peremptory challenges established by law which enable the attorneys to reject prospective jurors without cause. This decision is based on subjective considerations of the attorney when he feels a prospective juror would be detrimental to his side of the case.

After a prospective juror has been excused because of a peremptory challenge by an attorney, another prospective juror is called in his place. This continues until both sides have used all of their peremptory challenges or a sufficient number of jurors have been agreed upon by all attorneys. The jury is then empaneled.

§ 11.92　Request for Jury Trial

In most courts the attorney must request a jury well in advance of the trial date if he desires a jury. Usually, the request for a jury is accompanied by a jury fee. See Illustration 11–3 for jury request. Failure to make a timely request for a jury may later prevent the parties from having a jury trial, resulting in a trial before the judge as the trier of fact.

Illustration 11–3

NO. _____

JOHN W. BROWN,	)	IN THE DISTRICT COURT
Plaintiff	)	
v.	)	_____ JUDICIAL DISTRICT
	)	
CHARLES M. WHITE,	)	_____ COUNTY, TEXAS
Defendant	)	

DEMAND FOR JURY TRIAL

Now comes CHARLES M. WHITE, Defendant in the above-referenced cause, and demands a trial by jury.

_____

(Name and address of attorney)

ATTORNEY FOR DEFENDANT,
CHARLES M. WHITE

CERTIFICATE OF SERVICE

I certify that a true and correct copy of the foregoing Demand for Jury Trial was served on the attorney for Plaintiff, Mr. Jack Jones, 717 Main Street, Your town, Your State, by certified mail, return receipt requested, on this _____ day of _____, 199__.

_____

(Defendant's Attorney)

§ 11.93　Opening Statement

After the jury is empaneled, each side may present an opening statement. The plaintiff has the burden of proving that he was wronged and suffered damages from such wrong and that the defendant caused such damages. The plaintiff is allowed to present his statement first. This may be followed by the opening statement of defendant's attorney.

§ 11.94 Direct Examination

After the opening statements, the receipt of testimony and documents begins. The plaintiff sometimes is the first person to testify and gives his version of the incident involved, his injuries and damages, and other matters on questioning by his counsel. This is known as direct examination. The plaintiff's attorney may present additional witnesses to support or prove his case.

§ 11.95 Cross–Examination

The defense attorney has an opportunity to cross-examine the witness after the plaintiff's attorney has questioned him.

§ 11.96 Redirect Examination

The plaintiff's attorney then has an opportunity to requestion the witness on the points covered by the defense attorney. This requestioning process is known as redirect examination.

§ 11.97 Presentation of Defense

After the plaintiff's case is presented, the defense attorney may present his witnesses on direct examination and may introduce documents into evidence.

§ 11.98 Impeachment of Witnesses on Cross–Examination

Either party may cross-examine any witness called by opposing counsel. On cross-examination counsel may introduce documents to impeach or discredit the testimony of a witness. If a witness testifies to one fact and a statement or document in the files shows that testimony to be contradicted, the document can then be used to question the witness as to the accuracy of his statements.

§ 11.99 Trial Memorandum or Trial Brief

This is a written explanation to the judge of the law involved in the case.

§ 11.100 Motions During Course of Trial

Before the closing arguments and up until the time the case is sent to the jury for deliberation, certain motions may be made during the course of the trial.

§ 11.101   Motion in Limine

This motion is presented before jury selection and can be used to set out certain facts which the moving party requests the court to instruct opposing counsel and his client or other witnesses to refrain from mentioning. Such facts might include the existence of any insurance policies, subsequent marriages, criminal records (if applicable), issuance of traffic citations on either the incident in question or prior or subsequent traffic citations, and other matters which are either not relevant to the particular case involved or which might influence the jury unfairly.

§ 11.102   Trial Amendment

A short amendment or addition to the pleadings can be filed only after a motion is made to the court for permission to file an amendment and an order is entered by the judge granting the motion.

§ 11.103   Motion for Instructed or Directed Verdict

This motion usually is made by the defendant's attorney at the close of evidence presented by the plaintiff and is based on the premise that the plaintiff has failed to prove his case. If it is granted, the court instructs the jury to render a verdict for the defendant and against the plaintiff, and the trial is concluded in the defendant's favor. If the court denies the motion, the defendant may present it again following the presentation of his own evidence and again after closing arguments.

§ 11.104   Motion for Mistrial

Either party may petition the court to declare a mistrial at any time during the course of the trial if certain matters which are not admissible as evidence are presented by any witness either purposely or unintentionally in the presence of the jury. For example, the mentioning of any items set out in a motion in limine, if the motion previously was granted by the court, results in a mistrial. When the court grants a motion for mistrial, the jury is immediately dismissed and the trial ends. The case must then be set for a new trial with a new jury.

§ 11.105   Objections

An objection is a procedure taken during trial by either attorney by simply stating he objects to the preceding testimony. The purpose is to prevent the introduction of testimony or evidence which is about to be given and exclude it from the record. If the objection is sustained by the judge, that particular testimony or evidence is excluded. If it is overruled, the testimony or evidence is given. Often, the attorneys will approach the bench and present oral arguments for or against the objection. At this point, the judge usually sends the jury out while the arguments are heard. Rulings on objections are usually the basis for appeal. The objection must be made at the time testimony or evidence is introduced during the trial in order to preserve the right to later appeal on that point. The court reporter must also be asked to include the objection and arguments in the record. This is called "preserving the record."

§ 11.106   Rebuttal Testimony

After the defendant has presented his evidence, the plaintiff may be allowed to present rebuttal (response) testimony.

§ 11.107   Closing Arguments

Each side is given the opportunity to present closing arguments. Each party summarizes his case and his presentation in a closing argument to the jury, giving the reasons why the jury should find in his favor. Time limits are set by the court for closing arguments, and each side must adhere to the time allowed. The plaintiff's attorney presents his closing argument first and may choose to reserve some of his allotted time to use for rebuttal to the defendant's argument.

§ 11.108   Charge to the Jury

The presiding judge delivers the charge to the jury after both attorneys have completed their closing arguments. In some jurisdictions the charge is in a form of written instructions prepared in advance by the attorneys for both sides and approved and/or modified by the court. These instructions then become the charge to the jury, setting forth the jury's responsibility to render a verdict on the facts and applicable rules of law. Some jurisdictions permit the attorneys to prepare specific questions or issues that the jury is asked to answer. The answers of the jury to such issues or questions then constitute the verdict. Otherwise the jury would return a "general verdict," finding for the defendant or the plaintiff and awarding damages, if any, to the plaintiff.

§ 11.109   Mistrial

Following the court's charge, the jury retires (goes to the jury room) to deliberate the facts presented at the trial and reaches its verdict. The jury may find for the defendant or for the plaintiff, or it may be unable to reach a verdict. In this event the court declares a mistrial, and the case must be tried again before a new jury. A jury which cannot reach a verdict is usually referred to as a *hung jury*.

§ 11.110   Preparation of Judgment

Following the jury's verdict, either side may give notice of its intention to appeal. The judgment is prepared by the prevailing party and presented to the court for entry. There is a time set by the rules in which time the losing party may file post-trial motions before a judgment is entered. One such motion may include a judgment *non obstante veredicto* (notwithstanding the verdict), setting out the reasons why the court should disregard the jury verdict and render judgment for the movant. The losing party may object to the prepared judgment and present its own version of the judgment in keeping with the jury verdict.

§ 11.111   Nonjury Trials

In a nonjury trial the judgment is prepared by the prevailing party and presented to the court in much the same manner as in a jury trial. The judgment is based on the findings of facts and conclusions of law prepared by the prevailing attorney and approved by the court. The procedure for preparing the judgment in final form for court entry varies from state to state, and local adopted procedure should be followed.

§ 11.112   Costs

If the jury or the judge awarded costs to the prevailing party, it is necessary to prepare a bill of costs for approval by the court. Allowable costs are specified by rule or statute. Upon approval of the costs, the prevailing party is entitled to payment for those costs. If the plaintiff was the prevailing party, he is also entitled to receive the amount of damages awarded in the judgment.

As soon as possible after the trial, the attorney may wish to prepare a complete written report of the trial for his client, together with results and recommendations. In the event he was the prevailing party, the calendar should be marked with the final date for appeal. If no appeal is filed by the losing side, a closing report and final bill for services is prepared. If an appeal is filed by the losing party, the client should be notified immediately, advising him of the procedures and costs of an appeal.

At this point negotiations for a settlement may be renewed, as both parties must determine whether or not it is advantageous to continue expending more time and money on the case.

§ 11.113   Motion for New Trial

In most jurisdictions the first step to an effective appeal is the filing of a motion for new trial, setting out the grounds why a new trial should be granted. Any alleged error by the trial judge that prevented a fair trial, such as overruling objections or allowing testimony, is set out in the motion. If the motion is denied, the appealing party then files a notice of appeal, posts a bond for costs, requests the preparation of the record for appeal, and serves notice to all parties of his intent.

§ 11.114   Mediation

Mediation is a non-binding settlement discussion between the parties. A neutral, impartial third party assists with the negotiations and promotes reconciliation, settlement, or understanding among the parties. A mediator makes no decisions for the parties involved in the mediation process. The mediator must hold in confidence all information received during a mediation. Pre-suit mediation is not intended as a substitute for litigation or trial by jury, but as a method of settling a claim before filing suit.

§ 11.115   Appeals

A party who is dissatisfied with the trial court's decision or jury verdict may appeal to a higher court on the theory that error was committed during the trial procedure.

When an appeal is filed, the party filing the appeal becomes the appellant, and the party against whom the appeal is filed is the appellee.

The function of the appellate court is to ensure that the trial court acted properly in its conduct of the trial and that proper legal principles were recognized and applied correctly.

It should be noted that appeals are not based on the facts involved in the case but on questions of law. The appellate court considers whether the trial court committed error in conducting the trial, thus adversely affecting the outcome. Its review of the record is limited to determining whether the trial court erred in admitting or refusing to admit testimony that should have been allowed. The appellate court also determines whether the court's instructions to the jury correctly reflected the law, whether the court correctly sustained or overruled objections of the attorneys, and whether there was jury misconduct.

The appeal requires:

1. Notice of filing an appeal
2. Bond for costs and filing fees, if required
3. The record on appeal (transcript, statement of facts)
4. Briefs
5. Oral arguments

NALS, Car.Leg.Sec. 3rd Ed.—11

6. Appellate decision

Procedure for requesting the preparation of the record for the appellate court varies with different jurisdictions. However, the appealing party is responsible for initiating the requests to the proper parties. The record will consist of the statement of facts (transcription by the court reporter of the proceedings at the trial) and the transcript (requested documents from the court file prepared by the clerk of court).

The statement of facts: the appellant's attorney will notify the court reporter at the trial to prepare a transcription of the proceedings. This will be done by letter, along with payment for such transcription. The court reporter will forward the completed original transcription directly to the appellate court within the time allowed.

The transcript: the appellant's attorney will notify the clerk of court by letter of his request for the transcript. In his letter he will list the documents he wants included in the transcript (seldom will the whole file be requested). By copy of this letter request, the opposing counsel will be advised of the documents requested and given an opportunity to add any other documents he may want. The transcript is prepared, sealed, and forwarded to the appellate court by the court clerk.

§ 11.116 Communication With the Client

Effective communication between a client and his attorney is as necessary after the trial as it is before trial. After the trial the prevailing party is often under the mistaken impression that he will receive what was granted in the trial, whether money, land, objects, or rights, within a short period of time. While this may happen in some isolated instances, it is not usually the case. The losing party will usually appeal the decision. This will mean additional time and expenses before the decision can be final. Until an opinion is rendered by the appellate court, the execution of the terms of the judgment is on hold. The prevailing party in the trial court may be the losing party in the appellate court if the appeal is successful. Attorneys for both parties must explain all the possible results from an appeal so that everyone understands the risks involved.

§ 11.117 Time Limits

The applicable rules of procedure set out specifically the time limits within which each step on appeal must be taken. These rules are strictly enforced, and if a deadline is missed, the appeal may be invalid. The time limits are jurisdictional requirements and the appellate courts do not have the power to waive them. If a deadline has passed, the appellate court can only dismiss the appeal. Thus, a legal secretary's tickler file is of vital importance in an appeal. The time table begins with the date the judgment was entered in the trial court. The appellate court may, when good cause is shown in a written motion filed by either attorney, grant an extension of time to file the record or briefs. However, the request for extension of time must be filed prior to the time limit expiration and must state a specific requested time for extension.

§ 11.118 Briefs

Briefs are filed by both sides, with the appellant's brief due first. The appellee then responds with his brief. The appellant's brief is a written argument setting out the points of error alleged in the appeal. Relevant rules, statutes, and case law are cited and argued in the brief. The appellee's brief will respond to the appellant's points of errors and arguments.

§ 11.119 Oral Argument

Once the briefs have been filed, and if the attorneys have timely filed their requests, the appellate court may set a date for oral argument. It is, however, the court's discretion whether or not to allow oral argument in the case. Both attorneys may appear before the court and present oral statements to support their case. No further testimony or witnesses are allowed. The attorneys can only address the law involved in their case. The panel of judges hearing the arguments may question either or both attorneys during the oral argument or simply listen. Oral arguments are limited to a specific time set by the court. When oral arguments are not presented, the case is said to be submitted on the record.

§ 11.120 Opinion

The opinion of the appellate court either:

1. Upholds the judgment of the trial court

2. Reverses and remands (overturns the judgment and orders the trial court to retry the case or enter a new judgment)

3. Reverses and renders (overturns the judgment and enters new judgment)

4. Remands in part (some of the results were correct, but other points need to be clarified)

§ 11.121 Collecting a Judgment

Once all the appeals have been exhausted, the outcome of the suit is final. If the defendant has prevailed, the matter ends with no monetary payment from the defendant.

If the plaintiff has prevailed and was awarded a monetary sum from the defendant, he becomes a judgment creditor. The losing party becomes a judgment debtor.

Often, at this point, the amount of the judgment is paid by the judgment debtor, together with any interest accrued and court costs, if awarded. Upon such payment, satisfaction of judgment or release is entered.

Sometimes a judgment debtor is said to be judgment proof, meaning he has no assets with which to satisfy the judgment. Some assets, such as a homestead, are exempt from judgment. These exemptions vary according to the jurisdiction, as do the methods of seizing property to satisfy a judgment.

Local or state rules dictate the time limit for collecting a judgment, as well as whether this time limit may be renewed by refiling the judgment. The legal secretary should note the tickler file with the expiration date of all judgments for clients. She should advise the attorney of the time limits so judgments can be renewed in a timely manner.

The court provides for writs of execution and writs of garnishment to enforce collection of a judgment. A writ of execution instructs a court official, usually the sheriff, to seize the judgment debtor's property and sell it at auction. Any money collected from the sale is given to the judgment creditor. If this is not sufficient to satisfy the judgment, that judgment remains in force for the balance due until it can be paid or collected.

A writ of garnishment enables the judgment creditor to seize property from other people who hold assets belonging to the debtor. Funds from a bank account or wages, which may be subject to garnishment, may be seized in this manner. The bank would be forced to release the funds in that account, and the employer would withhold wages of the debtor until the judgment is satisfied.

§ 11.122 Billing

The method for billing a lawsuit depends upon the fee arrangement made with the client. Many plaintiffs' attorneys handle lawsuits on a contingent fee arrangement, either asking the client to pay expenses as they occur or advancing these costs for the client. When the case is either settled or tried, the attorney is first reimbursed from the award or settlement funds realized. Examples of these expenses would be court costs, service fees, witness or expert fees, or deposition costs. If costs have been taxed against the defendant, the plaintiff's attorney must ensure that a bill of costs to include all allowable expenses is filed with the court. After the attorney has recovered his expenses and all court costs are paid, his contingent fee is deducted from the balance of the judgment recovered. The remainder is then paid to the client.

If the plaintiff with a contingent fee agreement recovers nothing from the judgment, he is still liable to his attorney for expenses incurred or paid on his behalf. The attorney, in such instances, collects no fee.

If the fee arrangement is on an hourly basis, careful records of the time spent by the attorney are kept and maintained by the legal secretary. The client is billed according to the office procedure and agreement with the client, be it monthly, quarterly, annually, or at the conclusion of the case. The bill should include the time spent, rate charged for fees, and the expenses incurred and/or paid by the attorney for the client.

§ 11.123   The Team Concept in Litigation

In many law firms efforts have been made to introduce team strategy for handling cases. This concept can be very effective in litigation practice. Usually the team consists of one or more lawyers, one or more secretaries, one or more legal assistants, and a word processor. Proper use of the legal secretary and legal assistant can help keep the cost of litigation down. Each member of the team is important and contributes to the effective preparation and trial of the lawsuit.

§ 11.124   Duty of the Attorney

It is the attorney who first examines the claim and decides whether or not to accept the case. This may be based on several factors, one of which may involve a disqualification. He may be familiar with the case or have represented or talked with opposing party about the same case. The lawyer, at various stages while the case is pending, evaluates the case and offers the client an opinion of the possible outcome based on the law involved. His recommendations to the client are based on that opinion. The lawyer is responsible for the preparation of briefs and makes all necessary court appearances. He ultimately tries the lawsuit in court. He must be aware of the progress of his support staff assigned to the case. Since the ultimate responsibility for the case is his, he supervises all members of the trial team at all times, assigns tasks, and corrects their work when necessary.

§ 11.125   Legal Assistant or Paralegal

The legal assistant or paralegal always works under the supervision of the attorney. Based upon this supervision and upon his instructions, the legal assistant may question witnesses, prepare such discovery items as requests for admission and interrogatories, and obtain information with which to answer interrogatories. She can gather and index documentary materials for use as evidence, do basic legal research, and write a memorandum for the attorney as to statutes and cases pertaining to the case at hand. Additionally, the legal assistant may discuss cases with the attorney and on his instructions do further research. If the attorney uses a trial notebook, the legal assistant can gather the materials for the book, prepare indexes, and have it in ready form for the attorney's use at trial.

§ 11.126 Administrative or Executive Secretary

The legal secretary often may function as both a secretary and a legal assistant, performing some or all of the services listed under the paragraph on legal assistants. She works closely with each member of the team to maintain files and gather such information as is necessary for use at the trial. Often the docket control and tickler system are the responsibility of the administrative secretary. She reminds the attorney and the legal assistant of deadlines and appointments well in advance of the date they are scheduled. The legal secretary keeps time records for both the attorney and the legal assistant and either prepares or supervises the billing. The legal secretary makes appointments for the attorney for depositions with clients and witnesses. When a deposition is to be taken, the legal secretary arranges for a court reporter, a place for the deposition, and travel arrangements for witnesses and attorneys. When a legal assistant is not assigned to the team, the legal secretary assumes the dual role.

§ 11.127 Summary

Litigation is a particularly interesting field in the practice of law. The legal secretary or support staff member involved in litigation will find a varied and interesting career in this field. A legal secretary should develop an understanding of the various procedures involved in litigation in order to make a valuable contribution. An understanding of the process enables the legal secretary to maintain organized files and good relationships with the attorney, co-workers, clients, and the courts.

CHAPTER 12

CONTRACTS

Table of Sections

---

§ 12.1 In General

The law of contracts is a broad, general area upon which many other areas of law are hinged. It evolved from the Statute of Frauds passed in 1676 plus common law prior to that time. Because of its importance the Statute of Frauds required that certain contracts be in writing. It further provided that contracts could not be changed merely by an oral agreement. Some types of contracts covered by the Statute of Frauds are leases exceeding one year, contracts dealing with the sale of land, and executory contracts.

§ 12.2 Definition

Basically, a contract is an enforceable agreement between two or more competent parties which creates an obligation to do or not to do a particular thing. Contracts may be oral or written. However, prudence calls for contracts to be in writing whenever possible. Contracts affect the daily lives of all of us, whether we think of them as contracts or not. A written agreement to purchase a car or a house is a contract and makes us a party to that contract. Just by turning the lights on in the morning and taking showers, we are parties to contracts with both the light and water companies. They make utilities available, and we pay for the amount we use.

Much law relates to the sale of goods, either for cash or on credit. The Uniform Commercial Code (UCC), which has been enacted in all states except Louisiana (although Louisiana has enacted a code which includes many comparable provisions), governs many of these transactions and specifies the rules which the parties to such a contract must follow.

§ 12.3 Essential Elements

There are four elements essential to a valid contract. Unless all four are present, no contract exists.

1. Mutual consent (offer and acceptance)

2. Competent parties

3. Lawful consideration

4. Lawful subject matter

§ 12.4 Mutual Consent

There must be a meeting of the minds concerning the contract terms. In other words both parties must agree in every aspect concerning the performance required of each. To meet this requirement, there must be both a valid *offer* by one party (known as the offeror) and a valid *acceptance* by the party to whom it was made (the offeree).

EXAMPLES:

A offers to wash B's windows for $10. B agrees to pay $10 for that service. There is both an offer and an acceptance, so there is mutual consent.

A offers to wash B's windows for $10. B thinks the price is too high, but his friend C is willing to accept A's offer for the stated price. There is no mutual consent at this point, since A made the offer to B. He did not make the offer to C.

The offer must be clear and definite, and it must be made in such a way that it will be taken seriously. An offer made in jest is not an offer. An offer that is vague is not an offer.

EXAMPLES:

At a party one evening, A pulls out a very expensive ring and says, "Anyone who can guess what I actually paid for this ring can have it for $15." This would not be a serious offer.

B is very desirous of purchasing A's house at any price. A finally tells B, "Okay, I'll sell you my house someday." The word someday is too vague to consider the statement an offer.

Some contracts call for the offer to remain open for a specified period of time in exchange for which the offeree pays a sum of money. This is called an *option*.

EXAMPLE:

A wants to lease a portion of B's property to construct a new factory; however, he does not want to enter into the lease until he completes all of the details for financing and is assured the loan will materialize. In order to hold the property until he is ready, A agrees to pay $1,000 to B in exchange for B's promise that he will not lease the property to anyone else for a period of six months. This is an *option* to lease.

Offers can be made specifying a time limit during which the offer must be accepted. Usually, the time limit is quite short, and if the offer is not accepted within that period, the offer is automatically withdrawn. Offers for sale of real estate are good examples of this.

EXAMPLE:

An offer to buy real estate is made by a prospective buyer to the owner. The offer includes a provision that if it is not accepted within three days, the offer is automatically withdrawn. (This eliminates the possibility of the offer being open indefinitely.)

Where no time limit is specified, the offer remains open until any one of these events occur:

- Acceptance of the offer by the offeree
- Rejection of the offer by the offeree
- Revocation or withdrawal of the offer by the offeror
- Passage of a reasonable length of time

(Death or insanity of the offeror may also cause the offer to be withdrawn automatically, especially where personal services are part of the offer.)

EXAMPLES:

A offers to wash B's windows for $10; B accepts. There is no longer an offer, but rather mutual consent.

A offers to wash B's windows for $10 but B refuses. Later B changes his mind and wants to accept A's offer. Acceptance is not appropriate now, since the offer terminated when B originally refused it.

A offers to wash B's windows for $10, and B wants to think about it. In the meantime A withdraws the offer. There is no longer a valid offer, so there can be no acceptance.

A offers to wash B's windows for $10, but B wants to think about it. A year later, B decides it would be a good bargain. The offer would not generally be considered valid, since a year is more time than is reasonable to hold the offer open.

A offers to wash B's windows for $10, but before B has a chance to accept, A dies. The offer terminates, since it was based upon personal services being offered.

Advertisements by retailers, mail circulars, auctions, and the like are not generally valid offers. Instead they have been called "invitations to offer" and held in the same general classification as when the government issues an invitation to bid on a certain project or job. Persons who submit bids (offers) in response to the invitation to bid are the valid offerors, not the government.

The acceptance by the offeree must be in total agreement with the offer, point for point, or it is not an acceptance. If the acceptance changes any of the terms of the offer, it actually becomes an offer, frequently called a counteroffer.

EXAMPLE:

A offers to wash B's windows for $10. B is willing to accept but only if A will also wash the screens for that amount. There is no acceptance, since B has changed the terms of the offer and has made a counteroffer to A. If A agrees to the new terms, it is A who makes the acceptance.

Silence does not generally constitute acceptance. The exception to this rule is where prior dealings of the parties have incorporated silence as part of their normal method of acceptance.

EXAMPLES:

A offers to wash B's windows for $10, but B makes no response. His silence would not generally be taken as acceptance.

A and B have had a mutual understanding over the years that periodically A would leave a note stating that he would be in the neighborhood on Saturday and would wash B's windows at that time, for which B would then pay him the usual $10 fee. As a part of the understanding, B would then contact A only on those occasions when he knew he would not be home on the day indicated by the note. They would then set another day. Because of the understanding that had been reached over the years, silence on the part of B would constitute acceptance.

Unless the offer specifies the manner in which acceptance must be made, the acceptance is generally valid if communicated in the same way as the offer.

EXAMPLE:

An offer arrives by letter, stating that acceptance must be made within 24 hours. B immediately writes an acceptance letter and drops it in the mail during lunch. The letter is not received by the offeror until two days later.

In the above example the acceptance would be valid as soon as it had been deposited in the mail. Since this was done within the 24–hour period specified, the acceptance is valid even though it was not actually received until two days later.

Though both an offer and an acceptance have been made by the parties, lack of mutual consent may be claimed to avoid the contract where any of the following factors can be proved to have existed:

• Mistake

• Fraud

• Misrepresentation

• Duress

• Undue influence

§ 12.5   Mistake

It is possible that mutual consent may have been given on the basis of a genuine misunderstanding. This would not include misunderstandings created because a party failed to reasonably investigate or because a party was negligent in reading a document. Either of these events would certainly be a mistake, but they would not be mistakes the law would recognize. In both cases the mistake arose out of the person's failure to use reasonable care. A genuine misunderstanding occurs when, even after reasonable care, the end result of the contract is not what the parties intended.

EXAMPLES:

A offers to buy a lot on Poplar Street in Los Angeles and obtains the name of the owner from municipal authorities. The owner B agrees to sell the lot to A, and a contract is signed. Unknown to either party, there are two Poplar Streets in Los Angeles. A intended to purchase a lot on the other Poplar Street. There has been a mistake as to the subject matter, and the contract can be voided.

A has several cases of what he believes are apples in his warehouse. He sells them as apples to B. When the cases are opened, they are found to contain oranges. Again, there is no contract because of the parties' mutual mistake.

§ 12.6   Fraud

To prove fraud, there must have been (1) a false statement (2) of a material fact (3) with the intent to deceive (4) which is relied upon and is intended to be relied upon (5) to cause a loss to the victim. If all five elements can be proved, the contract can be voided because of the fraud.

EXAMPLE:

A, a jeweler, convinced B, a wholesale jeweler, that he was from St. Louis and that his credit was excellent. Relying on A's convincing representation, B delivered to him $5,000 worth of jewelry. B later learned that A was actually from Kansas City and that he had a very poor credit rating. Once proved, this fact situation would constitute fraud by A.

§ 12.7   Misrepresentation

Misrepresentation differs from fraud in only one way. Misrepresentation does not involve the intent to deceive. The other four elements are the same, however; and if they are proved, the contract can be voided. Because misrepresentation can be an honest mistake, it is often called innocent misrepresentation.

EXAMPLE:

A sells a block of stock in a certain corporation to B, representing it to be worth $10,000 based upon the corporation's net worth. It is later determined that losses of the corporation had reduced its net worth substantially, even though A honestly believed he had given the correct information to B. It is possible that the contract could be voided on the basis of misrepresentation.

§ 12.8 Duress

Duress is the use of force or threatened force to gain consent. In either case the consent would not be the voluntary act of the person giving consent, and that person could void the contract if duress were shown to exist. The person making the threat must be able to actually carry it out (or so it must appear to the person being threatened). The person being threatened must be sufficiently convinced the threat can be implemented so that he feels compelled to submit. Where duress is claimed, the claim must be made as soon as the force or threat of force is removed. Failure to make the claim promptly could be considered a waiver which would bar the claim entirely.

EXAMPLES:

A paid a ridiculously high freight charge in order to take possession of some goods shipped to him. Six months later he demanded a refund, claiming duress. Though duress was present, there may be some question of A's right to claim it since he let so much time pass.

A, a city official, threatened to turn off B's water unless B immediately paid an illegal license fee. B needed the water supply to operate his factory, so he paid the fee and immediately initiated an action to recover the money. Duress would apply, and B would probably recover his damages.

§ 12.9 Undue Influence

Undue influence is the dominance of a stronger-willed person over a weaker-willed one. Constant pressure and persuasion can impair the understanding of a victim so that the contract is not his voluntary act but, rather, is the expression of the will of the dominant person. A contract created under these circumstances is valid until the victim takes some action to avoid it. As with duress whatever action the victim takes must be done promptly.

Some relationships may create a presumption of undue influence because the parties are not on an equal plane in the transaction. In those relationships, one party is presumed to be in a position to take advantage of the other. Guardian-ward, physician-patient, and attorney-client are relationships which may give rise to the undue influence presumption.

§ 12.10 Competent Parties

Competent parties include all persons having the legal capacity to enter into a contract. Attention must be given, then, to those persons who do not generally have legal capacity. They include:

- Minors

- Mental incompetents

- Intoxicated persons

- Corporations (under certain circumstances)

- Married women (only in some states and only under some circumstances)

The claim of incompetent parties can be a little confusing simply because there are many instances where there is not a hard and fast rule. For instance, a minor can be held liable for certain necessities of life *provided* he could not obtain them from a parent or guardian. Those necessities would include food, shelter, clothing, and certain education. For all other contracts the minor has the choice of disaffirming or avoiding the contract once he has reached legal age, *provided* he does so within a reasonable length of time. If a minor marries, he is emancipated, and emancipation automatically makes him an adult for purposes of making a contract. A minor can be emancipated by a judicial proceeding and sometimes simply by leaving home and becoming self-supporting.

Contracts made by persons declared to be mentally incompetent or by persons who are so intoxicated that they are temporarily incompetent can be avoided but only if the person wishes to do so. Until the claim is made, the contract is valid.

Corporations are given certain powers under state statutes, as well as certain powers under their charters. Corporations can enter into contracts but only within the limitations set by state law and their individual charters. Some contracts of corporations which exceed the limitations of power (ultra vires contracts) can be voided. However, as long as the contract is not illegal and no claim for competency is made, the contract is valid.

A husband and wife cannot enter into a contract with each other in some states.

In summary, the element of competent parties can be complicated when that defense is claimed in a contract suit. Because there are as many exceptions as there are rules, the attorney reviews the facts of each case before he can determine what rule he thinks would apply.

§ 12.11 Lawful Consideration

Consideration is that thing (price, motive, or act) which leads one party to do something he would not be obliged to do otherwise. Basically, it is the thing of value being exchanged, and each party must receive some consideration for the contract to be valid. Common items of consideration include money, property, or a promise to do or not to do something.

Common law presumes that if the consideration is acceptable enough for the party making the contract, it is sufficient to bind that party to the contract terms. When the contract terms are reduced to writing, the existence of consideration is presumed.

The consideration must pass from one party to the other during the term of the contract. Past acts of either party cannot usually provide consideration for a new contract. If an individual makes a bad bargain, he cannot claim lack of consideration to avoid the contract.

§ 12.12 Lawful Subject Matter

A contract cannot be based upon anything that is illegal or against public interest. Examples of illegal subject matter are:

- Wagers
- Usury
- Unfair trade practices

Adverse public interest can include:

- Bribing a public official
- Agreement to conceal a crime
- Agreement to enforce a lawsuit

If a thing or act is illegal outside the realm of the contract, then no legal contract can be made concerning it.

§ 12.13 Types of Contracts

Once it is determined that all necessary elements are present and that a contract exists, the rights and duties of the parties are further clarified by determining the type of contract that exists. It can be either unilateral or bilateral; executory or executed; express or implied; valid, voidable, or unenforceable.

§ 12.14 Unilateral and Bilateral Contracts

A unilateral contract is one where a person makes a promise conditioned on the performance of another. The contract is not binding until the performance or act occurs.

EXAMPLE:

A promises B to pay B a commission if B will locate a buyer for A's house. When B finds a willing buyer, he has earned his fee.

A bilateral contract is one where both parties make a promise. If either party fails to keep the promise, the other may be entitled to recover damages.

EXAMPLE:

A promises to pay B 90¢ a dozen if B will deliver 50 dozen eggs by tomorrow morning. B promises to deliver them.

§ 12.15 Executory and Executed Contracts

Executory contracts are those that have been partially performed, but with something remaining to be done by one or both of the parties.

EXAMPLE:

Same as above. B delivers the 50 dozen eggs on time. At this point the bilateral contract is also executory.

Executed contracts are those that have been fully performed by both parties. The transaction is complete and nothing remains to be done.

EXAMPLE:

Same as above. Upon delivery of the 50 dozen eggs, B receives $45 from A. At this point we have an executed bilateral contract.

§ 12.16 Express and Implied Contracts

An express contract is one where the terms are specifically stated and agreed to by both parties. Express contracts are generally written. An insurance policy is an express contract because it is written and specifies terms and conditions. Leases are also express contracts; however, leases are not always in writing.

An implied contract is one created by law and imposed upon parties because of their actions or because of their relationship. The action of using electricity creates an implied contract with the power company. The relationship of husband and wife creates an implied contract of financial support.

§ 12.17 Formal and Informal Contracts

A formal contract is one where the format of the contract (the way it appears) must meet certain requirements established by law. Negotiable instruments, for instance, would fall into the formal contract category. Note that all checks follow the same basic format, since checks are negotiable instruments and formal contracts.

Informal contract is a term used to refer to all contracts which are not formal. A contract may be written and still be an informal contract if its format is not as prescribed by law.

§ 12.18 Valid, Voidable, and Unenforceable Contracts

A valid contract is one that contains all the necessary elements for the making of a contract:

1. Mutual consent
2. Competent parties
3. Consideration
4. Legality of subject matter

A voidable contract is one that is potentially defective in some respect. If the defect is asserted, the contract could be voided. Refer to the discussions on mutual consent and competent parties for examples of voidable contracts, and note that in each example illustrating a defect, one of the parties has the option of making a claim to void or invalidate the contract. Voidable contracts are treated as valid contracts until a defect is asserted.

An unenforceable contract is one that is neither void nor voidable; it is unenforceable because it does not comply with the law. Oral contracts for the sale of land are not enforceable because the law requires those contracts to be in writing. Assuming that all the elements making a contract are present and that there are no defects that would make a contract voidable by either party, the contract could not be enforced in court. The law (through use of courts) cannot enforce contracts that do not conform to the law. The same is true of a negotiable instrument that does not appear in the form prescribed by law. The instrument would be neither void nor voidable; however, because it does not conform to the law, it cannot be enforced by the law.

§ 12.19 Assignment of Contracts

To assign is to transfer. Contracts involving special skills, knowledge, or judgment cannot be assigned (transferred) to another without the consent of both parties to the original contract. Unless both parties consent, the assignment cannot be made.

Generally, contracts involving money or property may be assigned to third persons without the specific consent of the other party to the original contract. The third person is called the assignee. The person who transfers his interest in the contract to the assignee is called the assignor.

The assignee usually has responsibility for notifying the other party to the original contract that the assignment is being made and that he, as assignee, has the contractual rights and obligations previously belonging to the assignor.

EXAMPLE:

A leases an apartment to B for $300 a month. A, the landlord, subsequently sells the apartment building to C. As part of the sale A also assigns the apartment leases to C. C must notify B and any other tenants that the assignment has been made and that future rentals should be sent to C as assignee of A.

Assignment is simply a substitution of one party for another in a contractual relationship. The assignee "stands in the shoes" of the assignor. He has the same rights and duties as the assignor—no more and no less. If an assignee fails to perform under the contract terms, however, the responsibility falls back on the assignor to make that performance.

EXAMPLE:

Same as above. Within a few months, B decides to lease a larger apartment and to sublet his present apartment to D. D, then, has become the assignee of B, and C is properly notified of the assignment. D fails to pay the rent for two months in a row and leaves the city. B, as the assignor and original party to the contract, is liable (responsible) for D's nonperformance. B is ultimately responsible to live up to the original contract terms by paying the rent that is due.

Assignments are not always voluntary. Bankruptcy requires that property of the debtor be assigned to a trustee for the benefit of creditors. Probate proceedings have the effect of assigning property to the personal representative (sometimes called executor or administrator) of the deceased for distribution to heirs.

§ 12.20 Discharge of a Contract

Discharge in contract law means the cessation (termination) of the contract—the point at which the contractual duties are ended. There are many ways to discharge a contract, although only the ones used most often will be discussed.

§ 12.21 Performance

The most obvious method of discharge is performance of all the contractual terms by both parties. Most contracts are discharged by performance.

> EXAMPLE:
>
> A offers to wash B's windows for $10. B accepts. A washes the windows, and B pays the $10. The contract is discharged.

§ 12.22 Accord and Satisfaction

Accord is accepting another thing in place of the thing promised in the original contract (substitution). Once the substituted thing has been given or the substituted act performed, it satisfies the original contract and the agreement for substitution. Accord and satisfaction occurs at that point.

> EXAMPLE:
>
> After receiving $10 to wash A's windows, B becomes concerned about working on a ladder and offers to clean the garage instead. A agrees. B cleans the garage.

It is not correct to say accord and satisfaction occurred at any point before B completed cleaning the garage.

§ 12.23 Rescission

If both parties agree to cancel (rescind) a contract, it can be done by rescission. Rescission requires only the agreement to cancel or repeal the contract plus whatever is necessary to restore both parties to their original condition. In effect, rescission is a contract to cancel the original contract.

> EXAMPLE:
>
> A offers B $10 to wash A's windows. A changes his mind and asks B to agree to cancel the deal. B agrees.

§ 12.24 Novation

Discharge by novation involves the two original parties to a contract and a newcomer. One of the original parties is removed from the contract, and the newcomer takes his place absolutely. All three parties must consent. This should not be confused with assignment of contract, since the two have very different consequences.

461

EXAMPLE:

B agrees to wash A's windows for $10. B later realizes he doesn't want to wash windows and convinces C to do it. A, B, and C agree that A will pay C $10 to wash the windows.

In this situation, B is discharged from the contract by novation. His duty to A is ended. Because he has no legal duty, he cannot be held liable if C fails to wash the windows. Note, however, that if B had assigned only his duty to perform to C, and C later failed to wash the windows, B would have been ultimately liable to A for the failure to perform. Novation discharges B. Assignment does not.

§ 12.25   Account Stated

Suppose a debtor and creditor have had several transactions, and the creditor sends one statement as a summary of the transactions, with a price shown for each. If the debtor holds the bill for an unreasonable time, the creditor may use the summary statement as a basis for suit on "account stated." This has the effect of discharging the underlying transactions/contracts in favor of the "account stated." The debtor can object if he does so in a reasonable time. In that case the creditor would be required to justify each transaction listed.

§ 12.26   Release and Covenant Not to Sue

This method of discharge is used for contracts that are not fully performed but are too far along for rescission. In other words one party has performed all or part of his side, while the other has not. Yet, they both want to end the contract relationship.

EXAMPLE:

B agrees to wash A's windows for one year. Nine months later, B is transferred from the city. A releases B from the contract and agrees not to sue B for nonperformance. (Note that B may agree to pay a sum of money to A in exchange for the release and covenant not to sue.)

§ 12.27   Impossibility of Performance

If a contract has been made and an unforeseeable event occurs which makes performance of the contract impossible, the contract will be discharged. Impossibility means that no person could legally or physically perform the contract terms.

Using our window washing hypothesis, assume the city passes an ordinance requiring all those who wash windows to be licensed. While this places an unforeseen burden on B, it is not an impossibility. However, if the ordinance stated that no person could wash the windows of another, B would be discharged. Washing A's windows after the ordinance had passed would require him to do an illegal act.

Suppose that A's house burned down after the contract was formed. It would be impossible for B to wash windows after the house had been destroyed, and he would be discharged.

Suppose that B died before the windows were washed. Again, B's performance would no longer be possible, and he would be discharged.

This last situation may seem ridiculously obvious—one cannot perform an act after death—but not all legal obligations end at death. Recall the binding effect of a contract to sell land, for instance, on the estate of the deceased discussed elsewhere in this text. Contracts for personal services, such as B's window washing, are discharged at death. The legal effect of the discharge is to free B's estate from performing the balance of the contract.

Discharge for impossibility of performance only means the rest of the contract does not have to be performed. It does not cancel the contract obligations for prior performance. Suppose B washed A's windows for three months and then died. B's estate would be entitled to receive payment for three months, even though the remaining nine months were discharged for impossibility.

§ 12.28   Breach and Remedy for Breach

Once a contract has been formed, both parties have a duty to fully comply with its terms (performance). If either fails to do so, the noncomplying party is in breach of the contract. It is possible for each party to breach or break the contract terms and to have a claim against the other because of the respective breach.

The theory of contract law is simply to enforce binding promises people make to each other. If a person makes a binding promise and then fails to carry it out, the law will step in to require that person to either (1) keep the promise, or (2) pay for the damage caused by his broken promise. There are several methods of doing this, called remedies for breach of contract.

Remedies generally include:

• Specific performance

• Restitution

• Money damages

• Some combination of these

§ 12.29   Specific Performance

Specific performance is a legal remedy requiring the defendant to comply with the terms of an agreement. However, courts are usually reluctant to award specific performance unless no other remedy is adequate. Contracts for the sale of real estate are the most notable exception to the general rule.

§ 12.30   Restitution

Restitution is the act of restoring a thing to its rightful owner. Restitution lends itself to those situations where personal property has changed hands, but payment has not been made. The wrongful possessor of the property could be ordered to return the property to the rightful owner.

§ 12.31   Money Damages

Money damages is the term applied to a court proceeding seeking a money judgment. Money damages represent the largest percentage of remedies awarded, simply because most contracts can be reduced to a dollar value.

In assessing money damages, then, the loss must generally be mitigated (reduced) by the person making the claim. By doing this, he is compensated for his actual loss.

Under the ancient English case of *Hadley v. Baxendale,* damages cannot be awarded to a party merely because the result meant breach of the contract. The damages which resulted must have been foreseeable by the party breached or by a reasonable person in the same situation. In the *Hadley* case, a common carrier failed to deliver machinery which had been sent out by a factory for repair. When the carrier failed to return the machinery on time, the factory sued for lost profits. The court held that those damages were not foreseeable and therefore not recoverable.

Or suppose that before A was fired, his employer acted in some truly outrageous manner toward A (requiring him to work very late, harassing him at home about job questions, etc., to get him to quit so he wouldn't have to fire him). If the conduct was outrageous enough, it is conceivable that A could be awarded pecuniary damages in addition to his actual loss. The effect of pecuniary damages is to punish the wrongdoer in an effort to deter him from acting that way in the future. Generally speaking, punitive damages are more prevalently awarded in tort cases than in contracts.

EXAMPLE:

A is employed by B under an employment contract for one year at $2,000 per month. After eight months A is fired. A would not generally be permitted to sit at home during the remaining four months. He would be expected to seek other employment. Suppose he found another job two months later at a salary of $1,500 a month. His actual damages would be computed:

> $4,000 for two months unemployed and $1,000 ($2,000–$1,500) for two months employment at a lesser rate or a total of $5,000 actual damage for four months remaining under the contract.

Suppose A went to work the very next day at a greater salary. He sustained no actual loss; however, it is very possible that, in declaring a breach of the contract, A could be awarded nominal damages simply because the breach had occurred.

§ 12.32   Summary

Nothing in this material is intended to imply that the area of contracts is simple or cut and dried. It can be highly complex and is usually a far cry from the simple dilemma of having B's windows washed. It is presented here to give the beginning legal secretary a basic understanding of the concepts involved and to emphasize the importance of attorney involvement in such complex matters as contracts.

CHAPTER 13

TORTS

Table of Sections

§ 13.1   Definition

The law of torts is a broad general area of the law which is very difficult to define. Some legal scholars say that the law of torts cannot be defined, and the Restatement of the Law Second, Torts 2d [1] devotes many pages to its definition. The word *tort* comes from the Latin word *tortus* meaning twisted or crooked and from the French word *tort* meaning injury or wrong. Generally, a tort is an act or failure to act which causes an injury or wrong to someone else. A person so wronged or injured is provided a remedy or cure under the law. The law of torts, therefore, deals with injuries or wrongs for which society *permits* compensation or some kind of remedy or relief.

§ 13.2 Distinction Between Tort Law and Contract Law

Civil actions usually arise out of contracts or out of torts. Generally, persons are free to enter into agreements or contracts with other persons. These agreements form the bases of rights and obligations of the parties to the contract. By entering into such a contract, the parties commit to perform certain acts in return for which they usually acquire certain rights. Assuming the contract is valid, it has the force of law between the parties. Without a contract the only rights and obligations that exist between persons are found in the law of torts.

§ 13.3 Distinction Between Tort Law and Criminal Law

Torts are civil wrongs against individuals. Criminal wrongs are against the state. Tort law deals with conduct of individual society members with each other, and criminal law deals with conduct in relation to society as a group. An act may be both a tort and a crime, but a tort is not necessarily a crime, and a crime is not necessarily a tort.

EXAMPLE:

An automobile driver runs a traffic light. An accident results in which the other driver is injured. Under the law of torts the injured person could bring a civil action seeking compensation for his injuries, and the state could bring a criminal action against the driver for running a red light.

If such were the case, however, the civil action filed by the injured driver would probably not involve the action brought by the state for the traffic violation. They would probably be heard at different times by different courts, and the result in one case would not necessarily have any effect on the other.

§ 13.4 Kinds of Torts

Since the law of torts provides a remedy for any injury or wrong not covered by the law of contracts, there is a large variety of cases

---

1. American Law Institute, Restatement of the Law Second Torts 2d. West   Publishing Company, St. Paul, Minnesota, 1979.

encompassed within the law of torts. Some kinds, of course, are more common than others, but they all arise out of one of three kinds of torts categorized according to the kinds of liability involved. In other words, the tort or action is classified according to the legal responsibility which has been violated. The three categories are:

1. Intentional

2. Negligence

3. Strict liability

§ 13.5 Intentional Torts

Intentional torts are those resulting from the intentional interference with another's person or property. There are two broad categories of intentional torts:

1. Those interfering with the person, such as battery, assault, and false imprisonment;

2. Those interfering with property, such as trespass and conversion.

§ 13.6 Battery

DEFINITION:

A battery is a harmful, offensive touching of another's person.

RULE:

In our society a person may expect freedom from harmful or offensive bodily contact from another.

EXAMPLES:

A intentionally pushes B off a sidewalk. A is liable in tort if B proves that A intended for the pushing action to be offensive.

A punches B in the nose. A has committed a battery.

A taps B on the shoulder to get his attention. A has not committed a battery. Reasonable people would not be offended by this intrusion.

§ 13.7 Assault

DEFINITION:

An assault is an act which creates in the plaintiff immediate fear of an attempted battery.

RULE:

A person may expect freedom from apprehension of immediate contact, whether harmful or merely offensive.

EXAMPLES:

A throws a brick at B. B sees the brick coming at him and steps aside to avoid being hit. Although B is not injured (only very frightened), A may be liable in tort.

A puts his hand in his pocket so that it appears to B that A has a gun. A tells B to give him his money or his life. A has committed an assault. Any reasonable person would believe the danger was real and was likely to occur immediately.

A tells B that if it were not a holiday, he would punch him in the nose. A has not committed an assault. Threats alone are not an immediate danger.

A tells B he is going to punch him in the nose and then draws back his fist. A has committed an assault. B is concerned and believes that A has the ability to carry out his threat.

A, a small, elderly man, tells B, a tall, well-built football player, that he is going to punch B in the nose and then draws back his fist. A has not committed an assault. No reasonable person could believe that A would carry out the threat.

§ 13.8   False Imprisonment

DEFINITION:

False imprisonment is holding a person against his will without legal authority.

RULE:

One is free to choose his own location. If a person is held against his will by threats, intimidation, or physical force, he is entitled to be compensated for his time, physical discomfort and inconvenience, any resulting illness, mental anguish, or distress.

EXAMPLES:

A shopper in a department store triggers an alarm as he is leaving the store. He is detained by the security guard, who searches the shopper's packages. It is discovered that the clerk failed to remove a security tag from one of the shopper's purchases. The department store may be liable to the shopper.

A, a police officer, stops B's automobile, asks to see B's driver's license, and tells B not to leave until he is cleared through telephone contact with police headquarters. This is not false imprisonment. A is authorized to do this to preserve society's safety.

A offers B a ride home, and B accepts. A then refuses to take B to his house or to stop the car so B can get out of the car. This is false imprisonment. B is completely confined and cannot escape a moving auto without risking serious injury to himself.

§ 13.9 Trespass to Land

DEFINITION:

Illegal entry upon the land of another is trespass.

RULE:

A landowner has the right to keep his land intact (the surface, air space above it, and the minerals below it) so that anyone violating that right is liable in tort.

EXAMPLES:

If a person enters the land of another person without permission and cuts the timber, he is liable to the owner for the value of the timber.

The airline flight pattern of A calls for its plane to travel across B's land. This is not trespass.

§ 13.10 Conversion

DEFINITION:

Conversion is taking property which belongs to another and using it as one's own.

RULE:

Only the owner of a thing is entitled to possess it and use it.

EXAMPLE:

If a person finds, keeps, and uses a diamond ring, he is guilty of conversion and liable to the true owner, who may sue for the return of the ring or for its value (in which case the defendant or convertor becomes the new owner of the ring).

§ 13.11 Proving Damages

In intentional torts it is not necessary for the plaintiff to prove that he has been damaged. In other areas of tort law, it is usually necessary for a plaintiff to prove that he has suffered actual damage. Therefore, it is sometimes difficult for a layman to understand that there can be tort liability without damage. To recover for an intentional tort, the plaintiff need only prove *intent,* that is, he must convince the court that the defendant intended the act in question.

EXAMPLE:

If one person intentionally strikes another, a battery results. One can distinguish this from a person accidentally striking another by carelessly waving his arms.

As we pointed out earlier, however, only a court and/or jury can decide what the defendant's intent was, and in making the decision, the court must apply many technical elements.

§ 13.12 Negligence

Those torts which are unintentional and not controlled by the doctrine of strict liability (which will be discussed later) fall under the broad category of negligence. In establishing negligence a plaintiff must prove that the defendant owed a duty to the plaintiff. This duty falls into two categories:

1. That which a reasonable man owes to another in the particular circumstances—called "duty of due care"; and

2. A special duty or care required by a specific statute or by case law. This special duty may be in addition to or in place of the duty of due care.

The definition of *due care,* like the definition of *intent,* is very elusive. Ordinarily *due care* is that care which a reasonable, prudent person would exercise in a particular situation. What constitutes a reasonable action depends upon a balancing process. The court weighs the act's usefulness against the foreseeability and severity of any harm which might result. Society is constantly changing, and what constitutes an unreasonable act also changes. Therefore, an act that was unreasonable 20 years ago may be considered reasonable today. Although this balancing process is based upon practical considerations, in the final analysis the court must define an unreasonable act. The attorney must look to current case law to evaluate his client's claim. Examples of some of the most common kinds of torts resulting from negligence follow.

§ 13.13 Personal Injury Cases

DEFINITION:

Personal injury is the term usually applied to describe the kind of suit filed to recover damages for a physical injury.

RULE:

If one person's negligence causes injury to another, the negligent person is said to be liable in tort.

EXAMPLE:

A driver fails to obey a traffic signal, causing an accident. Someone is injured in that accident. The driver is said to be liable in tort to the injured person. The injured person is entitled to compensation for those injuries.

§ 13.14 Defamation (Libel and Slander)

DEFINITION:

Damage to a person's reputation caused by the repetition of false information is libel or slander. (The defamation is *libel* if the information is written or published and *slander* if the information is spoken.)

RULE:

A person who publishes an untruthful statement which is defamatory of someone is held liable for any damage to that person's reputation or business.

§ 13.15 Malpractice

Malpractice has become one of the most controversial areas of tort law. It applies to doctors, lawyers, ministers, counselors, teachers, realtors, and almost any other professionals or quasi-professionals. In general it is an action for negligence with the standard of performance measured by what is expected of a similar professional rendering professional services based on his geographical area, level of alleged expertise, and what was represented to the patient/client. A tremendous rise in many areas of malpractice insurance has prompted the creation by statute of many procedures prerequisite to suit, such as peer review boards, arbitration, and notice requirements.

§ 13.16 Strict Liability

Strict liability is imposed by the law to provide a remedy for injuries received as a result of certain kinds of accidents or situations regardless of the degree of care exercised by the defendant. Under the strict liability concept, neither negligence nor intent is a consideration. The plaintiff need only convince the court that his is a proper case to which strict liability should be applied.

§ 13.17   Products Liability

DEFINITION:

The term "products liability" is usually applied to cases in which a person is injured as the result of a defective product that was sold to him.

RULE:

Manufacturers are liable for damages caused by their defectively designed or manufactured products.

EXAMPLE:

An automobile accident occurs as a result of a defective steering mechanism in the car. The driver of the car is injured. The manufacturer of the car is said to be liable in tort to the injured person, who is entitled to compensation for those injuries. It is assumed that the product was fit to be used for its intended purpose.

§ 13.18   Animal Cases

DEFINITION:

For purposes of tort law these cases involve injuries or damages caused by animals, including all kinds of livestock, domesticated wild animals, household pets, or farm animals.

RULE:

An owner is liable for damage caused by his livestock, his domestic animals, or any wild animals he might keep regardless of whether he exercises due care.

EXAMPLE:

A child is playing with his neighbor's pet dog when the dog bites him. Regardless of whether the bite was playful, the neighbor is liable for it.

§ 13.19   Extra–Hazardous Activities

DEFINITION:

An extra-hazardous activity is one that carries the likelihood of causing some type of damage even if reasonable care is exercised.

RULE:

A person who maintains a dangerous thing or engages in a dangerous activity which produces a high risk of harm to other persons or property is liable to those damaged or injured regardless of whether he exercises due care.

EXAMPLE:

A demolition company is leveling a building by using carefully placed explosive charges. Every possible precaution is taken, but when the charges are detonated, some flying debris breaks some nearby windows. The demolition company is liable since explosives are inherently dangerous by nature.

It is important to note that some torts do not fall specifically into one of these broad categories. Recovery could be based on more than one kind of tort liability. A particular tort (for example, products liability or defamation) might sometimes be classified as falling under strict liability in one situation and as negligence in another. In those cases the kind of tort liability depends upon the circumstances of that particular case.

It is also important to note that the examples listed above are not all-inclusive and are given simply to provide the reader with a basic understanding of the most common types of torts that the legal secretary is likely to encounter. In fact our courts continue to expand the realm of tort law by applying it to types of claims for which there is no other legal remedy.

§ 13.20 Importance of Categorization to Legal Secretary

Why is the categorization of the tort important to the legal secretary? Having some knowledge of the bases for lawsuits and pleadings that are prepared in the law office enhances the performance of the legal secretary. If a person knows why he performs a particular task, he can usually do a better job. The single most important reason for classifying torts is for the purpose of defense. The types of defenses available to a defendant vary with the kind of tort liability. These defenses, of course, are very broad, and this discussion is limited to the most common defenses available.

§ 13.21 Defenses in Intentional Torts

The most important defenses available to a defendant charged with an intentional tort are (1) consent, (2) self-defense, (3) privilege, (4) defense of property, (5) legal process, and (6) recapture of chattels. Therefore, if a defendant were charged with an intentional tort, he might use one of the following examples as a defense in his attempt to convince the court that he was not responsible for the plaintiff's damages or injuries.

§ 13.22   Consent

A defendant sued for battery might take the position that although he did cause the plaintiff's injuries, the plaintiff agreed and consented to the fist fight which resulted in those injuries, so his consent bars his recovery.

§ 13.23   Self–Defense

Using the same example, the defendant could take the position that the plaintiff provoked the fight, attacked the defendant, and that the defendant injured the plaintiff in self-defense.

§ 13.24   Privilege

As a defense to an action for trespass, a defendant might assert privilege to enter upon the land, alleging that he had a written agreement authorizing the entry.

§ 13.25   Defense of Property

A defendant might also allege as a defense to an injury received by a plaintiff on the defendant's property that the defendant was forced to take such action for the purpose of protecting his property.

§ 13.26   Legal Process

A defendant sued for an injury could defend such an action if he were a police officer who used force to keep the plaintiff, who had been charged with a crime, in his custody.

§ 13.27   Recapture of Chattels

In an action by a plaintiff to recover for a personal injury, the defendant could assert that he injured the plaintiff while using force to recapture the money which the plaintiff stole from him a few minutes earlier.

§ 13.28   Defenses to Negligence

Two basic defenses to negligence are available—contributory negligence and assumption of risk.

Contributory negligence is a negligent act or action by a plaintiff that contributes to the cause of the accident. In many jurisdictions if a plaintiff is held to be contributorily negligent, he cannot recover from the defendant. Many jurisdictions have now modified the contributory negligence doctrine by adopting some variation of the comparative negligence doctrine. Under the comparative negligence theory, if the plaintiff is found to be contributorily negligent, the court makes a decision as to what percentage or portion each party was negligent and awards damages accordingly.

EXAMPLE:

In a suit involving an automobile accident where Driver A failed to obey a stop sign, but Driver B was traveling over the speed limit, the court might decide that Driver A was 80 percent at fault and Driver B was 20 percent at fault. If the court then determines that Driver B's injuries are worth $50,000, Driver B is awarded 80 percent of $50,000, or $40,000. Driver A is given a credit of $10,000.

The method of awarding damages varies in some jurisdictions. Contributory negligence is a defense only to negligence.

An assumption of risk defense is employed when the defendant takes the position that the plaintiff was aware of the risks involved and made a conscious decision to proceed in spite of them.

EXAMPLE:

If A slips and falls on B's icy driveway, is injured, and sues B, B can allege that A knew the driveway was icy but still took the risks involved.

§ 13.29   Defenses to Strict Liability Actions

Traditional defenses cannot be employed in a strict liability action. The whole concept of strict liability is such that liability is intended in those particular areas affected. That is not to say that a defendant cannot be successful in this kind of lawsuit. It merely means that the kinds of defenses available in other tort areas are not available in the strict liability cases, and a defendant must look to other ways to rebut the plaintiff's claim.

§ 13.30   Summary

Whether or not a defendant is found liable in tort depends upon whether or not the plaintiff can prove that the defendant's act or failure to act falls within one of those three areas of liability which we have discussed. In the general practice of law much of the litigation in an office involves torts, and the legal secretary should refer to the chapter on Litigation for an overview of trial procedures and a general description of her duties in litigation matters.

CHAPTER 14

CRIMINAL LAW AND PROCEDURE

Table of Sections

§ 14.1 Introduction

A secretary employed by an attorney who specializes in criminal law will find the job to be not only demanding and challenging but perhaps one of the most diversified, interesting, and sensitive in the legal field.

The defense of a person charged with a crime is one of the most important events in his life. If he is convicted, the punishment may include a substantial fine, a prison term, or even the death penalty. Even if he is acquitted, the fact that he has been accused of a crime will undoubtedly affect his personal and business relationships. A future business opportunity or political career may be ruined by the mere filing of a criminal charge. Frequently there are related civil suits and administrative proceedings which are being conducted at the same time as a criminal investigation.

§ 14.2 Definition

In the early days of England, every crime was a crime against the peace and dignity of the king since he owned everything, and it was the duty of his subjects to live in peace. To some extent, this concept remains the basis of criminal charges today, and charges are brought by the government because they are against the peace and dignity of the people of a political entity, such as a state.

A crime is usually defined as an act that violates the laws of a community, state, or country and for which a specific punishment is prescribed. A person convicted of a crime may be imprisoned, fined, or receive both a fine and imprisonment.

Criminal actions are prosecuted in federal cases by the United States. In state cases actions are brought by the state, generally in the county where the crime has occurred. The government is always the plaintiff in a criminal action.

§ 14.3 Jurisdictional Differences

Because of the differences among the federal, state, and local governments, specific matters and procedures outlined in this chapter may relate to the requirements of only some jurisdictions. Therefore, variations among the diverse jurisdictions must always be kept in mind.

§ 14.4 Criminal Law

Crimes are those offenses, either felonies or misdemeanors, considered harmful to the community.

EXAMPLE:

A man who murders another man threatens the safety of people in general, and therefore the community punishes him for his crime.

In early society, all crimes were considered torts or civil wrongs. Even murder was a private matter and was settled by the murderer and the family of the victim, either by the family's accepting payment from the murderer or by taking revenge on the murderer. Punishment remained primarily a matter of revenge until people began to consider punishment as a deterrent to committing crimes. Later, the idea of crime as an offense against society led to the development of criminal laws. There are some acts, however, such as vehicular homicides and wrongful deaths, which may constitute both a crime and a civil tort.

EXAMPLE:

After having consumed several alcoholic drinks, A drives through a stop sign and hits B, a male pedestrian, who later dies of injuries sustained in the accident. The state charges A with vehicular homicide. B's wife also files a civil lawsuit against A seeking monetary compensation from A for the wrongful death of B.

§ 14.5 Scope of Criminal Law

Criminal law includes matters involving the administration of criminal justice and encompasses such aspects as substantive criminal law, criminal procedure, and special problems in administering and enforcing criminal law.

§ 14.6 Substantive Criminal Law

Substantive criminal law is the law which defines what conduct is criminal and prescribes the type of punishment to be imposed for such conduct.

§ 14.7 Sources of Law

The rules which are enforced by the government are found in customs, constitutions, legislation by lawmaking bodies, decisions of judges, and orders of administrative agencies, which are enumerated below.

§ 14.8 The United States Constitution and Federal Statutes

The United States Constitution is the supreme law of the land and establishes the basic rights and liberties of the American people. The Supreme Court of the United States is the final authority in interpreting the Constitution and can set aside any law—federal, state, or local—that conflicts with any provisions of the Constitution. Congress enacts federal laws which prohibit certain conduct, *e.g.,* price fixing in violation of the federal antitrust laws, or counterfeiting United States currency, in which the federal government is deemed to have an interest.

§ 14.9   The State Constitutions and Statutes

The state constitutions and the statutes enacted by state legislatures comprise state laws and are found in the various state codes. State law governs the usual "street" crimes, such as robbery, murder, burglary, etc.

§ 14.10   Common Law

Common law rules are made by judges. These rules have developed from custom and usage and, as might be expected, can vary widely from state to state because of the differences in local customs.

§ 14.11   Administrative Rulings

Administrative rules are made by bureaus of the government called administrative agencies.

EXAMPLES:

The Federal Communications Commission is a federal agency that issues regulations and enforces certain statutes regarding use of the radio and television licenses on a nationwide basis.

A local board of health may regulate standards of cleanliness in restaurants within its jurisdiction.

§ 14.12   Classes of Crime

A person accused of a crime is entitled to certain rights under the Constitution of the United States and the constitutions of the individual states, as well as under federal and state statutes. The criminal charges must be filed in the proper court before the statute of limitations has expired, and the case must be brought to trial on a reasonably speedy basis.

The two major classes of crimes are:

1. Felony—a crime which generally carries a potential jail term of greater than one year, such as murder, grand larceny, arson, and rape. The penalty may include a fine or imprisonment, both a fine and prison term, or even the death penalty.

2. Misdemeanor—a crime which generally carries a maximum potential jail term of one year or less, such as petty larceny, drunkenness, disorderly conduct, and vagrancy. Like a felony, the penalty may include a fine, imprisonment, or both a fine and imprisonment.

§ 14.13 Commencement of Proceedings

Criminal proceedings are initiated by filing either a criminal complaint, an information, or an indictment. A complaint is usually filed under oath in order to secure an arrest warrant. An information is an accusation, filed in writing by the prosecutor, charging a person with a public offense. An indictment is an accusation, filed in writing by the grand jury, charging a person with a public offense which is usually more serious than those offenses prosecuted by a complaint or information.

§ 14.14 The Grand Jury

A grand jury is a body of citizens assembled to investigate complaints and accusations in criminal cases, to hear evidence, and to determine whether probable cause exists that a crime has been committed and whether an indictment should be returned against a person for such a crime. If probable cause does exist, the grand jury returns a "true bill." If probable cause does not exist, the grand jury returns a "no bill." A grand jury is usually comprised of a greater number of jurors than the ordinary trial jury or "petit jury." A grand jury does not decide guilt or innocence but decides only whether there was enough evidence, i.e., probable cause, to require an individual to stand trial. A grand jury's work is done in secrecy to avoid improper influence and to avoid harm to the reputation of those it may be investigating. The grand jury is assisted or directed by a prosecuting attorney.

§ 14.15 Arrest

An arrest is an actual restraint of the person arrested for submission to custody. An arrest may be made pursuant to a warrant signed by an appropriate judicial officer, such as a judge or magistrate. The arrest warrant indicates that the judge has found probable cause exists to believe the named individual has committed an offense. The warrant authorizes any law enforcement officer to arrest the individual and bring him before the court. Under proper circumstances, an officer may be authorized to make an arrest without a warrant. An officer may make an arrest:

1. Pursuant to an arrest warrant.
2. Without an arrest warrant:
    a. When he has reasonable cause to believe that a felony has been committed and that the person to be arrested has recently committed it.
    b. For a public offense, either a felony or misdemeanor, committed or attempted in his presence.

§ 14.16　Initial Client Interview

The initial interview of the criminal client is very important. At that time, the attorney must obtain from the client the details of the arrest to determine whether the client's rights were potentially violated or if any illegal acts may have been committed by the arresting officer.

The criminal client is frequently apprehensive, nervous, extremely distraught, and may even be irrational. Communicating with an illiterate client may be extremely difficult. He requires special handling and understanding, regardless of the type of crime with which he is charged or how reprehensible the secretary might personally find that particular offense. Although a crime with which a client is accused may be a high visibility crime with notoriety in the community, the secretary should never discuss the matter nor divulge information regarding the case to anyone.

§ 14.17　Bail

Usually a person charged with a crime is entitled to be released on bail pending trial. Bail is security given for the release of a jailed person which guarantees his attendance at all required court appearances. A person charged with an offense has a right to be admitted to bail in all cases except where the evidence of guilt is strong that he committed:

- A capital offense
- A felony while he was free on bail awaiting trial on a previous felony
- A felony while he was on probation or parole for a felony

Any person who is admitted to bail may likewise be released on his own recognizance, *i.e.,* released without posting bail at the discretion of the court. In setting bail, the following criteria are usually used:

- Financial condition of the accused
- Address of the accused and his employment history
- Occupation, name, and address of employer

• Family situation and history

• Prior criminal record and pertinent facts of the particular offense

At the discretion of the court, bail may be posted in cash or by a written guarantee called an undertaking or bail bond. The person who posts the bail bond is called a surety. A commercial surety is an insurance company which posts a bond for a premium. Individual sureties are persons who collectively own real or personal property within the state with a net worth of at least the amount set in the order for bail. In some jurisdictions the net worth of the sureties must be at least twice the amount of the undertaking. Each surety must sign an affidavit that his net worth is sufficient to pay the undertaking. Each may also be examined under oath by the court or by the prosecuting attorney in the presence of the court. The sureties who have signed the undertaking are then liable for all appearances required of the defendant up to and including the time when sentence, if any, is imposed. Upon approval of the undertaking by the court, the officer having custody of the arrested person releases him.

§ 14.18　Reduction of Bail

A motion is often filed to reduce the bail which has been initially fixed by the court. The motion is an application to the court for an order reducing the bail, stating the grounds upon which it is made. It must be filed within the time prescribed by law. The real purpose of bail is to ensure the attendance of the accused at all required court appearances. Therefore, if the attorney can show that the accused resides and works in the immediate area or perhaps owns property in that area, the likelihood of that person's being admitted to bail increases.

Sometimes the attorney feels that the amount set by the court is excessive, considering the accused person's financial status, the nature of the alleged offense, and other facts. If that is the case, the attorney files a motion to reduce bail. (See Illustration 14–1.)

The sample forms in this chapter are only a few of many which may be used during the course of a criminal proceeding. These are included primarily to acquaint the reader with some of the basic forms and should be used for guideline purposes only.

Illustration 14–1

[*NAME OF COURT*]

_____,)		
Plaintiff,)	MOTION FOR	
vs.)	REDUCTION OF BAIL	
_____,)	No. _____	
Defendant.)		

483

Defendant hereby moves the Court for an order reducing the bail which has been set in this matter in the sum of $_____ for the reason that said amount is excessive, and for the further reasons [*here the attorney will set out the facts concerning the defendant's financial condition, his ties in the community, his employment history and status, and his prior criminal record or lack of it*].

DATED this _____ day of _____, 19__

_____

JOHN SMITH
[*address*]
Attorney for Defendant

CERTIFICATE OF SERVICE

I hereby certify that a copy of the foregoing Motion for Reduction of Bail was mailed, postage prepaid, to [*name and address of attorney for plaintiff*] [*or was personally served on attorney for plaintiff*], this _____ day of _____, 19__

_____

§ 14.19   Misdemeanor Cases

At the first appearance in court by both the defendant and his attorney, a written entry of appearance may be filed. (See Illustration 14–2.)

Illustration 14–2

[NAME OF COURT]

_____,)
           Plaintiff,)
       vs.   )   ENTRY OF APPEARANCE
)   No. _____
_____,)
           Defendant.)

JOHN SMITH hereby enters his appearance as attorney for defendant in the above-entitled matter.

DATED this _____ day of _____, 19__

_____

JOHN SMITH
[*address*]
Attorney for Defendant

CERTIFICATE OF SERVICE

[Similar to Illustration 14–1]

§ 14.20 Arraignment

The initial appearance in a misdemeanor case is usually the arraignment. An arraignment is conducted in open court, where the judge reads the criminal charges to the defendant or states to him the substance of the charge and gives him a copy of the complaint or information before he calls on him to plead. At the arraignment, the defendant may plead not guilty or guilty. If the defendant enters a plea of guilty, he is sentenced by the magistrate. If the defendant enters a plea of not guilty, a trial date is set.

§ 14.21 Trial

In all cases the defendant has the right to appear and defend the charges against him in person or by counsel. Depending on the maximum potential sentence, misdemeanors in some jurisdictions may be tried without a jury unless the defendant makes written demand for a jury within the time prescribed by law prior to trial or unless otherwise ordered by the court. (See Illustration 14–3.)

Illustration 14–3

[NAME OF COURT]

```
_____, )
           Plaintiff, )
    vs.                 )   DEMAND FOR JURY TRIAL
                        )   No. _____
_____, )
           Defendant. )
```

Defendant hereby demands a trial by jury in the above-entitled matter.

DATED this _____ day of _____, 19__

```
                        _____
                        JOHN SMITH
                        [address]
                        Attorney for Defendant
```

CERTIFICATE OF SERVICE

[Similar to Illustration 14–1]

§ 14.22 Sentencing

Upon the entry of a plea or verdict of guilty, the court sets a time for imposing sentence. Pending sentence, the court may commit the defendant to jail or may continue or alter the bail. At the time of sentencing, the court imposes sentence and enters judgment of conviction. There are several purposes for a sentence, including:

- Prevention
- Restraint
- Rehabilitation
- Deterrence
- Education
- Restitution

§ 14.23   Felony Cases

When a person is arrested for a felony, the procedure is more complicated because the charge is more serious. After the arrest, the accused is brought before the court, who advises the defendant of his right to a preliminary hearing or examination and sets a date for the hearing unless it is waived or relinquished voluntarily by the defendant. The preliminary hearing is a hearing by the court to ascertain whether there is probable cause to believe that a crime was committed and the defendant may have committed it. If the court believes there is probable cause, the defendant is bound over or transferred to the appropriate trial court of general jurisdiction to answer the charges. If he is bound over to the trial court of general jurisdiction, the prosecuting attorney will either file an information within the prescribed time or seek an indictment from the grand jury if state law requires an indictment for that particular offense.

§ 14.24   Arraignment in Trial Court of General Jurisdiction

Upon the filing of an information by the prosecuting attorney or the return of an indictment by the grand jury, the defendant is arraigned in the trial court of general jurisdiction. As in a misdemeanor case, an arraignment is conducted in open court, where the charge is read to the defendant or the substance of the charge is stated to him, and he is given a copy of the indictment or information before he is called upon to enter his plea.

Upon arraignment, a defendant is usually represented by counsel, unless he waives counsel in open court. At this arraignment, or within a reasonably brief time thereafter, a defendant may enter one of the following pleas:

1. Guilty
2. Not guilty
3. No contest

If the defendant wants to plead guilty, the court should make the following findings:

1. If the defendant is not represented by counsel, he has knowingly waived his right to counsel and does not desire counsel.

2. The plea is voluntarily made.

3. The defendant knows he has certain rights including a right against compulsory self-incrimination, a right to a jury trial, and a right to confront and cross-examine in open court the witnesses against him, and that by entering the plea he waives all of those rights.

4. The defendant understands the nature and elements of the offense to which he is entering the plea; that at a trial the prosecution would have the burden of proving each of those elements beyond a reasonable doubt; and that the plea is an admission of all those elements.

5. The defendant knows the minimum and maximum sentences that may be imposed upon him for each offense to which a plea is entered, including the possibility of the imposition of consecutive sentences.

6. Whether the tendered plea is a result of a prior plea discussion and plea agreement, and if so, what agreement has been reached.

If the defendant pleads guilty, the court sets a date for sentencing.

If the defendant pleads not guilty or refuses to plead, the court enters a plea of not guilty for him and the case is set for trial.

§ 14.25   Discovery and Preparing for Trial

Even before a defendant's arraignment, the attorney should have begun preparing for trial by interviewing witnesses and preparing witnesses to be examined and cross-examined. He may gather exhibits and prepare them for presentation as evidence in the trial and may have investigations made and research done concerning the various issues pertinent to the case. The government is required, by statute or rule, in most jurisdictions to provide certain basic information or discovery to the accused, e.g., results of scientific tests such as drug analysis, the defendant's own statement made to the police, etc.

Only by thorough preparation can the attorney evaluate the nature and strength of the evidence which will be produced by the prosecution, and the attorney then will be able to prepare and to present properly the best possible defense of his client.

§ 14.26 Bill of Particulars

An indictment or information may contain, in addition to the formal accusation, certain details of the alleged crime. If the indictment or information does not provide these details, the defendant may file a written motion for a bill of particulars asking for details concerning the offense charged. This enables the defendant to prepare properly for his defense and to avoid double jeopardy, *i.e.*, being tried more than once for the same offense. (See Illustration 14–4.)

Illustration 14–4

[*NAME OF COURT*]

——————————————,)		
Plaintiff,)		MOTION FOR
vs.)		BILL OF PARTICULARS
——————————————,)		No. ———
Defendant.)		

Defendant hereby moves the Court to direct the State to file a bill of particulars in the above-entitled matter, particularly setting forth the following:

[*List items about which more particulars are sought, e.g., where and to whom does the State allege the defendant sold narcotics.*]

DATED this ——— day of ———, 19—

———————————————————

JOHN SMITH
[*address*]
Attorney for Defendant

CERTIFICATE OF SERVICE

[Similar to Illustration 14–1]

§ 14.27 Motion to Dismiss

After the attorney reviews the charging document, *i.e.*, the information or indictment, against the provisions of the statute alleged to have been violated, he may file a motion to dismiss based upon failure to have a speedy trial, lack of jurisdiction, or other grounds. Motions to dismiss must be filed within a specific time after the defendant is arraigned. Failure to file such a motion on time could result in a defendant's waiver of all such grounds other than lack of jurisdiction or failure of the charge to state an offense.

Whether a charge is sufficient to state an offense is governed generally by the rule that it is not sufficient unless it contains all necessary elements of the statute. In the event the statute does not specifically define the act or acts constituting the offense created thereby, the acts must be alleged sufficiently or the charge is deficient. Defenses and objections based on defects in the indictment or information other than that it fails to establish jurisdiction in the court or to charge an offense must usually be raised prior to trial by written motion. (See Illustration 14–5.)

Illustration 14–5

[NAME OF COURT]

————————————————,)	MOTION TO DISMISS THE IN-
Plaintiff,)	DICTMENT FOR FAILURE TO
vs.)	STATE AN OFFENSE
————————————————,)	No. ————
Defendant.)	

Defendant hereby moves the Court for an order dismissing the indictment in the above-entitled action on the grounds it fails to state a cause of action against defendant as set forth in [cite the relevant statute].

DATED this ———— day of ————, 19——

————————————————————

JOHN SMITH
[address]
Attorney for Defendant

CERTIFICATE OF SERVICE

[Similar to Illustration 14–1]

§ 14.28   Change of Venue

The attorney may also feel his client cannot receive a fair and impartial trial in the county where the crime was committed. In cases receiving much publicity and notoriety, the attorney may seek a change of venue by filing a motion for such change. A change of venue is a change in the location of the trial. This motion must be in writing supported by facts as to why the defendant cannot receive a fair trial in that county. (See Illustration 14–6.)

Illustration 14–6

[NAME OF COURT]

————————————————,)	
Plaintiff,)	MOTION FOR A
vs.)	CHANGE OF VENUE
————————————————,)	No. ————
Defendant.)	

Defendant hereby moves the Court for an order transferring this cause to a court of competent jurisdiction in any county other than the county of _____. In support of this motion, defendant sets forth the following facts showing that by reason of extensive and prejudicial publicity regarding the offense herein charged the defendant cannot receive a fair trial in the county of _____.

DATED this _____ day of _____, 19__

_____
JOHN SMITH
[*address*]
Attorney for Defendant

CERTIFICATE OF MAILING

[Similar to Illustration 14–1]

§ 14.29　Evidence Illegally Seized

If the attorney feels there was not probable cause for the arrest of the defendant or that the evidence was illegally seized, he should file a motion to suppress evidence illegally seized, such as drugs found on the defendant by the police or a statement given to the police after the defendant's arrest.　(See Illustration 14–7.)

Illustration 14–7

[*NAME OF COURT*]

_____,)		
Plaintiff,)	MOTION TO SUPPRESS EVI-	
vs.　　　　　　　)	DENCE	
_____,)	No. _____	
Defendant.)		

Defendant hereby moves the Court to suppress as evidence against the defendant in this case all items which were seized during the execution of a search warrant of the premises located at _____, executed on _____, including but not limited to the following items:

[*List items seized*]

and as a basis for this motion, defendant states the search and seizure of said evidence was illegal in the following respects:

    A.　The search warrant is insufficient on its face and fails to state probable cause for its issuance,

    B.　[*List other bases*]

Further, said search warrant is in violation of the rights of the defendant under the Fourth Amendment of the United States Constitution and a violation of [*here set forth state constitution section violated and section of the state statute violated*].

490

DATED this _____ day of _____, 19__

JOHN SMITH
[address]
Attorney for Defendant

CERTIFICATE OF SERVICE

[Similar to Illustration 14–1]

§ 14.30 Plea Bargaining

Plea bargaining agreements have received much attention in the administration of law and justice in our country. While the plea agreement system may need some reform, the United States Supreme Court expressly recognized the need for this system.

A plea agreement means that if there are numerous charges filed against the defendant, several may be dismissed with the acceptance of a plea of guilty to one of the charges. If there is only one charge filed against him, sometimes the charge is reduced to a lesser offense which provides for lesser punishment.

To protect the accused, the courts have held that there must be evidence in the record of the trial court that

1. The guilty plea is entered into knowingly and intelligently.

2. The defendant is aware of the maximum penalty which may be imposed.

3. The defendant is aware that by entering the plea he waives a number of important rights, including his rights against compulsory self-incrimination, to a trial, and to confront and cross-examine in open court the witnesses against him.

Although the client must make the final decision as to whether to plead guilty or go to trial, it is the defense attorney's duty to advise and inform his client so that the client may make the choice intelligently.

§ 14.31 Jury Trial

The defendant has the right to appear and defend himself in person or by counsel and to be personally present at his trial.

A defendant has a right to be tried by a jury of his peers. In capital cases, *i.e.,* felonies punishable by death, the jury is usually comprised of twelve persons, whereas in other felony cases the jury may consist of fewer persons. The number of jurors depends upon the jurisdiction. The prosecution and defense may proceed to trial or complete a trial then in progress with any number of jurors less than

NALS, Car.Leg.Sec. 3rd Ed.—12

otherwise required with the consent of the accused and the approval of the court.

After the jury has been impaneled and sworn, the trial proceeds in the following order:

1. The charge is read.

2. The prosecuting attorney makes an opening statement. The defense attorney may make an opening statement at that time or reserve it until the prosecution has rested.

3. The prosecution offers evidence in support of the charge, and the defendant may cross-examine the state's witnesses.

4. When the prosecution has finished his case or rested, the defense may present its case through witnesses.

5. Thereafter, the parties may offer only evidence to rebut or refute the other side's case, unless the court otherwise permits.

6. At the conclusion of the evidence, closing arguments are made by the defense attorney and the prosecuting attorney.

7. When the arguments are concluded, the court instructs the jury on what law to apply in deliberating on a verdict.

8. The jury deliberates or considers the case in secret and returns a unanimous verdict of guilty or not guilty.

If a judgment of not guilty, an acquittal, is returned by the jury, the defendant is discharged.

If a guilty verdict is returned, the court may order the defendant to be taken into custody to await judgment on the verdict, *i.e.,* sentencing, or may permit the defendant to remain on bail.

Upon the entry of a verdict of guilty, the court sets a time for imposing sentence.

§ 14.32 Sentencing

Before imposing sentence, the court affords the defendant an opportunity to make a statement in his own behalf and to present any information in mitigation (to make less severe) of punishment or to show any legal cause why sentence should not be imposed. The prosecuting attorney is also given an opportunity to present any information material to the imposition of sentence.

If the judgment calls for imprisonment, the sheriff of the county or other appropriate custodial officer designated by the court, upon receipt of a certified copy of the judgment, delivers the defendant to the appropriate place, *i.e.,* the state prison, for service of the sentence.

When judgment of death is rendered, a warrant signed by the judge is delivered to the sheriff of the county where the conviction is had. The sheriff delivers the warrant and a certified copy of the judgment to the warden of the prison at the time of delivering the defendant to the prison. The warrant states the conviction and judgment and the appointed day on which the judgment is to be executed.

In capital cases, where the sentence of death has been imposed, the case is automatically reviewed by the supreme court of the state.

§ 14.33   Post–Trial Proceedings

After a defendant has been convicted, he may file a motion for a new trial. This motion is made in writing within a specified time and should be accompanied by affidavits or evidence of the essential facts in support of the motion. (See Illustration 14–8.)

Illustration 14–8

[NAME OF COURT]

```
_____ , )
                 Plaintiff, )
        vs.                 )   MOTION FOR NEW TRIAL
                            )   No. _____
_____ , )
                 Defendant. )
```

Defendant hereby moves the Court for an order granting a new trial in the above-entitled matter, based on the grounds that [set forth grounds].

DATED this _____ day of _____, 19__

_____
JOHN SMITH
[address]
Attorney for Defendant

CERTIFICATE OF SERVICE

[Similar to Illustration 14–1.]

The court may, upon motion of a party or upon its own initiative, grant a new trial in the interest of justice if there is any error or impropriety which had a substantial adverse effect on the rights of a party.

If a new trial is granted, the defendant is in the same position as if no trial had been held, and the former verdict cannot be used or mentioned either in evidence or in argument.

493

§ 14.34 Appeals

Following imposition of sentence, the court advises the defendant of his right to appeal and the time within which any appeal must be filed.

After the court has imposed sentence, the defendant may file a motion for a correction or reduction of the sentence within the time period specified in the local rules. In considering a motion to reduce or correct the sentence, the court has virtually unlimited discretion to reduce or modify the sentence.

If the defendant takes an appeal from his conviction, he must file his brief setting forth the facts and law upon which he asserts his conviction should be reversed. After the defendant has filed his brief, the state is given an opportunity to file a brief in opposition to the defendant's brief. Thereafter, the defendant may file a reply brief to the state's brief in opposition.

§ 14.35 Collateral Attack

After the defendant has exhausted his so-called direct appellate remedies, he may still seek to attack the conditions of his confinement or otherwise "collaterally attack," *i.e.*, indirectly attack, his conviction. Many states and the federal government have provisions by which an inmate may seek to have his conviction set aside or his conditions of confinement changed. In some cases, a defendant convicted in a state court may also file a motion in federal court seeking to have a federal court review his conviction on constitutional grounds.

§ 14.36 Parole

At some point during his confinement, a defendant will come up for periodic review by the state or federal parole board. If the parole board determines to release the defendant upon certain conditions, the defendant will be released on parole. If the defendant commits another offense, or is even arrested for another offense during the period he is on parole, his parole may be revoked and he may be ordered back to the institution to complete his sentence. In certain cases, he will also face additional incarceration resulting from his parole revocation on top of his original sentence.

CHAPTER 15

FAMILY LAW

Table of Sections

---

§ 15.1 Definition

Family law is just what the name implies—all areas of the law pertaining to the family: abortion laws, adoption laws, child custody laws, duties to disabled persons laws, juvenile laws, civil and criminal support enforcement laws, parentage and paternity laws, and marriage and divorce laws. In many areas the term *domestic relations* is used to refer to family law.

Family law is a rapidly changing area of the law; if your office handles these types of cases, it will be necessary for you to keep current with the changes as they occur. Learn to watch for articles from bar associations and other publications to which your firm subscribes so that you can discuss any changes with your attorney.

§ 15.2 Influence of Uniform Acts

Although family law is controlled by state law, it is an area which has been greatly influenced by uniform acts. Many state legislatures use these acts as models and modify or expand them to suit their needs. There are probably as many variations as there are states, and the material in this chapter is very general. Therefore, you must refer to the pertinent statutes of your state to ascertain the applicable laws in your state. Some of the uniform acts pertinent to this chapter are the Uniform Marriage and Divorce Act, the Uniform Adoption Act, the Uniform Reciprocal Enforcement of Support Act (URESA), the Uniform Child Custody Jurisdiction Act, the Uniform Parentage Act, the Uniform Duties to Disabled Persons Act, and the Uniform Abortion Act.

§ 15.3 Definition of Marriage

Marriage is a legal union of a man and a woman as husband and wife. It is a civil contract governed by state law. All states have laws regulating the licensing, solemnization, and registration of the marriage.

§ 15.4 Types of Marriages

Generally, there are two types of marriages:

1. The ceremonial marriage authorized by legislative action and validated according to statutes for licensing, solemnization, and registration

2. The common law marriage (recognized in only a few states) which is an agreement to marry between two people, followed by their living together and representing themselves to the public as husband and wife

§ 15.5   Ceremonial Marriage

Each state has its own rules and regulations concerning application for a marriage license, the license itself, and the registration of the marriage.

§ 15.6   Prohibited Marriages

There are marriages which are prohibited by law. A marriage entered into by a person prior to a dissolution or invalidity of a previous marriage is prohibited. Also prohibited is a marriage between persons within specific degrees of blood relationship. The exact prohibitions are set out in state statutes. Very often, a prohibition of this type includes persons who are adopted, since in most cases they are treated as blood children of the adopting family. The licensing clerk requires satisfactory proof that the marriage is not prohibited.

§ 15.7   Application for License

The application for a marriage license usually requires certain biographical data of the marrying couple, such as:

- Names, ages, and sexes
- Addresses
- Birthdates and birthplaces
- Occupations
- Race
- Names and birthplaces of the respective parents
- Information on any previous marriages
- Method of termination of any previous marriages
- Whether or not the couple is related and, if so, how related
- Social Security numbers of the couple

§ 15.8   Blood Tests

Many states require applicants to have blood tests taken prior to applying for the license. The tests are for the purpose of assuring that neither person has a venereal disease and verifying immunity to rubella. Certification of these tests is supplied to the couple at the time they take the test on a form prescribed by the appropriate state agency.

This certification must be presented at the time of application for the license.

§ 15.9 Consent of Parents or the Court

In the event either person is a minor under the law of his or her state, that individual's parents or guardians must give their consent to the marriage. The consent of the court is also sometimes required. The minimum age at which a license may be obtained is commonly 16, but this varies from state to state. Pregnancy is not necessarily an automatic reason for obtaining a license by an underaged applicant.

§ 15.10 Premarital Counseling

Some states require the marrying couple to have professional counseling prior to issuance of the license if either of the couple is a minor. This counseling may be done by someone appointed by the court or by an ordained minister (depending upon state law). After the required counseling has been completed, the counselor then files with the court his written statement that the requirements of law have been met, together with any appropriate comments.

§ 15.11 The License

The marriage license is usually issued by the clerk of court or a deputy license clerk. There is a fee for the license, which must be paid before the license is issued.

§ 15.12 The Waiting Period

There is usually a minimum waiting period after issuance of the license before the marriage can be legally solemnized. Likewise, there is also usually a maximum period during which the license may be used before it expires (usually around 180 days). In some jurisdictions the court has the authority to shorten the waiting period or to waive it completely.

§ 15.13 Solemnization

The clerk explains at the time of issuance of the license that it can be used only within a designated geographic area. The marriage ceremony is performed by a minister, judge, or other authorized state official. At the time the marriage is solemnized, the license is signed by the marrying couple, the officiating minister or state officer, and the witnesses. The officiating minister or state official forwards a marriage certificate to the appropriate state office for registration. Once the marriage is registered, the original license is returned to the husband and wife.

§ 15.14 Common Law Marriage

A common law marriage is usually contracted by a couple cohabiting and representing to the public that they are husband and wife. This is the general basic requirement for a common law marriage relationship to exist in those states which recognize common law marriages.

A person who lives with another of the opposite sex and believes in good faith that he has a common law marriage is referred to as a *putative spouse* and is so known until he receives information to indicate that a marriage relationship does not in fact exist.

A putative spouse has the rights of a legal spouse; however, in the event there is more than one putative spouse or there is a legal spouse, the court in its discretion generally apportions marital assets, maintenance, and support among the parties making claim.

For some reason people are often under the impression that by living together for seven years, a couple contracts a common law marriage. This is not necessarily true. In some states that recognize common law marriages, the relationship of husband and wife is deemed to exist as soon as the parties represent to the public that they are husband and wife. On the other hand, in those states which do not recognize common law marriages, neither a representation that the couple are husband and wife nor their living together for any length of time constitutes a marriage.

In many cases where common law marriages are recognized, a couple sometimes wishes to make and file in the public records a declaration of marriage to protect the spouse's rights in the event of the other's death or disability. These are usually in the form of affidavits by persons who have known the couple for a number of years and know that a marriage relationship exists between the couple.

§ 15.15 Methods of Termination of Marriage

Although it is intended to last for the lifetime of the couple, since marriage is a civil contract governed by state law, it can be terminated by state law. There are several methods by which a marriage can be terminated:

• By death of one of the parties

• By divorce or dissolution

• By annulment or invalidity

§ 15.16   Grounds for Termination

The reasons for which the termination of a marriage by divorce/dissolution or annulment/invalidity may be sought are referred to as *grounds*. The grounds for termination are totally in the control of the state, and therefore grounds for termination do vary. It will be necessary for you to become familiar with the grounds in your state.

§ 15.17   Divorce or Dissolution and Annulment or Invalidity

Although annulment and invalidity are referred to as means of terminating marriages, in the strict sense of their definitions, that is not so. An *annulment* establishes that a marriage never existed, while a divorce or dissolution terminates a marriage. *Invalidity* is a term used for a marriage which is invalid (void) from its inception. In some states, however, the term *annulment* is used to include *invalidity*. In those states *annulment* would mean a declaration by a competent court that the marriage never existed, regardless of the reason.

§ 15.18   Grounds for Annulment/Invalidity

The general circumstances for a declaration for invalidity or annulment include:

- One or both parties lacked legal capacity to consent to the marriage
- One or both parties were under duress
- Fraudulent pretenses were used to entice the marriage
- Lack of capacity to physically consummate the marriage was not known to the other party prior to or at the time of the marriage
- One or both of the parties were under age and did not have proper consent or approval
- The marriage was prohibited under state laws

§ 15.19   Statute of Limitations

States have time limitations after the discovery of one or more of the above circumstances within which an annulment or invalidity action may be filed. Persons other than those to the marriage can file for the annulment. The classic example of this is a parent who institutes an annulment proceeding because his child is a minor and did not have consent. Special circumstances must exist, however, for another party to initiate the proceeding.

§ 15.20   Children of an Annulled or Invalid Marriage

Generally, it is recognized that children of a marriage declared invalid (or annulled) are legitimate children.

EXAMPLE:

> A and B have been married for twenty years. They have three children. A discovers that he was fraudulently induced to enter into the marriage; he files an action to have the marriage declared invalid. The three children are legitimate, although the marriage is declared invalid.

Whether or not the invalidity decree is retroactive to the date of the marriage usually depends upon the circumstances involved and the wishes of the parties. Since children of the marriage and property rights are often involved, the invalidity decree may be effective on the date it is rendered rather than retroactively.

§ 15.21   Definition of Divorce/Dissolution

Divorce or dissolution is the legal termination of a marriage relationship. For simplicity the terms *dissolution* and *divorce* are used interchangeably in this chapter although there is a technical difference between the two terms in some states.

§ 15.22   Grounds for Divorce/Dissolution

Since each state has control over its marriage and divorce laws, the grounds for divorce vary considerably. Traditionally, the grounds include:

- Cruel treatment of one spouse by the other;
- Abandonment of one spouse by the other (leaving home with no intention of returning);
- Living separate and apart from each other for a specified period of time;
- Adultery.

The foregoing list is by no means exclusive, but it is representative.

§ 15.23   No–Fault Divorce

No-fault divorce means that neither spouse is accused of the traditional grounds upon which divorces are granted—adultery, physical or mental cruelty, or the like. Therefore, neither spouse carries the stigma associated with these traditional grounds. Consequently, the no-fault concept relieves much of the mental and emotional stress experienced by the parties, their families, and their friends during a dissolution proceeding.

One of the purposes of the Uniform Marriage and Divorce Act is to make *irretrievable breakdown* a basis for dissolution. Many states have adopted irretrievable breakdown as the sole ground for filing a dissolution action. In some states the term *irreconcilable differences* is the term used to mean *irretrievable breakdown.*

§ 15.24   Dissolution of Common Law Marriage

A divorce is required to terminate a common law marriage in those states which recognize common law marriages.

§ 15.25   Division of Property

The termination of a marriage naturally requires division of the property accumulated during the marriage. The method by which a division of the couple's property is accomplished is another matter controlled by the state. Generally, a primary consideration is the contribution made by each, either monetary or otherwise, toward acquisition of any such property. This would not be the case, however, in states where the property of married couples is community property. In community property states the property of the couple is owned one-half by each. In many states a division of the property must be approved by the court; accordingly, it is an integral part of the proceeding for dissolution.

§ 15.26   Child Custody and Support

An action for separate maintenance, dissolution, or invalidity includes determination of which parent will be granted custody (control) of any minor children of the marriage. In addition, it is customary as part of the same proceeding to set an amount to be paid by the noncustodial parent to the other parent for support of the child.

§ 15.27   Jurisdiction Over Custody

For the most part, the court in which the action for dissolution is brought is the court which has jurisdiction over the custody of the children.

§ 15.28   Determination of Custody

Most parents are able to reach an amicable agreement on which parent is to have custody of the children. If the parents are unable to reach an amicable agreement as to custody, then the court makes that determination. It would be impossible to set out detailed criteria for the award of child custody. Therefore, the general rule is that in determining custody, the court is to act in the best interests of the minor.   This rule leaves the court with a great deal of discretion in reaching a decision on custody, but the best interests of the child is the primary consideration.

Traditionally, courts have favored the mother in granting custody. That tradition, however, is being eroded both by courts which are showing greater flexibility by exercising their discretion in favor of fathers and by the fathers themselves who are questioning the *right* of the mother to be so favored.   Therefore, a custody award to a father is not nearly so rare as it once was.

§ 15.29   Disputed Cases

In disputed cases, the court takes testimony of the parties and their witnesses just as in any other trial.   Sometimes the court considers reports from investigative agencies in reaching a decision.   The judge also has the discretion to interview the children to ascertain their wishes and their feelings, but the court is not bound to follow the wishes of the children.   Since the primary consideration is the best interests of the children, in some jurisdictions an attorney is appointed to represent the children in the custody hearing.

§ 15.30   Joint Custody

Some courts are resolving the custody dilemma by awarding *joint custody*, where both parents have custody of the child, often for specified periods of time during any one year.   In these instances, the terms of the custody agreement usually provide that the parents will keep each other informed of the health, education, welfare, and social development of the child.

§ 15.31   Visitation by the Noncustodial Parent

Regardless of which parent is awarded custody of the children, except in rare instances the noncustodial parent has the right to visit the children.   Therefore, the custody award is usually subject to the right of reasonable visitation by the noncustodial parent.   The intent of a reasonable visitation provision is that the parents will cooperate and act in the best interests of the children.   Specific times for visitation are established by the court if the parties cannot agree.

§ 15.32   Support

In determining support for the children, the resources of both the custodial and noncustodial parent, as well as the child's resources, are considered.   If the child has special problems—physical, emotional, or mental—these are also determining factors.   A child who is mentally, physically, or emotionally impaired may be entitled to a higher degree of support than other children, including support and maintenance for special or higher education which will allow the child to function independently in society.

§ 15.33   Agreements

When the parties are not in dispute as to custody and are able to agree upon a support figure, they enter into a written agreement concerning both custody and support. Often the agreement recites that while both parents are fit and proper persons to have the care, custody, and control of the children, they deem it in the best interests of the children to place them in the custody of one of the parties. Visitation privileges are also provided for in this agreement.

§ 15.34   Definition of Alimony and Separate Maintenance

Alimony or separate maintenance is an allowance which a spouse pays for the support of the other party, usually by court order. Most states have a provision for *alimony pendente lite* which is an allowance made during the pendency of an action. Then, whether or not the spouse is entitled to alimony after the divorce is granted may depend upon additional criteria. However, this is an area in which the trial judge is allowed great discretion. Generally in setting alimony the court considers the entire financial status of the parties, including their individual incomes and their debts.

§ 15.35   Who Is Entitled to Alimony

This is another area of family law where traditions are being eroded both by courts and by husbands. Traditionally, wives were the only spouses entitled to alimony and maintenance. Some state statutes providing alimony for wives only have been declared unconstitutional. Most states are therefore amending their statutes to provide for alimony and separate maintenance for either spouse.

Often if the parties reach an agreement on the division of property and child custody and support, they also reach an amicable agreement as to how much alimony or maintenance is to be paid.

Some states are allowing rehabilitative maintenance. This is support paid by one spouse to the other for a physical or vocational disability. In the case of a vocational disability, a sum of money would be paid to allow one spouse to finish school or training in order to reenter the working world.

§ 15.36   Tax Considerations

In setting alimony or maintenance and child support, there are tax consequences to be considered. Often, in an amicable settlement, a larger portion of the alimony and child support is classified as alimony in the agreement. This is because although alimony is considered income to the payee, it is deductible to the payor for income tax purposes. Child support is not deductible. Therefore, if the wife is in a much lower tax bracket than the husband, for example, a higher income might not result in a substantial increase in taxes for the wife, but it might result in a substantial deduction and savings for the husband. The attorney makes a careful study of the tax consequences facing his client in any such settlement and makes certain that the provisions of the decree or agreement will satisfy the requirements of the Internal Revenue Service.

§ 15.37   Procedures

While the difference between a divorce and a dissolution and the difference between an annulment and an invalidity are basically a matter of semantics in many states, the procedures as far as the legal secretary is concerned are generally the same regardless of whether or not her state has adopted the uniform acts or a variation of them.

The no-fault concept of dissolution of marriages has eliminated some of the paper work that is necessary for traditional divorce actions. It also makes the task of drafting the necessary legal pleadings simpler for both the legal secretary and the attorney, and the secretary can draft a simple petition of this type on her own initiative.

Procedures in termination actions follow the same course as in any other type of civil action. Since the procedural anatomy of an invalidity parallels that of a dissolution, the procedures are not repeated here. If you keep in mind the similarities between the two types of actions, you will have no problem conforming one to the other. In instances where the parties are in agreement, the procedure is simpler than in most civil litigation. However, when there is a dispute, the litigation follows the same course as any other litigation. There is a petition, an answer, discovery, and a trial.

§ 15.38   Requirements of Pleadings

Each state has varying requirements as to the pleadings in these actions, and it will be up to you to learn those in your state. You can learn many of the requirements by referring to the forms manual in use in your office. If there is none, you should begin immediately to develop your own. By having a good forms file, you can relieve your attorney of the burden of dictating the pleadings. However, be very careful not to use forms without individualizing them to the given situation. Each time a new situation arises or unique language is used, put a copy of the appropriate portion of the document in the forms manual for future reference.

§ 15.39   Client Interview Sheet

Here again is a type of proceeding which can be streamlined from the document preparation standpoint by the use of a detailed interview sheet. The secretary can soon learn what facts are necessary to prepare initial documents from the completed interview sheet.

§ 15.40   The Pleadings

In the traditional termination proceeding, just as in other civil litigation, the initiating party is the *plaintiff* and the spouse is the *defendant.* The caption is the same as in any other civil litigation. The initial document is a *petition* or a *complaint,* and a summons is issued as in any other civil litigation.

In no-fault proceedings, the initiating party is the *petitioner* and the spouse is the *respondent;* or there is no designation in the caption other than "In the Matter of Susie Que and Curley Que Applying for Dissolution." In some states where a joint petition for dissolution is allowed, the caption may read "Susie Que and Curley Que, Joint Petitioners." Even in no-fault dissolutions, however, it is still necessary to prepare a petition. Some jurisdictions do allow one of the spouses to waive service and legal delays in a no-fault proceeding.

§ 15.41   The Petition

The petition for a dissolution normally contains the following:

1. The age, address, occupation, and residence of each party and length of time residence has been continuously maintained within the state by each party is given.

2. There is a statement that at least one of the parties has resided within the state of jurisdiction for the required length of time.

3. The city, county, and state where the parties were married, the date of the marriage, and the office or governmental agency where the marriage was registered are given. This is particularly important under the uniform law, as a statistical report is sent to this office after the decree is entered, and in many jurisdictions the matter is also entered in the judgment docket.

4. A statement as to whether or not state conciliation laws apply to the action is made. If they do, a statement that the provisions thereof have been met by whatever action was taken is included.

5. There is a statement that the marriage is irretrievably broken (for whatever reason).

6. The names, ages, addresses, and birthdates of the children are given.

7. A statement that the wife is or is not pregnant may be required.

8. A reference to the division of property is made. If an amicable division has been reached, it is described.

9. A statement of custody, support, and visitation rights regarding minor children is required. If an agreement has been reached, refer to the provisions of the agreement. There may be an additional statement that the provisions of the agreement are not unconscionable and were made in the best interests of the children.

10. If the parties are in the process of negotiating an agreement, a statement to this effect and that the parties will make an effort to settle the property rights, custody, support, and visitation is given.

11. If the parties are not in agreement on property rights and child custody, they may request the court to make these determinations.

12. If the wife desires to retake her former name, a statement to that effect is included.

The prayer of the petition is typed just as in any other civil litigation and gives a summary of the relief sought by the petition:

1. That the marriage be dissolved

2. That the court approve the provisions of the agreement regarding the property rights or that the court determine the parties' respective property rights

3. That custody, support, and visitation be ordered as set forth in the petition or that these matters be determined by the court

4. That the wife's former name be restored

The petition is usually signed by the attorney for the petitioner. It may also be necessary that the petition be signed by the petitioner or verified. The actual form will depend upon the procedural law in your state.

Once the petition has been prepared and is ready to be filed, you will proceed just as you would in any other type of civil litigation. Refer to the chapter on Litigation for details regarding filing, summons, and service of the petition.

§ 15.42 Service

It is common in divorce proceedings for the defendant or respondent to accept service. This is usually done by a simple statement on the face of the summons acknowledging receipt of the summons on a certain date at a certain place. It is dated and signed by the defendant or respondent and returned to the originating attorney for filing with the court. Acceptance of service can be handled through the respondent's attorney, through the mail, or in person by the respondent.

Other jurisdictions require the serving party, *e.g.*, the sheriff's office, to complete the return of service on the summons.

§ 15.43 Answer or Response

Just as in any other civil litigation, the defendant or respondent has a specified period of time within which to answer the petition. If the parties are in agreement, the respondent may file a verified response admitting the allegations of the petition (including admission that the marriage is broken) and requesting that the decree be entered as prayed for in the petition. An alternative is that the respondent makes no appearance and the petitioner takes a default judgment. The procedure varies, and you must learn the accepted procedure in your state.

Note that in the traditional divorce action, the defendant's first appearance is usually an *answer*. In a no-fault action, the appearance is a *response*. Here, again, the terminology as well as the procedure may vary.

§ 15.44 Importance of Calendaring

It is important that you calendar the date that a response or an answer is due as well as the date when a default judgment can be taken. This is particularly crucial if your attorney represents the defendant or respondent, as a response of some type is essential to prevent a default judgment from being taken. If you have been instructed to prepare the entry of a default for your attorney, it is important to verify with him that he has not granted an informal extension of time for a response to be filed. Attorneys sometimes forget to make such notes in the file.

§ 15.45 The Decree

When the decree is entered, whether in an amicable action or a disputed one, it may set forth findings of fact, conclusions of law, and the decision of the court. Just as in any other litigation, if the matter is a disputed one, the attorney for the prevailing party drafts the judgment and submits it to the opposing attorney for approval before presenting it to the judge for his signature.

In a situation where there is no answer filed either by intent or otherwise, one of the parties appears to testify to obtain the decree. Testimony is taken by the court, and at the conclusion of the testimony, the judge signs the decree which has been prepared by the attorney prior to the court hearing.

Regardless of how the decree is obtained, it contains substantially the same information:

1. The names of those appearing at the hearing
2. That the summons was served and the default entered or that the summons was served and a response filed and whatever other action resulted
3. The date of the hearing and the date continued from (if applicable)
4. A statement that witnesses were sworn and testified and that from the evidence presented the court makes the findings of fact contained in the decree
5. The findings of fact (generally, a basic statement of the facts of the case)
6. A statement that from the findings the court draws the conclusions set out in the decree
7. The conclusions of law
8. The fact that the marriage is dissolved
9. That the parties have entered into an agreement regarding distribution and disposition of their property and that the agreement is incorporated by reference into the decree and approved
10. Full provisions for child custody, support, and visitation
11. Provisions regarding alimony or separate maintenance

It is also possible in some states to obtain the actual marriage dissolution, reserving for further consideration the property settlement, child custody, and support matters. The original decree should conform to this situation, with a final decree entered at such time as these other matters are settled or have been heard.

§ 15.46 Service of Decree

When the decree has been entered, copies should be served on the parties as required by appropriate state laws. Your state may require a notice of entry of decree, and it may be necessary that you prepare that notice, although it may be served by the clerk or by the sheriff. It is a good idea to see that each party receives a certified copy of the decree.

§ 15.47 Appeals

Appeals in these actions generally follow the same rules and procedures as in any other type of civil litigation.

§ 15.48 Other Special Considerations

There are several areas of special consideration in the divorce/dissolution action. Two of these which you are most likely to encounter are the rights of minor children and the rights of mentally incompetent family members.

§ 15.49 Appointment of Attorney to Represent Children

In some jurisdictions there are cases where there is a great deal of disparity over child custody and support. In some jurisdictions either parent may petition the court to appoint a disinterested attorney to represent the interests of the minor children or incompetent children who are affected by the custody, support, and property settlement of the parties. This attorney then enters the case with the best interest of his clients (the children) in mind.

§ 15.50 Petition to Appoint

The petition to appoint is a very simple one which merely requests that the court appoint an attorney to represent these special parties. Depending upon the procedural rules of the jurisdiction involved, probably the best interests of the children would be sufficient to seek the appointment. The fees of the attorney so represented are fixed by the court and taxed to the parties accordingly.

§ 15.51 Appointment of Guardian Ad Litem to Represent Incompetent Party

In a situation where one of the parties to the dissolution action is incompetent, the court may appoint a guardian ad litem to act in the place of the incompetent spouse. The guardian ad litem then retains the services of an attorney to represent the incompetent party (who is probably the defendant/respondent in the action).

§ 15.52 Incompetence as a Ground

In most states incompetence for a specific duration does constitute grounds for a divorce or dissolution. This type of action might be utilized when a spouse has become mentally incompetent to the point that the person must be institutionalized, placing a financial burden on the family. The dissolution action may enable the incompetent spouse to receive Medicaid or other subsidy to pay for the institutionalization and enable the family to remain financially intact.

§ 15.53 Definition of Uncontested Proceedings

In uncontested proceedings the couple have decided that they no longer wish to remain married, and they have reached an amicable decision on property, custody, child support, visitation, and alimony, if any.

§ 15.54 Agreement

Often the attorney prepares a proposed agreement for execution by the parties prior to filing the action. This agreement recites basically the following facts and provisions:

1. Names of the parties

2. Date and place of the marriage

3. That the parties now are husband and wife

4. That the parties have separated or will be separated for whatever reason

5. The names, ages, sex, and birthdates of any minor children

6. Name of each attorney representing each party; if one is not represented by an attorney, a statement that he understands he is free to seek legal representation and has been so advised

7. Statement that the parties intend by the agreement to set forth in writing their mutual promises

8. That the agreement is mutual

9. The provisions for the division of property and debts

10. Provisions for child custody, support, and visitation with a statement that the parties feel these are in the best interests of the children at this particular time

11. If joint custody, the controlling provisions

12. Alimony or separate maintenance provision

13. How tax returns for the year of dissolution will be handled, including who gets any refund and who pays any taxes due

14. Provisions for modification of the agreement

15. Provisions for attorney fees—current and future

16. Provisions for effecting transfer of title of the assets

17. Statement that the parties have fully disclosed all property, debts, and agreements to each other and to their attorneys

18. That the agreement has been read and is understood by the parties

19. That the agreement is voluntary

20. The name of the court having jurisdiction over the dissolution proceedings, any future modification of the agreement, and future child custody and support proceedings

The agreement, when finalized, is usually signed in triplicate by the parties and notarized. One triplicate original is then retained by each party and the third triplicate original is filed with the court when the petition for dissolution is filed. This eliminates the necessity of having to set forth the agreements in the petition. It also saves time when the decree is rendered, as the agreement can be made a part of the decree by reference if an original is in the court record.

§ 15.55   Modification of a Decree

State laws have usually recognized a minimum time within which a dissolution decree, including custody and support provisions, cannot be modified after it is entered. The uniform act recommends two years. During this time, the decree cannot be modified unless there is a substantial change in circumstances, such as severe disability of the custodial parent affecting the children; inability of noncustodial parent to continue support payments in the amount ordered; or circumstances which have changed greatly since the entry of the decree affecting the best interests of the minor children.

§ 15.56   Purpose of the Uniform Reciprocal Enforcement of Support Act (URESA)

The Uniform Reciprocal Enforcement of Support Act (URESA) provides a means for enforcing duties of support in foreign jurisdictions. In this context *foreign jurisdiction* means a state other than the one where the child and custodial parent live. URESA has now been adopted by a majority of states.

§ 15.57   Jurisdiction

Actions under URESA are initiated in the jurisdiction of the custodial parent and child to whom support is due. The action is then transferred to the county and state where the respondent lives for service on him.

§ 15.58   The Custodial Parent Can Initiate the Action

Sometimes a custodial parent initiates the petition on his own with the hope that by having support enforced, he will be able to avoid becoming dependent on state aid. The custodial parent may have custody as a result of a divorce proceeding in which he was awarded custody. Sometimes the parent seeks support even if the couple are not living apart under a formal court order. The noncustodial parent still has an obligation to support the child whether or not the parents are divorced.

§ 15.59   The State Department of Welfare Can Initiate the Action

The petition is often initiated by a state department of welfare which has provided support to the custodial parent. Usually, a condition to receiving financial aid for support from a state department is the assignment by the custodial parent of all support payments to which he is entitled. The state then initiates an action on behalf of the custodial parent to enforce support obligations and recover welfare payments made to the custodial parent. Sometimes the state is given custody of children because of emotional, physical, or mental disabilities or because of neglect by the parents. In those instances, the state often initiates a URESA action against the parents for support to offset the cost to the state for the child's care.

It is also common in cases where unwed mothers seek welfare aid for their children for the state department of welfare to file an action to enforce support from the father. In order to receive such aid, the unwed mothers are usually required to provide the name of the putative father of the child. The state then seeks to have the parentage of the child determined legally and seeks to enforce support obligations of the father. (Actions to establish paternity are discussed later in this chapter.)

§ 15.60   Verified Testimony

The verified testimony of the custodial parent containing the following information is an essential element to the URESA action:

    1.   Full names and addresses of both parties

2. Date and place of marriage and dissolution or separation

3. Names, ages, and addresses of the minor children

4. Amount of support ordered monthly

5. Amount of arrearages, together with date and amount of last payment

6. Respondent's employment, property, income, etc., as known to petitioner

7. Petitioner's monthly expenses, broken down into housing, food, utilities, health care costs, gasoline, and other expenses for the petitioner and the children

8. Whether the petitioner is currently on welfare and if petitioner will have to seek welfare assistance if support payments are not made

9. A description of the respondent, including age and distinguishing marks

10. Respondent's last known address and usual occupation as well as other occupations he has been engaged in or is capable of performing

11. Any other information which might aid authorities to find the respondent

§ 15.61　Certificate of Transfer

Another essential element to the URESA action is a request of the court to enter a certificate for the transfer of the action to the appropriate jurisdiction. Occasionally when the action is started by the state, the petition and testimony are a combined document; the important thing is that all information required is presented.

§ 15.62　Defenses to the Action

The respondent must present testimony as to the defenses for the alleged failure to provide support. In cases where the respondent has been unemployed or otherwise unable to meet the obligations of support, the court takes the circumstances under advisement and sometimes reduces the amount of support requested in the URESA action.

§ 15.63　Action by the Court

After consideration of the evidence and the respondent's testimony, the court having jurisdiction over the respondent enters its order. The order may require the respondent to make all payments through the clerk of court in the jurisdiction where the hearing is held. When that is done, that clerk of court then forwards the funds to the clerk of court in the originating jurisdiction for disbursement. Sometimes the court simply orders that regular support payments be made to the custodial parent and a specified amount reimbursed to the welfare department. In those instances there is a specific provision in the order rendered by the court.

§ 15.64 The Pleadings

The only pleadings generally required by the attorney for the petitioner are the petition, the verification of the testimony, and the certificate of the originating court to have the action transferred to the respondent's jurisdiction.

§ 15.65 The Petition

The petition is probably one for which your office has a standard form. If it does not, once the attorney has dictated one to you, it will be a simple matter for you to conform cases which follow to the same format. The petition is verified.

§ 15.66 The Verified Testimony

A very important aspect of the pleading is the sworn testimony of the petitioner which sets out the information recited in the section on verified testimony. A client interview sheet will prove an invaluable aid to you in this regard.

§ 15.67 The Certificate for Transfer

You will also prepare the certificate that the court must sign to have the matter transferred. Depending upon jurisdictional rules and local custom, it is usually not necessary for the petitioner to appear in person when the prosecuting or state attorney presents the matter to the court for issuance of the court certificate to transfer the case to the respondent's jurisdiction.

§ 15.68 Forwarding Pleadings to Respondent's Jurisdiction

The petition, testimony, and certified copies of URESA as adopted in the state of origin are forwarded to the respondent's jurisdiction. The clerk forwards the entire filing to the appropriate jurisdiction with the correct number of copies. How many copies you must prepare will depend upon several factors; but until you know how many you need for your particular jurisdiction, prepare several to be safe.

§ 15.69 Issuance of Citation

Upon receipt of the action in the responding jurisdiction, the matter is filed immediately and turned over to the prosecuting attorney. A citation for the respondent to appear is issued and served on him, together with a complete copy of the documents on file. Therefore, one set of documents is retained in the court file, one is retained by the prosecuting attorney, and one is used for service on the respondent.

§ 15.70   Service on Respondent

The citation is served on the respondent, together with the petition and supporting documents, advising him of the time when he must appear to present a defense to the URESA action.

§ 15.71   Failure to Appear

In the event the respondent does not appear at the time he is cited into court, he can be held in contempt and be punished accordingly. If previously the respondent has been known to flee after being served with process in a URESA action, the initiating court may request that he be arrested and held until such time as he can appear before the judge.

§ 15.72   Inability to Locate Respondent

In the event the parent against whom the action has been filed cannot be located within the county where the action has been transferred, the prosecuting attorney immediately notifies the initiating court asking for any information which will lead to the location of the respondent. In this event it may be necessary for you to help locate him. You can check telephone directories, police records, income tax offices, and the Social Security Administration to trace the respondent and to effect service. These agencies usually assist to the point which they legally can in a support matter.

§ 15.73   Transfer to Another Jurisdiction

If it develops that the respondent is in a county other than where the action is filed, the prosecuting attorney is notified, and he prepares an order for the court to issue transferring the action to the county where the respondent resides.

§ 15.74   For the Respondent

The secretary to the attorney for the respondent has a somewhat different approach to the URESA action. She will be involved in the defense preparation. The preparation which the secretary can provide is helping the client gather and categorize support payments made, employment records, income tax returns, and other financial records; this can be a time-consuming process and is more clerical than legal in many instances. The secretary should verify through the court where support was to be paid, the actual payments ordered, and the amount the client has paid.

All financial records of the respondent, medical records, and any other pertinent information which would show a change in circumstances of a client and substantially affect his ability to contribute to the support of the children should be categorized in a manner which can be presented to the court.

If paternity is denied, you should obtain copies of birth certificates and other public records which may substantiate the denial. You may also be responsible for seeing that blood tests are taken and made available for use at a hearing.

§ 15.75 The Secretary's Role in URESA Actions

Much of the routine work in these cases can be handled by the secretary under the supervision of the attorney. Once a workable form for the petition and the testimony are developed by the attorney, ordinary actions can be prepared; unusual circumstances, as always, will require more assistance from the attorney for special phrasing. The court certificate will always be the same. Requests for updates of information, notification of inability to locate, requests to transfer, and subsequent orders can all be handled on a routine basis by the secretary after she has done several proceedings.

§ 15.76 Civil Liability for Support

A Uniform Civil Liability for Support Act sets forth the duties of support between spouses and parents and children. This act and URESA were both enacted to help enforce support obligations required under court orders.

Civil actions against obligors for support may also be initiated by the custodial parent. These actions are filed much the same as any other civil suit with a complaint initiating the action and issuance of a summons. Judgments are obtained and enforced through execution and foreclosure proceedings. These, of course, will depend upon statutes applicable in the appropriate jurisdictions.

In the event the defendant to a civil support action resides in another state, the judgment entered may also be transferred to that state to ensure enforcement. It is also generally recognized that even when children have reached their majority, the noncustodial parent still owes the obligation to the custodial parent for support payments in arrears. State laws control these actions, and the procedural law for your state will have to be followed.

§ 15.77   Definition of Adoption

Adoption means taking into one's family the child of another and giving the child all the rights, duties, and privileges of a child and heir.

§ 15.78   Uniform Adoption Act

Although the Uniform Adoption Act has been adopted by only a few states, it still serves as a suitable basis for learning the requirements of adoption. Many of the states adopting the act have greatly modified it. As always, the secretary should be familiar with the requirements for her own state.

§ 15.79   Jurisdiction

Adoption matters are usually filed in the probate division of a state court. However, some jurisdictions have separate family courts or juvenile courts which have jurisdiction over adoption proceedings.

§ 15.80   Closed Hearings

Adoption files are sealed; that is, the public is not granted access to them. In the case of adoption from an agency, even the parents are not allowed access to these files. Discretion on the part of the secretary is imperative in adoption proceedings. Usually, adoption agencies request that the attorney somehow prevent the adoptive parent from even seeing the last name of the child when signing the requisite documents and pleadings. The adoption hearing itself is also a closed hearing. There is continuing controversy over whether or not an adopted child should be allowed to find his biological parents or whether parents should be allowed to find their children placed for adoption. Many times whether or not a child is allowed to see his adoption file is left to the discretion of the presiding judge.

§ 15.81   Adoption Procedure

The most common adoption proceeding is probably that of a spouse adopting stepchildren. The procedure in this type of case is relatively simple:

1. The stepparent files a petition in the proper court.

2. The spouse of the stepparent consents to the adoption by joining in the petition.

3. The noncustodial parent consents to the adoption releasing all his parental rights.

4. There is an investigation by a state agency, such as the Department of Social Services.

5. The agency reports to the court.

6. There is a closed court hearing, usually in the judge's chambers. Assuming the judge finds the record of the case to be in proper form, he renders the decree.

Adults may be adopted; however, the prospective adoptee and his spouse must also consent to the adoption.

From the initial client interview, the attorney determines the eligibility of the prospective adopting parent, who must receive notice, and who must consent to the adoption. If the office uses a detailed interview sheet, the secretary should have little difficulty drafting the petition. Generally, the following information is included in the petition. Again, there will be variations from state to state.

1. Full name, age, place of, and length of residence of the petitioner

2. Petitioner's interest (why he is petitioning for adoption, such as marriage to the natural, custodial parent)

3. Full name of the minor child, sex, date, and place of birth, relationship to petitioner, and request for name change

4. If petitioner is married to custodial parent, give date and place of marriage

5. How long child has been in physical custody of petitioner

6. That petitioner is a fit and proper person and has the capability, resources, and facilities to provide for the care, support, and maintenance of the child; that petitioner desires to do so and to establish the relationship of the natural parent and child

7. Name of natural parent of the child and any other person from whom consent might be necessary or the reason why consent from someone else is not necessary

8. Value and description of any property the child has

9. Signature of the petitioner with a verification

10. Name, address, and signature of petitioner's attorney

Usually the custodial parent joins in the petition for adoption. This joinder, with the consent, can be in affidavit form and should contain the following information:

1. Name of parent and relationship to child

2. Restatement of child's full name, age, sex, date, and place of birth

520

3. Former name of parent (as shown on birth certificate) if applicable

4. Name of natural father, if known, or statement that other parent is deceased or reason why consent from that parent is not necessary

5. Statement of free consent to adoption and of joining in petition to adopt

6. Statement that parent, by joining in adoption petition, does not relinquish rights as natural parent

When the petition and consent have been prepared and signed, they are filed in the proper court. A certified copy of the petition and attached consent are served on the appropriate state agency, such as the Department of Social Services or other applicable agency. Since this agency conducts an investigation regarding the proposed adoption, it must be served with the petition.

§ 15.82 Consent to Adoption

During the time that the investigation of the state department is being conducted, any required consents to the adoption can be obtained and filed. In the event the child is illegitimate, the natural father usually need not consent. Because of an increased recognition of the rights of the natural father, some attorneys still seek consent to avoid future actions by the natural father to invalidate the adoption. If consent from someone who cannot be located is required, an order to show cause why the adoption should not be granted may be served by publication in a newspaper of general circulation in the jurisdiction where that person was last known to reside. Service of this type will vary greatly among jurisdictions, but the attorney will supervise any such notice.

If the noncustodial parent or other person from whom consent is necessary refuses to give that consent, he may be personally served with an order to appear and show cause why the adoption should not be granted, especially if there may be a legal reason why his consent may not be necessary. Again, this is a determination that is solely in the discretion of the attorney, so he will make that decision.

After service of the petition and investigation by the investigative agency and a report by that agency to the court, the matter is set for hearing. Notice of the hearing is given in accordance with applicable state laws.

At the time of the hearing, the court, in its discretion, may enter a summary decree which waives all time requirements and declares the adoption final at that time. The court may also enter an interlocutory decree to be in effect for a specific period of time, usually six months, at which time another hearing is held prior to entry of a final decree of adoption.

It is important to know your local court rules and the attitudes of the presiding judge when time for the final hearing is set. Many times a certain judge will require that an interlocutory decree be entered in all adoptions, while another judge may usually enter a final decree at the initial hearing. As new secretaries soon learn, the judge expects a decree (of whatever nature) prepared and ready for him to sign at the time of hearing.

As the secretary is usually responsible for seeing that the parents and child are notified of the hearing date, she should also be aware of those whom the judge wishes to attend the hearing. Many judges like to have the parents and their other children present in order to assess the family situation and determine the feelings of other family members toward the adoption. Of course, the attorney should also be at the hearing. Since the hearings are closed, no one is allowed except those who are required to be present. In the event of a contested adoption, parties having a direct and vested interest are allowed to participate at the hearing.

When the adoption has been finalized, certified copies of the decree should be obtained. One copy should be given to the adoptive parent, one copy should be sent to the agency which conducted the investigation, and one copy should be sent (with appropriate fee) to the state bureau of vital statistics with the request to issue a new birth certificate for the child. This birth certificate should be delivered to the parents, with a copy retained in the office files. A copy of the final decree is likewise retained for the office files.

Special note should be given to private or non-agency adoptions. These adoptions have come under close scrutiny because of adverse publicity. Most states have adopted legislation which either outlaws private adoptions entirely or strictly regulates as to consents required and fees or costs which may be paid to the attorney, doctor, or natural mother.

§ 15.83   Child Custody Jurisdiction

The Uniform Child Custody Jurisdiction Act has been adopted in a majority of states. The main purpose of this act is the protection of the child in cases of child custody litigation or abduction of a child by the noncustodial parent establishing procedure on jurisdictional questions. The act sets forth how to determine the state which has jurisdiction of a child.

The actual law of child custody jurisdiction is applicable to the experienced legal secretary or legal assistant working in litigation of this nature. If the attorney specializes in this type of action, the secretary will soon become familiar with the procedures. This is still a changing area of the law, and new decisions are being rendered frequently in cases of this type.

§ 15.84 Child Custody Procedures

With certain exceptions, preparation of pleadings in a custody jurisdiction action is much the same as in any other civil suit. However, it is not uncommon in these types of cases for out-of-state service to be required. This is a decision that the attorney makes, as he does in any other special aspects of the case.

Litigation can sometimes be avoided by a designation in the custody and support agreement of the court that is to have jurisdiction over the child for custody and support purposes.

Child custody decrees entered by foreign (out of state) courts may be filed with the clerk in another state and transferred much the same as any other decree or judgment from a foreign jurisdiction. A decree filed in this manner has the same force and effect as a decree entered in the state where the foreign decree was entered, provided the state in which it is sought to be filed has adopted statutes recognizing foreign decrees.

It is important for the legal secretary to be aware of the existence of this uniform act in the event of a child custody action, especially if she must elicit initial information from a client prior to the client's being interviewed by the attorney. This information would include:

- The court where an original order of custody was entered
- How the client obtained custody of the child
- Who was awarded custody
- Residence of the child since the entry of the decree
- Any other information with regard to the custody of the child which might be helpful

Although more associated with visitation than with custody, more and more grandparents are seeking judicial determination of their rights of visitation with children subject to a custody agreement. Some states now statutorily recognize the rights of grandparents to visit with their grandchildren under custody and visitation privileges. If these rights are explained to the clients at the time of execution of the custody agreement, it might prevent future litigation by the grandparents. Setting out these rights in the original agreement, as well as in the decree, can save the client the time, money, and emotional stress involved in litigation for visitation privileges.

§ 15.85 Alternate Birth Options

Alternate options to birth, such as in vitro (test tube) babies, surrogate mothering, open adoption (where the natural parents know the adoptive parents), artificial insemination, and international adoptions are becoming increasingly popular and have raised a myriad of legal issues not yet fully resolved. Some of these issues are the rights of the surrogate mother who changes her mind, malpractice involving sperm donors, and forms of contracts between the various parties. While this is similar to adoption, it is presently approached in large part through aspects of contract law.

§ 15.86 Uniform Parentage Act

The Uniform Parentage Act defines, among other things, the parent/child relationship and how it is established. It also provides who may bring actions to establish paternity and when such actions may be initiated. The use of blood tests and the preservation of records are also provided for in this Act.

These actions are usually brought by state prosecuting attorneys on behalf of a mother receiving welfare aid against a putative father of a child to enforce support obligations.

The child is usually made a party to the action and represented by a guardian ad litem (a person other than either of the child's parents). The mother and the man purported to be the natural father are also made parties to the action.

§ 15.87 Parentage and Paternity Procedure

Ordinarily, the action is much the same as in any other civil suit, except—as in adoption proceedings—the proceedings are confidential and closed to the public. Initial pretrial proceedings are generally informal. Some attorneys prefer to contact the putative father informally; they try to keep the proceedings completely informal and avoid a formal court action by acting through the attorneys.

The secretary for either the prosecution or the defense may be responsible for collecting information in a paternity action. Her duties may include questioning the mother about the likelihood of sexual activity with another man during the period when conception most likely occurred. She may arrange for blood tests and locate experts to testify at the hearing.

The civil proceeding for determination of paternity brought by a mother or a child for support is usually also conducted in a closed courtroom with no jurors or spectators, but the evidence is similar to that brought by a prosecutor to enforce support obligations. The trial is closed because of the emotional stress and publicity which could seriously damage the reputation of a defendant, even if the court finds that he is not the father of the child.

Any judgment or order rendered by the court usually includes an order that the birth certificate be amended or reissued to conform to the order of the court.

Of course, after paternity is determined, support must be acted upon. As in other support proceedings, the abilities of both parents, the child's resources and any special needs, as well as other pertinent information, are used to determine the amount of support required by the child.

§ 15.88　Duties to Disabled Persons

A disabled person is one who lacks legal capacity or one who is physically or mentally disabled from acting in his own behalf or pursuing his normal occupation. The Uniform Duties to Disabled Persons Act provides for duties of police officers, medical practitioners, and others to disabled persons; also, it provides for the use of identifying devices for these persons.

Persons with specific disabilities—epilepsy, diabetes, allergies—are encouraged (but not required) to wear identifying devices to aid police, doctors, and others in the event the person is unable in an emergency to communicate these conditions.

On the other hand, police officers and medical practitioners especially have a duty to make reasonable searches of disabled or injured persons to ascertain whether or not they are in possession of such identifying devices.

The legal secretary is likely to become acquainted with this area of the law when a disabled person or his family brings suit against others for their failure to perform duties required under this act. Whether the attorney is prosecuting or defending the action, the pleadings (complaint, summons, discovery, etc.), as well as the procedures, are in much the same form as in any other civil action.

§ 15.89　Definition of Abortion

An abortion is, simply stated, intentional termination of a pregnancy. Abortion law is one which is changing rapidly amidst considerable controversy. The Uniform Abortion Act was developed in an effort to standardize abortion law.

Perhaps the most common cases with which the legal secretary is likely to work are those involving medical malpractice with regard to abortion, parental consent for abortion performed on minors, and the rights of the putative father in an abortion situation.

There are still, of course, criminal penalties for illegal abortions which vary from state to state.

§ 15.90 Summary

For professional advancement the beginning legal secretary may wish to read some of the uniform acts to become familiar with the subject. Both American Jurisprudence Second and Corpus Juris Secundum contain the uniform acts, and many of them are also published in Martindale–Hubbell Law Directory. If the law firm specializes in this area of the law, it may subscribe to The Family Law Reporter published weekly by The Bureau of National Affairs. This publication highlights important cases in all areas of family law; reading it will give the secretary an opportunity to have current information on decisions affecting the principal areas of family law.

CHAPTER 16

BUSINESS ORGANIZATIONS

Table of Sections

§ 16.1　Introduction

This chapter discusses the three principal ways of doing business in this country—by incorporation, by partnership, and by sole proprietorship.

§ 16.2 Distinction Among Corporations, Partnerships, and Sole Proprietorships

A corporation is a separate business entity, and for the most part, the people who own its stock have no liability for its debts or obligations. A partnership, which is an entity comprised of two or more persons, does not enjoy this limit of liability as the partners share in the losses as well as in the profits, although not necessarily on an equal basis. In a sole proprietorship the owner bears all the losses; and for all practical purposes, the legal obligations and liabilities of the owner's business are not separated from his personal ones. The most advantageous form of doing business is dependent upon many factors; and the attorney, with the help of a Certified Public Accountant (CPA) or a tax lawyer, often helps his client make the decision as to which method is best for him. By studying these concepts and understanding them, the legal secretary will be of more help to both the attorney and his clients.

§ 16.3 Definition

A corporation is a legal entity created by or under the authority of the laws of a state or a nation. For most legal purposes it is a person domiciled in its state of incorporation, and it is separate and distinct from the persons who own it. It can enter into contracts, own property, sell property, sue, and be sued.

§ 16.4 Domestic Corporation

A corporation that is created or organized in the state in which it does business is known as a domestic corporation.

EXAMPLE:

If a corporation was organized and is doing business in the state of Vermont, it is a domestic corporation insofar as Vermont is concerned.

§ 16.5 Foreign Corporation

A foreign corporation is a corporation that does business in a state or country other than the state or country in which it was created.

EXAMPLE:

The same corporation which is doing business in the state of Kentucky is a foreign corporation insofar as Kentucky is concerned.

§ 16.6 Types of Corporations

Generally, corporations are classified as one of the following types:

- Business corporations, which are organized for any lawful purpose to make a profit.

- Nonprofit corporations, which are organized for purposes other than making a profit, usually include charitable, religious, and educational purposes.

- Public corporations, which are organized for governmental purposes such as city or county governments.

- Professional corporations, which are organized to permit a professional man or group of professionals to practice a profession such as law or medicine.

In most states the laws differ for various types of corporations. Most of the corporations that you will be working on will be business corporations, and the discussion in this chapter is limited to business corporations.

§ 16.7   Advantages of Incorporating

One of the foremost reasons for incorporating is the aspect of limited liability with respect to persons contributing capital to the corporation and also to those who manage and control it. Usually this means that since the corporation is itself a legal entity, it is the corporation which is legally responsible for its acts and its debts—not the people who own it. Generally, the officers, the directors, and the shareholders of a corporation have no personal liability (legal responsibility) for debts incurred by the corporation provided they act in good faith and provided they keep their own personal business affairs completely separate from those of the corporation, treating the corporation as a separate entity at all times.

Since the corporation is a separate entity, it can continue to do business in the event one of its officers, directors, or shareholders dies. The ownership of the corporation can change without interrupting its day-to-day business operations.

Since the corporation has the power to hold property in its own name, it is sometimes advantageous for estate planning purposes, since an incorporated business may pass on from generation to generation through tax-free gifts of shares of stock in the corporation to family members.

Sometimes incorporation is advantageous for income tax purposes. In some instances the corporate tax rate is much lower than an individual's tax rate, and the corporation is allowed many tax deductions not available to individuals in business.

§ 16.8 Disadvantages of Incorporating

Disadvantages of incorporation include expenses of organization, governmental regulation, and sometimes tax disadvantages. While the income tax structure of a corporation might be advantageous to some individuals, it could create additional tax burdens for others. For this reason many attorneys who do not practice tax law urge their clients to discuss the advantages and disadvantages with a tax attorney or a CPA before drawing the incorporation papers.

§ 16.9 Corporate Structure and Operation

The government and operation of the corporation depend upon three groups of individuals: the shareholders, the board of directors, and the officers. A data sheet is helpful. (See Illustration 16–1.)

Illustration 16–1
CORPORATION DATA SHEET

Name of Corporation: _____

Date of Incorporation: _____

Directors:	Address:	Office:
_____	_____	
_____	_____	
_____	_____	
_____	_____	
_____	_____	

Maximum Number: _____ Quorum: _____ Terms: _____

Capitalization: _____

Authorized Shares: _____   Par Value: _____

Issued Shares:

   Name: _____ Number Issued: _____ Consideration: _____

   Address: _____ Soc. Sec. No.: _____

Any Preferred: _____

Principal Place of Business: _____

_____

Purpose: _____

_____

Registered Agent and Office: _____

_____

Accountant/CPA: _____

Preemptive Rights: _____

Indemnification Allowed: _____ How Broad: _____

Cumulative Voting Allowed: _____

Executive Committee: _____
Voting on Sale of All Assets: _____
Annual Meeting—Date: _____
             Place: _____
Fiscal Year: _____
First Meeting—Date: _____
             Place: _____
             Attendance: _____
Bank: _____

    Who Signs: _____

    Limitations: _____

    Limitations on Borrowing: _____

Salaries: _____

1244: _____

Subchapter S: _____

Employer ID #: _____

Actions Taken: _____

Documents: (strike any not needed)	Prepared	Executed	Filed
Reservation of Corporate Name			
Articles			
Bylaws			
Minutes of 1st Directors Meeting			
Minutes of 1st Shareholders Meeting			
1244 Plan			
Subchapter S Election			
Assumed Name Affidavit			
Certificate of Authority for Other States			
Cross Purchase Agreement			
Medical Reimbursement Plan			
Securities Filing			
Other			

Stock and Seal Ordered: _____

1st Meeting: _____

§ 16.10 Shareholders

The shareholders are the people who own shares in the corporation and therefore indirectly own the corporation. A share is the certificate issued by a corporation which evidences the shareholder's proportionate interest in the corporation. It is the sale of stock to the shareholders which provides the initial operating capital for the corporation. The prospective shareholders evidence their intent to purchase a specific number of shares before the corporation is formed by executing a subscription agreement. (See Illustration 16–2.) The shareholders have the right to vote on certain major issues related to the corporation, including the right to elect the board of directors and the right (through dividends) to share in the profits made by the corporation.

Illustration 16-2

SUBSCRIPTION AGREEMENT

THE UNDERSIGNED hereby subscribes to 2900 shares of the no par value common stock of A.B.C. Corporation, a _____ corporation. I agree to

(name of state)
pay the A.B.C. Corporation the sum of $_____ for said shares.

Dated: _____

_____

(name of subscriber)

§ 16.11   Board of Directors

The board of directors is the governing body of the corporation and is composed of the persons elected by the shareholders of the corporation. The board of directors establishes policies and oversees officers' actions.

§ 16.12   Officers

The officers of the corporation are elected by the board of directors and are subject to its control. The officers conduct day-to-day business affairs of the corporation and implement the policies established by the board of directors.

§ 16.13   Meetings

The articles of incorporation or the bylaws provide for meetings of both the shareholders and the board of directors to be held at specified times throughout the year. Additionally, there is provision for special meetings of both the shareholders and the board of directors. It is the duty of the secretary of the corporation to notify the shareholders or the board members of these meetings. The bylaws provide for the manner in which the notices must be sent, and if your office handles these notices for your corporate clients, be sure when you are asked to handle the notice that you follow carefully the provisions in the bylaws.

§ 16.14   Waivers of Notice

When you are dealing with small corporations with just a few shareholders and board members, it is not unusual for the shareholders or the board members to waive the notice of the meeting. This is perfectly acceptable as long as you remember to prepare the waiver and make certain that the waiver is signed. Many offices include the waiver in the minutes of the meeting, and this is acceptable if all people required to have notice actually sign the minutes. The method used will depend upon the preference of the attorney.

§ 16.15   Quorum

The bylaws provide for the number of persons required to constitute a quorum for both shareholders and board of directors meetings. A quorum is required for the transaction of business. In most corporations a majority constitutes a quorum. This means that if a corporation has 20 shareholders, five of whom own more than half of the stock, those five shareholders at a meeting would constitute a quorum. Meeting the quorum is not usually a problem for small corporations, since the people involved work together and find a time for the meeting that is convenient to all.

§ 16.16   Proxies

A proxy is the authority given by one shareholder to another to vote his shares of stock. This practice is particularly common in large corporations because it is impossible for all shareholders to attend meetings. In the case of those corporations listed on the exchange, the Securities and Exchange Commission (SEC) requires that a proxy form be sent with the notice of meeting so that the shareholder can name a proxy. The term "proxy" is used to mean both the authority given and the form used to accomplish it.

§ 16.17   Securities and Exchange Commission

Most of the corporations with which the average legal secretary deals are small business corporations involving local businessmen. However, since the formation of a business corporation which will have its shares of stock sold to the public on the open stock market must be handled by an attorney, the legal secretary should be aware that some aspects of such a corporation do differ from the corporations formed to do business locally. The most important difference is that the sale of shares to the public are governed by the rules and regulations of the Securities and Exchange Commission (SEC). The SEC is a federal agency which administers, among others, the Securities Exchange Act of 1934 which requires the publication of certain information concerning stocks which are listed on the exchange. Very often, the attorney engages the services of an SEC specialist for his client who is organizing this type of corporation.

§ 16.18   Initial Interview With Client

The lawyer generally meets with the client to determine his particular needs and to obtain all information necessary to begin incorporation proceedings. Most attorneys use a checklist for this purpose. (See Illustration 16–1.) One of the points of information that the attorney secures at the initial client interview is the name which the client proposes for the corporation.

§ 16.19　Reservation of Corporate Name

Since the name of the corporation is very important and most states do not allow a new corporation to have a name that is deceptively similar to an existing one, it is necessary to check the availability of the name in each state where the corporation will do business. Therefore, most states provide a method by which the proposed name of the corporation may be reserved for a specific time period. During that time period, no one else is allowed to use that name. Usually, you reserve the name by filing the proper form together with the reservation fee with the secretary of state or lieutenant governor. (See Illustration 16–3.) Reserving the name allows you time to prepare the necessary documents without fear of losing the name. Some states have a definite period of time for which a name may be reserved.

Illustration 16–3

APPLICATION FOR RESERVATION OF CORPORATE NAME

To the Secretary of State
State of _____:

Pursuant to the provisions of Section _____ of the _____ Business Corporation Act, the undersigned hereby applies for reservation of the following name for a period of _____ days: _____

DATED: _____, 19__

_____*
Its _____

(Street Address)

_____

(City and State)

Telephone: _____

*Signature of Applicant if an individual or name of Applicant if a Corporation.
Signature and title of officer if Applicant is a corporation.

Signature of the attorney alone is acceptable in some states.

Note that most states require the use of the word *Corporation, Incorporated,* or *Inc.,* in the name of the corporation. If the attorney fails to designate which is to be used, be sure to ascertain which it is to be before you write for the name reservation.

§ 16.20 Articles of Incorporation

The articles of incorporation is the legal document which forms the corporation and which states what a corporation is authorized to do. A corporation has legal authority to do only what the articles of incorporation specify that it will be able to do. However, in some states it is allowable to form the corporation for "any legal purpose." In states where such general authority is not allowed, the articles of incorporation go into great detail as to what the corporation may or may not do.

§ 16.21 Contents of Articles of Incorporation

Since corporations are governed by state law and laws vary from state to state, the incorporation procedure in each state varies considerably. The corporation laws of each state specify just what information must be contained in the articles of incorporation. Martindale–Hubbell Law Directory contains the requirements which must be met in each state. A set of typical articles would contain:

- The name of the corporation
- The date of incorporation
- The principal place of business from which the corporation intends to do business
- The duration of the corporation
- The capitalization of the corporation (how much money was paid for the stock by the original stockholders)
- The total number of shares which the corporation is allowed to issue, the classes of stock, and the par value of each share
- The registered agent and his office address

There are many other provisions which may be in the articles, depending upon state law. Some states require only a minimum of information in the articles while others require very detailed information about all matters pertaining to incorporation.

§ 16.22 Close Corporation

The incorporators may limit the sale or transfer of stock by having such a provision in the articles of incorporation. The purpose of such a provision is to give the initial shareholders the right to decide whether they want to allow any additional shareholders. Usually this provision specifies that in the event a shareholder has a proposed sale for his stock and wishes to sell his stock, he must first offer the stock on the same terms of the proposed sale to either the other shareholders or to the corporation itself. The corporation or the shareholders are allowed a specific period of time within which to exercise their right to buy the stock, and if they fail to do so, the selling shareholder has the right to sell his stock to the third person.

§ 16.23 Preemptive Right

A preemptive right provision gives the shareholders the right to maintain their original, proportionate share of the corporation in the event the corporation should later authorize the sale of additional shares of stock. Although the articles of incorporation specify the number of shares which the corporation may issue, it is possible for the corporation to increase that number at a later time either by amendment to the articles of incorporation or by any other method approved by state law. In the event of such an increase in the shares of stock, a preemptive right provision means that the original shareholders are given the first option to buy enough of those additional shares to maintain their proportionate share of ownership.

EXAMPLE:

If the corporation originally authorized 200 shares of stock with four shareholders each owning 50 shares and the corporation authorizes an additional 200 shares, then each shareholder has the right to buy another 50 shares. This will allow each shareholder to maintain a 25 percent interest in the corporation. (See Illustration 16–4.)

Illustration 16–4
ARTICLES OF INCORPORATION OF A.B.C. CORPORATION

We, the undersigned natural persons of the age of twenty-one years or more, acting as incorporators of the corporation under the Business Corporation Act, adopt the following Articles of Incorporation for the corporation.

FIRST: (The name of the corporation; *Corporation, Incorporated,* or *Inc.,* must be used in the name)

SECOND: (The period of the corporation's duration)

THIRD: (The purposes for which the corporation is organized)

FOURTH: (The capitalization structure of the corporation, *e.g.,* dollar amount of capital stock, aggregate number of shares authorized, par value per share, voting rights of shares, designation of class or classes of shares)

FIFTH: (The corporation will not commence business until consideration of the value of at least $1,000 has been received for the issuance of the shares)

SIXTH: (Provisions limiting or denying to shareholders the preemptive right to acquire additional or treasury shares of the corporation)

SEVENTH: (Provisions pertaining to the manner of voting in the election of directors)

EIGHTH: (The post office address of the corporation and the name of its initial, registered agent for service of process at said address)

NINTH: (The number, names, and addresses of the persons who shall serve as the initial Board of Directors of the corporation)

TENTH: (The name and address of each of the incorporators of the corporation)

DATED this _____ day of _____, 19__.

INCORPORATORS:

_____

_____

_____

STATE OF _____)
)   ss.
COUNTY OF _____)

On the _____ day of _____, 19__, personally appeared before me John Doe, George Doe, and Charles Doe, who duly acknowledged to me that they executed the foregoing Articles of Incorporation as the incorporators of A.B.C. Corporation.

_____
Notary Public
Residing at:

My Commission Expires:

§ 16.24   Execution and Filing of Articles

After the articles of incorporation have been prepared, you will schedule an appointment for your client to come in to execute (sign) the articles of incorporation. If you are in a state which requires more than one incorporator, all incorporators will have to come in to sign them. Many states require that the signatures be notarized. Once the articles are signed, they are filed with the secretary of state together with the appropriate filing fee. It may be necessary also to file duplicate originals in the office of the county clerk where the corporation is to do business and where it will own property. The appropriate filing fees must accompany the filings. The secretary of state issues a charter or certificate of incorporation which evidences the incorporation.

§ 16.25   First or Organizational Meeting of Shareholders

Although filing the articles of incorporation is the act which creates a corporation, as a practical matter there are other steps which must be taken in order for a corporation to be in a position to do business. In most states these matters are handled in an organizational meeting. The organizational meeting is known in some states as a shareholders' or stockholders' meeting or an incorporators' meeting or a subscribers' meeting. The term "subscribers" is used to describe both the signers of the articles of incorporation and the persons who have agreed to buy stock in the corporation. A few states do not hold an organizational meeting, and in those states the matters handled in the organizational meeting are handled by the board of directors in its first meeting. Since the matters handled in the organizational meeting are of a routine nature, you will probably prepare the minutes of the meeting when you prepare the articles of incorporation because usually the meeting is not actually held. Typical items that would be handled at this meeting include:

- Election of the initial board of directors

- Adoption of bylaws for the corporation

- Authorization to issue the capital stock

§ 16.26 First Meeting of the Board of Directors

The first meeting of the board of directors is usually held immediately following the time of the execution of the articles of incorporation and the organizational meeting if there is one. Typical items that are handled at this meeting include:

- Election of officers of the corporation

- Adoption of the corporate seal

- Approval of the form of stock certificate

- Approval for the purchase of an appropriate minute book by the secretary

- Selection of a bank for the corporation, together with a decision as to who will sign the checks for the corporation

- Action on whether the corporation wishes to be taxed as a subchapter "S" corporation

(See Illustration 16–5.)

Illustration 16–5

MINUTES OF FIRST MEETING OF BOARD OF
DIRECTORS OF A.B.C. CORPORATION

The first meeting of the Board of Directors of A.B.C. CORPORATION was held at _____ at _____ a.m. on _____, 19_, in accordance with the
     (city and state)
following Waiver of Notice:

NALS, Car.Leg.Sec. 3rd Ed.—13

WAIVER OF NOTICE FOR FIRST MEETING OF DIRECTORS

The undersigned, being all of the Directors of A.B.C. CORPORATION do hereby waive notice and publication of notice of the first meeting of the Directors of the Corporation. We do hereby assent and agree to the holding of the first meeting of the Directors of the Corporation at the offices of _____ at 10 a.m. on the 11th day of February, 1994, for the purpose of establishing the corporation in business, organizing the board of directors, electing officers, and the transacting of such other business as may properly come before this meeting, and we do further agree that any business transacted at this meeting shall be as valid and binding and of the same legal force and effect as though said meeting had been held after call and notice duly given.

_____

_____

_____

PROCEEDINGS

_____ called the meeting to order and upon motion duly made and seconded was appointed Temporary Chairman, and _____ was appointed Temporary Secretary.

The election of officers was thereupon declared to be in order. The following were named and duly elected:

President, TODD PAUL

Vice President, MYLES DAVID

Vice President, LOUIS BERNARD

Secretary, LISA WYNNE

Treasurer, LINDA GREEN

The Chairman announced that the Certificate of Incorporation had been filed in the office of the Secretary of State of _____ on the _____ day of _____, 19__, and that a certified copy thereof would be recorded in the office of the County Clerk and Recorder of _____ County, State of _____. The Secretary was instructed to cause a copy of the Certificate of Incorporation to be inserted in the Minute Book of this Corporation.

The Secretary presented a form of bylaws for the regulation of the internal affairs of the Corporation which were read by all present, section by section.

On motion duly made, seconded, and carried, it was:

RESOLVED That the Bylaws submitted to and read at this meeting be, and the same hereby are adopted as the Bylaws of this Corporation. The Secretary is instructed to cause said Bylaws to be inserted in the Minute and Bylaws Book of this Corporation which shall be held open for inspection by the shareholders at all reasonable times.

On motion duly made, seconded, and carried, it was:

RESOLVED That the seal, an impression of which is herewith affixed, be adopted as the Corporate Seal of this Corporation.

A form of stock certificate was presented and upon motion duly made, seconded, and carried, was unanimously approved.

The Secretary was authorized and directed to procure the proper Corporate Book.

On motion duly made, seconded, and carried, it was:

RESOLVED That the _____ Bank of _____ be designated as the depository of the Corporation and that funds deposited therein be withdrawn upon a check, draft, note, or order of the Corporation.

FURTHER RESOLVED That all checks, drafts, notes, or orders drawn against said account or evidencing indebtedness of this Corporation be signed by one of the five named officers of this Corporation.

It was agreed by the Board that each person desiring to transfer equipment and property in return for stock proceed to do so through the Secretary of this Corporation with the Secretary keeping a record of all property transferred, and its agreed valuation upon transfer, said agreed valuation to be consistent with the current market value attributed to each item transferred. The Board acknowledged that the acquisition of property and equipment would be necessary and essential for Corporate operations. Upon motion duly made, seconded, and carried unanimously, it was:

RESOLVED That the Corporation acquire property and equipment from those persons who desire to transfer property and equipment at market value as may be desired by the Corporation in exchange for the issuance of Corporate stock as payment in full, said stock to be without par value, and to constitute full payment; it being further stipulated that in the event any property transferred is encumbered by mortgage or other indebtedness, the Corporation assume such indebtedness, if any.

FURTHER RESOLVED That the Secretary be instructed to maintain a list of the property transferred and the valuation attributed thereto.

The Board then considered the issuance of capital stock in the Corporation, and upon motion duly made, seconded, and carried, it was:

RESOLVED That the Corporation will issue common stock, which stock shall qualify under § 1244 of the Internal Revenue Code of 1986 as amended.

FURTHER RESOLVED That the Treasurer of this Corporation cause to be issued § 1244 common stock of no par value to the following in the amounts indicated:

MYLES DAVID, 2900 shares;

TODD PAUL, 2900 shares;

LOUIS BERNARD, 2900 shares;

LISA WYNNE, 400 shares;

LINDA GREEN, 900 shares.

FURTHER RESOLVED That when such shares are issued by the Treasurer, they shall be deemed fully paid and nonassessable.

On motion duly made, seconded, and carried unanimously, it was:

RESOLVED That the proper officers of this Corporation be authorized and directed to take all steps necessary to execute and complete issuance of the stock and deliver all papers, including certificates of shares of stock of this Corporation, as such officer so acting may deem appropriate to effect the objectives and purposes of this Corporation, whether or not the same are subject to specific reference in this first meeting.

On motion duly made, seconded, and carried unanimously, it was:

RESOLVED That the Treasurer be authorized to pay all fees and expenses incident to the incorporation and organization of this Corporation.

On motion duly made, seconded, and carried unanimously, it was:

RESOLVED That _____, _____, _____, _____, and _____ constitute an executive committee in accordance with the Articles of Incorporation to act while the Board of Directors is not in session, said Executive Committee to have the same complete and unrestricted powers while so acting as would the Board of Directors acting in session.

There was discussion concerning salaries, following which, on motion duly made, seconded, and carried unanimously, it was:

RESOLVED That the following salaries be fixed to be paid to the individuals indicated until further action by the Board of Directors:

$1.00 per year to each officer.

There being no further business to come before the meeting, on motion duly made, seconded, and carried unanimously, the meeting adjourned at ___ a.m.

_____

Secretary

§ 16.27   Bylaws

The bylaws are the rules and regulations by which the business affairs of the corporation will be conducted. They are adopted by the shareholders at the organizational meeting. If there is no organizational meeting, they may be adopted by the directors. The officers, directors, and shareholders are bound by these bylaws which may contain any provisions for the regulation and management of the affairs of the corporation not inconsistent with law or with the articles of incorporation. Every corporation has the power to adopt, alter, and amend bylaws. The bylaws are usually a long, detailed document, and most offices have their own printed form of bylaws which they adapt to suit each corporation. (See Illustration 16–6 for the index of provisions usually contained in bylaws.)

Illustration 16–6
BYLAWS
TABLE OF CONTENTS

§ 16.28 Minutes and Minutes Book (Minute Book)

As part of the incorporation service to the client, you will be responsible for the preparation of the corporation minutes book (generally referred to as a minute book). The minute book should contain copies of the articles of incorporation, the bylaws, the minutes of the first meeting of shareholders, and the minutes of the first board of directors meeting, as well as any other documents which were prepared and executed in connection with the incorporation process. The minute book will be turned over to the secretary of the corporation so that it can be kept current. Minutes are simply a written record of who attended a meeting and what transpired at the meeting. However, it is essential that the minute book be kept up to date. In fact, some states impose a fine if the corporation fails to do so. Additionally, an incomplete minute book can result in serious tax consequences in the event of a tax audit.

§ 16.29 Corporate Seal

In some states it is necessary for a corporation to acquire a corporate seal, while in other states it is not. If you are in a state where a seal is required, it may be that your firm orders the seal as a part of the incorporation process. The corporate seal is an official impression utilized with the signature of an officer of the corporation to verify corporate authority.

§ 16.30   Issuance of Stock Certificates and Stockbook

In preparing the corporate files for your client, one of your duties will be to issue the original shares of stock and to open a stockbook. You may purchase a bound stockbook, or you may purchase individual blank stock certificates and insert the number you need in a binder of some type.

The articles of incorporation provide for the number of shares that the corporation is authorized to issue. The minutes of the organizational meeting lists the number of shares of stock purchased by each stockholder. From this list you should be able to prepare the stock certificates themselves. Each stock certificate should include:

- The name of the corporation;
- The domicile of the corporation (city and state);
- The name of the shareholder;
- The number of shares which he is purchasing;
- The par value of each share of stock;
- The number of the stock certificate (starting with the number 1);
- The notation that the stock is issued under Section 1244 of the Internal Revenue Code (if applicable).

Each stock certificate is attached to a receipt which contains the identical information as on the stock certificate, together with a notation that the stock being issued is the original issue. (See Illustration 16–7.) The shareholder signs the receipt, which is detached from the certificate. The shareholder is given the stock certificate, and the receipt is retained in the stockbook. The stockbook gives a continuing record of the stock ownership of a corporation. Anyone should be able to look at a corporation's stockbook at any time and tell who the shareholders of the corporation are and how many shares of stock each shareholder owns.

Illustration 16–7

The reverse of each stock certificate is equipped with an assignment; accordingly, the shareholder may transfer his shares of stock by simply executing the assignment on the reverse of his stock certificate. (See Illustration 16–7.1.) When that assigned stock certificate is handed to the secretary of the corporation, she issues a new stock certificate to the new shareholder, writes "canceled" across the face of the transferred share certificate, and attaches it to the receipt of that certificate in the stockbook. The receipt of the new share certificate shows that it is a transfer of the shares from the original certificate.

Illustration 16–7.1

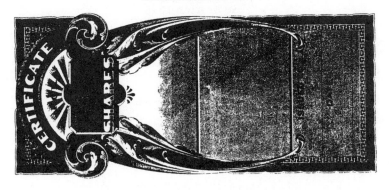

§ 16.31   Certificate of Assumed Business Name

If the corporation wishes to do business under a name other than its own, you will be asked to prepare a certificate of assumed business name. Your office probably has a form for this purpose.

§ 16.32   Application for Employer Identification Number, IRS Form No. SS–4

Depending upon the practice in your area, you may be expected to complete the corporation's application for an employer identification number. Once it is prepared and signed, it is filed with the Internal Revenue Service office where the federal tax returns of the corporation will be filed. The purpose of this form is to obtain the number the corporation will use for identification purposes on all Internal Revenue Service filings. (See Illustration 16–8.)

Illustration 16–8

Form **SS-4**	**Application for Employer Identification Number**	
(Rev. April 1991) Department of the Treasury Internal Revenue Service	(For use by employers and others. Please read the attached instructions before completing this form.)	EIN OMB No. 1545-0003 Expires 4-30-94

Please type or print clearly.

1	Name of applicant (True legal name) (See instructions.)

2	Trade name of business, if different from name in line 1	3	Executor, trustee, "care of" name

4a	Mailing address (street address) (room, apt., or suite no.)	5a	Address of business (See instructions.)

4b	City, state, and ZIP code	5b	City, state, and ZIP code

6	County and state where principal business is located

7	Name of principal officer, grantor, or general partner (See instructions.) ▶

8a Type of entity (Check only one box.) (See instructions.)

- ☐ Individual SSN ____
- ☐ REMIC   ☐ Personal service corp.
- ☐ State/local government   ☐ National guard
- ☐ Other nonprofit organization (specify) ____
- ☐ Other (specify) ▶ ____
- ☐ Estate
- ☐ Plan administrator SSN ____
- ☐ Other corporation (specify) ____
- ☐ Federal government/military   ☐ Church or church controlled organization
- If nonprofit organization enter GEN (if applicable) ____
- ☐ Trust
- ☐ Partnership
- ☐ Farmers' cooperative

8b	If a corporation, give name of foreign country (if applicable) or state in the U.S. where incorporated ▶	Foreign country	State

9 Reason for applying (Check only one box.)

- ☐ Started new business
- ☐ Hired employees
- ☐ Created a pension plan (specify type) ▶ ____
- ☐ Banking purpose (specify) ▶
- ☐ Changed type of organization (specify) ▶
- ☐ Purchased going business
- ☐ Created a trust (specify) ▶ ____
- ☐ Other (specify) ▶

10	Date business started or acquired (Mo., day, year) (See instructions.)	11	Enter closing month of accounting year. (See instructions.)

12	First date wages or annuities were paid or will be paid (Mo., day, year). Note: *If applicant is a withholding agent, enter date income will first be paid to nonresident alien. (Mo., day, year)* . . . . ▶			

13	Enter highest number of employees expected in the next 12 months. Note: *If the applicant does not expect to have any employees during the period, enter "0."* . . . . ▶	Nonagricultural	Agricultural	Household

14	Principal activity (See instructions.) ▶

15	Is the principal business activity manufacturing? . . . . ☐ Yes ☐ No If "Yes," principal product and raw material used ▶

16	To whom are most of the products or services sold? Please check the appropriate box. ☐ Business (wholesale) ☐ Public (retail) ☐ Other (specify) ▶ ☐ N/A

17a	Has the applicant ever applied for an identification number for this or any other business? . . . . ☐ Yes ☐ No Note: *If "Yes," please complete lines 17b and 17c.*

17b If you checked the "Yes" box in line 17a, give applicant's true name and trade name, if different than name shown on prior application.

True name ▶   Trade name ▶

17c Enter approximate date, city, and state where the application was filed and the previous employer identification number if known.

Approximate date when filed (Mo., day, year)	City and state where filed	Previous EIN

Under penalties of perjury, I declare that I have examined this application, and to the best of my knowledge and belief, it is true, correct, and complete | Telephone number (include area code)

Name and title (Please type or print clearly.) ▶

Signature ▶   Date ▶

Note: *Do not write below this line.   For official use only.*

Please leave blank ▶	Geo.	Ind.	Class	Size	Reason for applying

For Paperwork Reduction Act Notice, see attached instructions.   Cat. No. 16055N   Form **SS-4** (Rev. 4-91)

§ 16.33 Miscellaneous Forms

There are other forms such as applications for state and city sales tax licenses, withholding tax registration, unemployment insurance, and workers' compensation forms which are sometimes required. Most corporations handle the preparation and filing of these themselves, but there may be other agreements required to complete the legal work for the corporation. If this is the case, the attorney will probably dictate these to you.

§ 16.34 Professional Corporations

A professional corporation is a business corporation formed for the purpose of professional practice whose incorporator(s) or shareholder(s) can be only one or more natural persons, each of whom is duly licensed or admitted to practice his profession by a court, department, board, commission, or other agency of government. For example, attorneys, doctors, and certified public accountants must be licensed by the state in which they practice their profession.

The intent of the states that have enacted professional corporation statutes is to authorize licensed persons to render professional services in the corporate form.

§ 16.35 Formation, Structure, and Operation

The formation, structure, and operation of a professional corporation are similar to a business corporation as outlined earlier in this chapter.

§ 16.36 Differences

The articles of incorporation contain a specific statement that the corporation is a professional corporation, and the license number of the incorporator may be required by some states on the articles.

A professional corporation is formed only for the purpose of rendering the particular professional service and may not engage in any business other than the rendering of the professional service. Nevertheless, it may own real estate, make investments, and do other acts incidental to its primary purpose.

Each professional corporation must acquire a certificate of registration from the state board regulating that particular profession.

The shareholder(s) must be licensed in the profession, *i.e.,* only attorneys can be shareholders of a professional corporation organized for the practice of law. Shares in a professional corporation can be

549

delivered, issued, traded, etc., only to a third person licensed in the same profession in the same state or to the professional corporation.

Officers and directors of the corporation need not be licensed professionals.

A professional corporation may use any name not prohibited by law or the ethics of the profession in which the corporation is engaged or by a rule or regulation of the court, department, board, commission, or agency regulating such profession. For instance, a professional corporation engaged in the practice of law cannot use the name "Divorce Mill, Inc." because the Code of Professional Responsibility would not permit such a name.

Although "Corporation," "Incorporated," or "Inc." must be used in the name of a corporation (Section 16.21), the name of a professional corporation need not contain any of these words. The name may use the word "Associate" or consist solely of the name of one or more of the shareholders of the corporation. Some professional corporations use "P.C." in place of "Inc.," such as "Smith and Jones, P.C."

A shareholder may not give his proxy to another person unless it is to another licensed person who is a shareholder of the same corporation.

§ 16.37 Advantages and Disadvantages

The advantages and disadvantages of a professional corporation are similar to other types of corporations; however, the corporate entity will not shield the licensed professional from any actions against him for breach of professional ethical standards or liability for negligence in performing the services for the client.

§ 16.38 Partnerships

A partnership is a voluntary association of two or more persons to carry on a business for profit as co-owners. Partnerships in general are governed by uniform codes—the Uniform Partnership Act and the Uniform Limited Partnership Act. Nearly all states have adopted the uniform acts with modifications to conform the acts to their particular state laws.

§ 16.39 Types of Partnerships

There are two main types of partnerships—general partnerships and limited partnerships. Other similar associations are joint ventures, joint stock companies, syndicates, cooperatives, trading and non-trading associations, and mining partnerships. These are described more fully below.

§ 16.40 Legal Requirements

A partnership is a voluntary relationship based on the five elements of contract law:

1. Mutual agreement of the parties

2. Competency of the parties

3. Consideration

4. Lawful purpose

5. Meeting formal requirements

Partnerships are organized for profit and involve the contribution by their members of capital, labor, skills, property, or a combination thereof. The law governing formation, operation, and dissolution of partnerships is generally found in the corporation code of each state.

Partnerships must be formed for a lawful purpose. Otherwise, the partners may lose their rights under the law.

§ 16.41 General Partnerships

General partnerships are formed by two or more persons for the purpose of carrying on a business for profit as co-owners. The Uniform Partnership Act defines a person as including individuals, partnerships, corporations, and other associations. A partnership may be comprised of any two or more of the foregoing, provided that the entity is properly constituted and the individual is competent to enter into the partnership. The purpose for which the partnership is formed must be lawful and for the monetary gain of its partners.

§ 16.42 Partnership Agreement

While no formal written agreement is required by law to establish a general partnership, to avoid problems and misunderstandings among the partners as to their rights, duties, and liabilities, a written agreement is usually entered into and signed by all of the partners.

§ 16.43 Names of the Partners

The names and addresses of the partners are listed, and each partner also executes the agreement.

§ 16.44 Name of the Partnership

There are no restrictions on the name which the general partnership selects.

§ 16.45   Duration of the Partnership

Unlike corporations, partnerships cannot exist perpetually, and the partnership agreement generally states a termination date. However, the partners may desire the partnership to be formed for an indefinite period. In that event, the partnership agreement does not state a termination date and the partnership is "at will."

§ 16.46   Location and Nature of the Partnership Business

The nature of the business that the partnership will transact and the address from which it will operate are set forth. Sometimes there is no specific business address, and the address of one of the partners is used.

§ 16.47   Contributions Each Partner Will Make

These contributions may be in cash, property, skills, or services; and the initial contributions are recorded in the partnership agreement. The agreement may call for additional contributions to be made at a future date or additional services to be performed.

§ 16.48   Method for Sharing Profits and Obligation for Losses

When capital contributions are made in a different form, *i.e.*, cash or property, a value is assigned to the contribution. In the absence of different provisions, all of the partners share equally in the profits and losses of the partnership. However, provision may be made that some partners may receive a greater share of the profits (with a corresponding responsibility for a greater share of the losses). The agreement generally also sets forth the responsibilities of the partners in the event losses are sustained and additional moneys are required from the partners to sustain the partnership.

§ 16.49   Method of Accounting

The method of keeping the partnership account, who will be responsible for keeping the account, and where the partnership records will be located are set forth in the agreement. The method of valuing a partner's contribution or his partnership interest also may be set forth in this section.

§ 16.50   Withdrawals From Partnership Accounts

To avoid the problem that could be caused by several partners withdrawing money from the partnership at the same time, rules and procedures are set forth specifying when and in what amounts partners may withdraw moneys from the partnership account. All income is deposited to a central partnership account.

§ 16.51 Events Causing Dissolution and Procedure for Dissolution

The agreement may set forth specific actions of the partners which will cause dissolution of the partnership in addition to dissolution by operation of law. The agreement may also provide which of the partners is to be responsible for winding up the affairs of the partnership upon dissolution.

§ 16.52 Terms and Conditions for Admitting New Members to the Partnership

Additional partners may be admitted to the partnership on terms and conditions specified in the agreement and with the agreement of all of the existing partners. The incoming partner becomes a member upon execution of an amendment to the partnership agreement. To avoid dissolution of the partnership by operation of law, the partnership agreement must provide for its continuation in the event of the admission of a new member.

§ 16.53 Any Other Matters

Any other matters that the partners believe necessary for the smooth running of the partnership may be included in the agreement.

§ 16.54 Commencement of Existence

A general partnership commences at the time any one of the following occurs:

- Execution of the partnership agreement
- Commencement of the partnership business
- The filing or recording of any document required by state law to commence its existence

The partnership agreement may provide for a different event to cause commencement of the partnership business.

§ 16.55 Ownership of Partnership Property

Property brought into the partnership as a contribution becomes the property of the partnership, and a partner may not assign or encumber his interest in partnership property. Title to partnership property may be held in the partnership name or in the names of all of the individual partners.

§ 16.56 Partners' Liability

Unless the partnership agreement provides otherwise, all of the partners are equally liable for losses or damages arising out of the partnership. A new partner is responsible for liabilities incurred prior to his admission but only to the extent of his capital contribution. If a deficit occurs, the partners are required to satisfy the deficit. If one partner cannot completely satisfy his share, the other partners must make up the defaulting partner's share.

§ 16.57 Tax Returns

The partnership itself is not taxed, but an information return must be filed with state and federal tax authorities. The partners are taxed as individuals on the moneys deposited into their partnership accounts, and the partners are also entitled to the benefit of any partnership losses that may occur.

§ 16.58 Dissolution

Dissolution ends the right of a partnership to continue to do business. The partnership goes through a winding-up process and is then terminated as a legal entity. The partnership may be terminated by operation of law or by dissolution caused by the actions of the partners. Partnership agreements may express that certain actions do not automatically cause dissolution of the partnership. Actions of the partners which cause dissolution include:

• The express action of any one partner

• The consent of all of the partners

• The expulsion of a partner

Events which automatically cause dissolution of the partnership without the act of a partner or partners include:

• The occurrence of an event making it unlawful to continue the partnership business

• The death or bankruptcy of a partner or bankruptcy of the partnership

• Where it is in the best interests of the partnership that it be dissolved.

The partnership also automatically dissolves at the termination of the definite time for which it was formed.

After dissolution, the affairs of the partnership are wound up. Winding-up consists of collecting and preserving the partnership assets, paying debts, and distributing any profits. Creditors of the partnership have first claim on partnership assets, with the partners sharing any remaining assets after repayment of their capital contribution. After dissolution and during the winding-up process, the liabilities of the partners are not waived or forgiven but continue so that where dissolution of a partnership is caused by the death of a partner, his estate inherits that partner's liability. While liabilities remain, however, the authority of the partners ceases upon dissolution except for any acts they are required to perform to wind up the partnership.

Notice of dissolution must be given to the partners and to any persons who have dealt with the partnership.

§ 16.59 Limited Partnerships

Limited partnerships are considerably more regulated than general partnerships and must be evidenced by an agreement. Any two or more persons may form a limited partnership, but there must be at least one general partner and at least one limited partner. The general partner has unlimited liability for the obligations of the partnership; the limited partner's liability is limited to his initial contribution to the partnership. While a general partner may contribute management services but no cash or property, a limited partner may contribute only cash or property. A limited partner has no voice in the operation or management of the partnership except to any extent permitted in the limited partnership agreement. Limited partners performing acts outside of their scope as detailed in a limited partnership agreement may be considered general partners and thus forfeit their limited liability status.

The same requirements as to the competency of a person to contract apply to limited partners as in general partnerships. Accordingly, natural persons, partnerships, limited partnerships, trusts, estates, associations, or corporations may be partners.

Again, the partnership must be formed for a lawful purpose and may not be formed to carry out illegal purposes or purposes contrary to the law. Partnerships formed for illegal purposes are denied many of the rights granted to partners and to partnerships.

§ 16.60 Particular Requirements for Limited Partnerships

Limited partnerships differ from general partnerships in several areas covered by the limited partnership agreement.

§ 16.61 Partnership Name

There are restrictions on the name under which a limited partnership does business. The word or words "Ltd." or "Limited Partnership" must generally be included in the name, and the name must not be deceptively similar to another business so as to confuse those with whom the partnership has dealings. In some states, the limited partnership's name may not include the surname of the limited partner unless it is the same as a general partner's or unless, prior to becoming a limited partnership, the business had been carried on under a name in which the surname appeared.

§ 16.62 Existence

A limited partnership begins its existence on the filing or recording with the appropriate local agency of a Certificate of Limited Partnership listing specific information required by law. Generally, too, the name of the partnership must be registered or a statement filed with a local agency stating who is doing business under the partnership name and where the business is being carried on. The certificate must be amended whenever there is any change to the information contained in it. On dissolution of the partnership, a cancellation of the certificate must be filed for the public record alerting the public to the fact that the partnership will no longer continue its existence. Although all of the partners named in a Certificate of Limited Partnership must sign the certificate and have their signatures acknowledged if required, it may be necessary in the case of amendment for fewer signatures to be required (or merely those of the general partners).

§ 16.63 Right of Inspection of Books and Records

Because limited partners are not involved in the day-to-day activities of the partnership, they have the right to inspect and copy any of the partnership's records which it is required by law to maintain at the partnership office.

§ 16.64 Contributions

If under the terms of the limited partnership agreement, a limited partner promises to contribute certain sums or perform certain tasks, he must do so under any circumstances. If property or services are required but a limited partner is unable to contribute, he may be required to contribute cash equal to his portion of the required contribution.

§ 16.65 Sharing of Profits

The ratio in which the limited and general partners share in the profits of the corporation is set forth in the agreement. The agreement also states the amount of and manner in which future contributions will become due.

§ 16.66 Classification of Partners

Within a partnership the partners can be further classified as follows:

- A partner who takes no active part in the management of the business and is not known to the public as a partner is a dormant, sleeping, silent, or secret partner.

- A person who permits others to believe he is a partner of a partnership or behaves in such a manner that people believe he is such a partner is a nominal partner. Such a partner is also known as a partner by estoppel or ostensible partner.

§ 16.67 Joint Venture

A joint venture is similar to a general partnership in formation, but its duration is only for the accomplishment of the specific purpose for which it was formed such as construction of a building or performance of an act. The duties owed to each other by the joint venturers are the same as those owed by general partners. While one joint venturer might perform the major portion of the management duties, all joint venturers share in the profits, losses, and obligations.

§ 16.68 Syndicate

A syndicate is an association of persons formed to conduct a specific, generally financial business transaction. The most common type of syndicate is that formed by investment banks for the marketing of stocks and bonds.

§ 16.69 Cooperative

A cooperative is comprised of a group of people who pool their products or resources to their mutual advantage. Many states have enacted regulations concerning cooperatives. In some states incorporation is permitted in accordance with state statutes.

§ 16.70 Business or Massachusetts Trust

A business or Massachusetts trust permits the ownership of property to be transferred by the owners to trustees who run the business for the owners' benefit. To evidence the ownership of the property, the trustees issue shares or certificates to the trustors showing their original ownership or interest in the property. The shares or certificates may be freely transferred, but the trustors do not have the control over the trustees that shareholders have over the directors. One supposed benefit of this form of organization is that the trustors avoid liability by transferring responsibility for running the trust to the trustees.

§ 16.71　Joint Stock Company

A joint stock company is somewhat like a combined partnership and corporation. Shares of stock are issued to evidence each partner's ownership, and the shares are transferable. Management of the business is delegated to a small group of partners because generally there are many partners in a joint stock company. There is no restriction on the transfer of the shares or who may purchase them, and any person to whom such shares are transferred or sold becomes a member of the joint stock company upon such sale or transfer.

§ 16.72　Trading Partnership

A trading partnership is specifically engaged in buying and selling merchandise. The partners have authority to bind the partnership and obtain loans in the partnership name.

§ 16.73　Nontrading Partnership

A non-trading partnership is engaged in performing services such as legal, accounting, medical, etc. The partners have no authority to bind the partnership, and the success of the partnership is more dependent upon the results of the partners than on the capital they may contribute.

§ 16.74　Mining Partnership

A mining partnership is formed when two or more people join together to work a mining claim to extract minerals. While similar to a general partnership, a mining partnership is not dissolved when a partner's interest is transferred; and such interest is freely transferable. The partners share in the profits and losses in the ownership ratio.

§ 16.75　Unincorporated Associations

Unincorporated associations are formed when persons combine for a nonprofit purpose. Generally, unless a member ratifies or authorizes an act, such member is not liable for the association's actions. The association has no existence apart from its members and cannot sue or be sued in its name.

§ 16.76　Limited Liability Company

A limited liability company (LLC) is a new business form first created in Wyoming. It seeks to blend in one business form the advantages of limited liability for equity owners and control persons found in corporations with the tax advantages found in partnerships.

Though the rules differ in the various states that have LLC legislation, generally an LLC is formed by filing articles of organization with the state. The LLC is governed pursuant to an operating agreement. Equity holders in the LLC are referred to as members of the LLC. Members may or may not have management responsibility with respect to the LLC.

§ 16.77   Sole Proprietorship

A person who operates a business on his own and is solely responsible for its day-to-day operation is known as a sole proprietor. No formal documentation is required to form a sole proprietorship. The act of the individual conducting the business establishes the entity.

Depending on the type of business and local, state, and/or federal requirements, permits or licenses may be required to operate the business. If the business is conducted under a name different from that of the owner, it may be necessary to file or record documents asserting the ownership of that name.

Except for licenses or permits required because of the nature of the business, there are no restrictions on transfer of ownership of the business. Upon the death of the owner, the business ceases to exist.

CHAPTER 17

REAL ESTATE

Table of Sections

---

§ 17.1 Introduction

The field of real estate law offers to the legal secretary an almost unlimited opportunity to assist the attorney in the many details that are involved in a typical real estate transaction. Since the most common transaction in the law office of today may well be the transfer of residential real estate, it is likely that the legal secretary will encounter various types of real estate transactions. She is in a position to relieve the attorney of much of the detail work involved in the real estate transaction. In order for the secretary to progress to the point of handling all preliminary workup, preparing closing documents, and assembling all necessary information, she must understand the basic elements of real estate law.

The modern real estate transaction has its roots deep in American history. The ownership of land is one of the oldest and most coveted forms of ownership. Owning property is a right guaranteed by the United States Constitution to all citizens—not a right guaranteed to all citizens of the world. The dream of every American is to own his own home, and accordingly, the residential real estate transaction is one that touches most of us at one time or another. Regardless of whether the legal secretary is viewing the real estate transaction from a professional or personal viewpoint, she can expect to see innovative financing which will require that she continually update her knowledge.

§ 17.2 History of Real Estate Law

Many of our basic laws regarding property rights come to us from England. In medieval times, an English king would often grant real estate to an individual who supported him during a war or who performed some other valuable service for him. After the Revolutionary War, the United States found itself with a great deal of land and a large amount of debts. The government determined that it would sell land in order to retire those debts. A problem soon arose, however, for much of the land was undeveloped and in many cases totally unexplored and void of landmarks. The government had no way to describe adequately the property it was selling. Thus, in 1785 the government ordered a survey to be taken. This was the beginning of what we know as the rectangular survey system which is referred to in many legal descriptions of real estate as the United States Government Survey. A majority of the fifty states still use this system as the source of legal descriptions for real estate today. The remaining states retain control over original surveys of land which form the basis for all legal descriptions.

Legal descriptions as they relate to the preparation of real estate documents are described later in this chapter.

§ 17.3 Definition of Real Estate

Real estate, also called real property or realty, is defined as land and anything permanently attached to it. This includes items attached to the land naturally, such as grass, shrubs, or trees, and items attached to the land artificially, such as buildings, fences, certain fixtures, and other improvements.

§ 17.4 Fixtures

Fixtures are those items firmly affixed to buildings. Whether or not an item is a fixture has been the subject of much litigation.

EXAMPLE:

A built-in dishwasher is a fixture that has become a part of the real estate. Such an appliance has a specially created opening for its installation, and its removal would leave an obvious unfinished area in the kitchen not easily used for other purposes. On the other hand, a portable dishwasher that is moved about the kitchen on wheels would not be considered a fixture.

The distinction is often not so easily made as in this example, so great care is exercised by attorneys in defining the fixtures to be included in a given transaction.

§ 17.5 Improvements

Improvements include such items as curbs, gutters, sidewalks, street lights, and sewer systems constructed to enhance development of real estate. Items of a permanent nature are often referred to as improvements.

§ 17.6 Personal Property or Chattel Property

All property which is not real estate is known as personal property or chattel property. This includes everything from cars, boats, and appliances to jewelry and clothing.

§ 17.7 Comparison of Property

Real property is distinguished from personal property in that real property is generally immovable, while personal property is movable. Generally, reference to real property means real estate, while reference to personal property means easily movable property such as automobiles, furniture, or jewelry. In many states the term chattel property is used interchangeably with the term personal property. The legal requirements for the sale or transfer of personal property are much less stringent than those for real property. In fact, in most states the sale of personal property for cash is accomplished by the preparation of a very simple bill of sale. In many instances it is not even necessary to have a written bill of sale.

EXAMPLE:

If A wishes to sell his watch to B and B is agreeable to the price, the sale is accomplished by A's handing the watch to B and B's handing the agreed price to A.

This would not be the case if the sale were not for cash. If the seller were not paid the entire price, he would probably retain a security interest in the watch. To protect that interest, he would have to file the appropriate kind of instrument in the appropriate county or state office.

§ 17.8   General Principles and Concepts of Real Estate Law

In order for the legal secretary to attain her full potential in the field of real estate law, she must have a good understanding of the attorney's responsibilities in these transactions. The general principles and concepts of real estate law which play a significant role in the practice of real estate law are:

1. Ownership of real estate

2. Evidence of title to real estate

3. Examination of title to real estate

4. Encumbrances of real estate

5. Transfer of real estate

6. Preparation of real estate documents

7. Closing of real estate transaction

§ 17.9   Ownership of Real Estate

When a seller enters into a purchase agreement for the sale of his property with a prospective buyer, he takes the position that he owns the property. Since the form of ownership is controlled by state law and forms of ownership vary from state to state, the legal secretary will have to determine the types of ownership applicable in her state. Although there are many forms of ownership, this chapter deals only with the most common:

• Fee simple or fee simple absolute

• Joint tenancy

• Tenants in common

• Community property

• Tenancy by the entireties

§ 17.10   Fee Simple or Fee Simple Absolute

Ownership of real estate in fee simple or fee simple absolute is that which gives the owner the absolute legal possession of the property. The vast majority of real estate transactions involve ownership in fee simple, although there are other more complicated forms of lesser ownership. The phrase "in fee simple" means that the owner named owns it all without reservation. Fee simple ownership of real estate may be acquired by corporations, partnerships, individuals, trusts, or estates. Individuals may acquire fee simple ownership either alone or with others. If two or more individuals own real estate together, they may own it either as joint tenants or as tenants in common.

§ 17.11   Joint Tenancy

Joint tenancy is ownership by two or more persons, with the right of survivorship. It means that upon the death of one of the joint tenants, the property automatically and immediately becomes the property of the surviving joint tenant without the necessity of probate proceedings. This right of survivorship is considered by many to be the principal advantage of joint tenancy. A joint tenant may not change the right of survivorship in the other joint tenant by will. Neither can the heirs of a deceased joint tenant nor his creditors have any claim against property held in joint tenancy with others. The right of survivorship in joint tenancy property is absolute. Frequently, husbands and wives hold title to real estate in joint tenancy, but ownership in joint tenancy is not limited to married couples. On the other hand, just because a husband and wife have occupied certain premises jointly does not necessarily mean that they are owners in joint tenancy. The form of ownership is established not by the use of the property but by the form of ownership specified in the deed by which the owners bought the property. Therefore, it is clearly delineated in the records. There are circumstances when the joint tenancy form of ownership is not advisable for a husband and wife, and if that is the case, the attorney advises his client accordingly.

If it has been determined that the buyers will hold title as joint tenants, the deed contains language similar to the following:

> ... CONVEY and WARRANT to JOHN SMITH and MARY SMITH, husband and wife, as joint tenants, with right of survivorship ...

or

> ... CONVEY and WARRANT to JOHN SMITH and MARY SMITH, husband and wife, as joint tenants and not as tenants in common ...

or in the case when parties are not related:

> ... CONVEY and WARRANT to JOHN SMITH and MARY JONES, as joint tenants and not as tenants in common ...

If the deed does not clearly indicate how title is to be held, title passing only to "John Smith and Mary Smith" is presumed to be tenancy in common. In some states special forms are used for each form of tenancy. If this is the case, the legal secretary should be extremely careful to use the correct form.

§ 17.12   Tenants in Common

Tenants in common hold undivided fractional interests in the same property, with each tenant in common having the right to possess. The interest is a fraction of the whole, as there is no tangible division of the property. Therefore, none of the tenants in common can claim any specific portion of the property, such as the north half or the east half. Interests of tenants in common may be equal or unequal, and each tenant in common has a separate legal title to his undivided fractional interest. Hence, he can sell his interest or provide for its distribution by will. In the event a tenant in common dies without a will, his undivided interest passes to his heirs at law according to the laws of intestacy. These heirs become tenants in common with the other owners. The language in such a deed might read as follows:

> ... CONVEY and WARRANT to JOHN SMITH and MARY SMITH, husband and wife, as tenants in common, each to an undivided one-half interest, and not as joint tenants ...

§ 17.13 Community Property

Community property exists in some states, and it is the general rule that any property acquired during a marriage by either the husband or the wife, except the property acquired by gift or inheritance, belongs equally to husband and wife—one-half to each.

§ 17.14 Tenancy by the Entireties

Another form of ownership by a husband and wife is known as tenancy by the entireties. This form of ownership provides that neither party may convey his or her share of the property individually, and neither share can be attached by creditors. In some states this form of ownership has been abolished, while in others a conveyance to a husband and wife is presumed to be a tenancy by the entireties unless some other form of ownership is clearly indicated.

§ 17.15 Evidence of Title to Real Estate

Regardless of the form of ownership, when a parcel of real estate changes ownership, the owner, or in some instances the buyer, is required to furnish evidence of title. The form of title evidence varies from state to state, so the legal secretary must determine the methods used in her area. Most commonly, evidence of title is in the form of an abstract, a Torrens certificate, or a title policy.

§ 17.16 Abstracts

The abstract is a summary of all transactions pertaining to the parcel from the time of governmental entry (when the real estate was first recorded in formal land records) up to and including the current transaction.

Some areas deal almost exclusively with voluminous abstracts in real estate transactions. When such abstracts are used, they are updated for each transaction affecting the particular property covered by the abstract. The updating of an abstract is commonly referred to as a continuation or extension of abstract. The continuation may be attached to an existing abstract so that the abstract remains as one large document. On the other hand, the continuation might be done for each new transaction involving the real estate. The result would be several pieces of abstract, frequently referred to as stub abstracts. The cover sheet or first page of a continuation, called the caption, gives the legal description of the property covered by the abstract. The caption may sometimes describe a larger parcel of real estate from which the property involved in the transaction was taken. The final page of the continuation, called the certificate of the abstracter, contains several items of information needed for the real estate transaction. If the caption on the abstract refers to a larger parcel of land, the abstracter's certificate indicates the entry at which the legal description for which the abstract has been extended can be found.

The extension or continuation of an abstract may be done by an attorney. More commonly, it is done by a title company specializing in such work. In some states a title company can examine and assist in the search of records, insure the title to the property, and act as an escrow or closing agent. The extent to which a title company participates in these services depends upon the laws of that particular state, as well as the custom in the area. The legal secretary must become familiar with the information a title company must have in order to perform its services rapidly and efficiently. She must be aware of the special services which title companies have developed to provide specific limited title information to attorneys. Because the contribution and cooperation of the title company's staff are an integral part of the efficient real estate transaction, she should develop rapport with the staff members. The legal secretary's duties often include the responsibility of arranging for continuations of an abstract on pending real estate transactions. She must know whom to call and how to place an order for such a continuation.

An abstract must be treated as a valuable legal document, as it is very expensive and time-consuming to replace. Most firms require the use of receipts in all transfers of an abstract. The legal secretary should be able to draft such receipts. (See Illustration 17–1.)

Illustration 17–1

ABSTRACT RECEIPT

September 15, 1994

RECEIVED OF Jones and Jones, Attorneys, the Abstract of Title to the following real estate:

Lot 2, Block 1, Red Rose Addition, Any County, Any State.

_____

John K. Smith

Client/File Reference: <u>S–6948</u>

§ 17.17   Torrens Certificate or Owner's Duplicate Certificate of Title

Real estate having a Torrens certificate or owner's duplicate certificate of title is formally referred to as registered property. Under the Torrens Act, which has been adopted by some states, a county may establish a system of title registration indemnified by a security or assurance fund backed by assets of the county. All transactions concerning a parcel of real estate registered under the Torrens system must be recorded in the office of the registrar of titles. The registrar of titles issues a certificate of title for each parcel of real estate registered under the Torrens system. A Torrens certificate is considered to be conclusive evidence of the present ownership and state of title. Liens, mortgages, and other encumbrances in existence are listed on the certificates. These entries are called memorials. The original certificate of title is kept in the office of the registrar of titles and may not be removed for any reason. An owner's duplicate certificate of title is also issued and is delivered to the owner. This duplicate should be treated as an important legal document, as it must be surrendered to the registrar of titles upon change of ownership or when new encumbrances are memorialized (entered). If the owner cannot produce the owner's duplicate at such times, a court order must be obtained to have it replaced. Such proceedings are known as proceedings subsequent to registration. In a transaction involving registered property, the legal secretary may be requested to order a registered property abstract from a title company. This type of abstract summarizes the information contained on the certificate of title. In some instances the law firm may conduct an independent examination of Torrens records either in place of or as a supplement to a registered property abstract. At the request of a mortgagee (a creditor who holds property as security for a debt), a mortgagee's duplicate certificate of title may also be issued. Receipts should always be used in the transfer of duplicate certificates of title.

§ 17.18   Title Policy

A title policy is issued by a title insurance company and insures that title to a certain parcel of real estate is in certain parties. There are several kinds of title insurance available. In ordinary real estate transactions, however, the legal secretary will be dealing with owner's and mortgagee's insurance policies. An owner's title policy gives the owner the right to recover any loss he suffers from a title defect. (See the section on examination of titles for an explanation of title defects.) How much the owner can recover depends upon the amount of coverage afforded by the title insurance policy. The amount of coverage on an owner's policy is usually the purchase price of the real estate. A title insurance policy is usually issued in the form of a loan or mortgagee's policy when a lending institution requires title insurance up to the amount of its loan. Mortgagee's coverage does not insure an owner's interest but guarantees only that the mortgagee (creditor) will be paid in the event of any title defect. Mortgagee's coverage may be issued in conjunction with an owner's policy or by itself. If both an owner's policy and a mortgagee's policy are issued simultaneously, the insured parties are both the owner and the mortgagee, but a separate premium is charged for each insured party. A title insurance policy may be issued by itself even when no abstract of title exists or if the abstract of title has been lost or destroyed. Too, a title insurance policy may be issued in addition to an abstract if a title defect emerges and the company is willing to insure over such defect. Registered property may also be covered by title insurance.

In a transaction of this type, the legal secretary may be required to order the title insurance policy by telephoning or delivering the necessary information to the insurance company. In some cases this will be the same company which prepares the abstract. The legal secretary will need to know the practice of her office in ordering title insurance. Generally, she will need to provide the company with the names of the sellers, the names and marital status of the buyers, the amount of coverage, *i.e.*, purchase price, a legal description of the property, and in some cases the abstract of title, if one exists. The title insurance company issues a commitment of title for the attorney to examine prior to issuing the title insurance.

§ 17.19   Examination of Title

The buyer relies upon the attorney to certify that the evidence of title reveals that the prospective seller is in a position to convey a clear, merchantable, and marketable title. Clear and merchantable title is the term applied to ownership of property that is free from any type of legal defect or encumbrance. Therefore, when an attorney certifies to a buyer that the property has a clear and merchantable title, it means that a prudent person need have no fear of accepting it, as it would be readily transferable on the open market. If a defect in the title does exist, it is referred to as a cloud on the title or a defect in the title. Therefore, prior to the closing of a real estate transaction, the buyer has the evidence of title examined by an attorney. In lieu of or in addition to such an examination, the buyer may secure title insurance. At the conclusion of the title examination, the attorney issues a title opinion. In some areas, if title insurance is obtained, the attorney does not issue a title opinion. The title opinion and/or the commitment for title insurance advises the client as to the condition of the title. If there are defects or clouds on the title, the title opinion or title insurance commitment describes what action is required to correct them. Typically, the matters which would affect the title are:

- Encumbrances
- Easements
- Encroachments
- Tax sales
- Irregularities

§ 17.20 Encumbrances

An encumbrance is a recorded document placing the public on notice that a third person may have a claim against the property that might diminish the value of the property to a prospective buyer. In such cases the closing attorney would hold back sufficient funds to pay any such encumbrance so that the buyer ultimately gets full value for his purchase price. Mortgages, judgments, and liens are all encumbrances.

§ 17.21 Mortgages

A mortgage is a security instrument given by a debtor to a creditor to secure (guarantee) the payment of a debt. In granting a mortgage to a creditor, a debtor pledges his property to guarantee to the creditor that he will pay the debt. If the debtor does not pay, then under the terms of the mortgage the creditor may foreclose on the property. This means that upon meeting any legal requirements, the creditor may seize the property and have it sold to pay the debt owed him by the seller. Mortgages are quite common in real estate transactions, as most people who buy property do not have sufficient money to pay cash for the property. They borrow the money from a lending institution and grant a mortgage to secure the payment of the loan.

EXAMPLE:

The seller borrowed $10,000 against his home and has not paid back any of the money. He gave a mortgage as security for the loan. He immediately decided to sell the property and has found a buyer who has agreed to pay $80,000 for the property. In examination of the title, the buyer's attorney discovers the mortgage which is an encumbrance against the property. He contacts the creditor to determine how much money the seller owes and deducts that amount from the seller's proceeds.

§ 17.22 Judgments

A judgment is a court order or decree which represents the decision of a court. There are many kinds of judgments rendered by courts as a result of litigation. The type of judgment most likely to be encountered in real estate law is the money judgment which awards a sum of money due the plaintiff by the defendant. The plaintiff who is awarded the money judgment is the judgment creditor, and the debtor against whom the judgment is rendered is the judgment debtor. A certificate should be filed, making the judgment a lien on all of the debtor's real estate wherever located.

EXAMPLE:

The seller in the example above might also have a judgment recorded against him. The judgment creates a lien against the property. Its payment is handled much the same way as payment of a mortgage is handled. The closing attorney contacts the attorney for the judgment creditor to find out how much money is owed on the judgment. (Some judgments provide for the payment of attorney fees, interest, and court costs in addition to the principal amount owed.)

§ 17.23 Materialman's or Mechanic's Liens

A materialman's or mechanic's lien is a right created in a person who has done work on or delivered materials to property which, if perfected, creates a right enforceable against the property. (The manner in which liens are perfected is governed by state law.) If such a lien is found to be recorded against the property being sold, it must be paid by the seller if the buyer is to receive clear title and an appropriate formal satisfaction delivered at closing.

§ 17.24 Tax Liens

Local, state, and federal governments may utilize the tax lien as a vehicle to collect taxes. They attach by virtue of law; no action is necessary, unlike a judgment. These taxes are usually income taxes, sales taxes, federal unemployment taxes, etc. These tax liens attach to property just as judgments do. Therefore, a seller must pay any such lien to give his buyer a clear title and deliver a formal satisfaction at closing.

§ 17.25   Easements

An easement is a right granted to someone by a property owner to come upon his land. The terms "easement" and "servitude" are sometimes used interchangeably.

EXAMPLE:

A property owner grants to a utility company the right to enter his property to maintain its equipment, such as a telephone line.

§ 17.26   Encroachments

An encroachment is the unlawful intrusion of one's buildings or fixtures onto the land of another.

EXAMPLE:

If a neighbor builds a fence or a garage which extends over his property line onto his neighbor's property, that constitutes an encroachment.

The encroachment is usually discovered by the engineer who makes a survey of the property, and the buyer's attorney discovers the encroachment when he examines the survey in connection with his title examination. It can become a permanent right by virtue of adverse possession if unchallenged for the requisite number of years prescribed by law.

§ 17.27   Restrictive Covenants

When property is developed into a subdivision, the developer usually places on the property certain restrictions as to the use of the property. The restrictive covenants usually provide that the property will be used only for residential purposes and often provide for the size of the residences and the kinds of building materials permitted to be used. The reason for these covenants is to maintain the value of the property. By specifying the size and building materials, the developer ensures that the residences will cost generally the same to build.

EXAMPLE:

If it were possible for a homebuilder to build a $100,000 house next to a $600,000 house, the $600,000 house would lose some of its value based merely on the fact that it was located next to a $100,000 house.

§ 17.28   Tax Sales

As a rule, both state and local governing bodies levy taxes against property to obtain revenue. The tax is usually computed by multiplying a rate in mills ($1 per $1,000) times the assessed value of the property. (In some jurisdictions the assessed value may be some arbitrary percentage of the retail value.) Property taxes are collectible against the property. Therefore, if a property owner does not pay his taxes, the tax authority may seize the property and sell it to a purchaser who pays the taxes. The title attorney therefore routinely verifies that property taxes on the property have been paid. If they have not been paid and the property has been sold for taxes, it is necessary for the seller to redeem (reclaim) the property within a specified time. He does this by paying the taxes due as well as interest, penalties, and costs.

§ 17.29   Irregularities

There are numerous other problems that could result in some type of irregularity in the title. Errors or variations in legal descriptions, errors in divorce or probate proceedings, and other types of problems must sometimes be corrected.

In most jurisdictions the seller bears the cost of furnishing the evidence of title, while the buyer secures and pays for a title examination.

In the event that title insurance is to be used in lieu of or in addition to an attorney's opinion, the title company examines the title and issues its commitment or binder prior to the closing. This document contains a list of all defects or clouds on the title, such as those listed above. These defects are called exceptions to the policy. The title policy does not provide coverage for any loss resulting from the listed exceptions. The commitment also lists the requirements to be met prior to closing and the issuance of its final policy. The final policy is issued once all conditions are met and the transaction has been closed, subject only to customary exceptions and any approved by the buyer. Some exceptions to title are considered customary, and they appear on most title policies. Easements, for example, are essential to proper maintenance of utilities. The light company, water company, and telephone company must be able to enter upon residential property to service their lines. Therefore, most lenders accept this type of exception without question.

§ 17.30   Instruments of Conveyance

Since any legal entity may own property, an individual, a corporation, or a partnership may acquire an interest in real estate. There are a number of ways to acquire real estate. Only the most common will be discussed in this chapter:

- Sale or Deed
- Devise by will or by intestate succession (Probate Deed or Deed by Personal Representative)
- Gift or Donation
- Exchange

§ 17.31 Sale or Deed

In a transfer by sale or deed, the owner (called grantor, vendor, or seller) conveys title to the buyer (called grantee, vendee, or purchaser) by the delivery of a deed. A deed is a formal written contract between the parties by which the seller sells his property to the buyer for a consideration (price). There are a number of ways in which the price can be paid, and they are discussed later in this chapter.

The law of each state outlines the requirements of a deed. Printed forms containing these legal requirements are usually available through a legal stationer or through the county clerk's office. Some states require that only their forms be used, while other states allow general usage of various types of deeds. The legal secretary should use the most acceptable form in the state in which the property is located.

§ 17.32 The Warranty Deed

The warranty deed (sometimes called a general warranty deed) is the most widely used and desirable type of deed. The seller (party conveying his title) gives the following warranties to the buyer (party receiving the title):

1. That at the time of the making and delivery of the deed, the seller owned a fee simple interest in the property and had the full right to convey it
2. That the title is free of all encumbrances
3. That the buyer and his successors in interest have the right to quiet and peaceable possession of the premises and are indemnified against the claims of all persons who may lawfully claim an interest

§ 17.33 Special Warranty Deed or Limited Warranty Deed

A special warranty deed or limited warranty deed warrants the title to the property being conveyed against any claims by, through, or under the seller or his heirs. It does not guarantee against any claims that occurred prior to the time of the seller's acquisition.

§ 17.34   Quitclaim Deed

A quitclaim deed from the seller conveys any claim, right, title, or interest which he may have to the subject property. The seller on a quitclaim deed does not warrant the condition of the title. He does not even warrant that he has any interest in the property. He merely provides that if he does own any interest in the property, he is conveying that interest. Quitclaim deeds are often used to correct certain types of title defects.

§ 17.35   Probate Deed

If property is acquired from an estate or guardianship, the buyer receives a type of special warranty deed called a probate deed or a guardian's or personal representative's deed, which generally does not contain warranties. It is also possible, however, to obtain a deed with warranties.

A transfer by devise or testate succession occurs when the owner of real estate dies and leaves such property to person(s) by a will (devise). If the owner has left no will, it is distributed by operation of law to his heirs at law (intestate succession). Each state has statutes which provide for the distribution of a decedent's property to his nearest relatives. The method of conveyance is a decree from the court of jurisdiction in probate matters, which is then recorded with the appropriate county office for real estate documents.

§ 17.36   Gift or Donation

Property may be transferred by gift (also called donation)—a voluntary transfer made gratuitously by one person to another. Monetary consideration is not required, and the gift is usually made to a close relative in consideration of "love and affection" between the donor (the person transferring) and the donee (the person to whom the transfer is made). Gifts are very common in estate planning. This type of gift is usually effected by a quitclaim deed.

§ 17.37   Exchange

Just as the term implies, an exchange in real estate law is a swap of property. One property owner transfers his property to another and receives that person's property in return. The act of exchange accomplishes both transfers in the same transaction. It is often used by real estate investors for tax purposes.

§ 17.38   Legal Description of Real Estate

All real estate must have a means by which it can be uniformly described. This is known as the legal description. Do not confuse the legal description with the street address or tax identification number. A complete and accurate legal description is needed for every deed, mortgage, and other formal document required in a real estate transaction. The accuracy of a legal description is imperative, and proofreading is essential. After you have typed the description, you should check it while someone reads it to you. There are three basic types of legal descriptions:

1. Government Survey

2. Metes and Bounds Description

3. Recorded Plat or Subdivision

§ 17.39   The Government Survey

The Government Survey description is a description based upon the rectangular survey system which divides land into a system of squares within squares. The squares are six miles long and six miles wide. These squares are resubdivided into 36 sections (although there are some irregular sections) with each section being one mile square. Thirty-six sections make up one township. Each section contains 640 acres and is numbered from 1 to 36 running east to west. Townships are separated from each other by range lines which run north and south.

Illustration 17–2 is a diagram of the method of numbering a township.

Illustration 17–2

Township 8 South						
6	5	4	3	2	1	
7	8	9	10	11	12	
18	17	16	15	14	13	
19	20	21	22	23	24	
30	29	28	27	26	25	
31	32	33	34	35	36	

Township 9 South

Township 10 South

Range 7 West   Range 6 West   Range 5 West

N

[C4052]

The following shows the relationships involved when the rectangular survey system is used:

```
1 Check     = 16 Townships
1 Township  = 36 Sections
1 Section   = 640 Acres
1/4 Section = 160 Acres
```

Illustration 17–3 is a diagram of a Government Survey section, showing two methods of division.

Illustration 17–3

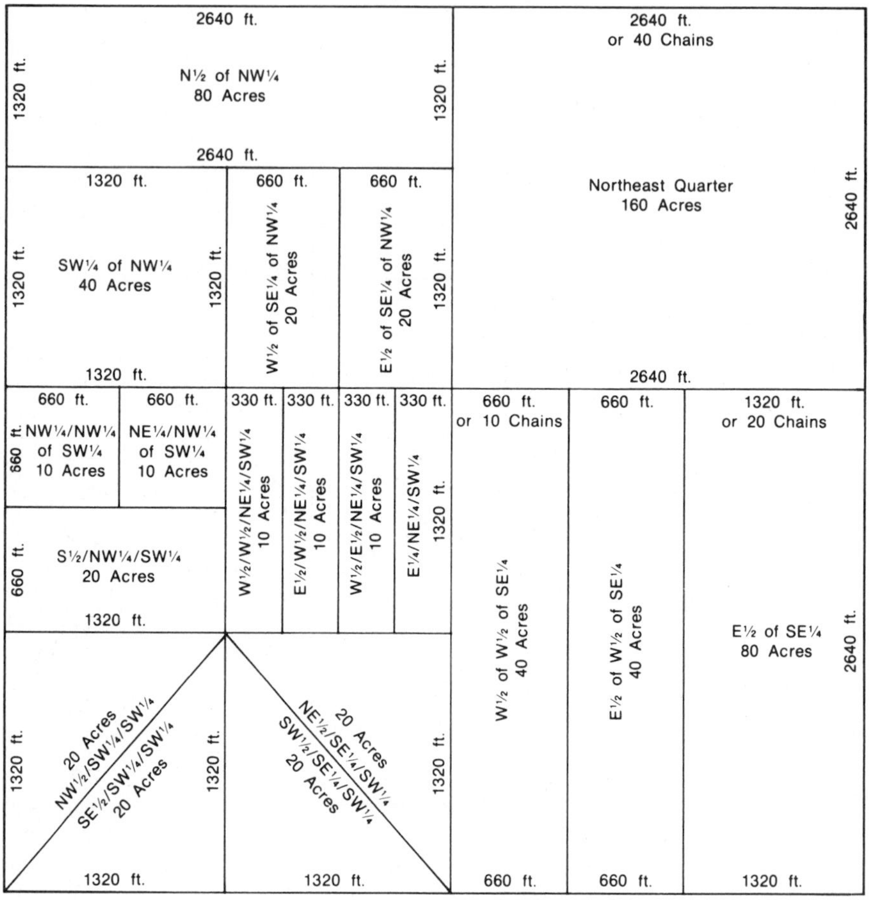

2640 ft.

1320 ft.

N½ of NW¼
80 Acres

2640 ft.

2640 ft.
or 40 Chains

1320 ft.

1320 ft.

1320 ft.

SW¼ of NW¼
40 Acres

1320 ft.

660 ft.

W½ of SE¼ of NW¼
20 Acres

660 ft.

E½ of SE¼ of NW¼
20 Acres

1320 ft.

Northeast Quarter
160 Acres

2640 ft.

2640 ft.

660 ft.

NW¼/NW¼
of SW¼
10 Acres

660 ft.

NE¼/NW¼
of SW¼
10 Acres

660 ft.

S½/NW¼/SW¼
20 Acres

1320 ft.

330 ft.

W½/W½/NE¼/SW¼
10 Acres

330 ft.

E½/W½/NE¼/SW¼
10 Acres

330 ft.

W½/E½/NE¼/SW¼
10 Acres

330 ft.

E¼/NE¼/SW¼
1320 ft.

660 ft.
or 10 Chains

W½ of W½ of SE¼
40 Acres

660 ft.

E½ of W½ of SE¼
40 Acres

1320 ft.
or 20 Chains

E½ of SE¼
80 Acres

2640 ft.

20 Acres
NW½/SW¼/SW¼

SE½/SW¼/SW¼
20 Acres

1320 ft.

1320 ft.

NE½/SE¼/SW¼
20 Acres

SW½/SE¼/SW¼
20 Acres

1320 ft.

1320 ft.

1320 ft.

660 ft.

660 ft.

1320 ft.

[C3799]

Illustration 17–3—Continued

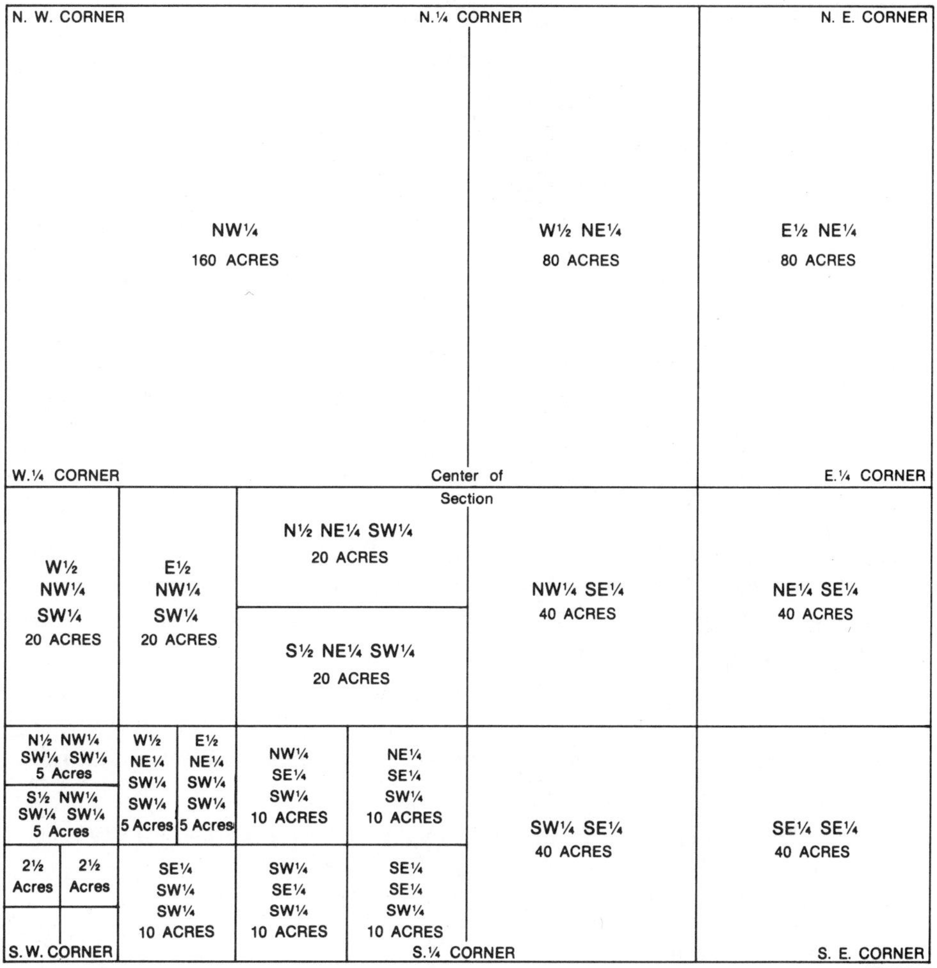

N. W. CORNER	N.¼ CORNER	N. E. CORNER
NW¼ 160 ACRES	W½ NE¼ 80 ACRES	E½ NE¼ 80 ACRES

W.¼ CORNER   Center of Section   E.¼ CORNER

W½ NW¼ SW¼ 20 ACRES	E½ NW¼ SW¼ 20 ACRES	N½ NE¼ SW¼ 20 ACRES S½ NE¼ SW¼ 20 ACRES	NW¼ SE¼ 40 ACRES	NE¼ SE¼ 40 ACRES

N½ NW¼ SW¼ SW¼ 5 Acres S½ NW¼ SW¼ SW¼ 5 Acres	W½ NE¼ SW¼ SW¼ 5 Acres E½ NE¼ SW¼ SW¼ 5 Acres	NW¼ SE¼ SW¼ 10 ACRES	NE¼ SE¼ SW¼ 10 ACRES	SW¼ SE¼ 40 ACRES	SE¼ SE¼ 40 ACRES
2½ Acres 2½ Acres	SE¼ SW¼ SW¼ 10 ACRES	SW¼ SE¼ SW¼ 10 ACRES	SE¼ SE¼ SW¼ 10 ACRES		

S.W. CORNER   S.¼ CORNER   S. E. CORNER

[C4051]

The description prescribed by these original surveys, whether government or state controlled, is the underlying basis for all legal descriptions in use today. For example, a typical original United States Government Survey description would be:

The Northwest Quarter (NW¼) of Section Five (5), Township Fifteen (15) North, Range Three (3) West, Jones County, Any State.

Illustration 17–4

Sec. 5, Twp 15N, Rge. 3W

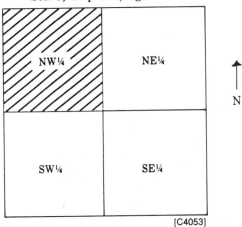

[C4053]

Illustration 17–4 shows the location of this property, a parcel which would consist of 160 acres (a quarter of a section or quarter section). Assume that this parcel is located in an urban area and is sold in increasingly smaller parcels.

EXAMPLE:

The description of a 40–acre tract in the northwest corner would be:

The Northwest Quarter of the Northwest Quarter (NW¼ of NW¼) of Section Five (5), Township Fifteen (15) North, Range Three (3) West, Jones County, Any State.

(See Illustration 17–5.)

Illustration 17–5

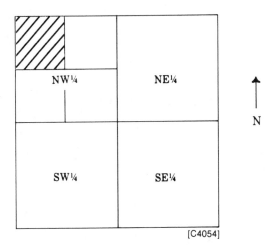

[C4054]

As increasingly smaller tracts are sold, particularly those having irregular boundaries, the legal descriptions become increasingly cumbersome. Simplified methods of describing real estate evolve. Also, as the tracts become smaller and irregularly shaped, it becomes very difficult to locate just where some of the parcels are. Therefore, it is often necessary to have a registered land surveyor actually locate the property and draw a map of the location. To do this, he makes "on site" measurements of the property being surveyed. If he is unable to find reference maps to help him determine the physical location of the property, he must often search property records to find all sales of parcels in a section and measure those "on site" before he is able to measure the property he is surveying.

In urban areas property is subdivided, measured, and mapped before sales are made. Descriptions refer to these subdivisions of property, as you will see from the discussion of subdivisions below.

§ 17.40 Metes and Bounds Description

The metes and bounds description is one that begins at a designated point and proceeds to describe the parcel of land by reference to units of measurement and direction.

Assume that the purchaser of the NW¼ of the NW¼ in the illustration above erected some fencing that encloses a portion of the "forty" and now wishes to sell that portion. A surveyor establishes a "point of beginning" and then follows the fencing around the property, carefully measuring distance and direction of each piece of fence until he returns to the point of beginning. His description of the property would be a "metes and bounds" description and would be as follows:

> Beginning at the Southeast corner of the Northwest Quarter of the Northwest Quarter (NW¼ of NW¼) of Section Five (5) Township Fifteen (15) North, Range Three (3) West, Jones County, Any State, according to the United States Government Survey thereof: thence proceed west along the south line of the NW¼ of NW¼ to an intersection with the east line of the west half of said NW¼ of NW¼; thence north along said east line 357.44 feet to a point and corner; thence south 66°07′24″ East to an intersection with the east line of said NW¼ of NW¼; thence south along the quarter quarter line 56.7 feet to the point of beginning.

Illustration 17–6 shows where this property is located. The entire quarter section is shown only for illustrative purposes so that the reader can "piece it all together." An actual survey plat would show only the property enclosed within the fence that is being sold.

Also note that there is an arrow on the illustration. This arrow indicates the direction of north for purposes of orienting the map. Unless otherwise indicated, the arrow always points north.

Illustration 17–6

Sec. 5, Twp 15 N, Rge. 3 W

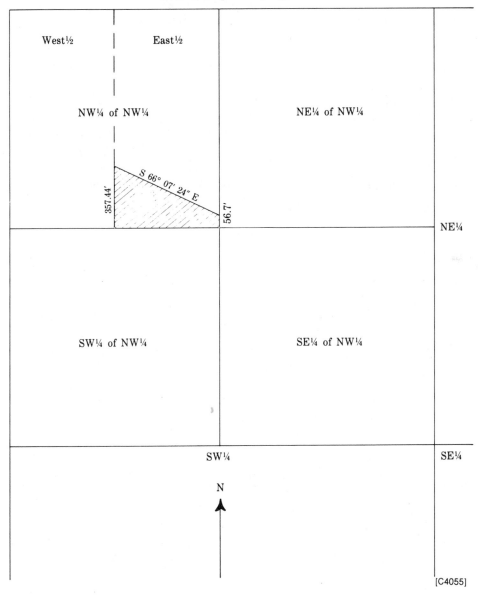

[C4055]

A metes and bounds description uses angles or vectors (a vector is a direction and distance of a line) to describe the line segments that represent the boundaries of the property being described. The description is actually a group of "calls," each call describing one line segment. Each call has length and direction. The length is usually given in feet, but it is not unusual to find other units of linear measurement. The direction is given in one of two ways. If the line segment's direction is exactly north, south, east, or west, then N, S, E, or W will accurately describe the direction of the line. If the direction is NE, NW, SE, or SW, then the angle between the line segment and the north-south line must be known. That angle is measured in degrees, minutes and seconds. One degree equals 60 minutes and one minute equals 60 seconds. If, for instance, the line direction is northwest and the angle between the line and the north/south line is 40, then the description of the line is N 40° W. Note that N 40° W generally describes the direction of the line, and by including "40°" the line is identified uniquely. There is only one line that fits the description. (See Illustration 17–7.)

Illustration 17–7

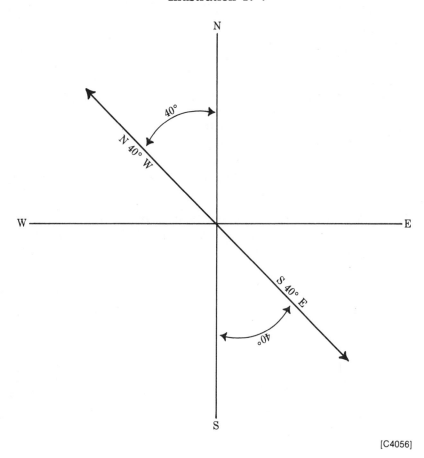

[C4056]

At this point it is interesting to note that a line can be described in either direction. The same line can also be described as S 40° E. A metes and bounds property description always proceeds from the point of beginning, around the property (usually clockwise) and back to the point of beginning, carefully and accurately describing each line segment. Once the direction of travel around the property is determined, then each line can no longer be described two ways. It must be described in the direction of travel.

In Illustration 17–6 the fencing that formed the northerly boundary of the property described made an angle of just over 66 degrees with the north/south line. Since we were going around the property clockwise, the call the surveyor used was S 66°07′24″ E. This call did not have a dimension in feet. Nevertheless, the distance can be found because it referred to a quarter-quarter (or one-eighth of forty) line which has a specific location.

§ 17.41 Recorded Plat or Subdivision

A subdivision is a division of one tract into two or more smaller lots or parcels. The word "subdivision" is also used to designate a development of similar lots for the purpose of constructing residences. A property owner who decides to subdivide property for this purpose is often called a developer. He engages the services of a civil engineer to map out the subdivision. The map is recorded in the county clerk's office, and the recorded map is then used as the basis for describing the lots in that subdivision.

Since most urban property is now subdivided, this is the predominant means used to describe urban real estate. It is much simpler and less cumbersome than describing property by metes and bounds or by Government Survey. A typical subdivision plat is shown in Illustration 17–8. A typical legal description in that subdivision would be:

Lot Twenty-five (25), Block Fourteen (14), Linden Park Addition Division No. 6 to the city of Idaho Falls, Idaho, according to the recorded plat or plan thereof.

Illustration 17–8

LINDEN PARK ADDITION

DIVISION NO. 6
TO
THE   CITY   OF   IDAHO   FALLS,   IDAHO
Part of
NE 1/4 of Sec. 20 T. 2 N., R. 38 E. B.M.

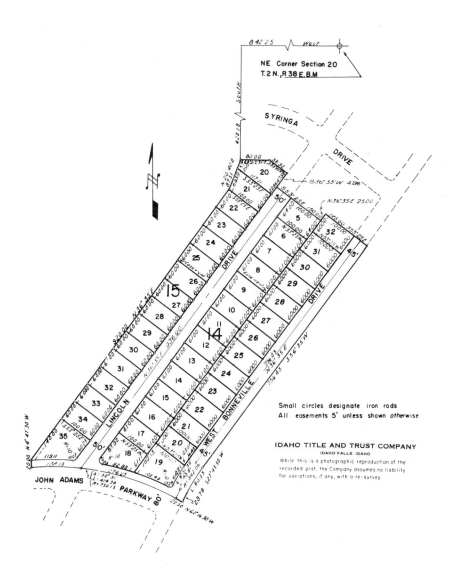

Small circles designate iron rods
All easements 5' unless shown *otherwise*

IDAHO TITLE AND TRUST COMPANY
IDAHO FALLS, IDAHO

While this is a photographic reproduction of the
recorded plat, the Company assumes no liability
for variations, if any, with a re-survey

§ 17.42   The Listing Agreement

A typical real estate transaction begins when someone decides to sell property he owns. The prospective seller may enlist the services of a real estate broker to help him locate a buyer. Additionally, the real estate broker often helps the seller arrive at a proposed selling price for his property. The broker charges a commission (fee) for his services, usually a fixed percentage of the sale price of the property, although a flat fee agreed upon by the parties is sometimes charged. Once the prospective seller and real estate broker reach an agreement, they enter into a contract, called a listing agreement, which describes in detail the real estate to be sold; the personal property to be included in the transaction, if any; the asking price; the terms of sale to which the seller is agreeable; and information concerning taxes, assessments, and existing encumbrances.

Ordinarily, this listing agreement is prepared by the real estate broker on a commercially printed form which contains the terms customary for the area involved. The seller may, however, engage an attorney to review the proposed listing agreement before he actually executes (signs) it.

Thereafter, the broker advertises, promotes, and shows the property to prospective buyers.

It is not unusual for prospective buyers to seek the services of a real estate broker to help them find property. This is particularly true in instances when people are moving to another state or are interested in a particular kind of property for investment purposes. In many areas, real estate brokers exchange information concerning all listings in the area (sometimes called a multiple listing service [MLS]), thus broadening the exposure of the property. If the property is ultimately sold to a client of another broker, that broker is said to be the selling broker while the original broker is the listing broker. The broker may act as the buyer's agent or as another agent of the seller. If no broker is involved, the seller must locate a buyer through his own efforts.

§ 17.43   The Purchase Agreement (Earnest Money Contract)

When a prospective buyer becomes interested in the property, he makes an offer to the seller. If the property is listed with a real estate broker, the prospective buyer makes the offer to the broker, who then relays the offer to the seller. The purchaser's offer usually includes the price he is willing to pay for the property and how he proposes to pay the sale price. If the prospective buyer and seller reach an agreement, that agreement is reduced to writing in the form of a purchase agreement, also referred to as a memorandum sale agreement, purchase offer, or earnest money contract. This document may be prepared by an attorney, a real estate broker, or by the parties themselves on a commercially prepared form. The purchase agreement is a contract, and it must meet all legal requirements for a contract. (See the chapter on Contracts.) It includes such information as:

- Full names and marital status of the seller
- Full names of the buyer
- Addresses of the parties
- Legal and common description of the property
- Property address
- Personal property to be included in the transaction (draperies, appliances, or similar items)
- Price
- Terms and conditions of the sale including financing arrangements
- Type of deed required
- Evidence of title to be provided

The closing and possession dates and any other special provisions or conditions of the transaction should be clearly set forth in the purchase agreement. A down payment, referred to as earnest money, is usually required of the buyer. The down payment typically is deposited in the trust account of either the attorney for the seller or the broker pending the closing of the transaction. As the parties negotiate the terms, the purchase agreement may be revised extensively before its final execution, since this document controls the consummation of the transaction. Frequently, attorneys for both parties review it and suggest changes. If a real estate broker is involved in the transaction, he can provide most of the basic information concerning the property. A broker may also assist the buyer with financing arrangements if the buyer is not able to pay for the property in cash. A purchase agreement should not be confused with a sale agreement or land contract, which fully sets out all responsibilities and obligations of each party to the sale and is executed at closing.

§ 17.44   Financing Arrangements

Once a seller and buyer have reached an agreement on the terms of the transaction, the buyer must get the money to buy the property. Ours is a credit-oriented society, and rarely is a prospective homeowner able to accumulate the substantial cash necessary to buy property. As a matter of fact, it is not uncommon for a purchase agreement to be conditioned upon the purchaser's ability to secure financing for the property. The buyer usually arranges his financing either through a commercial institution in the business of residential financing or through satisfactory arrangements with the seller. This chapter discusses only these two types of financing—commercial financing and private financing.

§ 17.45 Conventional Financing

There are many factors which control the availability of commercial money for residential financing, many of which are controlled by the general state of the economy. Local banks and savings institutions often have funds available for residential financing. Usually in this type of financing arrangement, it is necessary for the buyer to advance 20 to 30 percent of the purchase price. This type of financing is referred to as conventional financing.

§ 17.46 FHA and VA Financing

Assuming a buyer qualifies, he can secure certain types of financing through government agencies, such as the Department of Veterans Affairs (VA) or the Federal Housing Administration (FHA). These loans require little or no cash down payment and have less restrictive financial qualifications than conventional loans. VA loans are available only to veterans and surviving spouses of servicemen who died while they were on active duty.

VA and FHA loans are processed through local lending institutions, but the guarantee extended by the VA or FHA insures that the local lender suffers no financial loss in the event the buyer defaults on the loan. The Federal National Mortgage Association (FNMA) offers a similar guarantee to local lenders on qualified conventional loans.

§ 17.47 The Loan Application

Regardless of the type of loan, the buyer's application for the loan is processed through a local lending institution. To process a homebuyer's application, the lender accumulates financial and personal data about the buyer to determine whether he qualifies for the kind of loan for which he has applied.

§ 17.48 Private Financing

It is possible for the buyer to arrange for payment of the property without the necessity of securing commercial financing. Sometimes the seller is in a position to help with the financing. It is common for some type of financing to be in existence on the property. In such a case the buyer may be able to utilize the existing financing. The existing financing is probably in the form of a commercial loan which the seller made when he bought the property. That loan would be secured (guaranteed) by a mortgage on the property. A mortgage is a security instrument which allows a lender to foreclose on the property (seize it) and cause it to be sold at public sale if the loan is not repaid according to the terms of the mortgage.

The most common methods of private financing are:

• Assumption of an existing mortgage

• Installment real estate contract, either with or without an escrow

• Purchase money mortgage

• Deed of trust

§ 17.49　Types of Real Estate Transactions and Requisite Documents

The documents required in real estate transactions vary greatly. The legal secretary must learn to develop her own checklist of items that are required in various types of transactions. A commercial real estate transaction, such as an apartment complex or office building could easily require more than 25 different documents, while a transaction involving a home or vacant land could involve fewer than five documents. All real estate transactions require some form of conveyance document and closing statement. All except cash transactions require documents relating to the financing.

If a real estate broker is involved, his firm may have a closing department which submits drafts of documents to attorneys for both the buyer and the seller. The real estate firm may also act as an intermediary with any lending institution. In some states lending institutions or title insurance companies prepare the loan documentation, while in other states attorneys prepare all loan papers.

§ 17.50　The Cash Transaction

If a purchaser is buying the property for cash, it is not necessary to prepare any of the financing papers that would be necessary in real estate transactions involving financing. As was discussed earlier, most deeds are warranty deeds. Since this is a "fill in the blanks" form, preparation of the cash deed requires very little typing. The printed language in the form is important, but the attorney should verify that the form used is correct.

The other key document which you will need to prepare for the cash transaction is the closing statement. It will be a much simpler form than the example shown in Illustration 17–9 because this is a cash transaction, but the same principles apply to the preparation of all closing statements.

§ 17.51   The Sale With Assumption of Mortgage

In a transaction involving an assumption, the buyer pays cash down to the balance of the existing mortgage and thereafter makes all payments on it. For example, if a buyer buys for $50,000 a house having a $15,000 mortgage, his earnest money and cash at closing total $35,000. Each of these methods is explained more fully under "Preparation of Real Estate Documents."

If an assumption is planned, the attorney and/or broker (depending upon the practice in your area) verifies prior to the closing that an assumption is possible. Some mortgages specifically prohibit assumption, and even if the purchase agreement provides for assumption of the mortgage, the sale may not be possible if this is the case. Although the attorney often determines this fact in his examination of the title, it may come to light when your office or the realtor's office contacts the mortgage company for assumption information.

If you are responsible for helping to process the file to closing, you will contact the mortgage company for the necessary assumption information when you are given an assumption to process. Your office may have a form letter developed for this purpose, but if it does not, you should ask the attorney to help you develop such a form. In the letter you will ask the mortgage company for the balance due on the loan, the amount of the monthly payments, the balance being held by the company in the escrow account, and the status of both the monthly payment and the escrow accounts. Since you cannot prepare the sale papers until you have this information, you should do this as soon as possible. A good rule of thumb is to write the mortgage company when you open the file and order whatever abstract work must be done. (The attorney will probably order the abstract work until you are familiar with the procedures, or he will give you instructions on how to do this.) If the mortgage cannot be assumed, the mortgage company will advise you of this in response to your letter. In some mortgages the lender reserves the right to approve any prospective buyer in the event of a sale with assumption of mortgage. Most real estate brokers are familiar with the local lenders that make this requirement and often coordinate securing lender approval on the prospective buyer before the file reaches your office. If the realtor does not do this, the lender will notify you of this requirement in response to your letter asking for an assumption statement.

§ 17.52   The Assumption Closing Statement

In preparing the closing statement on an assumption, there are a few items peculiar to this type of sale.

- Most lenders charge an assumption fee or transfer fee. The amount of the fee varies greatly, and the lender's assumption statement will indicate the amount.

- It is very important to verify that the monthly installments on the loan are up to date, and if they are not, you must collect those payments from the seller.

- The escrow account is an account for the payment of property taxes and fire and extended insurance (protection against fire, wind damage, hail, and other perils of nature). The monthly payments include the amount of one-twelfth of the property taxes and one-twelfth of the insurance policy premium. Sometimes there is not enough money in the escrow account to pay the amount of the taxes or insurance, so the lender overdraws the account. This creates an escrow shortage, and the lender usually requires funds to bring this account current in the event of an assumption.

Although the buyer usually pays the transfer fee and attorney fees on assumption and the seller must pay to bring the loan and escrow account current, all closing costs in connection with an assumption of mortgage are negotiable; therefore, it is necessary for you to refer to the purchase agreement to determine who is paying which costs. Since insurance is usually paid in advance, sometimes the amount of the insurance premium is prorated, and the buyer pays the seller for the unused portion of the insurance premium if the insurance policy is being transferred in the sale. Property taxes are handled the same way; but in most areas, property taxes are paid after they have accrued, and the taxes will be prorated accordingly. In handling these items, you will need to become familiar with the practice in your area, and you will have to work very closely with the attorney on the preparation of this type of closing statement.

§ 17.53   Purchase Money Mortgage, Credit Sale, Sale With Mortgage

A purchase money mortgage is a mortgage given by a buyer to a seller in partial payment of the purchase price. Although the buyer pays an agreed portion of the price in cash, this kind of sale is generally referred to as a credit sale. Since the seller does not receive his money for the property until later, he has sold the property on credit. The transaction is directly between the buyer and seller. The seller gives a deed to the buyer at closing, and the buyer gives the seller a mortgage just as he would if he obtained his loan from a commercial lending institution.

If the financing on the transaction is being handled by the seller himself, you will prepare the documentation on both the deed and the mortgage. The kind of instrument which is used in this kind of transaction varies a great deal, but here again, your firm will already have on hand the kind of form it prefers to use. As was discussed earlier in this chapter, in this kind of sale the buyer pays some of the purchase price in cash and handles the remainder of the purchase price on credit with the seller. He pays the seller in monthly installments over a specified period of time just as if he were dealing with a commercial lender. The buyer executes a promissory note (promise to pay) and a mortgage (security instrument) in favor of the seller. These evidence the debt to the seller and also provide him security on the debt.

§ 17.54   General Closing Statements

The closing statement on a purchase money mortgage, credit sale, or sale with mortgage transaction is relatively simple, as only the buyer and seller are involved.

§ 17.55   Installment Real Estate Contract

An installment real estate contract (also called a land contract or a contract for deed) is an agreement between the seller and the buyer for the purchase of certain real estate over a period of time by making installment payments with interest. The contract buyer takes possession of the property and becomes responsible for payment of taxes, insurance coverage, maintenance of the property, and any other conditions set forth in the contract, but the contract seller retains title to the premises until the price is paid in full. At that time, the buyer receives a deed giving him title to the property. In some states to ensure the performance of the seller, the signed deed is placed in escrow until consummation of the contract.

The use of the installment contract provides the parties with a great deal of flexibility in structuring the financing of a real estate transaction. It often provides the seller the opportunity for more favorable income tax treatment. Advantages to the buyer may include a lower interest rate than that available from commercial lending institutions and lower payments in the early years of ownership through the use of a balloon payment. A balloon payment is a provision that provides for payment in full of any unpaid balance a certain number of years from the date of the contract, typically 5–10 years, but the payments are calculated as though the loan were for a longer period of time. Both parties benefit from low closing costs.

§ 17.56   Escrow Agreement

The escrow agent (usually a bank) serves as a trustee for certain documents (warranty deed executed by the seller, fire and extended coverage insurance policy, or abstract of title). The escrow agent collects payments from the buyer and puts them in the seller's account. When the total due the seller by the buyer has been paid, all documents are delivered to the buyer, and the warranty deed which the agent was holding in trust is recorded. The escrow agent charges a monthly fee for this service. Who pays the fee is negotiable, but it is often paid one-half by the seller and one-half by the buyer. If payments are not made as required, the escrow agent gives notice of default to the buyer upon the request of the seller. If an attorney is retained by the seller or the escrow agent, the buyer must pay the attorney fee.

All provisions of the agreement between the buyer and the seller are set out in an escrow agreement signed by all parties and acknowledged before a notary public.

The escrow agreement protects both the seller and the buyer. When the contract is paid, the buyer does not have to locate the seller for execution of a deed. The seller is protected because he retains title until he has received full payment for his property.

§ 17.57   Mortgage and Note

Once a buyer's loan application has been approved, the lender issues closing instructions which advise the closing attorney of its requirements in connection with the loan. Among the duties of the closing attorney is preparation of the security instruments required by the lender. The promissory note and mortgage are prepared on forms provided by the lending institutions or on commercially prepared forms. In the case of FHA or VA insured loans, the note and mortgage are prepared on forms provided by the FHA and the VA. Until she is able to differentiate among these various forms, the legal secretary should request the attorney to specify the kind of form needed for a particular transaction.

The person obligated to pay the amount specified in the promissory note is the maker, while the person or entity to whom the payment is made is the payee. Many of the terms are requirements of the lending institution and are provided to the attorney in writing. The mortgage is prepared using the information contained in the promissory note, as well as information provided by the deed as to the names of the parties and the legal description. The mortgage secures payment of the promissory note by the maker. The person executing the mortgage and granting the security in his real estate is called the mortgagor while the lending institution is the mortgagee. A lending institution usually requires that its mortgage be the first lien against the premises, so the mortgage is generally recorded immediately after the deed is recorded. Should the mortgagors grant a subsequent or second mortgage on the premises, they would again execute a promissory note and mortgage in compliance with the terms set forth by the lending institution or the individual taking the second mortgage.

The typewritten preparation of the mortgage follows the same principles as set forth below for the preparation of deeds. In addition, the mortgage contains the terms of the loan as they appear in the promissory note. A mortgage and promissory note are executed only by the mortgagor in the same manner as deeds are executed.

§ 17.58 Deed of Trust

Some lending institutions prefer to hold a deed to the property rather than a mortgage. They lend the money to the buyer. The buyer executes a deed of trust transferring title in trust to the lending institution. The title company can serve as trustee, but normally the trustee is either an officer of or the attorney for the lending institution. When the institution has been paid in full, the trustee executes a deed of reconveyance, returning title of the property to the buyer.

A deed of trust is similar to a mortgage, except that the lender holds title, rather than the buyer.

§ 17.59 Preparation of Deeds

In any transfer of real property, a deed (normally a warranty deed) is required. Regardless of the type of deed to be used in a given transaction, the typewritten preparation of deeds must be done precisely and with great attention to detail. Deeds should not contain any visible typographical corrections or "white-outs." In some jurisdictions, deeds containing such corrections are not recordable. The guidelines to be followed in the preparation of all deeds are:

1. The name of the seller must appear on the deed exactly as he took title to the property. If a seller appears in a different form on different documents, the preferred usage should be followed by the variant.

   EXAMPLE:

   John A. Smith a.k.a. Jon A. Smith; or Florence A. Jones formerly Florence A. Smith.

2. It may be necessary for the spouse of the seller to join in the conveyance and execute the deed. (This requirement may vary from state to state, depending upon whether the state recognizes rights of dower or curtesy, or the property is homestead or non-homestead.)

596

3. The marital status of the seller must be shown.

   EXAMPLE:

   John A. Smith and Florence A. Smith, husband and wife; or John A. Smith, a single person.

4. If the seller is a corporation or a partnership, its name should be used as set forth in its articles of incorporation or articles of partnership.

   EXAMPLE:

   A.B.C. Inc., an Any State corporation; or Jones and Smith Company, an Any State general partnership.

5. If the seller is a trust, that fact should be shown.

   EXAMPLE:

   Jack Smith, Trustee under Agreement with Donald Smith, dated January 15, 1986.

6. The buyer's name should appear exactly as he desires to take title. The legal secretary should verify the correct spelling of the names of all buyers. It is generally not necessary to state the marital status of the buyer(s).

7. The deed must contain the exact legal description of the property being conveyed. The legal description should be taken from the title opinion or title binder or commitment. Never rely upon a legal description taken from a tax statement. The legal description should be carefully proofread. Typewritten legal descriptions should have lot and block numbers written followed by the numerals in parentheses.

   EXAMPLES:

   Lot Two (2), Block One (1), Easy Street Addition to Jonestown, Any County, Any State;

   or in the case of a metes and bounds description:

   The Southwest Quarter of the Northwest Quarter (SW$\frac{1}{4}$ of NW$\frac{1}{4}$), Section One (1), Township Two (2) South, Range Three (3) West, Any County, Any State.

8. A deed is signed only by the seller. The name of the seller should be typewritten beneath the appropriate signature line. In some states this is mandatory.

9. Some states require that deeds have witnesses sign the deed as well.

10. A deed must be acknowledged by a notary public or other authorized person. The name of the grantor must appear in

the acknowledgment exactly as it appears in the body of the deed. The notary public must date, sign, and affix his official seal to the deed. Some states also require that the notary's area of commission and the expiration date of the commission also appear on the deed.

11. Many states require that the deed indicate the name and address of the person or firm drafting the deed and the name and address of the person or entity to whom future tax statements should be directed. (Since this is often the buyer, the address can be placed after the buyer's name.)

12. Some states require that the consideration shown on the warranty deed be the amount of the purchase price. In other states, a nominal consideration (usually $10) is stated along with the phrase "and other good and valuable consideration."

13. Consideration on a quitclaim deed is usually a nominal amount, such as $1.

§ 17.60   The Real Estate Closing

The closing is the formal meeting of all parties to the transaction at which documents are executed and funds disbursed. The location and mode of closing also vary greatly, depending upon local practice. In some states most closings are handled by title companies in their offices. In other states they are handled by law firms, lending institutions, or closers in the employ of the real estate broker. When all title matters are resolved, documents prepared, and financing arrangements finalized, a time for the closing is set. The attorney carefully explains the meaning of each of the documents, supervises the execution thereof, and sometimes disburses the sale funds to his client through his trust account if a closing or escrow agent is not involved.

The closing statement is a detailed accounting of the credits and charges to the buyer and seller. In preparing the closing statement, the purchase agreement serves as the guideline for determining pro-rations and payoff figures. Illustrations 17–9 and 17–10 are simple buyer's and seller's closing statement forms for study and use. It should be noted that the earnest money or down payment is deducted from the purchase price. It is held in the trust account of the real estate broker or by the attorney for the seller if no real estate broker is involved.

Illustration 17–9

BUYER'S CLOSING STATEMENT

Seller: John and Mary Doe
Buyer: David and Jane Smith
Property: Lot 1, Block 2, Marigold Addition
Date: September 15, 1994

Item	Debits	Credits
Purchase Price	$50,000.00	$
Earnest Money		5,000.00
First Mortgage Assumed		35,000.00
Interest		
15 days at $7.67		115.05
Transfer tax		33.00
Abstracting charges		56.00
1986 real estate tax adjustment		
$750.00 ÷ 365 × 107 days =		219.35
Cash at closing		9,576.60
	$50,000.00	$50,000.00

Accepted:

_____   _____
Buyer   Seller

Note: The foregoing represents a simple buyer's closing statement and accordingly would not reflect such items as broker's commissions, etc. These would be contained in a separate seller's closing statement.

Buyer's credits against the purchase price may include adjustments for:

- Accrued real estate taxes for the year in which the transaction occurs (formula to be used in making this computation designated in the purchase agreement)
- Special assessments (again as provided for in the purchase agreement)
- Unused rent for the remainder of the month (if the property is a rental unit)
- The amount to be carried on contract or the balance of the mortgage (if the transaction involves an installment contract or a mortgage assumption)
- Services rendered in repairing certain items on the premises or improvements made prior to closing
- Discount points which the sellers may be required to pay in order for buyers to obtain financing

Buyer's expenses (debits) may include adjustments for:

- Attorney's fees for examination of the title and opinion thereof
- Drawing a promissory note, mortgage, and other financing documents required for the closing
- Closing services

- Recording fees for the deed and mortgage
- Abstracting expenses
- Origination charge or service fee imposed by the lending institution according to the terms of the loan
- Interest on the new loan should the lending institution require it

EXAMPLE:

    A transaction is closed on January 20. The first mortgage payment is due on March 1. The lender may require that interest accruing on the loan from January 20 through January 31 be paid at closing. (February interest is paid in the March 1 payment.)

- Any other expenses incurred by the buyer prior to closing

Illustration 17–10

SELLER'S CLOSING STATEMENT

Seller: John and Mary Doe
Buyer: David and Jane Smith
Property: Lot 1, Block 2, Marigold Addition
Date: September 15, 1994

Item	Debits	Credits
Purchase Price	$	$50,000.00
Existing Mortgage Assumed	35,000.00	
Interest adjustment		
15 days at $7.67	115.05	
Transfer tax	33.00	
Abstracting charges	56.00	
1986 real estate tax adjustment		
$750.00 ÷ 365 × 107 days =	219.35	
Real estate commission	3,500.00	
Balance due Seller	11,076.60	
	$50,000.00	$50,000.00

Accepted:

_____   _____
Buyer   Seller

Note: Earnest money paid by buyer is normally held in the broker's trust account pending closing. In this example, the seller will receive $9,576.60 from the buyer and the balance from the broker's trust account after deduction is made for the real estate commission.

The seller might receive credit for:

- Unearned insurance premiums (should a buyer assume existing insurance coverage on the property)
- Insurance reserves or escrows being held by a lending institution (which the buyer assumes by virtue of a mortgage assumption)

The seller's expenses usually include:

- The broker's commission (usually a percentage of the purchase price unless a flat sum has previously been agreed upon) (earnest money deposit may have already been credited)
- Abstracting charges
- Recording charges for a release of mortgage or any documents necessary to clear title defects
- Attorney's fees applicable to seller for preparing a contract, deed, and closing
- Transfer tax, if required by the county or state in which the transaction is being closed
- The balance due on any outstanding contract, including interest up to the date of payment, or the balance due on a mortgage, including interest up to the date of payment
- Any other expenses or liens as outlined or required by the purchase agreement, such as inspection fees, repair costs, and similar items

A contract payoff is obtained from the contract seller or his agent, and a mortgage payoff with per diem (daily) interest is available at the lending institution holding the mortgage.

Other adjustments might be necessary to either closing statement, depending upon the particular transaction and the terms of the purchase agreement.

A settlement statement in compliance with the Real Estate Settlement Procedures Act (RESPA) can easily be prepared from the closing statement outlined above, and forms for its preparation are provided by the lending institution.

§ 17.61 Recording of Documents

Transfer of title occurs at the time an executed deed is delivered to and accepted by the buyer or his agent. A security interest (mortgage or other financing arrangement) becomes effective at the time the documents are executed and the funds disbursed. Recording is not necessary to complete the transfer of title; however, it is necessary to protect the buyer against a second fraudulent sale by the seller and against any liens which may accrue against the property while it is still recorded in the seller's name. Likewise, the mortgagee will want to have its security interest placed of record to protect it from subsequent security interests. Hence, the time of recording becomes essential in determining the priority of each of the liens or claims against the real estate. It is important, therefore, to record documents as soon as possible after the completion of a transaction.

The recording of documents is a function which will frequently be delegated to the legal secretary. The requirements for recording and fees charged for recording vary greatly from state to state. In some states documents are returned to the person filing them after the recording process is complete, while in other states they are not. Documents filed under the Torrens system are never returned to the filer.

§ 17.62   The Role of the Investor

Although the majority of residential financing is originated on the local level, unless the financing is arranged through a local savings and loan association (and sometimes certain banks), once the loan has been made and the legal work completed, the loan is sold to an investor who is in the business of buying these loans. This is particularly common with VA and FNMA loans. In this instance the investor usually, for a fee, retains the local lender to service the loan, that is, the local lender collects the monthly payment from the buyer and handles any day-to-day problems that might arise. Most buyers are not even aware that their loans are not owned by the lender servicing them.

§ 17.63   Miscellaneous Matters

The practice of real estate law is not limited to the representation of clients buying or selling property.

§ 17.64   Easements

On occasion, a property owner may wish to grant to another a limited right to make use of all or a portion of his land for a specific purpose or for a definite period of time. This grant is known as an easement. An easement may be created by the act of the parties involved through negotiation and agreement. Easements are usually custom-drafted by the attorneys of the respective parties. An example of an easement would be the right of a utility company to install a gas line across an individual's property and thereafter to enter the land to maintain, repair, and service the line. The utility would not have the right to enter the property for any other purpose.

§ 17.65   Leases

A lease is a contract between the landlord (lessor) and the tenant (lessee) whereby the landlord conveys the use of real estate to another for a specific term at a particular rent subject to certain conditions. Many commercially printed lease forms are available from legal stationers which may be used in their entirety or adjusted to use only particular sections in preparation of custom-drafted instruments, depending upon the needs of the client. An attorney drafts the lease to protect his client and includes those clauses and phrases beneficial to his particular client. Commercially printed lease forms generally favor the landlord. Certain statutory provisions and court decisions also govern the rights of the landlord and tenant in such contracts.

A lease also contains specific provisions relating to the permitted use(s) of the premises during the term of the lease, which vary depending upon the circumstances.

§ 17.66 Real Estate in Litigation

Real estate may also become the subject of litigation for a variety of reasons. One of the most common reasons is a lawsuit brought to establish the proper ownership of a parcel of real estate. Usually such a lawsuit has its basis in a title defect. A lawsuit of this kind is called an action to quiet title. Lawsuits may also result from boundary disputes, fraudulent conveyances, or misrepresentations made during a sale, as well as many other reasons.

§ 17.67 Summary

The foregoing is by no means exhaustive of all real estate matters that will confront the legal secretary. Additional information will be acquired from each transaction in which a legal secretary is involved, and as skill and knowledge increase, the legal secretary will become increasingly valuable in this area of law.

CHAPTER 18

ESTATE PLANNING

Table of Sections

§ 18.1   Introduction

The area of law dealing with the disposition of a person's property after his death is known as estate planning. There are many techniques available to the attorney to tailor a plan to achieve the client's desired distribution of his property while minimizing death taxes and expenses. The most common document utilized in estate planning is the last will and testament, or more simply, a will. However, many people are now creating living trusts that will enable them to avoid probate of their assets upon death and also avoid the necessity of having to establish a guardianship or conservatorship during their lifetimes should they become incapacitated. Of course, the trust agreement can have many technical features to minimize death taxes and take care of the special needs of the trustor or the trustor's family. Wills and trusts both have their places in the estate planning field, and even if a trust is executed and funded, it is still important for the testator to execute a will to take care of any assets that may not have been transferred to the trust.

§ 18.2   Importance of Accuracy and Proper Execution

A will or trust agreement is one of the most important legal documents that is prepared in the law office. Not only is it extremely important that it be prepared properly, but it must be executed with extreme care to protect the party making the will or trust. An error or omission could result in a lawsuit and expenditures of large sums for attorney's fees and court costs, and even more important, the wishes of the decedent might not be carried out.

§ 18.3   Definition

A will is a legal document in which a person provides for disposition of his property (estate) to take effect after his death. A male person making a will is referred to as the testator and a female person is called the testatrix.

A trust is a fiduciary relationship with regard to property in which the legal title is in the trustee, but the benefit of ownership is in another person. A trust must be intentionally created. The person who benefits from the trust is called the "beneficiary." The maker of the trust is often called a "grantor," "trustor," or "settlor." The relationship of the trust imposes "fiduciary" duties on the trustee.

§ 18.4   Power and Capacity to Make a Will

In order for a will to be valid, the testator must have both the power and capacity to make a will. In most states one has the power to make a will if he has reached legal age. (See the chapter on Courts for a more complete discussion of legal age.) Generally, minors and adults under legal disability (incompetent) do not possess the power to make a will. The age at which a minor may make a will varies from state to state. Possession of the capacity to make a will means that the testator is of sound mind, knows the extent of his assets, who his natural heirs are, and that he intends to make a will.

§ 18.5   Terminology

Those persons named in a will to receive property are beneficiaries. Gifts of real estate by will are devises, and the recipients of such gifts are devisees. A person may gift his personal property by will also, and personal property so transferred is known as a bequest. Money passing under a will is known as a legacy and the recipient as a legatee; however, the words "legacy" and "legatee" are commonly used to designate other kinds of personal property as well. In states which have adopted the Uniform Probate Code (UPC), all recipients of property under a will are referred to as devisees, regardless of whether they receive real or personal property. More information concerning the Uniform Probate Code is given in the chapter on Estates and Guardianships.

If a testator gives specific property in his will but he no longer owns the property at the time of his death, an ademption occurs. This simply means that the particular legacy is extinguished, and that provision of the will can be ignored.

In addition to the distribution of the property, the testator also names a person(s) or entity (usually a bank with a trust department) to administer the terms of his will and distribute his estate. That person or entity is called the executor (male or entity) or executrix (female). Under the Uniform Probate Code, the person or entity is referred to as the personal representative. If the testator has minor children, he may also designate a guardian for those children.

The supervision of an estate by an administrator or executor is called "administration."

§ 18.6   Characteristics of a Will

Regardless of the type of will you are preparing, there are certain requirements that control the preparation of all wills:

- Opening clause stating domicile and declaring document to be the testator's last will

- Clause(s) relating to the payment of testator's debts, death taxes, expenses of administration, etc.

- Clause(s) directing the disposition of the testator's property

- Clause nominating the estate's personal representative

- Signature and attestation clause (for testator and witnesses)

All wills prepared by attorneys will contain these basic elements. There may, of course, be many additional provisions, and these basic elements may be expanded to accommodate the testator's individual needs.

§ 18.7   Opening Clause of a Will

The opening clause of a will gives the testator's name and domicile, and it revokes any earlier wills or codicils he may have made. The revocation clause (revoking earlier wills and codicils) should be a part of every will whether or not the testator remembers executing a previous will. A will, of course, does not become effective until the death of the testator, and, until that time, the testator may take any action or make any changes he wishes.

§ 18.8   Domicile Clause of a Will

The place of the decedent's domicile should not be confused with his place of residence. It is quite possible to have several residences, but one may have only one domicile. The testator's place of domicile at the time of his death determines the location of the primary probate proceeding as well as the state which collects the major portion of state death taxes. A classic example of dilemma that can be created relating to domicile is the estate of the late billionaire, Howard Hughes. Mr. Hughes died without a will and lived in several states, apparently without firmly establishing domicile in any one. Three different states alleged that his domicile was in their state. Millions of dollars in state death taxes were at stake, and the matter was in litigation for several years.

§ 18.9   Payment of Debts Clause of a Will

The clause(s) relating to the payment of debts, expenses, and taxes give the estate's personal representative specific direction in that area. The direction relating to death taxes (inheritance, estate, etc.) is of particular importance, as it determines whether such taxes will be paid from estate funds or by the beneficiaries of the estate.

§ 18.10   Disposition of Property Clause of a Will

The disposition of property is divided into two basic kinds—specific bequests or devises and residuary bequests or devises.

§ 18.11   Specific Bequest Clause of a Will

A specific bequest is a gift of an identified asset or stated amount of money.

EXAMPLE:

> I give and bequeath to my daughter, Jane Doe, my sterling silver flatware.

> I give and bequeath to my friend, John Smith, the sum of $10,000.

§ 18.12   Residuary Bequest Clause of a Will

A residuary bequest is a gift of the remaining assets of the estate.

EXAMPLE:

> All of the rest, residue, and remainder of my property, real, personal, or mixed, wherever situated, I give, devise, and bequeath to my daughters, Jane Doe and Mary Doe, share and share alike, or to the survivor thereof.

The residue of an estate is what is left over after the payment of debts, expenses, taxes, and specific bequests. If the estate's assets are depleted entirely by payment of the debts, expenses, taxes, and specific bequests, there is no residue to distribute, so the residuary beneficiaries receive nothing.

§ 18.13   Appointment of Personal Representative

The clause relating to the testator's choice of personal representative (representative) (and frequently an alternate) may also include statements as to the specific powers granted to the representative. A testator may want to give the representative a great deal of leeway and may fully outline the powers. This enables the representative to go about the business of administering the estate without requesting the power from the court for each transaction. A will may designate that the representative need not provide a bond with surety. Some states now provide that representatives have statutory powers regardless of whether or not they are set forth in the will. (More information on the administration of wills is given in the chapter on Estates and Guardianships.)

§ 18.14 Signature Lines of a Will

The signature area of the will is an important one, since virtually all jurisdictions require that a will be signed by the testator. The date of the signing is also important since, if more than one will is found after the testator's death, the one bearing the most recent date controls.

§ 18.15 Attestation Clause of a Will

The attestation clause of the will is the section in which the witnesses are to sign the will. Most states require that wills be executed in the presence of at least two witnesses. In addition to the act of witnessing the execution, the witnesses also usually attest to the fact that the testator declared that this was his will and he requested them to witness it.

All wills drafted by attorneys contain these basic elements, although many are a great deal more sophisticated than the illustration in § 18.19.

§ 18.16 Self–Proved Affidavit

The trend in modern will writing is to add an affidavit at the end of the will which is signed by the witnesses and acknowledged by a notary. This affidavit, in most states, will allow the will to be admitted into probate without having to have one of the attesting witnesses file a separate affidavit or testify in court. In some states this may be accomplished by attaching a separate affidavit of attesting witnesses to the will.

§ 18.17 Possession of the Will

One important characteristic of a will is that it is the personal possession of the testator. The testator may designate who shall hold the will for him and may request possession of the document at any time. Because of the very personal nature of a will, should the testator desire to revoke the will, he must do so personally. A will may be revoked by mutilation, cancellation, destruction, or execution of a new will. A revoked will must, however, be destroyed by the testator.

§ 18.18 Types of Wills

There are many types of wills which are used for different purposes. Many of the more sophisticated wills are written to achieve favorable death tax consideration and involve the use of various kinds of trusts. A will may also contain trust provisions for minor children to avoid distributing estate assets to a child when the child attains majority (18 or 21 years of age, depending upon state law) because the testator may feel that a child is not ready to handle such sums of money at that age.

§ 18.19 Simple Will

Most wills which the legal secretary will prepare will be those drafted by attorneys and dictated to her. This chapter deals primarily with those types of wills, although the more unusual kinds of wills are defined. A typical simple will is shown in Illustration 18–1. This will contains all of the necessary elements mentioned earlier in the chapter.

Illustration 18–1

LAST WILL AND TESTAMENT OF JANE A. DOE

I, Jane A. Doe, domiciled in Any County, State of Anystate, do hereby make, with complete testamentary intent and capacity, my Last Will and Testament, hereby revoking all former wills and codicils.

ARTICLE I

I direct that all of my debts and my funeral expenses be paid from my estate as soon as practicable after my death.

ARTICLE II

I direct that all inheritance, estate, legacy, and death taxes imposed on account of my death, whether or not accruing against property or insurance proceeds not part of my probate estate, be paid from the residue of my estate passing under Article V, without apportionment. There shall be no obligation resting on anyone to contribute to the payment of said taxes, and my Personal Representative shall have no duty to secure reimbursement to my estate on account of taxes so paid.

ARTICLE III

I give and devise any homestead, including contiguous land used in connection therewith, which I may own at the time of my death to my husband, John J. Doe, outright. Should my husband not survive me, this devise shall lapse, and said homestead shall be added to and be distributed with the residue of my estate.

ARTICLE IV

I give and bequeath to my husband, John J. Doe, all of the household furniture and furnishings, automobiles, musical instruments, books, pictures, jewelry, watches, silverware, wearing apparel, and all other articles of household or personal use or adornment that I own at my date of death. In the event he shall not survive me, then I give all of said property to my children or to the survivor of them, in equal shares.

ARTICLE V

All the rest, residue, and remainder of my property, real, personal or mixed, wheresoever situated, I give and devise to my husband, John J. Doe; but if he does not survive me, I direct that my Personal Representative distribute said property to my children, Paula Doe, Elizabeth Doe, and Ryan Doe, in equal shares, or to their issue by right of representation.

ARTICLE VI

I nominate, constitute, and appoint my husband, John J. Doe, Personal Representative of my estate to serve without bond. If my husband predeceases me or is unable or unwilling to serve, then I appoint Brian Doe as Personal Representative. I grant my Personal Representative the power to do without court order any of the acts permitted a Personal Representative pursuant to the statutes of Anywhere state.

ARTICLE VII

In the event my husband and I die under such circumstances that the order of our deaths may not be conveniently determined, I direct that the distribution of my estate under this Will shall be made as if my husband predeceased me.

IN WITNESS WHEREOF, I have hereunto set my hand to this my Last Will and Testament this _____ day of _____, 19__.

_____
Jane A. Doe

This instrument, consisting of _____ typewritten pages, including this certificate, each bearing the signature of the above named, Jane A. Doe, was by her on the date hereof signed. We believe her to be of sound and disposing mind and memory and have hereunto subscribed our names as witnesses.

_____ Residing at _____

_____ Residing at _____

STATE OF _____
COUNTY OF _____

We, Jane A. Doe, _____, and _____, the Testatrix and the witnesses, respectively, whose names are signed to the attached or foregoing instrument, being first duly sworn, do hereby declare to the undersigned authority that the

Testatrix signed and executed the instrument as her last will and that she had signed willingly or directed another to sign for her, and that she executed it as her free and voluntary act for the purposes therein expressed; and that each of the witnesses, in the presence and hearing of the Testatrix, signed the will as witness and that to the best of his knowledge the Testatrix was at that time 18 or more years of age, of sound mind and under no constraint or undue influence.

_____

Testatrix

_____

Witness

_____

Witness

Subscribed, sworn to and acknowledged before me by Jane A. Doe, the Testatrix, and subscribed and sworn to before me by _____ and _____ witnesses, this _____ day of _____, 19__.

_____

Notary Public

The foregoing will is a sample of a simple will. Many times additional paragraphs will be added to wills to provide for the appointment of a guardian or a trust for minor children. Trust provisions for minor children do not have to be complicated and can continue beyond the time a minor child becomes of age. If funds are not left to a trust but are distributed to a guardianship for the estate of a minor child, then the funds must be distributed to said child upon attaining majority, even though that child may not have a full understanding of handling money, business, etc.

§ 18.20 Holographic Will

A holographic will is one completely handwritten by the testator and signed by him without the benefit of statutory formalities. State law regarding the circumstances under which holographic wills are valid vary greatly, although approximately half of the states make provision for holographic wills under certain circumstances.

§ 18.21 Oral Wills (Nuncupative and Soldier's and Sailor's)

Two kinds of oral wills are recognized by some states—nuncupative wills and soldier's and sailor's wills. A nuncupative will is a spoken will by a person in peril of imminent death. Usually, it must be reduced to writing within a limited time by the witnesses to whom it was spoken. Soldiers' and sailors' wills are oral dispositions made by soldiers in actual military service or sailors at sea.

Again, the requirements and recognition of these wills vary greatly in the states in which they are permitted. Since oral wills offer the open opportunity for fraud, all states in which they are recognized restrict severely the value of assets to pass under them and restrict it to personal property. In those states in which the Uniform Probate Code has been adopted only written wills are permitted.

§ 18.22 Contingent or Conditional Wills

Contingent or conditional wills do not take effect unless a specific event occurs. Therefore, if the event does not occur, it is as though there is no will. Most states do not recognize contingent wills.

§ 18.23 Joint Wills

Sometimes two or more persons execute a joint will, that is, two or more people execute the same document. These are not widely used since problems often arise if circumstances change and one testator desires to change the terms or revoke the instrument.

§ 18.24 Codicils

A codicil to a will literally means a "little will." It is an afterthought, postscript, addition, supplement, or change in the original will. It must be prepared, executed, and witnessed with all the formality of the original will.

§ 18.25 Preparation of Wills

Each person's will is a very personal matter, and it must be drafted to meet the individual needs of the client. Most law offices will have a compilation of standard will clauses in their computer forms file. Some clauses are not standard and need to be dictated by the attorney. The illustrated will in this chapter is an illustration only and should not be used without an attorney's approval.

§ 18.26 Will Paper

Many law firms use special paper, manuscript covers, and envelopes in preparing wills. If your office does not, you should prepare wills on bond paper of the non-erasable type.

§ 18.27   Printed Forms

Occasionally the legal secretary may encounter a homemade or printed form of will. Such wills should be used with caution as the forms available at the drugstore or through mail order houses obviously cannot be adapted carefully to a particular case. Such wills, by their very nature, must be general and may not be in accordance with the statutes of the state in which they are executed. It is very important that the will which is executed be entirely valid so that the testator's wishes will be honored after his death. A will which is successfully contested or proved invalid is inadmissible to probate, and the decedent's assets will be disposed of according to the law of descent in the state of his domicile.

§ 18.28   Corrections to Wills

Take special care in the spelling of names, figures, and words that could change the meaning of the will provisions. If you are setting forth percentages or fractions, make sure they equal 100 percent or a whole unit. If a correction must be made at the time the will is signed, the correction should be written out by the testator and then initialed. This type of correction could include changing the year at the beginning of a new year, a middle initial, etc. The best way to make corrections, however, is to revise and reprint the page before the testator signs.

§ 18.29   Numbering Paragraphs and Pages

Within the body of the will, each clause should be numbered with a Roman numeral or other designation used in your locality. The pages should be numbered. At the bottom of each page there may be a signature line for the testator or there may be places for the testator and witnesses to initial each page. If this is the practice of your firm, you should include the appropriate line(s) for the testator's signature, initials, etc., in the footer of your document.

§ 18.30   Ending a Page

Never complete an item at the bottom of a page or type the signature or attestation clause on a page separate from the remainder of the will. While no one anticipates that a person would attempt to substitute pages in a will after it has been executed, following this procedure will make such an attempt more difficult. The self-proved affidavit of attesting witnesses can be on a separate page as long as they will be signing the affidavit rather than just having the notary's signature.

§ 18.31   Execution of Wills

Wills must be executed under the supervision of an attorney. The legal secretary may, however, be called upon to serve as a witness. The number of witnesses necessary will vary from state to state as mentioned earlier.

The testator should declare that the instrument is, in fact, his will. It is preferable, and in some states mandatory, that none of the witnesses be beneficiaries or parties with a financial interest in the estate. Usually, they need not be aware of the contents of the will. Each witness should sign his name and write his address in the presence of the testator and should initial each page, if requested. Most states require that the witnesses and the testator sign in the presence of each other, so it is a good practice not to leave the room or attend to other business while executing a will. Only the necessary parties present, *i.e.*, the testator, the attorney, the witnesses, and the notary public should be in the room during the execution process. Once these people enter this room, the door should be closed, and no one should be permitted to leave until the task of execution is complete. The will should be dated correctly and checked after execution as to the accuracy and completeness of the execution. Only the original of the will should be executed, although file copies should be conformed to reflect the date of execution, witnesses, etc., or copies made for the attorney's file. The secretary should be aware that the procedures described here are merely illustrative and should learn the formal requirements for execution of wills in her state. The formal requirements do vary and are important, as a will could be contested for failure to meet those requirements.

§ 18.32   Intestate

Intestate means having made no will. A person who dies having made no will is referred to as having died intestate.

§ 18.33   Types of Trusts

There are two types of trusts—revocable and irrevocable. A revocable trust is one that can be revoked or amended by the trustor at any time prior to his death. An irrevocable trust cannot be revoked by the trustor and cannot be materially changed once it is executed. A trust is presumed to be irrevocable unless it is expressly stated to be revocable. A trust can be established between the trustor and the trustee during the lifetime of the trustor, or it can be established through the trustor's will to take effect upon his death. In order to establish a trust, the trustor must have legal capacity in order to transfer the property to the trustee.

Irrevocable trusts are generally made for tax reasons, and the trustor transfers all his ownership rights in and all his power over the property to the trustee so that the assets in the trust will not be included as part of his taxable estate for estate tax purposes at the time of his death.

In a revocable trust, the trustor generally maintains some power over the trust as long as he is alive and not incapacitated. Once the maker dies or becomes incapacitated, the terms of the trust become irrevocable and cannot be changed without court order.

The trustor can be more than one person, and the trustee can be more than one person, or it can be an entity, such as the trust department of a bank.

§ 18.34 Classifications of Trusts

Most trusts are active trusts in which the trustee has some additional duty other than just transferring the property to the beneficiary.

Testamentary trusts are created under a will, and inter vivos or living trusts are created during the lifetime of the trustor.

Express restrictions are usually included in a trust to limit the access to trust assets by a beneficiary and his creditors. These restrictions are referred to as spendthrift provisions.

In revocable trusts, standby trust provisions permit the trustor to retain control over the trust assets during his lifetime, unless he becomes disabled or requests the trustee to assume management of the trust. Income is taxed to the trustor, and the assets are included in the trustor's estate for federal estate tax purposes at the time of his death. No gift tax liability is created.

A joint interest trust is created when two trustors place jointly held assets in a trust. The income and principal are distributed by the trustee according to the terms of the trust. This type of trust is quite often used for a husband and wife so that they do not have to establish two separate trusts. When one of the trustors dies, that share of the trust property passes as the trust agreement dictates.

In a revocable trust where the trustor and trustee are the same person, the trust does not need to file separate fiduciary income tax returns, and the income is included on the trustor's individual income tax returns. If the trustor and trustee are not the same person, the Internal Revenue Code requires that the trust obtain a federal identification number and file its own fiduciary income tax returns.

A qualified terminable interest provision in a trust (or even in a will) permits property to qualify for a marital deduction, if the spouse has use of the property for life and other Internal Revenue Code

616

requirements are met. The personal representative or trustee is given the option to make this election, and the election is made on the decedent's federal estate tax return. If the election is not made on a return which is timely filed, the election is lost and not available.

§ 18.35   Powers and Duties of Trustee

The powers, duties, and liabilities of a trustee are interrelated. The trust instrument usually sets forth the trustee's powers. Most states have statutory laws that regulate a trustee's powers, duties, and liabilities. Generally it is not necessary for a trustee to post a bond or make accountings to a court, such as is required by a personal representative. A trustee is accountable to the trustor and beneficiaries during the trustor's lifetime and to the beneficiaries after the trustor's death.

§ 18.36   Funding the Trust

A trust agreement can be executed by the trustor, but until the assets are actually placed in the trustee's name and delivered to the trustee, the trust is not activated. In other words, if the trustor makes a trust agreement but does not deed his real property to the trust or place his bank accounts, securities, and other personal property in the trustee's name, then these assets remain in the individual's name and are not subject to the terms of the trust. If these assets have not been transferred to the trust, they are treated like any other asset at the time of the trustor's death and may have to be probated. That is why it is important that a trustor also execute a will, so that in the event there are any assets that are not in the trust they can be distributed to the trust and become a part of the trust estate. This type of will is often referred to as a "pourover" will because it simply pours the decedent's assets over to his trust.

It is a good idea for the attorney to keep in a client's file a letter, memorandum, or other written evidence of what assets the attorney has assisted the client in transferring to the trust and what assets the client is going to handle on his own. This could be very beneficial to the lawyer after the trustor's death if the beneficiaries bring a claim against the lawyer for not transferring estate assets to the trust.

§ 18.37   Trust Termination

A trust can be revoked by the trustor, so long as he possesses the power of revocation according to the trust terms. Generally a trust is terminated in accordance with the trust provisions, although it can be terminated differently, with the consent of all of the beneficiaries, if no material trust purpose is defeated by such termination.

§ 18.38 Other Estate Planning Documents

Many other documents may be executed by the client at the time he signs his will or trust agreement. Many people now desire to execute health care powers of attorney. This kind of power of attorney permits the attorney-in-fact to make health care decisions on behalf of the maker in the event the maker is unable to make these decisions on his own. A health care power of attorney should not be confused with a living will. In a living will, the maker instructs the physician or medical supplier not to keep the maker alive by the use of life-supporting procedures.

A durable power of attorney is used quite often in estate planning. A durable power of attorney is given to another, usually a spouse, child, or entity, which empowers that person to act on behalf of the maker, even if the maker has become incapacitated. If the maker has established a trust and has not transferred all of his assets to the trust, a general durable power of attorney would permit the agent to transfer the assets, so that the assets would become part of the trust estate and subject to the trust provisions. It is important that the power of attorney include language that it will be effective even if the maker is incapacitated, or it will not qualify as a durable power of attorney, and the agent will not be able to continue to act under the provisions of the power of attorney.

§ 18.39 Elder Law

The area of elder law developed as a response to the changing demographics of American society. It is sometimes defined as a practice of law focused on the unique concerns of a particular segment of the population over the age of 50. Attorneys who practice in this area are attuned to the social, medical, and legal aspects of complex issues facing the elderly and their families. Such issues include:

• Planning for disability

• Estate planning and management

• Estate tax and gift tax issues

• Medicaid and Medicare issues

• Age discrimination in housing and employment

• Personal injury

• Guardianships

• Living wills

• Durable power of attorney

• Health care power of attorney

§ 18.40   Meeting the Needs of Clients and the Community

As you can see, estate planning is not something to take lightly. The client trusts the lawyer to do what is best for him, and the lawyer needs to know what he is doing in order to help the client. If the lawyer is not trained in this area, the best thing he can do for the client and for the legal profession in general is to refer the client to a lawyer who can provide the client with the estate planning results he desires. Just like other areas of the law, because there are many things to be considered for some estate plans, it is impossible for all lawyers to know what will work best unless they specialize in estate and tax planning.

What can you do as a legal secretary to help the attorney? You can make sure that the documents are prepared as accurately as possible and that the file contains documents and written data as to what the lawyer is to do for the client and what he is not going to do. If you think a paragraph in a will or trust agreement does not make sense, bring this to the lawyer's attention. If you do not believe the will or trust agreement includes all of the provisions it should, ask the lawyer about it. This is just a way of double checking to make sure that the documents contain all of the necessary language in order to carry out the wishes of the client. Remember, most of the time these documents are not used until the client is either deceased or incapacitated, and then it is too late for him to make the corrections that should have been included prior to signing.

CHAPTER 19

ESTATES AND GUARDIANSHIPS

Table of Sections

---

§ 19.1 Introduction

When a person dies, it is necessary that an orderly disposition be made of that person's property. The person who dies is called the decedent or the deceased. The property which the decedent owned when he died is referred to as the decedent's estate or probate property.

Probate assets are those assets which generally require some type of proceeding in the appropriate court of jurisdiction to determine their proper distribution. Probate property consists of those items of property owned solely by the decedent or in which the decedent owned an interest as a tenant in common and life insurance proceeds payable to the executor, administrator, or personal representative of a decedent's estate.

Estate administration or probate proceedings are the terms most often used to refer to proceedings which are brought for the purpose of distribution of the estate. The persons or entities that become owners of the decedent's probate estate after the completion of probate proceedings are called the beneficiaries. The persons or institutions who manage money or property for another and who must exercise a standard of care imposed by law, *i.e.,* personal representative or executor of an estate, a trustee, etc., are called fiduciaries. It should be noted that fiduciaries also handle the affairs of living persons, *i.e.,* wards, minors, etc.

Non-probate property consists of those assets owned by the decedent and others in joint tenancy, life insurance, and other property payable under a contract to specific beneficiaries other than the decedent's estate, and property titled in inter vivos and Totten trusts, all of which are transferred automatically to the recipient without passing through probate. An inter vivos trust is one created by a decedent during his lifetime which becomes operative during his lifetime. A Totten trust is a trust created upon the deposit by the decedent of his own money in his own name as trustee for another. It may be revoked at will until his death, when it automatically becomes the property of the named beneficiary.

The legal process involved in handling a decedent's estate is one that laymen tend to find tedious and burdensome. In fact, laymen sometimes face estate administration with a great deal of apprehension because of the misinformation they have received that avoiding probate is desirable. Actually, the legal process is a very orderly one that can save the heirs many tax dollars. It is often the first contact that the survivors have with the court system. Also, the event that necessitates this kind of proceeding is one of the most traumatic in any of our lives—the death of a loved one. It is very important, therefore, that the legal secretary have an understanding of estate administration, so she can deal intelligently and compassionately with the client who is a member of the decedent's family.

§ 19.2 The Uniform Probate Code

The Uniform Probate Code (UPC) adopted by the National Conference of Commissioners on Uniform State Laws has been adopted by several states. Some states have adopted the Code with some modifications or have adopted only certain parts of it. The purpose of the UPC is to make it possible for estates to be administered in the same fashion in all states and to streamline the entire procedure. There has been a great deal of criticism from the public that the probate process is too involved and bureaucratic and permits the courts to become involved in matters in which they need not be involved.

The UPC provides for informal proceedings in some cases which can be handled without the assistance of an attorney or with only minimal attorney involvement. This greatly reduces the expenses of administering an estate. The UPC also provides for totally supervised court proceedings in the traditional manner. Accordingly, the heirs, the representative, and the attorney have the option of determining whether or not the estate should be administered under the informal proceedings or under the formal provisions of the Code.

§ 19.3   Classification

For purposes of handling the decedent's probate estate, the estate is classified in one of two ways: testate or intestate.

If the decedent had a will, he is said to have died testate. A will is a document by which an individual can provide for the disposition of his property after his death. Those persons named in the will to receive some portion of the estate are beneficiaries. Gifts of real estate by a will are known as devises, and the recipient of such gifts are devisees. A person may bequeath his personal property (movable property as distinguished from real estate) to another by will. Personal property so transferred is a legacy, and the recipient of the property is a legatee. The terms "legacy" and "devise" and "legatee" and "devisee" are now used interchangeably in many jurisdictions. Under the UPC all gifts made by will are known as devises, and the recipient is the devisee, regardless of whether or not the gifts consist of real or personal property.

§ 19.4   Locating the Will

If the decedent died testate, it is necessary to locate the original will so it can be presented to the appropriate court for probate. Probate of the will is its presentation to the court to have it declared valid. It is important to note, however, that the word "probate" is now used to mean all proceedings concerning the administration of estates.

If the decedent was a client of the law firm, you should review all his files, as they frequently contain information that will be necessary in the administration of the estate. The files may contain a copy of the decedent's will. If they do, you should have copies available at the initial conference, together with any information as to the location of the original.

It is the custom in some areas for the attorney to hold the original will for his client. Some attorneys are hesitant to do this, however, since a will belongs to the testator (person who makes the will), and one important characteristic of a will is that it is a personal possession of the testator. The testator may designate who will hold the will for him and may request possession of the document at any time. Because of the very personal nature of a will, should the testator desire to revoke the will, he must do so personally. A will may be revoked by mutilation, cancellation, destruction, or execution of a new will. It must, however, be destroyed by the testator. In many wills the first paragraph is a revocation of all prior wills. A will which was unintentionally destroyed by the testator may still be probated if the contents can be established to the satisfaction of the jurisdictional court. Marriage or divorce subsequent to the date of the will, however, may modify the terms of the will.

Some people place their wills in their safe deposit boxes, in home safes, or even in desk drawers at home. If the family believes that the decedent left a will, it is incumbent upon them to search through his personal belongings until they find it. Sometimes the decedent's will is stored in his safe deposit box, which may be sealed by state law upon his death, requiring that the attorney and family take special procedures to obtain access to the will.

An amendment, addition, or supplement to a will is known as a codicil or literally a "little will." If there are one or more codicils in existence, they will be subject to the same rules and treatment as wills in the probate proceedings.

If the decedent died without having left a will, he is said to have died intestate. His estate is then administered and distributed according to the laws of his state of domicile.

§ 19.5 Determination of Heirship

Proof of heirship is the judicial determination of the identity of those persons who are entitled to inherit the decedent's property under state law if the decedent dies intestate. In many states this proof is an essential part of the probate proceeding. It is also necessary in some states to notify these heirs of the pending probate proceeding regardless of whether or not they are named as beneficiaries in the will. This notice is extremely important, since it affords any heir at law not named as a beneficiary an opportunity to object to the admission of the will to probate. There is a statutory time period within which an objection to the will must be made. In the case of an intestate proceeding, the heirs at law must be notified, since they will ultimately share in the distribution of the estate.

§ 19.6   Proof of Heirship

In many jurisdictions heirship is proved by the filing of an affidavit of death and heirship. This is simply an affidavit executed by one or two family members (heirs are not allowed to sign this affidavit in some states) or close friends who attest their knowledge of:

- The date of the decedent's death;
- The decedent's address at the time of his death;
- The decedent's age at the time of his death;
- Facts about the decedent's marriages, surviving spouse, and children.

The affidavit is specific about the number of times the decedent was married and the children who were born of each marriage. Additionally, if there were any children who died before (predeceased) the decedent, the names of these children are listed as well as their issue. In an intestate estate, these children would probably inherit their parent's share.

§ 19.7   Minor Heirs

Should there be minor heirs, that is, persons who are under the statutory age of legal competence, the court in most states appoints a guardian to protect the minors' interests during any court proceedings. The court is concerned with the minor child or ward who cannot represent himself. The appointment of a guardian of the estate varies from jurisdiction to jurisdiction and may be an attorney disinterested in the proceeding, the natural guardian (parent), or the legally appointed guardian of the child.

§ 19.8   Functions of Estate Administration or Probate

Probate serves three main functions:

1. Identification of the assets so that they can be distributed to the beneficiaries
2. Protection of the creditors
3. Determination of the tax liability of the estate

§ 19.9   Protection of Creditors

Since distribution cannot be made to the heirs without paying the debts of the decedent, it is necessary also to determine what those debts are. Usually, the family members are aware of the debts, and if they are not, the creditors notify either the attorney for the estate or a family member of their claim. Most states also have a procedure by which creditors may protect their claims against estates.

All states make provisions in their laws to protect claims of creditors of an estate. While the method for making the claim varies from state to state, there is always a specific time period within which a creditor must assert his claim in order to protect it. Generally, a claim is filed by presenting it either to the court or to the executor or representative of the estate.

In some states a claim must be made for such items as funeral expenses and expenses of the last illness, as well as for ordinary debts. However, in other states funeral expenses and expenses of last illness are paid routinely as expenses of administration.

In some states the executor or representative may pay any debts presented to him routinely, while in other states the executor must advertise his intent to pay the debts and must have court approval. Generally, if an executor or representative wishes to disallow a particular debt submitted by a creditor, it is necessary for him to file his intent to disallow the claim with the court within a specific period of time after the claim is presented to him. The principal purpose of these provisions is to ensure that the creditor does not suffer a loss from having extended credit to the decedent.

§ 19.10 Death Taxes

The federal government, the District of Columbia, and most states have some form of death tax. This means that either the decedent's estate or its beneficiaries are taxed in connection with the distribution of the decedent's property. There are three types of death taxes:

1. Estate taxes, a tax on the property constituting the estate

2. Inheritance (or succession) taxes, a tax on the transfer of property

3. "Pickup" taxes

§ 19.11 Estate Tax

An estate tax is a tax imposed upon the privilege of transmitting property at death and thus is payable upon the entire amount of the taxable estate, that is, the gross estate consisting of probate and nonprobate assets less certain allowable deductions and exemptions. The federal government imposes an estate tax. As of 1987 no federal estate tax return is required if the gross estate is less than $600,000. If a return must be filed, it is filed within nine months from the date of death with the regional service center of the Internal Revenue Service in the area of the decedent's domicile. It is very important that the legal secretary calendar the date that the Federal Estate Tax Return is due because severe penalties are imposed if the estate tax return is not filed and the taxes paid timely. Deferral of payment and/or an extension of time within which to file the return are available in special circumstances upon proper application.

Some states also levy an estate tax, either alone or in conjunction with a "pickup" tax.

§ 19.12 Inheritance Tax

An inheritance tax is the most frequently encountered state death tax. Inheritance taxes are imposed upon the amount received by each beneficiary. Generally, each beneficiary is granted an exemption based upon his family relationship to the decedent (the closer the relationship the larger the exemption). The balance is taxed in accordance with a rate schedule provided by that state's laws. Frequently, the rates also vary depending upon the closeness of the relationship between the beneficiary and the decedent. The deadline for this return, if required, should also be calendared.

§ 19.13 "Pickup" Tax

Some states have what is commonly referred to as a "pickup" tax. In computing federal estate taxes, the government allows a credit for state death taxes which are paid. This credit is allowed regardless of what the state death taxes are. In the states having a "pickup" tax, this credit then becomes the amount of state death taxes.

§ 19.14 Final Personal Income Tax Return

The decedent's final personal income tax year ends on the date of his death. The decedent's spouse, if any, is entitled to file a joint return for the year in which the decedent dies if that spouse remains unmarried at the end of the year. The representative of the estate is responsible for filing this return with the spouse if one survives.

§ 19.15 Fiduciary Income Tax Returns

At the time of death, the decedent's estate becomes a separate entity for income tax purposes, and all income derived from probate assets must be reported on a Fiduciary Income Tax Return. The tax year starts on the date of decedent's death and may end on any date chosen by the representative; provided, however, that the tax year may be no more than 12 months in length and must end on the last day of a month. The choice of a tax year for the estate depends upon when the most favorable tax treatment of the income can be obtained.

§ 19.16   Identification of the Assets

The assets of the decedent are things of value which he owns. Not all of a decedent's assets are necessarily included in his probate estate. The decedent's property which forms his probate estate is specifically set forth by law. It is dependent also upon the form of ownership of the property.

EXAMPLES:

If a decedent owned property with anyone else in joint tenancy with right of survivorship, that property would automatically belong to the other owner upon the decedent's death. It would not form a part of the probate estate, but all or part of it may be a part of his gross estate for death tax purposes. On the other hand, if the decedent owned property as a tenant in common with someone else, then the undivided interest which the decedent owned in the property would form a part of his probate estate. If the decedent owned a life insurance policy payable to a named beneficiary upon his death, that policy would not be part of his probate estate. On the other hand, if the decedent owned a life insurance policy payable to his estate, that policy would form part of the probate estate. If the decedent owned property which was titled in beneficiaries other than his estate, particularly in certain types of trusts (property held by one party for the benefit of another), that property would not be included in his probate estate.

Regardless of whether the decedent died testate or intestate, it is necessary for the attorney to develop a list of the decedent's assets, both probate and non-probate. The attorney needs to know whether at the time of his death the decedent owned or had an interest in any of the following:

- Real estate, as well as the form of ownership of each parcel
- Mortgages, promissory notes, or real estate installment sale contracts payable to decedent
- Stocks, bonds, and other types of securities
- Life insurance on decedent's life
- Life insurance owned by decedent on the life of another
- Oil, mineral, timber, and gas interests
- Cash, bank accounts, savings certificates, etc.
- Interests in unincorporated businesses or partnerships
- Annuities, IRA, and Keogh plans
- Pension, profit sharing, and other employee benefit plans

- Assets in certain types of trusts

- Farm equipment, livestock, and crops

- Gifts made by decedent within three years of death in excess of $10,000 per year for each donee

- Powers of appointment

- Large amounts of jewelry

- Coin or stamp collections

- Antiques

- Art objects

- Household goods

- Vehicles

- Death benefits

- Uncashed checks in decedent's possession

- Payroll checks receivable

- Accounts receivable

- Tax refunds for decedent's final tax year

The foregoing is by no means inclusive of all types of assets that may be encountered but is shown to give some idea of the many different kinds of assets.

The form of ownership of each item must be ascertained to determine whether it is a probate asset or a non-probate asset. Often, compiling an accurate list of all assets of the decedent which comprise his gross estate is the most time-consuming step in the administration of an estate. It may be necessary to have several conferences with the family members before a complete list is compiled. It is also usually necessary to correspond with banks, savings and loan associations, stockbrokers, the former employer of the decedent, and insurance companies to get all of the information you need to handle the estate. Not only is it necessary to compile a list of assets, but it is also necessary to determine the values of the various assets as of the date of death. This process can become quite complicated. For some assets, such as bank accounts, this can be accomplished quite simply by writing to the bank and requesting that it furnish you with the date of death balance plus accrued interest to that date. However, many assets do not have such a clearly obtainable value and require the use of formulas and guidelines used by the Internal Revenue Service or professional appraisers. The exact procedures may also vary depending upon the jurisdiction and the size of the estate.

§ 19.17   The Estate Representative

The person who handles this administration is known as the personal representative (representative). This term is used in the Uniform Probate Code to mean anyone who handles the administration regardless of whether the appointment is by will or by the court in cases of intestacy. In many jurisdictions the formal designation of the personal representative depends upon whether the estate is testate or intestate or whether a representative is named in the will.

In the case of a testate succession the will usually designates someone to serve as the estate's representative. That person is referred to as the executor (male or entity) or executrix (female).

However, if the executor so named is unable or unwilling to serve, the court appoints a representative, and that representative is known as the administrator c.t.a. (or administratrix c.t.a.) (the Latin abbreviation for cum testamento annexo meaning *with will annexed*). If the decedent died intestate, then the representative appointed by the court is the administrator or the administratrix. However, each of these persons serves the same function and has basically the same duties. In the legal field, many use all of these terms interchangeably, although in the actual legal documents the appropriate designation should be used.

A testator may give the executor a great deal of leeway and fully outline in the will the powers accorded the executor. This enables the executor to go about the business of administering the estate without requesting authority from the court to handle transactions such as sale of estate assets. A will may also provide that the executor need not provide a surety bond. The surety bond is required for the protection of both the heirs and the creditors. The surety bond is often in the form of a commercial bond (similar to an insurance policy) issued by an insurance company which, for a premium, insures that the executor will properly perform his duties. The court may in some states override the waiver of the bond by the testator and require the executor to post bond. Some states now give executors certain statutory powers whether or not they are specifically set out in the will.

There are certain requirements (in addition to posting bond) that the representative must meet to be qualified to serve as the representative. Once he meets the requirements, the court issues letters testamentary (in testate matters) or letters of administration (in intestate matters) to the representative. These letters give the representative authority to act.

Usually, the representative acts under court supervision. The will or state statute may give the representative some freedom as to how much court authority is necessary to perform certain acts (such as paying bills or selling assets). However, it may be necessary for the representative to make periodic accountings to the court concerning the administration of the estate.

There are alternatives to probate that do not require the appointment of a representative. These kinds of proceedings are usually reserved for small estates passing to close relatives or having certain limited types of assets. It is not possible to discuss every conceivable alternative in this chapter, but the important thing for the student to realize is that there are many alternatives available to the beneficiaries in the administration of estates.

§ 19.18   Initial Client Interview

The initial contact with the law firm is generally made by one or more of the decedent's closest relatives. An appointment is usually scheduled for a time as soon as practicable following the funeral.

The initial interview generally includes the attorney, the decedent's spouse, children, or other close relatives. It may also include the person named as executor of the decedent's will if it is someone other than a family member. The executor is the person named in the will to carry out the terms of the will. The secretary or a legal assistant may also be included in the initial conference.

Most firms have developed client interview forms for probate matters which they use to ensure that they secure all needed information. (See Illustration 19–1.)

If the will is available for the initial conference, it is read at that time. The reading of the will, however, is not nearly so dramatic as is depicted in the movies. In fact, the family usually is familiar with the contents of the will before the conference with the attorney. At that time the attorney answers any questions any member of the family might have concerning the terms of the will.

It may also be useful for you to locate a copy of any printed obituaries appearing in the local newspapers, as they will list survivors and relationships. This will help both you and the attorney to become familiar with the family structure prior to the interview. Since it is necessary for the attorney to secure biographical data concerning the decedent's family, both the attorney and the decedent's family will be appreciative if some of the information can be obtained from the files.

Illustration 19–1

CLIENT INTERVIEW FORM

GENERAL INFORMATION

Estate of _____

Known aliases _____

Date of birth _____   Place of birth _____

Date of death _____   Place of death _____

Name of spouse _____   Date of birth of spouse _____

If spouse is deceased, state date of death _____

Decedent's social security no. _____

Spouse's social security no. _____

Date of marriage to surviving spouse _____

Domicile at date of marriage _____

Year domicile established in this state _____

For each devisee, heir or other interested person, state:

Full name and relationship to decedent	Address	Date of birth	Social Security #

Decedent's business or occupation _____

Employer identification number, if any _____

Name and address of personal representative _____

_____

Business phone _____   Home phone _____

Address of decedent at date of death _____

_____

Did the decedent have a safe deposit box? _____

If so, state: Name of bank _____ and joint depositor(s), if any

_____

ASSET INFORMATION

It is suggested sheets similar to the following should be prepared for each type of asset. In some cases you will need a separate sheet for every item of property within that category while for others you will be able to list several on the same sheet. These forms can be easily modified to meet specific information requirements of your state.

REAL ESTATE

Estate of _____

Probate _____

Non–Probate _____

* * * * *

Legal description of property _____

_____

_____

Name or names in which title stands and form of ownership _____

_____

Homestead? Yes _____   No _____

Abstract _____   Torrens _____

Location of abstract of title or Torrens certificate _____

_____

Date of death value $_____

Mortgages or other encumbrances:

Payee _____ Loan No. _____

Balance on date of death $_____

Property identification number _____

NOTE: It is helpful to obtain a copy of the most recent real estate tax
        statement and the deed to the present owner.

BANK ACCOUNTS

Estate of _____

Probate _____

Non–Probate _____

Name of bank _____

Type of account _____
No. of account _____

Approximate balance $_____
Date of death balance $_____

Name or names in which account stands and form of ownership _____

_____

LIFE INSURANCE

Estate of _____

Probate _____

Non–Probate _____

Name of company _____ Policy No. _____

Date of issuance _____ Face amount of policy _____

Date of death value _____

Beneficiary and relationship _____

Policy owner _____ Date established _____

Any known loans _____

NOTE: Form 712 should be requested from the insurance company for each
        policy of life insurance on the decedent's life.

STOCKS AND BONDS

Estate of _____

Probate _____

Non–Probate _____

* * * *

Name of company _____

Certificate No. _____ Dated _____

Issued to _____ for _____ shares

Transfer Agent _____

Date of death value $_____ Source _____

U.S. SAVINGS BONDS

Estate of _____

Probate _____

Non–Probate _____   Joint Owner _____

Date of issuance	Denomination	Serial number	Date of death value
_____	_____	_____	_____
_____	_____	_____	_____
_____	_____	_____	_____
_____	_____	_____	_____

MISCELLANEOUS SECURITIES & INVESTMENTS

Estate of _____

Probate _____

Non–Probate _____

Complete description of security, including type, numbers, date, approximate value, maturity date, if any, etc.

_____

_____

_____

Name or names in which security stands and form of ownership _____

_____

MISCELLANEOUS PERSONAL PROPERTY

Estate of _____

Probate _____

Non–Probate _____

Description	Joint owner or beneficiary, if any	Value
Federal income tax refund		
State income tax refund		
Household goods and furnishings		
Automobile		

Year and make

Vehicle ID or serial #

Final payroll check

Company _____

Cash in decedent's possession

Uncashed checks in decedent's possession (List)

633

Jewelry or other personal property of intrinsic value (List)

Retirement and/or deferred compensation plans (obtain copy of plan)

Interests in partnerships

IRA and Keogh Plans

PROPERTY TRANSFERRED WITHIN THREE YEARS

Estate of _____

Description _____

_____

_____

Transferee _____ Relationship to decedent _____

Date of transfer _____

Value of transfer _____

Were gift tax returns filed? _____

NOTE: If gift tax returns were filed, copies should be obtained.

EXPENSES OF ADMINISTRATION

Estate of _____

Expenses of last illness:

_____　$_____

_____　_____

_____　_____

_____　_____

Funeral expenses:

Mortuary _____　$_____

Cemetery _____　$_____

Flowers _____　$_____

Marker _____　$_____

Honorariums _____　$_____

Other _____　$_____

Debts of decedent:

_____　$_____

_____　_____

_____　_____

Taxes:

_____　$_____

Attorney's fees: _____　$_____

Miscellaneous: _____　$_____

§ 19.19　Method of Handling Estate Administration

In most jurisdictions there is usually a choice as to the type of probate proceeding to use to handle the estate. This is true of both testate and intestate successions. After the attorney has compiled a list of the items which comprise the estate of the decedent and determined who his heirs and beneficiaries are, he is then in a position to make a recommendation as to what he believes the most efficient method of probate is. Often, if some of the heirs or beneficiaries are minor children, there is less choice of the method of probate, and the proceedings may be more complicated. In some jurisdictions abbreviated or summary proceedings are available for estates that are valued up to a specific amount of money. It will be up to you to learn the methods which are available in your state. Ask the attorney or a senior secretary or legal assistant to help you find the applicable statutes for your state.

The value of the gross estate determines whether a state death tax return and a federal estate tax return are required. Based on the value of the gross estate, the attorney can also estimate what the tax liability is.

§ 19.20 Probate Procedures

The domicile of the decedent at the time of his death generally controls where a proceeding must be commenced. A domicile does not have the same legal meaning as a residence. A person may maintain many residences, but he can be domiciled at only one address. The necessary pleadings will depend upon whether you are dealing with a testate or intestate estate and whether informal proceedings may be utilized. The pleadings vary, too, with the jurisdiction. It is up to you, therefore, to familiarize yourself with the pleadings used in your state for each kind of proceeding. You probably will have sample forms of pleadings in a forms file or procedures manual.

In most instances, though, some kind of petition is necessary to begin the proceeding. Whether you utilize a printed form or have to type the complete pleading depends upon the procedures in your state. Probably the affidavit of death and heirship, if required, will be filed at the same time that the initial petition is filed. You may also file pleadings regarding the proof of the will and notice to creditors and heirs at that time.

In the event there is more than one validly executed will in existence at the time of a decedent's death, the will bearing the most recent date usually controls.

In most states at least one court hearing is required to admit the will to probate, establish heirship, and appoint a representative for the estate. The major exception to the hearing requirement is in informal proceedings under the UPC where only a conference with a registrar is necessary. The registrar is either a judge or a person such as the clerk of court designated as a registrar by the court.

§ 19.21 Proof of Will

Proof of will is that process by which a decedent's will is validated (proved) and admitted to probate. In some states this is done by one or more of the witnesses to the will filing an affidavit that they were in fact witnesses to the will and that the testator was of sound mind at the time he made the will. In other states it is necessary that one or more of the witnesses actually appear in open court and give oral testimony as to the circumstances under which they witnessed the execution of the will.

§ 19.22 The Self–Proved Will

The concept of the self-proved will was introduced by the UPC. A self-proved will contains not only the signatures of the testator and witnesses but also the acknowledgment of a notary public attesting to the signatures of the testator and witnesses, the soundness of the testator's mind, and his intention to declare the will to be his last will and testament. In those states in which the UPC has been adopted, a self-proved will needs no further proof. This does not mean that a state cannot make statutory provision for self-proved wills without adopting the UPC.

§ 19.23 Contesting the Will

Any heir who is disgruntled because he either was omitted from the will or did not receive the full bequest to which he thought he was entitled may file a petition to contest the will. Most states have a specific time period within which this must be done. Such a contest follows the standard procedures of civil litigation. Notice and service on the parties involved are required. The petitioner must allege to the court the reasons for the contest and must prove undue influence, fraud, or mistake in the making of the will. Should the petitioner receive a favorable decision in a will contest, the will is declared invalid, is not admitted to probate, and the laws of intestacy apply.

§ 19.24 Administering the Assets

The process of administering an estate is just what the name implies. The representative collects assets; liquidates assets if necessary or prudent; pays debts, funeral and administration expenses, taxes, and claims; and determines the distributions to be made. Liquidation is simply the process of converting assets of whatever form into cash for easier distribution when the estate is closed. If property is not liquidated and is distributed in the same form received, it is said to have been distributed in kind.

The estate of a decedent is generally administered in the state of his domicile; however, if the decedent owned any real estate or tangible personalty in another state, a probate proceeding must be opened there. This procedure is known as an ancillary proceeding.

As soon as feasible after appointment and prior to the statutory deadline date, the representative must file a complete inventory of the property owned by the decedent, including appraised or approximate values as required by law. An accurate inventory is important, as it serves as the basis for taxation purposes as well as subsequent accounting purposes. For this reason it is sometimes necessary to file an addendum to the inventory or to amend it if additional property is discovered after preparation and filing of the inventory.

§ 19.25 Accounting and Distribution

In all except informal probate matters, settlement of the estate is accomplished by the representative's filing a final account with the court; this account summarizes all of the transactions involved in the administration. This would include the payment of all claims, taxes, expenses of administration, liquidation of assets as necessary or prudent, and any other transactions that may have taken place. At the same time the representative petitions the court for distribution of the remaining assets. In some states a hearing is required on this account while in others the hearing may be waived by consent of the heirs. The court, after submission of these documents and the hearing (if required), approves the account and orders the distribution of assets. At the time distribution is made, the representative must obtain a receipt from each devisee or legatee to file with the court. Thereafter he is discharged from his responsibilities. If there was a surety bond required, it is ordered terminated.

§ 19.26 Guardianships or Conservatorships

You learned in the chapter on Litigation that minors do not have the legal capacity to act for themselves. Therefore the courts appoint someone to act for them concerning their legal affairs. The same is true of persons of adult age who do not possess either the mental or physical capacity to care for their own affairs. Someone must be appointed to handle their affairs for them. These persons are often considered as wards of the court, and the court appoints one or more guardians or conservators to protect the ward's personal needs and/or preserve his financial resources.

Terminology, when referring to these persons, varies from jurisdiction to jurisdiction. The term "minor" usually means someone under the age of legal majority in a particular state (usually 18 to 21 years of age). The term "incompetent" or "disabled adult" is applied to persons of adult age. Although state laws vary, guardianships generally may be initiated for both minors and adults while conservatorships are generally limited to disabled adults.

When it is necessary to appoint a guardian for a minor, the parent is usually appointed. The parent is usually referred to as the natural guardian. In some instances, however, if the court determines that the interests of the natural guardian may conflict with the interests of the minor, the court may appoint a guardian ad litem to represent the minor in that particular legal proceeding. It is for that particular purpose only.

When it is necessary to appoint a guardian or conservator for a disabled adult, it is necessary to present detailed proof to the court that the adult is in fact disabled. The disabled adult is usually served with a copy of the petition seeking the guardianship, or conservatorship, although in some states physically disabled adults may voluntarily petition for conservatorship on their own behalf. An attorney or a guardian ad litem may be appointed to represent the disabled adult. Once the statutory delays have run, the court receives testimony from a physician, as well as from the attorney appointed to represent the adult, as to the adult's inability to handle his own affairs and/or to care for his physical needs. Some states use the terms guardianship and conservatorship interchangeably. In other states guardianships and conservatorships are separate and distinct proceedings. The basic difference in these states is that a person under guardianship is declared incompetent to manage his own affairs. A person under conservatorship does not lose his civil rights and thus is free to execute a will, marry, vote, etc. Conservatorships and guardianships of adults terminate when the ward regains his mental or physical capacity or upon death. Guardianships of minors terminate when the ward reaches legal age.

In both guardianships and conservatorships, bonds are usually required of the guardian or conservator. These bonds are usually in the form of commercial insurance policies and guarantee that the guardian or conservator will properly perform his duties.

It is necessary for the guardian or conservator to file an inventory of the assets of the ward and to keep detailed accounts of his administration. He must file periodic accountings with the court; and when the guardianship or conservatorship terminates, he must file a final accounting before he is discharged and his bond terminated.

§ 19.27   Summary

The foregoing, very generally, covers the major steps to be taken in the administration of estates, guardianships, and conservatorships. A legal secretary's value will increase as she becomes familiar with procedures in her locale and establishes her own checklist of statutory requirements and steps to be taken.

CHAPTER 20

BANKRUPTCY

Table of Sections

---

§ 20.1   Definition

A bankruptcy is a proceeding under Title 11 of the United States Code whereby an individual or a legal entity requests protection under the terms of that law. The protection given a debtor under the Bankruptcy Code is the opportunity for financial rehabilitation.

§ 20.2   History

The Bankruptcy Code is a federal law. Under the Constitution, Congress has the power to establish "uniform laws on the subject of bankruptcies throughout the United States" (Article 1, Section 9). Five such national bankruptcy laws have been enacted. The present Bankruptcy Code, Public Law 95–598, was enacted November 6, 1978, with principal provisions effective October 1, 1979. The Bankruptcy Code has been amended by the Bankruptcy Amendments and Federal Judgeship Act of 1984 (Public Law 98–353) and the Bankruptcy Judges, United States Trustees and Family Farmer Bankruptcy Act of 1986 (Public Law 99–554).

§ 20.3   Options Available Under Code

Under the Bankruptcy Code, a debtor (including a business debtor) continues to have the option available since 1938 either to be declared a bankrupt or to have the protection of the bankruptcy court while he attempts to pay his debts from future earnings. These options are discussed in greater detail later in this chapter.

§ 20.4   Terminology Differences Under the 1978 Code

Since adoption of the first bankruptcy law, a person seeking relief under the law was known as a bankrupt, and the proceeding was known as bankruptcy. The 1978 Code abolishes both terms simply by not using them. A person filing for relief under the Bankruptcy Code is called a debtor. The proceeding is a *liquidation.* The relief the debtor seeks is a *discharge in bankruptcy.*

A person or entity may file for relief under chapter 7 (straight liquidation as discussed herein), chapter 11 (reorganization), chapter 13 (payment plan), or chapter 12 (Family Farmer plan). There is also a chapter for bankrupt municipalities (chapter 9).

§ 20.5   Definitions

Familiarity with the following terms should help the student better understand this chapter.

- Consumer Bankruptcy—a bankruptcy filed by an individual (or husband and wife) who is not in business

- Business Bankruptcy—a bankruptcy filed by a business entity—a sole proprietorship, a corporation, partnership, or other such business entity

- Claim—a debt owing by the debtor to another

- Debtor—the person or entity seeking relief under the Bankruptcy Code

- Consumer Debt—a debt incurred by an individual primarily for a personal, household, or family use

- Creditor—an entity to which the debtor owes money

- Entity—a person or legally recognized organization

- Insolvent—when the total debt of an entity is greater than the total value of its property

- Family farmer—an individual or corporation or partnership owned by one or more engaged in a farming operation with a regular annual income

- Lien—a legally enforceable claim against property of a debtor to secure repayment of a debt or obligation

- Judicial lien—a lien obtained by judgment or other judicial process

- Liquidation—the conversion by sale of all of a debtor's non-exempt property

- Exempt property—all of the property of a debtor which is, by virtue of the Bankruptcy Code or state statute, not attachable in a bankruptcy

- Trustee—the individual charged with the duty of liquidating a debtor's estate

- Estate—all of a debtor's non-exempt property

- Case—the entire bankruptcy proceedings of a debtor

- Adversary proceedings—any individual lawsuits brought within a case

§ 20.6 Purpose of Liquidation (Bankruptcy)

The purpose of liquidation (bankruptcy) is to grant the honest debtor who is overwhelmed by his debts a chance to make a fresh start in life and to remain a useful member of society by relieving him of the oppressive burden of his debts. As a condition for receiving this relief, however, the debtor must turn over to the bankruptcy court all property which he owns which is not exempt by law. (Exempt property is discussed more fully later in this chapter.) This property is converted into money and is used to pay costs of administration and creditors to the extent possible. Usually, however, there is so little money realized that creditors receive only a small fraction or none of the money owed to them.

§ 20.7   Need for an Attorney

A debtor contemplating filing for relief under the Bankruptcy Code normally requires the services of an attorney. He needs an attorney to:

1. Advise him whether liquidation or an alternative form of relief is the best solution to his financial problems, and if so

2. Prepare the necessary legal papers incident to filing bankruptcy

3. Represent him during the course of the bankruptcy proceedings

If a person encounters difficulty in securing the services of an attorney, he may be able to obtain a list of names of attorneys who accept bankruptcy cases from the bar association or Legal Aid Society serving the area in which he lives. The bankruptcy clerk of court, although he may not recommend any particular attorney, may be able to furnish the names of attorneys who regularly file bankruptcy petitions in that court.

§ 20.8   Bankruptcy Courts and Jurisdiction

There is a United States Bankruptcy Court for each United States District Court. This court has exclusive jurisdiction over the debtor, all of his property no matter where it is located, and over any and all lawsuits by or against the debtor. Like all federal courts, any lawsuit brought in this court can be heard by a jury.

§ 20.9   Venue

A debtor can file for bankruptcy only in the district where that debtor has resided or had his main place of business for the preceding six months or the majority of the preceding six months.

§ 20.10   Bankruptcy Court Officers

The bankruptcy court has, as its officers, certain persons whose job it is to administer an estate. They include:

• Bankruptcy Judge—The judge presides over the bankruptcy court and hears all litigation pertaining to the case. It is the bankruptcy judge who determines whether a debtor is entitled to a discharge.

- Clerk of Court—The clerk has the identical duties of a federal clerk of court; and in addition, in some districts he is the presiding officer at the first meeting of creditors of a debtor.

- Interim Trustee—An interim trustee is appointed at the commencement of a bankruptcy case and serves in the capacity of trustee until the first meeting of creditors of the debtor. Interim trustees in most districts are chosen from a panel of private individuals appointed by the United States courts.

- Trustee—A trustee is named upon the filing of the petition and is made permanent at the first meeting of creditors. The trustee is the representative of the estate. It is the duty of the trustee to recover all assets of the debtor not exempt under the law and to liquidate those assets for the benefit of the debtor's creditors.

§ 20.11　Kinds of Bankruptcy

There are two ways in which a bankruptcy case can be started:

1. By the filing of a voluntary petition or

2. By the filing of an involuntary petition

The terms *voluntary* and *involuntary* mean just that. In a voluntary case, a debtor decides to seek relief under the Code. In an involuntary case, creditors ask the court to place a debtor in liquidation. Of course, to accomplish that, the creditors must prove certain facts specified in the Code. Most bankruptcies are voluntary cases. Consequently, the information contained in this chapter is primarily applicable to the individual who voluntarily is seeking a discharge in bankruptcy from the court under the provisions of the Bankruptcy Code. These are generally referred to as straight chapter 7 bankruptcies (liquidation).

§ 20.12　Conditions to Be Met by Debtor in Voluntary Cases

An individual voluntarily seeking a discharge of his debts under chapter 7 in the bankruptcy court must meet certain conditions, although these conditions are not specified in the Bankruptcy Code.

- He must owe one or more debts, although there is no minimum or maximum as to the amount of debts which he must owe. (There is no requirement that the individual be insolvent. Normally, however, the individual seeking a discharge in bankruptcy is either insolvent—that is, his liabilities exceed his assets—or he is unable to pay his debts as they accrue.)

- He cannot file a petition to be adjudicated a bankrupt for the purpose of perpetrating a fraud.

- In addition, he may not file for bankruptcy if he previously has been granted a discharge in a proceeding commenced within six years prior to the date of the filing of the petition in bankruptcy.

§ 20.13   Filing the Petition in Voluntary Cases

Bankruptcy begins with the filing of a petition for an order for relief with the Clerk of the United States Bankruptcy Court having venue.

§ 20.14   Filing Fee in Voluntary Cases

A filing fee must be paid to the clerk at the time the petition is filed unless by local rule of court it may be paid in installments. This fee is in addition to the fees charged by the attorney for his services. The debtor may not receive a discharge unless the filing fee is paid in full. Under the Bankruptcy Code, a husband and wife may file under a single petition and pay one filing fee. (Local rules of court are very important in bankruptcy matters and must be followed very carefully. If your office does not have a copy of the rules, request a copy from the clerk of the bankruptcy court.)

§ 20.15   Significance of Filing a Petition in Voluntary Cases

The act of the debtor in filing a petition in bankruptcy has far-reaching significance:

- The petition serves as the application by the debtor for an order of relief, *i.e.*, for a discharge of his debts without further action on his part.

- The petition operates as an automatic stay, applicable to all creditors of the debtor, prohibiting further collection efforts.

- An estate is created by law consisting of any property and interests possessed by the debtor which are not exempt under applicable federal or state law. This estate is administered by a trustee for the benefit of creditors of the debtor.

§ 20.16   Dischargeable and Non-Dischargeable Debts

The filing of a petition for relief acts as a request for a discharge of all of a person's debts. A discharge frees the debtor from all of the debtor's pre-bankruptcy debts. If no objection to the discharge of a debt owed by the debtor is made by a creditor or by the trustee within the time set by the bankruptcy court, then the debtor is relieved of all of his debts except for those which are not dissolved by the bankruptcy.

§ 20.17   Non-Dischargeable Debts

Debts which are not discharged by the chapter 7 bankruptcy are itemized in the Code and include:

- Certain taxes

- Alimony, child support, or property settlement agreements incident to such

- Debts arising from fines, penalties, or forfeitures payable to a governmental unit

- Educational loans, if they first became due less than seven years before bankruptcy

- Debts not listed by the debtor on his schedules filed with the bankruptcy court

- Some of these may be discharged in a chapter 13 proceeding

§ 20.18   Complaint by Creditor to Have Debt Declared Non-Discharged

If a creditor believes that the debt owed him is not dischargeable, he has the right to file a complaint with the court to find that debt non-dischargeable. If the bankruptcy court, after a hearing, find this debt is not dischargeable, then it renders a judgment in favor of the creditor which is legally enforceable against the debtor. These petitions are usually filed by the creditors if the debtor obtained credit by fraudulent means, defrauded another, or owes another for willful or malicious injury.

§ 20.19   Secured and Unsecured Debts

Debts are also classified as secured or unsecured. Secured debts are those which are backed up by some kind of collateral.

EXAMPLE:

The debtor has a car for which he paid by borrowing the money from the bank. The bank made the loan and took a security interest in the car. The debtor purchased a home just as he did his car. He borrowed money from the bank, and the bank took a mortgage on the house as security. The debtor borrowed money from a finance company to consolidate his debts. The finance company loaned him the money and took a security interest in all his furniture and appliances.

These are secured debts, and the creditors are secured creditors. Unsecured debts are all of those which do not fit in the secured category, such as open accounts.

EXAMPLE:

The debtor has charge cards at a number of local department stores. The debtor has an American Express card and a Master-Card. The debtor has a charge account with his dentist and his family doctor.

These are unsecured debts and the creditors are unsecured creditors.

The debtor classifies (with his attorney's help) his debts accordingly when he files his schedules. If a creditor believes that he is a secured creditor, although he was listed as an unsecured creditor on the debtor's schedules, he may ask the court to be classified as a secured creditor.

As a technicality, a creditor is really secured only under bankruptcy definitions if the debt owed to it is equal to or less than the value of the collateral. It is unsecured for any deficiency. This does not apply to mortgages on real estate.

§ 20.20   Filing of Claims by Creditors

Creditors must file their claims with the bankruptcy court within the time set by the court or be barred from participating in any dividend which might be declared. There is a prescribed form for submitting proofs of claim which may be obtained from the bankruptcy court. If the creditor fails to file a claim, the trustee or a co-debtor may file a claim for the creditor.

§ 20.21   The Debtor's Estate

When a debtor files his petition, he actually surrenders all his property (except that which he is entitled to keep under the law) for the privilege of having his debts erased. At the time the petition is filed, the debtor's property comes under the control of the bankruptcy court. It is the responsibility of the trustee to liquidate the estate in the best interests of the creditors. There are many factors which the trustee must consider in his liquidation of the estate. The classification of debts is important, as secured creditors may be paid by priority over unsecured creditors. Also important is the fact that there is certain property which is exempt from the bankruptcy.

§ 20.22   Exempt Property

Although in theory the debtor surrenders all his property for the benefit of his creditors, he is entitled by law to keep certain items of his property. Such property is called exempt property. Until the 1978 Code there was no exempt property under federal law. Therefore, states made their own provisions as to exempt property. The federal exemption law permits the debtor to keep:

- Up to a maximum of $7,500 of equity in real estate or mobile home
- Up to $1,200 equity in a vehicle
- Up to $200 per item of personal property used in the household of the debtor up to $4,000
- Up to $500 equity in jewelry of the debtor
- Up to $750 in tools of trade of the debtor
- $400 plus any unused portion of the real estate exemption up to $3,750, which can be applied to any property of the debtor

There are various other exempt items—insurance, retirement, alimony, and the like—specifically itemized in the Code.

The Bankruptcy Code provides that if a state does not elect to replace these exemptions with its own, the federal exemptions apply to all bankruptcies filed in that state. However, the individual states have the right to "opt out" of the federal exemptions and set their own which may or may not be binding on all debtors filing for bankruptcy in that state depending on the law of the state. Many states have enacted their own exemptions. Generally, while each state has exemption statutes which vary from other states, some state exemptions are much more restrictive than the federal exemptions.

§ 20.23 Liquidation of the Estate

As discussed earlier, the trustee examines the economics of the debtor's entire financial situation. He is interested in how much money he can raise for the benefit of creditors. Important considerations are exempt property and equity in property.

§ 20.24 Equity

What is equity? Generally it is the difference between the value of a thing and what is owed on it.

EXAMPLE:

The debtor has a house worth $30,000. The mortgage balance is $15,000. His equity is $15,000.

It would seem as a practical matter that if the trustee sold the house, the debtor's estate would realize a profit of $15,000. However, that would be the case only if the state in which the debtor lives had overridden the federal exemption which provides for an equity exemption of $7,500 on a debtor's homestead. (Remember that the federal exemption applies if the state has not enacted its own exemption law to replace the federal one.) If a husband and wife own the home together and have filed a joint petition, they are each entitled to a $7,500 exemption or a total of a $15,000 exemption if the federal exemption applies. A bankruptcy court may not destroy the value of any valid security which a creditor has on property possessed by a debtor. Likewise, a debtor cannot expect to receive a discharge of his debts and at the same time keep the property without further liability. In other words, while the debtor may receive a discharge of the debt upon which the lien is based, the bankruptcy court may not destroy the lien itself. The trustee elects whether to take possession of the mortgaged property and sell it for the benefit of creditors or abandon it.

§ 20.25 Abandoned Property

Using the same example set out above, if a husband and wife had filed a joint petition and were entitled to the federal homestead exemption and if the trustee sold the property and paid the creditor $15,000 in payment of the mortgage and then paid the debtor and his wife $15,000 for their federal exemption, he would have no money left for creditors. Therefore, selling the property would serve no useful purpose, and the trustee usually abandons it. When the trustee abandons the property, the debtor becomes the owner again, subject only to valid liens.

§ 20.26 Reaffirmation of the Debt

If the trustee abandons the property, the debtor must decide whether he wishes to keep it subject to the mortgage. If he wishes to keep the house, he must continue to make the regular mortgage payments and pay any arrearage. The same is true for other debts secured by liens on property. He does not need to reaffirm the debt, since so long as he is making the payments and complying with the other terms of the mortgage, he is not in default, and the mere fact of bankruptcy is not a default.

Reaffirmation is appropriate only in limited situations, *i.e.*, where a credit card company offers to continue the line of credit, and the debtor for good reasons wishes to keep the credit card. But in such cases, either the attorney for the debtor must sign the reaffirmation stating that in his opinion the debtor fully understood what he was doing *and* that the attorney believes that the reaffirmation does not impose an undue hardship on the debtor or his dependents, *or* the debtor must appear in court and explain to the bankruptcy judge why it is in the debtor's best interests to do so. By not reaffirming the debt, if the debtor later defaults on his mortgage or car loan, etc., he will not be liable for any deficiency. See Illustration 20–1 for a form of a Reaffirmation Agreement.

Illustration 20–1

REAFFIRMATION AGREEMENT

B 240
(1/88)   REAFFIRMATION AGREEMENT

Debtor's Name	Bankruptcy Case No.

INSTRUCTIONS:

   1)   Write debtor's name and bankruptcy case number above.
   2)   Part A — Must be signed by both the debtor and the creditor.
   3)   Part B — Must be signed by the attorney who represents the debtor in
       this bankruptcy case.
   4)   Part C — Must be completed by the debtor if the debtor is **not** represented
       by an attorney in this bankruptcy case.
   5)   File the completed form by mailing or delivering to the Bankruptcy Clerk.
   6)   Attach written agreement, if any.

                                        COURT USE ONLY

PART A — AGREEMENT

Creditor's Name and Address	Summary of Terms of the New Agreement
	a) Principal Amount $ _____
	Interest Rate (APR) _____
	Monthly Payments $ _____
	b) Description of Security: _____
Date Set for Discharge Hearing (if any)	Present Market Value $ _____

The parties understand that this agreement is purely voluntary and that the debtor may rescind the agreement at any time prior to discharge or within 60 days after such agreement is filed with the court, whichever occurs later, by giving notice of recission to the creditor.

_____   _____
   Date   *Signature of Debtor*

_____   _____
  Signature of Creditor   *Signature of Joint Debtor*

PART B — ATTORNEY'S DECLARATION

   This agreement represents a fully informed and voluntary agreement that does not impose an undue hardship on the debtor or any dependent of the debtor.

_____   _____
   Date   *Signature of Debtor's Attorney*

PART C — MOTION FOR COURT APPROVAL OF AGREEMENT — Complete only where debtor is not represented by an attorney.

I (we), the debtor, affirm the following to be true and correct:

   1)   I am not represented by an attorney in connection with this bankruptcy case.
   2)   My current monthly net income is $ _____
   3)   My current monthly expenses total $ _____, including any payment due under this
       agreement.
   4)   I believe that this agreement is in my best interest because _____

Therefore, I ask the court for an order approving this reaffirmation agreement.

_____   _____
   Date   *Signature of Debtor*

                    _____
                    Signature of Joint Debtor

PART D — COURT ORDER

The court grants the debtor's motion and approves the voluntary agreement upon the terms specified above.

_____   _____
   Date   *Bankruptcy Judge*

                                                  [E7875]

---

§ 20.27   Sale of Property

There are many instances, of course, when there is sufficient equity in property over and above any exemptions to which the debtor is entitled to make a sale profitable for the estate. In those instances, the trustee offers the property for sale. Particularly in the case of chattels such as furniture and appliances, those items are much more valuable to the debtor himself than to third parties. Trustees therefore often sell those types of items to the debtor himself, since he can get a better price from the debtor than from someone else. The trustee often abandons those if their value is nominal.

§ 20.28   Closing Out the Estate

The administration of the estate is carried on by the trustee in accordance with specific duties which are set out in the Bankruptcy Code. Additionally, the trustee makes periodic accountings to the bankruptcy court as well as a final report to the bankruptcy court of the liquidation, including a detailed accounting of the money realized and disbursed and all property sold. At a final hearing, the trustee presents a final accounting to the court and disburses all funds on hand to the creditors in accordance with the bankruptcy court's order.

§ 20.29   Appointment of Interim Trustee

Promptly after filing of a petition in bankruptcy, an interim trustee is appointed. He serves in the capacity of trustee until the first creditors' meeting (discussed below) when the trustee is appointed.

§ 20.30   Notice to Creditors

Within a reasonable time after the petition is filed, normally at least 10 days but within 30 days, the bankruptcy court sends out notice by mail to all creditors listed by the debtor on his schedules of a meeting of creditors. The creditors are told they may (but are not required to) attend this meeting, elect a trustee, and question the debtor. In the same notice they are given information about filing claims. The creditors are also told that if they have a valid objection to the debtor's receiving a discharge, they must file a formal written objection within a specified number of days.

§ 20.31   First Meeting of Creditors

The debtor must attend this meeting (normally with his attorney) and answer any questions under oath which properly may be asked of him. The bankruptcy judge is not permitted to attend the meeting of creditors. A bankruptcy clerk or deputy clerk of court or a trustee presides at the meeting. At the first meeting of creditors, the debtor is questioned under oath by the presiding clerk or trustee and by any interested creditors who wish to do so. The debtor must be completely truthful and cooperative in answering questions concerning his financial status. Upon motion and order, the debtor may testify by written interrogatories.

§ 20.32 Election of Trustee

At the meeting of creditors, the creditors have the right to elect a trustee of their choice. When the creditors fail to elect a trustee, the interim trustee appointed by the court or by the United States Trustee, as the case may be, becomes the trustee.

§ 20.33 Administration by Trustee

The trustee, under the supervision of the bankruptcy clerk of court or United States Trustee, takes possession of all property owned by the debtor which is not exempt; converts such property into money by selling it; and on order of the bankruptcy judge, after costs of administration have been paid, distributes dividends to creditors to the extent money is available.

§ 20.34 Discharge Hearing

The Bankruptcy Code requires the bankruptcy court to hold a hearing to inform the debtor why a discharge has not been granted. If a discharge has been granted but the debtor desires to reaffirm one of the debts discharged, the court must inform the debtor that he is not required to do so but if he does do so, then he becomes legally liable for that debt.

Once a debtor has been granted a discharge, all creditors are enjoined from commencing or continuing any action against the debtor or his exempt property to collect their debt with the exception of debts reaffirmed which are subsequently defaulted on by the debtor or specific non-dischargeable debts.

§ 20.35 Preparation of the Petition, Schedules, and Supporting Documents

Just as in any other type of case, there are certain legal pleadings which must be filed by the debtor seeking relief under the Bankruptcy Code. The necessary forms are available from any office supply store which stocks legal forms. The debtor's attorney is responsible for proper preparation of the forms, but of course, he must get the information from the debtor. The legal secretary prepares these forms under the supervision of the attorney, and careful attention in preparation of the papers is very important. Errors or omissions often necessitate amendments to the pleadings and cause delays in the discharge—both expensive and time-consuming.

The number of copies of a petition and supporting documents that must be filed is a matter of local rule, which usually provides for filing sufficient copies for the court's files and for a trustee. The filing fee must accompany the petition at the time of filing or may be paid in installments upon application to the court by the debtor. A husband and wife may file a joint petition. The schedules and statements, other than the statement of intention, are filed with the petition in a voluntary case, or if the petition is accompanied by a list of all the debtor's creditors and addresses, they can be filed within 15 days thereafter (with some exceptions). Some bankruptcy courts may also require a separate listing of the names and addresses of creditors on a special form which is used by the clerk in preparing mailing labels.

An individual debtor in a chapter 7 case files the statement of intention (see Illustration 20–2) within 30 days after the filing of the petition or on or before the date of the meeting of creditors, whichever is earlier, and must serve a copy on the trustee and the creditors named in the statement on or before the filing of the statement.

Illustration 20-2

Form 8

CHAPTER 7 INDIVIDUAL DEBTOR'S STATEMENT OF INTENTION

Form B8
6/90

[Caption as in Form 16B]

CHAPTER 7 INDIVIDUAL DEBTOR'S STATEMENT OF INTENTION

1. I, the debtor, have filed a schedule of assets and liabilities which includes consumer debts secured by property of the estate.

2. My intention with respect to the property of the estate which secures those consumer debts is as follows:

    a. *Property to Be Surrendered.*

Description of Property	Creditor's name
1. _____	_____
2. _____	_____
3. _____	_____

    b. *Property to Be Retained. [Check applicable statement of debtor's intention concerning reaffirmation, redemption, or lien avoidance.]*

Description of property	Creditor's name	Debt will be reaffirmed pursuant to § 524(c)	Property is claimed as exempt and will be redeemed pursuant to § 722	Lien will be avoided pursuant to § 522(f) and property will be claimed as exempt
1. _____	_____	_____	_____	_____
2. _____	_____	_____	_____	_____
3. _____	_____	_____	_____	_____
4. _____	_____	_____	_____	_____
5. _____	_____	_____	_____	_____

3. I understand that § 521(2)(B) of the Bankruptcy Code requires that I perform the above stated intention within 45 days of the filing of this statement with the court, or within such additional time as the court, for cause, within such 45-day period fixes.

Date: _____

                                               _____

                                               Signature of Debtor   [G8605]

Rule 9009 of the Federal Rules of Bankruptcy Procedure provides that the Official Forms prescribed by the Judicial Conference of the United States shall be observed and used. However, Rule 9009 allows Official Forms to be altered as may be appropriate. A document that contains all of the information required by the Official Forms will generally meet the standard of substantial compliance.

This has lead to office supply companies in different parts of the country selling forms which are slightly different from competitors but contain the necessary information.

The Judicial Conference, however, has prescribed the format for certain forms because of the large volume of bankruptcy cases. For example, the Voluntary Petition must follow the format of the Official Forms to assist the bankruptcy court clerks in entering the case on the computer database and to ensure that all required information is available to the clerk and trustee at the beginning of the case.

Preparation of the petition, schedules, and other supporting documents should be completed with as much information as possible. The more detail and information presented in the filed documents, the less time the debtor will need to spend with the trustee, and the proceeding will run much smoother.

The Voluntary Petition (see Illustration 20–3) is completed for all types of bankruptcies with the appropriate type of proceeding indicated on the form, and it is signed and dated by the attorney and debtor.

Exhibit "A" to the Voluntary Petition is only used by corporations filing under chapter 11 of the Code and is signed by an authorized officer of the debtor corporation or a member or an authorized agent of the partnership debtor under penalty of perjury. (Note: a partnership may be comprised of corporations who are the partners.)

The first page of the debtor's schedules and the first page of any amendments thereto must contain the caption in the Petition, *i.e.,* name of the court, debtor, and case number. Subsequent pages should be identified with the debtor's name and case number. If the schedules are filed with the petition, the case number is left blank.

The Summary of Schedules indicates which schedules are attached and states the number of pages in each schedule. The total number of sheets of all schedules is added and inserted in the box at the bottom of the column entitled "No. of Sheets." The totals from each schedule are listed in the appropriate box and, except for Schedules I and J, are tabulated at the bottom of the form in the appropriate boxes.

Schedule A lists all real property in which the debtor has any legal, equitable, or future interest including all property owned as a co-tenant, community property, or in which the debtor has a life estate. The values of the property should reflect the best estimate of the debtor as to the property's true market value.

Schedule B lists all personal property of the debtor of whatever kind and is separated into 33 different categories. If the debtor does not own any property in a category, the column entitled "None" is checked. The values of the tangible property should reflect the best estimate of the debtor as to the true market value.

Schedule C lists the property claimed as exempt by the debtor. It is important that the correct law for exemptions be used. In some states, it may be in the best interests of the debtor to select the state exemptions instead of the federal exemptions. The legal secretary should check with the attorney to determine the correct exemption law to use. The property claimed as exempt should be listed individually, especially household furniture and effects, and each item should be valued separately.

Some bankruptcy courts take a stringent approach to exemptions, ruling that if all exemptions to which a debtor is entitled are not requested in the initial filing by the debtor, those not claimed will not be allowed to the debtor.

Schedule D lists all creditors holding secured claims. If the debtor has no secured creditors, the box provided on the form must be checked to indicate that there are no such creditors. If the continuation page is used, the number of continuation pages must be entered on the appropriate line at the bottom of the first page. At the bottom of each continuation page, the sheet number and the total of the number of continuation sheets must be completed. For example, if there are three continuation sheets, on the first continuation sheet you would insert "1 of 3," and on the second sheet you would insert "2 of 3," and so on.

Schedule E lists creditors holding unsecured priority claims. If the debtor has no unsecured creditors holding priority claims, the box provided on the first page must be checked to indicate that there are no such creditors. The first page also contains other statements that must be answered, and on the next page, or the continuation page, the creditors are listed. The number of continuation pages must be entered on the appropriate line at the bottom of the first page. Again, the sheet number and the number of continuation sheets must be inserted at the bottom of each continuation sheet.

Schedule F lists creditors holding unsecured nonpriority claims. If the debtor has no unsecured creditors, the box provided on the first page must be checked to indicate that there are no such creditors. If continuation sheets are used, the same numbering of continuation sheets must be used.

It is important that all creditors be listed on the appropriate schedules. Any creditor omitted from the schedule, by the debtor or by the attorney or staff, may not be discharged; and if the omission is a result of error in preparation by the attorney or the staff of the attorney, the error could result in a claim against the attorney.

Schedule G lists the executory contracts and unexpired leases. If the debtor owns no such contracts, the box must be checked to indicate this fact.

Schedule H lists codebtors, other than a spouse in a joint proceeding. Again, if there are no codebtors, the box must be checked to indicate this fact.

Schedule I lists the current income of the debtor.

Schedule J lists the current expenditures of the debtor.

The Summary of Schedules and the schedules include general instructions at the beginning of each form, which should be reviewed before starting to complete the forms to ensure that all the necessary information is available to the legal secretary.

The Declaration Concerning Debtor's Schedules is signed by the debtor or an officer or authorized agent of the debtor corporation or a member or authorized agent of a partnership debtor under penalty of perjury. If it is a husband and wife petition, both spouses must sign.

The Statement of Financial Affairs must be completed by every debtor. It contains instructions and definitions at the beginning of the form which should be reviewed prior to completion of the form. Each question must be answered. If the answer is "None" or the question is not applicable, mark the box labeled "None." If the answer space provided is not sufficient, attach a separate sheet properly identified with the case name, case number (if known), and the number of the question. It is signed by the debtor or an officer or authorized agent of the debtor corporation or a member or authorized agent of partnership debtor under penalty of perjury. If it is a husband and wife petition, both spouses must sign.

The Statement Pursuant to Rule 2016(b) form pursuant to Bankruptcy Rule 2016(b) is signed by the attorney and is filed and transmitted to the United States trustee within 15 days after the order for relief or at another time as the court may direct.

Illustration 20–3

Form 1

VOLUNTARY PETITION

FORM B1
(6/90)

United States Bankruptcy Court District of _____	VOLUNTARY PETITION

IN RE (Name of debtor - If individual, enter Last, First, Middle)	NAME OF JOINT DEBTOR (Spouse) (Last, First, Middle)
ALL OTHER NAMES used by the debtor in the last 6 years (Include married, maiden, and trade names)	ALL OTHER NAMES used by the joint debtor in the last 6 years (Include married, maiden, and trade names)
SOC. SEC./TAX I.D. NO. (If more than one, state all)	SOC. SEC./TAX I.D. NO. (If more than one, state all)
STREET ADDRESS OF DEBTOR (No. and street, city, state, and zip code)	STREET ADDRESS OF JOINT DEBTOR (No. and street, city, state, and zip code)

COUNTY OF RESIDENCE OR
           PRINCIPAL PLACE OF BUSINESS
	COUNTY OF RESIDENCE OR
	           PRINCIPAL PLACE OF BUSINESS

MAILING ADDRESS OF DEBTOR (If different from street address)	MAILING ADDRESS OF JOINT DEBTOR (If different from street address)

	VENUE (Check one box)
LOCATION OF PRINCIPAL ASSETS OF BUSINESS DEBTOR (If different from addresses listed above)	☐ Debtor has been domiciled or has had a residence principal place of business, or principal assets in this District for 180 days immediately preceding the date of this petition or for a longer part of such 180 days than in any other District. ☐ There is a bankruptcy case concerning debtor's affiliate, general partner, or partnership pending in this District.

INFORMATION REGARDING DEBTOR (Check applicable boxes)

TYPE OF DEBTOR
☐ Individual
☐ Joint (Husband and Wife)
☐ Partnership
☐ Other _____   ☐ Corporation Publicly Held
    ☐ Corporation Not Publicly Held
    ☐ Municipality
	CHAPTER OR SECTION OF BANKRUPTCY CODE UNDER WHICH THE PETITION IS FILED (Check one box)
	☐ Chapter 7 ☐ Chapter 11 ☐ Chapter 13
	☐ Chapter 9 ☐ Chapter 12 ☐ Sec. 304 - Case Ancillary to
	                          Foreign Proceeding

NATURE OF DEBT ☐ Non-Business/Consumer ☐ Business - Complete A & B below	**FILING FEE** (Check one box) ☐ Filing fee attached ☐ Filing fee to be paid in installments. (Applicable to individuals only.) Must attach signed application for the court's consideration certifying that the debtor is unable to pay fee except in installments. Rule 1006(b). See Official Form No. 3.
A. TYPE OF BUSINESS (Check one box) ☐ Farming ☐ Transportation ☐ Commodity Broker ☐ Professional ☐ Manufacturing/ ☐ Construction ☐ Retail/Wholesale Mining ☐ Real Estate ☐ Railroad ☐ Stockbroker ☐ Other Business	NAME AND ADDRESS OF LAW FIRM OR ATTORNEY
B. BRIEFLY DESCRIBE NATURE OF BUSINESS	Telephone No. NAME(S) OF ATTORNEY(S) DESIGNATED TO REPRESENT DEBTOR (Print or Type Names) ☐ Debtor is not represented by an attorney

STATISTICAL/ADMINISTRATIVE INFORMATION (28 U.S.C. § 604) (Estimates only) (Check applicable boxes)	THIS SPACE FOR COURT USE ONLY
☐ Debtor estimates that funds will be available for distribution to unsecured creditors. ☐ Debtor estimates that, after any exempt property is excluded and administrative expenses paid, there will be no funds available for distribution to unsecured creditors.	

ESTIMATED NUMBER OF CREDITORS

1-15	16-49	50-99	100-199	200-999	1000-over
☐	☐	☐	☐	☐	☐

ESTIMATED ASSETS (In thousands of dollars)

Under 50	50-99	100-499	500-999	1000-9999	10,000-99,999	100,000-over
☐	☐	☐	☐	☐	☐	☐

ESTIMATED LIABILITIES (In thousands of dollars)

Under 50	50-99	100-499	500-999	1000-9999	10,000-99,999	100,000-over
☐	☐	☐	☐	☐	☐	☐

EST. NO. OF EMPLOYEES - CH. 11 & 12 ONLY

0	1-19	20-99	100-999	1000-over
☐	☐	☐	☐	☐

EST. NO. OF EQUITY SECURITY HOLDERS - CH. 11 & 12 ONLY

0	1-19	20-99	100-499	500-over
☐	☐	☐	☐	☐

[G8567]

Name of Debtor _____

Case No. _____

(Court use only)

FILING OF PLAN

For Chapter 9, 11, 12 and 13 cases only. Check appropriate box.

☐ A copy of debtor's proposed plan dated _____ is attached.

☐ Debtor intends to file a plan within the time allowed by statute, rule or order of the court.

PRIOR BANKRUPTCY CASE FILED WITHIN LAST 6 YEARS (If more than one, attach additional sheet)

Location Where Filed	Case Number	Date Filed

PENDING BANKRUPTCY CASE FILED BY ANY SPOUSE, PARTNER, OR AFFILIATE OF THE DEBTOR (If more than one, attach additional sheet)

Name of Debtor	Case Number	Date
Relationship	District	Judge

REQUEST FOR RELIEF

Debtor requests relief in accordance with the chapter of title 11, United States Code specified in this petition.

SIGNATURES

ATTORNEY

X_____

Signature   Date _____

INDIVIDUAL JOINT DEBTOR(S)	**CORPORATE OR PARTNERSHIP DEBTOR**
I declare under penalty of perjury that the information provided in this petition is true and correct.	I declare under penalty of perjury that the information provided in this petition is true and correct and that the filing of this petition on behalf of the debtor has been authorized.
X_____ Signature of Debtor	X_____ Signature of Authorized Individual
Date _____	Print or Type Name of Authorized Individual
X_____ Signature of Joint Debtor	Title of Individual Authorized by Debtor to File this Petition
Date _____	Date _____

EXHIBIT "A" (To be completed if debtor is a corporation, requesting relief under Chapter 11.)

☐ Exhibit "A" is attached and made a part of this petition.

TO BE COMPLETED BY INDIVIDUAL CHAPTER 7 DEBTOR WITH PRIMARILY CONSUMER DEBTS (See P.L. 98-353 § 322)

I am aware that I may proceed under chapter 7, 11, or 12, or 13 of title 11, United States Code, understand the relief available under each such chapter, and choose to proceed under chapter 7 of such title.

If I am represented by an attorney, Exhibit B has been completed.

X_____

Signature of Debtor   Date _____

X_____

Signature of Joint Debtor   Date _____

EXHIBIT "B" (To be completed by attorney for individual chapter 7 debtor(s) with primarily consumer debts.)

I, the attorney for the debtor(s) named in the foregoing petition, declare that I have informed the debtor(s) that (he, she, or they) may proceed under chapter 7, 11, 12, or 13 of title 11, United States Code, and have explained the relief available under such chapter.

X_____

Signature of Attorney   Date _____

[G8568]

Form B1XA
6/90

Exhibit "A"

[If debtor is a corporation filing under chapter 11 of the Code, this Exhibit "A" shall be completed and attached to the petition.]

[Caption as in Form 16B]

Exhibit "A" to Voluntary Petition

1. Debtor's employer identification number is _____.

2. If any of debtor's securities are registered under section 12 of the Securities and Exchange Act of 1934, the SEC file number is _____.

3. The following financial data is the latest available information and refers to debtor's condition on _____.

		Approximate number of holders
a. Total assets	$ _____	
b. Total liabilities	$ _____	
Fixed, liquidated secured debt	$ _____	_____
Contingent secured debt	$ _____	_____
Disputed secured claims	$ _____	_____
Unliquidated secured debt	$ _____	_____

		Approximate number of holders
Fixed, liquidated unsecured debt	$ _____	_____
Contingent unsecured debt	$ _____	_____
Disputed unsecured claims	$ _____	_____
Unliquidated unsecured debt	$ _____	_____
Number of shares of preferred stock	_____	_____
Number of shares of common stock	_____	_____

[G8569]

659

Exhibit "A" continued

Comments, if any: _____
_____
_____
_____

4. Brief description of debtor's business: _____
_____
_____

5. List the name of any person who directly or indirectly owns, controls, or holds, with power to vote, 20% or more of the voting securities of debtor: _____
_____
_____
_____

6. List the names of all corporations 20% or more of the outstanding voting securities of which are directly or indirectly owned, controlled, or held, with power to vote, by debtor: _____
_____
_____
_____

[G8570]

Form 2

DECLARATION UNDER PENALTY OF PERJURY ON BEHALF OF A CORPORATION OR PARTNERSHIP

Form B2
6/90

Form 2. DECLARATION UNDER PENALTY OF PERJURY ON BEHALF OF A CORPORATION OR PARTNERSHIP

I, [the president *or* other officer *or* an authorized agent of the corporation] [*or* a member *or* an authorized agent of the partnership] named as the debtor in this case, declare under penalty of perjury that I have read the foregoing [list *or* schedule *or* amendment *or* other document (describe)] and that it is true and correct to the best of my information and belief.

Date _____

Signature _____

_____
(Print Name and Title)   [G8571]

FORM B6 - Cont.
(6/90)

United States Bankruptcy Court

_____ District of _____

In re _____,　　Case No. _____
　　　　　　　　Debtor　　　　　　　　　　　　　　　　　　　　　(If known)

SUMMARY OF SCHEDULES

Indicate as to each schedule whether that schedule is attached and state the number of pages in each. Report the totals from Schedules A, B, D, E, F, I, and J in the boxes provided. Add the amounts from Schedules A and B to determine the total amount of the debtor's assets. Add the amounts from Schedules D, E, and F to determine the total amount of the debtor's liabilities.

| | | | AMOUNTS SCHEDULED | | |
NAME OF SCHEDULE	ATTACHED (YES/NO)	NO. OF SHEETS	ASSETS	LIABILITIES	OTHER
A - Real Property			$		
B - Personal Property			$		
C - Property Claimed As Exempt					
D - Creditor Holding Secured Claims				$	
E - Creditors Holding Unsecured Priority Claims				$	
F - Creditors Holding Unsecured Nonpriority Claims				$	
G - Executory Contracts and Unexpired Leases					
H - Codebtors					
I - Current Income of Individual Debtor(s)					$
J - Current Expenditures of Individual Debtor(s)					$
Total Number of Sheets of ALL Schedules ▶					
Total Assets ▶			$		
Total Liabilities ▶				$	

[G8577]

662

FORM B6A
(10/89)

In re _____ .   Case No._____
           Debtor   (If known)

SCHEDULE A - REAL PROPERTY

Except as directed below, list all real property in which the debtor has any legal, equitable, or future interest, including all property owned as a co-tenant, community property, or in which the debtor has a life estate. Include any property in which the debtor holds rights and powers exercisable for the debtor's own benefit. If the debtor is married, state whether husband, wife, or both own the property by placing an "H," "W," "J," or "C" in the column labeled "Husband, Wife, Joint, or Community." If the debtor holds no interest in real property, write "None" under "Description and Location of Property."

Do not include interests in executory contracts and unexpired leases on this schedule. List them in Schedule G - Executory Contracts and Unexpired Leases.

If an entity claims to have a lien or hold a secured interest in any property, state the amount of the secured claim. See Schedule D. If no entity claims to hold a secured interest in the property, write "None" in the column labeled "Amount of Secured Claim."

If the debtor is an individual or if a joint petition is filed, state the amount of any exemption claimed in the property only in Schedule C - Property Claimed as Exempt.

DESCRIPTION AND LOCATION OF PROPERTY	NATURE OF DEBTOR'S INTEREST IN PROPERTY	HUSBAND, WIFE, JOINT OR COMMUNITY	CURRENT MARKET VALUE OF DEBTOR'S INTEREST IN PROPERTY WITHOUT DEDUCTING ANY SECURED CLAIM OR EXEMPTION	AMOUNT OF SECURED CLAIM

Total ► $_____   [G8578]

(Report also on Summary of Schedules.)

FORM B6B
(10/89)

In re _____ ,   Case No. _____
           Debtor   (If known)

SCHEDULE B - PERSONAL PROPERTY

Except as directed below, list all personal property of the debtor of whatever kind. If the debtor has no property in one or more of the categories, place an "X" in the appropriate position in the column labeled "None." If additional space is needed in any category, attach a separate sheet properly identified with the case name, case number, and the number of the category. If the debtor is married, state whether husband, wife, or both own the property by placing an "H," "W," "J," or "C" in the column labeled "Husband, Wife, Joint, or Community." If the debtor is an individual or a joint petition is filed, state the amount of any exemptions claimed only in Schedule C - Property Claimed as Exempt.

Do not list interests in executory contracts and unexpired leases on this schedule. List them in Schedule G - Executory Contracts and Unexpired Leases.

If the property is being held for the debtor by someone else, state that person's name and address under "Description and Location of Property."

TYPE OF PROPERTY	NONE	DESCRIPTION AND LOCATION OF PROPERTY	HUSBAND, WIFE, JOINT OR COMMUNITY	CURRENT MARKET VALUE OF DEBTOR'S INTEREST IN PROPERTY, WITHOUT DEDUCTING ANY SECURED CLAIM OR EXEMPTION
1. Cash on hand.				
2. Checking, savings or other financial accounts, certificates of deposit, or shares in banks, savings and loan, thrift, building and loan, and homestead associations, or credit unions, brokerage houses, or cooperatives.				
3. Security deposits with public utilities, telephone companies, landlords, and others.				
4. Household goods and furnishings, including audio, video, and computer equipment.				
5. Books, pictures and other art objects, antiques, stamp, coin, record, tape, compact disc, and other collections or collectibles.				
6. Wearing apparel.				
7. Furs and jewelry.				
8. Firearms and sports, photographic, and other hobby equipment.				
9. Interests in insurance policies. Name insurance company of each policy and itemize surrender or refund value of each.				
10. Annuities. Itemize and name each issuer.				

[G8579]

FORM B6B - Cont.
(10/89)

In re _____ ,   Case No. _____
            Debtor   (If known)

SCHEDULE B - PERSONAL PROPERTY
(Continuation Sheet)

TYPE OF PROPERTY	NONE	DESCRIPTION AND LOCATION OF PROPERTY	HUSBAND, WIFE, JOINT OR COMMUNITY	CURRENT MARKET VALUE OF DEBTOR'S INTEREST IN PROPERTY, WITH-OUT DEDUCTING ANY SECURED CLAIM OR EXEMPTION
11. Interests in IRA, ERISA, Keogh, or other pension or profit sharing plans. Itemize.				
12. Stock and interests in incorporated and unincorporated businesses. Itemize.				
13. Interests in partnerships or joint ventures. Itemize.				
14. Government and corporate bonds and other negotiable and non-negotiable instruments.				
15. Accounts receivable.				
16. Alimony, maintenance, support, and property settlements to which the debtor is or may be entitled. Give particulars.				
17. Other liquidated debts owing debtor including tax refunds. Give particulars.				
18. Equitable or future interests, life estates, and rights or powers exercisable for the benefit of the debtor other than those listed in Schedule of Real Property.				
19. Contingent and noncontingent interests in estate of a decedent, death benefit plan, life insurance policy, or trust.				
20. Other contingent and unliquidated claims of every nature, including tax refunds, counterclaims of the debtor, and rights to setoff claims. Give estimated value of each.				
21. Patents, copyrights, and other intellectual property. Give particulars.				
22. Licenses, franchises, and other general intangibles. Give particulars.				

[G8580]

FORM B6B - Cont.
(10/89)

In re _____,   Case No. _____
                      Debtor   (If known)

SCHEDULE B - PERSONAL PROPERTY
(Continuation Sheet)

TYPE OF PROPERTY	NONE	DESCRIPTION AND LOCATION OF PROPERTY	HUSBAND, WIFE, JOINT OR COMMUNITY	CURRENT MARKET VALUE OF DEBTOR'S INTEREST IN PROPERTY, WITHOUT DEDUCTING ANY SECURED CLAIM OR EXEMPTION
23. Automobiles, trucks, trailers, and other vehicles and accessories.				
24. Boats, motors, and accessories.				
25. Aircraft and accessories.				
26. Office equipment, furnishings, and supplies.				
27. Machinery, fixtures, equipment and supplies used in business.				
28. Inventory.				
29. Animals.				
30. Crops - growing or harvested. Give particulars.				
31. Farming equipment and implements.				
32. Farm supplies, chemicals, and feed.				
33. Other personal property of any kind not already listed. Itemize.				

_____ continuation sheets attached   Total ➔ $

(Include amounts from any continuation
sheets attached. Report total also on
Summary of Schedules.)
[G8581]

FORM B6C
(6/90)

In re _____,   Case No. _____
           Debtor   (If known)

SCHEDULE C - PROPERTY CLAIMED AS EXEMPT

Debtor elects the exemption to which debtor is entitled under

(Check one box)

☐ 11 U.S.C. § 522(b)(1) Exemptions provided in 11 U.S.C. § 522(d). Note: These exemptions are available only in certain states.

☐ 11 U.S.C. § 522(b)(2) Exemptions available under applicable nonbankruptcy federal laws, state or local law where the debtor's domicile has been located for the 180 days immediately preceding the filing of the petition, or for a longer portion of the 180-day period than in any other place, and the debtor's interest as a tenant by the entirety or joint tenant to the extent the interest is exempt from process under applicable nonbankruptcy law.

DESCRIPTION OF PROPERTY	SPECIFY LAW PROVIDING EACH EXEMPTION	VALUE OF CLAIMED EXEMPTION	CURRENT MARKET VALUE OF PROPERTY WITHOUT DEDUCTING EXEMPTIONS

[G8582]

FORM B6D
(6/90)

In re _____ ,   Case No. _____
                Debtor   (If known)

SCHEDULE D - CREDITORS HOLDING SECURED CLAIMS

State the name, mailing address, including zip code, and account number, if any, of all entities holding claims secured by property of the debtor as of the date of filing of the petition. List creditors holding all types of secured interests such as judgment liens, garnishments, statutory liens, mortgages, deeds of trust, and other security interests. List creditors in alphabetical order to the extent practicable. If all secured creditors will not fit on this page, use the continuation sheet provided.

If any entity other than a spouse in a joint case may be jointly liable on a claim, place an "X" in the column labeled "Codebtor," include the entity on the appropriate schedule of creditors, and complete Schedule H - Codebtors. If a joint petition is filed, state whether husband, wife, both of them, or the marital community may be liable on each claim by placing an "H," "W," "J," or "C" in the column labeled "Husband, Wife, Joint, or Community."

If the claim is contingent, place an "X" in the column labeled "Contingent." If the claim is unliquidated, place an "X" in the column labeled "Unliquidated." If the claim is disputed, place an "X" in the column labeled "Disputed." (You may need to place an "X" in more than one of these three columns.)

Report the total of all claims listed on this schedule in the box labeled "Total" on the last sheet of the completed schedule. Report this total also on the Summary of Schedules.

☐ Check this box if debtor has no creditors holding secured claims to report on this Schedule D.

CREDITOR'S NAME AND MAILING ADDRESS INCLUDING ZIP CODE	CODEBTOR	HUSBAND, WIFE, JOINT OR COMMUNITY	DATE CLAIM WAS INCURRED, NATURE OF LIEN, AND DESCRIPTION AND MARKET VALUE OF PROPERTY SUBJECT TO LIEN	CONTINGENT	UNLIQUIDATED	DISPUTED	AMOUNT OF CLAIM WITHOUT DEDUCTING VALUE OF COLLATERAL	UNSECURED PORTION, IF ANY
ACCOUNT NO.								
			Value $					
ACCOUNT NO.								
			Value $					
ACCOUNT NO.								
			Value $					
ACCOUNT NO.								
			Value $					

_____ Continuation sheets attached

             Subtotal ➔ $ _____
      (Total of this page)
                 Total ➔ $ _____
      (Use only on last page)

(Report total also on Summary of Schedules)   [G8583]

FORM B6D - Cont.
(10/89)

In re _____,   Case No. _____
                        Debtor   (If known)

SCHEDULE D - CREDITORS HOLDING SECURED CLAIMS
(Continuation Sheet)

CREDITOR'S NAME AND MAILING ADDRESS INCLUDING ZIP CODE	CODEBTOR	HUSBAND, WIFE, JOINT OR COMMUNITY	DATE CLAIM WAS INCURRED, NATURE OF LIEN, AND DESCRIPTION AND MARKET VALUE OF PROPERTY SUBJECT TO LIEN	CONTINGENT	UNLIQUIDATED	DISPUTED	AMOUNT OF CLAIM WITHOUT DEDUCTING VALUE OF COLLATERAL	UNSECURED PORTION, IF ANY
ACCOUNT NO.								
			VALUE $					
ACCOUNT NO.								
			VALUE $					
ACCOUNT NO.								
			VALUE $					
ACCOUNT NO.								
			VALUE $					
ACCOUNT NO.								
			VALUE $					

Sheet no. ____ of ____ continuation sheets attached to Schedule of Creditors Holding Secured Claims   Subtotal ► $ _____
(Total of this page)
Total ► $ _____
(Use only on last page)
(Report total also on Summary of Schedules)   [G8584]

FORM B6E
(6/90)

In re _____ ,   Case No. _____
                              Debtor   (If known)

SCHEDULE E - CREDITORS HOLDING UNSECURED PRIORITY CLAIMS

A complete list of claims entitled to priority, listed separately by type of priority, is to be set forth on the sheets provided. Only holders of unsecured claims entitled to priority should be listed in this schedule. In the boxes provided on the attached sheets, state the name and mailing address, including zip code, and account number, if any, of all entities holding priority claims against the debtor or the property of the debtor, as of the date of the filing of the petition.

If any entity other than a spouse in a joint case may be jointly liable on a claim, place an "X" in the column labeled "Codebtor," include the entity on the appropriate schedule of creditors, and complete Schedule H - Codebtors. If a joint petition is filed, state whether husband, wife, both of them, or the marital community may be liable on each claim by placing an "H," "W," "J," or "C" in the column labeled "Husband, Wife, Joint, or Community."

If the claim is contingent, place an "X" in the column labeled "Contingent." If the claim is unliquidated, place an "X" in the column labeled "Unliquidated." If the claim is disputed, place an "X" in the column labeled "Disputed." (You may need to place an "X" in more than one of these three columns.)

Report the total of claims listed on each sheet in the box labeled, "Subtotal" on each sheet. Report the total of all claims listed on this Schedule E in the box labeled "Total" on the last sheet of the completed schedule. Repeat this total also on the Summary of Schedules.

☐ Check this box if debtor has no creditors holding unsecured priority claims to report on this Schedule E.

TYPES OF PRIORITY CLAIMS (Check the appropriate box(es) below if claims in that category are listed on the attached sheets)

☐ **Extensions of credit in an involuntary case**

Claims arising in the ordinary course of the debtor's business or financial affairs after the commencement of the case but before the earlier of the appointment of a trustee or the order for relief. 11 U.S.C. § 507(a)(2).

☐ **Wages, salaries, and commissions**

Wages, salaries, and commissions, including vacation, severance, and sick leave pay owing to employees, up to a maximum of $2000 per employee, earned within 90 days immediately preceding the filing of the original petition, or the cessation of business, whichever occurred first, to the extent provided in 11 U.S.C. § 507(a)(3).

☐ **Contributions to employee benefit plans**

Money owed to employee benefit plans for services rendered within 180 days immediately preceding the filing of the original petition, or the cessation of business, whichever occurred first, to the extent provided in 11 U.S.C. § 507(a)(4).

☐ **Certain farmers and fishermen**

Claims of certain farmers and fishermen, up to a maximum of $2000 per farmer or fisherman, against the debtor, as provided in 11 U.S.C. § 507(a)(5).

☐ **Deposits by individuals**

Claims of individuals up to a maximum of $900 for deposits for the purchase, lease, or rental of property or services for personal, family, or household use, that were not delivered or provided. 11 U.S.C. § 507(a)(6).

☐ **Taxes and Certain Other Debts Owed to Governmental Units**

Taxes, customs duties, and penalties owing to federal, state, and local governmental units as set forth in 11 U.S.C. §507(a)(7).

_____ continuation sheets attached   [G8585]

FORM B6E - Cont.
(10/89)

In re _____ ,   Case No. _____
                   Debtor   (If known)

SCHEDULE E - CREDITORS, HOLDING UNSECURED PRIORITY CLAIMS
(Continuation Sheet)

TYPE OF PRIORITY

CREDITOR'S NAME AND MAILING ADDRESS INCLUDING ZIP CODE	CODEBTOR	HUSBAND, WIFE, JOINT OR COMMUNITY	DATE CLAIM WAS INCURRED AND CONSIDERATION FOR CLAIM	CONTINGENT	UNLIQUIDATED	DISPUTED	TOTAL AMOUNT OF CLAIM	AMOUNT ENTITLED TO PRIORITY
ACCOUNT NO.								
ACCOUNT NO.								
ACCOUNT NO.								
ACCOUNT NO.								
ACCOUNT NO.								

Sheet no. ____ of ____ sheets attached to Schedule of Creditors
Holding Unsecured Priority Claims

Subtotal ► $ _____
(Total of this page)
Total ► $ _____
(Use only on last page of the completed Schedule E)

(Report total also on Summary of Schedules)   [G8586]

Form B6F
(10/89)

In re _____ .   Case No. _____

         Debtor   (If Known)

SCHEDULE F - CREDITORS HOLDING UNSECURED NONPRIORITY CLAIMS

    State the name, mailing address, including zip code, and account number, if any, of all entities holding unsecured claims without priority against the debtor or the property of the debtor, as of the date of filing of the petition. Do not include claims listed in Schedules D and E. If all creditors will not fit on this page, use the continuation sheet provided.

    If any entity other than a spouse in a joint case may be jointly liable on a claim, place an "X" in the column labeled "Codebtor," include the entity on the appropriate schedule of creditors, and complete Schedule H - Codebtors. If a joint petition is filed, state whether husband, wife, both of them, or the marital community may be liable on each claim by placing an "H," "W," "J," or "C" in the column labeled "Husband, Wife, Joint, or Community."

    If the claim is contingent, place an "X" in the column labeled "Contingent." If the claim is unliquidated, place an "X" in the column labeled "Unliquidated." If the claim is disputed, place an "X" in the column labeled "Disputed." (You may need to place an "X" in more than one of these three columns.)

    Report total of all claims listed on this schedule in the box labeled "Total" on the last sheet of the completed schedule. Report this total also on the Summary of Schedules.

    ☐ Check this box if debtor has no creditors holding unsecured non priority claims to report on this Schedule F.

CREDITOR'S NAME AND MAILING ADDRESS INCLUDING ZIP CODE	CODEBTOR	HUSBAND, WIFE, JOINT OR COMMUNITY	DATE CLAIM WAS INCURRED AND CONSIDERATION FOR CLAIM, IF CLAIM IS SUBJECT TO SETOFF, SO STATE	CONTINGENT	UNLIQUIDATED	DISPUTED	AMOUNT OF CLAIM
ACCOUNT NO.							
ACCOUNT NO.							
ACCOUNT NO.							
ACCOUNT NO.							

_____ continuation sheets attached

Subtotal ➤ | $

Total ➤ | $

(Report total also on Summary of Schedules)

[G8587]

Form B6F - Cont.
(10/89)

In re _____ ,   Case No. _____
                  Debtor   (If known)

SCHEDULE F - CREDITORS HOLDING UNSECURED NONPRIORITY CLAIMS
(Continuation Sheet)

CREDITOR'S NAME AND MAILING ADDRESS INCLUDING ZIP CODE	CODEBTOR	HUSBAND, WIFE, JOINT OR COMMUNITY	DATE CLAIM WAS INCURRED AND CONSIDERATION FOR CLAIM, IF CLAIM IS SUBJECT TO SETOFF, SO STATE	CONTINGENT	UNLIQUIDATED	DISPUTED	AMOUNT OF CLAIM
ACCOUNT NO.							
ACCOUNT NO.							
ACCOUNT NO.							
ACCOUNT NO.							
ACCOUNT NO.							

Sheet no. _____ of _____ sheets attached to Schedule of   Subtotal ➤ $ _____
Creditors Holding Unsecured Nonpriority Claims   (Total of this page)
                                                        Total ➤ $ _____
(Use only on last page of the completed Schedule F)

(Report total also on Summary of Schedules)
[G8588]

Form B6G
(10/89)

In re _____ ,   Case No. _____
                 Debtor   (If Known)

SCHEDULE G - EXECUTORY CONTRACTS AND UNEXPIRED LEASES

Describe all executory contracts of any nature and all unexpired leases of real or personal property. Include any timeshare interests.

State nature of debtor's interest in contract, i.e., "Purchaser," "Agent," etc. State whether debtor is the lessor or lessee of a lease.

Provide the names and complete mailing addresses of all other parties to each lease or contract described.

NOTE: A party listed on this schedule will not receive notice of the filing of this case unless the party is also scheduled in the appropriate schedule of creditors.

☐ Check this box if debtor has no executory contracts or unexpired leases.

NAME AND MAILING ADDRESS, INCLUDING ZIP CODE, OF OTHER PARTIES TO LEASE OR CONTRACT	DESCRIPTION OF CONTRACT OR LEASE AND NATURE OF DEBTOR'S INTEREST, STATE WHETHER LEASE IS FOR NONRESIDENTIAL REAL PROPERTY. STATE CONTRACT NUMBER OF ANY GOVERNMENT CONTRACT

[G8589]

Form B6H
(6/90)

In re _____ .   Case No. _____
               Debtor   (If known)

SCHEDULE H - CODEBTORS

Provide the information requested concerning any person or entity, other than a spouse in a joint case, that is also liable on any debts listed by debtor in the schedules of creditors. Include all guarantors and co-signers. In community property states, a married debtor not filing a joint case should report the name and address of the nondebtor spouse on this schedule. Include all names used by the nondebtor spouse during the six years immediately preceding the commencement of this case.

☐ Check this box if debtor has no codebtors.

NAME AND ADDRESS OF CODEBTOR	NAME AND ADDRESS OF CREDITOR

[G8590]

Form B6I
(6/90)

In re _____ ,　　　　　　Case No. _____
　　　　　　　　Debtor　　　　　　　　　　　　　　　　　　　　　　　(If known)

SCHEDULE I - CURRENT INCOME OF INDIVIDUAL DEBTOR(S)

The column labeled "Spouse" must be completed in all cases filed by joint debtors and by a married debtor in a chapter 12 or 13 case whether or not a joint petition is filed, unless the spouses are separated and a joint petition is not filed.

Debtor's Marital Status:	DEPENDENTS OF DEBTOR AND SPOUSE		
	NAMES	AGE	RELATIONSHIP

EMPLOYMENT:	DEBTOR	SPOUSE
Occupation		
Name of Employer		
How long employed		
Address of Employer		

Income: (Estimate of average monthly income)　　　　　　　　　　　　DEBTOR　　　　SPOUSE
Current monthly gross wages, salary, and commissions
　(pro rate if not paid monthly.)　　　　　　　　　　　　　　　　$_____　$_____
Estimated monthly overtime　　　　　　　　　　　　　　　　　　$_____　$_____

SUBTOTAL　　　　　　　　　　　　　　　　　　　　　　　　　$_____　$_____

　LESS PAYROLL DEDUCTIONS
　a. Payroll taxes and social security　　　　　　　　　　　　　$_____　$_____
　b. Insurance　　　　　　　　　　　　　　　　　　　　　　　$_____　$_____
　c. Union dues　　　　　　　　　　　　　　　　　　　　　　$_____　$_____
　d. Other (Specify _____)　　　$_____　$_____

　SUBTOTAL OF PAYROLL DEDUCTIONS　　　　　　　　　　　$_____　$_____

TOTAL NET MONTHLY TAKE HOME PAY　　　　　　　　　　　$_____　$_____

Regular income from operation of business or profession or farm
(attach detailed statement)　　　　　　　　　　　　　　　　　$_____　$_____

Income from real property　　　　　　　　　　　　　　　　　$_____　$_____

Interest and dividends　　　　　　　　　　　　　　　　　　　$_____　$_____

Alimony, maintenance or support payments payable to the debtor for the
debtor's use or that of dependents listed above.　　　　　　　　$_____　$_____

Social security or other government assistance
(Specify) _____　　　　　$_____　$_____

Pension or retirement income　　　　　　　　　　　　　　　　$_____　$_____

Other monthly income　　　　　　　　　　　　　　　　　　　$_____　$_____

(Specify) _____　　　　　$_____　$_____

　　　　　_____　　　　　$_____　$_____

TOTAL MONTHLY INCOME　　　　　　　　　　　　　　　　$_____　$_____

TOTAL COMBINED MONTHLY INCOME $_____　　　(Report also on Summary of Schedules)

Describe any increase or decrease of more than 10% in any of the above categories anticipated to occur within the year following the filing of this document:　　　　　　　　　　　　　　　　　　　[G8591]

FORM B6J
(6/90)

In re _____ ,   Case No. _____
              Debtor   (If known)

SCHEDULE J - CURRENT EXPENDITURES OF INDIVIDUAL DEBTOR(S)

Complete this schedule by estimating the average monthly expenses of the debtor and the debtor's family. Pro rate any payments made bi-weekly, quarterly, semi-annually, or annually to show monthly rate.

☐ Check this box if a joint petition is filed and debtor's spouse maintains a separate household. Complete a separate schedule of expenditures labeled "Spouse."

Rent or home mortgage payment (include lot rented for mobile home) $ _____
Are real estate taxes included?   Yes _____   No _____
Is property insurance included?   Yes _____   No _____
Utilities   Electricity and heating fuel $ _____
           Water and sewer $ _____
           Telephone $ _____
           Other _____ $ _____
Home Maintenance (Repairs and upkeep) $ _____
Food $ _____
Clothing $ _____
Laundry and dry cleaning $ _____
Medical and dental expenses $ _____
Transportation (not including car payments) $ _____
Recreation, clubs and entertainment, newspapers, magazines, etc. $ _____
Charitable contributions $ _____
Insurance (not deducted from wages or included in home mortgage payments)
           Homeowner's or renter's $ _____
           Life $ _____
           Health $ _____
           Auto $ _____
           Other _____ $ _____
Taxes (not deducted from wages or included in home mortgage payments)
(Specify) _____ $ _____
Installment payments (In chapter 12 and 13 cases, do not list payments to be included in the plan)
           Auto $ _____
           Other _____ $ _____
           Other _____ $ _____
Alimony, maintenance, and support paid to others $ _____
Payments for support of additional dependents not living at your home $ _____
Regular expenses from operation of business, profession, or farm (attach detailed statement) $ _____
Other _____ $ _____

TOTAL MONTHLY EXPENSES (Report also on Summary of Schedules) $ _____

[FOR CHAPTER 12 AND 13 DEBTORS ONLY]
Provide the information requested below, including whether plan payments are to be made bi-weekly, monthly, annually, or at some other regular interval.
A. Total projected monthly income $ _____
B. Total projected monthly expenses $ _____
C. Excess income (A minus B) $ _____
D. Total amount to be paid into plan each _____ $ _____
                                     (interval)   [G8592]

FORM B6 - Cont.
(6/90)

In re _____ ,   Case No. _____
                        Debtor   (If known)

DECLARATION CONCERNING DEBTOR'S SCHEDULES

DECLARATION UNDER PENALTY OF PERJURY BY INDIVIDUAL DEBTOR

I declare under penalty of perjury that I have read the foregoing summary and schedules, consisting of _____ sheets,
and that they are true and correct to the best of my knowledge, information, and belief.   (Total shown on summary page plus 1)

Date _____   Signature _____
                                                                                                Debtor

Date _____   Signature _____
                                                                                       (Joint Debtor, if any)
                                                                      [If joint case, both spouses must sign]

- -

DECLARATION UNDER PENALTY OF PERJURY ON BEHALF OF CORPORATION OR PARTNERSHIP

I, the _____ [the president or other officer or an authorized agent of the corporation or a member or an
authorized agent of the partnership] of the _____ [corporation or partnership] named as debtor in this case,
declare under penalty of perjury that I have read the foregoing summary and schedules, consisting of _____ sheets, and that
they are true and correct to the best of my knowledge, information, and belief.   (Total shown on summary page plus 1)

Date _____

                                                        Signature _____

                                                        _____
                                                        [Print or type name of individual signing on behalf of debtor]

[An individual signing on behalf of a partnership or corporation must indicate position or relationship to debtor.]

- -

Penalty for making a false statement or concealing property.   Fine of up to $500,000 or imprisonment for up to 5 years or both. 18 U.S.C. §§ 152 and 3571.
                                                                                                                                [G8593]

Form 7

STATEMENT OF FINANCIAL AFFAIRS

FORM 7
(6/90)

UNITED STATES BANKRUPTCY COURT
_____ **District of** _____

In Re: _____ ,   Case No. _____
                     (Name)   (If Known)
                           Debtor

STATEMENT OF FINANCIAL AFFAIRS

      This statement is to be completed by every debtor. Spouses filing a joint petition may file a single statement on which the information for both spouses is combined. If the case is filed under chapter 12 or chapter 13, a married debtor must furnish information for both spouses whether or not a joint petition is filed, unless the spouses are separated and a joint petition is not filed. An individual debtor engaged in business as a sole proprietor, partner, family farmer, or self-employed professional, should provide the information requested on this statement concerning all such activities as well as the individual's personal affairs.

      Questions 1 - 15 are to be completed by all debtors. Debtors that are or have been in business, as defined below, also must complete Questions 16 - 21. **Each question must be answered. If the answer to any question is "None," or the question is not applicable, mark the box labeled "None."** If additional space is needed for the answer to any question, use and attach a separate sheet properly identified with the case name, case number (if known), and the number of the question.

DEFINITIONS

      "In business." A debtor is "in business" for the purpose of this form if the debtor is a corporation or partnership. An individual debtor is "in business" for the purpose of this form if the debtor is or has been, within the two years immediately preceding the filing of the this bankruptcy case, any of the following: an officer, director, managing executive, or person in control of a corporation; a partner, other than a limited partner, of a partnership; a sole proprietor or self-employed.

      "Insider." The term "insider" includes but is not limited to: relatives of the debtor; general partners of the debtor and their relatives; corporations of which the debtor is an officer, director, or person in control; officers, directors, and any person in control of a corporate debtor and their relatives; affiliates of the debtor and insiders of such affiliates; any managing agent of the debtor. 11 U.S.C. § 101(30).

---

      1. Income from employment or operation of business

None   State the gross amount of income the debtor has received from employment, trade, or
☐   profession, or from operation of the debtor's business from the beginning of this calendar year to the date this case was commenced. State also the gross amounts received during the **two years** immediately preceding this calendar year. (A debtor that maintains, or has maintained, financial records on the basis of a fiscal rather than a calendar year may report fiscal year income. Identify the beginning and ending dates of the debtor's fiscal year.) If a joint petition is filed, state income for each spouse separately. (Married debtors filing under chapter 12 or chapter 13 must state income of both spouses whether or not a joint petition is filed, unless the spouses are separated and a joint petition is not filed.)

         AMOUNT   SOURCE (if more than one)   [G8594]

2. Income other than from employment or operation of business

None
☐
State the amount of income received by the debtor other than from employment, trade, profession, or operation of the debtor's business during the **two years** immediately preceding the commencement of this case. Give particulars. If a joint petition is filed, state income for each spouse separately. (Married debtors filing under chapter 12 or chapter 13 must state income for each spouse whether or not a joint petition is filed, unless the spouses are separated and a joint petition is not filed.)

AMOUNT   SOURCE

---

3. Payments to creditors

None a. List all payments on loans, installment purchases of goods or services, and other debts,
☐   aggregating more than $600 to any creditor, made within **90 days** immediately preceding the commencement of this case. (Married debtors filing under chapter 12 or chapter 13 must include payments by either or both spouses whether or not a joint petition is filed, unless the spouses are separated and a joint petition is not filed.)

NAME AND ADDRESS OF CREDITOR	DATES OF PAYMENTS	AMOUNT PAID	AMOUNT STILL OWING

None b. List all payments made within **one year** immediately preceding the commencement of this case
☐   to or for the benefit of creditors who are or were insiders. (Married debtors filing under chapter 12 or chapter 13 must include payments by either or both spouses whether or not a joint petition is filed, unless the spouses are separated and a joint petition is not filed.)

NAME AND ADDRESS OF CREDITOR AND RELATIONSHIP TO DEBTOR	DATE OF PAYMENT	AMOUNT PAID	AMOUNT STILL OWING

---

4. Suits, executions, garnishments and attachments

None a. List all suits to which the debtor is or was a party within **one year** immediately preceding the filing
☐   of this bankruptcy case. (Married debtors filing under chapter 12 or chapter 13 must include information concerning either or both spouses whether or not a joint petition is filed, unless the spouses are separated and a joint petition is not filed.)

CAPTION OF SUIT AND CASE NUMBER	NATURE OF PROCEEDING	COURT AND LOCATION	STATUS OR DISPOSITION

[G8595]

None b. Describe all property that has been attached, garnished or seized under any legal or equitable
☐   process within **one year** immediately preceding the commencement of this case. (Married debtors
      filing under chapter 12 or chapter 13 must include information concerning property of either or both
      spouses whether or not a joint petition is filed, unless the spouses are separated and a joint petition is
      not filed.)

NAME AND ADDRESS OF PERSON FOR WHOSE BENEFIT PROPERTY WAS SEIZED	DATE OF SEIZURE	DESCRIPTION AND VALUE OF PROPERTY

5. Repossessions, foreclosures and returns

None List all property that has been repossessed by a creditor, sold at a foreclosure sale, transferred
☐   through a deed in lieu of foreclosure or returned to the seller, within **one year** immediately preceding
      the commencement of this case. (Married debtors filing under chapter 12 or chapter 13 must include
      information concerning property of either or both spouses whether or not a joint petition is filed, unless
      the spouses are separated and a joint petition is not filed.)

NAME AND ADDRESS OF CREDITOR OR SELLER	DATE OF REPOSSESSION, FORECLOSURE SALE, TRANSFER OR RETURN	DESCRIPTION AND VALUE OF PROPERTY

6. Assignments and receiverships

None a. Describe any assignment of property for the benefit of creditors made within **120 days** immediately
☐   preceding the commencement of this case. (Married debtors filing under chapter 12 or chapter 13 must
      include any assignment by either or both spouses whether or not a joint petition is filed, unless the
      spouses are separated and a joint petition is not filed.)

NAME AND ADDRESS OF ASSIGNEE	DATE OF ASSIGNMENT	TERMS OF ASSIGNMENT OR SETTLEMENT

None b. List all property which has been in the hands of a custodian, receiver, or court-appointed official
☐   within **one year** immediately preceding the commencement of this case. (Married debtors filing under
      chapter 12 or chapter 13 must include information concerning property of either or both spouses whether
      or not a joint petition is filed, unless the spouses are separated and a joint petition is not filed.)

NAME AND ADDRESS OF CUSTODIAN	NAME AND LOCATION OF COURT CASE TITLE & NUMBER	DATE OF ORDER	DESCRIPTION AND VALUE OF PROPERTY

[G8596]

7. Gifts

None
☐ List all gifts or charitable contributions made within **one year** immediately preceding the commencement of this case except ordinary and usual gifts to family members aggregating less than $200 in value per individual family member and charitable contributions aggregating less than $100 per recipient. (Married debtors filing under chapter 12 or chapter 13 must include gifts or contributions by either or both spouses whether or not a joint petition is filed, unless the spouses are separated and a joint petition is not filed.)

NAME AND ADDRESS OF PERSON OR ORGANIZATION	RELATIONSHIP TO DEBTOR, IF ANY	DATE OF GIFT	DESCRIPTION AND VALUE OF GIFT

8. Losses

None
☐ List all losses from fire, theft, other casualty or gambling within **one year** immediately preceding the commencement of this case **or since the commencement of this case.** (Married debtors filing under chapter 12 or chapter 13 must include losses by either or both spouses whether or not a joint petition is filed, unless the spouses are separated and a joint petition is not filed.)

DESCRIPTION AND VALUE OF PROPERTY	DESCRIPTION OF CIRCUMSTANCES AND, IF LOSS WAS COVERED IN WHOLE OR IN PART BY INSURANCE, GIVE PARTICULARS	DATE OF LOSS

9. Payments related to debt counseling or bankruptcy

None
☐ List all payments made or property transferred by or on behalf of the debtor to any persons, including attorneys, for consultation concerning debt consolidation, relief under the bankruptcy law or preparation of a petition in bankruptcy within **one year** immediately preceding the commencement of this case.

NAME AND ADDRESS OF PAYEE	DATE OF PAYMENT, NAME OF PAYOR IF OTHER THAN DEBTOR	AMOUNT OF MONEY OR DESCRIPTION AND VALUE OF PROPERTY

[G8597]

10. Other transfers

None
☐
a. List all other property, other than property transferred in the ordinary course of the business or financial affairs of the debtor, transferred either absolutely or as security within **one year** immediately preceding the commencement of this case. (Married debtors filing under chapter 12 or chapter 13 must include transfers by either or both spouses whether or not a joint petition is filed, unless the spouses are separated and a joint petition is not filed.)

		DESCRIBE PROPERTY TRANSFERRED
NAME AND ADDRESS OF TRANSFEREE, RELATIONSHIP TO DEBTOR	DATE	AND VALUE RECEIVED

11. Closed financial accounts

None
☐
List all financial accounts and instruments held in the name of the debtor or for the benefit of the debtor which were closed, sold, or otherwise transferred within **one year** immediately preceding the commencement of this case. Include checking, savings, or other financial accounts, certificates of deposit, or other instruments; shares and share accounts held in banks, credit unions, pension funds, cooperatives, associations, brokerage houses and other financial institutions. (Married debtors filing under chapter 12 or chapter 13 must include information concerning accounts or instruments held by or for either or both spouses whether or not a joint petition is filed, unless the spouses are separated and a joint petition is not filed.)

NAME AND ADDRESS OF INSTITUTION	TYPE AND NUMBER OF ACCOUNT AND AMOUNT OF FINAL BALANCE	AMOUNT AND DATE OF SALE OR CLOSING

12. Safe deposit boxes

None
☐
List each safe deposit or other box or depository in which the debtor has or had securities, cash, or other valuables within **one year** immediately preceding the commencement of this case. (Married debtors filing under chapter 12 or chapter 13 must include boxes or depositories of either or both spouses whether or not a joint petition is filed, unless the spouses are separated and a joint petition is not filed.)

NAME AND ADDRESS OF BANK OR OTHER DEPOSITORY	NAMES AND ADDRESSES OF THOSE WITH ACCESS TO BOX OR DEPOSITORY	DESCRIPTION OF CONTENTS	DATE OF TRANSFER OR SURRENDER, IF ANY

[G8598]

NALS, Car.Leg.Sec. 3rd Ed.—16

13. Setoffs

None
☐

List all setoffs made by any creditor, including a bank, against a debt or deposit of the debtor within **90 days** preceding the commencement of this case. (Married debtors filing under chapter 12 or chapter 13 must include information concerning either or both spouses whether or not a joint petition is filed, unless the spouses are separated and a joint petition is not filed.)

NAME AND ADDRESS OF CREDITOR	DATE OF SETOFF	AMOUNT OF SETOFF

14. Property held for another person

None
☐

List all property owned by another person that the debtor holds or controls.

NAME AND ADDRESS OF OWNER	DESCRIPTION AND VALUE OF PROPERTY	LOCATION OF PROPERTY

15. Prior address of debtor

None
☐

If the debtor has moved within the **two years** immediately preceding the commencement of this case, list all premises which the debtor occupied during that period and vacated prior to the commencement of this case. If a joint petition is filed, report also any separate address of either spouse.

ADDRESS	NAME USED	DATES OF OCCUPANCY
		[G8599]

The following questions are to be completed by every debtor that is a corporation or partnership and by any individual debtor who is or has been, within the two years immediately preceding the commencement of this case, any of the following: an officer, director, managing executive, or owner of more than 5 percent of the voting securities of a corporation; a partner, other than a limited partner, of a partnership; a sole proprietor or otherwise self-employed.

*(An individual or joint debtor should complete this portion of the statement **only** if the debtor is or has been in business, as defined above, within the two years immediately preceding the commencement of this case.)*

16. Nature, location and name of business

None a. If the debtor is an individual, list the names and addresses of all businesses in which the debtor was
☐   an officer, director, partner, or managing executive of a corporation, partnership, sole proprietorship, or was a self-employed professional within the **two years** immediately preceding the commencement of this case, or in which the debtor owned 5 percent or more of the voting or equity securities within the two years immediately preceding the commencement of this case.

     b. If the debtor is a partnership, list the names and addresses of all businesses in which the debtor was a partner or owned 5 percent or more of the voting securities, within the **two years** immediately preceding the commencement of this case.

     c. If the debtor is a corporation, list the names and addresses of all businesses in which the debtor was a partner or owned 5 percent or more of the voting securities within the **two years** immediately preceding the commencement of this case.

NAME	ADDRESS	NATURE OF BUSINESS	BEGINNING AND ENDING DATES OF OPERATION

---

17. Books, records and financial statements

None a. List all bookkeepers and accountants who within the **six years** immediately preceding the filing of
☐   this bankruptcy case kept or supervised the keeping of books of account and records of the debtor.

NAME AND ADDRESS	DATES SERVICES RENDERED

None b. List all firms or individuals who within the **two years** immediately preceding the filing of this
☐   bankruptcy case have audited the books of account and records, or prepared a financial statement of the debtor.

NAME	ADDRESS	DATES SERVICES RENDERED
		[G8600]

None ☐ c. List all firms or individuals who at the time of the commencement of this case were in possession of the books of account and records of the debtor. If any of the books of account and records are not available, explain.

NAME   ADDRESS

None ☐ d. List all financial institutions, creditors and other parties, including mercantile and trade agencies, to whom a financial statement was issued within the **two years** immediately preceding the commencement of this case by the debtor.

NAME AND ADDRESS   DATE ISSUED

18. Inventories

None ☐ a. List the dates of the last two inventories taken of your property, the name of the person who supervised the taking of each inventory, and the dollar amount and basis of each inventory.

                                                DOLLAR AMOUNT OF INVENTORY

DATE OF INVENTORY   INVENTORY SUPERVISOR   (Specify cost, market or other basis)

None ☐ b. List the name and address of the person having possession of the records of each of the two inventories reported in a., above.

                                   NAME AND ADDRESSES OF CUSTODIAN

DATE OF INVENTORY   OF INVENTORY RECORDS

19. Current Partners, Officers, Directors and Shareholders

None ☐ a. If the debtor is a partnership, list the nature and percentage of partnership interest of each member of the partnership.

NAME AND ADDRESS   NATURE OF INTEREST   PERCENTAGE OF INTEREST

[G8601]

None   b. If the debtor is a corporation, list all officers and directors of the corporation, and each stockholder
☐   who directly or indirectly owns, controls, or holds 5 percent or more of the voting securities of the
corporation.

NAME AND ADDRESS	TITLE	NATURE AND PERCENTAGE OF STOCK OWNERSHIP

___

20. Former partners, officers, directors and shareholders

None   a. If the debtor is a partnership, list each member who withdrew from the partnership within **one year**
☐   year immediately preceding the commencement of this case.

NAME	ADDRESS	DATE OF WITHDRAWAL

___

None   b. If the debtor is a corporation, list all officers, or directors whose relationship with the corporation
☐   terminated within **one year** immediately preceding the commencement of this case.

NAME AND ADDRESS	TITLE	DATE OF TERMINATION

___

21. Withdrawals from a partnership or distributions by a corporation

None   If the debtor is a partnership or corporation, list all withdrawals or distributions credited or given
☐   to an insider, including compensation in any form, bonuses, loans, stock redemptions, options exercised
and any other perquisite during **one year** immediately preceding the commencement of this case.

NAME & ADDRESS OF RECIPIENT, RELATIONSHIP TO DEBTOR	DATE AND PURPOSE OF WITHDRAWAL	AMOUNT OF MONEY OR DESCRIPTION AND VALUE OF PROPERTY

*   *   *   *   *   *

[G8602]

[If completed by an individual or individual and spouse]

I declare under penalty of perjury that I have read the answers contained in the foregoing statement of financial affairs and any attachments thereto and that they are true and correct.

Date _____   Signature _____
                                         of Debtor

Date _____   Signature _____
                                         of Joint Debtor
                                         (if any)

*   *   *   *   *   *

[If completed on behalf of a partnership or corporation]

I, declare under penalty of perjury that I have read the answers contained in the foregoing statement of financial affairs and any attachments thereto and that they are true and correct to the best of my knowledge, information and belief.

Date _____   Signature _____

                                         _____
                                         Print Name and Title

[An individual signing on behalf of a partnership or corporation must indicate position or relationship to debtor.]

_____ continuation sheets attached

Penalty for making a false statement: Fine of up to $500,000 or imprisonment for up to 5 years, or both. 18 U.S.C. § 152 and 3571

[G8604]

STATEMENT PURSUANT TO RULE 2016(b)

UNITED STATES BANKRUPTCY COURT FOR THE
_____ DISTRICT OF _____

In re	)
	)
	)
_____	) Case No. _____
Debtor [set forth here all names including trade names used by Debtor within last 6 years].	)
Social Security Number _____	)
	)

The undersigned, pursuant to Rule 2016(b) Bankruptcy Rules, states that:

(1) The undersigned is the attorney for the debtor(s) in this case.

(2) The compensation paid or agreed to be paid by the debtor(s) to the undersigned is: $_____
     (a) for legal services rendered or to be rendered in contemplation of and in $_____
         connection with this case $_____
     (b) prior to filing this statement, debtor(s) have paid
     (c) the unpaid balance due and payable is

(3) $ of the filing fee in this case has been paid,

(4) The services rendered or to be rendered include the following:
     (a) analysis of the financial situation, and rendering advice and assistance to the debtor(s) in determining whether to file a petition under title 11 of the United States Code.
     (b) preparation and filing of the petition, schedules, statement of affairs and other documents required by the court.
     (c) representation of the debtor(s) at the meeting of creditors.

(5) The source of payments made by the debtor(s) to the undersigned was from earnings, wages and compensation for services performed, and

(6) The source of payments to be made by the debtor(s) to the undersigned for the unpaid balance remaining, if any, will be from earnings, wages and compensation for services performed, and

(7) The undersigned has received no transfer, assignment or pledge of property except the following for the value stated:

(8) The undersigned has not shared or agreed to share with any other entity, other than with members of undersigned's law firm, any compensation paid or to be paid except as follows:

Dated: Respectfully submitted _____ _Attorney for Petition_
Attorney's name and address _____

REVISED STATEMENT OF COMPENSATION: RULE 2016(b)

§ 20.36   Chapter 13 Plans

A salaried person or wage earner who is temporarily overwhelmed by his debts but believes he could and would like to pay them off from future earnings or liquidation of certain assets within a reasonable period of time (three to five years) if given the opportunity to do so without harassment from creditors, might wish to consider the protection of chapter 13 of the Bankruptcy Code. Under this chapter of the Bankruptcy Code, the debtor files a plan whereby he agrees to pay a certain percentage of his future earnings or cash from sales of assets to a trustee to pay off his debts. If the court accepts the plan as being feasible, the debtor has the protection of the court while he pays off his debts and thus avoids the potential stigma of having to file chapter 7 and being involuntarily liquidated.

Further advantages in a chapter 13 plan are:

• Discharge of criminal fines and penalties (but not restitution)

• Discharge of debts for fraud and malicious injury

• Payment of tax arrearages without further penalties and interest

• Payment of mortgage arrearages over the objection of the mortgage lender

• Ability to "strip down" a mortgage to equal the property value

• Ability to change the terms of a secured loan (other than a mortgage secured only by the residence). A debtor can change the interest rate, length of loan, monthly payment, etc.

§ 20.37 Adjustment of Debts of a Family Farmer With Regular Annual Income (Chapter 12)

Under Bankruptcy Code chapter 12 which took effect November 26, 1986, under the terms of the Bankruptcy Judges, United States Trustees, and Family Farmer Bankruptcy Act of 1986 (Public Law 94–554), the family farmer with regular annual income may file for relief for the adjustment of his debts. Chapter 12 has been designed for use by true family farmers, including partnerships consisting of farmers and corporations consisting of owner farmers operating a farming operation. Only a "family farmer" with regular annual income may be a debtor under chapter 12. A chapter 12 case may only be initiated voluntarily by the debtor; there cannot be an involuntary chapter 12 proceeding.

Once a reorganization plan has been filed, a chapter 12 trustee will supervise the debtor's operation for a period of from three to five years, but once the plan has been confirmed the debtor retains possession of the assets of the estate, "including operating the debtor's farm."

BIBLIOGRAPHY

Black's Law Dictionary With Pronunciations, Sixth Edition, West Publishing Company, St. Paul, Minnesota, 1991.

Cline and Strong, *Law Office Management,* West Publishing Company.

Code of Professional Responsibility and Canons of Judicial Ethics, American Bar Association, Chicago, Illinois.

Cunningham, Wm. E., *The Para–Legal and the Lawyer's Library,* Shepards Citations, 1973.

Good, C. Edward, *Citing & Typing the Law, A Course on Legal Citations & Style.*

Hankinson, Marilyn, *I Can't Write Book,* Writing Services, Des Moines, Iowa.

Henderson, Greta LaFollette and Price R. Boiles; *Business English Essentials,* 6th ed., McGraw–Hill Book Company, New York, New York, 1980.

How to Find the Law, 7th ed., West Publishing Company, 1978.

Hutchinson, Lois Irene, *Standard Handbook for Secretaries,* 8th ed., McGraw–Hill Book Company, New York, 1977.

Kionka, Edward J., *Torts Injuries to Persons and Property,* West Publishing Company, 1977.

The Lawyer's Secretary, Fourth Edition, Practising Law Institute, New York, New York, 1972.

Malone, Wex S., *Torts Injuries to Family, Social and Trade Relations,* West Publishing Company, 1979.

Martindale–Hubbell Law Directory, Reed Publishing (USA), Inc., 1992.

Miles, Norma Jean, Certified PLS, *Citations Manual,* National Association of Legal Secretaries.

Miller, Besse May, *Legal Secretary's Complete Handbook,* 3rd Edition, Prentice–Hall, Inc., Englewood Cliffs, New Jersey, 1980.

Price, Miles O., *A Practical Manual of Standard Legal Citations,* Second Edition, Oceana Publications, Inc., Dobbs Ferry, New York, 1958.

The Reader's Digest Great Encyclopedia Dictionary, The Reader's Digest Association, Inc., Pleasantville, New York, 1966.

BIBLIOGRAPHY

Restatement of the Law, Second Edition, American Law Institute, West Publishing Company, 1979.

Sabin, William A., *The Gregg Reference Manual*, 7th ed., Macmillan/McGraw-Hill, 1992.

A Uniform System of Citation, 15th ed., The Harvard Law Review Association, Gannet House, Cambridge, Massachusetts, 1991.

United States Government Printing Office Style Manual, Superintendent of Documents, Government Printing Office, Washington, D.C., 1984.

West's Law Finder, West Publishing Company, 1987.

GLOSSARY

This Glossary consists of words, terms, and phrases used in this volume, and the explanations and definitions are restricted to those discussions found in the text.

A

Abandoned property	In bankruptcy, property belonging to the debtor which a trustee decides would bring in no money for creditors in a bankruptcy proceeding.
Abortion	Intentional termination of a pregnancy.
Abstract extension	The act of having the abstract of title brought to a current date through search of title records.
Abstract of title	A condensed history of the title to the land.
Abstracter's certificate	A certificate which is made a part of the abstract and signed by the abstracter verifying what the abstract covers.
Acceptance	In contracts, the situation occurring when the offeree is in total agreement with the offer.
Accord and satisfaction	Accord is accepting another thing (substitution) in place of the thing promised in the original contract. Satisfaction occurs when the substitution is accepted.
Account stated	A summarized statement of a debtor's account.
Accounting cycle	The steps involved in handling all of the transactions completed during the fiscal period beginning with recording in a book of original entry and ending with a post-closing trial balance.
Accounting equation	Assets = liabilities + owner's equity.
Accounts payable	All accounts owed.
Accounts receivable	Amounts owed by the clients to the law firm.
Accrual basis	Recording revenue in the period in which it is earned.
Acknowledgment	(1) A formal declaration by the person who executed the instrument before an authorized official that it is his free act and deed. (2)

693

	The certificate of the official on such instrument attesting that it was so acknowledged.
Acquittal	(1) A release, absolution, or discharge of an obligation or liability. (2) In criminal law the finding of not guilty.
Action to quiet title	Legal action taken by a property owner to have a court declare him the owner of a particular parcel. This action is usually taken when the merchantability of a land title has been questioned.
Active files	Files in which there is work to be done and in which there may be unbilled time.
Adjudicate	To settle controversies and disputes between parties.
Adjust	A text-editing typewriter feature in which the machine automatically adjusts the right-hand margin if one inserts or deletes copy during the playback or changes margins in any way.
Administration	In estates, the supervision of an estate by an administrator or executor.
Administrative agencies	Agencies created by the legislative branch of government to administer laws pertaining to specific areas, such as taxes, transportation, and labor.
Administrator	A male person appointed by a court to administer an intestate estate. See personal representative, executor, executrix.
Administratrix	A female person appointed by a court to administer an intestate estate. See personal representative, executor, executrix.
Adoption	The legal process under a state statute by which a child is taken into one's family and given all rights and privileges of a natural child and heir.
Advance sheets	Paperback pamphlets published weekly or monthly which contain reporter cases, including correct volume number and page number. When there are sufficient cases, they are replaced by a bound volume.
Adversary proceeding	(1) One having opposing parties, such as a plaintiff and a defendant. (2) Individual lawsuit(s) brought within a bankruptcy proceeding.

694

GLOSSARY

Adverse possession	A method of acquiring title to real property under certain conditions by possession for a statutory period.
Affiant	The person who makes and subscribes to an affidavit.
Affidavit	A written or printed declaration of facts made voluntarily and confirmed by oath of the maker to a person with authority to administer the oath.
Affirmation	A solemn and formal declaration that an affidavit is true. This is substituted for an oath in certain instances.
Affirmative defense	A defense raised in a responsive pleading (answer) relating a new matter as a defense to the complaint.
Agreement	Mutual consent.
Alien	A foreign-born person who has not qualified as a citizen of the country.
Alimony	Allowance which a spouse pays for the support of the other spouse after final divorce decree.
Allegations	Numbered paragraphs setting forth the background and reasons for filing a suit.
Alphanumeric filing	A combination of an alphabetic filing system and a numeric system where numbers are assigned to files in blocks according to the letter of the alphabet which identifies the client.
American Bar Association	A national association of lawyers whose primary purpose is improvement of lawyers and the administration of justice.
American Law Reports	Reports cases from all United States jurisdictions by subject matter.
Ancillary	Describes a proceeding which is auxiliary or subordinate to another proceeding.
Annotations	Remarks, notes, case summaries, or commentaries following a statute which describe interpretations of the statute.
Annulment	(1) The act of making void. (2) That which establishes that marital status never existed.
Answer	A formal, written statement by the defendant in a lawsuit which answers each allegation contained in the complaint.

695

Answers to interrogatories	A formal, written statement by a party to a lawsuit which answers each question or interrogatory propounded by the other party. These answers must be acknowledged before a notary public.
Appeal	A proceeding brought to a higher court to review a lower court decision.
Appeal bond	A guaranty by the appealing party insuring that court costs will be paid.
Appearance	Coming into court as a party to a suit, either in person or by an attorney.
Appellate jurisdiction	Authority of a court to review cases tried in lower courts.
Archive	In computer terminology, the procedure of transferring text from the on-line system diskette to an off-line storage diskette.
Archive diskette	A storage medium used to store text off line. Each sector holds bytes of information.
Arithmetic capability	The ability of a word processing system to be used as a calculator or adding machine. Some of the more sophisticated systems have the ability to do arithmetic tasks; a small number can do such tasks as part of word processing routines with totals embedded in text, etc.
Arraignment	The hearing at which the accused is brought before the court to plead to the criminal charge in the indictment. He may plead "guilty," "not guilty," or where permitted "nolo contendere."
Articles of incorporation	The basic instrument filed with the appropriate government agency to form a corporation.
Assault	An act which creates in the plaintiff immediate fear of an attempted battery.
Assets	In bookkeeping the entries on a balance sheet that express in terms of money the value of tangible things or intangible rights which constitute the resources of a person or business as of a given date. In estates, the property owned by the decedent.
Assignee	A person to whom an assignment is made.
Assignor	A person who assigns a right, whether or not he is the original owner thereof.

Assumed business name	A name other than its own by which a person or entity does business. Also known as a fictitious name.
Assumption of risk	The legal rule under which a person may not recover for an injury he receives when he voluntarily exposes himself to a known danger.
At issue	The term used when the complaint and a responsive pleading have been filed.
Attestation clause	The clause of a will immediately following the signature of a testator and usually beginning "Signed, sealed, published, and declared...."
Auto centering	The ability to center a word or text segment automatically. This function is usually implemented by a keystroke(s) that instructs the system to center the previously typed or next text segment. Text may be centered between margins or at a designated point. Also some systems can center between tab settings for the centering of column headings of tabular material.
Auto headers/footers	The ability to place header/footer text at the top or bottom of each page of a multi-page document. The operator specifies the text once, and the header/footer (usually document title, company name, or confidential requirements) is automatically added during printout. Changes may be made to the main document text without affecting the headers and footers.
Auto pagination	The ability to take a multi-page document and divide it into pages of a specified length (in number of lines). Often such ability is joined with the capability to generate page numbers automatically.
Auto repagination	The ability to change page endings automatically if text is inserted or deleted within a document or if a new page length is desired. Text is removed from or added to pages, as required, to maintain page length.
Automatic letter writing	A method of producing a "personalized" form letter. Each time a boilerplate or standard letter is printed out, variable information (name, address, etc.) is automatically inserted in the appropriate places.

697

Automatic measured review	A feature of certain dictation systems which permits the machine to back up a certain number of words so that the dictator can hear what he has just dictated.
Automatic word wraparound	A feature which automatically moves a word to the beginning of a new line when the current line becomes full during text entry, thereby freeing the operator from the necessity of estimating a full line, touching return, or hyphenating words.

B

Bail	Security given for the release of a jailed person which guarantees his attendance at all required court appearances.
Bail bond	A written guaranty executed by a defendant and a surety to ensure the defendant will appear and make himself available to the court.
Bailiff	The peace officer of the court responsible for keeping order and maintaining appropriate courtroom decorum.
Balance	In bookkeeping, the difference between the total debits and credits in an account.
Balance sheet	Provides information regarding the status of assets, liabilities, and owner's equity as of a specified time or date.
Bankruptcy	The means by which a person may gain protection under the law for unpaid debts.
Bankruptcy judge	The judge who determines whether a debtor is entitled to a discharge in bankruptcy.
Bankruptcy law	The area of federal law dealing with persons or businesses who file for protection under the Bankruptcy Code.
Battery	A harmful offensive touching of another's person.
Beneficiary	(1) A person who benefits from the act of another. (2) A person named to receive property in a will or trust.
Bequest	A gift by will of personal property; a legacy.
Bidirectional printout	The capability of a word processing system to print line one from left-to-right and line two from right-to-left, saving time by avoiding unnecessary carriage (or element) movement.

GLOSSARY

Bilateral contract	One where both parties make a promise.
Bill of costs	A certified, itemized statement of the amount of costs in an action or suit.
Bind over	Transfer of jurisdiction of an accused person from one court to another court.
Bit	The smallest unit of information recognized by a computer. Also, an abbreviation for "binary digit."
Black box	Refers to the operating unit or "brains" of an electronic system; slang term for a central processor unit.
Block move/copy	The ability to designate a block of text (generally with some maximum number of characters and related to buffer size) and to move it within the document or to another document. Most systems which can access and move blocks of text can also copy blocks to another storage location (for editing) without erasing the original text.
Board of directors	Governing body of a corporation elected by the shareholders.
Boilerplate	An initial prerecorded document combined with variable information to produce a second document. It contains that section of the final document which remains constant, *e.g.,* the body of a form letter or provisions of a will.
Bond	A written agreement by which a person says he will pay a certain sum of money if the person bonded does not perform certain duties properly.
Bound supplement	A supplement to a book or books to update the service bound in permanent form.
Breach	(1) The breaking or violating of a law, right, or duty, either by commission or omission. (2) The failure of one party to carry out any condition of a contract.
Brief	A memorandum of material facts, points of law, precedents, etc., prepared to familiarize the court with the facts and the law of a particular case.
Bureau of Land Management (BLM)	A federal agency which administers federally owned public lands.
Burglary	The act of illegal entry with the intent to steal.

Business bankruptcy	The proceeding under the Bankruptcy Code filed by a business entity.
Bylaws	Rules or laws adopted by an association or corporation to govern its actions.
Byte	A sequence of adjacent binary digits operated upon as a unit and usually shorter than a word (eight adjacent binary digits).

C

Canons of ethics	Standards of ethical conduct for attorneys.
Capacity	Having legal authority or mental ability; being of sound mind.
Capital case	A felony case punishable by death.
Caption	The title of the case.
Cash basis	In bookkeeping, the method by which no record is made of revenue until cash is received and expenses are not recorded in the records until they are paid.
Cash journal	Book of original entry for recording daily transactions.
Cathode ray tube (CRT)	Also, video display unit (VDT). A visual terminal resembling a television screen displaying up to a page of printed material, depending on make of equipment.
Cause of action	The incident or facts which give a person a right to relief in court.
CD–ROM	Compact Disk–Read Only Memory
Central Processor Unit (CPU)	The part of a computer or a word processing system where all computations, sorting, selecting, and all data manipulation take place; oversees the use of the main memory and monitors input and output operations. The CPU is often referred to as the computer's "brains."
Central recording system	A dictation system with the recorder located in one main area but with dictating and transcribing units in several locations.
Certificate of abstracter	See abstracter's certificate.
Certificate of title	See title insurance.
Certiorari	A writ of review issued by a higher court to a lower court.

Cessation	Termination.
Challenge for cause	A request by a plaintiff or a defendant to a judge that a certain prospective juror not be allowed to be a member of the jury because of specified causes or reasons. See peremptory challenge.
Change of venue	A change in the location of a trial.
Chapter 13 Plan	A plan in bankruptcy which gives a salaried debtor or wage earner the protection of the court from creditors while he pays a percentage of his wages to a trustee who pays off his debts.
Chart of accounts	An outline of the business accounts used in the bookkeeping system.
Chattel	An article of personal property; not real estate.
Checklist	A list of items to be used as a means of reference, comparison, or verification.
Chronological	Arranged in the order in which events happened; according to date.
Circular E—Employer's Tax Guide	A booklet published periodically by the Internal Revenue Service as a guide for the bookkeeper regarding tax law.
Citation	A legal authority, such as a constitution, statute, case, or other authoritative source, which is used to support a written legal document.
Citators	A set of books which provide the subsequent history of reported decisions through a form of abbreviations or words. Most widely used are Shepard's Citations.
Civil	Relating to private rights and remedies sought by civil actions as contrasted with criminal proceedings.
Civil action	An action brought by one party against another to resolve a controversy.
Civil Law	The legal system prevailing in the European, Asiatic, Central American, and South American countries which inherited their legal systems from Rome.
Civil Service Commission	A federal agency which regulates the hiring of government employees.
Claim	A debt owing by a debtor to another person or business.

Clear and merchantable title	The term used to indicate that there are no outstanding liens or encumbrances of record against the property.
Clerk of court	Administrator or chief clerical officer of the court.
Close corporation	A corporation whose shares are held by a single shareholder or a closely-knit group of shareholders.
Closed hearing	Hearings at which members of the general public are not allowed as spectators.
Closing agent	A person who handles a closing of sale of real estate.
Closing entries	Bookkeeping totals made to close out accounting entries at the end of a given time period.
Code of Federal Regulations	Published annually and contains the cumulative executive agency regulations.
Code of Professional Responsibility	Rules of conduct that govern the legal profession.
Codicil	An amendment to a will, either to add provisions or delete provisions of a will, which is executed with all the formalities of a will.
Codification	The process of collecting and arranging the laws (federal, county, or state) into a code.
Collate	The process of placing the pages of a document in proper sequence.
Combined cash journal	Multicolumn cash journal in which items that have a great number of entries are placed in an appropriate titled column and only the total is posted to the general ledger at the end of the month.
Common law	Law that has evolved from earlier decisions of courts; law based on precedent; case law. The legal system prevailing in English-speaking countries; originated in England and its form of development was different from that of civil law.
Common stock	A class of corporate stock which represents the ownership of the corporation and normally has voting rights.
Community property	Property acquired during a marriage which is owned by husband and wife, each having an undivided one-half interest.
Comparative negligence	The rule under which negligence is measured by percentage and damages are diminished in proportion to the amount of negligence attributable to the person seeking recovery.

702

Compatibility	A characteristic of word or data processing equipment which permits one machine to accept and process data prepared by another machine without conversion or code modification.
Complaint	The original or initial pleading by which an action is filed in court.
Concurrent jurisdiction	Jurisdiction granted in different courts at the same time over the same matters and within the same territorial limit.
Conditional will	Also, contingent will. One which does not take effect unless a specific event occurs. If the event does not occur, it is as though there is no will. Most states do not recognize this type of will.
Conforming	The process of typing on all copies of a document the information shown on the original so the copy will reflect dates, signatures, and corrections which were placed on the original.
Consent	Agreement; voluntary acceptance of the wish of another.
Conservator	A person appointed by a court to manage the estate of a protected person.
Consideration	In contracts, the price bargained for and paid for a promise, goods, or real estate.
Constitution	The fundamental law of a nation or state which establishes the character and basic principles of the government.
Constitutional law	Law set forth in the Constitution of the United States and in state constitutions.
Consumer bankruptcy	A proceeding under the Bankruptcy Code filed by an individual (or husband and wife) who is not in business.
Consumer debt	A debt incurred for personal, household, or family debt.
Consumer Product Safety Commission	Commission which protects against unreasonable risks of injury from consumer products.
Contempt of court	The term applied to an individual who refuses to obey either a written or oral order of the court.
Contested	Challenged; opposed.
Contingent will	See conditional will.

703

Continuation or extension of abstract	See abstract extension.
Continuous form	One set of forms is joined to another in a series of accordion-pleated folds.
Contra account	Name for an account or item in an account which balances a corresponding account or item on the opposite side of the ledger.
Contract	An enforceable agreement between two or more competent parties which creates an obligation to do or not to do a particular thing.
Contract for deed	A contract to sell real estate upon installment payment. See land contract.
Contributory negligence	An affirmative defense which means that the injuries and damages complained of by the plaintiff were caused in whole or in part, or were contributed to as a result of plaintiff's own negligence.
Conversion	Taking property which belongs to another and using it as one's own.
Conveyance	Transfer of title to land from one person or entity or group of persons or entities to another by deed.
Cooperative	An organization comprised of a group of people who pool their products or resources to their mutual advantage.
Copy	A feature which duplicates a designated section of text, then moves the duplicated text to an operator-specified location and inserts it. May be used either within a document or among documents.
Copy revision	Includes console preparation, automatic playback when making corrections due to editorial changes, and actuating of various playback controls. Console adjustments are included, if required.
Corporate seal	A seal used by a corporation for authenticating its corporate acts and executing legal instruments.
Corporation	A legal entity created by authority of the laws of a state or nation.
Costs advanced	Costs paid by the attorney on the client's behalf.
Counterclaim	A claim presented by a defendant in opposition to or for deduction from the claim of plaintiff.

Counteroffer	Response to an offer with different terms than the original offer; counterproposal.
Court	Tribunal with judicial authority to handle the administration of justice.
Court-appointed attorney	An attorney appointed by the court to represent a defendant, usually with respect to criminal charges and without the defendant's having to pay for the representation.
Court of original jurisdiction	A court where a matter is initiated and heard in the first instance.
Court reporter	A person who usually sits in court while it is in session and records all proceedings verbatim.
Credit	In bookkeeping, (1) to record on the right or credit side of an account; (2) those items recorded on the right side of an account.
Credit sale, sale with mortgage, or purchase money mortgage	Sale of real estate for credit. The seller receives a mortgage on the property to secure the unpaid portion of the purchase price.
Creditor	A person or entity to whom a debt is owed by another.
Crime	An act in violation of the penal laws of a state or the United States and for which a specific punishment is prescribed.
Criminal action	Generally brought by the people through a government (either federal or state) against the person or persons accused of a crime.
Criminal justice system	The network of courts and tribunals which deal with criminal law and its enforcement.
Cross-claim	A pleading filed by a defendant which asserts a claim against another defendant arising out of the same action as the original complaint.
Cursor	A lighted position indicator, usually shown as a blinking underline or a reversed character. Indicates position where next typed character will be.
Cursor positioning	Describes the motion of a cursor. Most systems employ a series of arrow keys for up, down, left, and right movement. Some systems use a home key to position the cursor at the upper-left corner of the screen. A few systems also offer a "reverse home" to move the cursor to the lower-right corner of the screen. Some systems use a key code plus alphanumeric or function keys for cursor

movement. A number of systems permit cursor movement only horizontally, along a fixed line.

Custody
The care and keeping of anything; in divorce (dissolution), the physical care and control of minors.

D

Daisy wheel
The print wheel for a daisy wheel printer. Print wheels are interchangeable, allowing the operator to select an appropriate font. A flat disk resembling a daisy wheel with characters around the circumference; may be either 10 or 12 pitch in a variety of type styles.

Debit
In bookkeeping, to record an amount on the left or debit side of an account; those items recorded on the left side of an account.

Debtor
One who owes a debt to another; a person or entity filing for relief under the Bankruptcy Code.

Decedent
Also, deceased. A person who has died.

Decimal tab
A feature which automatically keeps decimal points in vertical alignment while columns of numbers are being typed. Aligns whole numbers on the right-most digit.

Decision
The opinion of the court.

Declaratory judgment
The result of litigation in which the plaintiff seeks a determination by the court as to the rights and obligations of the parties; distinguished from other litigation because no relief is sought other than the above; such a determination is sought in an effort to avoid a controversy, for example, the meaning of a contract provision.

Decree
Document issued by a court evidencing final judgment.

Deed
A formal written document by which a person or entity conveys title to real property.

Deed of trust
An instrument given to a lending institution to secure a loan whereby the institution holds title to the property until the debt has been paid; it is similar to a mortgage, but the lender holds title to the property rather than the property owner.

706

Default	(1) Failure of the defendant to appear and answer the summons and complaint. (2) Failure to comply with the terms of a contract.
Defendant	(1) The person or entity defending or denying a suit. (2) The party against whom recovery is sought or the accused in a criminal case.
Defense of property	Affirmative defense in criminal law or tort law where force was used to protect one's property.
Deficient	Incomplete; defective; not sufficient in quantity or force.
Defunct	With reference to corporations, a corporation no longer operative; having ceased to exist.
Delete	A feature which removes a specified section of text (either a space, character, group of words, paragraph, or page) from the storage medium.
Department of Veterans Affairs (VA)	A department of the executive branch of the United States Government which administers veterans' benefits. Formerly known as the Veterans Administration.
Deposition	Testimony of a witness or a party taken under oath outside the courtroom.
Depository resolution	A resolution by a corporation which designates a bank to be the depository of the corporate funds.
Devise	A gift of real property by will. Under the Uniform Probate Code, a gift of personal or real property by will.
Devisee	The person to whom lands or real property is given by will.
Digest	A detailed index by subject on points of law covered by reported cases.
Directed verdict	In a case in which the plaintiff has failed to present on the face of his case proper evidence for jury consideration, the trial judge may order the entry of a verdict without allowing the jury to consider it.
Directors	Persons appointed or elected by shareholders who are authorized to manage and direct the affairs of the corporation.
Disabled person	One who lacks legal capacity; one who is physically or mentally unable to act in his own behalf or pursuing his normal occupation.

GLOSSARY

Disbursement	The act of paying out; money paid out; expenditure.
Disciplinary rules	Rules stating the minimum level of conduct below which no lawyer shall fall without being subjected to disciplinary action.
Discharge	In bankruptcy, the relief sought by a person who files a petition in bankruptcy.
Disclaimer	The refusal, or rejection, of an estate or right offered to a person.
Discovery	The vehicle by which a party to a lawsuit is entitled to obtain facts, documents, and information about the case.
Discreet (discrete) media	Term applied to recording media that are individually distinct—that can be filed, mailed, moved, and otherwise separately handled. In dictation equipment, for example, belts, disks, cartridges, and cassette media are "discrete"; endless loop media are not.
Discretionary hyphen	A semi-permanent hyphen inserted by the operator in words that may require a hyphenation decision. Upon printout the word processor can retain the hyphen or ignore it if no hyphen is required. Also called ghost or soft hyphen.
Diskette	See storage media.
Display	(1) Term applied to the screen of a CRT-equipped WP typing system as well as the textual images appearing on that screen. (2) The act of commanding a CRT-equipped WP system to produce specified text on its screen.
Display highlights	The ability of the system to intensify or blink certain portions of the display screen—either the characters themselves or the screen area behind the characters—to emphasize a text segment designated for some special activity such as delete or move.
Disposition	In estate and probate matters, the handling of a person's property in accordance with the terms of his will.
Dispositive provisions	The provisions of a will or trust agreement relating to the disposition and distribution of property in the estate or trust.
Dissolution	(1) Dissolving the business entity and winding up its affairs. (2) The termination process of

dissolving or winding up something. (3) Legal termination of a marriage.

Diversity of citizenship A term used to mean that the party on one side of a lawsuit is a citizen of one state and the other party is a citizen of another state. Diversity of citizenship is one of the jurisdictional requirements of federal courts.

Dividends Payments designated by the board of directors of a corporation to be distributed pro rata among shareholders.

Docket (1) An abstract or brief entry or the book containing such entries. (2) Trial docket is a list or calendar of cases to be tried in a certain term of court.

Docket control A system for keeping track of deadlines and court dates for both litigation and non-litigation matters.

Doctrine of stare decisis That doctrine requiring courts to stand by earlier court decisions when hearing cases with similar fact situations.

Document assembly/merge (1) The manner in which a system assembles new documents from previously recorded text. Most systems can combine prerecorded text with keyboarded text. Many systems can combine selections from prerecorded text to form a new document. (2) The system's ability to join a document to such variable information as names and addresses to create a number of nearly identical documents.

Domestic corporation Corporation created or organized in the state in which it does business.

Domicile The place where a person has his true, fixed, and permanent home and principal establishment, and to which whenever he is absent he has the intention of returning.

Donation A gift; something given to another in which no consideration was given or accepted.

Dormant partner Either known or unknown partner who takes no active part in the business.

Double-entry bookkeeping A bookkeeping system where each entry has a dual effect. A change in any asset, liability, or in owner's equity is always accompanied by an off-setting change within the basic accounting elements.

709

Drawing account	Account of withdrawals by owner for personal use.
Due care	That care which a reasonable, prudent person would exercise in a particular situation.
Duplicate original	A term frequently used when an original and duplicate copy are both executed as originals.
Durable power of attorney	A power given to another which empowers that person to act on behalf of the maker, even if the maker has become incapacitated.
Duress	Use of force or threatened force to gain consent.

E

Earnest money	Deposit made by buyer indicating he is entering a contract in good faith.
Earnest money contract	Purchase agreement accompanied by earnest money to guarantee performance of buyer.
Easement	A right to use the lands of another. (See right of way.)
Editing	(1) Reading back, scanning, deleting, inserting, and reformatting. (2) The act of revising and correcting text of a manuscript prior to its production as a final document or publication. (3) The act of operating the function and alphanumeric keys of a WP typewriter to alter the recorded text which will eventually be played out automatically.
Elder law	A practice of law focused on the unique concerns of a segment of the population over the age of 50.
Element	(1) Golf-ball sized sphere that holds all type characters on magnetic keyboards. (2) In WP usually a reference to the typing component on an automated typewriter such as the Diablo or Qume printwheel or the Selectric "golf ball."
Emancipated	One who is set free and made his own master. The term principally used as an emancipated minor, a person under legal age who is given legal capacity by court order or by operation of law.
Employer identification number	A number assigned to an employer by the Internal Revenue Service which must be used on all reports submitted to the IRS.

Encroachment	An intrusion on the property of another.
Encumbrance	A claim or lien on real property (real estate).
Encyclopedia	In law, a series of topics in book form arranged alphabetically containing information on legal matters.
Endless loop media	A very long loop of magnetic tape (usually sealed in a large tank) on which a dictator records dictation for transcription.
Entity	A person or legally recognized organization.
Entrapment	The act of inducing a person to commit a crime so that a criminal charge will be brought against him.
Entry	In practice, a statement of conclusion reached by the court and placed in the court record.
Environmental Protection Agency (EPA)	A federal agency which works to abate and control pollution.
Equity	In bookkeeping, the difference between the value of something and the balance owed upon it.
Escrow	Something of value delivered to a disinterested third party to be held pending performance of certain conditions and delivered upon performance.
Escrow agent	The person designated to hold escrow property.
Esquire	In the United States, the title commonly appended after the name of an attorney.
Estate	A person's property.
Estate planning	The area of the law dealing with arranging a person's property and estate by taking into account the laws of wills, taxes, property, and trusts to gain a maximum benefit under all laws while carrying out the person's own wishes for disposition of his property upon his death.
Estate tax	A tax imposed by the federal government and some states on the right to transfer property by death based upon decedent's assets on date of death or an alternate valuation date.
Ethical considerations	(1) Objectives toward which attorneys should strive. (2) Principles upon which the lawyer can rely for guidelines in specific instances.

711

Ethics	Of or relating to moral action and conduct; professionally right; conforming to professional standards.
Evidence of title	A document establishing title to property.
Ex parte	A court order rendered without the presence of an attorney from both sides of the case.
Exceptions to title	Those things that are not included in a title policy or title opinion letter, *e.g.*, taxes not yet due, instrument affecting title not yet of record.
Exclusive jurisdiction	The authority granted to a court to hear certain matters to the exclusion of all other courts.
Execute	To complete; to sign; to carry out according to its terms.
Executed contract	A contract which has been fully performed by both parties.
Executor	A male person or an entity appointed by a person to administer the terms of his will. Called *personal representative* under the Uniform Probate Code.
Executory contract	A contract which has been partially performed but with something remaining to be done by one or both parties.
Executrix	A female person appointed by a person to administer the terms of his will. Called *personal representative* under the Uniform Probate Code.
Exempt property	All the property of a debtor which is not attachable under the Bankruptcy Code or state statute.
Express contract	A contract in which the terms are specifically stated and agreed to by both parties.
Extra-hazardous activity	One that carries that likelihood of causing some type of damage even if reasonable care is exercised.

F

Facsimile	Also, fax. An exact reproduction of a document or image sent or received to and from any location where there is phone service and a compatible fax machine.
Fair Labor Standards Act	Minimum wage laws.

712

Family law	Those areas of the law pertaining to families, *e.g.,* marriage, divorce, child custody, juvenile, paternity, etc.
Federal Aviation Administration (FAA)	A federal agency which regulates air commerce to promote aviation safety.
Federal Bureau of Investigation (FBI)	A federal agency which investigates all violations of federal laws, except those assigned to other federal agencies.
Federal Communications Commission (FCC)	A federal agency which licenses and regulates interstate and foreign communications by radio and television broadcast, wire, telephone, telegraph, cable television operation, two-way radio and radio operators, and satellite communications.
Federal Deposit Insurance Corporation (FDIC)	An independent agency within the executive branch of the federal government, which insures, up to statutory limitations, the deposits in national banks, in state banks which are members of the Federal Reserve System, and in state banks which apply for Federal Deposit Insurance and meet certain prescribed qualifications.
Federal Employment Tax Form	A booklet containing a supply of the routine forms needed to report taxes, an order blank for more forms, and instructions for filling out forms.
Federal estate tax	A federal tax imposed upon the privilege of transmitting property at death—IRS Form 706.
Federal Insurance Contributions Act (FICA)	Commonly known as Social Security tax, it funds the Social Security and Medicare programs.
Federal Mediation and Conciliation Service	A federal agency which provides mediators to assist in labor-management disputes.
Federal Register	Published daily and contains federal administrative rules and regulations.
Federal Reporter	Reports of decisions of the United States Courts of Appeals.
Federal Savings and Loan Insurance Corporation (FSLIC)	A federal agency which provides insurance coverage for savings and loan depositories in the event of financial failure.
Federal Supplement	Contains reported decisions of the United States District Courts.

713

Federal Trade Commission (FTC)	A federal agency which promotes free and fair competitive enterprise in interstate commerce.
Federal Unemployment Tax Act (FUTA)	A federal unemployment tax based on wages.
Fee simple	Absolute ownership of real property (real estate).
Felony	(1) A serious criminal offense. (2) Under federal law any offense punishable by death or imprisonment for a term exceeding one year.
Fiduciary	A person or institution who manages money or property of another and who must exercise a standard of care imposed by law, *e.g.,* personal representatives or executor of an estate, a trustee, etc.
Fiduciary income tax return	A federal tax return filed by the fiduciary for an estate or trust—IRS Form 1041.
Field	Pre-defined areas on the word processing/computer screen where one or more characters of specific information may be entered or modified.
Files management	The control of each file in the office from the time it is opened to the time that it is ultimately closed and destroyed.
Filing fee	The fee required for filing various documents.
Final individual tax return	Final return for a decedent due on April 15 of year following taxable year—Form 1040.
Findings of fact and conclusions of law	A court's decision is a finding of facts in a case. The judge's written reasons for the findings are conclusions of law.
Fiscal year	A period of 12 consecutive months chosen as an accounting period for a business or year from date of death for an estate.
Fixture	An article of personal property permanently attached to real estate.
Floppy disk	See storage media.
Font	The typing or printing element of a word processor/computer available in different type styles.
Food and Drug Administration (FDA)	A federal agency which sets safety and quality standards for food, drugs, cosmetics, and household substances.

714

Foreign corporation	A corporation that does business in a state or country other than the state or country in which it was created.
Form letter	A standard means of communicating information to replace many letters that have similar content. Also known as a repetitive letter, standard letter, or guide letter.
Form paragraphs	Paragraphs which are typed, stored on a medium (cassette, disk, or diskette), and coded for easy access. They may be retrieved and arranged appropriately to produce a document or letter tailored for a particular response. Also known as canned paragraphs, boilerplate paragraphs, or guide paragraphs.
Format	Includes margin and tab settings, line length and spacing, page length, etc.
Fraud	A false statement of a material fact with the intent to deceive, which statement is relied upon and is intended to be relied upon to cause a loss to the victim.

G

General jurisdiction	Court with no limitation as to the types of cases it can hear and no limitation as to monetary jurisdiction (sometimes referred to as unlimited jurisdiction).
General ledger	A group of accounts.
General partnership	A partnership in which the parties carry on their trade or business for the joint benefit and profit of all parties.
Geographic filing	A system of filing by geographic area, such as state or region. This would be rare in a law office, except in those cases where a law office has several branches.
Global hyphenation	A final editing procedure used in conjunction with an operator-established hot zone which searches for every instance where hyphenating a word is necessary to equalize the length of lines in a document. Aids the operator by highlighting the characters on the succeeding line which would properly fill out the line and suggesting the division of the word by the cursor position.
Government Printing Office (GPO)	A federal agency in charge of printing, binding, and sales of all government communications.

Government survey	System adopted by government in 1785 for mapping out tracts of ground in townships and sections.
Grand jury	A body of citizens assembled to receive complaints and accusations in criminal cases, to hear evidence, and to determine whether probable cause exists that a crime has been committed, and whether an indictment should be issued.
Grantee	Person who receives a grant of property; the buyer.
Grantor	Person who transfers property; the seller; maker of a trust.
Guardian of the estate	Also, conservator. Person appointed by the court to be responsible for preserving the estate of a minor or incompetent person.
Guardian of the person	Person appointed by the court to be responsible for the physical well-being, education, and general welfare of a minor or incompetent person.

H

Hard copy	Written, typed, or printed matter; a document.
Hardware	The electrical, electronic, magnetic, and mechanical devices which are combined with software (programs, instructions, etc.) to create a word processing system.
Headnote	A brief statement of fact and the rule or law applied to those facts.
Health care power of attorney	A power given to another permitting that person to make health care decisions on behalf of the maker.
Hearing	A formal proceeding (generally less formal than a trial) with definite issues of law or of fact to be tried. Hearings are used extensively by legislative and administrative agencies.
Heir	One who inherits property, either real or personal, from a relative.
Highlighting	Display screen intensifies or blinks certain areas of the screen—either the characters themselves or the screen behind the characters—to emphasize a text segment designated for a system activity such as delete or move.

Holographic will	Also, olographic. A will that is entirely hand-written, dated, and signed by the testator himself.
Homestead property	The dwelling house and the adjoining land where the head of the family lives.
Horizontal scrolling	Ability of the system to move horizontally along a line of text to access more characters than may be shown on the screen at one time. Several methods may be used. The system can move horizontally across the line, adding one character at a time, or it may display the text as overlapping left, center, and right segments, etc. Some systems display wide lines by condensing character size so that a large number of characters may be displayed.

I

Illegitimate	Term applied to children born out of lawful wedlock.
Immigrant	Person who comes into a foreign country or region to live.
Immigration	The entry of foreign persons into a country to live permanently.
Immigration and Naturalization Service (INS)	A federal agency which regulates immigration and naturalization of aliens.
Implied contract	A contract created by law and imposed upon parties because of their actions or because of their relationships.
Imprest fund	Petty cash fund. See petty cash fund.
Improvements	Such items as curbs, gutters, sidewalks, street lights, and sewer systems constructed to enhance development of real estate. Often items of a permanent nature attached to the land are referred to as improvements.
Inactive files	Files in which there will be no activity for some time but for which all time has been billed.
Incarceration	Imprisonment in a jail or penitentiary.
Income statement	Profit and loss statement.
Income tax	A tax levied by the federal (and in some cases, state and local) government on the income of individuals which an employer may be re-

717

quired to withhold from the wages of an employee.

Incompetent   One who lacks ability, legal qualification, or fitness to manage his own affairs.

Incorporation   The act or process of forming a corporation.

Incorporator   Each person signing the articles of incorporation.

Indictment   A written accusation issued by a grand jury against a defendant.

Information   A written accusation against the defendant.

Information management   A system of processing all types of information (written text, statistics, voice communications and any other form of data) at top speed with the highest accuracy, least effort, and lowest cost utilizing automated equipment, standardized procedures, and specialized personnel.

Inheritance tax   A tax imposed by some states upon persons receiving property from an estate based upon individual shares, less exemptions, depending upon familial relationship between the decedent and recipient.

Ink jet   A printing method by which alphanumerics are electronically "squirt printed" onto paper.

Input   (1) Information or ideas in raw form. (2) Term used when referring to the submission of work to a word processing center. (3) To keyboard material.

Insolvent   When the total debt of an entity is greater than all of its property.

Installment real estate contract   Agreement between seller and buyer for the sale and purchase of certain real estate over a period of time by making installment payments with interest.

Intent   (1) A clearly formulated or planned intention. (2) That which a plaintiff must prove to recover damages for an intentional tort.

Intentional tort   Wrong perpetrated by one who intends to break the law.

Interim trustee   The individual who serves until a trustee is appointed.

Interlocutory   Temporary; provisional; interim, not final.

718

Internal Revenue Ser-
vice (IRS)
A federal agency which administers the tax laws of the United States, except tax on alcohol, firearms, explosives, and tobacco.

Interrogatories
A set or series of written questions propounded to a party, witness, or other person having information or interest in a case; a discovery device.

Interstate Commerce
Commission (ICC)
A federal agency which regulates all transportation in interstate commerce.

Intestate
Having died without making a will.

Intestate succession
The statutory acquisition of title to property when the deceased left no will or an invalid will.

Invalidity
In marriage, one which is invalid from its inception.

Inventory
In estates, a list of the assets which comprise the estate, including values.

Involuntary bankrupt-
cy
A proceeding initiated by creditors requesting the bankruptcy court to place a debtor in liquidation.

Irrevocable trust
A trust which may not be revoked by the maker after its creation; generally made for tax reasons.

J

Joint custody
In a divorce/dissolution, the situation occurring when both parents are awarded custody of a child, often for specified periods of time during any one year.

Joint interest trust
A trust that is created by two persons placing their jointly held assets in trust.

Joint stock company
An unincorporated business enterprise with ownership represented by shares of stock.

Joint tenancy
Property held by two or more persons, each with the same undivided interest in the property.

Joint venture
A legal entity in the nature of a partnership engaged in a joint undertaking of a commercial enterprise.

Joint will
A single will made by two or more persons.

Journal
In bookkeeping, a chronological record of all transactions completed, showing date, titles of accounts to be debited or credited, and

amounts of the debits and credits; contains the first formal double-entry record of a transaction.

Journalizing — In bookkeeping, the act of recording transactions in a journal.

Judgment — The written decision of a court to an action or suit submitted to the court for determination.

Judgment debtor — One who owes money as a result of a judgment in favor of a creditor.

Judicial lien — A lien obtained by judgment or other judicial process against a debtor.

Judiciary — The branch of government vested with judicial power to interpret and apply the law; the court system; the body of judges; the bench.

Jurat — Certification of person or officer before whom writing was sworn to.

Jurisdiction — (1) The power and authority of a court to hear and try a case. (2) The geographic area in which a court has power or the types of cases it has power to hear.

Jurisdiction in personam — The authority of a court to render a judgment against a person or to subject the disputing parties to the decisions and rulings made by it.

Jurisdiction in rem — The authority of a court to render a judgment concerning property over which it has jurisdiction.

Jurisdiction over the subject matter — The authority of a court to render judgment over the matter in dispute.

Jury — A certain number of men and women selected according to law and sworn to try a question of fact or indict a person for public offense.

Justification — The term used in automated typing to define the adjustment of a line of type so that it fills the line flush from left to right to a special measure. This may be achieved by interword spacing (leaving extra white space between words) or by intercharacter spacing with proportionally spaced characters which provides output with a more print-like appearance.

K

Key number system — A research aid developed by West Publishing Company which divides the law into primary

720

sections, subsections, and topics. The key number for a given topic will help the researcher find all references to that subject quickly.

Keyboarding   Inputting information into a computer.

L

Land contract

Contract for purchase and sale of real property.

Landlord

Also, lessor. The owner of property who leases it to a person or business entity.

Last will and testament

Also, will. An instrument by which a person makes a disposition of his property, to take effect after his death, and which by its own nature is ambulatory and revocable during his lifetime.

Law blank

A printed legal form available for preparing documents.

Law of descent

Controls who shall inherit under a will which has been proved invalid or when there is no will.

Lawsuit

(1) An action or proceeding in a civil court. (2) Term used for a suit or action between two private parties in a court of law.

Lease

(1) A contract between owner and lessee for possession and use of property. (2) An agreement which gives rise to a landlord and tenant relationship.

Leave of court

Permission of court to take some action.

Ledger

The book of final entry in bookkeeping, where a complete record of all assets, liabilities, and proprietorship items are kept.

Legacy

A disposition of personal property by will; a bequest.

Legal back

Heavy paper longer than a legal document used as a backing sheet for court papers or other documents.

Legal cap

Bond writing paper in $8\frac{1}{2} \times 14$–inch size used for preparation of legal documents.

Legal capacity	Refers to whether a person may sue in his own right without being represented by someone else.
Legal description	A detailed specification of real property which must be complete enough that the parcel can be located and identified (by metes and bounds or lot numbers of a recorded plat).
Legal process	(1) A formal paper that is legally valid. (2) Something issuing from the court, usually a command such as a writ or mandate.
Legal texts	Books that cover specific areas of the law, usually dealing with a single topic.
Legatee	The person to whom a legacy is given in a will.
Legislation	(1) The act of giving or enacting laws. (2) The power to make laws via legislation in contrast to court-made laws.
Legitimate	That which is legal, lawful, recognized by law, or according to law. A child or children born of persons in lawful wedlock.
Lessee	Also, tenant. Person who rents property from another.
Lessor	Also, landlord. Owner who rents his property to another.
Letters of administration	Formal document issued by probate court appointing the administrator of an estate.
Letters testamentary	Also, letters of authority. The formal instrument of authority and administration given to a personal representative by the court in a testacy situation, empowering the personal representative to enter upon the discharge of his office as the personal representative.
Liabilities	In bookkeeping the debts or other financial obligations of a business for money, goods, services, etc., received.
Liability	(1) A debt or obligation to another person or entity. (2) Legal responsibility to another.
Libel	In torts, damage to a person's reputation by written or published information.
Licensing boards	State agencies created to regulate the issuance of licenses, *e.g.*, contractors, cosmetologists, realtors, etc.
Lien	An encumbrance or legal burden upon property.

Limited jurisdiction	Where a court is restricted in the type of case it can hear or in the amount of money involved in the litigation.
Limited liability company (LLC)	A business entity giving advantages of limited liability to equity owners and control persons.
Limited partnership	A partnership consisting of one or more general partners who conduct the business and one or more special partners who contribute cash payments as capital and who are not liable for the debts of the partnership beyond the amount each contributes.
Limited warranty deed	Also, special warranty deed. Guaranty clause in deed by which grantor pledges that he has done nothing to cloud or encumber the title. He does not guarantee against any defects which occurred before he owned the property.
Liquidation	The conversion by sale of all of a debtor's non-exempt property in a bankruptcy proceeding.
Listing agreement	Agreement whereby owners of real estate agree to have a broker represent them in the sale of real estate.
Litigation	A lawsuit; a legal action, including all proceedings therein.
Living will	The document by which the maker instructs the physician or medical supplier not to keep the maker alive by use of life-supporting procedures.
Loose-leaf services	Loose-leaf replacement pages provided by a publisher in areas of the law where changes occur at a rapid rate.

M

Magistrate	An official or officer with limited judicial authority; a public officer.
Magnetic media	Any of a wide variety of belts, cards, disks, cassettes, or tapes coated or impregnated with magnetic material, on which dictation or keystrokes are recorded and stored, for use with appropriate WP equipment.
Malpractice	Professional misconduct or unreasonable lack of skill.
Marriage	A legal union of a man and a woman as husband and wife.

723

Martindale–Hubbell Law Directory	A publication of several volumes which contains names, addresses, specialties, and ratings of lawyers; also includes digest of state and foreign statutory law and includes text of uniform laws, such as the Uniform Probate Code.
Massachusetts trust	A business organization wherein property is conveyed to trustees and managed for the benefit of the holders of certificates similar to corporate stock certificates.
Materialman's lien	Also, mechanic's lien. An instrument filed by a materialman or a mechanic who has furnished material or performed labor for improvements to property but has not been paid for that work. Such a lien creates a security interest in the property.
Media	In general, the term used by the word processing industry to identify recording material such as magnetic belts, cards, disks, and tapes in cassettes or cartridges.
Medium	(1) Singular form of the plural word "media." (2) A paper or magnetic entry for recording used with a WP device.
Mega (M)	(1) Abbreviation denoting one million units. (2) In "computerese" 10M bytes denotes 10 million bytes of storage.
Memorial	In real estate, an entry on a Torrens certificate which describes an encumbrance (such as a mortgage or lien) in existence on the property.
Metes and bounds	A way of describing land by listing compass directions and distances of boundaries.
Mining partnership	An association of several mine owners for cooperation in working the mine.
Minor	A person under the age of legal competence.
Minute book	The official book of corporate minutes kept by the secretary of the corporation.
Minute clerk	The person who sits in court while it is in session and keeps track of files, exhibits, and proceedings and administers oaths.
Minutes	Memorandum of a transaction or proceeding.
Misdemeanor	A criminal offense lesser than a felony and generally punishable by fine or by imprisonment other than in a penitentiary.

Misrepresentation — A false statement of material fact which is relied upon and is intended to be relied upon to cause a loss to the victim.

Mitigation — Reducing money damages to the amount of the actual loss.

Model Rules of Professional Conduct — The guidelines to define the relationship of the lawyer to the legal system.

Modification of decree — A procedure whereby a decree can be changed after a period of time due to a substantial change in circumstances.

Monetary jurisdiction — The limitation on dollar amount that a court may award.

Mortgage — A written instrument granting an interest in land to provide security for the repayment of a debt. Such interest becomes void upon repayment of the debt.

Mortgagee — Person who receives the mortgage (the creditor).

Mortgagor — Person with legal title who gives a lien on property to secure a loan (the debtor).

Motion — An application made to a court or judge which requests specific relief.

Movant — The moving party.

Mutual and reciprocal will — Sometimes also called a double will. A will executed jointly by two persons containing reciprocal provisions and language to the effect that the devises are made one in consideration of the other.

N

NALS — National Association of Legal Secretaries.

National Labor Relations Board (NLRB) — A federal agency which prevents and remedies unfair labor practices by employers and labor organizations.

Naturalization — Process by which a person acquires nationality after birth and becomes entitled to privileges of citizenship.

Negligence — Failure to use care which a reasonable and prudent person would use under similar circumstances.

Net income — Total income less expenses equals net income.

Net loss — If total expenses exceed net income, a net loss results.

No-fault divorce	The dissolution of a marriage on the grounds that it has irretrievably broken down or because of irreconcilable differences. Fault on the part of either spouse need not be proved.
Nominal partner	One whose name appears in connection with the business as a member of the firm but who has no actual interest in it.
Noncustodial parent	The parent who does not have physical care and control of the child.
Nonjury trial	Trial before the court but without a jury.
Non-probate assets	Assets owned by decedent and others in joint tenancy, life insurance, and other property payable to others instead of to the estate, and property held in inter vivos and Totten trusts.
Nontrading partnership	A partnership engaged in performing services; dependent on the work results of the partners rather than on capital they contribute.
Notary public	A public officer whose function it is to administer oaths, to attest and certify documents, and to take acknowledgments.
Notice	Written notification to parties in a lawsuit of the date, time, place, and subject matter of a hearing.
Notice to creditors	A notice given by the bankruptcy court to all creditors of a meeting of creditors.
Novation	In contracts, the removal of one of the original parties to a contract and the substitution of a newcomer (all parties must consent).
Nuncupative will	A will spoken by a person in peril of imminent death. Must usually be reduced to writing within a limited time by the witnesses to whom it was spoken; invalid in some states.

O

Oath	A solemn pledge by which a person signifies that he is bound in conscience to perform an act faithfully and truthfully.
Occupational Safety and Health Act (OSHA)	A federal act which develops and regulates occupational safety and health standards.
Occupational Safety and Health Review Commission	A federal agency established by the Occupational Safety and Health Act to adjudicate enforcement actions under the Act.

Offeree	The party to whom the offer is made.
Offeror	The party making the offer.
Officers	In corporations, the persons elected by the directors of said corporation to be responsible for the day-to-day operation and management of the corporation.
Open court	Hearings conducted in the courtroom at which members of the general public may be present as spectators.
Optical Character Reader	A device or scanner which can read printed or typed characters and convert them into a digital signal for input in a data or word processor. OCR units in word processing applications usually read special machine-readable type fonts (OCR–A, OCR–B, or the IBM Courier font). The use of such equipment allows an ordinary typewriter fitted with such a font to serve as an input station for a word processing system. Pages produced on the typewriters are fed into the OCR and converted into a digital form. Such digitized text may either be entered directly for text edit and format or stored on mag media for future processing.
Optical Character Recognition (OCR)	A form of data input employing optical scanning equipment.
Oral argument	Presentation of case before a court by spoken argument; usually with respect to a presentation of a case to an appellate court where a time limit might be set for oral argument.
Order	Direction of a court or judge made in writing.
Ordinance	A rule established by authority; may be a municipal statute of a city council regulating such matters as zoning, building, safety, matters of municipality, etc.
Original jurisdiction	The authority granted to a court to hear and determine a matter for the first time.
Output	In word processing, (1) the final results after recorded "input" is processed, revised, and printed out; (2) the final documents or other information produced by an automated system.
Owner's equity	The amount by which the assets of a business exceed the liabilities of a business (assets − liabilities = owner's equity).

Owner's title policy	Policy of insurance issued by a title insurance company to a property owner insuring title to his land.

P

Page scrolling	In word processing, where the system can "flip" through the pages of a document, usually in both forward and backward directions, allowing access to all text of a multi-page document.
Partnership	A voluntary contract between two or more persons to place their money, effects, labor, and skill in lawful commerce or business and to have a proportional share in profits and losses between them.
Patent and Trademark Office	A federal agency which examines and issues patents and registers trademarks.
Payroll records	The records which are the accounting of employees' earnings and deductions.
Pegboard system	A bookkeeping system that requires placing figures in the system only once and still records cash disbursements, cash receipts, and payroll records without the danger of transposing numbers during posting.
Peremptory challenge	Request by a party that a judge not allow a certain prospective juror as a member of the jury. No reason or cause need be given.
Performance	The doing of all the contractual terms by both parties.
Periodical	A publication which appears regularly but less often than daily.
Peripherals	In word processing, devices (such as printers, OCR readers, and communications) which may be configured with word processing systems as options, extending their capabilities. More sophisticated systems can frequently share a peripheral among multiple stations, making the use of a high-speed printer or other expensive pieces of equipment cost effective.

Personal injury	The term which usually describes the kind of suit filed to recover damages for a physical injury.
Personal representative	Term used by the Uniform Probate Code to designate the representative of an estate, replacing the terms executor, administrator, etc. (See executor, executrix, administrator, and administratrix.)
Petition	First pleading filed in any lawsuit; also called complaint.
Petition for dissolution	Initial document in a dissolution of marriage proceeding.
Petitioner	Initiating party in a dissolution of marriage proceeding.
Petty cash	Fund for paying small expenses to eliminate necessity of writing checks for small amounts. Sometimes referred to as an imprest fund.
Petty cash ledger	A subsidiary ledger in which all expenditures and reimbursements of the petty cash fund are listed.
Plaintiff	A person or entity who brings the action; the party who complains or sues in a civil action.
Plat	A map of a subdivided area, usually drawn to scale.
Playback	(1) The process of listening to recorded dictation. (2) The automatic typing out of recorded text.
Plea	The first pleading by a criminal defendant.
Plea bargaining	Process where the accused in a criminal case and the prosecutor work out a satisfactory disposition of the case, usually by the defendant's agreeing to plead guilty to a lesser offense.
Pleading	Written statement made by each side of a lawsuit concerning the various claims and defenses to be decided in court.
Pocket parts	Supplements to law books in pamphlet form which are inserted in a pocket inside the back cover of the books to keep them current.
Posting	The process of recording information in the ledger from the journal.
Post-trial	Refers to items happening after the trial, *e.g.*, post-trial motions or post-trial discovery.

Prayer

A summary in the complaint or petition which states what the plaintiff or petitioner is asking the court to do.

Preemptive right

The original shareholders are given the first option to buy enough of additional issued shares of stock to maintain their proportionate share of ownership.

Preferred stock

Class of stock given preference or priority with respect to dividends over the common stock of the corporation and normally has no voting rights.

Preliminary hearing

Also, preliminary examination. A hearing by a judge to determine whether a person charged with a crime should be held for trial.

Pretrial conference

Conference among the opposing attorneys and the judge called at the discretion of the court to narrow the issues to be tried.

Primary authority

Constitutions, codes, statutes, ordinances, and case law.

Printout queuing

In word processing the method which allows a number of documents to be lined up or queued for subsequent printout while the operator goes on to perform other tasks.

Printwheel

A typing element, daisy-like or cylindrical in shape, used on certain WP typewriters and printer units.

Privilege

A benefit or advantage to certain persons beyond the advantages of other persons, *e.g.,* an exemption, immunity, power, etc.

Pro se

Term used to designate a person who represents himself in court.

Probable cause

Justification for believing that the crime charged was committed.

Probate

Court proceeding by which a will is proved valid or invalid. Term used to mean all proceedings pertaining to the administration of an estate.

Probate assets

Those items of property owned by the decedent which must pass through the probate process.

Probate deed

An instrument by which property is acquired from an estate or guardianship, generally without warranty. Sometimes referred to as executor's, fiduciary's, or trustee's deed.

GLOSSARY

Probate proceeding	The actions and pleadings required by law to administer a person's estate.
Procedural law	That body of law which defines and describes the process to be followed to enforce substantive law.
Procedures manual	Guide used by technicians and processors in a word processing center setting forth a step-by-step process for completing a particular job.
Product liability	Legal responsibility of manufacturers and sellers to buyers, users, and bystanders for damages or injuries suffered because of defects in goods.
Professional corporation	A corporation of licensed professionals rendering personal service to the public, *e.g.,* attorneys, physicians, surgeons, dentists, certified public accountants, etc.
Professional Legal Secretary (PLS)	One who has passed the comprehensive examination conducted by the National Association of Legal Secretaries.
Promissory note	A promise in writing to pay a certain sum of money at a future time.
Proportional spacing	Typed, printed, or displayed text where each alphanumeric character is given a weighted amount of space. For instance an "I" might be two units wide, an "L" four units wide, and a "W" five units wide. Such output has a print-like appearance, especially when combined with a character spacing scheme employing sophisticated intercharacter spacing.
Proprietor	Owner; person who has legal right or title to anything.
Proxy	The instrument authorizing one person to represent, act, and vote for another at a shareholders' meeting of a corporation.
Public law	Law which applies to the public, such as traffic ordinances or zoning laws.
Public service commission	Also, public utilities commission. A state agency which regulates utilities.
Punitive damages	An award in addition to the actual loss.
Purchase agreement or purchase offer	Also, sales agreement. Agreement between buyer and seller of property which sets forth in general the consideration and terms of a proposed sale.
Putative	Alleged; supposed; reputed.

GLOSSARY

Q

Qualified terminable interest property (Q–TIP) A type of property which is permitted to qualify for a marital deduction under federal estate tax if the spouse has use of the property for life and other Internal Revenue Code requirements are met.

Queue A set of documents waiting to be processed sequentially by a printer or other device. Most systems provide a means for putting documents into and out of queue.

Quitclaim deed A deed without warranty of title which passes whatever title the grantor has to another.

Quorum (1) A majority of the entire body of directors or shareholders. (2) The number of members who must be present to conduct business.

R

Random access memory (RAM) In computer/word processing terminology, the storage or memory which allows data (such as documents) to be stored randomly and retrieved directly by an address location. The system accesses the addressed material with no need to read through intervening data. Information may be retrieved more speedily from random access memory than from serial media such as tape.

Reaffirmation agreement An agreement whereby the debtor agrees to continue payments to the creditor as before bankruptcy.

Real estate Land and whatever is attached or affixed to it. Generally synonymous with the words "real property."

Realty A collective brief term used to designate real estate.

Recapture of chattels A defense to personal injury claims by asserting that the defendant was attempting to recover his own property which had been taken from him.

Reconcile To make agree, as a bank statement and a check register.

Rectangular survey system System adopted in 1785 by the government for dividing tracts of land into townships and sections.

Registered property	Real property registered upon application of the owner under the Torrens title system.
Registered property abstract	Abstract used in sale of registered property which summarizes information contained on the certificate of title and tax and other information.
Rehabilitative maintenance	Support paid by one spouse to the other for a physical or vocational disability.
Release and covenant not to sue	An agreement by both parties to end the contract even though both parties have not fully performed the terms of the contract.
Replace	In computer/word processing, a feature which searches for and stops at every occurrence of a specified section of text, thereby giving the operator the option to alter or accept the text.
Replacement volumes	Volumes which replace a book and its pocket parts when it becomes too bulky.
Reply to counterclaim	The answer filed by plaintiff in response to the allegations contained in defendant's claim against plaintiff.
Reporters	Books which contain published court decisions.
Request for admissions	Also, requests to admit. Written statements of facts concerning a case which are submitted to an adverse party which that party must admit or deny.
Request for production of documents	A direction or command served upon another party, witness, or other person for production of specific documents for review with respect to a suit; a discovery device.
Res judicata	The principle which states that once there has been a judicial decision the matter cannot be litigated again.
Rescission	Agreement to cancel or repeal the contract plus whatever is necessary to restore both parties to their original condition.
Residue	Pertains to what is left after the payment of specific bequests, devises, expenses, and taxes.
Resolution	A formal expression of the will of a public assembly, official body, or a corporation which is adopted by vote.
Resolution Trust Corporation (RTC)	A federal agency established to manage and resolve failed savings associations that were insured by the FSLIC.

733

Respondent	The party against whom a dissolution of marriage proceeding is initiated.
Response	Initial pleading of a respondent in a no-fault divorce proceeding.
Restatement	A publication which tells what the law is in a particular field as compiled from statutes and decisions.
Restitution	Act of restoring a thing to its rightful owner.
Restrictive covenant	Regulations of record setting forth those things that are allowed and not allowed affecting property such as minimum building lines, etc.
Retrieve	In computer/word processing, a system filing operation which brings a document from the archive diskette to the system diskette.
Revocable trust	A trust in which the maker generally maintains some power over the trust as long as he is alive and not incapacitated; can be amended or revoked during maker's lifetime.
Revocation clause	Clause in a will revoking all former wills and codicils made by the testator.
Right of way	The right of a party to pass over the land of another.
Rules of Court	Procedures and requirements adopted by all courts which must be followed when filing legal pleadings.

S

Sale with assumption of mortgage	A sale of real estate whereby the purchaser pays a portion of the sales price in cash and agrees to hold the seller harmless from the payment of the mortgage which the seller placed on the property.
Seal	(1) To mark a document with a seal. (2) To authenticate or make binding by affixing a seal.
Search capability	The method employed by a WP system to search for an editing point. Unsophisticated systems usually search for document, page, or paragraph number (reference code), or by line number. More sophisticated systems can also search by character string, having the ability to access the occurrences of a set number of sequential characters.

Secondary authority	(1) Legal encyclopedias, treatises, legal texts, law review articles, citators, and case law from other jurisdictions. (2) Writings which set forth the opinion of the writer as to the law.
Secret partner	A partner who takes no active part in the business and is not known to the public as a partner.
Secured debts	Debts for which the debtor has pledged something of value to guarantee payment.
Securities and Exchange Commission (SEC)	A federal agency which monitors the securities industry.
Self-defense	The right of a person to defend his person, property, home, or family against anyone who intends to commit a forcible felony.
Self-proved clause	A clause in a will signed by the testator and witnesses before a notary public for the purpose of allowing the will to be admitted to probate without the affidavit of the witnesses at the time of probate.
Sentence	Judgment on the verdict; usually in a criminal action.
Separate maintenance	An allowance which a spouse pays for the support of the other spouse.
Service of process	The delivery of writs, summonses, and subpoenas by handing them to the party named in the document.
Settlor	The maker of a trust.
Share certificate	A certificate of a corporation or joint stock company that the named person is the owner of a designated number of shares of stock.
Shared logic system	A word processing system with several input and output devices linked to a host computer which controls recording of input, editing functions, and generation of output. This system is the opposite of a standalone system which accomplishes all text processing in one unit.
Shareholders	The persons or other entities who own shares in a corporation and therefore indirectly own the corporation.
Shepardizing	Checking the subsequent history of a reported court decision to make sure it has not been overturned by a higher court.

735

Show cause	An order granted ex parte stating a date and time the opposing side may appear before the court to present evidence against the court taking certain action.
Silent partner	A partner who takes no active part in the business but is known publicly as a partner.
Simple will	A will containing only certain required basic elements.
Simultaneous printout	The ability of a WP system to print one document while simultaneously recording new text or revising previously recorded text. Some systems accept one page or one document at a time for simultaneous (also called background) printing; others queue the documents to be printed. If the system creates a print queue, printout may occur on a first-in, first-out basis, or the operator may be allowed to make priority assignments.
Slander	Damage to a person's reputation by spoken information.
Small Business Administration (SBA)	A federal agency which provides assistance of all kinds, including loans to small businesses.
Social Security	A system of federal old-age pensions for employed persons begun in 1935. A portion of the payment is deducted from the employee's salary and an equal portion is contributed by the employer.
Social Security Administration	A federal agency which administers the national social security and Medicare programs.
Social Security number	A number obtained from the federal government. All employees must have this number so that Social Security and Medicare taxes can be deducted from earnings and applied to the employee's account.
Software	All materials or machine programs needed to instruct, control, and operate the "hardware" of a computer system such as flowcharts, manuals, programs, routines, training, and the like.
Soldier's or sailor's will	An oral will (nuncupative) which the law allows soldiers or sailors to make disposing of personal property.
Sole proprietorship	A business owned and operated by a person who is solely responsible for its day-to-day operation.

Source paper	Any document or paper that provides information about cash received, cash disbursed, fees charged, or purchases charged.
Special warranty deed	See limited warranty deed.
Specific bequest	A gift in a will of an identified asset or stated amount of money.
Speedy Trial Act	A federal act establishing time limits for carrying out major events in the prosecution of federal criminal cases, *e.g.*, indictment, arraignment, etc.
Spouse	One's wife or husband.
Standalone automated system	A self-contained word processing system which consists of a keyboard, printer, storage console, and magnetic media recorder such as a card or diskette.
Standalone visual display system	A self-contained word processing system with a cathode ray tube (CRT) screen located above a keyboard, a storage console, and a separate printer. The magnetic storage media provides unlimited storage capabilities.
Standing	A concept requiring that the person injured be the one who must sue.
Statute of limitations	A statute which limits the right of a plaintiff to file an action unless it is done within a specified time period after the occurrence which gives rise to the right to sue.
Statutory law	Law enacted by Congress, state legislatures, and local governments.
Stepchild	The child of one of the spouses by a former marriage not adopted by the other spouse.
Stipulation	An agreement between the parties involved in a suit regulating matters incidental to the trial.
Stock certificate	See share certificate.
Storage media	Computer systems generally use one or more of the following types of media:
	Cassette. Magnetic tape loaded into a reel-to-reel cassette that holds a number of pages or paragraphs.
	Cartridge. Magnetic tape loaded into a cartridge that holds multiple pages of text.
	Diskette or Floppy Disk. A $3\frac{1}{2}''$ or $5\frac{1}{4}''$ disk of magnetic-coated mylar enclosed in a protective envelope.

Strict liability	Concept applied by the courts in product liability cases that when a manufacturer presents his goods for public sale he is representing that they are suitable for their intended use.
Subchapter S corporation	A small business corporation taxed as if it were an individual proprietorship. Sometimes referred to as an S corporation.
Subdivision	The division of a tract or parcel of land or lot into two or more tracts, parcels, or lots for sale or development.
Subjective filing	A system where files are filed alphabetically by the subject matter involved, *e.g.*, accounting, insurance, personnel, etc.
Sublease	A transaction where a tenant leases to another a whole or part of the premises during the term of the tenant's lease.
Subpoena	A command to appear at a certain time and place to give testimony upon a certain matter.
Subpoena duces tecum	A command to appear at a certain time and place to give testimony and to bring items specified therein.
Subsidiary ledger	A ledger which contains a complete breakdown of a subsidiary account and which must balance with the appropriate account in the general ledger.
Substantive criminal law	(1) Law with the purpose of prevention of harm to society which prescribes punishment for specific offenses. (2) The basic law of rights and duties as opposed to "remedial law" which provides methods of enforcement.
Substantive law	The statutory or written law that governs rights and obligation of those who are subject to it.
Sub/superscript printout	The ability of the printer to print characters a fractional increment (sometimes adjustable) above and below the baseline; useful for footnotes, formulas, equations, etc.
Surety	A person or entity who posts bond for another.
Survey	Actual ground measurement of a parcel of property giving the location of the property as well as its boundary lines.
Syndicate	An association of individuals formed for the purpose of conducting and carrying out some

particular business transactions, usually of a financial character, in which the members are mutually interested.

T

Tax lien	A lien filed for nonpayment of property taxes or for nonpayment of federal, state, or local taxes such as income taxes, FICA, sales taxes, etc.
Tax sale	The sale of property which results when the property owner has failed to pay the property taxes assessed on the property.
Teleconferencing	Transmitting and receiving video and audio signals over standard communication channels.
Temporary restraining order	An emergency remedy of brief duration issued by a court only in exceptional circumstances, usually when immediate or irreparable damage or loss might result before the opposition could take action.
Tenancy by the entireties	Type of ownership by which a husband and wife hold title to the entire property with the right of survivorship should one spouse die.
Tenancy in common	The type of ownership by which each owner holds an undivided interest in the entire property with no right of survivorship to the parties. The owner's interest passes on to his heirs upon his death.
Tenant	Also, *lessee.* One who holds lands of another during the term of a lease.
Terminal	A device that consists of a keyboard and some type of display that is connected to a word processor or computer used for the input and output of data. Often a reference to a communicating typewriter.
Territorial jurisdiction	The actual geographic area over which the court has authority.
Testamentary trust	A trust created in a will, which takes effect upon the death of the decedent.
Testate	Having died leaving a valid will.
Testator	A male person who makes a will.
Testatrix	A female person who makes a will.

Testimonium clause	The clause of a deed or a legal instrument immediately preceding the signatures which reads: "In witness whereof the parties hereunto have caused this instrument to be properly executed the day and year first above written."
Text editing	An application of magnetic typewriters which speeds retyping of revised texts. The typist keyboards only new material and instructs the machine to skip unwanted text already recorded. The revised document is then played out automatically from the magnetic media.
Third-party complaint	A complaint filed by defendant against a third party (not presently a party to the suit) which alleges that the third party is liable for all or part of the damages plaintiff may win from defendant.
Tickler system	A reminder system used in offices to supplement diaries in docket control.
Timekeeping	A system for reporting time spent by attorneys in various cases so that the attorney can bill the clients for the time spent.
Title commitment or binder	Certificate issued by a title insurance company setting forth the status of real estate and any requirements which must be completed before title can be insured.
Title company	A business organization which searches a title to determine facts and encumbrances and sells the buyer or mortgagee an insurance policy of title.
Title examination	An investigation of the title history made for a prospective purchaser of property to determine the condition of the title and whether marketable title exists.
Title insurance	Insurance against loss or damage resulting from defects in the title to a parcel of real estate.
Title opinion	A written opinion by an attorney as to the marketability of land title based on his review of the abstract of title and other land records.
Title policy	A policy issued by a title insurance company insuring a title to land.
Torrens Act	An act adopted by 11 states establishing a system for registration of land—as distinguished from recording evidence of title.

Tort	A private or civil wrong or injury for which the court provides a remedy through an action for damages.
Trading partnership	A business whose nature is that of buying and selling.
Transcript	Usually refers to a verbatim record of a trial, hearing, or other proceeding.
Treatise	A book or writing prepared by a legal scholar or practice expert that covers a specific area of the law.
Trespass	Illegal entry upon the land of another.
Trial	A judicial examination of issues between parties to an action.
Trial balance	In bookkeeping, a list of all debit and credit balances prepared to check equality of accounts.
Trial brief	A written document prepared for and used by the attorney at trial containing the issues to be tried, synopsis of evidence and witnesses to be presented, and case and statutory authority to back a legal position, and presented to the judge at trial.
Tribunal	A court or forum of justice.
Trust	A fiduciary arrangement whereby property is transferred with the intention that it be administered by a trustee for another's benefit.
Trust account	Also, "special" account. An account held by a law firm in which clients' money is deposited and kept separate from the attorney's account.
Trust under will	See testamentary trust.
Trustee	(1) An individual charged with the duty of liquidating a debtor's estate under the Bankruptcy Code. (2) A person who administers a trust.
Trustor	The maker of a trust.

U

Ultra vires contract	Contract of a corporation which exceeds the limitations of its power.
Undue influence	Dominance of a stronger-willed person over a weaker-willed person.
Uniform Commercial Code (UCC)	A uniform law governing commercial transactions. The UCC has been adopted by all states except Louisiana.

Uniform Laws Annotated

A publication of case law from various states with annotations.

Uniform Probate Code (UPC)

Promulgated by the National Conference of Commissioners on Uniform State Laws and adopted by several states (with modifications or only in part) to make it possible for decedents' estates to be administered in the same fashion in all states and to streamline the entire probate procedure.

Uniform Reciprocal Enforcement of Support Act (URESA)

An act adopted by the majority of states to enforce duties of support in foreign jurisdictions.

Unincorporated association

An organization formed for a nonprofit purpose which has no existence apart from its members and cannot sue or be sued in its name.

United States Attorney

An attorney appointed by the President to prosecute all offenses against the United States and to defend the government in civil actions in which it is concerned in the district to which he is assigned.

United States Customs Service

A federal agency which enforces customs laws and collects revenues from imports.

United States Marshals Service

A federal agency which provides protection to witnesses whose testimony endangers their lives and that of their families. It also maintains custody of prisoners after their arrest and during their transport and maintains custody and control over evidence seized.

United States Postal Service

A federal agency which provides mail delivery to individuals and businesses within the United States.

United States Reports

Publication of court decisions of the United States Supreme Court.

Unsecured debts

Debts for which the debtor has not pledged collateral to guarantee payment, such as open accounts at department stores.

V

Valid contract

One which contains the four essential elements of a contract.

Variable

A segment of a prerecorded document that is subject to change. Examples would be the name and address listings that are merged

	with form letters or the specific information that is merged to produce a complete will or other legal document.
Vector	The direction and distance of a line used in a metes and bounds description.
Vendee	A purchaser or buyer of property; generally used to refer to the purchaser of real estate.
Vendor	The person who sells property; generally used to refer to the seller of real estate.
Venue	Authority of a court to hear a matter based on geographical location.
Verdict	Finding of the jury as to the guilt or innocence of a defendant in a criminal trial.
Verification	A statement that the allegations are true and correct.
Vertical scrolling	The ability to move vertically, a line at a time, up and down through a display page or more of text. Allows text which will not fit on a video display screen to be accessed for review or editing. Many systems have a display buffer (memory area) larger than the display screen capacity (*e.g.*, the screen might be 66 lines, while the display buffer holds and may vertically scroll through 99 lines).
Video display terminal	A CRT or gas plasma tube display screen terminal or keyboard console that allows keyed or stored text to be viewed for manipulation or editing.
Visa	An official endorsement on a document or passport denoting that the bearer may proceed.
Voice mail	Verbal electronic mail, similar to an answering machine, made possible by a computerized telephone system.
Voice operated relay (VOR)	A feature of some dictation systems that stops the forward motion of the dictation media when the dictator stops speaking and activates the unit at the sound of the dictator's voice.
Voidable contract	One that is potentially defective in some respect (treated as a valid contract unless the defect is asserted).
Voir dire	The preliminary examination made in court of a witness or juror to determine his compe-

	tency or interest in a matter. Literally, to speak the truth.
Voluntary bankruptcy	A proceeding by which a debtor voluntarily asks for a discharge of his debts under the Bankruptcy Code.

W

Waive	Relinquish rights voluntarily.
Warranty	A promise that a proposition of fact is true.
Warranty deed	A deed which guarantees that the title conveyed is good and its transfer rightful.
Will	See last will and testament.
Will envelope	A heavy stock envelope which opens at the narrow end and is used to hold a will.
Will paper	Heavy bond paper used for typing wills. May be ruled and may have "Last Will and Testament" or "Will" engraved at the top.
With prejudice	A judgment barring the right to bring or maintain an action on the same claim or cause; a declaration which dismisses all rights.
Withholding taxes	Funds withheld by the employer from the employee's payroll check for payment of federal, state, and local income taxes and Social Security and Medicare taxes.
Without prejudice	A declaration that no rights or privileges of the party concerned are waived or lost. In a dismissal these words maintain the right to bring a subsequent suit on the same claim.
Witness	One who personally sees or perceives a thing and who testifies to what he has seen, heard, or otherwise observed.
Word processing (WP)	A method of producing written communications at top speed, with the greatest accuracy, the least effort, and the lowest possible cost through the combined use of proper procedures, automated equipment, and trained personnel.
Word processor	An automated system used for generating letters and documents. A word processor stores the documents permitting access for editing and plays them out according to operator specifications.

Words and Phrases Legally Defined	A set of books in dictionary form which list judicial determinations of a word or phrase.
Workstation	(1) An identifiable work area for one person. (2) In an office a desk and the associated furnishings required for a worker to accomplish her assigned responsibilities. (3) A component of the system containing a CRT and keyboard at which an operator keys in and edits a document. The workstation works in conjunction with the master processor and printer.
Workers' compensation board	A state agency which handles claims of workers injured on the job.
Writ of execution	An order of the court evidencing debt of one party to another and commanding the court officer to take property in satisfaction of the debt.
Writ of garnishment	An order of the court whereby property, money, or credits in the possession of another person may be seized and applied to pay a debtor's debt. It is used as an incident to or auxiliary of a judgment rendered in a principal action.

Z

Zoning commission	Local agency with jurisdiction to regulate use of properties within its geographic area.

*

INDEX

References are to Sections

747

INDEX

ACCUMULATED DEPRECIATION, § 5.25

ACE
See American Council on Education

ACKNOWLEDGMENT(S), §§ 3.31, 7.5, 18.16, 19.22, Illus. 3–1 through 3–9
By telephone, § 3.33

ACTIVE FILES, §§ 3.86, 3.94

ADDRESSES, §§ 6.133–6.137
Number usage, § 6.98

ADEMPTION, § 18.5

ADJECTIVES, §§ 6.43, 6.45–6.48
Clause, § 6.60
Compound, § 6.46
Degrees of comparison, § 6.47
Proper, § 6.45

ADJUSTING ENTRIES, § 5.25

ADJUSTMENT COLUMN(S), § 5.24

ADMINISTRATION (Bankruptcy), § 20.33
Costs of, §§ 20.6, 20.33

ADMINISTRATION, ESTATE, §§ 18.5, 18.13, 19.16
See also Personal Representative
Expenses of, §§ 18.6, 19.9

ADMINISTRATIVE AGENCIES, §§ 9.21, 9.39, 9.46, 10.1–10.4, 14.7, 14.11, 18.5
Contact with, § 10.4
Directories, § 10.4
Federal, local branches of, § 10.2
Local, § 10.3
Rules, § 14.11
State, § 10.4

ADMINISTRATOR
See also Personal Representative
C.T.A., § 19.17

ADMIRALTY MATTERS, §§ 9.36, 9.39, 9.40

ADOPTION(S), §§ 9.48, 9.61, 15.1, 15.77–15.82
Closed hearing, §§ 9.61, 15.80, 15.82
Consent of natural father, § 15.82
Definition, § 15.77
International, § 15.85
Joinder by custodial parent, § 15.81
Jurisdiction, § 15.79
Notice of hearing, § 15.82
Of adult, § 15.81
Open, § 15.85
Private (non-agency) proceedings, § 15.82
Procedure, § 15.81
Sealed files, § 15.80

ADULTERY, §§ 15.22, 15.23

ADVANCE SHEETS, § 8.35

ADVERBS, §§ 6.20, 6.43–6.44, 6.46, 6.48, 6.56
Clause, § 6.60

748

INDEX

INDEX

753

INDEX

INDEX

INDEX

INDEX

INDEX

INDEX

INDEX

INDEX

777

INDEX

INDEX

NALS, Car.Leg.Sec. 3rd Ed.—18

INDEX

793

INDEX

INDEX

INDEX

807

INDEX

INDEX

†